Information and Meaning

Connecting Thinking, Reading, and Writing

Information and Meaning

Connecting Thinking, Reading, and Writing

Jennifer M. Ivers, Ph.D.

Upper Saddle River, New Jersey 07458

Library of Congress Cataloging-in-Publication Data

Information and meaning : connecting thinking, reading, and writing / [compiled by] Jennifer M. Ivers
p. cm.
Includes bibliographical references.
ISBN 0-13-099526-6
1. College readers. 2. English language--Rhetoric--Problems, exercisdes, etc. 3. Reading comprehension--Problems, exercises, etc. 4. Though and thinking--Problems, exercises, etc. 5. Report writing--Problems, exercises, etc. I. Ivers, Jennifer.

PE1417.I525 2004
808'.0427--dc22 2003022492

Senior Acquisitions Editor: Corey Good
Editor-in-Chief: Leah Jewell
Editorial Assistant: Steve Kyritz
Executive Marketing Manager: Brandy Dawson
Marketing Assistant: Allison Peck
Executive Managing Editor: Ann Marie McCarthy
Production Liaison: Fran Russello
Permissions Supervisor: Kathleen Karcher
Manufacturing Buyer: Mary Ann Gloriande
Cover Design: Robert Farrar-Wagner
Composition/Full-Service Project Management: John Shannon/Pine Tree Composition, Inc.
Printer/Binder: Hamilton Printing Company
Cover Printer: Phoenix Book Tech

Credits and acknowledgments borrowed from other sources and reproduced, with permission, in this textbook appear on pages 761–762.
Cover: *Untitled,* c.1942-44 (oil, pen, ink, w/c, paper) by Jackson Pollock (1912–56) © Scottish National Gallery of Modern Art, Edinburgh, UK/Bridgeman Art Library.

Pearson Education LTD, London
Pearson Education Singapore, Pte. Ltd
Pearson Education, Canada, Ltd
Pearson Education—Japan
Pearson Education Australia PTY, Limited
Pearson Education North Asia Ltd
Pearson Educación de Mexico, S.A. de C.V.
Pearson Education Malaysia, Pte. Ltd
Pearson Education, Upper Saddle River, New Jersey

10 9 8 7 6 5 4 3 2 1
ISBN 0-13-099526-6

For MM, RBM, and SBM

Contents

Preface

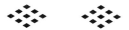

In our media-rich society, companies buy and sell information, adventurers cruise the "information superhighway," and experts have emerged to provide "architecture" and "systems" for "managing" information. *Information and Meaning* explores the ways we encounter, assess, and create meaning using the vast landscape of information available to us. It provides students with models of and tools for critical reading, thinking, and writing that will not only benefit them during their college years, but will teach them to be discerning consumers of information

For decades, scholars, critics, and consumers alike have been looking closely at the means by which we process information in contemporary society. When media critic Marshall MacLuhan argued in 1964 that "the medium *is* the message," he suggested that content is irrelevant and that our nervous systems respond more to the electricity coming from a television set than to the programming. Almost forty years later, we are more comfortable with new media, and conscious enough of the physical effects to redirect ourselves to the challenge of "the message," as well as how the medium and the message interact. The works in this anthology—whether from the humanities, the social sciences, or the natural sciences—all interest themselves in such interaction, and in the complicated struggle for meaning in this information age.

In the college environment, the relationship between information and meaning is even more fraught. The college student is asked to absorb unfathomable amounts of information and simultaneously to be skeptical of it. Composition students especially must learn to filter, shape, reject, revise, present, deconstruct, support, and sell information in the context of the essays they write. They must consciously create meaning in contexts and via delivery methods new to them. The first step toward being able to do this successfully is learning to read actively and critically. *Information and Meaning* functions on the premise that difficult material with adequate support provides the most enriching instruction in this regard. Critical reading skills can only be acquired through challenging reading experiences, so none of the essays in this anthology presents simple arguments with definitive answers to the questions raised. The readings all analyze or illustrate what struggle there is in *knowing* something, especially in a culture that seems to resist the very concept of knowledge. So in addition to raising questions that will inspire critical inquiry, these authors present models of intellectual work for students—work that is always ambiguous, always difficult, and limitless in its implications.

In the midst of such complexity and difficulty, it is important for students to feel competent and autonomous. This text is designed to familiarize students with critical reading, thinking, and writing skills by offering both challenging texts *and* comprehensive support. The support offered is intended to show students the value of active reading rather than to provide a "crutch." In order to experience the intellectual delight in createing one's own meaning by synthesizing a text with the contexts, communities, and traditions that text has alluded to or been built upon, a student must be given ample illustration of, and practice with, such work. The following is an overview of the features of this book that provide this practice and illustration to help students internalize the intellectual process of critical analysis.

The texts are drawn from a range of perspectives, genres, styles, and disciplines. They cover a wide range of themes and offer a diversity of arguments; still, almost all of the texts can be shown to relate to each other and to the problem of making meaning out of information. Familiar subjects are addressed in fresh ways so that students do not recycle old ideas, but create new ones. And generally, the selections have not been previously anthologized, so it is unlikely students have read or written about them in previous classes.

The **organization** is alphabetical by author to avoid overly directed interpretations based on unit "themes." The texts do not have to be used sequentially, and each text is lengthy enough to provide many class periods of discussion. The texts can be used in just about any combination, depending on the needs of the particular course/curriculum.

Glosses of unfamiliar terms, names, dates, historical events, texts, and subtle allusions are bolded in the text and defined or described in the margins and in footnotes. The bolding facilitates easy navigation between text and gloss material, but students may choose to disregard glosses to avoid having to pause in their reading.

In Your Journal prompts in the margins feature note-taking suggestions, which may ask students to connect a passage to the main argument; to analyze a piece of evidence, the author's tone, or use of language, etc.; to remember a previous passage in the text for comparison; simply to paraphrase a difficult point; or to look for deeper meaning. Instructors may choose to require or encourage **In Your Journal** responses, which are numbered in each text for ease of use.

Introductions to each text provide biographical information, significant works and professional achievements of the author. For some students, this information will help place the supplied text in a larger context.

Questions about Substance encourage students to think about a text's main topic, argument, uses of evidence, and logic; to do close readings of quoted material and footnotes; to analyze or compare specific passages; and to formulate judgments about specific ideas presented in the text.

Questions about Structure and Style point students to sentence and paragraph organization, stylistic techniques, repeated themes or tropes, use of tone or emphasis, titles, introductions and conclusions, level of detail, imagery, or word choice—all to facilitate understanding of the relationship between a text's form and content.

Multimedia Suggestions provide short lists of films, television programs, Web sites, music, or other media to help students make interesting thematic or other connections across genres and subcultures. The suggestions are not meant to substitute for further reading, but to demonstrate that intertextual connections exist in all forms and that research can include myriad sources.

Suggestions for Writing and Research are not recipes for papers; they are meant to provoke deep thinking and complicated analysis, allowing for the development of original arguments. Students should think of these suggestions as springboards for their work, rather than quantitative questions that have "right" or "wrong" answers. There are various types of assignments here—from close reading exercises to more abstract argument assignments to full-blown research papers. An instructor may want to assign just one of the topics or to give students a choice of many, or even to assign a series of connected assignments. No one assignment is meant to take precedence over the others—they appear in no particular order of importance.

The **Working with Clusters** section at the end of the anthology presents lists of texts organized around concepts that will provide enriched reading and writing experiences. Each cluster includes a brief description of the ideas around which it is built and a series of questions called "Suggestions for Writing" that, in addition to providing paper topics, could also be used for purposes of discussion or to enhance the reading experience. Related clusters are also listed as potential unit partners, so that an instructor might build a whole course around the suggested cluster groups. The list of clusters here is by no means exhaustive, and instructors may use them as models for developing their own thematic or conceptual groups of texts. Finally, a short list of discipline- and genre-related clusters is provided without additional apparatus.

Combined, the book's apparatus gives students opportunities to practice:

- Active reading
- Intertextual inference/synthesis

- Interdisciplinary thinking
- Analysis of point of view, tone, purpose, and creative language
- Finding main ideas
- Exploring style choices
- Looking at themes and patterns
- Testing theoretical ideas
- Assessing evidence
- Examining logic
- Critical thinking about context
- Research

First, though, the **Introduction for Students** will describe for students some of the contexts in which they will use this book and some of the expectations it is meant to help them fulfill.

Acknowledgments

The hundreds of students who have taken my Rhetoric 101 and Rhetoric 102 courses at Boston University's College of General Studies (CGS) inspired and shaped this text at every stage—from conception to completion. I would especially like to thank Elaine Estano (who still owes me a paper . . .), Chandler Means, and Anne McCullough for their superhuman efforts on several of the chapters herein.

I have learned more in my eight years of teaching at CGS than in several decades of my own reading, writing, and research, and for that I am also indebted to many of my CGS colleagues, whose feisty opinions and tireless wit staves off insanity and exhaustion (most of the time). Most notably, Joellen Masters, Megan Sullivan, Davida Pines, Natalie McKnight, Adam Sweeting, Robert Emery, Matt Parfitt, and Lauren Henry all had a hand (whether they know it or not) in shaping my pedagogical theories and practices.

Tracy Slater, content maven extraordinaire, for your deluxe emergency research and writing services, I am eternally grateful. Margaret K. Anderson's ad hoc contributions were likewise indispensable (I wish you were the project manager for my whole life). In the home stretch, Monica Mahoney offered truly invaluable help as well. To John Shannon at Pine Tree Composition, many thanks for the extreme make-over of this ugly little duckling.

I also would like to thank the following reviewers: Mary Peters Rodeback, University of Oregon; Jane Kuenz, University of Southern Maine; Kathleen Kelly, Northeastern University; Janikka Charlton, Purdue University; Diane Thonpson, Harrisburg Area Community College; Pamela J. Colbert, Marshalltown Community College; Marlene Miner, University of Cincinnati; Elizabeth Teare, University of Dayton; Marianne Taylor, Kirkwood Community College; Martk James Morreale, Marist College; Jeannette E. Riley, Kent State University—Stark; Dr. Lisa Williams, Ramapo College; Robin Visel, Furman University; Michael Berstrom, UC Davis; Elizabeth Fifer, Lehigh University; and Will Hochman, Southern Connecticut State University.

Finally, Corey Good (I can't be the first to think his name is a true *mot juste*) trusted and encouraged me with the lightest touch. Thank you for taking a chance on my ideas, for selling them to the folks at Prentice Hall, and for pretending you didn't notice how behind schedule I was.

Introduction for Students

IDEAS, INFORMATION, MEANING

Most students come to college thinking a lot about what they need in order to succeed in their new setting. Good study habits, a computer, cool roommates, and "a major" are the main things students worry about having when they arrive on campus. It can be a shock to find out that the only things your professors want you to have are *ideas.* "What do you *think?*" they want to know, about what you read, see, hear, and experience—both in the classroom and in the world around you. For some, the professors' questions are daunting: Are "ideas" opinions, memorized facts, feelings? You wonder if your ideas are "right" or "wrong." For others, the question of ideas is liberating: You are excited at the prospect of expressing yourself, being an individual, making a statement. In either case, ideas come from a more complicated calculus than you may be accustomed to working with. They are both more and less about you than you think. Your ideas are the sum of your knowledge—derived from facts, experiences, or opinions—plus the information all around you—in textbooks, world and local news, your environment, and in the expressed ideas of others. Having ideas is not synonymous with either "knowing what the teacher wants" or merely thinking out loud. Good ideas are the product of hard intellectual work that involves reading, criticizing, synthesizing, writing, re-evaluating, revising, theorizing, and testing hypotheses. Producing ideas is certainly not a neat or simple process, especially in the context of our information-saturated society, but it is an essential skill for you to develop in your academic career.

How do you choose from, evaluate, and use the information around you effectively? No one is an expert in all fields, lots of information is unverifiable, and sometimes there seems to be *no* information available on a given topic. Most importantly, what does the information you find *mean?* Meaning, like ideas, is not a concrete, readily available substance labeled clearly for your convenience. Meaning is something you interpret, infer, coax, tweak, and sometimes embellish in the service of your ideas. You and I would likely find very different meanings in the same text, statistic, or historical event, and neither of us would necessarily be incorrect in our inferences. In fact, by evaluating and trying to synthesize our ideas, we would produce a stronger interpretation than either of us could independently. For example, the media repeatedly informs us that one in two marriages in the United States will end in divorce. What does this mean to you? Does it mean that people marry too young? Does it mean that divorce is too easy to obtain? Does it mean that the institution of marriage is outdated? What if it can mean all of those things? What if we synthesize all of these meanings? Then we might argue that marriage must soon be redefined or risk further dissolution.

Meaning, ideas, and arguments are thus *created;* they do not lie in wait or exist without us—we make them out of the raw material of information as a sculptor would make a figure out of clay. Information, like clay, can be manipulated, shaped, honed, and reconfigured. It can be made to express one meaning or its opposite, it can inspire us with new thoughts as we play with it, and the figures we thus create can be interpreted variously and repeatedly. The marriage statistic cited above may inspire some to think about the ways families have changed over the past several decades. Now that so many women work outside the home, perhaps less attention is being paid to priorities within the home, such as childrearing, household chores, or even the marriage relationship itself, causing stress and unhappiness for couples. Does this mean women shouldn't work? Does it mean that men aren't picking up enough of the domestic responsibilities women have had to abandon? Or is it all a matter of perception? Do both men and women need to change their fundamental expectations about what marriage is and does? If women weren't expected to take charge of domestic chores and men weren't expected to be primary wage earners, how would this change the definition of marriage as we know it? And what other changes would that shift precipitate?

Occasionally, if one is lucky, the sculpted meaning resonates strongly with others and takes on a life of its own; it can *become* information. If the definition of marriage changed as a result of the divorce rate, perhaps that new definition would become the foundation for subsequent interpretations of other issues. For example, if men and women became true equals (indistinguishable in their roles) in the newly defined institution of marriage, would that pave the way for same-sex marriages? If the social and legal institution of marriage placed less emphasis on traditional gender roles, would religious institutions change their perspective on marriage and want to disassociate themselves from it? The intellectual domino effects that one piece of information (e.g., one in two marriages will end in divorce) can have is really quite remarkable. This kind of layered interaction between meaning and ideas and the existing informational landscape is the primary preoccupation of academia.

READING AND WRITING FOR IDEAS

"What did *you* think of the reading?" your professor asks. This is not a question about what is there on the page, but what you have done with it in an intellectual sense. You are not being asked to summarize the text, or to merely defend or oppose it, but to interpret it. When we read, we bring identity, perspective, and experience to bear on the ideas of a text. And while we may speculate about what the author means, it is ultimately what we infer that matters. In the Kenneth Cole advertisements (123) one ad for handbags makes a provocative reference to reproductive choice, as it states: "After all, she's the one carrying it." Regardless of Kenneth Cole's intentions, you will have a response to this image based on your own beliefs, knowledge, and exposure to the issue of reproductive choice. However, a "response" is not merely an opinion. Whether or not you "like" the ad is less important than how you interpret the conditions and point of view that make such an ad possible. Whereas a simple opinion or preference can shut down dialogue, interpretation and inference lead unavoidably to further development of ideas.

"Do you have an *idea* for your paper?" your professor will eventually probe. This is not a call to regurgitate the paper topic sheet, but a request for some genuine response or original concept that you might develop in concert with, or apply to, the text(s) you have read in preparation for the assignment. Often, your ideas will come only after you have reread the text(s) multiple times, molding and honing the information you see there. Often your paper effectively presents those ideas only after you have rewritten it several times. If you were asked to write a paper about Sven Birkerts's "MahVuhHuhPuh," (47) for example, you may notice only after quoting and paraphrasing from his essay several times that the style he uses is a direct example of the argument he is making. His title, complex sentences, and apparently wandering exposition seem designed to make you pause, to disorient you a little, or to give you the opportunity to be distracted and daydream intermittently in your reading process, which is the very experience he advocates. This deferred observation could give you a much better idea for your paper than you had in the first place (in your first draft), and you might change the paper's whole focus as a result. In this sense, your ideas are read and written into existence, usually after some amount of trial and error. It is a long and somewhat mysterious process that brings truly articulate ideas into being, and you should learn to be as aware of finding ideas through writing as you are of worrying about your ideas before you write.

These texts provide examples of how writing for ideas can lead to insight. Many of the texts in this anthology seem to *resist* meaning at first glance. They do not present thesis statements; they circumnavigate their subject matter rather than "getting to the point"; and they specialize in tangents, pondering more than clearly explaining, retracing thoughts and restarting multiple times rather than progressing in an orderly linear fashion. "The Bone Garden of Desire" by Charles Bowden (71), for example, describes the deaths of several of the author's close friends. His descriptions of each of those deaths fade in and out, overlapping each other and seeming to appear in no particular order. Bowden further complicates his exposition by weaving recipes and descriptions of plants into his narrative. It can take multiple readings of this essay even to begin to understand what Bowden is trying to express about death and grief. But like the authors of all of these texts, Bowden values the complexity of his subject matter and resists forcing one clear or simple line of meaning onto readers. These writers want to engage their readers in a dialogue, and assume a kind of audience participation in the creation of their ideas.

The writing that results requires an active reader—one who marks up the text with questions, comments, and connections to other texts. An active reader rereads passages and entire texts in an effort to uncover additional implications and test the inferences she made the first time around. An active reader also takes notes that do not merely summarize and regurgitate the text, but that evaluate, deconstruct, and respond to the text, setting the groundwork for the critical writing that will eventually be expected of her.

When an active reader embarks on the writing process, she has more questions than answers, and she allows herself to experience the discomfort of *not knowing* what she wants to say long enough to allow her ideas to develop fully and with fairness to the text and its author. She knows that her draft material is again like the sculptor's clay: Much of it will be cut away or moved or reshaped entirely. Most important, she knows her writing *leads to* the formation of ideas; it does not merely present prefabricated notions. Reading and writing share this exploratory quality, though many of you have probably come to believe that reading is a passive act and writing is a means of controlling or manipulating the passive reader. Of course a writer wants to have influence on her readers; she wants to make an impression on them, to communicate with them. But readers are not mere vessels for information; they too are part of the machinery that creates a text. Though you may think of yourself as a novice reader of academic work, you do bring preferences, experiences, knowledge, memories, and personalities to your reading, which all constitute a very legitimate kind of reading authority. You do not need to be an expert in epidemiology to read Cindy Patton's essay about AIDS information (441), for example, where she argues about different types of politics that interfered with the dissemination of that information. Based on your present understandings and exposures to the subject of AIDS, you will have a means *into* the essay, and thus the author's argument. Even if you fail to grasp the argument exactly, your failure may lead you to further reading, research, or discussion that will enable other productive insights. In fact, the only real "failure" in reading is the failure to act upon the text, the failure to have your own response, no matter how tentative or changeable.

Oftentimes, you will respond more strongly to an author's tangent or subpoint than you will to the main argument. You might find yourself drawn to the content of a quoted passage or a lengthy footnote—feeling more compelled by a "distraction" than the primary focus. Awareness of and reaction to these kinds of responses are strongly encouraged. The subtler points of an essay can lead to insights as fruitful and complicated as the main topic's revelations. In fact, merely "getting the point" of the author's general argument is not a signal that you are "finished" with an essay. The interplay between the main ideas and the subtler points of an essay often yields the greatest satisfaction. Similarly, what is *not* in an essay can be almost as revealing as what is presented. Speculation about why an author excluded an illustration that you see as central can be a terrific starting point for written analysis of a text. You may find that because Patrick Tierney (681) is so critical of his anthropologist colleague Napoleon Chagnon's subjectivity, he ought to make a better attempt to address his own subjective motives. Your speculation about that omission is as legitimate a topic as your interpretation of what the essay does in fact present. Sometimes information withheld is as significant as information provided.

USING THIS TEXT

The contents of *Information and Meaning* were designed for the typical first-year college student—a student eager for new challenges and a higher level of difficulty, but who has not yet had to work so independently. This book wants to lead you to a higher level of critical reading, writing, and thinking by balancing the degree of difficulty with an appropriate level of support. Thus, you will be reading very complicated texts with the assistance of a comprehensive apparatus. The readings are difficult and provocative, the guidance is extensive, and the assignments are challenging. As you develop intellectual expertise, you can choose to depend on the apparatus less and less frequently. Whatever your reading needs, *Information and Meaning* provides the following supports:

- Embedded in-text glossing of unfamiliar terms, events, people, and textual allusions
- Note-taking suggestions—labeled *In Your Journal*—prompt you to slow down your reading process and help you to analyze the texts thoroughly
- Engaging and challenging discussion questions, writing assignments, and multimedia connections, designed with an awareness that while in some academic contexts there may be "correct answers," in the composition class there is no such thing as one "right meaning" of a text

As you embark on this challenge to think for yourself, to analyze the thoughts of others, and to write your way to insightful syntheses of both, you will not only lay the groundwork for a successful college career, but prepare yourself to be a discerning consumer of information and producer of meaning in the world at large.

Information and Meaning
Connecting Thinking, Reading, and Writing

A Natural History of the Senses

by Diane Ackerman

Diane Ackerman—poet, essayist, and nature writer—was born in Waukegan, Illinois. During her twenties, she published three books of poetry while earning an M.F.A. and a Ph.D. in English from Cornell University. Her nonfiction works include A Natural History of the Senses *(excerpted here),* Deep Play, A Slender Thread, The Rarest of the Rare, A Natural History of Love, The Moon by Whale Light, *and* On Extended Wings. *Her poetry has been collected into six volumes, among them* Jaguar of Sweet Laughter: New and Selected Poems *and* Praise My Destroyer. *Ackerman has received many prizes and awards, including the John Burroughs Nature Award and the Lavan Poetry Prize. She has been Visiting Professor at the Society for the Humanities at Cornell University and the National Endowment for the Humanities Distinguished Professor at the University of Richmond. She also has a molecule named after her: dianeackerone.*

A MAP OF SMELL

1. In Your Journal: What does Ackerman mean by "the lather of one's life"? How does this phrase relate to one's sense of smell?

2. In Your Journal: Why does Ackerman call words "fabrications"? How does language compare to the senses, given her word choice?

Breaths come in pairs, except at two times in our lives—the beginning and the end. At birth, we inhale for the first time; at death, we exhale for the last. In between, through all the lather of one's life, each breath passes air over our olfactory sites. Each day, we breathe about 23,040 times and move around 438 cubic feet of air. It takes us about five seconds to breathe—two seconds to inhale and three seconds to exhale—and, in that time, molecules of odor flood through our systems. Inhaling and exhaling, we smell odors. Smells coat us, swirl around us, enter our bodies, emanate from us. We live in a constant wash of them. Still, when we try to describe a smell, words fail us like the fabrications they are. Words are small shapes in the gorgeous chaos of the world. But they are shapes, they bring the world into focus, they corral ideas, they hone thoughts, they paint watercolors of perception. Truman Capote's *In Cold Blood* chronicles the mischief of two murderers who collaborated on a particularly nasty crime. A criminal psychologist, trying to explain the event, observed that neither one of them would have been capable of the crime separately, but together they formed a third person, someone who was able to kill. I think of metaphors as a more benign but equally potent example of what chemists call hypergolic. You can take two substances, put them together, and produce something powerfully different (table salt), sometimes even explosive (nitroglycerine). The charm of language is that, though it's human-made, it can on rare occasions capture emotions and sensations which aren't. But the physiological links between the smell and language centers of the brain are pitifully weak. Not so the links between the smell and the memory centers, a route that carries us nimbly across time and distance. Or the links between our other senses and language. When we see something, we can describe it in gushing detail, in a cascade of images. We can crawl along its surface like an ant, mapping each feature, feeling each texture, and describing it with visual adjectives like red, blue, bright, big, and so on. But who can map the features of a smell? When we use words such as smoky, sulfurous, floral, fruity, sweet, we are describing smells in terms of other things (smoke, sulfur, flowers, fruit, sugar). Smells are our dearest kin, but we cannot remember their names. Instead we tend to describe how they make us feel. Something smells "disgusting," "intoxicating," "sickening," "pleasurable," "delightful," "pulse-revving," "hypnotic," or "revolting."

My mother once told me about a drive she and my father took through the Indian River orange groves in Florida when the trees were thick with blossom and the air drenched with fragrance. It overwhelmed her with pleasure. "What does it smell like?" I asked. "Oh, it's delightful, an intoxicating delightful smell." "But what does that smell *smell* like?" I asked again. "Like oranges?" If so, I might buy her some eau de cologne, which has been made of neroli (attar of oranges), bergamot (from orange rind), and other minor ingredients since its creation in the eighteenth century, when it was the favorite of **Madame du Barry.** (Although the use of neroli itself as a perfume probably goes back to the days of the **Sabines**.) "Oh, no," she said with certainty, "not at all like oranges. It's a delightful smell. A wonderful smell." "Describe it," I begged. And she threw up her hands in despair.

Sabines: fifth century people of central Italy

Try it now. Describe the smell of your lover, your child, your parent. Or even one of the aromatic clichés most people, were they blindfolded, could recognize by smell alone: a shoe store, a bakery, a church, a butcher shop, a library. But can you describe the smell of your favorite chair, of your attic or your car? In *The Place in Flowers Where Pollen Rests,* novelist Paul West writes that "blood smells like dust." An arresting metaphor, one that relies on indirection, as metaphors of smell almost always do. Another engagingly subjective witness is novelist Witold Gombrowicz, who, in the first volume of his diary, recalls having breakfast at the Hermitage "with A. and his wife. . . . The food smells of, forgive me, a very luxurious water closet." I presume it was the fried kidneys for breakfast he didn't care for, even if they were expensive and high-class kidneys. For the **cartography** of smell, we need sensual mapmakers to sketch new words, each one precise as a landform or cardinal direction. There should be a word for the way the top of an infant's head smells, both talcumy and fresh, unpolluted by life and diet. Penguins smell starkly *penguin,* a smell so specific and unique that one succinct adjective should capture it. *Pinguid,* which means oily, won't do. *Penguinine* sounds like a mountain range. *Penguinlike* is the usual model, but it just clutters up the language and labels without describing. If there are words for all the pastels in a hue—the lavenders, mauves, fuchsias, plums, and lilacs—who will name the tones and tints of a smell? It's as if we were hypnotized en masse and told to selectively forget. It may be, too, that smells move us so profoundly, in part, because we cannot utter their names. In a world sayable and lush, where marvels offer themselves up readily for verbal dissection, smells are often right on the tip of our tongues—but no closer—and it gives them a kind of magical distance, a mystery, a power without a name, a sacredness.

cartography: science or art of making maps

3. In Your Journal: Why does Ackerman call the distance between us and our sense of smell "magical" and "sacred"?

Madame du Barry: (Jeanne Bécu, Comtesse) (1743–1793) King Louis XV's mistress; known for her beauty, love for life, and extravagant collections of fine things; arrested for treason and guillotined during the French Revolution

THE FALLEN ANGEL

Smells spur memories, but they also rouse our dozy senses, pamper and indulge us, help define our self-image, stir the cauldron of our seductiveness, warn us of danger, lead us into temptation, fan our religious fervor, accompany us to heaven, wed us to fashion, steep us in luxury. Yet, over time, smell has become the least necessary of our senses, "the fallen angel," as Helen Keller dramatically calls it. Some researchers believe that we do indeed perceive, through smell, much of the same information lower animals do. In a room full of businesspeople, one would get information about which individuals were important, which were confident, which were sexually receptive, which in conflict, all through smell. The difference is that we don't have a trigger response. We're aware of smell, but we don't automatically react in certain ways because of it, as most animals would.

4. In Your Journal: Why does Helen Keller refer to smell as "the fallen angel"? How does this relate to the lack of "trigger response" Ackerman discusses?

One morning I took a train to Philadelphia to visit the Monell Chemical Senses Center near the campus of Drexel University. Laid out like a vertical neighborhood, Monell's building houses hundreds of researchers who study the chemistry, psychology, healing properties, and odd characteristics of smell. Many of the news-making **pheromone** studies have taken place at Monell, or at similar institutions. In one experiment, rooms full of housewives were paid to sniff anonymous underarms; in another study, funded by a feminine hygiene spray manufacturer, the scene was even more bizarre. Among Monell's concerns: how we recognize smells; what happens when someone loses their sense of smell; how smell varies as one grows older; ingenious ways to control wildlife pests through smell; the way body odors can be used to help diagnose diseases (the sweat of schizophrenics smells different from that of normal people, for example); how body scents influence our social and sexual behavior. Monell researchers have discovered, in one of the most fascinating smell experiments of our time, that mice can discriminate genetic differences among potential mates by smell alone; they read the details of other animals' immune systems. If you want to create the strongest offspring, it's best to mate with someone whose strengths are different from yours, so that you can create the maximum defenses against any intruder, bacteria, viruses, and so on. And the best way to do that is to produce an **omnicompetent** immune system. Nature thrives in **mongrels**. *Mix well* is life's motto. Monell scientists have been able to raise special mice that differ from one another in only a single gene, and observe their mating preferences. They all chose mates whose immune systems would combine with theirs to produce the hardiest litters. Furthermore, they did not base their choices on their perception of their own smell, but on the remembered smell of their parents. None of this

pheromone: chemical substance produced by an animal, which stimulates behavioral responses in individuals of the same species

omnicompetent: able to handle any situation

mongrel: result of mixed breeding; not pure

5. In Your Journal: What does Ackerman mean when she says, "Nature thrives in mongrels"?

was reasoned, of course; the mice just mated according to their drive, unaware of the subliminal **fiats**.

fiat: command

SPEAKING OF TOUCH

6. In Your Journal: Why does it make sense to "call our emotions feelings"?

Language is steeped in metaphors of touch. We call our emotions feelings, and we care most deeply when something "touches" us. Problems can be thorny, ticklish, sticky, or need to be handled with kid gloves. Touchy people, especially if they're coarse, really get on our nerves. *Noli me tangere,* legal Latin for "don't meddle or interfere," translates literally as "Don't touch me," and it was what Christ said to Mary Magdalen after the Resurrection. But it's also one term for the disease lupus, presumably because of the disfiguring skin ulcerations characteristic of that illness. A toccata in music is a composition for organ or other keyboard instrument in a free style. It was originally a piece intended to show touch technique, and the word comes from the feminine past participle of *toccare,* to touch. Music teachers often chide students for having "no sense of touch," by which they mean an indefinable delicacy of execution. In fencing, saying *touché* means that you have been touched by the foil and are conceding to your opponent, although, of course, we also say it when we think we have been foiled because someone's argumentative point is well made. A touchstone is a standard. Originally, touch-stones were hard black stones like jasper or basalt, used to test the quality of gold or silver by comparing the streaks they left on the stone with those of an alloy. "The touchstone of an art is its precision," Ezra Pound once said. D. H. Lawrence's use of the word touch isn't **epidermal** but a profound penetration into the core of someone's being. So much of twentieth-century popular dancing is simultaneous solo gyration that when people returned to dancing closely with partners again a couple of years ago, we had to call it something different—"touch dancing." "For a while there, it was touch and go," we say of a crisis or precarious situation, not realizing that the expression goes back to horse-and-carriage days, when the wheels of two coaches glanced off each other as they passed, but didn't snag; a modern version would be when two swerving cars brush fenders. What seems real we call "tangible," as if it were a fruit whose rind we could feel. When we die, loved ones swaddle us in heavily padded coffins, making us infants again, lying in our mother's arms before returning to the womb of the earth, ceremonially unborn. As Frederick Sachs writes in *The Sciences,* "The first sense to ignite, touch is often the last to burn out: long after our eyes betray us, our hands remain faithful to the world. . . . in describing such final departures, we often talk of losing touch."

epidermal: relating to the skin

FIRST TOUCHES

Although I am not a portly middle-aged gentleman with nothing else to do, I am massaging a tiny baby in a hospital in Miami. Often male retirees volunteer to enter preemie wards late at night, when other people have families to tend or a nine-to-five job to sleep toward. The babies don't care about the gender of those who **cosset** and cuddle them. They soak it up like the **manna** it is in their wilderness of uncertainty. This baby's arms feel limp, like vinyl. Still too weak to roll over by itself, it can flail and fuss so well the nurses have laid soft bolsters on its bed, to keep it from accidentally wriggling into a corner. Its torso looks as small as a deck of cards. That this is a baby boy lying on his tummy, who will one day play basketball in the summer Olympics, or raise children of his own, or become a **heliarc** welder, or book passage on a low-orbital plane to Japan for a business meeting, is barely believable. The small life form with a big head, on which veins stand out like river systems, looks so fragile, feels so temporary. Lying in his incubator, or "Isolette," as it's called, emphasizing the isolation of his life, he wears a plumage of wires—electrodes to chart his progress and sound an alarm if need be. Reaching carefully scrubbed, disinfected, warmed hands through the portholes of the incubator with pangs of protectiveness, I touch him; it is like reaching into a **chrysalis**. First I stroke his head and face very slowly, six times for ten seconds each time, then his neck and shoulders six times. I slide my hands down his back and massage it in long sweeping motions six times, and caress his arms and legs six times. The touching can't be light, or it will tickle him, nor rough, or it will agitate him, but firm and steady, as if one were something a crease from heavy fabric. On a nearby monitor, two turquoise EKG and breath waves flutter across a radiant screen, one of them short and saw-toothed, the other leaping high and dropping low in its own improvisatory dance. His heartbeat reads 153, aerobic peak during a stiff workout for me, but calm for him, because babies have higher normal heart rates than adults. We turn him over on his back and, though asleep, he scrunches up his face in displeasure. In less than a minute, he runs a parade of expressions by us, all of them perfectly readable thanks to the **semaphore** of the eyebrows, the twisted code of the forehead, the eloquent India rubber of the mouth and chin: irritation, calm, puzzled, happy, mad. . . . Then his face goes slack and his eyelids twitch as he drifts into REM sleep, the blackboard of dreams. Some nurses refer to the tiny preemies, sleeping their sleep of the womb, as fetuses on the outside. What does a fetus dream? Gently, I move his limbs in a mini-exercise routine, stretching out an arm and bending the elbow tight, opening the legs and bending the knees to the chest. Peaceful but alert; he seems to be enjoying it. We turn him onto his tummy once more, and again I begin caressing his head and shoulders. This is the first of three daily touch sessions for him—it may seem a shame

cosset: treat as a pet; pamper

manna: unexpected or divine food source

heliarc: type of magnesium seam and joint welding

chrysalis: pupa of an insect, especially a moth or butterfly

semaphore: method for signaling with flags or lights

7. In Your Journal: How are eyebrows like a "semaphore"?

8. In Your Journal: Why does Ackerman go into such great detail when describing the preemie wards?

to interrupt his thick, druglike sleep, but just by stroking him I am performing a life-giving act.

Massaged babies gain weight as much as 50 percent faster than unmassaged babies. They're more active, alert, and responsive, more aware of their surroundings, better able to tolerate noise, and they orient themselves faster and are emotionally more in control. "Less likely to cry one minute, then fall asleep the next minute," as a psychologist, detailing the results of one experiment, explained in *Science News* in 1985, they're "better able to calm and console themselves." In a follow-up examination, eight months later, the massaged preemies were found to be bigger in general, with larger heads and fewer physical problems. Some doctors in California have even been putting preterms on small waterbeds that sway gently, and this experiment has produced infants who are less irritable, sleep better, and have fewer apneas. The touched infants, in these studies and in others, cried less, had better temperaments, and so were more appealing to their parents, which is important because the 7 percent of babies born prematurely figure disproportionately among those who are victims of child abuse. Children who are difficult to raise get abused more often. And people who aren't touched much as children don't touch much as adults, so the cycle continues.

9. In Your Journal: Why do you think "massaged babies gain weight" so much faster than other babies?

TABOOS

Despite our passion, indeed our need, to touch and be touched, many parts of the body are taboo in different cultures. In the United States, it isn't acceptable for a man to touch the breasts, buttocks, or genitals of a woman who doesn't invite him to do so. Because a woman tends to be shorter than a man, when he puts an arm around her shoulder her arm falls naturally around his waist. As a result, a woman often ends up touching a man's waist and pelvis without its becoming a necessarily sexual act. When a man touches a woman's pelvis, though, it immediately registers as sexual. Women touch other women's hair and faces more often than men touch other men's hair and faces. Females, in general, have their hair touched more by everyone—mothers, fathers, boyfriends, girlfriends—than males do. It's taboo to touch a Japanese girl's **nape**. In Thailand, it's taboo to touch the top of a girl's head. In Fiji, touching someone's hair is as taboo as touching the genitals of a stranger would be in, say, Iowa. Even primitive tribes, in which men and women walk around naked, have taboos about touching parts of the body. In fact, there are only two situations when the taboos disappear: Lovers have complete access to the body of another person, and so does a mother with her baby. Many of the encounter groups that blossomed during the sixties were little more than organized touch sessions, often "aided" by drugs, in which people tried to break down

10. In Your Journal: Does Ackerman's analysis suggest that women touch each other's hair and have their hair touched more than men do for cultural or biological reasons?

nape: back of the neck

some of the social inhibitions and taboos that left them feeling pent-up, rigid, and alien.

There are also gender and status taboos. We look at, talk with, and listen to all sorts of people every day of our lives, but touch is special. Touching someone is like using their first name. Think about two people talking in a business meeting: One of them touches the other lightly on the hand while making a point, or puts an arm around the other's shoulder. Which one is the boss? The one who initiates a touch is almost always the person of higher status. Researchers observing hundreds of people in public settings in a small town in Indiana and in a big city on the East Coast, found that males touch females first, that females are more likely to touch females than males are to touch males, and that people of higher status generally touch lower-status people first. Lower-status people wait for the go-ahead before they risk an increased intimacy—even a subconscious one—with their presumed superiors.

11. In Your Journal: Why do you think bosses are more likely to touch their subordinates than the other way around?

12. In Your Journal: Ackerman lists a lot of taboos related to touch. Can you think of any taboos related to our other senses?

SUBLIMINAL TOUCH

At Purdue University Library, a woman librarian goes about her business, checking out people's books. She is part of an experiment in subliminal touch, and knows that half the time she is to do nothing special, the other half to touch people as insignificantly as possible. She brushes a student's hand lightly as she returns a library card. Then the student is followed outside and asked to fill out a questionnaire about the library that day. Among other questions, the student is asked if the librarian smiled, and if she touched him. In fact, the librarian had not smiled, but the student reports that she did, although he says she did not touch him. This experiment lasts all day, and soon a pattern becomes clear: those students who have been subconsciously touched report much more satisfaction with the library and life in general.

In a related experiment staged at two restaurants in Oxford, Mississippi, waitresses lightly and unobtrusively touch diners on the hand or shoulder. Those customers who are touched don't necessarily rate the food or restaurant better, but they consistently tip the waitress higher. In yet another experiment in Boston, a researcher leaves money in a phone booth, then returns when she sees the next person pocket the money; she casually asks if they've found what she lost. If the researcher touches the person while asking for their help, touches them insignificantly so that they don't remember it later, the likelihood that the money will be returned rises from 63 to 96 percent. Despite the fact that we're territorial creatures who move through the world like small **principalities**, contact warms us even without our knowing it. It probably reminds us of that time, long before deadlines and banks, when our mothers cradled us and we were en-

principality: domain or territory of a prince

thralled and felt perfectly lovable. Even touch so subtle as to be overlooked doesn't go unnoticed by the **subterranean** mind.

subterranean: below the surface

13. In Your Journal: Are you surprised by the effect of touches "so subtle as to be overlooked"?

THE SOCIAL SENSE

The other senses may be enjoyed in all their beauty when one is alone, but taste is largely social. Humans rarely choose to dine in solitude, and food has a powerful social component. The **Bantu** feel that exchanging food makes a contract between two people who then have a "clanship of porridge." We usually eat with our families, so it's easy to see how "breaking bread" together would symbolically link an outsider to a family group. Throughout the world, the stratagems of business take place over meals; weddings end with a feast; friends reunite at celebratory dinners; children herald their birthdays with ice cream and cake; religious ceremonies offer food in fear, homage, and sacrifice; **wayfarers** are welcomed with a meal. As **Brillat-Savarin** says, "every . . . sociability . . . can be found assembled around the same table: love, friendship, business, speculation, power, importunity, patronage, ambition, intrigue . . ." If an event is meant to matter emotionally, symbolically, or mystically, food will be close at hand to sanctify and bind it. Every culture uses food as a sign of approval or commemoration, and some foods are even credited with supernatural powers, others eaten symbolically, still others eaten ritualistically, with ill fortune befalling **dullards** or skeptics who forget the recipe or get the order of events wrong. Jews attending a **Seder** eat a horseradish dish to symbolize the tears shed by their ancestors when they were slaves in Egypt. **Malays** celebrate important events with rice, the inspirational center of their lives. Catholics and Anglicans take a communion of wine and wafer. The ancient Egyptians thought onions symbolized the many-layered universe, and swore oaths on an onion as we might on a Bible. Most cultures embellish eating with fancy plates and glasses, accompany it with parties, music, dinner theater, open-air barbecues, or other forms of revelry. Taste is an intimate sense. We can't taste things at a distance. And how we taste things, as well as the exact makeup of our saliva, may be as individual as our fingerprints.

Bantu: ethnic and linguistic group inhabiting much of Southern Africa

wayfarer: traveler especially on foot

dullard: stupid or unimaginative person

Seder: event customary during the Jewish Passover, commemorating the struggles the Israelites endured on the quest for freedom

Malay: inhabitant of the Malay Peninsula in southeast Asia

14. In Your Journal: What does Ackerman mean when she says that taste is "an intimate sense"

Food gods have ruled the hearts and lives of many peoples. Hopi Indians, who revere corn, eat blue corn for strength, but all Americans might be worshiping corn if they knew how much of their daily lives depended on it. Margaret Visser, in *Much Depends on Dinner,* gives us a fine history of corn and its uses: livestock and poultry eat corn; the liquid in canned foods contains corn; corn is used in most paper products, plastics, and adhesives; candy, ice cream, and other goodies contain corn syrup; dehydrated and instant foods contain cornstarch; many familiar objects are made from corn

---

Brillat-Savarin: (Jean) (1912–1992) French lawyer and politician; famous for writing *Physiologie du Goût,* a book on gastronomy products, brooms and corncob pipes to name only two. For the Hopis, eating corn is itself a form of reverence. I'm holding in my hand a beautifully carved Hopi corn kachina doll made from cottonwood; it represents one of the many spiritual essences of their world. Its cob-shaped body is painted ocher, yellow, black, and white, with dozens of squares drawn in a cross-section-of-a-kernel design, and abstract green leaves spearing up from below. The face has a long, black, rootlike nose, rectangular black eyes, a black ruff made of rabbit fur, white string corn-silk-like ears, brown bird-feather bangs, and two green, yellow, and ocher striped horns topped by rawhide tassels. A fine, soulful kachina, the ancient god Maïs stares back at me, tastefully imagined.

Throughout history, and in many cultures, *taste* has always had a double meaning. The word comes from the Middle English *tasten,* to examine by touch, test, or sample, and continues back to the Latin *taxare,* to touch sharply. So a taste was always a trial or test. People who have taste are those who have appraised life in an intensely personal way and found some of it sublime, the rest of it lacking. Something in bad taste tends to be obscene or vulgar. And we defer to professional critics of wine, food, art, and so forth, whom we trust to taste things for us because we think their taste more refined or educated than ours. A companion is "one who eats bread with another," and people sharing food as a gesture of peace or hospitality like to sit around and chew the fat.

15. In Your Journal: How is taste a kind of "trial" or "test"?

The first thing we taste is milk from our mother's breast,* accompanied by love and affection, stroking, a sense of security, warmth, and well-being, our first intense feelings of pleasure. Later on she will feed us solid food from her hands, or even chew food first and press it into our mouths, partially digested. Such powerful associations do not fade easily, if at all. We say "food" as if it were a simple thing, an absolute like rock or rain to take for granted. But it is a big source of pleasure in most lives, a complex realm of satisfaction both physiological and emotional, much of which involves memories of childhood. Food must taste good, must reward us, or we would not stoke the furnace in each of our cells. We must eat to live, as we must breathe. But breathing is involuntary, finding food is not; it takes energy and planning, so it must tantalize us out of our natural **torpor**. It must decoy us out of bed in the morning and prompt us to put on constricting clothes, go to work, and perform tasks we may not enjoy for eight hours a day, five days a week, just to "earn our daily bread," or be "worth our salt," if you like, where the word *salary* comes from. And, because we are omnivores, many tastes must appeal to us, so that we'll try new foods. As children grow, they meet regularly throughout the day—at mealtimes—to hear grown-up talk, ask questions, learn about customs, language, and the world. If language didn't arise at mealtimes, it certainly evolved and became more fluent there, as it did during group hunts.

torpor: sluggishness in bodily functioning; stupor

* This special milk, called colostrum, is rich in antibodies, the record of the mother's epidemiologic experience.

We tend to see our distant past through a reverse telescope that compresses it: a short time as hunter-gatherers, a long time as "civilized" people. But civilization is a recent stage of human life, and, for all we know, it may not be any great achievement. It may not even be the final stage. We have been alive on this planet as recognizable humans for about two million years, and for all but the last two or three thousand we've been hunter-gatherers. We may sing in choirs and park our rages behind a desk, but we patrol the world with many of a hunter-gatherer's drives, motives, and skills. These aren't knowable truths. Should an alien civilization ever contact us, the greatest gift they could give us would be a set of home movies: films of our species at each stage in our evolution. Consciousness, the great poem of matter, seems so unlikely, so impossible, and yet here we are with our loneliness and our giant dreams. Speaking into the perforations of a telephone receiver as if through the screen of a confessional, we do sometimes share our emotions with a friend, but usually this is too disembodied, too much like yelling into the wind. We prefer to talk *in person,* as if we could temporarily slide into their feelings. Our friend first offers us food, drink. It is a symbolic act, a gesture that says: *This food will nourish your body as I will nourish your soul.* In hard times, or in the wild, it also says *I will endanger my own life by parting with some of what I must consume to survive.* Those desperate times may be ancient history, but the part of us forged in such trials accepts the token drink and piece of cheese and is grateful.

16. In Your Journal: Compare the meaning and effects of feeding oneself and feeding others.

THE HEARING HEART

In Arabic, absurdity is not being able to hear. A "surd" is a mathematical impossibility, the core of the word "absurdity," which we get from the Latin *surdus,* "deaf or mute," which is a translation from the Arabic *jadr asamm,* a "deaf root," which in turn is a translation from the Greek *alogos,* "speechless or irrational." The assumption hidden in this **etymological** nest of spiders is that the world will still make sense to someone who is blind or armless or minus a nose. But if you lose your sense of hearing, a crucial thread dissolves and you lose track of life's logic. You become cut off from the daily commerce of the world, as if you were a root buried beneath the soil. Despite Keats's observation that "Heard melodies are sweet, but those unheard/Are sweeter," we would rather hear the world's **Niagara** of song, noise, and talk. Sounds thicken the sensory stew of our lives, and we depend on them to help us interpret, communicate with, and express the world around us. Outer space is silent, but on earth almost everything can make sound. Couples have favorite songs, even a few bars of which bring back sweet memories of a first meeting on the boardwalk in Atlantic City, or the steamy summer nights in a Midwestern town when, as teenagers, they sat in their Chevies at the A & W Root Beer stand, burning up hours like so many dried leaves. Mothers sing their babies to sleep with lullabies that rock and soothe, not just cradlesongs, but cradles *of* song. Music rallies

etymological: study of the history and structure of a word

Niagara: (Falls) in western New York State and Ontario, Canada; pair of 160-foot and 167-foot waterfalls

cadence call: rhythmic song sung by the military during marching or running

people to action, as civil rights marches, Live Aid concerts, political demonstrations, Woodstock, and other mass communions have shown. Work songs and military **cadence calls** make long marches or repetitive tasks less boring. Solo joggers, fast-walkers, people schussing on cross-country ski machines, astronauts pedaling stationary bikes in space, leotard-clad aerobics classes, all get psyched up from exercising to loud music that has a regular, pounding beat. A campfire wouldn't be as exciting if it were silent. And, when the campers launch their floating candles upon the lake at sunset at the end of the summer, they usually accompany the ritual with a hymnlike song of devotion to camp and one other. People want certain foods (potato chips, pretzels, cereals, and the like) to crunch; noise is an important ingredient in the marketing of such foods. Music accompanies weddings, funerals, state occasions, religious holidays, sports, even television news. Paid choirs sing poignant anthems to homeowner's insurance, laundry soap, and toilet paper. On a busy street at rush hour, despite the growl of traffic and the gyrations of thousands of hurrying strangers, we can still recognize the voice of a friend who comes up behind us and says hello. As we stroll along the reimagined streets of Williamsburg, Virginia, we hear a melodic clanging and recognize at once the sound of a blacksmith hammering on an anvil. Sitting in a chair in the living room, idly stroking the cat while sunlight streams through a window rimmed with frost, may be relaxing, but when we hear the cat purr loudly we feel even more contented. Most restaurants serve obligatory music with every course; some even hire violinists or guitarists to stand at your table and ladle out enormous helpings of music as you chew. In the lobbies of hotels in India, and on the slate patios of Houston, wind chimes tinkle in the breeze. During so-called silent hours, the inmates of Alcatraz managed to whisper into the empty water pipe that led from sink to sink and then put an ear to the pipe to hear. Hikers llama-trekking along Point Reyes National Seashore in California, or climbing the boulder face of Mount Camelback in Pennsylvania, revel alike in the sounds of birds, river rapids, swirling wind, dry seedpods rattling on the trees like tiny gourds. In the robust festivity of a dinner party, a waiter pours a luscious Liebfraumilch, whose apricot blush we behold, whose bouquet we inhale, whose savory fruitiness we taste. Then, wishing one another well, we clink our glasses together because sound is the only sense missing from our full enjoyment of the wine.

DEAFNESS

John Cage once emerged from a soundproof room to declare that there was no such state as silence. Even if we don't hear the outside world, we hear the rustling, throbbing, whooshing of our bodies, as well as incidental

---

John Cage: (1912–1972) American composer, known for his work in percussion orchestra and his invention of the "prepared" piano buzzings, ringings, and squeakings. Deaf people often remark on the variety of sounds they hear. Many who are legally deaf can hear gunfire, low-flying airplanes, jackhammers, motorcycles, and other loud noises. Being deaf doesn't protect them from ear distress, since humans use their ears for more than hearing. As anyone who has had an inner-ear infection knows, one of the ear's most important jobs is to keep balance and equilibrium; the internal workings of the ear are like a biological **gyroscope**. In the inner ear, semicircular canals (three tubes filled with fluid) tell the brain when the head moves, and how. If you were to half fill a glass with water and swirl it in a circle, the water would spin around, and, even after you stopped, the water would continue swirling for a little while. In a similar way, we feel dizzy even after we've gotten off of a merry-go-round. Not all animals hear, but they all need to know which way is up. We tend to think of the deaf as people minus ears, but they're as much prey to ear-related illnesses as hearing people are.

gyroscope: rotating wheel or spinning mass

Despite all the folk wisdom about how important hearing is (including **Epictetus the Stoic**'s 2,000 year-old axiom: "God gave man two ears, but only one mouth, that he might hear twice as much as he speaks"), most people, given a choice, would rather lose their hearing than their sight. But people who are both deaf and blind often lament the loss of their hearing more than anything else, perhaps none so persuasively as Helen Keller:

> I am just as deaf as I am blind. The problems of deafness are deeper and more complex, if not more important, than those of blindness. Deafness is a much worse misfortune. For it means the loss of the most vital stimulus—the sound of the voice that brings language, sets thoughts astir and keeps us in the intellectual company of man.
>
> . . . If I could live again I should do much more than I have for the deaf. I have found deafness to be a much greater handicap than blindness.*

17. In Your Journal: Why does Helen Keller mourn the loss of her hearing more than her sight?

The literature of deafness is extraordinarily rich. Writers and thinkers from **Herodotus to Guy de Maupassant** have written about their own deaf-

---

- **Epictetus the Stoic:** (A.D. 50–138) Roman philosopher and former slave who provided guidelines for life through stoicism, which asserts that true goodness is inside oneself and not dependent on any external circumstances

---

- **Herodotus:** (485?–420? B.C.) Greek historian; named the Father of History, as he was the first to use the past to gain knowledge into human behavior

---

- **Guy de Maupassant:** (1850–1893) French author of short stories; used everyday life to reveal hidden aspects of people; known for a charming anecdotal writing style

---

* From a letter to Dr. J. Kerr Love, March 31, 1910, from the souvenir program commemorating Helen Keller's visit to Queensland Adult Deaf and Dumb Mission in 1948.

ness or the deafness of friends and loved ones with poignancy, eloquence, and charm. The interested reader may turn to Brian Grant's anthology, *The Quiet Ear,* a fine sampler of writings on deafness that spans the centuries and many different cultures. Mark Medoff has written a powerful play called *Children of a Lesser God,* which was recently made into an equally powerful movie. My two favorite books about deafness are *Deafness: A Personal Account,* an autobiography by the poet David Wright, and *Words for a Deaf Daughter,* a classic memoir by the novelist Paul West. From Wright, we learn that his world, though it has little sound in it, "seldom *appears* silent," because his brain translates movement into a gratifying sense of sound:

> Suppose it is a calm day, absolutely still, not a twig or leaf stirring. To me it will seem quiet as a tomb though hedgerows are full of noisy but invisible birds. Then comes a breath of air, enough to unsettle a leaf; I will see and hear that movement like an exclamation. The illusory soundlessness has been interrupted. I see, as if I heard, a visionary noise of wind in a disturbance of foliage. . . . I have sometimes to make a deliberate effort to remember I am not "hearing" anything, because there is nothing to hear. Such non-sounds include the flight and movement of birds, even fish swimming in clear water or the tank of an aquarium. I take it that the flight of most birds, at least at a distance, must be silent. . . . Yet it appears audible, each species creating a different "eye-music" from the nonchalant melancholy of sea-gulls to the staccato of flitting tits . . .

maudlin: tearfully or drunkenly sentimental

18. In Your Journal: What does it mean to "be heard"?

Ameslan: American Sign Language

West's *Words for a Deaf Daughter* frequently appears in college syllabuses, but not, as one might imagine, only in courses for or about the deaf. Lavishly written, with much wit and phenomenological devotion, it also appeals to students of philosophy and literature as a jubilant hymn to language and life. Told in the second person throughout, it addresses and at times impersonates West's deaf daughter Mandy. And, unlike many memoirs about handicapped children, it isn't at all **maudlin**, but rompy, poetic, and concerned with the struggle we all wage to know ourselves and to make ourselves known. These books allow one to eavesdrop on the inner life of the deaf, a special privilege, since many people assume the deaf, especially if they don't read or write, think differently, dwelling in a no-man's-land between concept and word. But, as the literature of the deaf makes clear, ideas and emotions find their way through with surprising ingenuity, whether in English, **Ameslan**, or some other language, from silence to the inner world where words can be "heard."

MUSIC AND EMOTION

One of the most soothing things in the world is to put your tongue to the roof of your mouth right behind the teeth and sing *la, la, la, la, la, la, la.* When we sing, not only do our vocal cords vibrate, but so do some of our bones. Hum with your mouth closed, and the sound travels to your inner ear directly through the skull, not bothering with the eardrum. Chant "om," or any other **mantra**, in a solid, prolonged tone, and you will feel the bones in your head, as well as the cartilage in your sternum, vibrate. It's like a massage from the inside, very soothing. Another reason it may be so conducive to meditation is that it creates an inner **white noise**, which cancels out extraneous noises, making your body a soundproof booth. Hebrew **davening**, in which the faithful bend and chant, bend and chant, has a similar effect. The drumbeat in a **macumba** ceremony seizes one in a crescendo of fury that climbs higher and higher, as if scaling the Himalaya of one's belief. All these sounds repeat hypnotically. Every religion has its own liturgy, which is important not just in its teachings but also because it forces the initiate to utter the same sounds over and over until they are ingrained in memory, until they become a kind of aural landscape. We are a species capable of adding things, ideas, and creative artifacts to the world, even sounds, and when we do, they become as real a fact as a forest.

mantra: mystical formula of invocation or incantation

white noise: mixture of sound waves spreading over a wide frequency range

davening: reciting prescribed prayers set forth in the Jewish custom

macumba: religion of African origin

The odd thing about music is that we understand and respond to it without actually having to learn it. Each word in a verbal phrase tells something all by itself; it has a history and nuances. But musical tones mean something only in relation to one another, when they're teamed up. You needn't understand the tones to be moved. Say the words "It's a gift to be simple. It's a gift to be free. It's a gift to come down where we ought to be," and nothing much happens. You might even disagree with its minimalist doctrine. Yet if you add the tuneful Shaker music that goes with it (which Aaron Copland adapted so beautifully in *Appalachian Spring**), its haunting melody, full of enough ebullience, joy, and conviction to inspire a whole village to put up a neighbor's barn in one afternoon, will truly captivate you. When I was in Florida, at an artist's colony on a tidal **estuary**, one of my writing students, also a professional whistler, regaled us one evening with a whistle concert, including this Shaker tune, "Simple Gifts," and for the next week you could hear people humming, whistling, or singing its gaily hammering rhythm. *Catchy* is the right word for such a melody; it hooks onto your subconscious and won't let go. Many hymns would thrill us even if they didn't have words, but, with words, they're a double score: emotional music tied to emotional messages. It works particularly well if the hymn has a dying fall in it, a musical swoon. In Blake's "Jerusalem," that swoon

estuary: place where a river current meets ocean tides

* He wrote this music for Martha Graham while living in a Hollywood block house with no windows.

comes in the third stanza, in the second syllable of the word "desire," which you have to sing as a sigh to a lower note:

> *Bring me my bow of burning gold!*
> *Bring me my arrows of de-sire!*

Few desires sound as smoldery and secular as that one, especially if you're reminded of Cupid's arrow and the double meaning of a word like "quiver." In the Christmas hymn "O Holy Night," the swoon comes right after the word "fall," in the line "Fall on your knees," and just singing it enacts the supplication. Most often hymns soar steadily in slow sweeping steps, from lower to higher notes, as the singer climbs a mystical staircase onto progressively higher planes of feeling. "Amazing Grace" is a good example of that lighter-than-air sort of hymn, full of musical striving and stretching, as if one's spirit itself were being elongated. Think lofty thoughts and sing that elevating tune, and soon enough you will feel uplifted (even despite having to sing such unmelodious words as "wretch"). Hypnotists use a similar technique when they put people into a deeply suggestive meditative trance: They often count from one to ten a few times over, telling patients to imagine themselves climbing deeper and deeper down with each number.

Like pure emotions, music surges and sighs, rampages or grows quiet, and, in that sense, it behaves so much like our emotions that it seems often to symbolize them, to mirror them, to communicate them to others, and thus frees us from the elaborate nuisance and inaccuracy of words. A musical passage can make us cry, or send our blood pressure soaring. Asked to define the feeling, we say something vague: *It made me sad.* Or: *It thrilled me.* In *Great Pianists Speak for Themselves, Vol. II,* Paul Badura-Skoda says of Mozart's Fantasy in C minor:

> What about the *emotional* content? What does the work *say* to you and me? Surprisingly, when I ask such questions in my master classes, I get rather tepid answers such as, "It is a serious work," or none at all. Then I am forced to exclaim, "Don't you realize, my dear fellows, that music is a *language* which *communicates* experience? And what experience! Life and death are involved in this *Fantasy.* May I tell you my personal interpretation of this work? The opening phrase is a death symbol: *The hour has struck—there is no escape!* The rest of the Fantasy is shock and anxiety, pages one and two, giving way then to a series of recollections: happy, serene ones, like the Adagio in D and the Andantino in B-flat major, or violent ones, full of anguish, like the two fast, modulating sections, until finally the original call returns. The **inexorable** fate seems to be now accepted, were it not for the heroic gesture of defiance at the very end.

inexorable: unyielding

Not all composers care for listeners to find such a clear program in their work, but people get so frustrated by the abstractions of music they try to elicit from it landscapes of emotions and events.

We find a profound sense of wholeness in the large, open structure of a classical composition, but it is a unity filled with tumult, with small comings and goings, with obstructed quests, with bouts of yearning and uncertainty, with insurpassable mountains, with interrupted passion, with knots that must be teased apart, with great washes of sentimentality, with idle ruminations, with strident blows to recover from, with love one hopes to consummate, with abruptness, disorder, but, ultimately, with reconciliation. One can re-create the emotional turmoil of an affair, a disappointment, a religious ecstasy, in as small a space as a concerto. *Show, don't tell!* writing teachers counsel their students. Say what one will, words rarely capture the immediate emotional assault of a piece of poignant music, which allows the composer to say not "It felt something like this," but rather "Here is the unnamable emotion I felt, and even my obsession with structure, proportion, and time, *inside of you.*" Or, as T. S. Eliot puts it in "The Dry Salvages," here is:

> *music heard so deeply*
> *That it is not heard at all, but you are the music*
> *While the music lasts.*

There are still many questions to be answered about music and emotion. In his fascinating book on music theory, *The Language of Music,* Deryck Cooke, for example, offers a musical vocabulary, spelling out the emotional effects a composer knows he can create with certain sounds. But why is this so? Do we tend to respond to a minor seventh with "mournfulness" and to a major seventh with "violent longing" and to a minor second with "spiritless anguish" because we've formed the habit of responding to those sounds in that way, or is it something more intrinsic in our makeup? Listen to **Wagner**'s *Tristan und Isolde,* and you'll hear pent-up, soaring, frustrated emotion of an intensity that may drive you to distraction. *Yearning* overflows the music like the **meniscus** on a too-full glass of wine, and this is how Wagner himself described the work:

meniscus: curved upper surface of liquid in a container

> . . . a tale of endless yearning, longing, the bliss and wretchedness of love; world, power, fame, honour, chivalry, loyalty, and friendship all blown away like an insubstantial dream; one thing alone left living—longing, longing, unquenchable, a yearning, a hunger, a anguishing forever renewing itself; one sole redemption—death, surcease, a sleep without awakening.

Wagner: (Richard) (1813–1883) German romantic opera composer; known for his ability to evoke strong emotion through music and for placing an emphasis on dramatic unity

Another question we might ask, along with Cooke, is: If we transform music into emotion, "how closely does this emotion . . . resemble the original emotion of Beethoven? . . . There can only be one answer to this . . . about as closely as the emotions of one human being can ever resemble those of another." And, because we're not Beethoven, we hear his joyous "Gloria" in the *Missa Solemnis* and feel joy, but probably not as passionately as he did when he wrote it. I suppose part of what's fascinating about creativity in any field is the author's necessity to share it with—or impose it on—the world. When he wrote the "Gloria," Beethoven underwent a volcanic, shriek-to-the-heavens joy, but instead of dancing around in delight, he "felt the need to convert it into a permanent, stored-up, transportable, and reproducible form of energy," as Cooke describes it, "a musical shout for joy, as it were, that all the world might hear, and still hear over and over again after he was dead and gone." The notes he jotted down "only ever were and only ever will be a command from Beethoven to blow his eternal shout for joy, together with a set of instructions . . . exactly how to do so." When we proclaim that artists live on in their work, we're usually referring to the emotional steppingstones that lead through their lives, their disembodied moods and obsessions, but most of all their senses. Beethoven may be dead, but his sense of life at that moment lives in his score at this moment, at any moment.

THE BEHOLDER'S EYE

19. In Your Journal: According to Ackerman, why are our eyes on the front of our heads rather than the sides?

Look in the mirror. The face that pins you with its double gaze reveals a chastening secret: You are looking into a predator's eyes. Most predators have eyes set right on the front of their heads, so they can use binocular vision to sight and track their prey. Our eyes have separate mechanisms that gather the light, pick out an important or novel image, focus it precisely, pinpoint it in space, and follow it; they work like top-flight stereoscopic binoculars. Prey, on the other hand, have eyes at the sides of their heads, because what they really need is peripheral vision, so they can tell when something is sneaking up behind them. Something like us. If it's "a jungle out there" in the wilds of the city, it may be partly because the streets are jammed with devout predators. Our instincts stay sharp, and, when necessary, we just decree one another prey and have done with it. Whole countries sometimes. Once we domesticated fire as if it were some beautiful temperamental animal; harnessing both its energy and its light, it became possible for us to cook food to make it easier to chew and digest, and, as we found out eventually, to kill germs. But we can eat cold food perfectly well, too, and did for thousands of years. What does it say about us that, even in refined dining rooms, our taste is for meat served at the temperature of a freshly killed antelope or warthog?

Though most of us don't hunt, our eyes are still the great monopolists of our senses. To taste or touch your enemy or your food, you have to be unnervingly close to it. To smell or hear it, you can risk being farther off. But vision can rush through the fields and up the mountains, travel across time, country, and **parsecs** of outer space, and collect bushel baskets of information as it goes. Animals that hear high frequencies better than we do—bats and dolphins, for instance—seem to see richly with their ears, hearing geographically, but for us the world becomes most densely informative, most luscious, when we take it in through our eyes. It may even be that abstract thinking evolved from our eyes' elaborate struggle to make sense of what they saw. Seventy percent of the body's sense receptors cluster in the eyes, and it is mainly through seeing the world that we appraise and understand it. Lovers close their eyes when they kiss because, if they didn't, there would be too many visual distractions to notice and analyze—the sudden close-up of the loved one's eyelashes and hair, the wallpaper, the clock face, the dust motes suspended in a shaft of sunlight. Lovers want to do serious touching, and not be disturbed. So they close their eyes as if asking two cherished relatives to leave the room.

parsec: unit of measure for interstellar space; 3.2616 light years

Our language is steeped in visual imagery. In fact, whenever we compare one thing to another, as we constantly do (consider the country expression: "It was raining harder than a cow pissing sideways on a rock"), we are relying on our sense of vision to capture the action or the mood. Seeing is proof positive, we stubbornly insist ("I saw it with my own eyes . . ."). Of course, in these days of relativity, feats of magic, and tricks of perception, we know better than to trust everything we see (". . . a flying saucer landed on the freeway . . ."). See with our naked eyes, that is. As **Dylan Thomas** reminds us, there are many "fibs of vision." If we extend our eyes by attaching artificial lenses and other accessories to our real ones (glasses, telescopes, cameras, binoculars, scanning electron microscopes, CAT scans, X-rays, magnetic resonance imaging, ultrasound, radioisotope tracers, lasers, DNA sequencers, and so on), we trust the result a little more. But Missouri is still called the *Show Me!* state, which, as a kind of visual pun, I guess, it displays on its license plates for motorists to see. "The writing is on the wall," a politician says sagely, forgetting temporarily that it could be a forgery nonetheless. We quickly see through people whose characters are transparent. And, heaven knows, we yearn for enlightenment. "I see where you're coming from," one woman says to another in a café, "but you'd better watch out, he's bound to see what you're up to." *See for yourself!* the impatient exclaim to disbelievers. After the Bible's first imperative—"Let there be light"—God viewed each day's toil and "saw that it was good." Presumably, He, too, had to see it to believe it. Ideas dawn on us, if we're

---

Dylan Thomas: (1914–53) controversial Welsh poet who made frequent use of complex and difficult imagery bright enough, not dim-witted, especially if we're visionary. And, when we flirt, though the common phrase sounds quite ghoulish and extreme, we give someone the eye.

We may pretend that beauty is only skin deep, but **Aristotle** was right when he observed that "beauty is a far greater recommendation than any letter of introduction." The sad truth is that attractive people do better in school, where they receive more help, better grades, and less punishment; at work, where they are rewarded with higher pay, more prestigious jobs, and faster promotions; in finding mates, where they tend to be in control of the relationships and make most of the decisions; and among total strangers, who assume them to be interesting, honest, virtuous, and successful. After all, in fairy tales, the first stories most of us hear, the heroes are handsome, the heroines are beautiful, and the wicked **sots** are ugly. Children learn implicitly that good people are beautiful and bad people are ugly, and society restates that message in many subtle ways as they grow older. So perhaps it's not surprising that handsome cadets at West Point achieve a higher rank by the time they graduate, or that a judge is more likely to give an attractive criminal a shorter sentence. In a 1968 study conducted in the New York City prison system, men with scars, deformities, and other physical defects were divided into three groups. The first group received cosmetic surgery, the second intensive counseling and therapy, and the third no treatment at all. A year later, when the researchers checked to see how the men were doing, they discovered that those who had received cosmetic surgery had adjusted the best and were less likely to return to prison. In experiments conducted by corporations, when different photos were attached to the same résumé, the more attractive person was hired. Prettier babies are treated better than homelier ones, not just by strangers but by the baby's parents as well. Mothers snuggle, kiss, talk to, play more with their baby if it's cute; and fathers of cute babies are also more involved with them. Attractive children get higher grades on their achievement tests, probably because their good looks win praise, attention, and encouragement from adults. In a 1975 study, teachers were asked to evaluate the records of an eight-year-old who had a low IQ and poor grades. Every teacher saw the same records, but to some the photo of a pretty child was attached, and to others that of a homely one. The teachers were more likely to recommend that the homely child be sent to a class for retarded children. The beauty of another can be a valuable accessory. One particularly interesting study asked people to look at a photo of a man and a woman, and to evaluate only the man. As it turned out, if the woman on the man's arm was pretty, the man was thought to be more intelligent and successful than if the woman was unattractive.

sot: habitual drunkard

20. In Your Journal: How does beauty affect the way one is treated by others?

Aristotle: (384–322 B.C.) Greek philosopher, who studied under Plato and believed that form is inherent in matter

We are not just lovers of one another's features, of course, but also of nature's. Our passion for beautiful flowers we owe entirely to insects, bats, and birds, since these pollinators and flowers evolved together; flowers use color to attract birds and insects that will pollinate them. We may breed flowers to the pitch of sense-pounding color and smell we prefer, and we've greatly changed the look of nature by doing so, but there is a special gloriousness we find only in nature at its most wild and untampered with. In our "sweet spontaneous earth," as **e. e. cummings** calls it, we find startling and intimate beauties that fill us with ecstasy. Perhaps, like him, we

notice the convulsed orange inch of moon
perching on this silver minute of evening

and our pulse suddenly charges like cavalry, or our eyes close in pleasure and, in a waking faint, we sigh before we know what's happening. The scene is so beautiful it deflates us. Moonlight can reassure us that there will be light enough to find our way over dark plains, or to escape a night-prowling beast. Sunset's fiery glow reminds us of the warmth in which we thrive. The gushing colors of flowers signal springtime and summer, when food is plentiful and all life is radiantly fertile. Brightly colored birds turn us on, sympathetically, with their sexual flash and dazzle, because we're **atavists** at heart and any sex pantomime reminds us of our own. Still, the essence of natural beauty is novelty and surprise. In cummings's poem, it is an unexpected "convulsed orange inch of moon" that awakens one's notice. When this happens, our sense of community widens—we belong not just to one another but to other species, other forms of matter. "That we find a crystal or a poppy beautiful means that we are less alone," John Berger writes in *The Sense of Sight,* "that we are more deeply inserted into existence than the course of a single life would lead us to believe." Naturalists often say that they never tire of seeing the same mile of rain forest, or of strolling along the same paths through the **savanna**. But, if you press them, they inevitably add that there is always something new to behold, that it is always different. As Berger puts it: "beauty is always an exception, always *in despite of*. This is why it moves us." And yet we also respond passionately to the highly organized way of beholding life we call art. To some extent Art is like trapping nature inside a paperweight. Suddenly a locale, or an abstract emotion, is viewable at one's leisure, falls out of flux, can be rotated and considered from different vantage points, becomes as fixed and to that extent as holy as the landscape. As Berger puts it:

atavist: an organism in which a characteristic reappears after several generations of absence

savanna: tropical or subtropical grasslands containing few trees

---

E.E. Cummings: (Edward Estlin) (1894–1962) American poet, known for use of experimental diction and unorthodox typography and punctuation

> All the languages of art have been developed as an attempt to transform the instantaneous into the permanent. Art supposes that beauty is not an exception—is not *in despite of*—but is the basis for an order. . . . Art is an organized response to what nature allows us to glimpse occasionally. . . . the transcendental face of art is always a form of prayer.

Art is more complex than that, of course. Intense emotion is stressful, and we look to artists to feel for us, to suffer and rejoice, to describe the heights of their passionate response to life so that we can enjoy them from a safe distance, and get to know better what the full range of human experience really is. We may not choose to live out the extremes of consciousness we find in **Jean Genet** or **Edvard Munch,** but it's wonderful to peer into them. We look to artists to stop time for us, to break the cycle of birth and death and temporarily put an end to life's processes. It is too much of a **whelm** for any one person to face up to without going into sensory overload. Artists, on the other hand, court that intensity. We ask artists to fill our lives with a cavalcade of fresh sights and insights, the way life was for us when we were children and everything was new.* In time, much of life's spectacle becomes a polite blur, because if we stop to consider every speckle-throated lily we will never get our letters filed or pomegranates bought.

whelm: cover with water; submerge

FOR USE IN DISCUSSION

Questions about Substance

1. "Smells are our dearest kin, but we cannot remember their names," Ackerman writes (2). She also says that smells may "move us so profoundly, in part, because we cannot utter their names" (3). What does she mean by these comments? Are they true of other senses as well?
2. How are smell and memory related, according to Ackerman? Can you think of any instances when something you smelled has triggered a memory?

* As Laurens van der Post observed among the Bushmen of the Kalahari, "I saw the reason why poetry, music and the arts are matters of survival—of life and death to all of us. . . . The arts are both guardians and makers of this chain; they are charged with maintaining the aboriginal movements in the latest edition of man; they make young and immediate what is first and oldest in the spirit of man."

Jean Genet: (1910–1986) French writer who glorified the lives of social outcasts in his work; leading figure in avant-garde theater

Edvard Munch: (1863–1944) Norwegian painter; known for use of contrasting colors to convey strong emotion; greatly influenced impressionism

3. Ackerman makes a lot out of the fact that massage helps babies gain weight (7). Why does she see this as such an important example of the power of touch?
4. Taste "has always had a double meaning," Ackerman writes (10). What is that double meaning? How do each of the two meanings relate to each other?
5. What role does heartbeat play in the experience of hearing?
6. Ackerman quotes David Wright, a deaf man, on how his sight can "translate" what he sees into a kind of sound (14). How are sight and hearing related in this passage? Can you think of other pairs of senses that influence each other significantly?
7. "We find a profound sense of wholeness in the large open structure of classical compositions," Ackerman writes (17). She goes on to list the kinds of visions and feelings she perceives in this kind of music. Can you connect any of the specific metaphoric experiences (e.g., "insurpassable mountains") listed in this passage with any specific kinds of musical instruments or effects?
8. Ackerman suggests that "abstract thinking evolved from our eyes' elaborate struggle to make sense of what they saw" (19). What do you think she means by this?

Questions about Structure and Style

1. On pages 11–12, Ackerman presents a long list of hearing experiences. Can you discern any logic in the way they are presented? Read the long paragraph out loud to yourself. How does it sound?
2. At times, Ackerman likes to provide quantitative information (e.g., the number of breaths we take per day) and scientific study results (e.g., "massaged babies gain weight as much as 50 percent faster than unmassaged babies"). What do these numbers have to do with the subjectivity of sensory experience that Ackerman is primarily interested in? Why does she sometimes turn to data rather than description to articulate the senses? Is this an effective technique?
3. Describe Ackerman's writing style and technique—the types of sentences, paragraphs, language, etc. How does the style connect to the content of what she is trying to say?
4. Ackerman uses the rhetorical technique of description quite a lot in this series of excerpts. Some paragraphs seem exclusively devoted to the enumeration of the details of sensory experience. Are these descriptions Ackerman's evidence for some theoretical conclusion or are they themselves her conclusions?

Multimedia Suggestions

1. Listen to Aaron Copeland's *Appalachian Spring* or a recording of the Shaker song "Simple Gifts." Try to describe the sounds you hear in your own words. Can you hear what Ackerman values in these works? Can you see how the words in "Simple Gifts" are enhanced by the sound?
2. View Errol Morris's 1998 documentary film, *Stairway to Heaven,* which features Temple Grandin, who designed a "squeeze machine" that comforts animals on

the way to slaughter; she based the device on her experience with extrasensory sensitivity related to autism. Can you imagine what it would be like for one or more of your senses to be exponentially more sensitive?

SUGGESTIONS FOR WRITING AND RESEARCH

1. Ackerman is convinced that words, which come from the thinking rather than the feeling part of our brains, are ultimately incapable of describing sensory experience (see pages 3,45). But she is also interested in the way that language uses the senses (e.g., it is "steeped in visual imagery," see page 19). Is language so separate from the senses? If words come from our mouths don't we feel and hear them as much as we think them? Write an essay about the relation between language and the senses, using Ackerman's analyses as a guide. Are you ambivalent about the relationship like Ackerman, or do you see the relationship more clearly?
2. What does Ackerman mean by the phrase "aural landscape" (15)? Aren't landscapes usually visual? What non-visual landscapes does Ackerman present in her writing? Write an essay that examines some of those examples or write your own non-visual landscape, choosing instead smell, touch, hearing, or taste to provide the features of your composition.
3. Compare and contrast two of the five senses as Ackerman presents them. Do you think she is more precise, clinical, emotional, or fanciful about one than the other? Would you add anything to either of the descriptions? Or do the selections complement each other effectively, presenting a richer picture of the senses in combination?

WORKING WITH CLUSTERS

Cluster 1: Sensory Knowledge

Cluster 16: Imagination and Experience

Discipline: The Natural Sciences

Rhetorical Mode: Description

"Circular Reasonings: The Story of the Breast" (from *Woman: An Intimate Geography*)

by Natalie Angier

Natalie Angier began her journalism career as a staff writer for Discover *magazine. After joining* The New York Times *as a science reporter, she won a Pulitzer Prize in the beat reporting category. Angier's first book,* Natural Obsessions: The Search for the Oncogene, *won the Lewis Thomas Award for excellence in writing about the life sciences and was cited as one of the best biology books of the year by* The New York Times, *the American Association for the Advancement of Science, and* Library Journal. *Her second book,* The Beauty of the Beastly: New Views on the Nature of Life, *was cited by the* Library Journal *as one of the best science books of the year. Angier's third book,* Woman: An Intimate Geography *(from which this selection is drawn), was a finalist for the National Book Award and a* New York Times *bestseller, as well as a* New York Times *Notable Book of the Year.*

Nancy Burley, a professor of evolution and ecology at the University of California in Irvine, plays Halloween with birds. She takes male zebra finches and she accessorizes them. A normal, pre-Burley finch is a beautiful animal, red of beak and orange of cheek, his chest a zebra print of stripes, his underwings polka-dotted in orange, and his eyes surrounded by vertical streaks of black and white, like the eyes of a mime artist. One thing the zebra finch does not have is a **crest**, as some species of birds do. So Burley will give a male a crest. She will attach a tall white cap of feathers to his head, turning him into Chef Bird-o-Dee. Or she'll give him a tall red Cat-in-the-Hat cap. His bird legs are normally a neutral shade of grayish beige, so she gives him flashy anklets of red, yellow, lavender, or powder blue. And by altering the visual **pith** of him, his finchness, Burley alters his life. As she has shown in a series of wonderful, amusing, important experiments, female zebra finches have decided opinions about the various **accouterments**. They love the tall white chef caps, and they will clamor to mate with a male so **haberdashed**. Zebra finches ordinarily couple up and abide by a system of shared parental care of nestlings, but if a female is paired with a white-hatted male, she gladly works overtime on child care and allows him to laze—though he doesn't laze but spends his free time philandering. Call the **benighted** wife the bird who mistakes a hat for a mate.

crest: any growth on the head of an animal, such as a comb or a tuft

pith: essential part; gist

accouterment: accessory

haberdasher: professional dealer in men's apparel

benighted: ignorant

1. In Your Journal: What does Angier mean when she refers to "the bird who mistakes a hat for a mate"? What are the reactions of the females to the various adornments of the males?

2. In Your Journal: Through the addition of unnatural adornments, how is Burley able to change the finches' natural lifestyle? Are these changes positive?

But put a male in a tall red cap, and the females turn up their beaks. No trophy he: you can have him, sister. If a red-capped male manages to obtain a mate, he ends up being so busy taking care of his offspring that he has no time for extramarital affairs, and there are no demands for his moonlighting services anyway.

The opposite holds true for leg bands. Dress a male in white ankle rings and he's of scant appeal. Put him in red and he's a lovebird.

Zebra finches have no good reason for being drawn to white toques and red socks. We cannot look at the results of Burley's costume experiments and say, Ah, yes, the females are using the white crest as an indicator that the male will be a good father, or that his genes are robust and therefore he's a great catch. A zebra finch with a white crest can hardly be said to bear superior finch genes when he's not supposed to have a crest in the first place. Instead, the unexpected findings offer evidence of the so-called sensory exploitation theory of mate choice. By this proposal, the white hat takes advantage of a neurophysiological process in the zebra finch's brain that serves some other, unknown purpose but that is easily coopted and aroused. The hat stimulates an **extant** neural pathway, and it lures the female, and the female does not know why, but she knows what she likes. We can understand that impulse, the enticement of an object we deem beautiful. "Human beings have an exquisite **aesthetic** sense that is its own justification," Burley says. "Our ability to appreciate impressionistic painting cannot be called functional. In my mind, that's what we're seeing with the zebra finches. The preferences are aesthetic, not functional. They don't correlate with anything practical."

extant: not destroyed; intact

aesthetic: related or sensitive to beauty

3. In Your Journal: Summarize the "sensory exploitation theory" of mate choice.

Nevertheless, the evidence suggests that if a male finch someday were born with a mutation that gives him a touch of a white thatch, the mutation would spread rapidly through finchdom, possibly becoming accentuated over time, until a bird had the toque by nature that Burley loaned by contrivance. No doubt some researchers in that hypothetical future would assume that the finch's white cap had meaning and was an indicator of zebra finch mettle, and they'd speculate about the **epistemology** of the trait.

epistemology: study or theory of the nature of knowledge

A woman's breasts, I argue, are like Burley's white crests. They're pretty, they're flamboyant, they're irresistible. But they are arbitrary, and they signify much less than we think. This is a contrarian view. Evolutionary theorists have proposed many explanations for the existence of the breast, usually according it a symbolic or functional value, as a signal to men of information they need to know about a potential mate. How can we not give the breast its evolutionary due when it is there in our faces, begging for narrative. "Few issues have been the focus for a wider range of speculation based on fewer facts than the evolutionary origin and physiological function of women's breasts," the biologist Caroline Pond has written. The stories about the breast sound real and persuasive, and they may all have a germ of validity, because we ascribe meaning wherever and however we choose; that is one of the **perquisites** of being human. As the actress Helen Mirren said in the movie *O Lucky Man,* "All religions are equally true."

4. In Your Journal: What is the difference between the aesthetic and the functional? Does the comparison between the aesthetic choices of finches and humans make sense to you?

5. In Your Journal: What does the phrase "begging for narrative" mean?

perquisite: bonus

Still, I will argue that breasts fundamentally are here by accident. They are sensory exploiters. They say little or nothing about a woman's inherent health, quality, or **fecundity**. They are accouterments. If we go looking for breasts and for ways to enhance and display our breasts, to make them stand out like unnatural, almost farcical Barbie-doll missile heads, then we are doing what breasts have always done, which is appeal to an irrational aesthetic sense that has no function but that begs to be amused. The ideal breasts are, and always have been, stylized breasts. A woman's breasts welcome illusion and the imaginative opportunities of clothing. They can be enhanced or muted, as a woman chooses, and their very substance suggests as much: they are soft and flexible, clay to play with. They are funny things; really, and we should learn to laugh at them, which may be easier to do if we first take them seriously.

fecundity: productivity; fertility

6. In Your Journal: What is the relationship between humor and seriousness, according to Angier's logic here?

The most obvious point to be made about the human breast is that it is unlike any other bosom in the primate order. The breasts of a female ape or monkey swell only when she is lactating, and the change is usually so modest that it can be hard to see beneath her body hair. Once the mother has weaned her offspring, her breasts flatten back. Only in humans do the breasts inflate at puberty, before the first pregnancy occurs or could even be sustained, and only in humans do they remain engorged throughout life. In fact, the swelling of the breasts in pregnant and lactating women occurs quite independently of pubertal breast development, and in a more uniform manner: a small-breasted woman's breasts grow about as much during pregnancy, in absolute terms, as a busty woman's breasts do, which is why the temporary expansion is comparatively more noticeable on a small-breasted woman. For all women, maternal **augmentation** results from the proliferation and **distention** of the cells of the ducts and lobules (the dairy equipment), increased blood flow, water retention, and the milk itself. Small-breasted women have the same amount of lactogenic tissue as large-breasted women do—about a teaspoonful per nonlactating breast—and when they lactate, they can make as much milk. Given the functional nature of lactation, it is under selective pressure to follow fairly standardized rules of behavior.

augmentation: make or become larger

distention: stretching; swelling

7. In Your Journal: Why does the human breast "stand out" from those of other primates?

The growth of the aesthetic breast is another thing altogether. Here, it is development of the fatty and connective tissues of the breast that accounts for its mass. As tissues with few cellular responsibilities or functional restrictions, fat and its fibrous netting can follow the whim of fashion and the consequences of sensory exploitation. They can be enlarged, exaggerated, and accentuated without exacting a great cost to their possessors, at least up to a point. In **Philip Roth**'s novel *Sabbath's Theater,* the following exchange occurs between the **eponymous dilettante** of the sewer, Mickey Sabbath, and a small-breasted patient in a mental hospital:

eponymous: giving one's name to a place, tribe, etc.

dilettante: one who dabbles in art, literature, etc. in a superficial way

> "Tits. I understand tits. I have been studying tits since I was thirteen years old. I don't think there's any other organ or body part that evidences so much variation in size as women's tits."
>
> "I *know,*" replied Madeline, openly enjoying herself suddenly and beginning to laugh. "And why is that? Why did God allow this enormous variation in breast size? Isn't it amazing?

Phillip Roth: (1933–) American novelist; author of *Good-bye Columbus* (1959), *Portnoy's Complaint* (1969), *The Breast* (1972), *My Life as a Man, The Counterlife* (1987), *American Pastoral* (1997, Pulitzer Prize), among other books; chiefly concerned with middle class Jewish-American life, the distinction between truth and fiction, and the intellectual details of interpersonal relationships.

> There are women with breasts ten times the size of mine. Or even more. True?"
>
> "That is true."
>
> "People have big noses," she said. "I have a small nose. But are there people with noses ten times the size of mine? Four or five, max. I don't know why God did this to women. . . .
>
> "But I don't think size has to do with milk production," said Madeline. "No, that doesn't solve the problem of what this enormous variation is *for*."

8. In Your Journal: How does the exchange between Mickey Sabbath and Madeleine fit into Angier's discussion of the breast?

As mad Madeline says, the aesthetic breast that is subject to such wide variation in scale is not the mammalian breast gland that ranks as an organ, a necessary piece of anatomy. On the contrary, the aesthetic breast is nonfunctional to the point of being counterfunctional, which is why it strikes us as so beautiful. We are not enticed by the practical. We understand the worthiness of the practical, but we rarely find it beautiful. The large, nonlactating female breast has so much intrinsic, irrational appeal that it almost sabotages itself. We love the hemispheric breast for itself, independent of, and often in spite of, its glandular role. We love it enough that we can be made squeamish by the sight of a breastfeeding woman. It is not the exposure of the breast in public that makes us uncomfortable, for we welcome an extraordinary degree of **décolletage** and want to walk toward it, to gaze at it. Nor is it the reminder of our animal nature, for we can eat many things in public and put pieces of food in a baby's mouth—or a bottle of breast milk, for that matter—without eliciting a viewer's discomfort at the patent display of bodily need. Instead, it is the convergence of the aesthetic and the functional that disturbs and irritates us. When we find the image of a breastfeeding mother lovely or appealing, we do so by negating the aesthetic breast in our minds and focusing on the bond between mother and infant, on the miraculous properties that we imagine human milk to have, or on thoughts of warmth, comfort, and love recalled from our childhood. The maternal breast soothes us and invites us to rest. The aesthetic breast arouses us, grabs us by the collar or the bodice, and so it is used on billboards and magazine covers and everywhere we turn. The two conceptual breasts appeal to distinct pathways. One is ancient and logical, the love of mama and mammary. (Sarah Blaffer Hrdy has written: "The Latin term for breasts, *mammae,* derives from the plaintive cry 'mama,' spontaneously uttered by young children from widely divergent linguistic groups and often conveying a single, urgent message, 'suckle me."') The other pathway is much newer, specific to our species, and it is noisier and more gratuitous. Being strictly human, the aesthetic breast puts on airs and calls itself divine.

9. In Your Journal: Angier suggests that the aesthetic breast is almost self-sabotaging. What does she mean by this?

décolletage: low

10. In Your Journal: Why does the convergence of the aesthetic and the functional disturb and irritate us?

11. In Your Journal: How do the differing tones and words Angier uses to describe functional and aesthetic breasts reveal her perspective on this dichotomy?

Because the display of the beckoning breast is aggressive and **ubiquitous** in the United States, we are said to be unusually, even

ubiquitous: present everywhere at the same time

pedestrian: dull; ordinary

pathologically, breast-obsessed. In other cultures, including parts of Africa and Asia, breasts are **pedestrian.** "From my research in China, it's very clear that the breast is much less sexualized there than it is in American culture," Emily Martin, the cultural historian and author of *Flexible Bodies,* said to me. "It's neither hidden nor revealed in any particular way in women's dress or undergarments. In many villages, women sit in the sun with their breasts exposed, and older women will be out washing clothes with their breasts exposed, and it's all completely irrelevant to erotic arousal." Yet if breast obsession varies in intensity from country to country and era to era, it nonetheless is impressively persistent, and it is not limited to men, or to strictly sexual tableaux. "Everybody loves breasts," Anne Hollander, the author of *Seeing Through Clothes,* told me. "Babies love them, men love them, women love them. The whole world knows that breasts are engines of pleasure. They're great treasures of the human race, and you can't get away from them." The first thing that women did in the fourteenth century, when they broke free of the shapeless drapery of the Christian era, was to flaunt their bosoms. Men shortened their outfits and exposed their legs, women lowered the neckline and tightened the bodice. They pushed their breasts together and up. They took the soft and floppy tissue of the breasts and molded it with corsets and whalebones into firm, projecting globes. "As a fashion gimmick, you can never go wrong with breasts," Hollander says. "They may be deemphasized for a short period, as they were in the sixteenth century, when tiny breasts and thick waists were in vogue, and during the flapper era of the 1920s. But breasts always come back, because we love them so much."

12. In Your Journal: Compare the views of Anne Hollander and Emily Martin. Do they share any logic?

What we love is not the breast per se but the fantasy breast, the aesthetic breast of no practical value. At a recent exhibition of Cambodian sculpture spanning the sixth through fifteenth centuries, I noticed that most of the female deities depicted had breasts that might have been designed by modern plastic surgeons: large, round, and firm. **Helen of Troy**'s breasts were said to be of such flawless, curved, suspended substance that goblets could be cast from their form, as **Ezra Pound** told us in Canto 120: "How to govern is from **Kuan Tze**/but the cup of white gold in Petera/Helen's breast gave that." In the art of ancient India, Tibet, Crete, and elsewhere, the cups never runneth over, and women are shown with

---

Helen of Troy: reputed to be the most beautiful, perfect woman in the world; also the cause of the Trojan War, a ten-year battle waged by the confederated Greeks under Agamemnon against the Trojans (to avenge the abduction of Helen)

Ezra Pound: (1885–1972) American poet, critic, and translator, Pound's major works are "Homage to Sextus Propertius" (1918), *Hugh Selwyn Mauberley* (1920), and the *Cantos* (1925–1960)

celestial breasts, zero-gravity planet breasts, the sorts of breasts I've almost never seen in years of using health-club locker rooms. On real women, I've seen breasts as varied as faces: breasts shaped like tubes, breasts shaped like tears, breasts that flop down, breasts that point up, breasts that are dominated by thick, dark nipples and areolae, breasts with nipples so small and pale they look airbrushed. We erroneously associate floppy breasts with older breasts, when in fact the drooping of the breast can happen at any age; some women's breasts are low-slung from the start. Thus the high, **cantilevered** style of the idealized breast must be considered more than just another expression of a taste for youth.

cantilever: projecting structure anchored to a wall

We don't know why there is such a wide variety of breast sizes, or what exactly controls the growth of the breast, particularly the fat tissue that gives the human breast its bulk. As mammary glands, human breasts follow the standard mammalian pattern. A mammary gland is a modified sweat gland, and milk is highly enriched sweat. Prolactin, the hormone responsible for milk production, predates the evolution of mammals, originally serving to maintain salt and water balance in early vertebrates such as fish—in essence, allowing fish to sweat. In **monotremes,** an order of egg-laying mamals the platypus and the spiny anteater, which are considered the most primitive of living mammals, the milk simply seeps from the gland onto the nippleless surface of the mother's skin, rather as sweat does, and is licked off by the young.

monotreme: an order of egg-laying mammals

Breast tissue begins to develop early, by the fourth week of fetal life. It grows along two parallel milk ridges, ancient mammalian structures that extend from the armpits down to the groin. Males and females both have milk ridges, but only in females do they receive enough hormonal stimulation later in life to achieve complete breastiness. If we were rats or pigs, our twin milk strips would develop into a total of eight teats, to meet the demands of large litters. Mammals such as elephants, cows, goats, and primates, which give birth to only one or two offspring at a time, require only two mammary glands, and so the bulk of the milk strip regresses during fetal development. Among four-legged grazing animals, the teats that grow are located at the hindquarters, where the young can suckle beneath the protective awning of a mother's powerful hind legs and rib cage. In at least one primitive primate, the aye-aye, the twin teats also are situated at the rear end of the mother. But among monkeys, apes, and humans, who either hold their young or carry them clinging to their chests (the better to navigate **arboreally**), the nipples graced with milk are the uppermost two, closest to the armpits.

13. In Your Journal: Why does Angier provide descriptions of the breasts/mammary glands of other mammals?

arboreally: by way of trees

Our potential breasts do not entirely abandon us, though. The milk ridge reminds us of our lineage subcutaneously: breast tissue is distributed

---

⁂ **Kuan Tze**: Chinese poet circa 500 B.C.; famous for the proverb: If you are planning for a year, sow rice./If you are planning for a decade, plant trees./If you are planning for a lifetime, educate the person.

far more extensively than most of us realize, reaching from the collarbone down to the last two ribs and from the breastbone, in the middle of the chest, to the back of the armpit. In some people the milk ridge expresses itself graphically, as extra nipples or entire extra breasts. Recalling her years as a lingerie saleswoman, an essayist in the *New York Times Magazine* wrote about a customer looking for a bra that would fit her unusual figure. The woman bared her breasts to the essayist, Janifer Dumas. The woman was a modern-day Artemis, the goddess of the hunt, who often is portrayed with multiple breasts. In this case, Artemis had three equal-sized breasts, the standard two on either side of her thorax and the third directly below the left one. Dumas found the perfect item, a "bralette," similar to a sports bra but with a more relaxed fit, no underwire, and a wide elastic band to hug the rib cage. "It occurred to me that this was also the type of bra I sold to women with recent mastectomies," Dumas wrote, "a piece of lingerie designed for comfort, and, as it turned out, able to accommodate more or less."

primordial: first created or developed; existing in its original state

Primordial breast tissue arises early in embryogenesis, yet the breast is unusual among body parts in that it remains primordial until puberty or later. No other organ, apart from the uterus, changes so dramatically in size, shape, and function as the breast does during puberty, pregnancy, and lactation. It is because the breast must be poised to alter its contours repeatedly throughout adulthood, swelling and shrinking with each new mouth to feed, that it is prone to turning cancerous. The genetic controls that keep cell growth in check elsewhere in the **corpus** are relaxed in the breast, giving malignancy an easy foothold.

corpus: (Latin) body

14. In Your Journal: Are you surprised by the relationship between breast function and cancer?

The aesthetic breast develops in advance of the glandular one. Early in adolescence, the brain begins secreting regular bursts of hormones that stimulate the ovaries. The ovaries in turn discharge estrogen, and estrogen encourages the body to lay down fat "depots" in the breast. That adipose tissue is suspended in a gelatinous matrix of connective fibers that extend from the muscle of the chest wall to the underside of the breast skin. Connective tissue can stretch and stretch, to accommodate as much fat as the body inserts between its fibers; the connective tissue's spring gives the breast its bounce. Estrogen is necessary to the aesthetic breast, but it is not sufficient; the hormone alone does not explain the wide variability in breast size. A woman with large breasts does not necessarily have higher estrogen levels than a small-breasted woman. Rather, the tissue of the breast is more or less responsive to estrogen, a sensitivity determined in part by genetic makeup. Among the sensitive, a very small amount of estrogen fosters an impressive bosom. Estrogen-sensitive women who take birth control pills may discover that they need bigger bras, while the estrogen-insensitive can swallow oral contraceptives by the foilful and find their breasts unmoved. Even some children are extremely sensitive to estrogen. Berton Roueche, the great medical writer, recounted the story of a six-year-old boy who began growing breasts. Eventually, the source of the **hypertrophy** was traced to his vitamin tablets. A single stamping machine had been used to punch out the vitamins and estrogen pills. "Think of the minute amount of estrogen the stamping machine passed on to the vitamin tablets," Roueche wrote. "And what a profound effect it had." The boy's breasts retreated on cessation of the vitamin tablets, and his parents could breathe again.

hypertrophy: excessive development of a body part

Conversely, **androgens** such as testosterone can inhibit breast adiposity. Women who are genetically insensitive to androgen may grow very large breasts. Men whose gonads fail to produce enough testosterone sometimes suffer from **gynecomastia.** Without testosterone to keep breast growth in check, the men's small amount of estrogen has the opportunity to lay down selective depots of fat hurriedly, demonstrating once again that the line between maleness and femaleness is thin—as thin as the fetus's **bipotential genital ridge,** as thin as the milk ridge in all of us. Yet androgens don't entirely explain discrepancies in breast size among women either. Many women with comparatively high testosterone levels, women whose visible mustaches and abundant armpit hair make it clear that they are not insensitive to the androgens coursing through them, nonetheless have full frontal shelves. Thyroid hormones, stress hormones, insulin, growth hormone—all leave their smudgy fingerprints on **mammogenesis.** In sum, we don't know what makes the aesthetic breast. We don't have the hormonal recipe for the universal **Mae West** breast. If science fiction television is any indication, though, in the future, the heartbreak of "micromastia" (plastic-surgeon-speak for small breasts) will be surmounted, and if our brains don't get bigger, our breasts surely will. Today, the average nonlactating breast weighs two thirds of a pound and measures about four inches across and two and a half inches from chest wall to nipple tip. The average brassiere size is a 36B, and it has been since the modern bra was invented about ninety years ago. On television shows like *Star Trek,* however, every woman of every race, whether human, Vulcan, Klingon, or Borg, is as bold in bust as in spirit, and no cup less than C will be cast. Estrogen also helps spur the elaboration of the practical breast, the glandular tissue that presumably will soon secrete its clouded, honied sweat. A series of firm, rubbery ducts and lobes begin threading their way through the fat and ligamentous glue. Each breast usually ends up with between five and nine lobes, where the milk is generated, and each lobe has its independent duct, the conduit that carries the milk to the nipple. The lobes are subdivided into about two dozen lobules, which look like tiny clusters of grapes. The lobes and lobules are distributed fairly evenly throughout the breast, but all the ducts lead to a single destination, the nipple. As the ducts

androgen: steroid hormone that maintains masculine characteristics

gynecomastia: abnormal enlargement of the breast in males

bipotential genital ridge: fold in an embryo that eventually becomes a gonad—a male or female sex organ; at the bipotential stage, the sex of the embryo is indeterminate

mammogenesis: breast development

15. In Your Journal: Angier presents a lengthy discussion of the various aspects and science of breast size. Why?

Mae West: (1892–1980) buxom American stage and movie comedienne; famous for the quip "Come up and see me sometime" converge on the nipple, curling and bending like snakes or strands of ivy, their diameters widen. The circuitry of lactation follows the hydrodynamic pattern that we recognize from trees, or the veins in a leaf, or the blood vessels in the body. The lobes and lobules are the foliage, the fruits and leaves, while the ducts are the branches, thickening into a braid of trunks. But while in a tree or the body's vasculature the fluid of life is pumped from the widest conduit out to the narrowest vessel or vein, here the milk is generated in each tiny lobular fruit and pulsed to the spacious pipeline below. The ducts perforate the skin of the nipple, and though these portals ordinarily are concealed by the warty folds of the nipple tip, when a woman is nursing her nipple balloons out and looks like a watering can, each ductal hole visible and visibly secreting milk.

16. In Your Journal: Does the descriptive analogy "dairy farmers" enhance the reader's understanding of Angier's scientific explanation?

17. In Your Journal: Angier suggests that the functional and aesthetic breasts are separate from each other. Why?

bon vivant: hedonist

kiosk: refreshment booth or newsstand

The ducts and lobules do not fully mature until pregnancy, when they proliferate, thicken, and differentiate. Granular plugs the consistency of ear wax, which normally keep the ducts sealed up, begin breaking down. The lobules sprout microlobules, the alveoli. The dairy farmers commandeer the breast. They push fat out of the way to make more room for themselves. The breast gains as much as a pound while lactating. The areola, that pigmented bull's-eye surrounding the nipple, also changes markedly in pregnancy. It darkens and seems to creep down the hillock of the breast, like lava spreading slowly from the peak of a volcano. The areola is permeated by another set of modified sweat glands, the little goosebumps called Montgomery's glands, and the bumps multiply in the maternal breast and exude lubricating moisture to make the sensation of suckling bearable. After weaning, the lobules atrophy, the ducts regress, the areola retreats, and the fat reclaims dominion over the breast—more or less. Women who breastfeed their children often complain that their breasts never recover their former bounce and bulk. The fat grows lazy and fails to reinfiltrate the spaces from which it was edged out by the gland. The aesthetic breast is a **bon vivant,** after all, a party favor. For reliability, look to the ducts and lobules. They'll return when needed, and they're not afraid to work up a sweat.

Breasts weigh a few ounces in fact and a few tons in metaphor. As Marilyn Yalom describes admirably in her cultural study *A History of the Breast,* the breast is a communal **kiosk,** open to all pronouncements and cranks, and the endorsements of the past are easily papered over with the homilies of today. The withered tits of witches and devils represented the wages of lust. In Minoan statues dating from 1600 B.C., priestesses are shown with bare, commanding breasts and snakes wrapped around each arm. The snakes strain their heads toward the viewer, their extended tongues echoing the erect nipples of the figurine, as though to warn that the powerful bosom they bracket might as soon dispense poison as love. The breast is a bralette, able to accommodate more or less. The multi-breasted goddess seen in many cultures projects tremendous strength. So too do the Amazons, those mythical female warriors who lived apart from men, consorting with them once a year solely for the sake of being impregnated, and who reared their daughters but slayed, crippled, or abandoned their sons. The Amazons are most famed for their self-inflicted mastectomies, their willingness to cut off one breast to improve their archery skills and thus to resist conquest by the male hordes surrounding them. For men, Yalom writes, "Amazons are seen as monsters, **viragos,** unnatural women who have misappropriated the masculine warrior role. The missing breast creates a terrifying asymmetry: one breast is retained to nurture female off-spring, the other is removed so as to facilitate violence against men." For women, the Amazon represents an **inchoate** wish, a nostalgic longing for the future. "The removal of the breast and the acquisition of 'masculine' traits suggests this mythic Amazon's desire to be bisexual, both a nurturing female and an aggressive male, with the nurturance directed exclusively toward other women and the aggression directed exclusively toward men." A softened variant of the Amazon icon occurred in eighteenth-century France, when the figure of Liberty often was shown with one breast clothed, the other bared, her willingness to reveal her breast (or at least her indifference to her temporary state of **dishabille**) evidence of her commitment to the cause. More recently, women who have had a breast surgically removed for the treatment of cancer have assumed the mantle of the Amazon warrior and proudly, angrily publicized their naked, asymmetrical torsos on magazine covers and in advertisements. Where the breast once was, now there is a diagonal scar, crossing the chest like a bow or a **bandolier**, alarming, thrilling, and beautiful in its fury.

virago: domineering woman

inchoate: being only partly in existence or operation

18. In Your Journal: How do the Amazons use their breasts to emphasize their power and way of life?

dishabille: state of being dressed in a careless manner; half-dressed

bandolier: belt worn by a soldier that carries cartridges

The breast has been used like a cowbrand, to denote possession. In Rembrandt's famous portrait *The Jewish Bride,* the husband, considerably the elder of the two, is shown with his right hand covering the bride's left breast, claiming her, including her within his gentle, paternal jurisdiction, and her hand reaches up to graze his groping one—though whether as an expression of modesty, concurrence, or hesitation is left gorgeously unclear. In nineteenth-century America, female slaves being put up for auction were photographed barechested, to underscore their status as beasts to be bought. In driving a metaphor home, breasts were beaten, tortured, and mutilated. In the seventeenth century, women accused of witchcraft often had their breasts hacked off before they were burned at the stake. When Anna Pappenheimer, a Bavarian woman who was the daughter of gravediggers and latrine cleaners, was condemned as a witch, her breasts were not merely cut off but stuffed into her mouth and then into the mouths of her two grown sons, a grotesque mockery of Pappenheimer's maternal role.

19. In Your Journal: Why do you think that Angier would refer to the absence of the breast and the presence of the scar as "alarming, thrilling, and beautiful in its fury"? What does this statement reflect about the functional and the aesthetic roles of the breast?

20. In Your Journal: Why does Angier include such violent anecdotes in her discussion?

Early scientists too had to have their say on the breast. In the eighteenth-century, Linnaeus, the ever-colorful Swedish taxonomist, paid the breast a dubious honor by naming an entire class after it: Mammalia, literally "of the breast," a term of Linnaeus's invention. As Londa Schiebinger has described, Linneaus could have chosen from other features that mammals were known at the time to have in common. We could have been classified as Pilosa, the hairy ones, or as Aurecaviga, the hollow-eared ones (a reference to the distinctive three-boned structure of the mammalian middle ear), or as bearers of a four-chambered heart (term uncoined and perhaps uncoinable). But despite the derision of some of Linnaeus's contemporaries, we and our fuzzy, **viviparous** kin became mammals. It was the **Enlightenment**, and Linnaeus had a point to make, and so again the breast was called upon to service metaphor. Zoologists accepted that humans were a type of animal, as uncomfortable as the notion was and remains. A taxon was needed that would link humans to other species. Whatever feature Linnaeus chose to highlight as the bond between us and them inevitably would become the **synecdoche** of our beastliness. All mammals are hairy, but men are hairier than women, so Pilosa wouldn't do. The structure of the ear is too dull to merit immortalization through **nomenclature**. The breast, however, has romance and resonance, and best of all, it is most highly articulated in women. In the same volume in which Linnaeus introduced the term *Mammalia,* he also gave us our species name, *Homo sapiens,* man of wisdom, the category distinguishing humans from all other species. "Thus, within Linnaean terminology, a female characteristic (the lactating mamma) ties humans to brutes, while a traditionally male characteristic (reason) marks our separateness," Schiebinger writes. Thinkers of the Enlightenment advocated the equality and natural rights of all men, and some women of the time, including Mary Wollstonecraft and Abigail Adams, John's wife, argued that women too should be given their due rights—enfranchisement, for example, or the rights to own property and divorce a brutal spouse. The husbands of the Enlightenment smiled with tolerance and sympathy, but they were not prepared to peep over that political precipice. Through zoology and the taxonomic reinforcement of woman's earthiness, rational men found convenient justification for postponing matters of women's rights until woman's reason, her *sapientia,* was fully established. (Interestingly, though, human milk has often been characterized as the purest and most ethereal of body fluids, the least brutish aspect of a woman.)

viviparous: producing living young from within the body rather than from laying eggs

synecdoche: figure of speech in which a part is used for the whole or the whole for a part, the special for the general or the general for the special (e.g., to call a single police officer "the law")

nomenclature: system of names

In the nineteenth century, some scientists used the breast as **phrenologists** have used the skull, to demarcate and rank the various human races. Certain breasts were more equal than others. The European breast was drawn as a hemisphere standing at full attention—meet the smart and civilized breast. The breast of an African woman was portrayed as flabby and pendulous, like the udder of a goat. In abolitionist literature,

phrenologist: one who believes character traits can be discerned from the contours of the skull

21. In Your Journal: What does Angier mean by the statement: "Certain breasts are more equal than others"?

Enlightenment: scientific and intellectual trend of the 17th century that fostered the belief in natural law, universal order, and confidence in human reason that spread to influence all of 18th-century society, contributing to a secular view of the world and a general sense of progress and perfectibility; also known as the Age of Reason illustrations of female slaves gave them high, round, sympathetic breasts—the melanized counterparts to the pop-up breasts of the slaves' tightly cinched mistresses.

Linnaeus hog-tied us to other mammals by our possession of teats, but our breasts, we know, are ours alone. Evolutionary thinkers have known it too, and they have given us a wide selection of justifications for the human breast. As Caroline Pond says, there is little evidence to support any of the theories. We don't have a clue when in human evolution breasts first began their rise. Breasts don't fossilize. We don't know if they appeared before we lost our body hair or after, and in any event we don't know when—or why—we lost our body hair. But breasts are such a prominent feature of a woman's body that scientists keep staring at them, looking for clues. They are baffled by breasts, and they should be.

Men don't have breasts, but they like to stake their claim on breasts, to grope their Jewish bride, and to feel they had a hand in inventing them. We must not be surprised if many evolutionary theories assume that breasts arose to talk to men. By far the most famous explanation in this genre comes from Desmond Morris, the British zoologist, who in 1967 wrote a spectacularly successful book, *The Naked Ape,* in which he presented a metaphor **nonpareil**, of breasts as buttock mimics. You've probably heard this theory in some form. It's hard to escape it. Like the Rolling Stones, it refuses to retire. As originally conceived, the theory rested on a sequence of assumptions, the first being that men and women needed to form a pair bond—better known as marriage—to raise children. The pair bond required the cultivation of sustained intimacy between partners, which meant intercourse was best done face to face rather than in the anonymous doggy-style position presumed to be the copulatory technique of our prehuman ancestors. To that end, the clitoris migrated forward, to give early women the incentive to seek frontal sex. For the gentlemen, the breast arose as an inspiration to modify their technique, offering a **recapitulation ventrally** of a body part they had so coveted from behind. In subsequent books, Morris has repeated the theory, illustrating it with photos comparing a good set of female buttocks with a good set of cleavaged knockers.

nonpareil: having no equal; peerless

22. In Your Journal: What is the purpose of Angier's analogy between Morris's theory and the Rolling Stones?

recapitulate: restate briefly

ventral: of or relating to the belly

Maybe he's right about breasts looking somewhat like buttocks, but who's to say that rounded buttocks didn't develop to imitate breasts, or that the two developed in tandem for their intrinsic aesthetic appeal? The high, rounded human buttocks are unlike the flat and narrow rump of many other primates. Morris and others argue that the gluteal hemisphericity surely came first, because the evolution of upright posture demanded greater musculature in the rump. The vertical configuration also created an area where energy could be stored as fat without interfering with basic movements, Timothy Taylor writes in *The Prehistory of Sex.* Moreover, upright posture introduced a need for alluringly shaped female

23. In Your Journal: Why does Morris feel that "gluteal hemisphericity" must have preceded the development of breasts?

buttocks, Taylor says. When a woman stands up, you can't see her vulva. The presentation of the vulva serves as an important sexual signal in many other primate species. If a woman isn't going to be flashing her vagina, she requires some other sexual signal rearguard, and the buttocks thus became accentuated. To ensure that she caught men's attention coming and going, the woman's breasts soon swelled too. Which is fine, except that women find a high, rounded butt on a man as alluring as a man does on a woman, and women notice it on women, and men on men. Beautiful buttocks are a thing to behold, but they need not have assumed their globular contours to provide a home for a large muscle. Instead, the curviness of the human rump on both sexes could well have been selected as another example of sensory exploitation, and of our preference for the curved and generous over the straight and narrow. The breast might not imitate the buttock so much as the two converge on a common theme.

There are other reasons to be skeptical about the development of breasts as an encouragement to pursue frontal sex. Several other primates, including bonobos and orangutans, also copulate face to face, and the females wear no sexual badges on their chests, no clever replicas of their narrow rumps or swollen vulvas. Nevertheless, they are sought after—in the case of bonobos, many times a day. What is ***P. paniscus***'s secret, and does she have a catalogue?

P. paniscus: bonobo ape species

Because breasts, when not serving as visual lures, play an essential role in reproduction, many theorists have assumed that they developed to advertise to men some aspect of a woman's fecundity. Breasts certainly proclaim that a female is of reproductive age, but so do many other things—pubic hair, the widening of the pelvic bone, the wafting of hormonally activated body odors. A woman needs a certain percentage of body fat to sustain a pregnancy. Breasts are two parcels of fat. Perhaps they proclaim that a woman is nutritionally well stocked and so can bear and suckle children, a point that a prehistoric man, surveying the options among a number of calorically borderline women, conceivably would want to know. Yet breasts, for all their prominence, represent a small fraction of the body's total fat mass—4 percent, on average—and their size generally changes less in proportion to a woman's weight gain or loss than other fat depots of the body, like the adipose of the thighs, buttocks, and upper arms; thus breast fatness is not a great indicator of a woman's health or nutritional status. And as we saw above, breast size has nothing to do with a woman's reproductive or lactational capabilities and so is a poor signal of her maternal worth. Others suggest that breasts evolved to deceive, to confuse a man about a woman's current ovulatory status or whether she is pregnant or not, the better to mask issues of paternity and inhibit the tendency of men to kill infants they know are not their own. Why a man would be attracted to such devious commodities is unclear, unless we assume that he is predisposed for another reason to love the look of a breast.

24. In Your Journal: What does Angier mean by "calorically borderline women"?

Women have laid claim to breasts too. Meredith Small recasts the idea of breasts as mobile pantries, but sees them as designed to help women rather than to assure men that they are fertile. "A large breast might be simply a fat storage area for females who evolved under nutritional stress," she writes. "Ancestral humans walked long and far in their search for food, and they needed fat for years of lactation." Again, though, breasts are not the most liquid of fat assets, and they are surprisingly stingy about releasing their energy stores on demand. When a woman is lactating, lipid energy from the hips and thighs is far more readily mobilized than the fat of the breasts, even though the breast fat is much closer to the means of milk production. Helen Fisher proposes that breasts are a woman's pleasure chests, the swollen scaffolding beneath the erotogenic nipples ensuring that the breasts are caressed, sucked, and pressed against for maximum stimulation. Yet not all women have sensitive breasts, nor do they necessarily adore chronic fondling. "I've had a lot of experience in life," says a seventy-five-year-old woman in *Breasts: Women Speak*. "I've come to the conclusion that women get breast cancer because men handle their breasts *too much*." At the same time, many men have very sensitive nipples, and they only wish women were more inclined to take a lick now and then.

If not for the woman, then maybe for the child. Elaine Morgan, an original and brave thinker who continues almost single-handedly to push the aquatic ape theory of human evolution, has submitted several breast lines. She believes that humans spent part of their evolutionary development immersed in water, that we are part **pinniped**, part ape. One excuse for breasts, then, might be that they were Mae Wests, as the British soldiers of World War II called their life jackets—flotation devices that infants could cling to as they nursed. More recently, Morgan has suggested that hairlessness, another presumed legacy of our nautical phase, gave birth to the breast. Young monkeys and apes can cling to their mother's chest hair while they suckle, she says. Human infants have nothing to grab. In addition, they're so helpless, they can't lift their heads up to reach the nipple. The nipple has to come to them. Consequently, the nipple of the human breast is situated lower on the chest than the teat of a monkey is, and it is no longer anchored tightly to the ribs, as it is in monkeys. "The skin of the breast around the nipple becomes more loosely-fitting to make it more maneuverable, leaving space beneath the looser skin to be occupied by glandular tissue and fat," Morgan concludes. "Adult males find the resulting species-specific contours sexually stimulating, but the instigator and first beneficiary of the change was the baby." It's the empty-closet theory of the breast: if it's there, it will be stuffed. Apart from the lack of any evidence to support the aquatic ape theory, the **putative** benefits of the loosened nipple to nursing are not obvious. A woman must hold her baby to her breast, or prop the baby up with pillows, or strap the infant in place with a baby

pinniped: aquatic mammal that uses fin-like flippers to move

25. In Your Journal: Do some of the provided explanations for the use/existence of breasts seem far-fetched to you? Which ones? Are any of them more credible than the others?

putative: commonly accepted

sling (which is how the vast majority of women in the developing world nurse their infants). If a mother were to spend much time hunched over a baby in her lap like Daisy the cow, her nipple dangling in the infant's mouth, she might find it difficult ever to straighten back to bipedalism again.

The aesthetic breast won't lift a finger to help you.

26. In Your Journal: What rhetorical strategy is served in this sentence: "The aesthetic breast won't lift a finger to help you"?

Plato called the psyche a sphere. **Carl Jung** said that the circle symbolizes the self. The Buddha sat on a lotus of eight radially symmetrical petals. The circular **mandala** signifies the unity of the conscious and unconscious minds. In the great Gothic cathedrals of Europe, where every window is stained with the tears and hymns of every pilgrim and atheist to behold it, the highest artistry is displayed in the rose windows, the symbolic circles of heaven. The crowning achievement of **Filippo Brunelleschi**, father of the Renaissance, was the **Duomo**, which returned to the world the forgotten joy of the dome, the conjoiner of the sacred and the humane. To encircle is to love and to possess, as we acknowledge today with a wedding ring. Shakespeare's theater was constructed around a circular stage, and it was named the Globe.

mandala: representation of the universe, featuring a configuration of geometric shapes and a deity or deities

Duomo: cathedral in Florence designed by Brunelleschi

We live life **vertiginously**, attending to the round. Who knows why. It may have all started with the face. The first thing that a newborn pays visual attention to is not the breast, which the infant cannot adjust its focus to see from its ringside position, but the mother's face. Human faces are round, much rounder than those of other adult apes. The white of the human eye, which is absent in our simian cousins, serves to emphasize the roundness of the iris. When we smile, our cheeks become round, and the uplifted corners of the mouth and the downturned corners of the eyebrows create an image of a circle within a circle. Only humans universally interpret the smile as a friendly gesture. Among most primates, a smile is a grimace, an expression of threat or fear.

vertiginously: in a revolving manner; in a dizzy state

27. In Your Journal: Why does Angier spend so much time discussing the circular attributes of the human body and the general human affinity for roundness? How does this discussion relate to the title of the essay?

Or it may have all begun with fruit, the mainstay of our foraging years, the brass rings we reached for, the fantasy of abundance. Fruit is round, and so are nuts and tubers and most of the edible parts of plants. Or was it our reverence for light? The sources of all light, the sun and the moon, are round, and the rounder they are, the brighter they shine. They die in each cycle by the degradation of their celestial geometry. As long as we have been human, we have observed the preponderance of the circle and the link

---

Plato: (427?–347 B.C.) Greek philosopher and student of Socrates who emphasized the unity of virtue and knowledge

Carl Jung: (1875–1961) Swiss psychiatrist influenced by Freud and founder of analytical psychology; coined the term "collective unconscious"

Filippo Brunelleschi: (1377–1446) first great architect of the Italian Renaissance between that which is round and that which defines us. The circle illuminates and delimits. We can't escape it. We can't get enough of it.

The breast is the body's most transparent way of paying homage to the circle. Over the centuries, the human breast has been compared to all the round things we know and love—to apples, melons, suns, moons, cherries, faces, eyes, Orient pearls, globes, mandalas, worlds within worlds. Yet to focus exclusively on the breast is to neglect the other ways in which the human body commemorates and resonates with roundness. The buttocks, of course, are round and conspicuous. Our long human necks curve into our shoulders, a parabola of grace when seen from behind. Our muscles too assume a species-specific roundness and prominence. Other animals become extremely, densely muscular without forming the projecting curves seen on human athletes. Many creatures can outrun us, but none have our distinctive calf muscles, which, like the buttocks, are curved on men and women alike. The biceps of the arms can look breastlike. So too can the deltoids, the muscles of the shoulders. Highly developed chest muscles give the impression of cleavaged breasts. The curvaceous sensuality of the muscular male was not lost on the ancient Greeks, nor on Michelangelo, nor on the photographer Bruce Weber, who in his pictures for Calvin Klein underwear gave us a nude male chest as **vociferous** as the conventional female cleavage shot. Dancers of both sexes, who have radiant, muscular bodies that are as if drawn with spirographs, emphasize and consecrate the curve through movement. To defy the choreographed curve is to renounce, mock, or affront the pretty.

vociferous: causing or given to loud outcry

We are attracted to well-defined curves. It has been suggested that humans shed their body hair better to reveal the curviness of female breasts and hips, but why then would we not have had a more targeted hair loss around the areas in question? Instead, the aesthetic benefits of **depilation** must be viewed globally. The entire body becomes the **proscenium**, to expose whatever curves we have to offer. Our options are in part determined by our physiology and our hormonal **milieu**. Women are rich in estrogen, the hormone that controls the maturation and release of the egg each month, and estrogen is adept at laying down fat depots. The primate breast was capable of supporting expansion; it was primed to be curved. Men are moneyed in testosterone, which is necessary to sperm production, and testosterone helps lay down muscle. In neither case do we need our curves. We can be strong and fertile, swift and milky, without them. Still, mysteriously, we have curves and we are drawn to curves, and to those who wave them in our faces. We are drawn to rounded breasts and rounded muscles. We are drawn to prominent cheekbones, those facial breasts, or are they facial buttocks, or minibiceps, or apples, or faces within faces?

depilation: hair loss/removal

proscenium: part of a stage in front of the curtain

milieu: environment; setting

Here I must note that the benefits of being considered attractive are not limited to the ability to attract mates. Attractive people attract allies. As an extremely social species, dependent on the group for survival, we can accrue advantages to ourselves and our offspring in a series of harmonics that reinforce and amplify one another. If you have friends, you have defenders, and your children have defenders. Attractiveness is as often used for the purposes of displaying to the members of your own sex as it is to arouse the interest of the opposite sex. Display can be extremely competitive, but it can also be solicitous. Women display for each other, and dress for each other, and are concerned about what other women think of their appearance. We conventionally interpret such preening as competitive, a bit catty, and we assume that the ultimate goal is to show the gals who can win the boys. But female display also can be affiliative, implying the possibility of an alliance. In that sense, women may have "chosen" breasts on each other as much as men chose them on women. And the breast of choice for exhibition and persuasion is not the soft, sloping maternal breast or the virginal rose-bud breast, but the strong, prominent breast, the breast that can practically be flexed like a muscle, the breast that stands out in a crowd.

28. In Your Journal: What does Angier mean when she says that "women may have 'chosen' breasts"?

The zebra finch is a natural aesthete, but the bird has its structural and intellectual limitations. It can't fabricate its own hats. If it could, it might become reckless. It might start building crests as high as the hair of Marie Antoinette. Or it might thread the crest with strands of Lycra, to abet its bounce and waggle and to leave no finch's visual cortex unexploited. A crest would be a perfect trait to accentuate. There's not much you can do with a leg band, but a feather cap can be made to crow: Look at me! No, look at *me*.

We have not only taste but the wherewithal to indulge, inflect, and abuse it. Breasts, like crests, lend themselves to manipulation. They are ideal accessories, and we have exploited our sensory exploiters. Breasts are much easier to work with than any other body part. They are soft and compressible. They can be lifted up, squeezed together, thrust forward, padded out, prostheticized. Cinching in the waist is hard, though women have done it, and have fainted and died from the effort; hoisting up the breasts is relatively painless. The fetishization of the breast goes hand in hand with our status as clothinged apes. Not only did necklines plunge in the fourteenth century, the first corsets elevated the breasts to the occasion. More often than not, the ideal breast is an invented breast. Decolletage, the tushy breast, is an artifact of clothing. Naked breasts don't dance cheek to cheek—they turn away from each other. Breasts vary in size and shape to an outlandish degree, but they can be whipped into an impressive conformity, and because we are human and we can't leave anything alone, we have whipped away. We have played on the eye's tendency to follow the round, to be attracted by the hemisphere, and we have inflated and mollycoddled it.

29. In Your Journal: How is it that the "ideal breast is an invented breast"?

We can take some comfort from the fact that men's curves are under increasing pressure to expand as well. The introduction of the Nautilus machine has ushered in the era of the attainable **David**, whose chest and arms are breaking out with breasts all over. We can wring our hands raw in **priggish** despair over the contemporary emphasis on surface and our homogenized appraisal of beauty, but though the technology is new, the obsession is congenital. We've been scolded for our vanity since **Narcissus** discovered the reflective properties of water. We have been threatened with visions of withered witches' tits if we refuse to mend our ways and stop worrying about our bodies or staring at the moons and melons of others.

priggish: acting as one who irritates through rigid observance of propriety

To say that all breasts are pretty is like saying that all faces are pretty: it's true but false. Yes, we all have our **winsome** components, and we are genotypically and anatomically unique and uniqueness has its merit. At the same time, we know beauty when we see it. Beauty is a **despot**, but so what? Our mistake is in attributing grander meaning to a comely profile than it already has. High cheekbones, a high butt, and a high bosom are nice, but none should be viewed as the **sine qua non** of womanliness. If breasts had something important to say, they would be much less variable and whimsical than they are. They would be like mere mammary glands, a teaspoon per breast per woman. If breasts could talk, they would probably tell jokes—every light-bulb joke in the book.

winsome: charming

despot: ruler with absolute power and authority; person exercising power tyrannically

sine qua non: (Latin) indispensable condition, element, or factor; something essential

FOR USE IN DISCUSSION

Questions about Substance

1. Caroline Pond is quoted as saying that, "Few issues have been the focus for a wider range of speculation based on fewer facts than the evolutionary origin and physiological function of women's breasts"(27). Does Angier's essay contribute to such speculation or does it intend to rise above it? Explain.
2. Angier argues that, "we ascribe meaning wherever and however we choose; that is one of the perquisites of being human"(27). Angier follows up her point with a quote from the movie *O Lucky Man*: "All religions are equally true"(27).

David: 1504 sculpture of *David* by Michelangelo Buonarroti, who portrayed David in a classical style, giving him a perfectly proportioned body and musculature

Narcissus: in classical mythology, a boy who fell in love with his own image reflected in a pool, and was transformed into a flower

Is Angier comparing science to religion? How can scientific method be related to religious belief?

3. On page 29, Angier shifts from using the term "functional" to using the term "maternal" to describe the non-aesthetic breast. Examine this substitution. Are these terms synonyms?
4. Angier is interested in some of the metaphoric ways breasts are described. In society at large, what sorts of metaphors are used to describe breasts? What do these metaphors imply about breasts? What do they imply about the society that uses them?
5. How can it be both true and false to say that "all faces [or breasts] are pretty"(43)?

Questions about Structure and Style

1. Why would Angier open an essay about human breasts with anecdotes about finch mating patterns?
2. Why does Angier announce her view as a "contrarian"(27)? What does this announcement suggest is her target audience for this essay?
3. Note Angier's pattern of presenting, exemplifying, and then knocking down theories about the function of the breast throughout this essay. What does she accomplish with this method? Discuss some specific examples and rate their effectiveness.
4. "If breasts could talk, they would probably tell jokes— every light-bulb joke in the book" (43). How fitting is this sentence as the last word of Angier's essay?

Multimedia Suggestions

1. A&E premiered a documentary about the breast called *Cleavage* in December 2002, which is now available on VHS and DVD. View the film and think about how Angier would respond to this cultural history of the aesthetic breast.
2. Most women's magazines feature breast augmentation ads in their back pages. Survey some of these ads and see how they frame society's apparent *need* for the aesthetic breast. Do they mask the aesthetic purpose of breast implants with self-esteem rhetoric or promises for an improved sex life? What would such advertisers make of Angier's argument?
3. The "La Leche League" (*http://www.lalecheleague.org/*) is an organization that provides information on and support for breast-feeding women. Compare the way it talks about and presents the functional breast with the way Victoria's Secret (*http://www.victoriassecret.com*) celebrates the aesthetic breast.

SUGGESTIONS FOR WRITING AND RESEARCH

1. The breast—especially the functional breast—is an embarrassing topic to read about or discuss for just about anyone but a gynecologist or mammography technician. Many women are discouraged from breastfeeding in public, mas-

tectomy patients get prosthetic breasts or implants to cover up the evidence of their surgeries, and girls are rushed to a department store for a bras as soon as they begin to develop breasts. Simultaneously, the aesthetic breast is everywhere. Victoria's Secret ads exaggerate the aesthetic breast to ridiculous proportions, breast augmentation is common even among teenagers now, and breasts are used to sell everything from yogurt to carburetors. Discuss your own observations of this phenomenon and write an essay about the "social life" of breasts that is informed by Angier's scientific study. Using her primary distinction between the aesthetic and functional, address the ways that mainstream culture mirrors the theories of evolutionary biologists.

2. Compare the breast to another body part that seems to have both an aesthetic and a functional role (e.g., hair, ears, buttocks, etc.). Compare and contrast your choice with breasts. While borrowing concepts and vocabulary from Angier will be helpful, you may also find it helpful to do some outside research so that you know what the evolutionary theories about your choice of body part are.
3. Angier is a science writer, drawing heavily from scientific studies (from both human and animal biology, among other disciplines). She also uses literature, anecdotes, and social science material in her work. Describe how her style affects your response to her argument. Is she too much a scientist for you? Not enough? Do you find one type of her evidence to be more compelling than another? What writing goals do you think she has, based on the techniques you see in her writing style?

WORKING WITH CLUSTERS

Cluster 2: Constructing and Corrupting the Feminine

Cluster 8: Metaphor and Truth

Cluster 9: Bodies of Knowledge

Cluster 14: Epistemologies

Discipline: The Natural Sciences

Rhetorical Mode: Definition

"MahVuhHuhPuh" (from *The Gutenberg Elegies: The Fate of Reading in an Electronic Age*)

by Sven Birkerts

Sven Birkerts is the author of several books, including American Energies: Essays on Fiction, The Electric Life: Essays on Modern Poetry, An Artificial Wilderness: Essays on Twentieth Century Literature, *and* The Gutenberg Elegies: The Fate of Reading in an Electronic Age, *from which this essay is taken. He is the recipient of various awards, most notably a Guggenheim Fellowship in 1994. While some reviewers have accused Birkerts of "Chicken Little-ism," others have praised his elegiac sketches that argue on behalf of the pleasures of reading in an age that worships the shortcut. In 2002, Birkerts became editor of* Agni, *a literary journal published at Boston University.*

oblique: not straightforward; roundabout

1. In Your Journal: Based on your understanding of Albert Einstein's theory of relativity (which explores the relationship between space and time), examine the way Birkerts uses it in relation to thinking.

2. In Your Journal: Examine this statement: "Thinking is now something I partake in, not something I do." What is Birkerts saying about the nature of thinking?

3. In Your Journal: How does Birkerts distinguish between **thinking** and **ideas?**

It was **Virginia Woolf** who started me thinking about thinking again, set me to weighing the relative merits of the abstract analytical mode against the attractions of a more **oblique** and subjective approach. The comparison was ventured for interest alone. Abstract analysis has been closed to me for some time—I find I can no longer chase the isolated hare. Problems and questions seem to come toward me in clusters. They appear inextricably imbedded in circumstance and I cannot pry them loose to think about them. Nor can I help factoring in my own angle of regard. All is relative, relational, Einsteinian. Thinking is now something I partake in, not something I do. It is a complex narrative proposition, and I am as interested in the variables of the process as I am in the outcome. I am an essayist, it seems, and not a philosopher.

I have had these various distinctions in mind for some time now, but only as a fidgety scatter of inklings. The magnet that pulled them into a shape was Woolf's classic essay, *A Room of One's Own*. Not the *what* of it, but the *how.* Reading the prose, I confronted a paradox that pulled me upright in my chair. Woolf's ideas are, in fact, few and fairly obvious—at least from our historical vantage. Yet the *thinking,* the presence of animate thought on the page, is striking. How do we sort that? How can a piece of writing have simple ideas and still infect the reader with the excitement of its thinking? The answer, I'd say, is that ideas are not the sum and substance of thought; rather, thought is as much about the motion across the water as it is about the stepping stones that allow it. It is an intricate choreography of movement, transition, and repose, a revelation of the musculature of mind. And this, abundantly and exaltingly, is what I find in Woolf's prose. She supplies the context, shows the problem as well as her relation to it. Then, as she narrates her growing engagement, she exposes something more thrilling and valuable than any mere concept could be. She reveals how incidental experience can encounter the receptive sensibility and activate the mainspring of creativity.

❖ **Virginia Woolf:** (1882–1941) one of England's most well-known and often-taught writers, Woolf is famous for her particular use (in fiction) of the "stream-of-consciousness" technique. Woolf put this technique work in her explorations of the inner experiences of memory, time, and perception in her major novels: *Orlando, Mrs. Dalloway,* and *To the Lighthouse.* Her most well known non-fiction is *A Room of One's Own,* an important feminist literary text

I cannot cite enough text here to convince you of my point, but I can suggest the flavor of her musing, her particular way of intertwining the speculative with the reportorial. Woolf has, she informs us at the outset, agreed to present her views on the subject of women and fiction. In the early pages of her essay she rehearses her own perplexity. She is a writer looking for an idea. What she does is not so very different from the classic college freshman maneuver of writing a paper on the problem she is having writing a paper. But Woolf is Woolf, and her stylistic **verve** is unexcelled:

verve: energy; vitality

> Here then I was (call me Mary Beton, Mary Seton, Mary Carmichael or by any name you please—it is not a matter of any importance) sitting on the banks of a river a week or two ago in fine October weather, lost in thought. That collar I have spoken of, women and fiction, the need of coming to some conclusion on a subject that raises all sorts of prejudices and passions, bowed my head to the ground. To the right and left bushes of some sort, golden and crimson, glowed with color, even it seemed burned with the heat, of fire. On the further bank willows wept in perpetual lamentation, their hair about their shoulders. The river reflected whatever it chose of sky and bridge and burning tree, and when the undergraduate had oared his boat through the reflections they closed again, completely, as if he had never been. There one might have sat the clock round lost in thought. Thought—to call it by a prouder name than it deserved—let its line down into the stream. It swayed, minute after minute, hither and thither among the reflections and the weeds, letting the water lift it and sink it, until—you know the little tug—the sudden conglomeration of an idea at the end of one's line: and then the cautious hauling of it in, and the careful laying of it out? Alas, laid on the grass how small, how insignificant this thought of mine looked; the sort of fish that a good fisherman puts back into the water so that it may grow fatter and be one day worth cooking and eating.

Soon enough, Woolf will rise and attempt to cross a patch of lawn, only to encounter a zealous **beadle**, who will not only shoo her back toward authorized turf, but will initiate her reverie on male power and privilege. This is her triumph: the trust in serendipity, which proves, when unmasked, to be an absolute faith in the transformative powers of the creative intellect. *A Room of One's Own,* whatever it says about women, men, writing, and society, is also a perfect demonstration of what might be called "**magpie aesthetics**." Woolf is the **bricoleuse**, cobbling with whatever is to hand; she is the **flâneuse**, redeeming the slight and incidental by creating the context of its true significance. She models another path for mind and sensibility, suggests procedures that we might consider implementing for ourselves

beadle: usher; minor official

magpie: indiscriminate collector

aesthetics: study or theory of beauty or art

bricoleuse: (French) tinker (tinsmith)

flâneuse: (French) stroller; rambler

now that the philosophers, the old lovers of truth, have followed the narrowing track of abstraction to the craggy places up above the timberline.

By now the astute reader will have picked up on my game—that I am interested not only in celebrating Woolf's cunningly sidelong approach, but that I am trying, in my own ungainly way, to imitate it. Woolf had her "collar" (women and fiction) thrust upon her; I have wriggled into mine—let's call it *reading and meaning*—of my own volition. I know that I face an impossible task. Who can hope to say anything conclusive on so vast a subject? But I opted for vastness precisely because it would allow me to explore this unfamiliar essayistic method. A method predicated not upon conclusiveness but upon exploratory **digressiveness**; a method which proposes that thinking is not simply utilitarian, but can also be a kind of narrative travel that allows for picnics along the way.

digressiveness: quality of straying from the main point or line of thought

I invoke Woolf as the instigating presence. Her example sets the key signature for an inquiry into the place of reading and sensibility in what is becoming an electronic culture. Within the scheme I have in mind, Woolf stands very much at one limit. Indeed, her work is an emblem for some of the very things that are under threat in our age: differentiated subjectivity, **reverie**, verbal articulation, mental passion . . .

reverie: daydreaming; having wandering thoughts

Before I go on, I must make a paradoxical admission: I was spurred to read *A Room of One's Own* by watching a televised adaptation of the book. On the program, Eileen Atkins, playing the part of Woolf, soliloquized for a full hour. Her address, supposedly directed at an audience of women at Girton College, was composed of extracted passages from the text. Armed with minimal props and a rather extraordinary repertoire of gestures, Atkins held forth. And I, wedged into my corner of the couch, was mesmerized. By the acting, sure, but more by the sheer power and beauty of the spoken word. Here, without seeming **archaic** or excessively theatrical, was a language such as one never hears—certainly not on TV. I was riveted. And as soon as the show was over I went to find the book.

archaic: having characteristics of the past; antiquated

A Room of One's Own, I'm happy to say, stood up to its television rendition—indeed, galloped right past it. And it has spent many nights since on my bedside table. But the paradox remains: Just as Woolf's charged prose shows us what is possible with language, so it also forces us to face the utter impoverishment of our own **discourse**. And as we seek to explain how it is that flatness and dullness carry the day, we have to lay at least part of the blame at the feet of our omnipotent media systems. And yet, and yet . . . here I found myself reintroduced to the power of Woolf by the culprit technology itself.

discourse: formal expression associated with a specific subject

This is the sort of thing I tend to think about. I ponder the paradox—stare at it as if it were an object on the desk in front of me. I stare and wait for ideas and intuitions to gather, but I do not unpack my instruments of reason. For, as I see it, this little triad—of me, TV, and book—potentially touches every aspect of our contemporary lives and our experience of meaning. To think about the matter analytically would be to break the filaments of the web.

I will therefore set down what amount to a few anecdotal provocations and go wandering about in their midst. All of my points of focus have, as you will see, some connection to my immediate daily experience; they are embedded in the context of my life. But they also have a discernible link. For I *have* been going around for quite some time with a single question—a single imprecisely general question—in my mind. The interrogation mark has been turned upside down and, to follow Woolf, lowered into the waters of my ordinary days. It is always there, and, from time to time, for whatever reason, it captures the attention of some swimming thing. I feel a tug: The paper is produced, the note gets scribbled, and the hook is thrown back out.

The question, again, is, "What is the place of reading, and of the reading sensibility, in our culture as it has become?" And, like most of the questions I ponder seriously, this one has been around long enough to have become a conspicuous topographical feature of my mental landscape. In my lifetime I have witnessed and participated in what amounts to a massive shift, a wholesale transformation of what I think of as the age-old ways of being. The primary human relations—to space, time, nature, and to other people—have been subjected to a warping pressure that is something new under the sun. Those who argue that the very nature of history is change—that change is constant—are missing the point. Our era has seen an escalation of the rate of change so drastic that all possibilities of evolutionary accommodation have been short-circuited. The advent of the computer and the astonishing sophistication achieved by our electronic communications media have together turned a range of isolated changes into something **systemic**. The way that people experience the world has altered more in the last fifty years than in the many centuries preceding ours. The eruptions in the early part of our century—the time of world wars and emergent modernity—were premonitions of a sort. Since World War II we have stepped, collectively, out of an ancient and familiar solitude and into an enormous web of imponderable linkages. We have created the technology that not only enables us to change our basic nature, but that is making such change all but inevitable. This is why I take reading—reading construed broadly—as my subject. Reading, for me, is one activity that inscribes the limit of the old conception of the individual and his relation to the world. It is precisely where reading leaves off, where it is supplanted by other modes of processing and transmitting experience, that the new dispensation can be said to begin.

systemic: pertaining to a whole structure

4. In Your Journal: What is Birkerts saying about change in isolation versus change of a system?

None of this, I'm afraid, will seem very obvious to the citizen of the late twentieth century. If it did, there would be more outcry, more debate. The changes are keyed to generational transitions in computational power; they come in ghostly increments, but their effect is to alter our lives on every front. Public awareness of this expresses itself obliquely, often unconsciously, as nostalgia—a phenomenon which the media brokers are all too aware of. They hurry to supply us with the necessary balm: media productions and fashions that harken back reassuringly to eras that we perceive as less threatening, less **cataclysmic.** But this is another subject. We are, on a conscious level, blinkered to change. We adapt to the local disturbances. We train ourselves to computer literacy, find ways to speed up our performance, accept higher levels of stress as a kind of necessary tax burden, but by and large we ignore the massive transformations taking place in the background. This is entirely understandable. The present hastens us forward, at every moment sponging up what preceded it. Only when we wrench ourselves free and perform the ceremony of memory do we grasp the extent of the change. In our lives, in the world. Then indeed we may ask ourselves where we are headed and what is the meaning of this great metamorphosis of the familiar.

cataclysmic: causing total upheaval

I was recently reading a novel by **Graham Swift** entitled *Ever After.* At one point, the narrator, an adult looking back upon his youth, recalls how he used to race on his bike to a private lookout post from which he could watch the great steam engines go hurtling past. Calling upon the privileged hindsight of his narrator, Swift writes:

> Between Aldermaston Wharf and Midgham, where the Reading-to-Newbury line clipped the side of the hill and entered a short cutting—a favorite spot for these enthralled vigils, so limply known as "train-spotting"—I could look out on a vista which might have formed the model for one of those contrived scenes in a children's encyclopedia, depicting the theme of "Old and New." River, canal and railway line were all in view. At a single moment it would have been perfectly possible to see, in the background, the old watermill on the Kennet, with a horse working the field before it; in the middle distance, a barge on the canal; and in the foreground, a train racing for the cutting; while no less than three road bridges provided a fair opportunity for some gleaming motor car (complete with an inanely grinning couple in the front seats) to be brought simultaneously into the picture.

I must have seen it once—many times—that living **palimpsest.** And no doubt I should have been struck by some **prescient, elegiac** pang at the sight of these great expresses steaming only to their own oblivion, and taking with them a whole lost age.

palimpsest: something having diverse layers beneath the surface

prescient: omniscient; having foreknowledge of events

elegiac: expressing of sorrow for the past

Graham Swift: (1949–) contemporary British novelist whose works include *Waterland* (1983) and *Last Orders* (1996 winner of the Booker Prize), which have earned him comparisons to William Faulkner, Günter Grass, and Gabriel Garcia Marquez; *Ever After,* referred to here by Birkerts, is a novel about a contemporary suicidal scholar who comes across some Victorian diaries that express much of his own angst

I found the passage a compelling analogy of our own situation, only instead of modes of transport in the palimpsest I would place book, video monitor, and any of the various interactive hypertext technologies now popping up in the marketplace. Looking up from Swift's page, I wondered what it would be like to look back upon our own cultural moment from a vantage of, say, thirty years. Are we not in a similar transitional phase, except that what is roaring by, destined for imminent historical oblivion, is the whole familiar tradition of the book? All around us, already in place, are the technologies that will render it antiquated.

In the fall of 1992 I taught a course called "The American Short Story" to undergraduates at a local college. I assembled a set of readings that I thought would appeal to the tastes of the average undergraduate and felt relatively confident. We would begin with Washington Irving, then move on quickly to Hawthorne, Poe, James, and Jewett, before connecting with the progressively more accessible works of our century. I had expected that my students would enjoy "The Legend of Sleepy Hollow," be amused by its caricatures and ghost-story element. Nothing of the kind. Without exception they found the story over-long, verbose, a chore. I wrote their reactions off to the fact that it was the first assignment and that most students would not have hit their reading stride yet. When we got to Hawthorne and Poe I had the illusion that things were going a bit better.

But then came **Henry James**'s "Brooksmith" and I was completely derailed. I began the class, as I always do, by soliciting casual responses of the "I liked it" and "I hated it" sort. My students could barely muster the energy for a thumbs-up or -down. It was as though some **pneumatic** pump had sucked out the last dregs of their spirits. "Bad day, huh?" I ventured. Persistent questioning revealed that it was the reading that had undone them. But why? What was the problem? I had to get to the bottom of their stupefaction before this relatively—*I thought*—available tale.

pneumatic: works by use of pressurized air or gas

I asked: Was it a difficulty with the language, the style of writing? Nods all around. Well, let's be more specific. Was it vocabulary, sentence

---

Henry James: (1843–1916) one of American literature's greatest novelists; his "psychological realism" features concentrated attention to the subtleties of character (particularly among Americans abroad), which paved the way for modernism's emphasis on representing consciousness; his most famous novels include *The Portrait of a Lady* (1881), *Wings of the Dove* (1902), and *The Golden Bowl* (1904). Here is a passage from "Brooksmith":

> I remember vividly every element of the place, down to the intensely Londonish look of the grey opposite houses, in the gap of the white curtains of the high windows, and the exact spot where, on a particular afternoon, I put down my tea-cup for Brooksmith, lingering an instant, to gather it up as if he were plucking a flower. Mr. Offord's drawing-room was indeed Brooksmith's garden, his pruned and tended human parterre, and if we all flourished there and grew well in our places it was largely owing to his supervision.

length, syntax? "Yeah, sort of," said one student, "but it was more just the whole thing." Hmmmmm. Well then, I said, we should consider this. I questioned whether they understood the basic plot. Sure, they said. A butler's master dies and the butler can't find another place as good. He loses one job after another—usually because he quits—then falls into despair and disappears, probably to end it all. "You don't find this moving?" One or two students conceded the **pathos** of the situation, but then the complaints resurfaced, with the original complainer chiming in again that it was not so much the story as "the whole thing."

pathos: representation that evokes pity

The whole thing. *What* whole thing? My tone must have reflected my agitation, my impatience with their imprecision. But then, after endless going around, it stood revealed: These students were entirely defeated by James's prose—the medium of it—as well as by the assumptions that underlie it. It was not the vocabulary, for they could make out most of the words; and not altogether the syntax, although here they admitted to discomfort, occasional abandoned sentences. What they really could not abide was what the vocabulary, the syntax, the ironic indirection, and so forth, were communicating. *They didn't get it,* and their not getting it angered them, and they expressed their anger by drawing around themselves a **cowl** of ill-tempered **apathy.** Students whom I knew to be quick and resourceful in other situations suddenly retreated into glum illiteracy. "I dunno," said the spokesman, "the whole thing just bugged me—I couldn't get into it."

> ***5. In Your Journal:*** What do Birkerts's students mean when they refer to "the whole thing"? Can you relate to this complaint?

cowl: long, hooded cloak

apathy: indifference; lack of concern

Disastrous though the class had been, I drove home in an excited mood. What had happened, I started to realize, was that I had encountered a conceptual ledge, one that may mark a break in historical continuity. This was more than just a bad class—it was a corroboration of something I had been on the verge of grasping for years. You could have drawn a lightbulb over my head and turned it on.

What is this ledge, and what does it have to do with the topic I've embarked upon? To answer the second question: Everything. As I wrote before: the world we have known, the world of our myths and references and shared assumptions, is being changed by a powerful, if often intangible, set of forces. We are living in the midst of a momentous paradigm shift. My classroom experience, which in fact represents hundreds of classroom experiences, can be approached diagnostically.

This is not a simple case of students versus Henry James. We are not concerned with an isolated clash of sensibilities, his and theirs. Rather, we are standing in one spot along a ledge—or, better, a fault line—dividing one order from another. In place of James we could as easily put **Joyce** or Woolf

---

✧ **James Joyce:** (1882–1941) Ireland's most famous and renowned novelist, whose works include *Portrait of the Artist as a Young Man* (1916) and *Ulysses* (1922); a high modernist maverick known for his non-linear portrayal of the interior complexities of identity or **Shakespeare** or **Ralph Ellison.** It would be the same. The point is that the collective experience of these students, most of whom were born in the early 1970s, has rendered a vast part of our cultural heritage utterly alien. *That* is the breaking point: it describes where their understandings and aptitudes give out. What is at issue is not diction, not syntax, but everything that diction and syntax serve. Which is to say, an entire system of beliefs, values, and cultural aspirations.

In Henry James are distilled many of the elements I would discuss. He is inward and subtle, a master of ironies and indirections; his work manifests a care for the range of moral distinctions. And one cannot "get" him without paying heed to the least twist and turn of the language. James's world, and the dramas that take place in that world, are predicated on the idea of individuals in an organic relation to their society. In his universe, each one of those individuals are still surrounded by an aura of importance; their actions and decisions are felt to count for something.

> ***6. In Your Journal:*** How does the example of Henry James figure into the initial expression of Birkerts's main idea?

I know that the society of James's day was also repressive to many, and was, further, invested in certain now-discredited assumptions of empire. I am not arguing for its return, certainly not in that form. But this was not the point, at least not in the discussions I then pursued with my students. For we did, after our disastrous James session, begin to question not only our various readings, but also the reading act itself and their relation to it. And what emerged was this: that they were not, with a few exceptions, readers—never had been; that they had always occupied themselves with music, TV, and videos; that they had difficulty slowing down enough to concentrate on prose of any density; that they had problems with what they thought of as archaic diction, with allusions, with vocabulary that seemed "pretentious"; that they were especially uncomfortable with indirect or interior passages, indeed with any deviations from straight plot; and that they were put off by ironic tone because it flaunted superiority and made them feel that they were missing something. The list is partial.

All of this confirmed my longstanding suspicion that, having grown up in an electronic culture, my students would naturally exhibit certain aptitudes and lack others. But the implications, as I began to realize, were rather staggering, especially if one thinks of this not as a temporary

---

Shakespeare: (William) (1564–1616) singular Renaissance playwright and poet whose works were concerned with the most fundamental aspects of humanness throughout his prolific career; he used a multiplicity of voices and themes to investigate simultaneously all levels of human motivation: individual, social, and universal

---

Ralph Ellison: (1914–1944) one of the most influential American writers of the 20th century, Ellison brought the techniques of his influences—Joyce, Proust, and Faulkner—to bear on the realities of black American life. *Invisible Man* (1952), Ellison's crowning achievement, traces the journey of a nameless black everyman from innocence to experience, and employs the non-linear narrative and attention to consciousness characteristic of literary modernism generational disability, but rather as a permanent turn. If this were true of my twenty-five undergraduates, I reasoned, many of them from relatively advantaged backgrounds, then it was probably true for most of their generation. And not only theirs, but for the generations on either side of them as well. What this meant was not, narrowly, that a large sector of our population would not be able to enjoy certain works of literature, but that a much more serious situation was developing. For, in fact, our entire collective subjective history—the soul of our societal body—is encoded in print. Is encoded, and has for countless generations been passed along by way of the word, mainly through books. I'm not talking about facts and information here, but about the somewhat more elusive soft data, the expressions that tell us who we are and who we have been, that are the record of individuals living in different epochs—that are, in effect, the cumulative speculations of the species. If a person turns from print—finding it too slow, too hard, irrelevant to the excitements of the present—then what happens to that person's sense of culture and continuity?

7. In Your Journal: How does Birkerts begin to suggest that print is related to culture? What do you perceive to be the relationship?

These are issues too large for mere analysis; they are **over-determined**. There is no way to fish out one strand and think it through. Yet I think we must, even if we have to be clumsy and obvious at times. We are living in a society and culture that is in dissolution. Pack this paragraph with your own headlines about crime, eroded values, educational decline, what have you. There are many causes, many explanations. But behind them all, vague and menacing, is this recognition: that the understandings and assumptions that were formerly operative in society no longer feel valid. Things have shifted; they keep shifting. We all feel a desire for connection, for meaning, but we don't seem to know what to connect with what, and we are utterly at sea about our place as individuals in the world at large. The maps no longer describe the terrain we inhabit. There is no clear path to the future. We trust that the species will blunder on, but we don't know where *to*. We feel imprisoned in a momentum that is not of our own making.

over-determined: having many determining psychological factors; over-saturated with meaning

I am not about to suggest that all of this comes of not reading Henry James. But I will say that *of* all this comes not being *able* to read James or any other emissary from that recent but rapidly vanishing world. Our historically sudden transition into an electronic culture has thrust us into a place of unknowing. We have been stripped not only of familiar habits and ways, but of familiar points of moral and psychological reference. Looking out at our society, we see no real leaders, no larger figures of wisdom. **Not a brave new world** at all, **but a fearful one**.

"not a brave new world, but a fearful one": allusion to Aldous Huxley's novel *Brave New World;* though he wrote many novels, Huxley (1894–1963) is most famous for this nightmarish depiction of a future "utopia," characterized by a vision of "natural man" in an "unnatural world," where efficiency and soullessness prevail

The notion of historical change compels and vexes me. I am not so much interested in this war or that treaty or invention, although obviously these are critical factors. What I brood about has more to do with the **phenomenology** of everyday life. How it is that the world greets the senses differently—is experienced differently—from epoch to epoch. We know about certain ways in which the world has changed since, say, 1890, but do we know how the *feeling* of life has changed? We can isolate the more

phenomenology: study of human consciousness and self-awareness objective sorts of phenomena, cite improvements in transportation, industrial innovations, and so on, but we have no reliable access to the subjective realm. When older people sigh and say that "life was different back then," we may instinctively agree, but how can we grasp exactly what that difference means?

> ***8. In Your Journal:*** Why is the author so preoccupied with **how life feels?** How is this different from what events happen in life or what we see as the meaning of life?

On the other hand, we all inhabit multiple time zones. We have the world of our daily present, which usually claims most of our attention, but we are also wrapped in shadowy bands of the past. First, we have the layers of our own history. The older we get, the more substantial grows the shadow—and the greater the gap between the world as we know it now and the world as it used to be. At the outer perimeter, that indistinct mass of memories shades together with another mass. These are the memories we grew up among. They belong to our parents and grandparents. Our picture of the world, how it is and how it used to be, is necessarily tinged with what we absorbed from innumerable references and anecdotes, from the *then* that preceded us.

Thus, as a man in my early forties, I already carry a substantial **temporal** baggage. I am a citizen of the *now,* reading the daily paper, sliding my embossed card into the money machine at the bank, and renting a video for the evening's relaxation. But I am also other selves: a late starter, a casualty of the culture wars of the 1960s, an alienated adolescent sopping up pop culture and dreaming of escape, an American kid growing up in the 1950s, playing touch football and watching "I Love Lucy." An American kid? I should say a kid trying very hard to be an American kid. For although I was born here, both my parents were from the old country, Latvia, and my childhood was both subtly and overtly permeated by their experience—their stories of growing up in Riga, of war and dispersal. And how it was for them naturally became a part of how it was for me.

temporal: time-related

Nor did it end there. I also grew up with grandparents. And from them I imbibed still another sense of time. Visiting their home, I circulated among their artifacts, heard their reminiscences. Through them I made contact, however indirectly, with a world utterly unlike anything I know now: a world at once more solid and grim, a world that held gaps and spaces and distances. Although my grandparents both grew up in towns, they had roots in rural places. Their stories were filled with farm and country lore. Indeed, until quite late in their lives they had no car, no TV. Even the telephone had something newfangled about it. Their anecdotes unfolded in a different order, at a different pace. They had one foot in the modern era and one foot back in the real past. By that I mean the past that had seen generation upon generation living more or less in the same way—absorbing incremental change, yes, but otherwise bound to a set of fundamental rhythms.

There is a difference between this sort of reflection and that more-piercing awareness we call nostalgia. Nostalgia is immediate, and tends to be more localized. As often as not, it is triggered by an experiential short-circuit; our awareness of the present is suddenly interrupted by an image, a feeling, or a sensation from the past. A song on the radio, an old photograph discovered in the pages of a book. The past catches us by surprise and we are filled with longing: for that thing, that person, that place, but more for the selves that we were then.

Like everyone else, I am subject to these intrusions. I distinguish them from the more sustained sorts of excavations that I have been undertaking recently. I am not in search of private sensation, but of a kind of understanding. I want to know what life may have been like during a certain epoch, what daily living may have felt like, so that I can make a comparison with the present. Why? I suppose because I believe that there is a secret to be found, a clue that will help me to solve the mystery of the present.

It happened that while I was in this season of thinking about time and the life of the past I rented a video of a film called *Fools of Fortune,* based on a novel by **William Trevor.** It was a desperate grab, really, a bid to cancel the residue of an enervating day. But as soon as I popped the cassette into the player I felt my obsessions again coalesce. The opening moments of the film reproduced what were meant to be bits of old 8-mm footage. Jerky, erratic, bleached and pocked by time. A child toddling forward across a grand lawn, a manor house in the background. A woman in a garden chair with period clothing and hairstyle. All cinematic artifice, of course, but I was entirely susceptible to it.

The film depicted Ireland in the early years of our century, during the time of the civil war. I was most struck by what seemed its real sensitivity to the conditions of the provincial life it recorded. Lingering shots of silent rooms, of people working in uninterrupted solitude, of people walking and walking, carts slowly rolling. I may be tailoring my memory of the film to fit my need, but never mind. And never mind the fact that I was sitting in my 1990s electronic cottage, watching actors in a commercial production on my videocassette player. For a few moments I succumbed to the intended illusion: I was looking through a window at the actual past, at things as they had once been. I was overwhelmed, really, by the realization of change. In a matter of decades—from the time of my grandparents to the time of the present—we have, all of us, passed through the looking glass.

> ***9. In Your Journal:*** How do you think these references to Lewis Carroll's *Alice in Wonderland* and *Through the Looking Glass* relate to Birkerts's larger argument?

At one point in the film the main character walks along the side of a brick building, toward the town square. An unremarkable scene, transitional filler. Yet this was, for some reason, the moment that awakened me. I thought: If I could just imagine myself completely into this scene, see my surroundings as if through the eyes of this person, then I would know

⁂ **William Trevor:** (1928–) Irish novelist and essayist, who captures the complexities of love within the Anglo-Irish conflict in his *Fools of Fortune* something. I tried to perform the exercise in different ways. First, by taking a blind leap backward, restricting myself to just those things he might have encountered, imagining for myself the dung and coal-smoke scent of the spring air, the feel of rounded cobblestones under my shoes, a surrounding silence broken by the sounds of hammers, cartwheels, and hooves. A nearly impossible maneuver, but attempting it I realized how much has to be forcibly expunged from awareness.

I have also tried working myself back gradually from present to past, peeling off the layers one by one: taking away televisions and telephones (all things "tele-"), airplanes, cars, plastics, synthetic fibers, efficient sanitation, asphalt, wristwatches, and ballpoint pens, and on and on. The effect is quite extraordinary. I feel a progressive widening of space and increase of silence, as well as a growing specific gravity in objects. As I move more deeply into the past, I feel the encroachment of place; the specifics of locale get more and more prominent as the distance to the horizon increases. So many things need to be reconstituted: the presence of neighbors; the kinds of knowledge that come from living a whole life within a narrow compass; the aura of unattainable distance that attaches to the names of faraway places—India, Ceylon, Africa . . . And what was it like to live so close to death? And what about everything else: the feel of woven cloth, the different taste of food, drink, pipe tobacco? From the center of the life I imagine, a life not even a century old, I find it impossible to conceive of the life I am living now. The looking glass works both ways.

The chain of association is the lifeline, or fate, of thought. One thing leads to another; ideas gather out of impressions and begin to guide the steps in mysterious ways. After my experience of watching *Fools of Fortune,* I decided that I should find a novel from the period. To read it with an eye for those very "background" features—to derive some further sense of the feel of life in a pre-electronic age. I picked up **Thomas Hardy**'s *Jude the Obscure.*

Read this way, with as much attention paid to the conditions of life as to the lives themselves, *Jude* becomes another window opening upon *how it was.* From the very first sentences, the spell of the past is woven:

> The schoolmaster was leaving the village, and everybody seemed sorry. The miller at Cresscombe lent him the small white tilted cart and horse to carry his goods to the city of his

---

∴ **Thomas Hardy:** (1840–1928) English novelist and poet, whose most well known novels are *The Mayor of Casterbridge* (1886), *Tess of the d'Urbervilles* (1891), and *Jude the Obscure* (1896), quoted here by Birkerts; the novels are generally naturalistic in their style, meaning that they examine the sometimes inevitably destructive relationship between individuals and their environments; *Jude the Obscure* is a story about a stonemason who struggles with intellectual and sexual desire, and the novel caused an uproar for its frank treatment of carnal love

> destination, about twenty miles off, such a vehicle proving of quite sufficient size for the departing teacher's effects.

pedagogue: teacher

To enter the work at all we need to put our present-day sense of things in suspension; we have to, in effect, reposition the horizon and reconceive all of our assumptions about the relations between things. Hardy's twenty miles are not ours. The **pedagogue** does not pile his belongings into the back of a Jeep Cherokee. His "effects" fit easily into a small horse-drawn cart he has borrowed. The city, called Christminster in the novel, is within walking distance of the village of Marygreen, but the distance means something. Soon enough, Hardy's Jude will stand on a nearby hill straining to catch a glimpse of that city's spires. He will dream of one day going there: to Jude it is the far edge of the world. Not because he could not with some pluck walk there to see it himself, but because he knows, as does everyone, that places are self-contained. Christminster is not just a point on a grid, it is a small world with its own laws, its own vortex of energies; it is *other.* And reading *Jude* we begin to grasp distinctions of this sort.

It would take too long to address as they deserve the myriad ways in which Jude's world is different from ours. But as we read we are gradually engulfed by a half-familiar set of sensations. Because the characters walk, we walk; because they linger by roadsides or in market squares, we do too. And by subtle stages we are overwhelmed. Overwhelmed by the size of the world. If Christminster is a trip, then London, hardly even mentioned, is a journey. And America, or any other country, is a voyage. The globe expands, and at the same time our sense of silence deepens. No background hum, no ambient noise. When people communicate, it is face to face. Or else by letter. There are no telephones or cars to hurriedly bridge the spatial gaps. We hear voices, and we hear footsteps die away in the distance. Days pass at a pace we can hardly imagine. A letter arrives and it is an event. The sound of paper unfolding, of wind in the trees outside the door. And then the things, their *thingness.* Jude's little hoard of Greek and Latin grammars, the smudgy books he had scrimped to buy—books he carried with him until his dying day. His stoneworking tools: well cared for, much prized. I suddenly think of lines from **Elizabeth Bishop**'s poem "Crusoe in England." The castaway has returned "home" after his long years on the island:

10. In Your Journal: What does Birkerts mean by "thingness"?

Elizabeth Bishop: (1911–1979) American poet known for descriptive attention to commonplace detail and precision; Bishop's book *Poems: North and South—A Cold Spring* won a Pulitzer Prize in 1955. "Crusoe in England," quoted here by Birkerts, revises the story of Daniel Defoe's Robinson Crusoe, exchanging an investigation of personal and cultural memory for Defoe's emphasis on Christianity and empiricism

Now I live here, another island,
that doesn't seem like one, but who decides?
My blood was full of them; my brain
bred islands. But that archipelago
has petered out. I'm old.
I'm bored, too, drinking my real tea,
surrounded by uninteresting lumber.
The knife there on the shelf—
it reeked of meaning, like a crucifix.
It lived. How many years did I
beg it, implore it, not to break?
I knew each nick and scratch by heart,
the bluish blade, the broken tip,
the lines of wood-grain on the handle . . .
Now it won't look at me at all.
The living soul has dribbled away.
My eyes rest on it and pass on.

This is it, no? The densities of meaning once conferred, since leached out. Our passage into bright contemporaneity has carried a price: The more complex and sophisticated our systems of lateral access, the more we sacrifice in the way of depth. Read *Jude the Obscure* and you will be struck, I think, by the material particularity of Hardy's world. You will feel the heft of things, the solidity. You will also feel the stasis, the near-intolerable boredom of boundedness.

Advantages and disadvantages—how could it be otherwise? I speak as if longingly of those times, but would I trade the speed and access and comfort of my life for the rudeness and singularity of that? I doubt it. But then, I have the benefit of hindsight. I am in the position of the adult who is asked if he would return once and for all to his childhood. The answer is yes and no.

And the purpose of this rambling excursion? Am I simply lamenting the loss of something I could not bear to recover—a gone world? No. What I intended, in the obscure way one intends these things when writing, was to wander away from the specter of my American short story class, wander until the reader's memory traces should have all but faded, and then to bring the image of those students forward again. To try one more time to make something of my intuition: that their unease before Henry James's "Brooksmith" has a larger significance, that it is not just another instance of young minds being put off by James's assumptions of civilization, but rather that that unease illuminates something central about our cultural condition and its prospects.

Obviously it is too simplistic to blame the students' discomfiture, not just with James but with demanding texts in general, upon any one thing, such as television, video games, inadequate secondary schools, or what have you. To do so would be to miss the larger point: that the situation is total and arises from systemic changes affecting the culture at every level.

watershed: crucial dividing point

And while the situation thus defies ready analysis, it nevertheless has the greatest consequences for all of us and must somehow be addressed. We are at a **watershed** point. One way of processing information is yielding to another. Bound up with each is a huge array of aptitudes, assumptions, and understandings about the world.

We can think of the matter in terms of gains and losses. The gains of electronic postmodernity could be said to include, for individuals, (a) an increased awareness of the "big picture," a global perspective that admits the extraordinary complexity of interrelations; (b) an expanded neural capacity, an ability to accommodate a broad range of stimuli simultaneously; (c) a relativistic comprehension of situations that promotes the erosion of old biases and often expresses itself as tolerance; and (d) a matter-of-fact and unencumbered sort of readiness, a willingness to try new situations and arrangements.

In the loss column, meanwhile, are (a) a fragmented sense of time and a loss of the so-called duration experience, that depth phenomenon we associate with reverie; (b) a reduced attention span and a general impatience with sustained inquiry; (c) a shattered faith in institutions and in the explanatory narratives that formerly gave shape to subjective experience; (d) a divorce from the past, from a vital sense of history as a cumulative or organic process; (e) an estrangement from geographic place and community; and (f) an absence of any strong vision of a personal or collective future.

These are, granted, enormous generalizations. But they record what a great many of my students have said of themselves and their own experiences. For, apart from talking about their responses to texts, we talked a good deal about their lives. They were as interested as I was in discussing how their sense of the world had bearing on their reading. What surprised me was the degree to which their own view of themselves was critical.

But these are all abstract considerations while the pressure that compels me to write this is very much rooted in daily experience and in my own fears. I worry not only that the world will become increasingly alien and inhospitable to me, but also that I will be gradually coerced into living against my natural grain, forced to adapt to a pace and a level of technological complexity that does not suit me, and driven to interact with others in certain prescribed ways. I tried to live without a telephone answering machine for a time and was made to feel like a pariah. I type these words on an IBM Selectric and feel positively **antediluvian**: My editors let me know that my quaint **Luddite** habits are gumming up the works, slowing things down for them.

antediluvian: before the flood; ancient

❖ **Luddite:** originally, Luddites were groups of laborers in early 19th century England fighting against the threats of industrialization, especially textile machines, which they believed were directly responsible for high unemployment and low wages; the word is now used to refer to people who are generally skeptical of any technological advance

These are trivial examples, but they are indicative. On one level or another we make our adjustments; we shrug and bow to progress. But the fact is that with each capitulation we are drawn more deeply into the web. True, none of the isolated changes make that much difference—but the increasing enmeshment does. The more deeply we are implicated, the more we forfeit in the way of personal initiative and agency; the more we become part of a species-organism. Every acquiescence to the circuitry is marked by a shrinkage of the sphere of autonomous self-hood.

As a writer I naturally feel uneasy. These large-scale changes bode ill for authorship, at least of the kind I would pursue. There are, we know this, fewer and fewer readers for serious works. Publishers are increasingly reluctant to underwrite the publication of a book that will sell only a few thousand copies. But very few works of any artistic importance sell more than that. And those few thousand readers—a great many of them, it turns out, are middle-aged or older. The younger generations have not caught the habit.

I **rue** all of this, but I can take it. Reading and writing will last long enough to cover my stay here below. Indeed, I have resolved to make the crisis—I see it as such—my subject. But I also look toward the future as a father. I have a five-year-old daughter and cannot but think of the ways in which her life will be different than mine. And when, in my darker moods, I contemplate the forces that will determine so much of her experience, her subjective outlook, I feel a sharp sense of regret. Then it seems to me that unless her mother and I are able to equip her with an extraordinary doggedness and with a strong appetite for what is unique and vital, she will be swept up in the tide of the homogeneous. If she goes to a school where reading is not prized, if she follows the non-reading horde of her peers, where will she find the incentive, the desire to read on her own? And if she does not read on her own, where will she find the nutrients she needs in order to evolve an independent identity?

rue: feel strong regret

We do what we can, and we try to do it in a noncoercive way. We promote the pleasures of the book by example, by forever reading. And we try to make the encounter enjoyable. We buy books, borrow them from the library, and read to her regularly. But we also try to avoid any association of the medicinal—that books are good for her and that reading is a duty. So far it seems to be working. She is eager; she recognizes that books are a place away from routine, a place associated with dreams and fantasies.

On the one side, then, is the reading encounter, the private resource. On the other is the culture at large, and the highly seductive glitter of mass-produced entertainment. We are not so foolish as to prohibit it, but I sometimes wonder if we are being as wise as we might be in not curtailing it more. We have entered the world of Disney, and I am seized by the fear that there might be no way out. This past season it was *Beauty and the Beast*. I don't just mean that we saw the movie in the theater once or twice, which would have been the beginning and end of it when I was a child; we saw the movie three, four, five times. We bought the book, illustrated with stills from the movie, and we read that, and looked through it, half a hundred times. The cassette of the songs was purchased and played until the emulsion on the tape wore thin. Then, for Christmas, the video. Another thirty viewings, maybe more. And then the ice show with the *Beauty and the Beast* theme, and the accessories (flashlight, cup) that can perch on the shelf alongside the plastic *Beauty and the Beast* toys given out at Burger King.

Today as never before in human history the child lives in an entertainment environment, among myriad spinoffs and products and commercial references, all of which reinforce the power, or should I say tyranny, of the movie. I relent in the face of it. I was raised quite strictly so I am, in my turn, lenient. I don't have the heart to deny my daughter what she covets and what all her friends have. I see the pleasure she takes in occupying this vivid universe and I want her to have it. I tell myself that it will feed her imagination and that she will soon enough grow into more intricate and demanding fantasies.

And then I despair. I conjure up a whole generation of children enslaved by a single carefully scripted, lushly animated narrative. Not even a narrative created by a single artist, but a team product. A studio job. And I wonder what tale or rhyme or private fantasy will be able to compete with the high-powered rendition from Hollywood's top talents. Is her imagination being awakened, or stultified, locked forever on a kind of assembly-line track? What is the effect of these dozens and dozens of repetitions? What are the overt and subliminal messages she is taking in? What is she learning about men, women, love, honor, and all the rest? Is she incorporating into her deepest subjective structure a set of glib clichés? Will she and her millions of peers, that huge constituency that comprises our future and that is underwriting the global growth of the Disney empire—will all of these kids march forward into adulthood as Disney automatons, with cookie-cut responses to the world they encounter?

I have these fears, and yet I remain permissive. I suppose that is in part because I believe that mass culture is so pervasive these days that it is folly to try to hide from it; that if I do curtail it I will invest it with all that much more appeal. But my permissiveness also depends upon a kind of wager, or a profession of faith. I let the rivers of popular culture (the less-polluted ones) flow freely around my daughter. But at the same time I do everything I can to introduce her to books and stories. I trust that in the free market of the child's imagination these more traditional goods are interesting and unique enough to hold their own. No less important, I stake myself on the basic vitality and independence of that child's soul. I cannot allow that we are so limited, so acquiescent in our basic makeup that we can be stamped to shape like identical cogwheels by the commercial machinery, however powerful that machinery may be.

The good and the true, I believe, will win out. But for that to happen there must be exposure. The child needs to know the range of pleasures. There is room for *Beauty and the Beast* à la Disney, but only when the field includes the best that has been imagined and written through the ages. I believe, I believe—help mine unbelief.

The form of my meditation has been—as I warned—loose. Liberated by the example of Woolf, I have at times let the line of thought go trailing away. But there is also a point to these musings. To put it simply: We have, perhaps without noticing, slipped over a crucial threshold. We have rather abruptly replaced our time-honored and slow-to-evolve modes of communication and interaction with new modes. We have in significant ways surmounted the constraints imposed by nature, in the process altering our relation to time, space, and to each other. We have scarcely begun to assess the impact of these transformations—that will be the work of generations. What I have tried to suggest is that some of our fundamental assumptions about identity and subjective meaning need to be examined carefully. For, by moving from the order of print to the electronic, we risk the loss of the sense of obstacle as well as the feel of the particular that have characterized our experience over millennia. We are poised at the brink of what may prove to be a kind of species mutation. We had better consider carefully what this means.

I have been accused of being alarmist and conservative and prey to excessive nostalgia. And I accuse myself of cowardly pessimism. Why can't I embrace the necessity of historical progress? I have my reasons.

1. I believe that what distinguishes us as a species is not our technological prowess, but rather our extraordinary ability to confer meaning on our experience and to search for clues about our purpose from the world around us.

2. I believe, too, that meaning of this kind—call it "existential" meaning—has from the beginning been the product of our other great distinguishing aptitude: the ability to communicate symbolically through language. Indeed, language is the soil, the seedbed, of meaning. And the works of language, our literatures, have been the repository of our collective speculation.

3. Literature holds meaning not as a content that can be abstracted and summarized, but as experience. It is a participatory arena. Through the process of reading we slip out of our customary time orientation, marked by distractedness and **surficiality**, into the realm of duration. Only in the duration state is experience present as meaning. Only in this state are we prepared to consider our lives under what the philosophers used to call "the aspect of eternity," to question our origins and destinations, and to conceive of ourselves as souls.

I am not going to argue against the power and usefulness of electronic technologies. Nor am I going to suggest that we try to turn back or

11. In Your Journal: How does this author's argument distinguish between the production of things and the production of meaning? Do you see the same distinction?

12. In Your Journal: How is literature synonymous with experience, in Birkerts's opinion?

surficiality: preoccupation with or interest in occurrences on the Earth's surface dismantle what we have wrought in the interests of an intensified relation to meaning. But I would urge that we not fall all over ourselves in our haste to filter all of our experience through circuitries. We are in some danger of believing that the speed and wizardry of our gadgets have freed us from the sometimes arduous work of turning pages in silence.

I keep a file at home entitled "The Reading Wars"—there I save newspaper clippings and relevant notes I've jotted down. The title captures my sense of urgency, my sense that there is a battle going on. On bad days I think it's hopeless, that the forces pulling us away from print—and from ourselves—are too strong; that it is inevitable that generation by generation all independence and idiosyncrasy and depth will be worn away; that we will move ever more surely in lockstep, turning ourselves into creatures of the hive, living some sort of diluted universal dream in a perpetual present. When that fear threatens to lay me low, I try to remember to turn my head. There, pinned to my bulletin board, is a sheet of white paper covered with crayon marks. Crude letters, **runes** on a cave wall. M's and V's and H's and P's—repeated over and over. My daughter's work. She came to it by herself. One afternoon she marched into my study with the page extended proudly. She wanted to know what she had written. How to answer? You wrote "MahmahmahVuhvuhvuhHuhhuhhuhPuhpuhpuh"? Or act the indecipherable adult and say: "You just helped your dad finish something he's been working on for weeks"? I said neither. I complimented her work and let her help me pin it to the bulletin board.

rune: ancient letter

13. In Your Journal: Examine the author's response to what his daughter wrote. Do you have the same reaction?

FOR USE IN DISCUSSION

Questions about Substance

1. Sven Birkerts claims he is not as interested in the *what* of Virginia Woolf's essay so much as he is interested in the *how* (48). What does he mean by this? Do you think the what and the how can be so separated? Explain.
2. "[Virginia Woolf] reveals how incidental experience can encounter the receptive sensibility and activate the mainspring of creativity" (48). What does this statement say about the writing of Woolf and Birkerts's response to her prose? Do you think ideas are generally accidental or intended?
3. Birkerts calls Woolf's method "exploratory digressiveness; a method which presupposes that thinking is not simply utilitarian, but can also be a kind of narrative travel that allows for picnics along the way." Examine the following passage from *Mrs. Dalloway* to see an illustration of this method: "She had a perpetual sense, as she watched the taxi cabs, of being out, far out to sea and alone; she always had the feeling that it was very, very dangerous to live even

one day. Not that she thought herself clever, or much out of the ordinary. How she had gotten through life on the few twigs of knowledge Fraulein Daniels gave them she could not think. She knew nothing; no language, no history, she scarcely read a book now, except memoirs in bed; and yet to her it was absolutely absorbing; all this; the cabs passing; and she would not say of Peter, she would not say of herself, I am this, I am that" (50). How does this passage avoid the "utilitarian" in favor of "picnics" (50)?

4. What does Birkerts mean when he says Woolf's writing evokes a kind of "magpie aesthetics" (49)? How has the way you have been taught to write discouraged such a method?
5. Several times Birkerts suggests that he is less interested in analysis than description. What reason could he have for being so? Do you think this claim is ultimately true of the essay he has written?
6. "Our era has seen an escalation of the rate of change so drastic that all possibilities of evolutionary accommodation have been short-circuited" (51). Do you agree or disagree with this assessment? Is this problem related at all to what Birkerts calls "collective subjective history—the soul of our societal body" (56)? Explain your answer.
7. The author is particularly troubled by his students' assertion that "the whole thing" is what they dislike or are uninterested in when it comes to Henry James's story. Is he fair in his frustration about and criticism of this response? Do you think this is a lazy response on the part of the students or a telling commentary on generational difference?
8. Birkerts says quite matter-of-factly that "we are living in a society and culture that is in dissolution" (56). Do you agree? Why or why not?
9. How are Birkerts's Latvian parents relevant to his discussion about reading and technology? Why does he take the time to discuss of their daily lives (57)? How do those details compare with the use Birkerts makes of Elizabeth Bishop's "Crusoe" (61)? What are the sentiments in the quoted stanza, and how do they contribute to Birkerts's argument?

Questions about Structure and Style

1. How does the title of this essay, "MahVuhHuhPuh," set an immediate tone and indicate—however subtly—the subject matter of this essay? How does your understanding of the title eventually crystallize? Why is the meaning deferred so long?
2. Virginia Woolf could be called the catalyst of this essay. Does it make sense to you why her presence would fade as the essay progresses? Why or why not?
3. On page 61, the author admits that he would probably not trade the efficiency of technology for the clarity and singularity of the past. How does this confession affect the voice of this essay? Why do you think it comes at the point it does, rather than sooner or later in the essay?
4. A fishing metaphor recurs throughout the essay. Find some examples of this imagery. What it is intended to illustrate? Why is the metaphor so recurrent?

5. Both page 62 and page 65 feature ***lists,*** though the rest of the essay is in standard paragraph form. Speculate on the reason these two sections appear in list rather than paragraph form.
6. Towards the end of his essay, Birkerts uses a three-item list to distill his criticism of technological progress. How would his criticism change in its persuasiveness if written in narrative form? Examine the list, paraphrase it, and explain whether you think electronic texts (and other non-paper texts) are necessarily excluded from his vision.

Multimedia Suggestions

1. Review films with similar cautionary tales about "progress": *1984* (1955, 1984), *2001: A Space Odyssey* (1968), *Blade Runner* (1982), *Terminator* (1984), *A Handmaid's Tale* (1990), *The Brave New World* (1998), *Matrix* (1999), *Minority Report* (2002); *AI* (2001), or any others that you are familiar with. See if you can apply Birkerts's ideas about selfhood and "collective subjective history" to the films as you watch them.
2. Read the article "Think," about the meaning of Techno music at: *http://ravehousetech.about.com/gi/dynamic/offsite.htm?site=http://www.ele%2Dmental.org/ele%5Fment/think./.* It argues among other things that: "the origins of techno and electronic music, then, lie deep in the hearts and minds of humanity; the way we interact with our environment, the way we interact with each other, and especially, the way we shape and improve our world through technology." Can you use this history/defense of techno music to challenge Birkerts's skeptical view of technology? Is this new genre relevant to Birkerts's argument? Explain why or why not.
3. Recently many classic novels have been made into films. Some interpretations (e.g., *Clueless* as a version of Jane Austen's *Emma* or *O* as a version of William Shakespeare's *Othello*) even bring the stories into entirely new contexts. Watch the film version of a novel or play you *have* read and discuss whether you think the novel's ideas hold up despite the transformation. Also consider the different experiences of reading and viewing. What is gained and lost in each of the genres? Compare your reaction to the film of your choice to Birkerts's reactions after he watches both *A Room of One's Own* and *Fools of Fortune.*
4. Check out the writing on *Slate.com, Salon.com,* and/or *Nerve.com,* paying attention to how the reading experience changes with the introduction of various navigation bars, menus, hypertext, and other technological intrusions. How is this a more enriching reading experience? How is it a more impoverished experience? What would Birkerts's reaction be to these types of texts?
5. Read the interview with Sven Birkerts at *http://www.nea.gov/artforms/Lit/Birkerts.html,* which focuses on his latest book project, *Tolstoy's Dictaphone: Technology and the Muse.* Would you say that his thinking about technology has shifted at all since the publication of "MahVuhHuhPuh"?

SUGGESTIONS FOR WRITING AND RESEARCH

1. Birkerts is surprised that his students find Henry James's story so impenetrable when he had thought it relatively ***available*** (53). What does it mean for a text to be "available"? Is that meaning different for teachers and students? Should texts be immediately available or should they encourage excavation? Explore the subject in reference to Birkerts himself. Is "MahVuhHuhPuh" available or unavailable? Explain your answer in an essay, quoting Birkerts as necessary.
2. Birkerts talks a good deal about selfhood and autonomous thinking in this essay. Do you agree with him that society has become more of a "species-organism" than a collection of autonomous beings, or do you think society has become more individualistic with the rise in technology? Explore the theme of selfhood in Birkerts's argument.
3. Read Virginia Woolf's essay, "A Room of One's Own," to examine the inspiration of Birkerts's ideas. Compare and contrast the structure of the two essays, keeping in mind that Birkerts aspires to mimic Woolf in this regard. Do you think he succeeds? Why or why not? Which essay is ultimately more persuasive to you? Why?

   Alternately, read Henry James's "Brooksmith," the story that illustrates the gap Birkerts perceives between himself and his students. Try to get beyond "the whole thing" complaint of the students and examine the details of the story. What elements of James's story and prose do you think are ***specifically*** responsible for the resistance of the students? Write the essay as a letter to Birkerts that tries to explain more specifically than his students what "the whole thing" entails.
4. One aspect of technology that Birkerts does not explore in this essay is its application in the delivery of education. Using Birkerts's ideas and language, write an essay that explores the ways that that technology could change not only the *content* of education (texts, assignments, etc.), but also the ***form*** of it (e.g., T.V. courses and online learning). Are there formal considerations in this application that could contribute to Birkerts's argument or challenge it?

WORKING WITH CLUSTERS

Cluster 3: Reading Meaning, Achieving Literacy
Cluster 19: Structuring Chaos
Cluster 20: The Burdens of Modernity
Discipline: The Humanities
Rhetorical Mode: Illustration

"The Bone Garden of Desire" (from *Esquire*, August 2000)

by Charles Bowden

Charles Bowden, a resident of Tucson, Arizona, writes primarily about living in the Southwest and on the U.S.-Mexico border, describing life on what he calls "the edge," often including photographs in his creative non-fiction style. His books include Blue Desert, Juarez: The Laboratory of Our Future, *and* Blood Orchid: An Unnatural History. *Bowden writes regularly for* Harper's, Esquire, *and* GQ. *He has won several awards, including the Lannan Foundation Literary Award for Non-fiction in 1996. This essay was first published in* Esquire *magazine and was included in* Best American Essays 2000.

When everyone dies on you, keep the recipe simple. As long as you are alive be alive. Taste deeply. Trust the senses. Forget advice. Drink something. Cook. Eat.

Rossini, the great opera composer, could recall only two moments of real grief in his life. One, when his mother died. And the second time was out on a boat when a chicken stuffed with **truffles** fell into the water and was lost.

truffle: rare and prized mushroom-like tuber

Sometimes, when he was nearing death, I'd go over to help Art cook. I'm down on my knees on the patio, and Art is sitting in a chair with a beer. He has grilled steaks to a cinder and caught the juice. And now I pound the meat with a claw hammer until it's infused with cloves of garlic and peppercorns. Then I shred it with my fingers, put it all in a bowl with the saved juice and herbs, and then simmer. This is machaca according to his late wife's recipe and it takes hours, and this is life, or the best part, he believes as he sits in the chair while I bend and pound to spare his battered old joints. It is a deep taste of something within his bones.

We are outside in the old downtown **barrio** while I pound in the desert sun, and nearby are the justicia flaming-orange flowers and the chuparosa with the buzz of hummingbirds and the nicotiana reaching up twelve, fourteen feet, the pale-green leaves, the spikes of yellow flowers, the Costa hummingbirds with purple gorgets that seem to favor it, and Art beams and says, "My birds, my plants."

barrio: Spanish-speaking neighborhood or district

1. In Your Journal: "Maybe it is the mouth," Bowden writes about Art's mood. What do you think the mouth has to do with approaching or accepting death?

He takes another swig of beer, and beads of cold moisture fleck the can. Maybe it is the mouth, I think, as I sit down in the garden, swirling red wine in my mouth, dry wine, the kind that reaches back toward the throat and lasts for maybe half a minute on the tongue.

2. In Your Journal: List or summarize the references to sensory experience in the first five paragraphs of this essay.

Anyway, when we made the machaca, Art was alive then, and being alive is gardening and cooking and birds and green and blue, at the very least. He was relaxed. I pounded the garlic and pepper, and grilled flesh hung in the air. He told me that during the Korean War, his Navy ship made a run from Philadelphia to Europe, and during the Atlantic crossing five officers went over the side and nobody ever writes about stuff like that. But he knows, he was there and all fell overboard at night. They were all assholes, he said.

3. In Your Journal: Why do you think Bowden includes Art's anecdote about his experiences in the Navy?

The beef was tender, the chiles hot, but not too hot, just enough to excite the tongue, and the seasonings bite, the garlic licks the taste buds, and I began to float on the sensations as Art drank his beer and the plants grew and stirred, the hummingbirds whizzed overhead and then hovered before my face, my tongue rubbed against the roof of my mouth, and it is all a swirl of sensation as I remember that summer day cooking.

I also remember Art (died February 11) sitting down in my garden in a chair on a Sunday in January, the last day he left home under his own power. He could barely walk then, his chunky body dwindling as the cancer snacked on various organs, and his skin was yellow from the jaundice. He held on to my arm as we crept through the garden, down from the upper bench, past the bed of trichocereus, under the thin arms of the selenicereus snaking through the tree overhead. He looked over by the notocactus, with their dark-green columns, their tawny rows of bristles and small bubbles of white down on their crowns where the yellow flowers would finally emerge; he looked over there where I'd scattered Dick's bone and ash and he said brightly, Hi, Dick (died August 23).

4. *In Your Journal:* Bowden uses the word "snacked" to describe progression of Art's cancer. To what effect?

We sat in plastic chairs surrounded by garden walls that were purple, yellow, and pink, colors to fight back all the nights. He knew he'd be dead in two or three weeks, and he was. He knew he'd never see this spring, just as Dick had never made it to the previous fall. And five months before Dick had been Paul (died March 9). And five months after Art would come Chris (died August 6).

5. *In Your Journal:* Why does Bowden include the specific dates of his friends' deaths?

The cooking had begun earlier, like the gardening, but both took hold of me around the time my friends started dying. I remember walking to the market, coming home and flipping through books for recipes, and then cooking. While the sauce simmered, I would open a bottle of red wine and begin drinking. There was never enough red wine, never. I was always cooking from Italian recipes because they were simple and bold and I loved the colors, the red of the tomatoes, the green skin of the zucchini, and because I like peeling garlic and chopping onions and tearing basil. The oil mattered also, the thought of olives, and I preferred the stronger, cheaper oils with their strong tastes. I used iron pans coated with green enamel on the outside. There would be scent in the air.

The garden also went out of control. I put in five or six tons of rock. Truckloads of soil. I built low terraces and planted cactus and a few herbs. I had no plan and the thing grew from someplace in my mind.

6. *In Your Journal:* The author reports that he has brought "tons" of rock and "truckloads" of soil into his garden, but that he has "no plan." What could this extravagance mean in the context of his subject matter?

I must tell you about this flower, Selenicereus plerantus. It opens only in the dark; it begins to unfold around 9:00 P.M. and it closes before dawn, slams shut at the very earliest probes of gray light. When it blooms, no one can be alone at night, it is not possible, nor can anyone fear the night, not in the slightest. This flower touches your face, it kisses your ear, its tongue slides across your crotch. The flower is shameless, absolutely shameless. When it opens its white jaws, the petals span a foot and lust pours out into the night, a lust as heavy as syrup, and everything is coated by the carnality of this plant. It opens only on the hottest nights of the year, black evenings when the air is warmer than your body and you cannot tell where your flesh ends and the world begins.

7. *In Your Journal:* *Selenicereus plerantus*, according to Bowden, is "shameless, absolutely shameless." Why do you think he uses this term? Does it seem to be a positive or negative characteristic?

A month, maybe a month and a half, before Chris died, he came over in the evening. He could not control his hiccuping then—the radiation, you know. And he found it better to stand in his weakness than to sit. He wore a hat; his hair was falling out. So we were out in the darkness, him hiccuping and not drinking—he just did not want that beer anymore—and the flower opened and flooded the yard with that lust, the petals gaping shamelessly, and we watched it unfold and felt the lust caress us and he hiccuped and took it all in.

8. In Your Journal: How does Chris's hiccupping contribute to the scene of one of his last nights in Bowden's garden?

He understood that flower, I'm sure of it.

Blind old **Homer** wrote that no part of us is more like a dog than the "brazen belly, crying to be remembered." By the twentieth century, there were fifty or sixty thousand codified recipes in Italian cooking alone. By the mid-twentieth century, Italians were eating seven hundred different pasta shapes, and one sauce, Bolognese, had hundreds of variations.

9. In Your Journal: "What can death mean in the face of all this drive?" Try to answer this question yourself.

What can death mean in the face of this drive? What can death say at this table? I tell you: Art called up when things had gotten pretty bad and said he had this craving for strawberry Jell-O.

There must be something about the mouth, about the sucking and the licking and the chewing and the sweet and the sour. The pepper also, and the saline. An English cookbook of 1660 suggests a cake recipe that consumes a half bushel of flour, three pounds of butter, fourteen pounds of currants, two pounds of sugar, and three quarts of cream. There is a leg of mutton smeared with almond paste and a pound of sugar and then garnished with chickens, pigeons, capons, cinnamon, and, naturally, more sugar.

The dark-green flesh of the cactus glows with life from the ash and ground human bone. I've come to depend upon the garden, and so I stare at the Madagascar palms, their thorny trunks bristling under the canopy of the mesquite tree. Red wine swirls against my tongue because this bone gardening, this wall of green flesh, has all become hopelessly oral with me. I eat, therefore I am. I appreciate nothing, devour everything.

Art found out about the cancer after Thanksgiving. He couldn't really eat. It wasn't the chemotherapy, since he'd passed on that after having a first bout with the colon cancer, and to be honest, the doctors didn't recommend chemo or any other therapy. They gave him prescriptions for opiates and advised him to take lots of them and not to worry. But he didn't like them, didn't like having his mind turn to mush, and besides, he was an old narc, and I think pill popping didn't quite sit right with him. But he couldn't eat, just had no appetite, and when he ate, he felt kind of sick. The cancer was everywhere, of course, with the liver just being the signature location.

Homer: principal figure and epic poet of ancient Greece; author of *The Odyssey* and *The Iliad*, which emphasize the concepts of tragedy and fate

So I took him over some marijuana brownies and that evening he took two and then spent half the night in the kitchen-frying steaks and potatoes, whipping up this and that, and gorging. And after that, he refused ever to take another brownie.

Art said they upset his stomach.

But, Lord, that one night, he came alive and tasted deeply.

She has the gift of writing exactly the way she speaks and speaking exactly the way she thinks. For years I have gotten letters from Barbara, and they are always fresh and clear and without any of the filters we generally use to guard our hearts. When she writes of her son's death, her words remain the same. Paul was not a surprise to her. She is an artist, her father was an artist, his father was an artist. And it has never been easy—art is not made by the easy, but it has been in the house for generations and felt as a part of life. She told me that's what she put on his tombstone: ARTIST.

At first she was very angry. Not at Paul, at least not in a way she was ready to say, but at the people around him who introduced him to heroin and then did nothing as the drug took over his soul. Shouldn't they have done something? Didn't they realize what they had unleashed? Aren't they responsible? And, of course, the questions were sound and the answers were deserved and Paul was still dead.

She works, she organizes his papers, letters, his art work. She revisits the studio, the pipe, the rope, a boy hanging there. She writes me, "Found out Paul hung for over 8–9 hours. That would not have happened had I been there. 8–9 hours after he was found. Fuck the criminal codes. My baby hung by his neck for as long as 14 hours. I didn't think there could be more pain."

They take away the mints because the case is metal. They scrutinize the carton of cigarettes also and then I'm allowed on the ward. Dick is puzzled by the shower, why the head is buried up some kind of funnel in the ceiling. It takes him weeks to figure out they are trying to prevent him from hanging himself. Of course, he cannot think clearly, what with the steady dose of electroshock treatments. He'd checked himself in after the suicide attempt failed. He had saved up his Valiums, taken what he figured to be a massive dose, and then, goddammit, still woke up Monday morning when by any decent standards he ought to have been dead. It was the depression, he told me, the endless blackness. He could handle the booze, and when he was rolling, that was a quart or two of vodka a night, plus coke, of course, to stay alert for the vodka. There was that time he'd checked into detox with blood oozing from his eyes and ears and ass. But he could handle that. He was working on the smoking, didn't light up in the house, you know.

But he couldn't take the depression, never tasted blackness like that. I'd go out in the evening to the ward and we'd sit outside in the walled yard, kind of like a prison, and for two days I tried to get him to pitch

10. In Your Journal: Why do you think Art "refused ever to take another brownie"?

11. In Your Journal: Bowden speaks of a "she" who writes him letters before he names his friend Barbara. Why do you think he does this?

12. In Your Journal: What does Barbara put on her son Paul's tombstone? Why?

13. In Your Journal: Speculate about why the author would follow his introduction of Paul's completed suicide with Dick's failed attempt. How do these two men's lives compare and contrast?

horseshoes. Finally, on the third night, he tried but couldn't make the distance between the two pits. The shoes, of course, were plastic, lest the patients hurt one another. But we worked on it, and he got to tossing okay.

We'd been friends for a good long time, business partners once, and we'd survived being in business together, so we must've really been friends, and he'd always been like me, riding a little roughshod over the way life was supposed to be lived, but he'd kept his spirits up. Not now.

When he got out, I'd go over and take him to the store. He could not move. I'd walk him from the car into the market and then walk with him up and down the aisles. He could not connect with food. I'd buy him bananas because his potassium was low, and lots of green vegetables. He couldn't abide this; he told me he'd never eaten anything green since he was five. Then I'd take him through the checkout and home. The place was a wreck. One day I showed him how to clean off one square foot of the kitchen counter. He watched me do it. I said, Look, you do a foot a day and if you don't do a damn thing else, you'll feel like you did something. His face remained passive.

I'd bring him over and cook dinner and make him eat it. Then we'd sit in the yard, he'd stare out at the cactus and trees, and his eyes would glaze at the twisting paths and clouds of birds. He could hardly speak. The blackness, he'd say by way of explaining.

My huge Argentine mesquite arced over the yard. Nobody believed I'd planted it myself, dug the hole and everything, and that when I put it in the ground, it did not come up to my knee. I remember when I planted it, a woman was over and I told her what this little sapling would become and she said, Nope, it ain't gonna happen. But it did.

I kept trying to get Dick to plant trees. But it was like the horseshoes. It came hard.

In 1696, Mme. de Maintenon, Louis XIV's longtime mistress, writes, "Impatience to eat [peas], the pleasure of having eaten them, and the anticipation of eating them again are the three subjects I have heard very thoroughly dealt with. . . . Some women, having supped, and supped well, at the king's table, have peas waiting for them in their rooms before going to bed."

lascivious: lusty, lecherous

stoic: indifferent to pleasure and pain

stalwart: one who is sturdy, resolute

14. In Your Journal: What does the discussion of peas in 17th century France have to do with the general ideas presented in this essay?

Peas are new to the French court and all those **lascivious** mouths and expert tongues are anxious for this new sensation. I applaud this pea frenzy. Who would want a **stoic** as a cook? Mme. de Maintenon, sixty-one years old, now secretly wed to the king, **stalwart** of court etiquette, she likes her pea pods dipped in a sauce, and then she licks them. Yes, she does.

Going up the stairs, I instantly miss the sunlight. Outside, Brooklyn in January is brilliant and the sea is in the air. The stairs feel narrow and dim and cold and dank, and it is like leaving childhood behind for the grave. In my memory, Paul is a child, permanently around the age of, say, ten. I've seen his later photographs on driver's licenses, and the face seems gaunt, the eyes hollow. I'm afraid of finding the room those eyes came from, finding it upstairs at the end of these seemingly endless flights of stairs, with almost no light, a chill in the air, and that dampness that says no one cooks in the kitchen and the woman is never in the bed.

But the machinery standing in the gray light of the big room comforts me. I have stumbled into a surviving pocket of the nineteenth century, that time when people still believed that they could throw themselves at problems and wrestle with materials and fabricate solutions. The morning bleeds through the large windows and glows against the shrink-wrap machine. He had a thing about shrink-wrap—the more you stressed it, the stronger it became. I soak up the room and feel at peace. This is a proper shop for a craftsman and his craft. His craft was pretty simple: He was going to be the best fucking artist in the world and show that all the other stuff was shit. He was going to cut through the fakery and the fashion and get to the ground floor, the killing floor, the factory floor. He was not about tricks or frills or style. He was brutally simple and industrial-strength. I can feel him here, his mouth a firm line, his hair carelessly framing his totally absorbed face, his body bent over slightly as he tinkers with some project, oblivious to everything, including himself, pushing on relentlessly toward mastering a riddle that only he sees or feels or can solve. He's forgotten to eat for a day, his dog watches him silently from a corner of the big room, a stillness hangs over everything and is only slightly broken by the careful movements he makes.

Over in a corner of the shop is the apartment he carved out of the vast cavern of the old factory, and sketched on his door is an arrow pointing down to the floor and a message to slide the mail under here. It has the look of something a twelve-year-old would do. And enjoy doing. I half expect Orville and Wilbur Wright to tap me on the shoulder, or to hear old Henry Ford **laconically** announcing **idiot-savant** theses about the coming industrial age. I'm in the past, a place Paul picked to find the future. There is a feeling of grime everywhere, an oil-based grime that has come off machines as they inhaled and exhaled in the clangor of their work. I stand over a worktable and open a cigar box of crayons and carefully pluck two for myself, a blue and a red. I ask a friend of Paul's a question, and he visibly tightens and says suddenly that he can't stay in here anymore. He says he is still upset. So I go alone and look down the narrow hallway to the door to this loft/studio/factory floor and glance up at the stout pipe; it looks to be six or eight inches in diameter. Then I come back to the factory room and see a piece of a black doormat that Paul had nailed to the wall. It says quietly, GET HOME. I think, Well, shit, so this is where he hung himself.

laconically: succinctly, tersely

idiot-savant: intellectually disabled person who exhibits extraordinary ability in a highly specialized area

15. In Your Journal: According to Bowden, Paul used the past to "find the future." What does this mean in terms of art? In terms of death?

King Solomon's palace was probably one warm home. He lived with seven hundred wives and three hundred girlfriends and somehow everybody tore through ten oxen a day, plus chunks of gazelles and hartebeests.

16. In Your Journal: Compare the way King Solomon's life is described to the way Paul's life is.

The Bible said the wise old king had twelve thousand horsemen charging around the countryside scaring up chow for the meals back home.

Money does not replace the lust for food. Or the flesh. Nothing replaces it, nothing. Sometimes it dies, this appetite, sometimes it just vanishes in people. But it is never replaced. By 1803, one restaurant in Paris had kept its stockpot bubbling twenty-four hours a day for eighty-five years. Three hundred thousand **capons** had gone into the pot over the decades. This is what we like to call a meaningless statistic. Until we open our mouths. Or catch the scent of a woman. Or lean over into a bloom raging in the night.

capon: rooster castrated to improve the taste of its flesh

I'd come out to the ranch, a two-hundred-acre remaining fragment of the fifty to eighty square miles that once wore his family's brand, and we'd sit on the porch and have a beer. Chris worked as a carpenter and enjoyed life. He knew every plant and rock for miles around. He didn't seem to give a damn about being born into money and now living without it. I never heard him say a word about it. He cared about when one of his cows was going to calf. And he liked not owning a horse—he prided himself on getting along without one and in wearing sensible boots instead of narrow, highheeled cowboy boots like every other person in a western city.

He'd show me things. The foundations of a settler's cabin down the hill. The little collapsed house he and his first wife lived in along the **arroyo.** An old Indian village.

arroyo: deep gully with little water

I remember the village clearly. We walked for an hour or two or more and then hit a steep incline under the **palisades.** Chris paused and pointed out the hawk and falcon nesting sites. Then his legs went uphill at a steady pace, like pistons. At the top, we slid through a narrow chute and were upon a small village on a **mesa.** At the entrance was a low wall and piles of rocks for throwing at invaders. This was clearly a fort people fled to in some time of trouble five hundred years or more ago.

palisades: steep lofty cliffs along a river

mesa: flat elevation with cliff-like sides

Chris had been coming here since he was a boy. The place, like almost everything else in the area, was his secret. We sat up there in the sunshine, swallowing a couple hundred square miles of scenery and saying little. He was like that. I hardly ever heard him complain. Things just are. And if you look around, they're pretty good. Have a cold beer, a warm meal. And take in the countryside.

In the first century **Apicius** put together a manuscript that lets us visit the lust of the Roman palate. The empire made all things possible—Apicius once outfitted a ship because he'd heard some good-sized shrimp were being caught off North Africa. The emperor **Vitellius,** said to be somewhat

---

-:- **Apicius**: (Marcus Gabius) Roman gourmet of the 1st century

-:- **Vitellius**: (Aulus) (A.D. 15–69) Roman emperor

of a pig at table, favored a dish of pike liver, pheasant brains, peacock brains, flamingo tongues, and lamprey roe. Apicius is supposed to have killed himself when he was down to his last couple of million bucks because he could not bear to lower his standard of living. Before there was a language of words on paper, there must have been a language of food. Speech begins with the fire and the kettle. I am sure of this.

17. In Your Journal: What does Bowden mean in connecting speech and cooking here?

When I was drinking at the grave, I didn't feel quite right. I'd been uneasy about leaving Dick, worried about two days away. I'd gone down and gotten him bailed out a few days before, done the shopping trips, talked to him about the importance of cleaning a counter. All of that. We had sat in the yard and watched the woodpecker eat insects in the throb of the August air. His speech was very slow and nothing seemed to ever lift, nothing. He'd been fired, the drinking had come back, the electroshock didn't seem to do much good, and the gambling dug in deep until he had about a hundred thousand on the credit cards. So we'd sit in the yard and I'd explain that you can't beat a slot machine, that you can't win. He'd say, That's it, that's it, you can't win.

So when I left for a memorial mass in a distant city for a murder victim named Bruno Jordan who'd crossed my path, I felt ill at ease. Out at the cemetery after the mass, we stood around the grave drinking beer and talking, and then we went back to the house in the barrio for dinner, one cousin looking down at the grave and saying, Hey, Bruno, see you back at the house.

The next day, when I came through the door, the phone was ringing. They'd found the body. Dick had been dead two days. He'd died clean, nothing in his body. He'd accidentally tripped on the rug, hit his head on the dining-room table, that was it. He'd been working on a book about the drinking life.

Dick had always had one terror: that he would die drunk.

So God smiled on him.

I feel surprisingly at peace. Walking the few blocks from the subway, I took in the Brooklyn street, warming to its resemblance to the endless warrens of houses and factories I knew in Chicago. It looked just like the places Paul lived as a boy, and I thought, You cagey guy, you found the Midwest in New York. Behind the factory-now-loft stands a Russian church, thrown up in the 1920s by those determined to keep the lamp of faith lit on a distant shore. Across from that is a small park with beaten grass, the kind of sliver of light our urban planners have always tossed to the inmates of our great cities. It all felt very comfortable to me. When Paul was a small boy, I can remember walking across the tundra of Chicago to visit his parents' apartment and passing scenes just like these in this pocket of Brooklyn. And the workspace itself, with its **patina** of grime from machines, its workman's bench, its **monastic** sense of craft, hard work, and diligence, recalls the various places Paul toiled as a boy—his room, the cellar, the corner

patina: brown-green sheen produced by age or corrosion

monastic: characterized by contemplative seclusion

grabbed in some cottage in the country. That's part of the sense of peace I feel pervading me. I think to myself, Paul, you kept the faith.

I've gotten up before dawn and gone over his letters, which I've brought with me, and the bank statements, all the while sipping coffee in a mid-Manhattan hotel. The numbers on the statements blurred as I sat amid businessmen who were studying CNN on the lounge television, and then I'd look back down at the bank statements and feel as though I were watching the spinning dials of a slot machine, only this machine always comes up with the same result: a hundred dollars a day. December, January, February, the steady withdrawals are punctual and exact. I thought to myself, Paul, you create order even in your disorder. So later when I stand in the big room where he tore at the limits of what he called art and plunged into some place he hoped was behind that name, when I touch his row of tools on the workbench and admire his shrinkwrap machine in one corner, whirring in my head is this blur of numbers as he swallowed his earnings in a grim, orderly fashion. I look over at the wall, the one punctured by the hallway leading to the doorway and the stout pipe against the ceiling, and read once more the doormat still whispering GET HOME. I reach up and rip the black message from the wall. This one I am taking home.

Paul was up to something here. I know this in my bones.

He kind of scowls and comes limping across the kitchen at me, saying, No, no. He takes the knife and says, Here, see, you gotta do this rocking motion, and with that he chops the hell out of the cilantro. Art will be dead in three weeks, and this is his last hurrah, teaching me how to make salsa cruda. He's real yellow now, wheezing all the time, and beneath the yellow is the color of ash.

He's got these papers to straighten out, and we go over them. He's going to do a bit of writing, and so I bring the office chair and computer. But then he can't sit up anymore, and we try to **jury-rig** something in the easy chair. And then that's too much and the damn fluid is building in his body, he's all bloated and distended, and, by God, he tells the nurse who comes to the house each day, he's gotta get the swelling drained at the hospital. And she says, That won't do any good, you're not sick, you're dying. He listens without so much as a blink, I'm sitting right there, and then he pads down the hall to his bedroom, lies down, and sleeps. In twenty-four hours, he goes into a coma. The next day, he's dead after a night of family praying and shouting over him—ancient aunts hollering messages in his ear for other family members that have gone to the boneyard ahead of him. His cousin, the monsignor, says the funeral mass.

jury-rig: set up for special emergency use

I can still taste the salsa and smell the cilantro and feel that rocking motion as he tries to show me the right way to wield the knife. And to make salsa, his salsa, as he learned it from his wife, Josie, who learned from her parents and back into the brown web of time. Like everything that matters to the tongue, it is simple.

> ***18. In Your Journal:*** Do you agree with Bowden's claim that "everything that matters to the tongue . . . is simple"?

Put five or six sixteen-ounce cans of whole TOMATOES into a big pot, reserving the liquid. Coarse-grind the tomatoes in a food processor, a short pulse so they come out in chunks and not puree. Now add them to the reserved juice.

Cut up two or three bunches of GREEN ONION, in very thin slices so that you end up with tiny circles. Now very finely cut up a bunch of CILANTRO.

Add five cans of diced GREEN CHILES, a teaspoon of GARLIC POWDER, and the onion and cilantro to the tomatoes and their juice. Sprinkle a teaspoon or two of OREGANO. Taste it and adjust seasoning.

Now start crushing CHILTEPINS (*Capsicum annuum* var. aviculare) and add to taste. Add salt. Taste again. Keep crushing chiltepins until it is right for your tongue.

That was the last time I really saw him move, when he was trying to teach me how to make salsa cruda. He knew some things can't be allowed to end.

The bottom line is always simple, and the way to this line is to get rid of things. I stand at a hot stove and make risotto, a rice dish of the Italian north:

Melt some butter in oil, then saute some CHOPPED ONION, toss in the RICE, and coat it with the oil; add the liquid (make the first ladle white wine, then go with broth) a half cup at a time, constantly stirring.

In twenty minutes, the rice is ready, the center of each kernel a little resistant to the tooth, but ready. Each grain is saturated with the broth and onion and oil flavor.

Then spread the rice on the plate to cool and eat from the edge inward. Pick a brilliant plate with rich color—I like intense blues and greens, you know—to play off the white. Some mix in A HALF OR FULL CUP OF GRATED PARMESAN to the rice to make it stickier. I just sprinkle some on top and usually favor Romano, because it has more bite. But that is your choice.

> ***19. In Your Journal:*** Why are recipes included in this essay? Do you think they are meant to be followed?

The rest is not. After all, we are in Paul's workshop, a thing to be kept clean and simple and direct. The difference between good art and good cooking is you can eat cooking. But the important part, the getting rid of things, it is always there and the kid knew it.

The kid worked. Like most products of the Midwest, I can't abide people who fuck off and don't do things. I can remember my father sitting at a kitchen table in Chicago with his quart of beer, telling me with a snarl that in Chicago we make things, but in New York they just sell things.

I look up at the torn drywall. When Paul didn't answer the phone, his uncle flew from Chicago to New York and took a cab over here to Brooklyn.

Clawed his way through the drywall—I look up at the hole he made—and found Paul swinging from the big pipe. He'd left a note and neat accounts on the table, plus his checkbook, so everyone would be paid off proper.

I hum to myself as I look up at that pipe. Hum that song by **John Prine** about the hole in Daddy's arm where all the money goes.

It got so he couldn't do much. One day his ex-wife, Mary, stopped by the ranch to check on him, and he was sprawled in the doorway, half in the house and half out, surrounded by the dogs and cats.

20. In Your Journal: As the author promotes the pleasure and value of eating, he also describes cancer as something that eats. Why?

So Mary took him into town. He'd been busy at the ranch despite his weakness as the cancer ate. He'd been building check dams to cure a century of erosion; he planted a garden, put the boots to the cattle, and let the hills come back. He said ranching was over and it was time for the earth to get some other kind of deal. I'd run into him a week or so before at the feed mill and he was chipper. His hair had just about all fallen out because of the radiation, but he said he felt good. He was in town to get a part for the pump.

He was real lean by then, and when I went down to see him at Mary's place, he was stretched out in bed. He wanted to talk Mexico, the people, the plants; the cattle, the way the air felt at night. I brought down some pictures of Mexico and we hung them around the room. He was having some kind of magic tar shipped down from Colorado that was supposed to beat back the cancer, and he was tracking the pennant race also. People would drop by at all hours to see him, since the word was out that he was a goner. He'd smoke a joint with them, talk about this and that, especially Mexico, which he knew was color and sound and smell and taste and a wood fire with a kettle on the coals. Some of the time he lived down there in a shack with a **campesino** family. When he fell in the doorway at the ranch, half in and half out, he was pretty much set to go back to Mexico. That was on hold at the moment as he tackled dying.

campesino: farm worker in Latin America

21. In Your Journal: How can Chris be excited about two inches of rain at his ranch when he is just days away from death?

He lasted about a week. I went over one day, and he was propped up in bed so that the tumor blocking his throat didn't pester him too much. He said, Chuck, I got some great news. We just got two inches of rain at the ranch.

Yes. I can smell the sweet grass as the clouds lift.

She is at war with herself, the life within her fighting the death without her. And she knows this. And she writes me this. She says, "So after I talked to you, I went out to the cemetery. The sun was out here and it was a beautiful day. Snow in patches hugging the earth in lovely patterns making me realize the earth has temperatures of variation, like a body. I had not realized that before. Then as I drove back, a rage overtook me and I raped and pillaged. I went to where I used to live along the beach and cut

---

John Prine: (1946–) contemporary blues/country/rock singer and songwriter, known for artful lyrics and rhythmic guitar playing branches from bushes I know will bloom (not in obvious places or so they would hurt the bush or tree). Many, many branches that filled up the trunk of the car and the backseat. It took an hour and a half to get them all recut and into water all over my house and closed porch. I've been cutting forsythia and 'forcing' it, but haven't tried these others—redbud, cherry, baby's breath, flowering almond, weigela (probably too late a bloomer), lilac (doubt this one will work). . . ."

22. In Your Journal: Why does Paul's mother want to "force" so many plants that she has "pillaged" from the beach where she used to live?

As she writes this to me, it is March, a month when boys hang themselves, a month when winter has stayed too long. A month when spring is near and force may be applied.

I don't trust the answers or the people who give me the answers. I believe in dirt and bone and flowers and fresh pasta and salsa cruda and red wine. I do not believe in white wine; I insist on color. I think death is a word and life is a fact, just as food is a fact and cactus is a fact.

23. In Your Journal: Respond to Bowden's claim that "death is a word, and life is a fact."

There is apparently a conspiracy to try to choke me with words. There are these steps to death—is it seven or twelve or what? fuck, I can't remember—and then you arrive at acceptance. Go toward the light. Our Father who art in heaven. Whosoever shall believe in me shall not perish. Too many words choking me, clutching at my throat until they strangle any bad words I might say. Death isn't the problem. The words are, the lies are. I have sat now with something broken inside me for months, and the words—death, grief, fear—don't touch my wounds.

I have crawled back from someplace where it was difficult to taste food and where the flowers flashing their crotches in my face all but lacked scent. My wounds kept me alive; my wounds, I now realize, were life. I have drunk a strong drug and my body is ravaged by all the love and caring and the colors and forms and the body growing still in the new silence of the room as someone I knew and loved ceased breathing.

I remember standing in the room with Art's corpse, so warm, his heart had stopped beating maybe a hundred and twenty seconds earlier, and I stood there wondering, What has changed now, what is it that just took place? And I realized that I had advanced not an inch from where I stood as a boy when I held my dying dog and watched life wash off his furry face with a shudder. I do not regret this inability to grow into wisdom. I listen to Chris saying, Good news, two inches of rain at the ranch. Look up at the stout pipe Paul picked for the rope. Hear Dick slowly trying to explain—in words so soft I must lean forward to hear them—why he cannot pick up a plastic horseshoe in the evening light at the nuthouse. Then these pat words show up that people offer me and these pious words slink away like a **cur** flinching from this new stillness on the wind.

cur: mongrel dog

Almost every great dish in Italian cooking has fewer than eight ingredients. Get rid of things or food will be complex and false. In the garden, there is no subtlety. A flower is in your face and is never named Emily. Be careful of the words; go into the bone garden and then taste desire. So it

24. In Your Journal: "If you go toward that light and find it, piss on it for me." Does this sentence surprise you? How would you characterize the tone of it? What do you think it means?

polenta: corn meal mash, usually served grilled or fried

has taken months and it is still a matter of the tongue and of lust. And if you go toward that light and find it, piss on it for me.

I would believe in the words of solace if they included fresh **polenta** with a thickened brown sauce with shiitake and porcini mushrooms. The corn must be coarse-ground and simmered and stirred for at least forty minutes, then spread flat on a board about an inch thick and cooled in a rich yellow sheet. The sauce, a brew of vegetable broth, white wine, pepper, salt, some olive oil, and minced garlic, is rich like fine old wood in a beloved and scarred table. When you are ready, grill a slab of the polenta, having first lightly brushed it with olive oil, then ladle on some sauce. And eat. The dish is brutally simple. But it skirts the lie of the words of solace; it does not deny desire.

Never deny desire. Not once. Always go to the garden and the kitchen. Whatever death means, the large white cactus flower still opens in the evening and floods the air with lust and hot wet loins. The mushroom sauce on the corn mush will calm no one, either. That is why they are better than the words.

25. In Your Journal: If the mushroom sauce "will calm no one," then why is it "better than words"?

As I sit here, Chris is to the south, Art is to the west, Paul is back east, and Dick is in the backyard by the fierce green flesh of the cactus. These things I know. The answers I don't know, nor am I interested. That is why food is important and plants are important. Because they are not words and the answers people offer me are just things they fashion out of words. A simple veal ragu is scent and texture and color and soft on the tongue. It is important to cut onions by hand. The power of the flower at night is frightening, the lust floods the air and destroys all hope of virtue.

There will be more blooms this spring—the cactus grew at least ten feet last year. They will open around nine in the evening and then close at the first gray light of dawn. I'll sit out there with a glass of red wine and the lights out.

When I tell people about the blooms, about how they open around nine and close before sunrise and do this just for one night, they always ask, Is that all?

Yes. That's all.

SIDEBAR

Cook. Eat.

CIBREO IS SMALL and maybe six or eight blocks from Dante's old house in Florence. The night air was cool and flavored with the roasting chestnuts of street-corner vendors. The place has an open kitchen, low-key help, and high prices. The wine ran fifty a bottle, dinner for two passed two hundred.

It was about YELLOW-PEPPER SOUP.

Mince some CELERY, ONION, AND CARROTS, this is the good part, the slow part with just a constant chop, chop, chop and the feel and color of vegetables.

Now put them into the kettle with TWO TABLESPOONS OF GOOD OLIVE OIL and stir them over a moderate heat for maybe ten minutes, until they get soft.

Earlier you've grilled, say, HALF A DOZEN YELLOW BELL PEPPERS skinned and seeded and cut into strips.

Add the peppers and let them flavor everything for four or five minutes. Then put in A COUPLE OF PEELED AND DICED AVERAGE-SIZED POTATOES.

Next, a quart of water and A COUPLE CUPS OF GOOD CHICKEN STOCK you've made in the by and by.

Now let it simmer for about twenty-five minutes until the potatoes are soft. Puree it all, and then you might add some BAY LEAVES and MILK to knock down any acidity. Or you might let well enough alone.

AS A DISH it is very simple; most things that matter are. Certainly that is true of flowers, smells, colors, and the fresh breath of sky. At Cibreo they were insistent that you should never cut up the onions with a machine. It kind of mushes them, they say. I believe them. I have swallowed the $E = mc^2$ of cooking.

By the time I got to the restaurant that night, everybody had died on me. And I carried this fact around with me like a stone. But it did not hurt my appetite.

FOR USE IN DISCUSSION

Questions about Substance

1. Bowden's friend Art has little time left to live, and yet he will spend hours on a recipe he has presumably made or had hundreds of times before (72). Does this make sense to you? Why or why not?
2. The author juxtaposes the pain in Art's joints with the hunger in Art's bones (72). What is the purpose of this juxtaposition?
3. How do cooking and gardening represent different aspects of dying?
4. How does Bowden's description of the mouth seem to create a connection between excess and joy?
5. There are several references to red wine in this essay. Examine those references and speculate about the meaning of this theme.

6. Bowden's guest didn't believe that his Argentine mesquite would grow. "But it did" (76). How does this relate to the author's investment in Dick's will to live?
7. Paul is described as pursuing a riddle that "only he sees or feels or can solve" (77). Is there a value in solving a riddle that no one else can see? How does this image relate to Paul's difficulty in life and eventual suicide?
8. "This is what we like to call a meaningless statistic. Until we open our mouths. Or catch the scent of a woman. Or lean over into a bloom raging in the night" (78). How does this statement emphasize the relationship between the abstract and the concrete? How does it speak to the relationship between the collective and the individual?

Questions about Structure and Style

1. Why do you think Bowden opens in part with the Rossini anecdote? Is his tone in the second paragraph more or less serious than what follows?
2. In his discussion about the plant "*selenicereus plerantus*," the author makes connections between flowers, flesh, sex, and the life cycle (73–74). Describe the way his use of language (word choice, tone, imagery, etc.) also connects to these things.
3. Homer is neither Italian, nor a cook. Why do you think the quote from Homer about the "brazen belly [like a dog], crying to be remembered" (74) is followed by a discussion about Italian recipes and ingredients? What does this connection reveal about the author's main idea?
4. How does the role of place develop over the course of this essay? How does place relate to the more overt themes of food and nature and death?
5. The deaths of Bowden's various friends seem to blend into each other as a result of the structure of his essay. What effect and/or point about their dying do you think this structure is meant to facilitate?
6. The conclusion to this essay emphasizes a minimalistic theory of "getting rid of things" (in cooking especially). At the same time, it urges the reader to "Never deny desire." Do these ideas contradict each other? Is desire simple or complicated, in your estimation? Why is the lustful nighttime cactus symbolic of these ideas and Bowden's connecting them?

Multimedia Suggestions

1. View one of the following films: *Babette's Feast* (1987), *Big Night* (1996), *Like Water for Chocolate* (1991), or *Eat, Drink, Man, Woman* (1994), *Chocolat* (2000), or *Tampopo* (1986), and explore the ways the film uses food to communicate.
2. Visit some of the following grief-centered Web sites and describe the way they are consistent with or in conflict with Bowden's ideas:
   - *http://www.journeyofhearts.org/*
   - *http://www.growthhouse.org/*
   - *http://www.grief-recovery.com/*
   - *http://www.grow.com/*

- *http://www.webhealing.com/*

3. In the film *Smoke Signals* (1998), two young Native American men must journey to retrieve their father's body for burial. Compare the way these characters cope with grief to the way Bowden does.

SUGGESTIONS FOR WRITING AND RESEARCH

1. Write an essay about how you coped with death in some way and try to describe how all of your senses were affected. Compare this experience with Bowden's style of coping, and model the style of your essay on Bowden's, using descriptive language and a non-linear structure.
2. "Death isn't the problem. The words are, the lies are . . . don't touch my wounds . . . my wounds . . . were life" (83). Analyze Bowden's logic here. What is so inadequate about language that it makes grief worse? Trace the way Bowden criticizes the language of grief and sympathy in his essay. Does Bowden's own writing fall into the category he criticizes? Why or why not? To add an element of research, look at some sympathy cards or books about coping with grief to see how they do or don't illustrate the falseness Bowden criticizes.
3. Write an essay about the recipes and emphasis on cooking in this essay about death. What do Bowden's meals and recipes all have in common? How do they illustrate his theory of grief? To add an element of research, Read *A Year in Provence* by Peter Mayle, or *Tender at the Bone* by Ruth Reichl. Compare the symbolic use of food in the book you choose to the symbolism in Bowden's essay.
4. Research the history of a recipe that is meaningful to your family. Write an essay describing how the different steps of the recipe represent different aspects of your family's history or traditions.

WORKING WITH CLUSTERS

Cluster 1: Sensory Knowledge
Cluster 4: Conceiving Death
Cluster 8: Metaphor and Truth
Cluster 15: Spatial Realities
Discipline: The Humanities
Rhetorical Mode: Narration

"Free Press, Free Voyeurs?" (from *Voyeur Nation: Media, Privacy and Peering in Modern Culture*)

by Clay Calvert

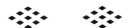

Clay Calvert is Associate Professor of Communications and Law and Associate Dean of The Schreyer Honors College at The Pennsylvania State University, and Co-Director of the Pennsylvania Center for the First Amendment. He is also a member of the State Bar of California. He holds both a J.D. from the University of the Pacific's McGeorge School of Law and a Ph.D. in Communication from Stanford University. Calvert's research and teaching focus on issues involving the freedoms of speech and press. He is the author of the book Voyeur Nation: Media, Privacy, and Peering in Modern Culture *(from which this selection is drawn) and has published more than 30 law journal articles.*

"Congress shall make no law . . . abridging the freedom of speech, or of the press," reads the First Amendment to the United States Constitution. Ratified in 1791, the First Amendment was drafted by **James Madison** long before the advent of the sophisticated electronic technology that makes mediated **voyeurism** possible. Today, that amendment increasingly safeguards, or at least is called on to safeguard, mediated voyeurism—our right to peer and to gaze into places typically forbidden to average citizens and to facilitate our ability to see and to hear the innermost details of others' lives without fear of legal repercussion. Why? The increase in the offering of reality television programs and news magazines has resulted in a surge of lawsuits filed by persons featured on those shows.[1] The First Amendment, in turn, is trotted out by the media as a defense against those suits.

voyeur: observer who enjoys watching the sordid or sensational acts of others

1. In Your Journal: What sort of tone do you see in the last sentence of this paragraph? Does the tone give you any indication of Calvert's point of view?

Whether the First Amendment protects mediated voyeurism ultimately is left to the courts that interpret its meaning and, in particular, to the United States Supreme Court. The nine justices who sit on the nation's high court are the final **arbiters** of its meaning. Their word determines the scope of freedom of expression in the United States. To the extent that the First Amendment press freedom is construed expansively by the judiciary, our right to be voyeurs is enhanced. To the extent that it is narrowly interpreted, our ability to watch others' lives unfold voyeuristically is limited.

arbiter: someone in a position to resolve a dispute

If press freedom is viewed broadly to serve mediated voyeurism, then several propositions must be supported by courts construing the First Amendment. First, they must provide journalists, photographers, and camerapeople with enhanced protection in both their ability to *gather* voyeuristic images—to enter buildings, use telephoto lenses and hidden cameras, and lie if necessary to procure information—and to *disseminate* private but titillating and embarrassing true facts about others. The media must, in other words, receive special protection that other people would not normally possess to go places, see things, and tell stories if the voyeurism value is to carry the day in First Amendment **jurisprudence**.

jurisprudence: body of law created by court decisions in cases where legal doctrine, such as the Constitution, must be interpreted to determine how it should apply to different sets of facts

Second, the public's so-called right to know—a right that is not explicitly mentioned in the First Amendment, or anywhere else in the

James Madison: (1751–1836) fourth president of the United States; known as the "Father of the Constitution" because he wrote the Virginia Plan, which formed the basis for the U.S. Constitution; also drafted the Bill of Rights, the first ten Amendments to the Constitution

Constitution for that matter—must be the official, judicially accepted battle cry to defend voyeuristic media practices. Journalists already heartily embrace the right-to-know mantra. As Christopher Meyers, a philosophy professor at California State University, Bakersfield, writes, "An appeal to the public's right to know serves as the core element of the journalism **ethos**."[2] Courts too must adopt the right-to-know claim if the voyeurism value is to be privileged under the First Amendment. Why? If the public has a right to know, then the public has a right to watch so that it can know. Concomitantly, if the public has a right to know, then the press must have a right to gather the same images the public has a right to watch.

2. In Your Journal: Did you think that "the right to know" was a constitutionally protected right? Does it surprise you that it's not a formal extension of the First Amendment?

ethos: guiding principles of a person or group

The media themselves also must push the envelope of the First Amendment to guard their ability both to gather the visuals and videotape we like to watch and then to publicize and broadcast those images. Put more bluntly and perhaps cynically, the First Amendment must be pushed by large media conglomerates and corporations to protect the kinds of high profits and ratings that often are generated by relatively low budget voyeuristic techniques such as hidden camera reportage and ride-along journalism. Not only, then, does the voyeur benefit from an expansive reading of the First Amendment, but so do the corporate entities that feed us voyeurism. They reap the monetary rewards of large audiences, which translate into hefty advertising revenue.

But this is still not enough if the voyeurism value is to be privileged by the First Amendment. The audience's right to receive speech—a right, in particular, to receive voyeuristic video images and others' personal information—must triumph over individuals' ability to control the flow of information about themselves. In other words, the rights of one person—the person who is the object or focus of the voyeur's gaze—must be sacrificed to privilege the rights of another person—the voyeur. The right to watch must trump the right not to be watched. It is an essential trade-off of rights if the voyeurism value is to prevail in the new millennium.

3. In Your Journal: Is there no way to protect both the rights of individuals to know and the rights of individuals to their privacy? Do someone's rights always have to be "sacrificed"?

For example, the right of the audience of a television news magazine such as *PrimeTime Live* to watch hidden camera footage of employees at Food Lion supermarkets allegedly repackaging spoiled meat must trump the right of the unsuspecting employees caught on tape either to suppress or to punish its dissemination. Likewise, the right of the audience to watch police officers raid a home during the execution of a search warrant must take precedence over the right of the home owner to keep journalists and media cameras out of his or her home when the police enter.

If, alternatively, press freedom is viewed narrowly under the First Amendment, then the access of the press to both the places and the information that make for mediated voyeurism will be curtailed. The press would be granted no special immunity from laws such as trespass and fraud that would otherwise hinder its news-gathering (read, *image*-gathering) ability. As a general rule, in fact, the United States Supreme Court has held

4. *In Your Journal:* Does it surprise you that journalists don't have any special protections with respect to violating the laws that might get in the way of their professional activities?

that journalists receive no greater protection than other citizens when it comes to violating general laws that apply to all people, such as trespass and general principles of contract law.

For instance, the Court ruled in 1991 that when a reporter breaches a promise of confidentiality to a source—in essence, violates a contract not to reveal the source's name—the reporter can be held liable to the source for damages incurred by the violation.[3] In the particular dispute, the source lost his job as a result of two newspapers breaking their promises to protect his identity. Justice Byron White wrote for the majority of the Court in that case, *Cohen* v. *Cowles Media*, that "enforcement of such general laws against the press is not subject to stricter scrutiny than would be applied to enforcement against other persons or organizations."[4] The First Amendment does not, in other words, exempt the press from liability for breaking promises.

Despite its language in a 1972 decision that "without some protection for seeking out the news, freedom of the press could be **eviscerated**,"[5] the United States Supreme Court has not been willing to provide extensive First Amendment protection for the press to gather images. As the communications law scholar Matthew D. Bunker and his colleagues observed in a 1999 law review article, "First Amendment protection for newsgathering has remained largely **inchoate**."[6] Courts and juries today, in fact, are more willing to punish the press for how it gathers information than for how it reports information. A country that privileges interests such as an individual's concern for privacy over an audience's voyeuristic proclivities clearly will pull in the reins on mediated voyeurism by imposing legal liability for both intrusive news gathering and invasive news reporting.

eviscerate: take the guts out of something; remove an essential part of it

inchoate: not well developed

Of course, the situation is not as black and white as this description would have it. It seldom is with the law, a fact that is just as frustrating for the general public as it is aggravating for first-year law students. The Supreme Court does not provide blanket support to voyeurs' rights to watch others under the First Amendment, just as it does not give absolute protection to the privacy interests of celebrities and others who are the frequent subjects of mediated voyeurism. More often than not, courts engage in the time-honored tradition of balancing interests, weighing the merits of one right or claim against another to reach a solution. In the case of mediated voyeurism, they must balance First Amendment interests in free speech and press—interests that directly serve the audience's right to receive voyeuristic speech and images—against concerns such as the privacy of the individual whose property is trespassed to acquire voyeuristic images or whose personal information is disclosed to titillate the audience. The legal issues that affect voyeurism often are couched in such terms of balancing.

5. *In Your Journal:* How does this concept of "balance" relate to the concept of "sacrifice" mentioned on page 91?

For instance, in its 1998 decision in *Shulman* v. *Group W Productions*[7], the California Supreme Court faced a question involving the voyeuristic dissemination of a videotape showing a woman rendered paraplegic by a car accident begging to die. As the high court of California framed the overriding issue in *Shulman*,

> At what point does the publishing or broadcasting of otherwise private words, expressions and emotions cease to be protected by the press's constitutional and common law privilege—its right to report on matters of legitimate public interest—and become an unjustified, actionable invasion of the subject's private life?[8]

How courts resolve the tension between the audience's interest in voyeurism and an individual's interest in privacy is a key issue that is explored here. Initially, I suggest three ways in which courts protect the audience's voyeuristic First Amendment interests. First, courts tend to adopt an expansive definition of "newsworthiness." This is extremely important because newsworthiness is a complete defense to an invasion of privacy lawsuit that would otherwise punish the media for the dissemination of truthful, private, and embarrassing facts about an individual.

Second, and closely related to the first point, courts are wary of second-guessing the editorial control and discretion of journalists, providing them instead with wide latitude to bring us voyeurism masquerading as news. Courts are extremely deferential to journalists' choices about content, having repeatedly held that under the terms of the First Amendment, editing should be left to editors. This breathing room allows profitable voyeuristic content to flourish.

> ***6. In Your Journal:*** Do you get a sense of Calvert's opinion of journalism's ability to edit its own content when he refers to "voyeurism masquerading as news"?

Third, a perhaps more subtle legal force leading to the propagation of mediated voyeurism is the United States Supreme Court's well-established decision to give large, megamedia corporations the same First Amendment rights as individuals. As will be suggested later, these corporations simultaneously use the First Amendment as a sword to make money and deploy it as a shield to protect their voyeuristic practices.

PRIVACY LAWS AND VOYEURISM

The concepts of voyeurism and privacy are related. As our expectations of what is or should remain private *decrease*, our expectations about what information is fair game for public consumption and mediated voyeurism *increase*. In the terms often used by social scientists, this is known as an "inverse," or "negative," relationship. An inverse relationship exists when one item—in this case, voyeurism—increases or goes up while another item—here, privacy—decreases or goes down.

> ***7. In Your Journal:*** Why does Calvert emphasize the "inverse" nature of the relationship?

The legal system today protects privacy in its many forms. For instance, a woman's right to choose to have an abortion is protected, the United States Supreme Court held in 1973's still-controversial *Roe* v. *Wade* decision,[9] by an unenumerated, or implied, right to privacy found in the United States Constitution. Privacy is this sense refers to the ability to make one's own autonomous choice, free from government control or interference.

statutory: based on statute, or written law

Privacy can also take the form of **statutory** protection of information designed to prevent others from voyeuristically peeping at our lives. For instance, after Robert Bork was nominated in the 1980s by former President Ronald Reagan to the United States Supreme Court and during his ill-fated confirmation hearings, a Washington, D.C., weekly paper published a list of 146 videos Bork allegedly had recently rented. Although Bork's cinematic tastes came up clean—he primarily rented Westerns and family films—the threat to privacy was clear. Shortly after this transpired, Congress quickly passed—perhaps for the sake of some of its own members' more carnal tastes—a piece of federal legislation restricting access to movie rental information known as the Video Privacy Protection Act of 1988.[10]

8. In Your Journal: If Robert Bork's video rental history was "clean," why would Congress pass a law restricting a journalist's access to such records?

Protection against mediated voyeurism can also take the form of civil remedies that allow one person to sue another under various privacy "torts" or theories of legal relief. One privacy **tort**, known as *public disclosure of private facts*, is particularly relevant here. Under this theory, a reporter or media entity may be held legally liable for giving publicity to truthful but otherwise private and embarrassing information about an individual if the publication of that information would be highly offensive to a reasonable person.

tort: body of law dealing with injuries to the person and providing a way for injured parties to sue for fair compensation

9. In Your Journal: What do you think it means for a piece of information to be "highly offensive to a reasonable person"?

This theory is significant in terms of mediated voyeurism because it suggests that there are some images and information that society believes should remain private, sheltered from the prying eyes and ears of a voyeuristic nation. Publicizing an embarrassing fact that an individual has kept secret deserves punishment, according to this theory. As the law professor Robert C. Post of the University of California–Berkeley observes, this privacy tort recognizes and embodies civility rules that suggest there are "information preserves" that are integral to individuals and that deserve respect.[11] Courts too acknowledge this important interest. The Supreme Court of the state of Washington observed in a 1998 case that "every individual has some phases of his life and his activities and some facts about himself that he does not expose to the public eye, but keeps entirely to himself or at most reveals only to his family or to close personal friends."[12]

But there is a critical caveat, or exception, to the public disclosure of private facts tort that allows us to play the role of voyeur and to discover the facts that others want to keep secret. It is a defense that the media often raise when sued for publicly disseminating private and embarrassing information about a person. The defense is *newsworthiness* and it is described below.

Newsworthiness: The Voyeur's Legal Defense

One critical legal standard with a direct bearing on the voyeurism value is newsworthiness. Newsworthiness, as noted above, is a defense to the invasion of privacy theory known as public disclosure of private facts. If published information or images are considered by a court to be newsworthy—courts often use the phrase "of legitimate public concern" interchangeably with newsworthiness—there can be no liability for the media.

Newsworthiness also is a defense for a legal theory called appropriation. Appropriation occurs when a person or corporation uses the name or likeness or image of another person—usually a celebrity—for commercial gain without the consent of the person. For instance, if a cereal company places an image of the golfer Tiger Woods on its boxes without Woods's permission, Woods can claim appropriation. If the photograph or name is used in connection with a newsworthy story, however, there is no liability, even if the person did not consent to the use of the photograph or name. Thus a newspaper that uses a picture of Woods to accompany a story about the golfer winning a tournament would be protected from liability.

> ***10. In Your Journal:*** Do you think there is a difference between "legitimate public concern" and "newsworthiness"?

Journalists often have trouble defining news. Many times it amounts to whatever the public is interested in watching or reading and whatever will boost advertising revenues. The definitional problem is exacerbated when courts—not journalists—are asked to provide a definition of what is newsworthy.

Courts, unfortunately for the targets and victims of mediated voyeurism, often defer to journalistic judgment when deciding whether a particular story is newsworthy.[13] They generally adopt what the law professor Diane Zimmerman aptly describes as the Leave-It-to-the-Press Model for defining news.[14] In other words, journalists often are awarded, by judicial default, the power to provide the legal definition of news. As Zimmerman observes, "The vast majority of cases seem to hold that what is printed is by definition of legitimate public concern."[15] Courts, in turn, have "gradually increased the scope of the newsworthy defense since its initial formulation in 1890."[16] As the veteran legal scholar Donald M. Gillmor and his colleagues wrote in 1996, "The news media have for the most part been able to persuade the courts to accept their standards of what is newsworthy."[17]

This legal definition promotes and serves the voyeurism value. How? Many broadcast journalists, as described earlier in the book, are increasingly driven by economic and entertainment concerns—not concerns over whether they are serving some abstract public good or democracy with a product they call news. They are, in turn, driven to provide sensationalistic

> ***11. In Your Journal:*** Why does the "Leave-It-to-the-Press Model" worry Calvert

videotape that captures and holds the attention of a large audience. In other words, broadcasters are compelled to provide videotape that the public *wants* to watch, not necessarily what it *needs* to watch to engage in wise and informed decisionmaking. If the public wants to watch something, news shows will keep serving it up to the audience on behalf of the advertisers who want to reach that audience with their commercials. As Kathleen Hall Jamieson, dean of the Annenberg School for Communication at the University of Pennsylvania, writes, "The primary function of the mass media is to attract and hold large audiences for advertisers."[18]

12. In Your Journal: How do economic concerns affect the definition of "newsworthiness" applied by "the mass media"? What kind of relationship does there seem to be between network news and the advertising industry?

It should be clear by now, then, that both the legal and journalistic definitions of news ultimately are shaped by economic marketplace forces. Broadcast news programs and television newsmagazines will keep feeding us whatever it is that we *want* to watch. The legal scholar and law professor C. Edwin Baker writes, "Market-based incentives will lead media producers to provide audiences with what they want."[19]

Most courts, in turn, will continue to trust the news judgment of broadcasters in determining what is newsworthy. The courts will protect what we want to watch if it is chosen by journalists who know that we want to watch it. The power of the media to define newsworthiness for the courts thus protects their ability to pander to our desires to voyeuristically watch others, provided the videotape and facts are packaged as news. The deep bow that courts give to journalistic judgment in defining what is newsworthy is topped by the even deeper bow that members of the media, in turn, give to public tastes and preferences in determining newsworthiness.

It is critical to note that when courts actually do attempt to define newsworthiness, they often do so with nebulous and expansive concepts such as "matters of public interest"[20] and "legitimate public interest."[21] Almost anything can be said to be of public interest, of course, if the public is interested in it. In turn, broadcast journalists will produce whatever it is that the public is most interested in at the time—whatever it is, in other words, that we want to watch.

13. In Your Journal: How would you define "public interest"?

mores: values or principles

The judicial admonition to consider "community **mores**"[22] in determining whether something is newsworthy does little to stop a community that likes to watch from watching. In other words, as we become a nation of mediated voyeurs, and more and more people watch reality TV shows and become accustomed to hidden camera investigative news shows, the community standards issue is rendered **moot**. If the community wants to watch, then that is the community's value and norm.

moot: legally obsolete; of only academic importance

It is this kind of logic that allowed a federal court in California in 1997 to hold, in the context of a cause of action for appropriation, that "the scope of newsworthiness is extremely broad" and includes photographs of "sexual touchings" between the erstwhile couple Pamela Anderson Lee of *Baywatch* fame and Motley Crüe bad-boy drummer Tommy

Lee.[23] A year later, in a 1998 case involving another videotape of the overexposed Anderson Lee having sex (this time with a different man), the same federal court observed that California courts "have consistently held that newsworthiness is not limited to high minded discussion of politics and public affairs" and instead have established "that the romantic connections of celebrities are newsworthy."[24] This time, the newsworthiness defense precluded Anderson Lee from recovering for both an action for appropriation and one for public disclosure of private facts. This same type of logic also extends the newsworthiness defense outside of the area of newscasts, newsmagazine, and reality television shows like *Cops* to talk shows that cater to voyeuristic audiences that crave the public revelations of embarrassing facts such as *The Sally Jessy Raphael Show*[25] and *Donahue*.[26]

> ***14. In Your Journal:*** How can it be "in the public interest" to know about the "romantic connections of celebrities"?

Beyond these cases, however, a 1998 decision handed down by the Supreme Court of California involving a reality television show illustrates the broad scope of the newsworthiness defense to the public disclosure of private facts tort. That case—*Shulman* v. *Group W Productions*[27]—is described in the next section.

"I Just Want to Die"

"I just want to die," forty-seven-year-old Ruth Shulman told a nurse, Laura Carnahan, as she was being hoisted on a stretcher into an air ambulance helicopter. Shulman had just been riding in a car driven by her daughter on Interstate 10 in smoggy Riverside County, California. She was returning home to Palos Verdes from the desert resort town of Palm Springs along with her husband, son, and daughter, when the car suddenly spun off the side of the highway. It landed upside down in a drainage ditch. Emergency personnel were forced to use the jaws-of-life rescue machine to pry Shulman free.

Carnahan tried to reassure Shulman. She told her that she was "going to do real well." But Shulman sensed she was not going to do real well—she would, in fact, be rendered paraplegic by the accident—and she repeated her death wish to Carnahan. "I just want to die. I don't want to go through this."

Unfortunately for Shulman, she had no idea that those words, uttered during moments of intense pain, suffering, and confusion, would be broadcast three months later to all of greater Los Angeles on a reality-based television show called *On Scene: Emergency Response*. Shulman had no idea that at the accident scene and in the air ambulance, the consoling and beneficent Nurse Carnahan was wearing a tiny wireless microphone that picked up and recorded their conversations. What is more, Shulman did not know that Joel Cooke, a cameraman for the company that produced *On Scene*, was recording the events inside and outside of the helicopter. Of course, even had Shulman somehow realized that her words and image

15. In Your Journal: Why do you think *Emergency Response* didn't tell Shulman that she was being taped or that her accident was going to appear on television?

were being recorded, she was in no mental condition to consent in an informed manner to the tapings. At one stage, in fact, she asked Nurse Carnahan whether she was dreaming.

Shulman would not learn about the media voyeurism until the program aired. She was still in her hospital room and received a call from her son, Wayne, who told her to turn on the television set. "Channel 4 is showing our accident," Wayne told her. Ruth Shulman was shocked and angered. As she would later tell a reporter for the *Los Angeles Times*, "They took one of the most tragic moments of my life and made it entertainment for the nation."[28]

Rather than sit back and be a passive victim of mediated voyeurism, Shulman filed a lawsuit against Group W Productions, the producers of *On Scene*. Like many disputes against the media, it would prove to be lengthy, **protracted** litigation. In fact, it took nearly eight years from the date of the accident—June 24, 1990—before the California Supreme Court issued its critical ruling in the case on June 1, 1998.

protracted: drawn-out in time

One of Ruth Shulman's legal theories against Group W Productions was based on public disclosure of private facts, an invasion of privacy theory described earlier. Shulman argued that the broadcast of her appearance and words while she was riding in the rescue helicopter constituted the disclosure of private and embarrassing facts that would be highly offensive to a reasonable person. The facts certainly were private, given that the inside of the helicopter was equivalent to a private hospital room, and they definitely were embarrassing based on her state of confusion, physical distress, and mental anguish.

But the case would ultimately hinge on something else—whether the facts were newsworthy. As the California Supreme Court wrote, "The element critical to this case is the presence or absence of legitimate public interest, i.e., newsworthiness in the facts disclosed."[29] How the court would resolve that issue—its reasoning and analysis—tells us much about the legal forces that allow voyeurism to propagate with the law's consent.

The California Supreme Court began by attempting to define newsworthiness. It initially acknowledged that the concept is difficult to explicate and that there is "considerable variation in judicial descriptions of the newsworthiness concept."[30] In an opinion written by Justice Kathryn Mickle Werdegar, the court noted that if every piece of information or image that found its way into a newspaper or newscast was considered newsworthy— "if all coverage that sells papers or boosts ratings is deemed newsworthy" as the court put it—then the newsworthiness defense would essentially "swallow the publication of private facts torts."[31] In other words, the newsworthiness defense would always apply, the defendants would always succeed and the plaintiffs would always lose. Mediated voyeurism thus would prevail and the public disclosure of private facts tort would be rendered a meaningless remedy.

On the other hand, the court wrote, "If newsworthiness is viewed as a purely normative concept, the courts could become to an unacceptable degree editors of the news and self-appointed guardians of public taste."[32] Such a purely normative definition would raise serious First Amendment questions about whether courts were usurping press freedom from the media. The court thus attempted to seek a middle ground between the extremes of the hands-off, leave-it-to-the-press model of newsworthiness described earlier and what might be called the hands-on, judge-as-editor model.

16. In Your Journal: Why do the courts struggle so much to define newsworthiness?

In its endeavor to locate a point in between the two poles, the California Supreme Court came down much closer to the leave-it-to-the-press model of newsworthiness. It made it clear that judges and justices should not act as editors looking over the shoulder of journalists. "The courts do not, and constitutionally could not, sit as superior editors of the press," Justice Werdegar wrote for the court, adding that "in general, it is not for a court or jury to say how a particular story is best covered."[33] Werdegar's reference to the Constitution illustrates a clear example of how the First Amendment rises to the defense of mediated voyeurism.

Whether a publication, then, is newsworthy is not governed by "the tastes or limited interests of an individual judge or juror." A publication is newsworthy instead, the court wrote, if "*some* reasonable members of the community *could* entertain a legitimate interest in it."[34] The words "some" and "could" are emphasized here because they provide critical space for mediated voyeurism to breathe and to masquerade as news. Majoritarian tastes, in other words, do not control what is news. If *some* person out there *could* find voyeuristic videotape newsworthy, then it must be protected.

17. In Your Journal: What is the logic behind the idea that "newsworthy" should be defined as that which "*some* people *could*" find newsworthy? Why is the definition so broad?

The court did not stop there, however, in showing deference to the press. It expressly emphasized that newsworthiness is "not limited to 'news' in the narrow sense of reports of current events" but must include the "use of names, likenesses or facts in giving information to the public for purposes of education, *amusement* or enlightenment, when the public may reasonably be expected to have a legitimate interest in what is published."[35] Quoting an earlier California case, the court added, "The constitutional guarantees of freedom of expression apply with equal force to the publication whether it be a news report or an entertainment feature." With those statements, the court made it clear that the lines between amusement, entertainment, and news are slippery, if not nonexistent, and that the newsworthiness is not destroyed by amusing or entertaining features of a story or broadcast.

18. In Your Journal: Does it surprise you that "amusement" is considered to be "in the public interest"? What do you think constitutes "amusing news"?

But the court did not fully adopt a leave-it-to-the-press model of newsworthiness or abandon the concern for privacy. It recognized a line previously acknowledged by other courts between newsworthiness and information that constitutes "a morbid and sensational prying into private lives for its own sake." The court quoted an earlier decision that suggested that voyeurism was the opposite of newsworthiness. It noted that private facts were not newsworthy "when the community has no interest in them beyond the voyeuristic thrill of penetrating the wall of privacy that surrounds a stranger."[36] Finally, the Supreme Court of California articulated a number of factors that determine whether information is newsworthy, including its social value, the degree of the intrusion into the privacy interest of the plaintiff, and the extent to which the plaintiff voluntarily brought attention to himself or herself.

With those principles in mind, the court proceeded to analyze whether the newsworthiness defense would protect Group W Productions from liability for its broadcast of Ruth Shulman's image and words. To resolve this question, the court engaged in a two-step process.

First, it considered whether the subject matter itself—the rescue and medical treatment of auto accident victims and the work of emergency rescue personnel—was newsworthy. It quickly concluded that the subject was indeed newsworthy, noting that "automobile accidents are by their nature of interest to the great portion of the public that travels frequently by automobile." It added that videotape of the rescue and medical treatment of car crash victims such as Ruth Shulman also was newsworthy because it demonstrated "a critical service that any member of the public may someday need."[37]

19. In Your Journal: Why do you think that "demonstrating "a critical service" like emergency medicine is "newsworthy"?

But the court recognized that just because a particular *event* may be newsworthy does not necessarily mean that the identification of the plaintiff as the *person* involved in that event is also newsworthy. The court thus turned to the second and more difficult part of its inquiry: deciding whether Ruth Shulman's own words and appearance were newsworthy.

Attorneys for Shulman argued that her image and words were "not *necessary* to enable the public to understand the significance of the accident or the rescue as a public event."[38] It might have been possible, for instance, to screen out or block out Shulman's face and to omit the audio portion that contained her voice. The Supreme Court of California, however, squarely rejected this argument. It reasoned that the fact that "the broadcast *could* have been edited to exclude some of Ruth's words and images and still excite a minimum degree of viewer interest is not determinative." That decision was one of editing, one better left to Group W Productions than to the judicial system, the court reasoned. Indeed, the court remarked that "it is difficult to see how the subject broadcast could have been edited to avoid completely any possible identification [of Ruth Shulman] without severely undercutting its legitimate descriptive and narrative impact." Shulman's words and images were vital, the court reasoned, because they helped to demonstrate the importance of Nurse Carnahan's work. The court thus concluded that images and audio of Shulman were substantially relevant to the show's newsworthy subject matter—the rescue of accident victims and work of medical personnel. Shulman's lawsuit for public disclosure of private facts was thrown out.

The decision marks a victory for voyeurism. What the television show did was to give the entire nation—not just drivers on that particular stretch of Interstate 10 in Riverside County, California—the chance to **rubberneck** at Ruth Shulman's grave medical conditions. *New technologies, operating in the name of newsworthiness and corporate profits, extend our voyeurism, giving us the right to watch a grown woman's life nearly end.* The fact that Shulman was not a public figure was not enough in this case to render her images and words non-newsworthy. The fact that she was rendered paraplegic made no difference as well. It was just "too bad, so sad" for Shulman. It just happened to be her turn that day—her tragic dumb luck—to be the unfortunate and unwitting victim of mediated voyeurism. She was newsworthy under the law.

rubberneck: strain to stare at something as you pass it

20. In Your Journal: Why was Shulman's identity deemed "newsworthy"?

EDITING IS FOR EDITORS

A second force beyond newsworthiness that allows mediated voyeurism to thrive in contexts other than privacy claims was hinted at in the California Supreme Court's decision in Ruth Shulman's case—the vast **deference** given under the First Amendment to journalists' decisions. In particular, the United States Supreme Court has made it clear that editing is best left to editors.

deference: allowance for decision-making power to reside with another

This journalistic independence, of course, is essential if the press is to be an independent watchdog on the government rather than a government lapdog. If the government controlled editorial judgment and told journalists what images to broadcast and what information to print, the press no longer would be able to serve as the unofficial fourth branch of government that checks abuses of power by the legislative, executive, and judicial branches. A state-controlled media would operate merely as a public relations organ, only providing the official and favorable government view. The public, in turn, would be left to itself to **ferret** out government corruption.

21. In Your Journal: Can you see why the journalism industry might be considered the "unofficial fourth branch of government"?

ferret: drive out, bring to light

But an obvious yet important side effect, or cost, of this deep deference to journalistic freedom is its abuse in the name of corporate profit. Economic forces determine much of what passes for "news" these days, and there is much indeed that passes for news that seemingly has very little to do with wise and informed decisionmaking in a self-governing democracy, education, or other matters that affect the collective well-being of society. When the economic realities of the media are coupled with the judicial deference granted to the press, the low-cost videotape voyeurism format will flourish while the watchdog role of the press, which could generate expensive and time-consuming lawsuits, will dissipate. Ironically, of course, the video **vérité** voyeurism that is so cheap to create has produced

vérité: realism; truth

a rash of expensive and time-consuming lawsuits like Ruth Shulman's and others described.

The University of Michigan president Lee Bollinger's "fortress model" of freedom of expression is useful in understanding how abuse of journalistic freedom occurs.[39] This model suggests that one way to prevent government intrusion on speech or the press is "to secure the boundary of protected speech at some considerable distance from the speech activity we truly prize."[40]

> ***22. In Your Journal:*** What do you think is the purpose of the "fortress model" of freedom of expression?

Using this fortress model, we might consider news that affects self-governance or politics as a speech activity that we truly prize. But to protect this type of core speech, the United States Supreme Court has placed the boundary of protected speech, as Bollinger might put it, some considerable distance away from that core speech. To take Bollinger's metaphor a step further, the wall of the fort is placed far from the building that we want to protect within it. Voyeurism falls in the protected gap between the wall and core political speech. How is this reflected in First Amendment jurisprudence?

Historically, the United States Supreme Court has recognized a broad definition of the press, not confining it to newspapers and periodicals but instead letting it sweep up "every sort of publication which affords a vehicle of information to the public."[41] In other words, the protection granted to the press extends far beyond hard news shows to include other programs that blur distinctions between news and entertainment. The Court made it clear as well in a 1972 decision "that liberty of the press is the right of the lonely pamphleteer who uses carbon paper or a mimeograph just as much as of the large metropolitan publisher who utilizes the latest **photocomposition** methods.[42]

photocomposition: sophisticated printing technique using electrophotographic machines

false dichotomy: unrealistic or unnecessary division into two opposing sides

The United States Supreme Court also has refused to engage in drawing sketchy lines between inherently ambiguous concepts like "good" and "bad" journalism. In refusing to create such a **false dichotomy**, the Court has suggested that even shoddy journalism merits First Amendment protection. The Court made this clear in its 1931 decision in the case of *Near v. Minnesota*.[43] Jay Near's newspaper, *The Saturday Press*, had printed articles that, the Court observed, "charged, in substance, that Jewish gangsters were in control of gambling, boot-legging, and racketeering in Minneapolis, and that law enforcing officers and agencies were not energetically performing their duties."[44] The local district attorney had attempted to permanently enjoin publication of the newspaper as a nuisance and was successful. Near eventually appealed to the United States Supreme Court, which by a narrow majority—the nine justices split five to four—reversed in his favor. Chief Justice Hughes observed in writing the majority opinion,

> ***23. In Your Journal:*** How can "even shoddy journalism" be granted protection from the First Amendment?

> Some degree of abuse is inseparable from the proper use of everything, and in no instance is this more true than in that of

> the press. It has accordingly been decided by the practice of the States that it is better to leave a few of its noxious branches to their luxuriant growth, than, by pruning them away, to injure the vigor of those yielding the proper fruits.[45]

What is most striking about this language is not the rather flowery, Shakespearian prose but rather that the Court is willing to tolerate an irresponsible press in order to protect a **meritorious** one. The majority was not willing to mandate or protect only responsible journalists or a responsible press. As it said later in its opinion, "The fact that the liberty of the press may be abused by **miscreant** purveyors of scandal does not make any the less necessary the immunity of the press from previous restraint in dealing with official misconduct."[46] The Court's language in *Near* would be echoed decades later in *Miami Herald Publishing Co* v. *Tornillo*.[47]

meritorious: having merit; valuable

miscreant: having characteristics of a scoundrel; villainous

24. In Your Journal: Why do you think the court tolerates abuse of the Constitutional protections of the press?

In *Tornillo*, the United States Supreme Court considered whether a state right-of-reply statute granting a political candidate free access to newspaper space to reply to criticism and attacks on his character and record by a newspaper violated that newspaper's First Amendment right of freedom of the press.[48] In holding that the statute was unconstitutional, the Supreme Court discussed the role and responsibility of journalists in a self-governing democracy.[49] The Court, in an opinion authored by Chief Justice Warren Burger, observed that "a responsible press is an undoubtedly desirable goal, but press responsibility cannot be mandated by the Constitution and like many other virtues it cannot be legislated."[50]

25. In Your Journal: The Supreme Court argues that "virtue cannot be legislated." What is the difference between journalistic "virtue" and journalistic "practices" or "activities"? Can practices and activities in journalism be legislated?

The Court has extended this sentiment of journalistic deference beyond the print medium to the realm of broadcasting. In *Columbia Broadcasting System* v. *Democratic National Committee*,[51] for instance, the Court observed,

> For better or worse, editing is what editors are for; and editing is selection and choice of material. That editors—newspaper or broadcast—can and do abuse this power is beyond doubt, but that is no reason to deny the discretion Congress provided. Calculated risks of abuse are taken in order to preserve higher values. The presence of these risks is nothing new; the authors of the Bill of Rights accepted the reality that these risks were evils for which there was no acceptable remedy other than a spirit of moderation and a sense of responsibility—and civility—on the part of those who exercise the guaranteed freedoms of expression.[52]

26. In Your Journal: If the *Sally Jesse Raphael Show* involves "bona fide news interviews," what definition of "news interview" is the Supreme Court using?

In addition to the United States Supreme Court, the Federal Communications Commission has recognized a broad definition of news.[53] It has held, for instance, that the syndicated nightly tabloid program, *Hard Copy*, is a **bona fide** newscast and that the daytime talk show, *The Sally Jessy Raphael Show*, involves bona fide news interviews.[54]

bona fide: genuine; without fraud

The bottom line is that although the broad deference that courts extend to the media and journalistic judgment may be necessary for an independent press to play a watchdog role, today the profit-driven concerns of media companies may trump the desire to perform that important function. The breathing space given to the press for that role may be abused to disseminate sensationalistic mediated voyeurism.

THE CORPORATE MEDIA AND THE FIRST AMENDMENT SHIELD

"Trusts with the capacity for overbearing power are being merged and acquired into existence as if there were nothing at stake but stock values. Today's deals may weigh on the culture for decades."[55] So writes Todd Gitlin, a professor of sociology at New York University, describing what he perceives as a relentless conglomeration **juggernaut** in the communications and media industries.

juggernaut: large force that seems to destroy anything in its path

The speech and images propagated by the conglomerates about which Gitlin writes are protected by the First Amendment. Corporations are protected by the Constitution as if they were people rather than the legally created entities that they are. This is not too surprising at first glance, of course, given that the First Amendment specifically calls for protection of "the press." As C. Edwin Baker, a professor at the University of Pennsylvania Law School writes, "The 'press' is the only business to receive explicit constitutional protection," a decision premised largely on the assumption that "the press should provide the public with information and opinion uncensored by government."[56]

27. In Your Journal: Why do you think the press, as opposed to doctors, retailers, or educators, receives "explicit constitutional protection"?

More than 200 years after the First Amendment was ratified, however, it is clear that many of the corporate entities that engage in speech activities are controlled, directly or indirectly, by other corporate entities that may be engaged in distinctly *non-press*-oriented activities. General Electric owns NBC. Disney owns ABC. What is more, newspaper chains such as Gannett and Knight-Ridder that own large numbers of papers across the United States must attempt to walk a fine line between the often-conflicting goals of generating corporate profit and providing the public with information and speech that enlightens and serves the public interest. The politics of ownership **deregulation** embodied in the **Telecommunications Act of 1996** has increased concentration of ownership in the broadcast industry and has facilitated the growth of the "trusts" about which Gitlin writes.

deregulation: elimination of restrictive regulations

Telecommunications Act of 1996: law that removed many of the regulations barring competition in the telecommunications industry; Once enacted, it allowed anyone to enter the communications business and it allowed communications businesses to compete with other types of businesses

It is in this atmosphere that the low-cost, high-profit mediated voyeurism format of the television newsmagazine and reality-based program businesses flourishes. The First Amendment can be used as a shield, in turn, by corporate entities to ward off attempts to dictate or control this content. The First Amendment might be employed, for instance, to blunt any attack on shows that pander to our sensationalistic and voyeuristic thirst for vérité video. If these shows are criticized as trash and in need of some government supervision, then the First Amendment provides a ready response. Media-related corporations would simply argue that their autonomy as speakers in the metaphorical marketplace of ideas—their ability to freely choose and to decide for themselves what images are worthy of being viewed—would be violated by government intervention.

> ***28. In Your Journal:*** What does the phrase "metaphorical marketplace of ideas" mean?

Those same corporations, of course, have a loud and increasingly dominant voice in the marketplace of ideas. Put simply, they control access to the avenues of communication production and information distribution that nonlegal entities—read, *real people*—do not possess. Although a growing number of us may have a page on the World Wide Web, most of us do not own newspapers. Family newspapers are a dying breed. But corporations—newspaper chains or groups, in particular—own newspapers. Many newspapers. In 1986, for instance, about 63 percent of daily newspapers in the United States were owned by chains. By 1998, that figure had reached 80 percent.[57]

The premise of providing individuals with the autonomy necessary to choose their own speech, free from government intervention, writes the Yale Law School professor Owen Fiss, is that this "will lead to rich public debate."[58] The danger, however, as Fiss points out, is that when profit-driven corporations are the speakers in question, the exercise of autonomy "might not enrich, but rather impoverish, public debate."[59] Although there are examples of well-intended public debate on the mainstream media today—so-called town hall meetings conducted from time to time by the major networks, for instance, on shows such as *Nightline*—it seems evident that much of what we watch today does not enrich public debate. Speech often is viewed by corporations more as a **salable** commodity than as a public or social good.

> ***29. In Your Journal:*** How might public debate be "impoverished" rather than "enriched" by the corporations that own mainstream media outlets?

salable: something that can be sold; marketable

The hands-off corporate-speech doctrine, nurtured and protected by the First Amendment, largely presumes that any government intervention must be feared and is evil. But as many scholars today argue, perhaps we have almost as much to fear from corporate entities that control the means of production and transmission of speech and images as we do from the government. If it is true, as the late communications professor Herbert Schiller wrote, that "the bulk of cultural work provided to the American public is organized and controlled by a handful of giant business,"[60] then perhaps it is time for some of what Kathleen Sullivan, dean of the Stanford Law School, calls "cultural **trustbusting**."[61] Perhaps, in other words, it is time to roll back some First Amendment protection for corporate entities that engage in the speech-and-image businesses in order to promote deliberative democratic discourse and improve the quality of information flow.

> ***30. In Your Journal:*** Why does Calvert compare corporate entities to the government?

trustbusting: destroying large business conglomerates to increase competition

The standard argument for reduced First Amendment protections for corporate speech usually proceeds along the following lines. If media-

31. In Your Journal: There are four "ifs" and one "then" in this paragraph. What does this if-then logic imply about the legal standard that must apparently be met by corporations seeking First Amendment protection?

related corporations are merely legally created entities as compared to real people, if their First Amendment press protection is premised on serving the collective needs of all citizens in a democracy as opposed to generating profits for the private wants of a few shareholders, if access to the marketplace of ideas is radically skewed in favor of wealthy corporations as opposed to private individuals, and if the airwaves on which much mediated voyeurism appears are held in public trust rather than privately owned, then the door is open for increased government intervention and regulation of the corporate media.

Such intervention, of course, would potentially jeopardize the freedom of the press to serve as a watchdog on the government. If the government is telling the press what to do, how can it possibly expose government abuse? That is the standard defense against such intrusion on corporate speech rights. One thing is clear, however. In the absence of such intervention, there is little to stop the proliferation of sensationalistic mediated voyeurism. The First Amendment provides a shield behind which corporate-produced mediated voyeurism may seek protection. With this in mind, let us turn to some recent examples in which the government—at the federal and state levels—has taken steps to curb mediated voyeurism, including that disseminated by media corporations.

LEGAL BACKLASH AGAINST MEDIATED VOYEURISM

For those of us in the television audience to play the role of voyeur, there necessarily must be something to watch. We cannot, after all, be voyeurs without receiving any videotape, photographs, or other forms of the reality-based visual images that we like to consume. This means, in turn, that videotape and photographs must be gathered for us by the media.

A host of different laws now exist in most states, however, that place limits on the ability of the media to gather photographs and videotape of the sights and sounds that make up mediated voyeurism. Some of these laws are age-old remedies that have evolved over time with the common law and can be applied, with varying degrees of difficulty, to the modern image-gathering methods of the media. Others can be found in statutes created by state legislative bodies. Three common-law remedies against the tactics of mediated voyeurism—trespass, intrusion into seclusion, and fraud—are discussed below. As will become clear, they are not always successful in precluding or punishing mediated voyeurism.

Trespass: Forgive Not the Press for Its Trespasses

The common law of *trespass* can be used to punish individuals, including journalists, who intentionally enter the property of another person without his or her consent or permission. If a journalist thus runs across the property of a celebrity to take his or her picture and the celebrity has not consented to the entry, then a trespass has likely occurred and a remedy to voyeuristic news gathering has been put into play. The United States Supreme Court, as noted earlier in this chapter, has held that the press receives no special First Amendment protection when it violates generally applicable laws—laws that apply to everyone and do not single out or target journalists or other members of the media—such as trespass. As one federal **appellate court** wrote in 1995, "There is no journalists' privilege to trespass." [62]

appellate court: court of review by appeal for the decisions of trial courts

But the trespass tort does not always provide an absolute remedy against undercover, hidden camera media voyeurism. The case of *Desnick* v. *American Broadcasting Companies Inc.*,[63] involving a 1993 *Prime Time Live* report on an eye care facility that allegedly performed unnecessary cataract surgeries to collect Medicare reimbursements, makes this clear. As part of its segment on the Desnick Eye Center—a business that at the time had twenty-five offices in four states and performed more than 10,000 cataracts operations each year—ABC rounded up seven "test patients." The test patients, wearing hidden cameras on behalf of ABC, secretly videotaped their visits to Desnick offices in Wisconsin and Indiana.

At the offices, each of the ABC confederates requested an eye examination. The results? The two test patients who were *under* sixty-five and thus ineligible for Medicare reimbursement were told they did not need cataract surgery, whereas four of the five patients who were *over* sixty-five were told they needed the procedure. Suffice it to say, the *Prime Time Live* report, narrated by the **irascible** Sam Donaldson, did not paint the Desnick Eye Center in a flattering light.

irascible: easily angered; hotheaded

Desnick sued for trespass. The contention? That ABC committed a trespass by insinuating the test patients, equipped with the hidden cameras, into the Wisconsin and Indiana offices. Desnick's argument was relatively straightforward—it never would have consented to the entry by ABC's test patients into its offices had it been aware in the first place that their real purpose was to gather voyeuristic and secretive videotape to expose the center's alleged problems. In a stunning victory for voyeurism, however, Judge Richard A. Posner of the U.S. Court of Appeals for the Seventh Circuit rejected Desnick's argument and kicked out the trespass lawsuit.

How did Posner and the other members of the appellate court reach the conclusion that trespass had not occurred? Bending over backward to protect the hidden camera reporting, Posner began by looking at the original intent and purpose of the law of trespass—to protect "the inviolability of the person's property." [64] In plain English, the purpose of trespass law is to prevent others from interfering with one's ownership or use of his or her own property. With that in mind, Posner wrote,

> There was no invasion in the present case of any of the specific interests that the tort of trespass seeks to protect. The test

> patients entered offices that were open to anyone expressing a desire for ophthalmic services and videotaped physicians engaged in professional, not personal, communications with strangers (the testers themselves). The activities of the office were not disrupted. [65]

Business went on as usual, in other words, at the eye care center. There was no interference with Desnick's property by the camera-equipped patients. Whether other courts will follow this logic is unclear. As Jonathan D. Avila, litigation counsel for CBS Broadcasting in Los Angeles, emphasized in a 1999 law review article, "The laws of the various states are not in accord as to whether an undisclosed intent to conduct hidden-camera taping may give rise to a claim for trespass, where the landowner has consented to the physical presence of the camera person." [66] Trespass, however, is not the only legal theory that may be used against mediated voyeurism. The next section discusses one privacy theory that may provide a remedy in some, but not all, cases of video vérité voyeurism.

Intrusion into Seclusion: The Current Battleground for Hidden Cameras

Another legal remedy against mediated voyeurism is a privacy theory commonly known as *intrusion into seclusion*. Designed to protect an individual's "zone of privacy," this remedy holds that an individual such as a journalist who intrudes, physically or otherwise, on the solitude or seclusion of another person is liable for damages to that other person if the intrusion would be highly offensive to a reasonable person. To succeed in an intrusion lawsuit, the person filing the claim must possess a *reasonable* expectation of privacy in the place, location, or information in question. In general, there is no reasonable expectation of privacy if one either is in a public place or, if on private property, can be seen from a public place. For instance, if a celebrity is sunbathing in his or her front yard, and the yard and celebrity are plainly visible from the public sidewalk or street running in front of the house, there is no reasonable expectation of privacy and taking a photograph would not constitute an intrusion. If, however, there is a ten-foot tall solid stone wall surrounding the front yard, then the celebrity is more likely to possess a reasonable expectation of privacy. A photographer who decided to scale the wall to capture a picture would intrude on the celebrity's seclusion. If the photographer repeated the actions, he or she might also be charged under stalking and harassment statutes that exist in many states.

There has been, in line with the rise of the voyeurism value and the development of sophisticated recording devices, a dramatic increase in recent years in the number of lawsuits based on intrusion into seclusion. As the media attorney Victor Kovner and his colleagues write, this increase "derives principally from advances in surveillance technology, as the equipment becomes more compact and more powerful. Today, hardly a news cycle passes without word of some intrusion claim or potential claim."[67]

Intrusion into seclusion lawsuits, however, will not stop the deceptive and voyeuristic use of hidden cameras if those cameras are recording events that occur in a public place. This principle recently saved NBC and its newsmagazine *Dateline* from liability for hidden camera reportage in a 1999 decision handed down by a California appellate court. In *Wilkins* v. *NBC*,[68] producers from *Dateline* were investigating the practice of some companies—often adult entertainment or so-called dial-a-porn businesses—of charging for services on supposedly toll-free "800" telephone numbers. The "800" numbers, in fact, would provide access to pay-per-call "900" numbers.

A company called SimTel Communications leased and programmed "800" number and "900" number phone lines and then sold the leases to investors. After SimTel placed an ad for its services in *USA Today*, producers from *Dateline* arranged for a meeting with representatives from the company at a Malibu, California, restaurant. The *Dateline* producers did not reveal their affiliation with the newsmagazine. They also did not reveal that they were wearing hidden cameras that would capture images of the lunchtime encounter, some of which would later be broadcast by *Dateline* on a report called "Hardcore Hustle" and would spark a lawsuit by the SimTel employees for intrusion into seclusion.

The lunch, along with the surreptitious taping, took place at an outside table. The table was located in the middle of a crowded patio, close to other tables. One of the SimTel employees spoke freely about the business and its services while waiters were standing next to the table. Given the public setting—the appellate court noted that the SimTel employees "were not seated in a private dining room of a restaurant"[69]—the employees did not possess a reasonable expectation of privacy. The appellate court thus held that they could not maintain a lawsuit based on intrusion into seclusion. There simply was no "seclusion" into which to intrude on the outdoor patio. The use of hidden cameras in this case was protected.

But what about a slightly different situation? What if the hidden camera videotaping by the news media takes place *inside* the business establishment that is under investigation? Does the intrusion into seclusion tort provide a remedy in this situation? Unfortunately, the law of hidden cameras is unsettled today, and the answer appears to be either "sometimes yes, sometimes no" or "it depends on the facts of the case."

Courts have made it clear, however, that expectations of privacy are substantially lower inside a business establishment than they are inside a person's private home or residence. Busting businesses with hidden camera videotape, of course, is favorite fodder for television newsmagazines. A December 1998 decision handed down by a federal court in Arizona called

Medical Laboratory Management Consultants v. *American Broadcasting Companies, Inc.*[70] illustrates how the intrusion theory may provide little relief against such business-place mediated voyeurism.

That case involved a report by ABC's now-defunct newsmagazine *Prime Time Live* (it was essentially rolled into 20/20 along with coanchors Diane Sawyer and Sam Donaldson) called "Rush to Read" on allegedly faulty pap smear testing. Medical Laboratory Management Consultants performed pap smear testing in Phoenix, Arizona. An ABC employee named Robbie Gordon contacted one of the owners of the facility, John Devaraj. Rather than reveal her true identity, however, Gordon lied. She said she was a medical laboratory technologist who wanted to find out more details about the costs of running such a laboratory herself. In fact, as the federal court would later observe, Gordon's "only interest in Medical Lab was as a possible source of information for an upcoming episode of *Prime Time Live*."[71]

When the owner agreed to meet with Gordon at the business in March 1994, Gordon brought along Jeff Cooke. Cooke, an undercover camera specialist, wore a camera hidden in his wig. Like Gordon, Cooke also lied to the owner of the laboratory. He claimed to be a computer expert. Cooke captured the entire two-hour visit to the laboratory on videotape.

The group primarily talked in a conference room that had windowed French doors and was visible to a nearby accounting clerk. Devaraj also took Gordon and Cooke on a tour of the facility. As the court described it, "The conversation and office tour took place in a laboratory that was at least partially open to the public and was accessible to employees."[72] In fact, other employees were present for portions of the conversations during the tour. The discussion itself focused on the pap smear testing industry as a whole as well as the general practices at Devaraj's business. There was no effort made to ensure that the conversations were confidential.

32. *In Your Journal:* Does Calvert think that Deveraj deserved legal remedy in his lawsuit against *PrimeTime Live*?

After the negative *Prime Time Live* report aired—Devaraj was not named in the report but his face was shown during the broadcast—the owner sued for intrusion into seclusion. He claimed that his privacy was invaded by the use of false pretenses to secure entrance to the laboratory and by the secret videotaping of the conversations. Unfortunately for Devaraj—fortunately, however, for ABC and mediated voyeurs everywhere—the federal court concluded that there had been no intrusion. Why?

First, the court observed what it called a "diminished expectation of privacy in the workplace." Citing prior case law, it emphasized that "when courts have considered claims in the workplace, they have generally found for the plaintiffs *only* if the challenged intrusions involved information or activities of an intimate nature."[73] The court gave an example of an actual case involving such "intimate" information. It involved an employer who had searched through and read an employee's personal medical records that were sitting on that employee's desk. But where "the intrusions have merely involved unwanted access to data or activities *related to the workplace*, claims of intrusion have failed." Applying these principles to the facts given above, the court concluded that Devaraj "can claim no reasonable expectation of privacy in the location or contents of the conversation." As in the *Wilkins* case, then, there was no solitude or seclusion that was intruded on, despite the fact that this time around the hidden camera taping took place *inside* the plaintiff's place of business instead of *outside* at a public restaurant.

But the court in the *Medical Laboratory* case did not stop its analysis there. It gave a second, independent reason to deny Devaraj's claim for intrusion into seclusion. The conduct by the ABC employees simply was not highly offensive to a reasonable person. As noted earlier, a person who files a lawsuit for intrusion must prove both that there was a reasonable expectation of privacy in the place or thing intruded on *and* that the intrusive conduct would be highly offensive to a reasonable person. How could the court reach the conclusion that lying in order to use hidden cameras to secretly videotape conversations inside someone else's business was not highly offensive? The court simply pulled out another shield that sometimes protects mediated voyeurism—the alleged motive for the intrusion. Under the law in most states, the question of offensiveness is determined, in part, by the intruder's motive or reason for engaging in the intrusive conduct.

33. In Your Journal: Why does motive have a bearing on whether or not someone has committed a privacy offense?

In this case, the media claimed a noble motive for its lying and use of hidden cameras. ABC was reporting on an important health issue that could impact millions of women. As the court stated, "The information was clearly in the public interest." In contrast, the court noted that it is only when the intrusion is "**gratuitous**, threatens the safety of anyone involved, or unnecessarily intrudes on a target of the news in his private capacity"[74] that it is likely to be considered highly offensive. Because the intrusion by ABC was not gratuitous but instead was done to tell an important story, and because no one got hurt during the taping and Devaraj was acting in his business capacity, the factors that would indicate "highly offensive" conduct simply were not present. ABC's conduct thus was protected and the intrusion claim was tossed out.

gratuitous: without purpose; unwarranted

But as mentioned earlier, the law of hidden cameras is extremely volatile today. Different courts may reach very different conclusions depending on the unique factual situation in question. A much-anticipated decision handed down by the Supreme Court of California in June 1999 in a case called *Sanders* v. *American Broadcasting Companies, Inc.*[75] makes this clear. That opinion appears, at least on the question of privacy expectations in the workplace, to contradict the *Medical Laboratory* ruling. Unlike the federal court in Arizona in the *Medical Laboratory* case, which threw out a claim for intrusion based on the media's use of a hidden camera in the workplace, the high court of California allowed a **plaintiff** to proceed with a

plaintiff: person who initiates a lawsuit to assert a legal claim lawsuit for intrusion that also featured hidden camera taping inside a business establishment under media investigation. The *Sanders* decision, if followed by courts in other states, could deal a serious, but probably nonfatal, blow to mediated voyeurism and, in particular, to hidden camera voyeurism in the workplace.

The *Sanders* case grew out of a 1992 *Prime Time Live* investigation of the telepsychic industry. Chances are that if you are an insomniac or night owl, you have probably seen so-called infomercials—thirty-minute commercials thinly masquerading as television shows—for telepsychic hot lines. You have probably also questioned whether the people at the other end of the telephone line were "real" psychics. ABC too apparently had its doubts about the industry and it decided to investigate.

An ABC employee named Stacy Lescht obtained employment for a few days as a telepsychic in the Los Angeles office of a company known as the Psychic Marketing Group (PMG). While working for PMG, Lescht sat at one of about 100 cubicles in a large room taking phone calls and giving psychic readings. Each cubicle had three sides, and each side was five feet high. Access to the room in which the telepsychics worked was generally restricted to employees only. When she was not on the phone, Lescht talked with the other psychics. She could easily overhear their conversations in the surrounding cubicles.

Unknown to her fellow employees, however, Lescht wore a small hidden camera in her hat—a "hat cam" as the California Supreme Court fittingly put it—and an audio microphone attached to her brassiere. She taped the conversations that she had with her unsuspecting fellow employees. One of those other telepsychics was a man named Mark Sanders. In one taped conversation with Sanders, Sanders was standing in the aisle just outside Lescht's cubicle. Two other employees also joined in that conversation, which, according to the court, was conducted in "moderate tones of voice."[76] A second taped conversation occurred in Sanders's cubicle. Both Lescht and Sanders were seated in the cubicle while they discussed Sanders's personal aspirations in what the court described as "relatively soft voices." Portions of the second conversation aired on the *Prime Time Live* broadcast. Sanders ultimately sued Lescht for intrusion into seclusion based on her secretive video and audio recordings made in the PMG offices.

> *34. In Your Journal:* Why doesn't Calvert reveal the content of Lescht and Sanders's conversation?

By the time the case reached the Supreme Court of California, it faced a very narrow but important issue—"whether a person who lacks a reasonable expectation of *complete* privacy in a conversation because it could be seen and heard by coworkers (but *not* the general public) may nevertheless have a claim for invasion of privacy by intrusion based on a television reporter's covert videotaping of that conversation."[77] The court would ultimately answer that query in the affirmative—a person such as Mark Sanders could still maintain a claim for intrusion in this situation. It would reject ABC's argument that because other employees could hear the conversations there was no expectation of privacy.

To reach this conclusion, the unanimous court rejected the notion that there must be "absolute or complete privacy" to successfully pursue a cause of action for intrusion into seclusion. "Mass media videotaping may constitute an intrusion even when the events and communications recorded were visible and audible to some limited set of observers," Justice Kathryn Mickle Werdegar wrote for the court. Werdegar, it will be recalled, wrote the majority opinion in Ruth Shulman's case.

35. In Your Journal: Compare Werdegar's rulings in the Shulman and PMG cases. Is there a contradiction here?

In allowing a claim for intrusion based on covert media taping to proceed in a place of business, the court observed that privacy "is not a **binary**, all-or-nothing characteristic. There are degrees and nuances to societal recognition of our expectations of privacy."[78] In this case, the circumstances that suggested there *was* a reasonable expectation of privacy included (1) the fact that the room in which the recordings were made was not regularly open to observation by the press or public but instead was generally limited to employees only; (2) the fact that the conversations recorded were not between a proprietor and a customer but rather between one employee and a member of the media posing as an employee but who "acted solely as an agent of ABC when she talked with and secretly recorded the other psychics";[79] and (3) the fact that the only other people who could overhear the taped conversations were fellow coemployees. As the court emphasized, "There was no evidence the public was invited into the PMG Los Angeles office, or that the office was visited by the press or public observers on a routine basis or was ordinarily subject to videotaped surveillance by the mass media."[80] The court thus concluded that Sanders indeed possessed a reasonable expectation of privacy against being videotaped by an "ABC employee planted to collect videotape for use in a national television broadcast."[81]

binary: concerning two opposing forces, choices, or concepts

The *Sanders* decision clearly is a blow to hidden camera voyeurism conducted by the media inside workplace or business settings. But the Supreme Court of California was careful *not* to create an absolute, or "per se," rule that there *always* is an expectation of privacy in the workplace. "We hold *only* that the possibility of being overheard by coworkers does not, as a matter of law, render unreasonable an employee's expectation that his or her interactions within a nonpublic workplace will not be videotaped in secret by a journalist," the court wrote.[82]

36. In Your Journal: How does the PMG case compare to the Desnick and Deveraj cases?

The Supreme Court of California also made it clear that it was not ruling on whether the intrusion by Lescht was or was not highly offensive. It will be recalled from the *Medical Laboratory* case that the person bringing a lawsuit for intrusion must show not only that there was a reasonable expectation of privacy but also that the intrusion would be considered highly offensive to a reasonable person. Offensiveness, in turn, is determined in part by the intruder's motive. The California Supreme Court wrote in

Sanders, "Nothing we say here prevents a media defendant from attempting to show, in order to negate the offensiveness element of the intrusion tort, that the claimed intrusion, even if it infringed on a reasonable expectation of privacy, was justified by the legitimate motive of gathering news."[83] In other words, ABC could still make a claim that Mark Sanders's intrusion case should be thrown out because ABC had a legitimate motive—showing and telling the public about the practices of the for-profit telepsychic industry—for using a hidden microphone and cloaked camera.

It should be clear from this brief review of current case law that intrusion into seclusion claims may be used to punish mediated voyeurism but they are far from a complete remedy. In fact, as the *Wilkins* and *Medical Laboratory* cases suggest, intrusion often fails to provide a remedy for hidden camera voyeurism, even when the media lie or fail to reveal their true identities or purposes. The *Sanders* decision, in contrast, may cast a chilling effect over video vérité voyeurism captured by undercover media operatives in the workplace. The key issues are the reasonableness of one's expectation of privacy in the location or information captured by cameras and microphones and the offensiveness of the conduct engaged in by the media. The unique set of facts in each case will prove critical in resolving these questions. Two things are clear, however, as of the writing of this essay. The law of hidden cameras is far from settled, and the extent to which intrusion claims will prevent or hinder mediated voyeurism remains to be seen.

Fraud: Food Lion Roars Back, Then Goes Out with a Whimper

The law of *fraud* can be invoked—sometimes successfully, sometimes not—when the media use deceptive news-gathering techniques to obtain voyeuristic videotape. Fraud generally occurs when an individual knowingly makes a false statement about an important fact to another person who, in turn, relies on that statement and is harmed by it. In addition, the person who makes the false statement must do so with the intent to deceive or induce the reliance by the unsuspecting individual.

The law of fraud most often applies in distinctly *non*–media-related cases. For instance, consider the used car dealer who represents to a potential customer that a particular vehicle has never been in an accident. In fact, the car has been in a major collision that affects its steering and the dealer knows this. If the customer relies on the false information and the car later breaks down because of the earlier accident, the duped buyer may have an action for fraud. As the case described below suggests, the law of fraud can be stretched from this typical scenario to apply to fraudulent conduct by members of the media seeking voyeuristic videotape.

The ABC television newsmagazine *PrimeTime Live*—it should be clear from this and some of the earlier examples that the law of hidden cameras might just as well be called the law of *PrimeTime Live* investigations—conducted a voyeuristic hidden camera report in the early 1990s to expose alleged food-mishandling practices at the then fast-growing Food Lion grocery store chain. Its producers deliberately lied on résumés to gain access to the store as employees. The producers submitted false references, false employment histories, and false reasons for wanting to work in a Food Lion store. For instance, one ABC employee wrote on her Food Lion job application, "I love meat wrapping. I would like to make a career with the company."[84]

Relying on these misrepresentations, Food Lion hired one of the producers. Once on the inside, the ABC employee proceeded to shoot some hidden camera footage and tape some audio behind the food counters and in the butcher shop. The network eventually broadcast a very negative report by Diane Sawyer about Food Lion's allegedly unsanitary food-handling practices on November 5, 1992. After the report aired, the supermarket chain's market value and profits plummeted, and it was forced to close eighty-eight stores. Food Lion blamed this disastrous turn of events on the *PrimeTime Live* report. It sued Capital Cities/ABC[85] under several legal theories based on how the network gathered its information, including fraud and trespass.

In December 1996, just over four years after the report first aired, a federal jury in North Carolina found that ABC's deception amounted to fraud and trespass. It later ordered ABC to pay nearly $5.5 million in damages. The verdict sent shock waves through the journalism world, with a Chicken Little "the sky is falling" type of outrage. It was the end of voyeuristic journalism as we knew it. The public's right to watch hidden camera footage would be irreparably harmed.

But the supermarket chain's victory would not last too long and as always seems to happen despite the doomsayers' prognostications, the sky did not come crashing down on journalism. Instead, the multimillion-dollar damage award was reduced significantly by the trial judge to $315,000. But the cutting did not stop there. On appeal in October 1999, the sum was pared down again, this time to a paltry **nominal** damages award of two dollars.[86]

nominal: small in amount; insignificant; existing in name only

The Fourth Circuit Court of Appeals, in a split two-to-one decision in favor of ABC, concluded that the fraud verdict could not stand because it was "an **end-run**" around the First Amendment protection of the press.[87] Although the majority acknowledged that ABC employees had used deceptive practices to obtain its voyeuristic videotape, it concluded that this deception "did not harm the consuming public" and that ABC's intent, in fact, was "to benefit the consuming public by letting it know about Food

end-run: short-cut maneuver meant to avoid meaningful obstacles by some type of trick

Lion's food handling practices."[88] All that was left for the supermarket chain to collect was one dollar to compensate it for ABC's trespass and one dollar for the breach of loyalty owed by the ABC-turned-Food-Lion employees to their deceived employer, Food Lion. Not a bad cost-of-doing-business price for ABC to collect the materials of mediated voyeurism.

It should be noted that it was not the hidden cameras per se that got ABC in trouble with the jury but rather the trespass, deception, and fraud. Although the fraud did not stand up on appeal, the split decision from one federal appellate circuit court does not resolve the issue in other appellate courts. The Fourth Circuit did *not* conclude that fraud could never be used in a similar case as means of attacking news-gathering practices. The **viability** of a fraud cause of action to attack deceptive news gathering thus remains unsettled without a decision from the United States Supreme Court.

viability: ability to succeed or survive

There are, then, a number of potential legal avenues available to victims of mediated voyeurism, such as trespass, intrusion into seclusion, and fraud. But today, apparently, those remedies are not always enough to check mediated voyeurism. The confluence of three recent developments in the law suggests there may be a stepped-up movement against mediated voyeurism. These developments include (1) a 1999 United States Supreme Court decision that limits the media's ability to capture voyeuristic videotape during so-called police ride-alongs; (2) a wave of anti-paparazzi legislation that cropped up after the 1997 death of Princess Diana; and (3) a small but growing number of states passing laws that make videotape voyeurism a criminal offense. The common thread that unites them is an interest in and concern for privacy and the control of information flow that contradicts mediated voyeurism.

NOTES

1. Eve Klindera, "Qualified Immunity for Cops (and Other Public Officials) with Cameras: Let Common Law Remedies Ensure Press Responsibility," *George Washington Law Review* 67 (1999): 401.
2. Christopher Meyers, "Justifying Journalistic Harms: Right to Know vs. Interest in Knowing," *Journal of Mass Media Ethics* 8 (1993): 133, 134.
3. *Cohen* v. *Cowles Media*, 501 U.S. 663 (1991).
4. Ibid., p. 670.
5. Branzbrug v. Hayes, 408 U.S. 665, 681 (1972).
6. Matthew D. Bunker, Sigman L. Splichal, and Sheree Martin, "Triggering the First Amendment: Newsgathering Torts and Press Freedom," *Communications Law and Policy* 4 (Summer 1999): 290.
7. *Shulman* v. *Group W Productions*, 955 P.2d 469 (Cal. 1998).
8. Ibid., p. 474.

9. *Roe* v. *Wade,* 410 U.S. 113 (1973).
10. 18 U.S.C. §2710 (2000).
11. Robert C. Post, *Constitutional Domains: Democracy, Community, Management* (Cambridge, MA: Harvard University, 1995), p. 73.
12. *Reid* v. *Pierce County,* 961 P.2d 333 (1988).
13. Sean M. Scott, "The Hidden First Amendment Values of Privacy," *Washington Law Review* 71 (1996): 683, 700.
14. Diane L. Zimmerman, "Requiem for a Heavyweight: A Farewell to Warren and Brandeis's Privacy Tort," *Cornell Law Review* 68 (1983): 291, 353.
15. Ibid., p. 353.
16. Geoff Dendy, "The Newsworthiness Defense to the Public Disclosure Tort," *Kentucky Law Review* 85 (1996): 147, 152.
17. Donald M. Gillmor, *Fundamentals of Mass Communication Law* (Minneapolis, MN: West, 1996), p. 92.
18. Kathleen Hall Jamieson and Karlyn Kohrs Campbell, *The Interplay of Influence,* 4th ed. (Belmont, CA: Wadsworth Publishing, 1997), p. 4.
19. C. Edwin Baker, "Giving the Audience What It Wants," *Ohio State Law Journal* 58 (1997): 311, 313.
20. *Anonsen* v. *Donahue,* 857 S.W.2d 700, 702 (1993).
21. *Sipple* v. *Chronicle Pub. Co.,* 154 Cal.App.3d 1040, 1048 (1984).
22. Ibid.
23. *Lee* v. *Penthouse International Ltd.,* 25 Media Law Reporter (BNA) 1651, 1655 (1997).
24. *Michaels* v. *Internet Entertainment Group, Inc.,* 27 Media Law Reporter (BNA) 1097, 1101 (1998).
25. *Weber* v. *Multimedia Entertainment Inc.,* 26 Media Law Reporter (BNA) 1377, 1380 (S.D.N.Y. 1988) (holding that the newsworthiness defense, under New York law, can apply to television talk shows).
26. *Anonsen* v. *Donahue,* 857 S.W.2d 700 (1993) (extending the newsworthiness defense in the context of a cause of action for public disclosure of private facts arising from a revelation on *Donahue*).
27. *Shulman* v. *Group W Productions, Inc.,* 955 P.2d 469 (Cal. 1988).
28. Maura Dolan, "The Right to Know vs. the Right to Privacy," *Los Angeles Times,* August 1, 1997.
29. *Shulman* v. *Group W. Productions,* 955 P.2d 469, 478 (Cal. 1998).
30. Ibid., p. 481.
31. Ibid.
32. Ibid.
33. Ibid., p. 485.
34. Ibid.
35. Ibid. Emphasis added.
36. Ibid.

37. Ibid., p. 488.
38. Ibid.
39. Lee C. Bollinger, *The Tolerant Society* (Oxford, UK: Oxford University Press, 1986).
40. Ibid., p. 77.
41. *Lovell* v. *Griffin*, 303 U.S. 444, 452 (1938).
42. *Branzburg* v. *Hayes*, 408 U.S. 665, 704 (1972).
43. *Near* v. *Minnesota*, 283 U.S. 697 (1931).
44. Ibid., p. 704.
45. Ibid., p. 718.
46. Ibid., p. 719.
47. *Miami Herald Publishing Co.* v. *Tornillo*, 418 U.S. 241 (1974).
48. Ibid., p. 243.
49. Ibid., p. 258.
50. Ibid., p. 256.
51. *Columbia Broadcasting System* v. *Democratic National Committee*, 412 U.S. 94 (1973).
52. Ibid., pp. 124–125.
53. "In 1959, the Federal Communications Commission—a federal regulatory agency—was directed by Congress to define 'bona fide news' programs, a definition broadcast journalists were to follow to be excluded from certain equal-time regulations." Samuel P. Winch, *Mapping the Cultural Space of Journalism: How Journalists Distinguish News from Entertainment* (Westport, CT: Praeger, 1997), pp. 73–74. *See* 47 U.S.C. §315(a) (1988) (providing that bona fide newscasts, bona fide news interviews, bona fide news documentaries, and spot coverage of bona ride news events do not trigger the equal opportunities requirements imposed on broadcasting stations for legally qualified candidates for public office).
54. Winch, *Mapping the Cultural Space*, p. 92.
55. Todd Gitlin, "Not So Fast," *Media Studies Journal* (Spring-Summer 1996): 6.
56. C. Edwin Baker, "Turner Broadcasting: Content-Based Regulation of Person and Presses," *Supreme Court Review* (1994): 80.
57. "Ticker," *Brill's Content*, September 1998, p. 148.
58. Owen M. Fiss, "Free Speech and Social Structure," *Iowa Law Review* 71 (1986): 1410.
59. Ibid.
60. Herbert I. Schiller, *Information Inequality: The Deepening Social Crisis in America* (New York: Routledge, 1996), p. 7.
61. Kathleen M. Sullivan, "Free Speech and Unfree Markets," *UCLA Law Review* 42 (1995): 958.
62. *Desnick* v. *American Broadcasting Companies, Inc.*, 44 F.3d 1345 (1995).
63. Ibid.
64. Ibid., p. 1352.

65. Ibid.
66. Jonathan D. Avila, "Food Lion and Beyond: New Developments in the Law of Hidden Cameras," *Journal of Media, Information, and Communications Law* 16 (Winter 1999): 22.
67. Victor Kovner et al., "Recent Developments in Newsgathering, Invasion of Privacy, and Related Torts," in *Communications Law 1997* (New York: Practicing Law Institute, 1997), p. 539.
68. *Wilkins* v. *NBC*, 71 Cal.App.4th 1066 (1999).
69. Ibid., p. 1078.
70. *Medical Laboratory Management Consultants* v. *American Broadcasting Companies, Inc.*, 30 F.Supp.2d 1182 (1998).
71. Ibid., p. 1185.
72. Ibid., p. 1188.
73. Ibid.
74. Ibid., p. 1190.
75. *Sanders* v. *American Broadcasting Companies, Inc.*, 978 P.2d 67 (Cal. 1999).
76. Ibid., p. 70.
77. Ibid., p. 71.
78. Ibid., p. 72.
79. Ibid., p. 76.
80. Ibid., p. 78.
81. Ibid., p. 76.
82. Ibid., p. 77.
83. Ibid.
84. Robert A. Bertsche, "$5.5M Ruling Against ABC Highlights Growing Risks of Undercover Reports," *TIPS Committee News* 4(1) (Winter 1997): 7.
85. *Food Lion* v. *Capital Cities/ABC*, 194 F.3d 505 (4th Cir. 1999).
86. Felicity Barringer, "Appeals Court Rejects Damages Against ABC in Food Lion Case," *New York Times*, October 21, 1999.
87. Ibid.
88. Lisa de Moraes, "ABC Won't Pay Food Lion's Share," *Washington Post*, October 20, 1999.

FOR USE IN DISCUSSION

Questions about Substance

1. Calvert suggests that there are three parts to the issue of the public's "right to know": the right to know; the right to watch in order to know; and the right to gather the images to be watched (91). Do any of these rights seem to you more

intrinsic to the First Amendment than the others, or are they all equally essential? Do you think that any of the parts is more complicated than the others?

2. Is there a clear difference between the definition of "newsworthy" as that which "*some* people *could*" find newsworthy" even for purposes of "amusement" (99) and the definition of "not newsworthy" as being something that the "community has no interest in . . . beyond the voyeuristic thrill" (100)? Or is the distinction somewhat ambiguous?
3. Why does Calvert have a problem with corporate, "*non-press*-oriented" entities owning large segments of the press (104)? Why does this complicate the protections of the press offered by the Constitution?
4. While corporations that own press outlets receive constitutional protection analogous to that afforded individual citizens, individual citizens do not possess the ability to own so much of a "voice in the marketplace of ideas" (199). In other words, media corporations get individual protection, but have much greater public access than individuals. Is this disparity logical? Is there any way for individuals to have greater access to "avenues of communication"? Or should media corporations have less constitutional protection?
5. How does the "intrusion into seclusion" theory (108) compare to the "public disclosure of private facts" tort described earlier (94)? How do both compare to trespass law (106–107)? And how are the examples Calvert uses to illustrate these legal concepts similar to, and/or different from, each other?
6. Concrete physical space seems to be an important factor in the determination of privacy as a legal concept. In the Shulman, Desnick, Deveraj, and PMG cases, the location of the alleged violation was a key factor in how the courts decided the outcome. Why can't the *abstract* concept of privacy (the "privacy" of one's personal space, for example) be given more legal weight?
7. In the Food Lion case, ABC was found not to have "[harmed] the consuming public" by trespassing on and defrauding the supermarket. How is the public involved in this case between a supermarket and a news show?

Questions about Structure and Style

1. Calvert writes: "For those of us in the television audience to play the role of voyeur, there necessarily must be something to watch. We cannot, after all, be voyeurs without receiving any videotape, photographs, or other forms of reality-based visual images that we like to consume. This means, in turn, that videotape and photographs must be gathered for us by the media" (106). Describe the structure and pace of this passage. What might the speed and logic of Calvert's exposition have to do with the content of his message? How might it relate to his perspective as a lawyer?
2. Calvert spends a significant amount of time describing cases to illustrate each potential legal violation of freedom of the press (e.g., trespass, intrusion into seclusion, and fraud). Why does he insist on examining each of these aspects

of the First Amendment law as it relates to freedom of the press? How would this essay be different if he generalized more, since so many of the outcomes are similar?

Multimedia Suggestions

1. Read the story *Dateline NBC* did on a lawsuit involving Sears and telemarketing at *http://www.msnbc.com/news/761700.asp*. How does the thrust of Dateline's story, which is presented from the point of view of the plaintiff bringing the suit against Sears for their invasion of her privacy, contradict in any way *Dateline*'s actions in the cases Calvert describes?
2. Shortly following the death of Princess Diana, the press (specifically the "paparazzi," freelance photographers who specialize in celebrity photos) was blamed for the tragedy by many celebrities and ordinary citizens, and even by some members of the press itself. The paparazzi defended itself by arguing that celebrities are by definition newsworthy, and that public exposure even of their private lives is something they implicitly agree to as professional entertainers and public figures. Examine some tabloid magazines and newspapers (those that specialize in celebrity sightings, such as the *National Enquirer* at http://www.nationalenquirer.com/ or the *Daily Mirror* at http://www.mirror.co.uk/. Do you think you have a right to know any of the information presented in those papers? Why or why not?
3. The movie *Minority Report* (2002) presents a parallel version of the "dystopia" Calvert so fears. View this film and compare its setting and background to that of Calvert's illustrations of voyeurism. Alternately, watch *1984* (1955, 1984), *Handmaid's Tale* (1990), *The Truman Show* (1998), or *EdTV* (1999), additional examples of the anxiety created by invasions of privacy in a technological age.

SUGGESTIONS FOR WRITING AND RESEARCH

1. What is your definition of "newsworthy"? What does it mean for a story to be in the "public interest"? Is getting a "newsworthy" story delivered to the public more important than protecting an individual's right to privacy? Explain your answer by relating it to at least two of the cases Calvert presents in his essay.
2. Are you surprised by the level of involvement of large corporations in the delivery of "news" to the public? What is Calvert's position on this trend? What is your own position? Can large corporate entities produce unbiased news that is in "the public interest" more than their own financial interest? Discuss this growing trend in an essay, and suggest ways the public interest can be served within this corporate context.
3. Discuss the boundary between news and entertainment as you perceive it in today's media. In what ways has the news become more "entertainment," and in what ways do you think that "reality T.V." wants to be more like the news?

WORKING WITH CLUSTERS

Cluster 5: The Law and the Public
Cluster 20: The Burdens of Modernity
Discipline: The Social Sciences
Rhetorical Mode: Illustration

"Where Would We Be without Our Rights?"

by Kenneth Cole New York

Kenneth Cole has been in business for over twenty years. Initially, the company (and its eponymous CEO) sold shoes out of the back of a truck in Manhattan during the city's annual shoe convention, making use of a special parking permit provided to filmmakers. While shooting "The Birth of a Shoe Company," Kenneth Cole Productions, Inc. sold 40 thousand pairs of shoes in a little over two days. The company is known for its provocative and sometimes political advertising, and it supports causes such as handgun control, the ACLU, and AIDS research. Kenneth Cole's products now include handbags, apparel, and fragrances, in addition to shoes, selling its products under the brand names Kenneth Cole New York, Kenneth Cole Reaction, and Unlisted. In 2002, the company's net income was $17.7 million dollars. The ads featured here are drawn from a 1998 Kenneth Cole New York catalogue.

1. In Your Journal: Where does this image suggest we would be "without our rights"? Do the advertised products relate in any way to the caption on the front of this catalogue?

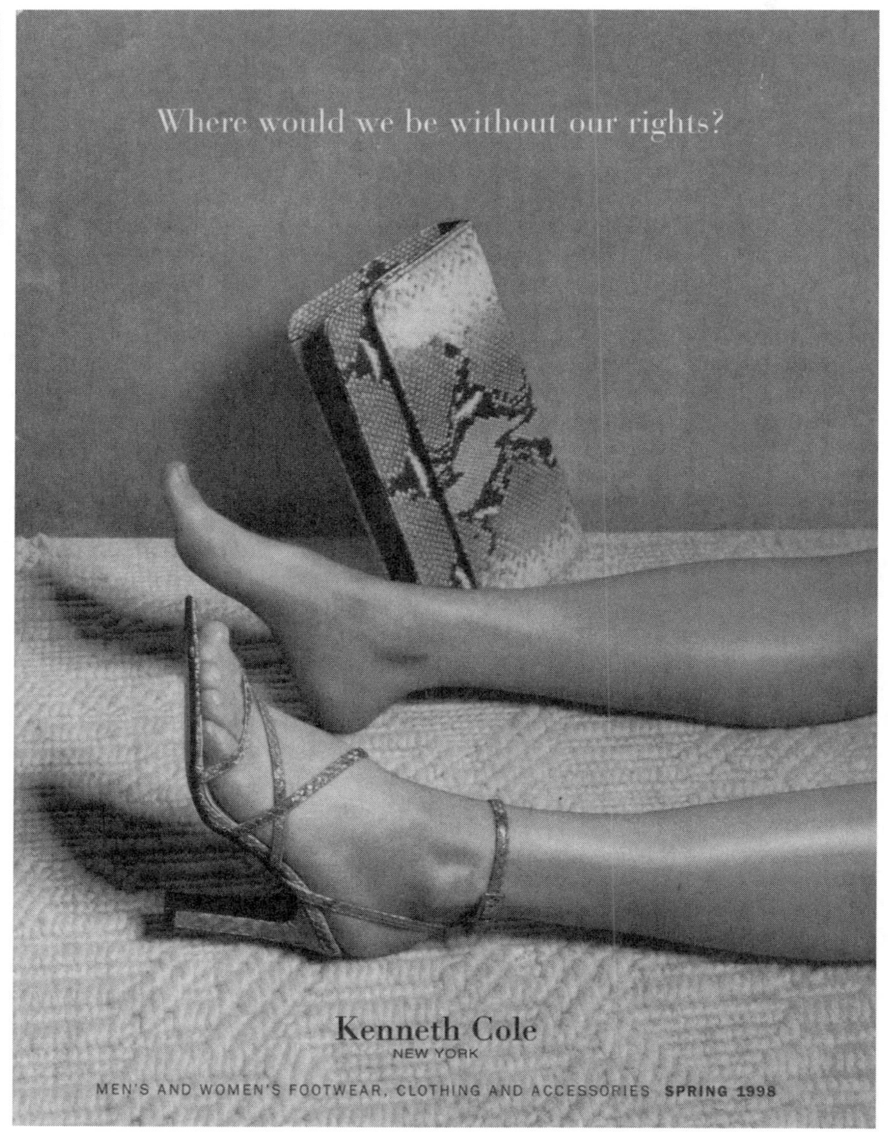
Where would we be without our rights?
Kenneth Cole
NEW YORK
MEN'S AND WOMEN'S FOOTWEAR, CLOTHING AND ACCESSORIES SPRING 1998

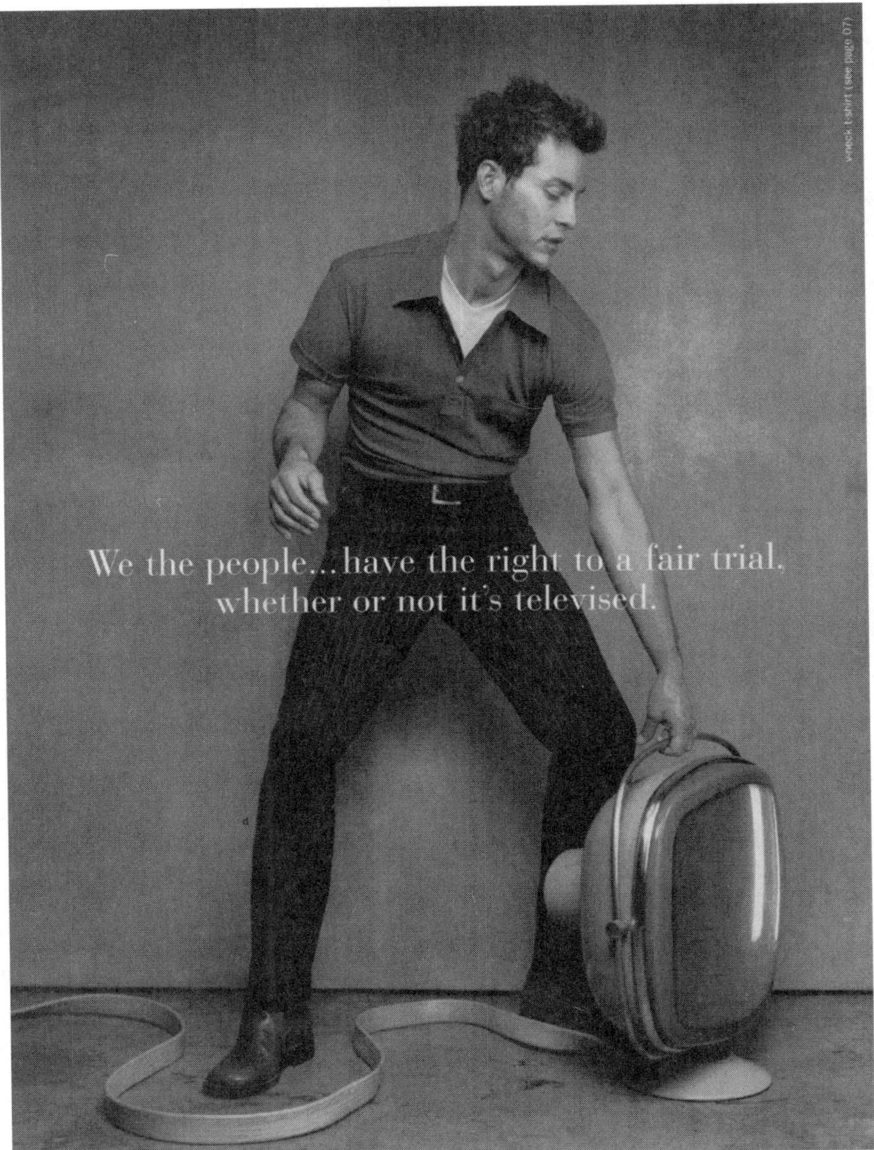
We the people...have the right to a fair trial,
whether or not it's televised.
V-neck t-shirt (see page 07)

right to a fair trial: Amendment VI of the Constitution states: "In all criminal prosecutions, the accused shall enjoy the right to a speedy and public trial, by an impartial jury of the State and district wherein the crime shall have been committed, which district shall have been previously ascertained by law, and to be informed of the nature and cause of the accusation; to be confronted with the witnesses against him; to have compulsory process for obtaining witnesses in his favor, and to have the Assistance of Counsel for his defence"

2. In Your Journal: What effect does this question suggest television has on a trial?

right to bear arms: Amendment II of the Constitution states: "A well regulated Militia, being necessary to the security of a free State, the right of the people to keep and bear arms, shall not be infringed"

3. In Your Journal: Does the pun presented here ("bear" to "bare") seem based in any kind of logic? What position do you think this ad takes on our "right to bear arms"?

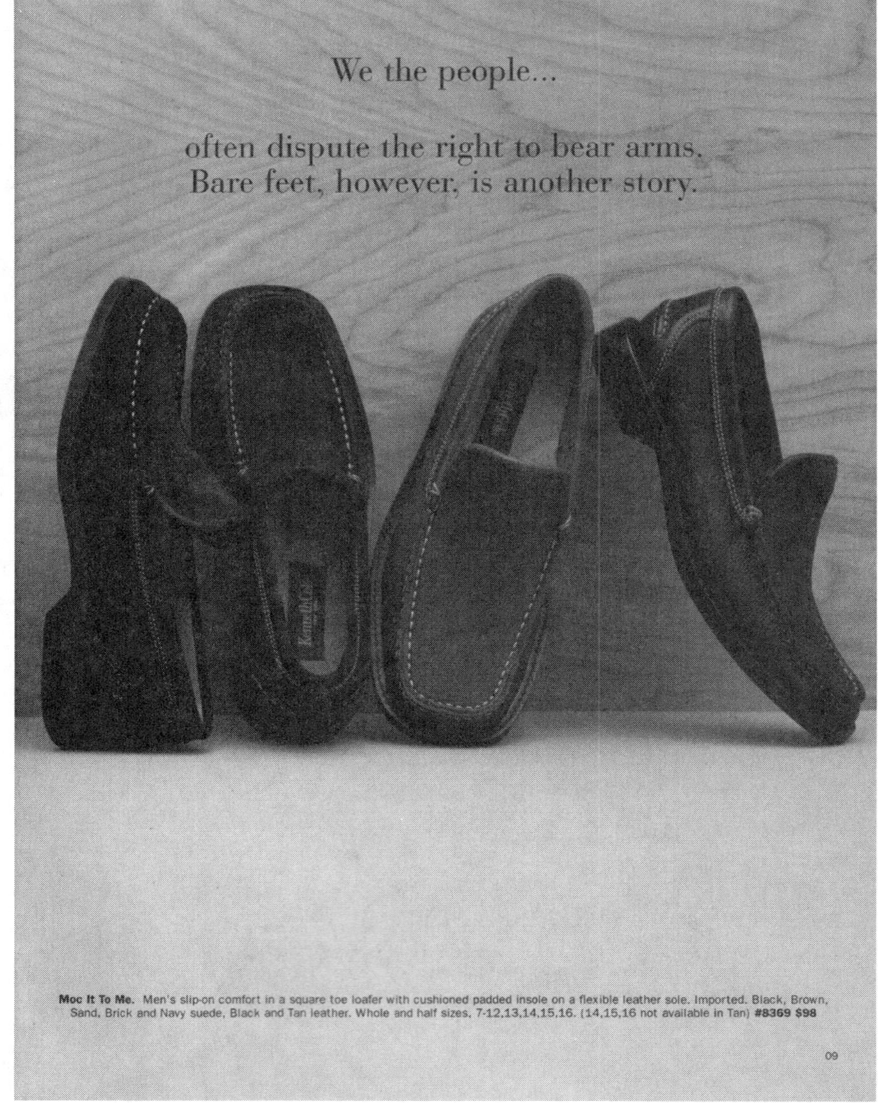
We the people...
often dispute the right to bear arms.
Bare feet, however, is another story.
Moc It To Me. Men's slip-on comfort in a square toe loafer with cushioned padded insole on a flexible leather sole. Imported. Black, Brown, Sand, Brick and Navy suede, Black and Tan leather. Whole and half sizes, 7-12,13,14,15,16. (14,15,16 not available in Tan) **#8369 $98**
09

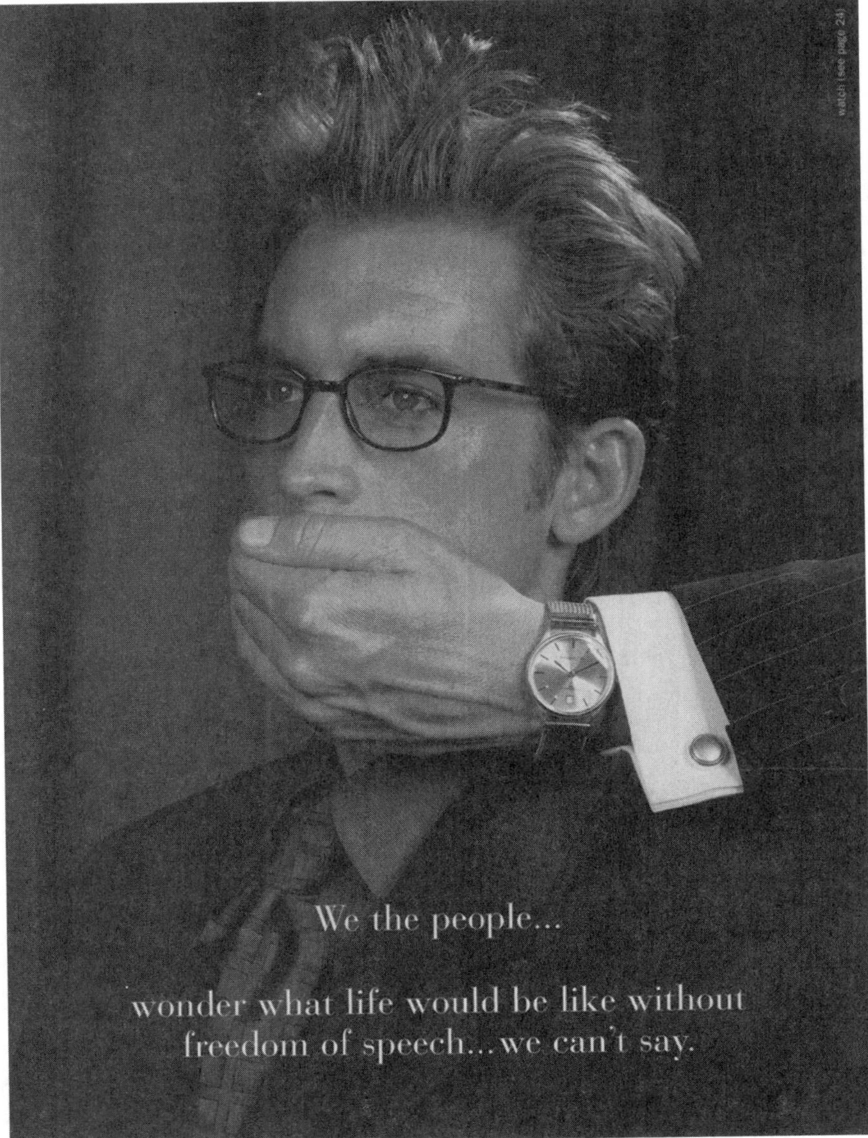
watch (see page 24)
We the people...
wonder what life would be like without
freedom of speech...we can't say.

freedom of speech: Amendment I of the Constitution states: "Congress shall make no law respecting an establishment of religion, or prohibiting the free exercise thereof; or abridging the freedom of speech, or of the press; or the right of the people peaceably to assemble, and to petition the Government for a redress of grievances"

4. In Your Journal: Does freedom of speech have any particular relevance in the context of this ad series?

freedom of the press: see **freedom of speech**

5. In Your Journal: Does Kenneth Cole implicate itself in any way with this image? How are advertisements related to "the press"?

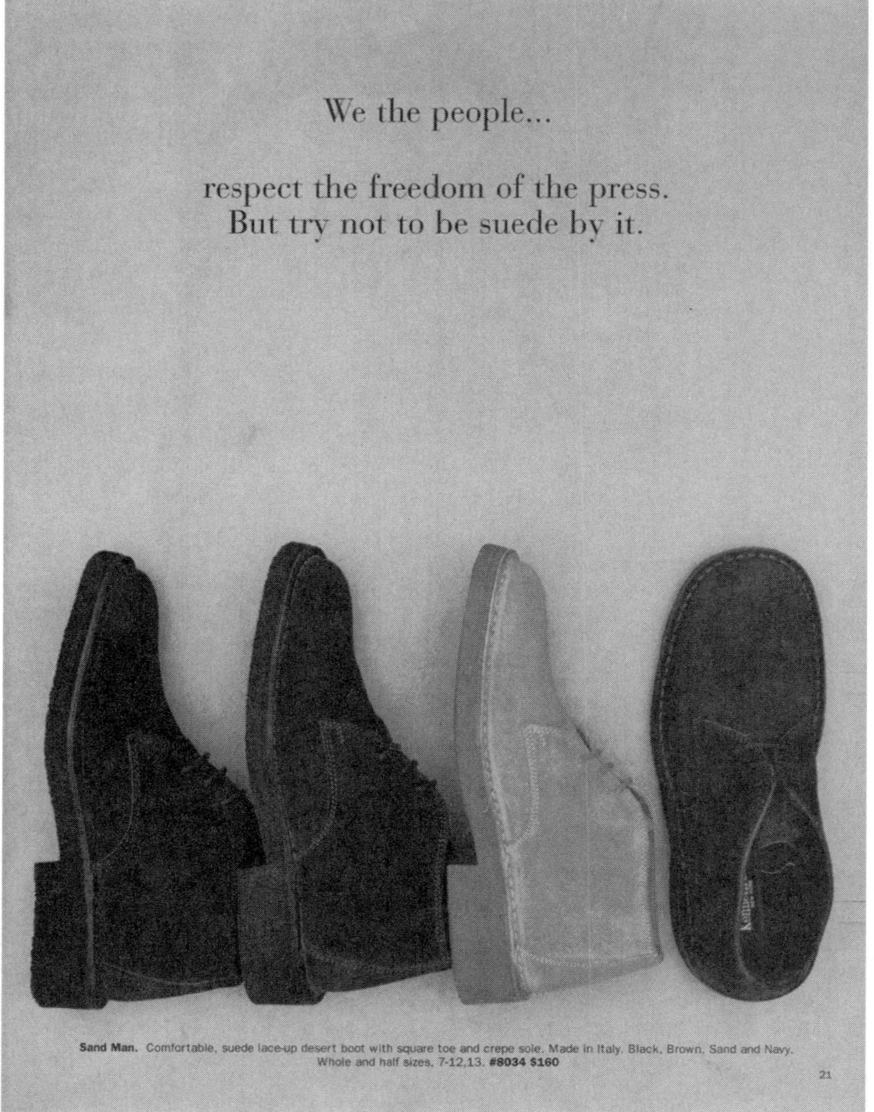
We the people...
respect the freedom of the press.
But try not to be suede by it.
Sand Man. Comfortable, suede lace-up desert boot with square toe and crepe sole. Made in Italy. Black, Brown, Sand and Navy.
Whole and half sizes, 7-12,13. #8034 $160
21

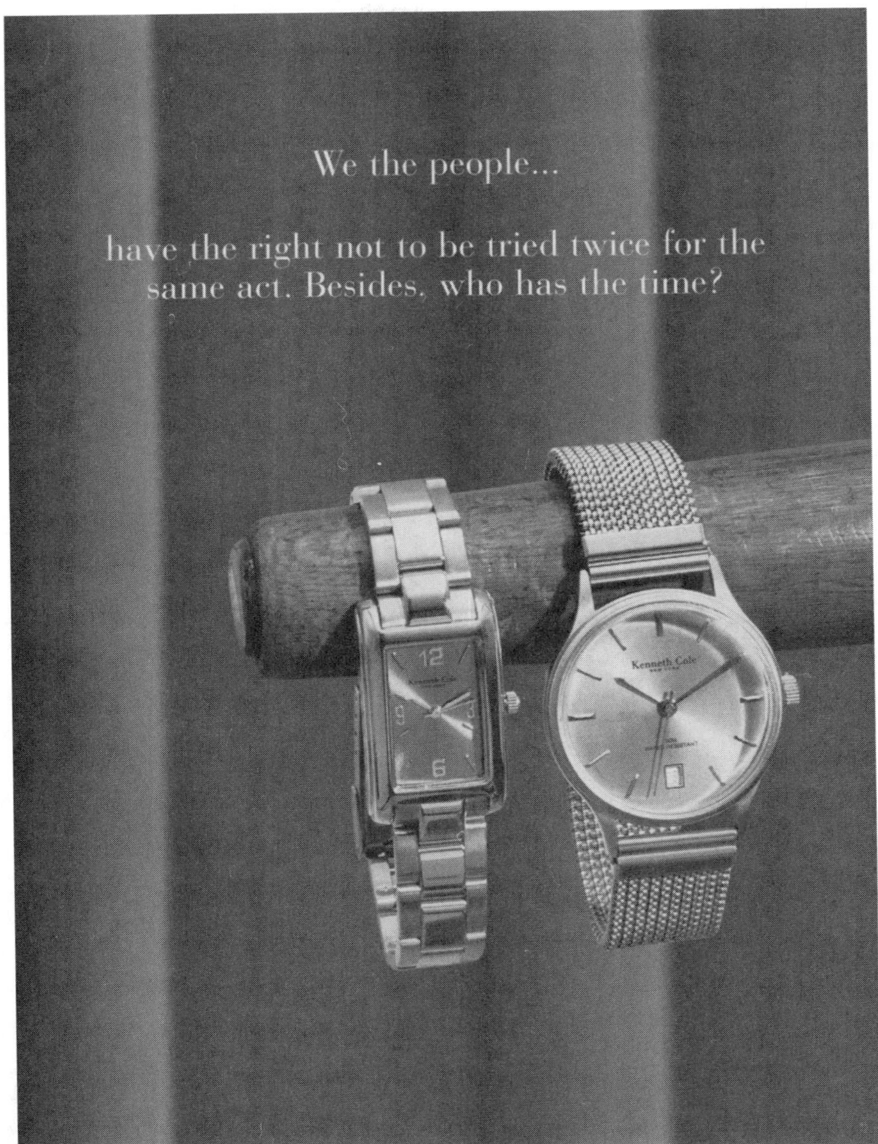

right not to be tried twice for the same act: Amendment V of the Constitution partially states: "No person shall be . . . subject for the same offence to be twice put in jeopardy of life or limb . . ."

6. In Your Journal: Is this question merely a joke or does it contain a critique of any kind?

right to privacy: Amendment XIV of the Constitution partially states: "No State shall make or enforce any law which shall abridge the privileges or immunities of citizens of the United States; nor shall any state deprive any person of life, liberty, or property, without due process of law; nor deny to any person within its jurisdiction the equal protection of the laws"; the right to privacy is generally protected by this amendment, in terms of the right to "life, liberty, [and] property" as well as in terms of the "due process" clause

7. In Your Journal: Does it surprise you that the phrase "right to privacy" is never specifically mentioned in the Constitution? How do you think it has been construed from the 14th amendment?

We the people...
have a right to privacy, if we see fit.

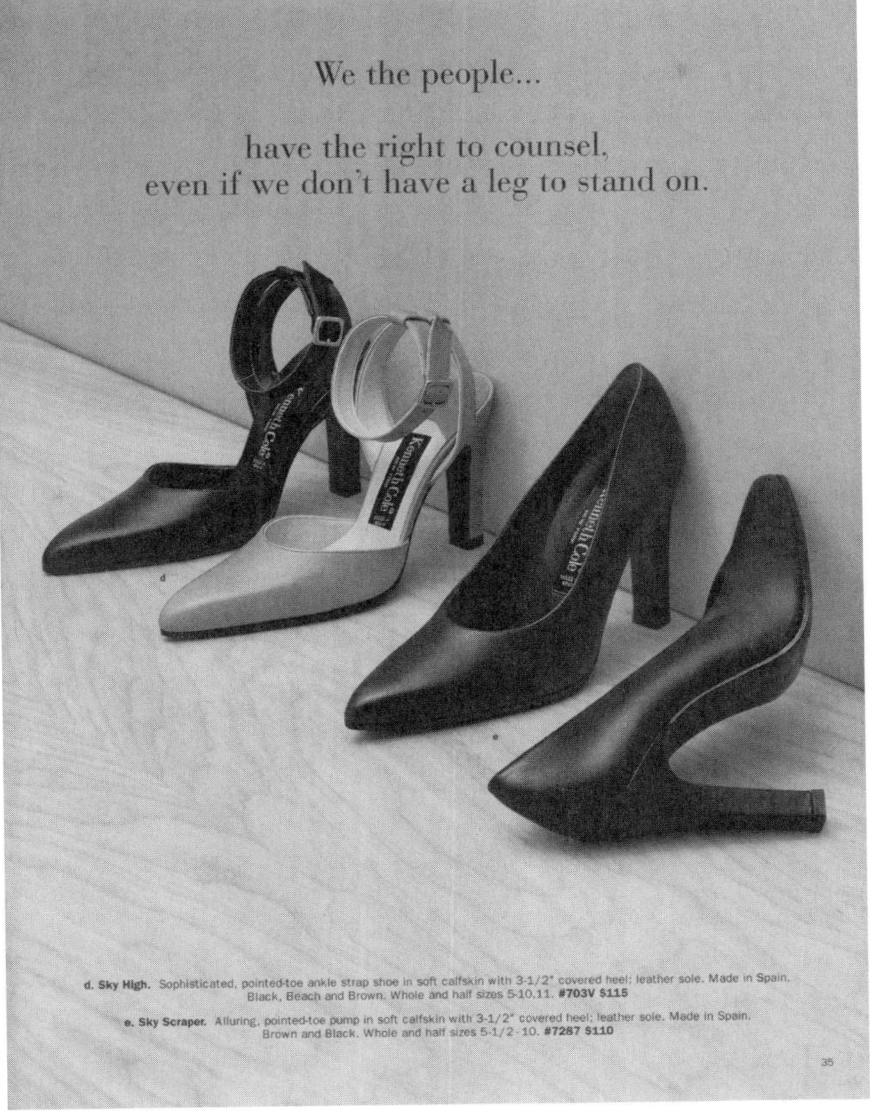
We the people...
have the right to counsel,
even if we don't have a leg to stand on.
Kenneth Cole
d. Sky High. Sophisticated, pointed-toe ankle strap shoe in soft calfskin with 3-1/2" covered heel; leather sole. Made in Spain. Black, Beach and Brown. Whole and half sizes 5-10,11. #703V $115
e. Sky Scraper. Alluring, pointed-toe pump in soft calfskin with 3-1/2" covered heel; leather sole. Made in Spain. Brown and Black. Whole and half sizes 5-1/2-10. #7287 $110
35

right to counsel: see **right to a fair trial**

8. In Your Journal: Does this image/question seem contemptuous of the "right to counsel"? Why or why not?

right to seek elective office: Article I of the Constitution determines the powers and processes of Congress; Amendment XVII provides for direct popular election for Senators

9. In Your Journal: With regard to the "right to seek elective office," what does this question mean by "cover our backs"?

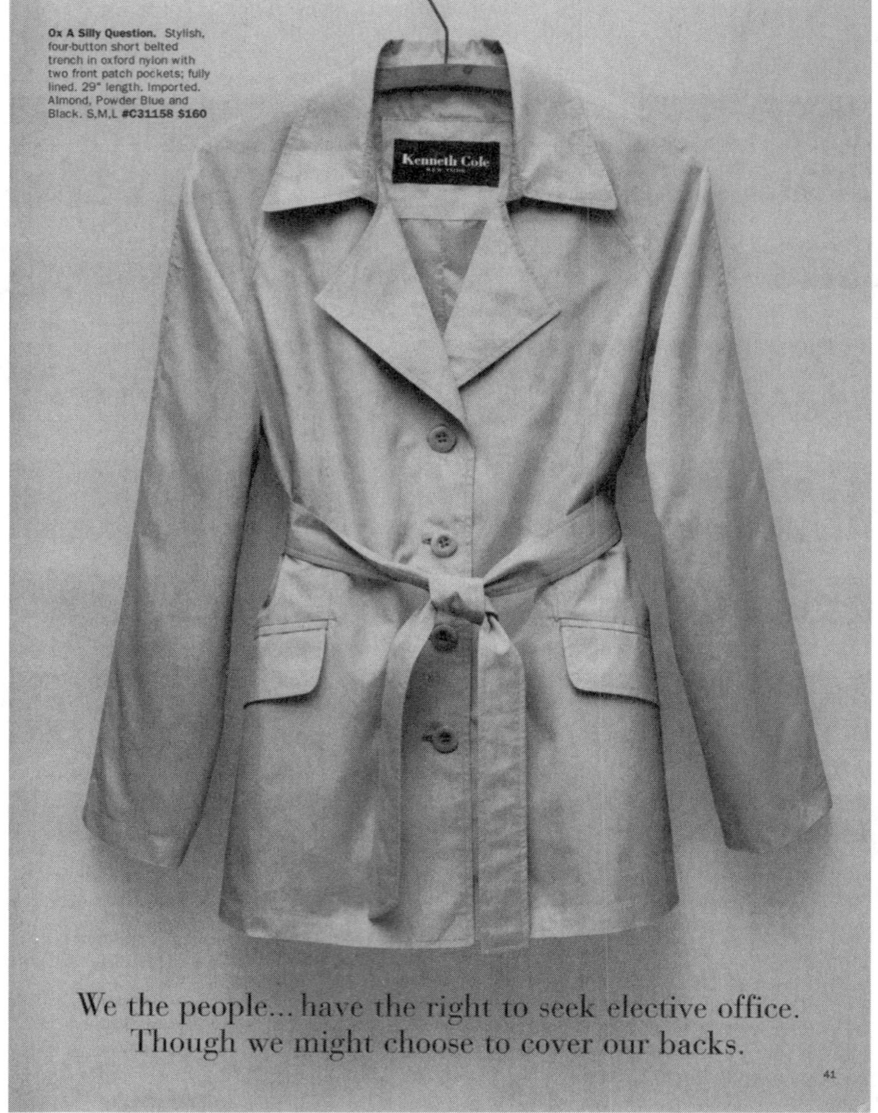
Ox A Silly Question. Stylish, four-button short belted trench in oxford nylon with two front patch pockets; fully lined. 29" length. Imported. Almond, Powder Blue and Black. S,M,L **#C31158 $160**
Kenneth Cole
We the people... have the right to seek elective office.
Though we might choose to cover our backs.
41

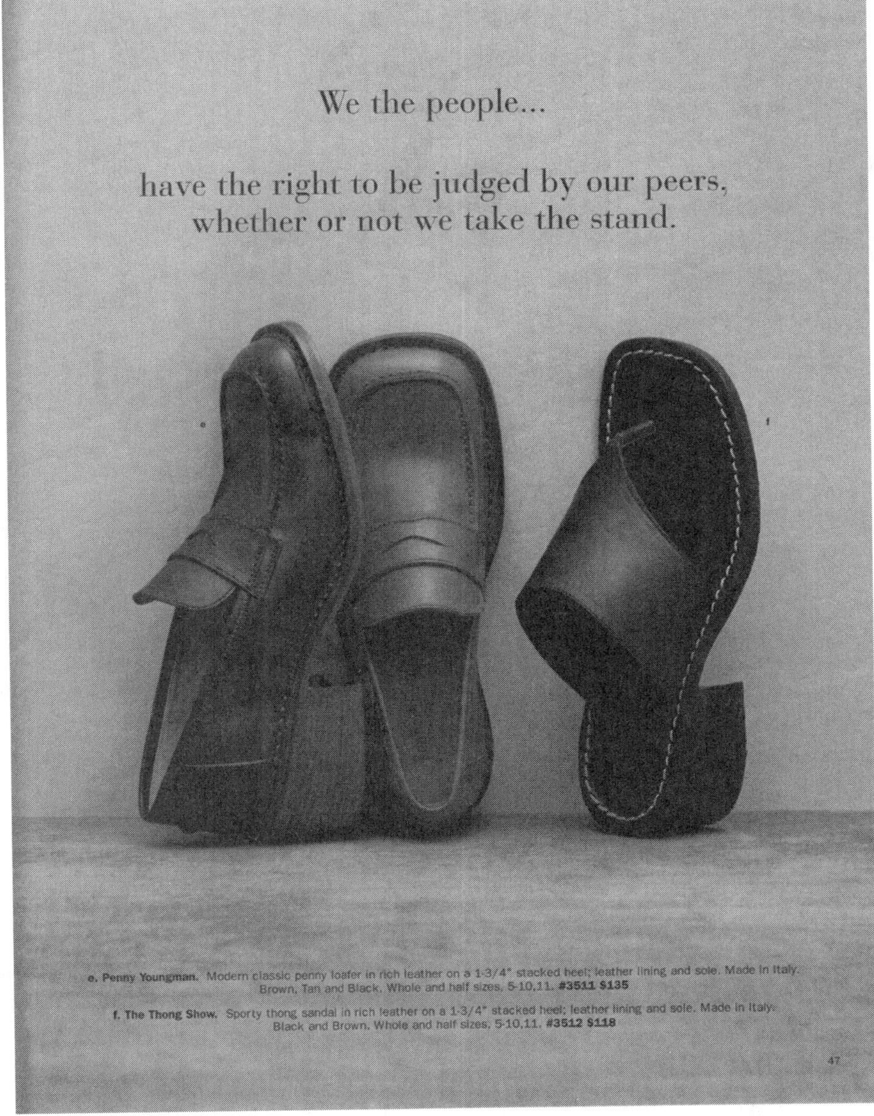
We the people...
have the right to be judged by our peers, whether or not we take the stand.
e
f
e. Penny Youngman. Modern classic penny loafer in rich leather on a 1-3/4" stacked heel; leather lining and sole. Made in Italy. Brown, Tan and Black. Whole and half sizes. 5-10,11. #3511 $135
f. The Thong Show. Sporty thong sandal in rich leather on a 1-3/4" stacked heel; leather lining and sole. Made in Italy. Black and Brown. Whole and half sizes. 5-10,11. #3512 $118
47

right to be judged by our peers: see **right to a fair trial**

10. In Your Journal: Why do we value the right to be "judged by our peers" if put on trial? Why are peers more desirable than professionals when it comes to the jury system.

right to choose: see **right to privacy.** The "right to choose" is generally protected by this amendment, both in terms of a person's right to "liberty" and in terms of the "due process" clause.

11. In Your Journal: What is your reaction to the tone of this image and its corresponding rhetorical question? What reaction do you think Kenneth Cole wants from readers?

12. In Your Journal: How directly does the Constitution seem to protect abortion rights, given the Amendment that the "right to choose" invokes?

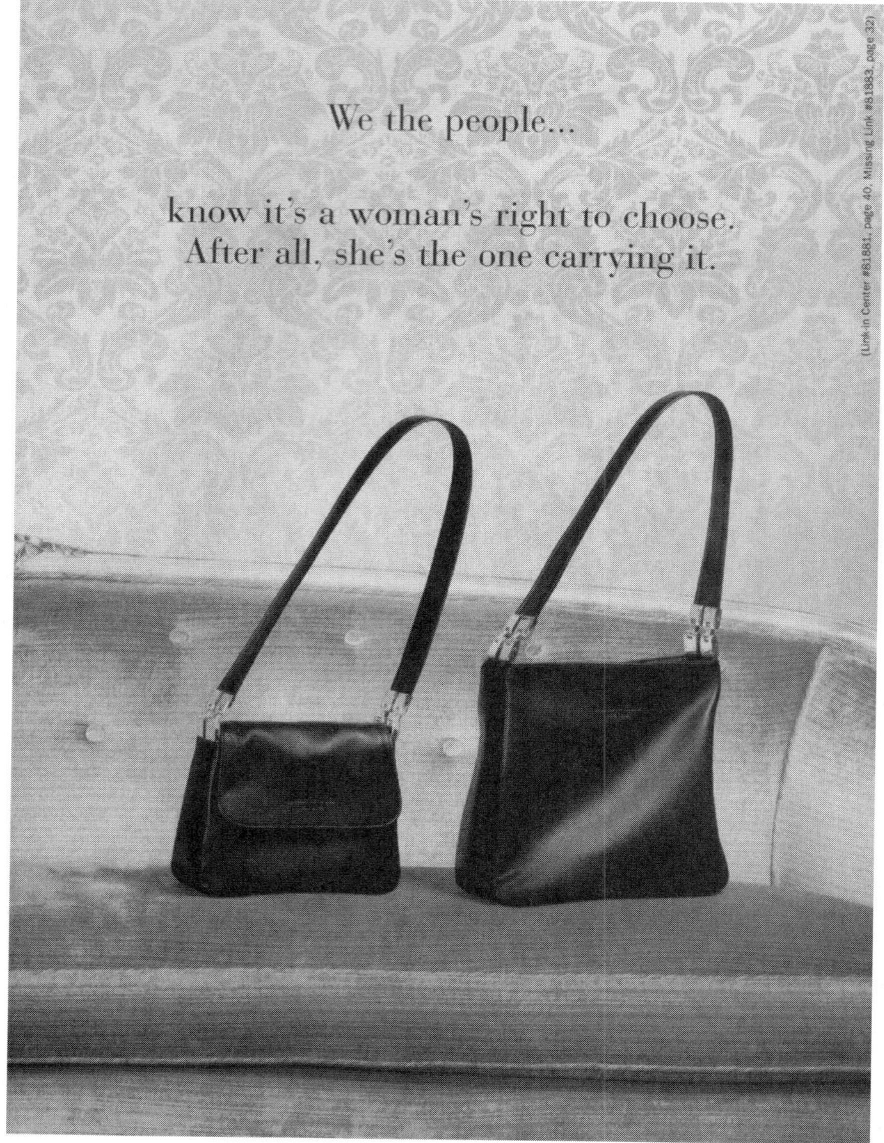

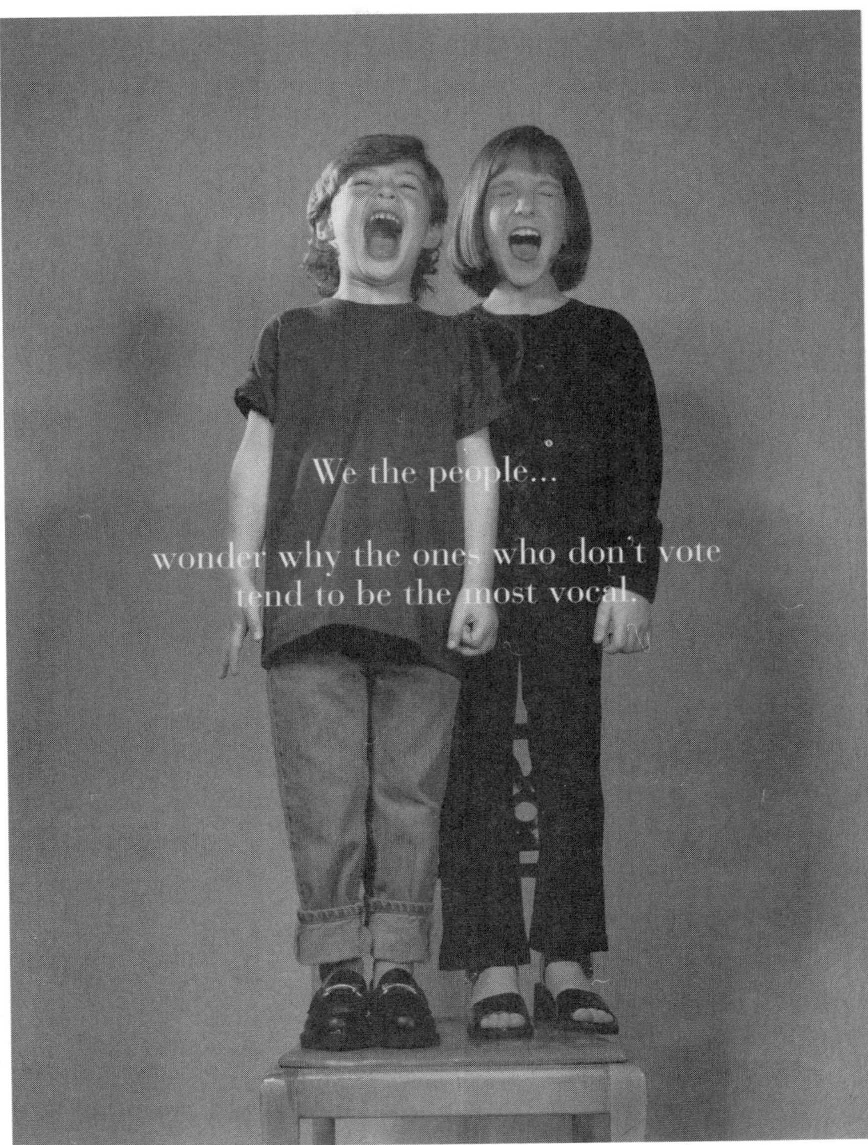
We the people...
wonder why the ones who don't vote
tend to be the most vocal.

vote (right to vote): Amendment XV of the Constitution states: "The right of citizens of the United States to vote shall not be denied or abridged by the United States or by any State on account of race, color, or previous condition of servitude"; Amendment XIX of the Constitution states: "The right of citizens to vote shall not be denied or abridged by the United States or by any State on account of sex"

13. In Your Journal: Whom do you suppose the children in this ad are meant to represent? Who or what is being criticized in this ad?

14. In Your Journal: How are the image and question meant to interact in this image?

FOR USE IN DISCUSSION

Questions about Substance

1. What is the purpose of a catalogue? How well do you think this catalogue serves that purpose? Cite examples to support your answer.
2. Do you get a sense of a specific ideology behind these ads? Are they simply meant to raise awareness about Constitutional issues, or is there an implicit political agenda in the ads?
3. Does it seem particularly important to you that this is a catalogue of *accessories* rather than more necessary items? How does the concept of accessories relate to the subject of the Constitution?
4. Discuss the role of humor in this ad catalogue. What's so funny about Constitutional rights?

Questions about Structure and Style

1. Is there any logical difference between the images that feature models and the images that feature only products?
2. Do you think this catalogue must have a target audience? What characteristics do you think, would define that audience?
3. How are catalogues different from billboards or magazine ads? What are the apparent advantages and disadvantages of advertising in a catalogue?

Multimedia Review

1. Look at some of the satirical ads at *www.adbusters.org*. These ads are intended to criticize the advertising industry rather than to sell products. How are they similar to the Kenneth Cole ads? How are they different? Do you think the Kenneth Cole ads are meant to criticize the advertising industry as well? Why or why not?
2. "Product placement" (the incidental use of specific brands in a film or television show) is an increasingly common practice. The next time you go to a movie, watch for specific brands. Are the brands trying to associate themselves with particular lifestyles or politics or are they merely trying to get noticed? Do you have any opinion of this practice?
3. Look for additional Kenneth Cole ads in whatever fashion magazines you can find. Are they all so provocative? Do different magazines feature different approaches? Bring your findings to the class for discussion.
4. Compare these Kenneth Cole ads to the ads found on the United Colors of Benetton Web site, *www.benetton.com*, or the anti-smoking Web site for The Truth campaign, *www.thetruth.com*. Which are more similar in composition and/or tone to Kenneth Cole's?

5. Read the article "Risky Kenneth Cole Ad Becomes Fashion Faux Pas" by Candace Murphy at *http://www.ccchronicle.com/back/2001-10-15/ arts11.html*. What disadvantages are there in using politics in advertising? How do financial considerations threaten to undermine Kenneth Cole's provocative advertising campaigns?

SUGGESTIONS FOR WRITING AND RESEARCH

1. Pay attention to all of the advertisements that you come across in one day. Keep a log of what they are for, where you see them, and how noticeable they were to you. Which ones stood out the most? What did the standouts have in common: size, recognizable faces, intriguing compositions, etc.? Where does this Kenneth Cole spread fit into the range of what you have recorded? Is it commonplace or does it stand out even from the standouts?
2. Write a letter to the Kenneth Cole in response to this catalogue. Whether you think it's effective or offensive, explain why by citing specific examples from the catalogue.
3. Research one of the Constitutional amendments this catalogue refers to. Describe the history and current case law regarding this amendment, and assess Kenneth Cole's reference to it. Does the ad present an accurate picture of the amendment's legal uses?

WORKING WITH CLUSTERS

Cluster 5: The Law and the Public

Cluster 12: Visual Language

Cluster 20: The Burdens of Modernity

Discipline: The Humanities

Rhetorical Mode: Illustration

"Whose Story Is It, Anyway? Feminist and Antiracist Appropriations of Anita Hill" (from *Race-ing Justice, En-gender-ing Power: Essays on Anita Hill, Clarence Thomas, and the Construction of Social Reality,* Toni Morrison, Ed.)

by Kimberlé Crenshaw

Kimberlé Williams Crenshaw is a professor at the UCLA Law School and Columbia University School of Law, where she teaches courses in civil rights and constitutional law. Her articles have appeared in Harvard Law Review, Stanford Law Review, University of Chicago Law Review, National Black Law Journal, *and* Southern California Law Review, *and many anthologies. A founding member of the Critical Race Theory workshop and co-editor of* Critical Race Theory: The Key Writings That Formed the Movement, *she serves on the governing board of the Law and Society Association and the Society of American Law Teachers. Professor Crenshaw has been honored twice as Professor of the Year at UCLA Law School. She received a B.A. from Cornell in 1981, a J.D. from Harvard in 1984, and an LL.M. from University of Wisconsin in 1985, where she was also a William H. Hastie Fellow. This essay is drawn from the anthology* Race-ing Justice, En-gendering Power: Essays on Anita Hill, Clarence Thomas, and the Construction of Social Reality, *edited by Toni Morrison, and Crenshaw wrote it after assisting Anita Hill's legal team during the Thomas hearings.*

The Twilight Zone: 1960s science fiction television series suggesting the existence of parallel universes

"exploitation of the mythic black rapist": refers to the 1988 presidential election campaign ads featuring Willie Horton, a convicted murderer who had received a 48-hour furlough under a program supported by Massachusetts Governor Michael Dukakis, the democratic candidate for president; Horton, an African American, never returned from his 1986 furlough, and was later found to have brutally attacked a young white couple in their home, stabbing and beating the man and raping the woman; anti-Dukakis ads ominously alluded to Horton and the furlough program, and were widely thought to have shored up the victory for Bush by exploiting stereotypes of black male sexual aggression

stymie: block; thwart

As television, the **Clarence Thomas/Anita Hill** hearings played beautifully as an episode right out of **"The Twilight Zone."** Stunned by the drama's mystifying images, its misplaced pairings, and its baffling contradictions, viewers found themselves in a parallel universe where political allegiances barely imaginable a moment earlier sprang to life: an administration that won an election through the shameless **exploitation of the mythic black rapist** took the offensive against stereotypes about black male sexuality; a political party that had been the refuge of white resentment won the support, however momentary, of the majority of African Americans; a black neoconservative individualist whose upward mobility was fueled by his unbounded willingness to **stymie** the advancement of other African Americans was embraced under the wings of racial solidarity; and a black woman, herself a victim of racism, was symbolically transformed into the role of a would-be white woman whose unwarranted finger-pointing whetted the appetites of a racist lynch mob.

But it was no "Twilight Zone" that America discovered when Anita Hill came forward. America simply stumbled into the place where African-American women live, a political vacuum of erasure and contradiction maintained by the almost routine polarization of "blacks and women" into separate and competing political camps. Existing within the overlapping margins of race and gender discourse and in the empty spaces between, it is a location whose very nature resists telling. This location contributes to black women's ideological disempowerment in a way that tipped the scales against Anita Hill from the very start. While there are surely many dimensions of the Thomas-Hill episode that contributed to the way it played out, my focus on the ideological plane is based on the idea that at

---

❖ **Clarence Thomas:** 1990 nominee of President George Bush (Senior) to replace retiring Supreme Court Justice Thurgood Marshall in July 1991; after allegations of sexual harassment made by his former colleague, Anita Hill, and widely televised hearings on the matter, Thomas was confirmed by a 52–48 margin

---

❖ **Anita Hill:** lawyer, professor, writer, and political activist; accepted a job as the personal assistant to Clarence Thomas in 1981 (and held it for two years); co-editor of *Race, Gender, and Power in America: The Legacy of the Hill–Thomas Hearing* with Emma Coleman Jordan, and author of *Speaking Truth to Power,* an account of the events before, during, and after the Thomas hearing least one important way social power is mediated in American society is through the contestation between the many narrative structures through which reality might be perceived and talked about. By this I mean to focus on the intense interpretive conflicts that ultimately bear on the particular ways that realities are socially constructed. Ideology, seen in the form of the narrative **tropes** available for representing our experience, was a factor of social power to the extent that Anita Hill's inability to be heard outside the rhetorical structures within which cultural power has been organized hampered her ability to achieve recognition and support. Thus, Anita Hill's status as a black female—at the crossroads of gender and race hierarchies—was a central feature in the manner in which she was (mis)perceived. Because she was situated within two fundamental hierarchies of social power, the central disadvantage that Hill faced was the lack of available and widely comprehended narratives to communicate the reality of her experience as a black woman to the world.

trope: figure of speech; figurative use of a word or expression

1. In Your Journal: Crenshaw refers to the "empty spaces between" different types of discourse as the place "where African-American women live." Why do you think she uses this metaphor of *location* to express the social and political predicaments of black women?

The particular experience of black women in the dominant cultural ideology of American society can be conceptualized as intersectional. Intersectionality captures the way in which the particular location of black women in dominant American social relations is unique and in some senses unassimilable into the **discursive** paradigms of gender and race domination. One commonly noted aspect of this location is that black women are in a sense doubly burdened, subject in some ways to the dominating practices of both a sexual hierarchy and a racial one. In addition to this added dimension, intersectionality also refers to the ways that black women's marginalization within dominant discourses of resistance limits the means available to relate and conceptualize our experiences as black women.

discursive: digressive, covering a wide range; in the context of narrative, can mean intentionally deceptive

2. In Your Journal: Discuss the ways Crenshaw sees ideology (beliefs that directly reflect the needs or aspirations of an individual or social group—for example, conservative ideology or feminist ideology) as means to social power.

In legal doctrine this idea has been explored in terms of doctrinal exclusion, that is, the ways in which the specific forms of domination to which black females are subject sometimes fall between the existing legal categories for recognizing injury.[1] Underlying the legal parameters of racial discrimination are numerous narratives reflecting discrimination as it is experienced by black men, while the underlying imagery of gender discrimination incorporates the experiences of white women. The particularities of black female subordination are suppressed as the terms of racial and gender discrimination law require that we mold our experience into that of either white women or black men in order to be legally recognized.

3. In Your Journal: What is the "double burden" with which Crenshaw describes the social plight of black women?

The marginalization of black women in antidiscrimination law is replicated in the realm of oppositional politics; black women are marginalized in feminist politics as a consequence of race, and they are marginalized in antiracist politics as a consequence of their gender. The consequences of this multiple marginality are fairly predictable—there is simply silence of and about black women. Yet black women do not share the burdens of these elisions alone. When feminism does not explicitly oppose racism,

4. In Your Journal: How is it that black men and white women seem to be more aptly represented in anti-discrimination law than black women?

and when antiracism does not incorporate opposition to patriarchy, race and gender politics often end up being antagonistic to each other and both interests lose. The Thomas/Hill controversy presents a stark illustration of the problem as evidenced by the opposition between narratives of rape and of lynching. These tropes have come to symbolize the mutually exclusive claims that have been generated within both antiracist and feminist discourses about the centrality of sexuality to both race and gender domination. In feminist contexts, sexuality represents a central site of the oppression of women; rape and the rape trial are its dominant narrative trope. In antiracist discourses, sexuality is also a central site upon which the repression of blacks has been premised; the lynching narrative is embodied as its trope. (Neither narrative tends to acknowledge the legitimacy of the other; the reality of rape tends to be disregarded within the lynching narrative; the impact of racism is frequently marginalized within rape narratives.) Both these tropes figured prominently in this controversy, and it was in this sense that the **debacle** constituted a classic showdown between antiracism and feminism. The tropes, whether explicitly invoked, as lynching, or implicitly referenced, as rape, served to communicate in shorthand competing narratives about the hearings and about what "really" happened between Clarence Thomas and Anita Hill. Anita Hill was of course cast in both narratives, but because one told a tale of sexism and the other told an opposing tale of racism, the simultaneity of Hill's race and gender identity was essentially denied. In this sense, both feminist and antiracist told tales on Anita Hill, tales in which she was **appropriated** to tell everybody's story but her own.

> *5. In Your Journal:* Why does there seem to be an "opposition between narratives of rape and of lynching" according to Crenshaw, especially when sexuality is central to "both race and gender domination"?

debacle: sudden collapse or disaster

appropriate: steal

These competing appropriations of Anita Hill within feminist and antiracist discourses represent a persistent dilemma that confronts black women within prevailing constructions of identity politics: dominant conceptions of racism and sexism render it virtually impossible to represent our situation in ways that fully articulate our subject position as black women. While Thomas was able to invoke narratives that linked his situation to the sexual oppression of black men and thus have his story understood as relevant to the entire black community, Hill remained unable to represent even herself, much less other similarly situated black women.

> *6. In Your Journal:* What does Crenshaw mean when she states that Hill was "appropriated to tell everybody's story but her own"?

> *7. In Your Journal:* What do you think is meant by the expression "identity politics"?

In this essay I want to elaborate how the cultural dynamics surrounding the Thomas-Hill conflict are better understood in terms of Hill's intersectional disempowerment. My argument proceeds as follows. Addressing first the dominant paradigm for understanding the exercise of gender power, the narrative trope of the raped (white) woman, I discuss how Hill's experience in fact partly fit this rhetorical structure, and how her lack of power can be understood in part through the ways that white feminists have articulated gender domination. Second, however, I highlight Hill's intersectional identity by likewise showing the ways that the rape-trial analogy didn't fit, and how the limitations of traditional feminist discourse worked to suppress the more nuanced experience that Hill was communicating. In the second part of the essay I turn to race discourse and discuss how Hill's experience was partially explicable in terms of the dominant discourse of racial liberation. But this same discourse, embodied in the image of the lynched black man, also worked to disempower Hill in relation to Clarence Thomas.

I. ANITA HILL AS A VICTIM OF SEXUAL DOMINATION—THE RAPE TROPE

Anita Hill was primarily presented to the American public as simply a woman complaining about sexual harassment. Her plausibility in that role was dependent upon the degree to which she could be fit within the dominant images of sexual victimization. Those images, in turn, have been heavily critiqued in the feminist articulation of gender politics. My argument here is that one consequence of the feminist movement's tendency to think about gender power and dynamics in terms of what we might call a **universalist or essentialist** form is that it depicts the structural forms that gender power plays in the white community as representing gender pure and simple. While many elements of the dominant feminist discourse about gender power and sexuality clearly did apply to Anita Hill—for example, the tradition of **impugning** charges of sexual aggression with baseless allegations of psychic delusions or vengeful spite—the grounding of the critique on white women meant that, in a sense, Hill (and Thomas) had to be deraced, so that they could be represented as actors in a recognizable story of sexual harassment. While white feminists were in general the most consistent and vocal supporters of Hill, the fact remains that both her lack of fit into the dominant imagery of the violated madonna and, more specifically, the feminist movement's inability to develop alternative narratives comprehending the ways that women of color experience gender power, led to the particular dynamics that many of her supporters themselves were unable to understand, dynamics that included the rejection of Hill by the majority of black women as well as white women.

> ***8. In Your Journal:*** Why would Hill need to fit into the "dominant images of sexual victimization"?

universalist or essentialist: espousing a theory of identity based on *essence* rather than social construction (e.g., an essentialist would argue that there is an essence of femininity that all women innately possess, whereas a social constructivist would argue that women are taught by society how to be feminine)

impugn: criticize; brand as false

> ***9. In Your Journal:*** Why did Hill and Thomas have "to be deraced" for this story to be understood by the white mainstream?

Feminist legal scholars have frequently used rape as a framework to capture both the way women experience sexual harassment and the way the law shapes the claims of the few courageous women who come forward. Feminist scholars and activists have long criticized the way the adjudication of sexual aggression is animated by myths about women, about assumptions regarding their veracity and their integrity, and by doubts about their grasp on reality. In both rape and sexual-harassment cases the inquiry tends to focus more on the woman's conduct and character rather than on the conduct and character of the defendant. As a consequence, rape law does less to protect the sexual autonomy of women than it does to reinforce established codes of female sexual conduct.

Part of the regulation of sexuality through rape law occurs in the perception of the complaining witness at the rape trial. Building on the idea that reality is socially constructed in part through ideologically informed images of "men" and "women," feminist legal work has emphasized the ways that perceptions of the credibility of witnesses, for example, are mediated by dominant narratives about the ways that men and women "are." Within this framework, the vast disparity between male and female characterizations reflects a gendered zero-sum equation of credibility and power. The routine focus on the victim's sexual history functions to cast the complainant in one of several roles, including the whore, the tease, the vengeful liar, the mentally or emotionally unstable, or, in a few instances, the madonna. Once these ideologically informed character assignments are made, "the story" tells itself, usually supplanting the woman's account of what transpired between the complainant and the accused with a fiction of villainous female intentionality that misleads and entraps the "innocent" or unsuspecting male in his performance of prescribed sexual behavior. Such displacing narratives are overwhelmingly directed toward interrogating and discrediting the woman's character on behalf of maintaining a considerable range of sexual **prerogatives** for men. Even the legal definitions of the crime of rape itself are inscribed with male visions of the sexual sphere—the focus on penetration, the definitions of consent (with the once-conventional requirement of "utmost resistance"),[2] the images of female provocation and spiteful false accusation, and the links between desirability, purity, chastity, and value.[3]

10. In Your Journal: How do narratives about gender inform "witness credibility" in rape trials?

11. In Your Journal: When Crenshaw remarks that, "the story tells itself" once characters are established, to what *story* does she refer?

prerogative: exclusive privilege

The feminist narrative of the rape trial did in many ways account for the dynamics that Anita Hill put into play. For example, a good deal of the hearings was allegedly devoted to determining the credibility of the parties. Anita Hill's subordination through the notion of credibility is revealed in the relatively wide range of narratives that Thomas's defenders could invoke by simply describing events and impressions that had little to do with what transpired between Hill and Thomas in private. For example, the conversation that Anita Hill allegedly had with **John Doggett** was deemed relevant within a narrative that presented Hill as an undesirable woman who constructed relationships with men who rejected her. Testimony that she was aloof, ambitious, and hard to get along with was relevant within a narrative that presented her as calculating and careerist. The continuous focus on failure to resign after the harassment began fit into a narrative that presented her as a woman who did not meet the utmost-resistance standard because she was apparently unwilling to exchange her career for her "honor"; she was thus unworthy to make the claim.

John Doggett: friend of Clarence Thomas who alleged that Anita Hill had trouble accepting that he (Doggett) had no romantic interest in her

Yet there were many narratives that could have been told about Thomas that bore on his credibility. For example, his quite startling shift in philosophy during the eighties and his subsequent "confirmation conversion" could have been understood as bearing on his reputation for truthfulness;[4] his derogatory public references to his sister could be seen as further evidence of his willingness to bend the truth;[5] his participation in an administrative position paper recommending reduced enforcement of sexual harassment could have been interpreted as suggesting a dismissive attitude toward the problem of sexual harassment. Moreover, the testimony of **Angela Wright** and two other corroborating witnesses could have been used to suggest that there was in fact a pattern of harassment,[6] and most obviously, evidence relating to his consumption of pornography could have been used to suggest a source for the elusive Long Dong Silver. That none of these narratives were seriously pursued while countless narratives about Anita Hill were—though they were arguably less relevant—demonstrates how the interpretive structures we use to reconstruct events are thoroughly shaped by gender power.

12. In Your Journal: What does Crenshaw mean by "interpretive structures"? How are they shaped "by gender power"?

II. RACE AND CHASTITY: THE LIMITATIONS OF THE FEMINIST PARADIGM

Feminist discourse speaks to the particular way in which Anita Hill was disempowered through the very structuring of the inquiry, yet it could account for only part of the context within which Anita Hill acted. The particular intersectional identity of Hill, as both a woman and an African American, lent dimensions to her ideological placement in the economy of American culture that could not be translated through the dominant feminist analysis.[7] Again using the parallel between rape and sexual harassment, these race-specific aspects of black women's experiences are accessible.

Rape and other sexual abuses in the work context, now termed sexual harassment, have been a condition of black women's work life for centuries. Forced sexual access to black women was of course institutionalized in slavery and was central to its reproduction. During the period when the domination of white women was justified and reinforced by the **nineteenth-century separate-spheres ideology,** the few privileges of separate spheres were not available to black women at all. Instead, the subordination of African-American women recognized few boundaries between public and private life. Rape and other sexual abuses were justified by myths that black women were sexually voracious, that they were sexually indiscriminate, and that they readily copulated with animals, most fre-

nineteenth-century separate-spheres ideology: refers to the general middle-class understanding of gender roles in the nineteenth century, where men dominated the public sphere, and women dominated the private sphere

Angela Wright: former co-worker of Clarence Thomas at the EEOC (who did not know Hill) who corroborated Hill's characterization of Thomas's workplace behavior in an interview with the Judiciary Committee quently imagined to be apes and monkeys. Indeed, their very anatomy was objectified. Patricia Hill Collins notes that the abuse and mutilation that these myths inspired are memorialized to this day in a Paris museum where the buttocks and genitalia of Sara Bartmann, the so-called **Hottentot Venus,** remain on display.[8]

The stereotypes and myths that justified the sexual abuse of black women in slavery continue to be played out in current society. They are apparent in the experiences of women who are abused on their jobs and in the experiences of black women elsewhere in society. For example, in many of the sexual-harassment cases involving African-American women, the incidents they report often represent a merging of racist myths with the victims' vulnerability as women. Black female plaintiffs tell stories of insults and slurs that often go to the core of black women's sexual construction. While black women share with white women the experience of being objectified as "cunts," "beavers," or "pieces," for them those insults are many times prefaced with "black" or "nigger" or "jungle." Perhaps this racialization of sexual harassment explains why black women are disproportionately represented in sexual-harassment cases. Racism may well provide the clarity to see that sexual harassment is neither a flattering gesture nor a misguided social overture but an act of intentional discrimination that is insulting, threatening, and debilitating.

13. In Your Journal: Why does the author refer to the relationship between the sexual harassment of black women and the institution of slavery?

Pervasive myths and stereotypes about black women not only shape the kinds of harassment that black women experience but also influence whether black women's stories are likely to be believed. Historically, a black woman's word was not taken as truth; our own legal system once drew a connection—as a matter of law—between lack of chastity and lack of veracity. In other words, a woman who was likely to have sex could not be trusted to tell the truth. Because black women were not expected to be chaste, they were likewise considered less likely to tell the truth. Thus, judges were known to instruct juries to take a black woman's word with a grain of salt. One judge admonished jurors not to apply the ordinary presumption of chastity to black women, for if they were to do so, they "would be blinding themselves to actual conditions."[9] In 1971 a judge was quoted as saying, "Within the Negro community, you really have to redefine rape. You never know about them." Lest it be believed that such doubts have been banished to the past, a very recent study of jurors in rape trials revealed that black women's integrity is still very deeply ques-

Hottentot Venus: (b. Sara Baartman) South African woman kidnapped from her home in South Africa to Europe in 1810 to become a curiosity of scientists studying race and sexual difference (and attributing a sexual voraciousness and savagery to black women); her sexual organs and brain were preserved and displayed in a French museum until 1985 tioned by many people in society. One juror, explaining why a black rape victim was discredited by the jury, stated, "You can't believe everything they say. They're known to exaggerate the truth."[10]

> *14. In Your Journal:* How does chastity seem to be related to veracity in terms of gender role stereotyping?

Even where the facts of our stories are believed, myths and stereotypes about black women also influence whether the insult and injury we have experienced is relevant or important. One study concluded, for example, that men who assault black women are the least likely to receive jail time; when they do, the average sentence given to black women's assailants is two years; the average for white women's assailants is ten years. Again, attitudes of jurors seem to reflect a common belief that black women are different from white women and that sexual aggression directed toward them is less objectionable. In a case involving the rape of a black preteen, one juror argued for acquittal on the grounds that a girl her age from "that neighborhood . . . probably wasn't a virgin anyway."

These responses are not exceptional, as illustrated by the societal response to the victimization of **Carol Stuart,** the Boston woman whose husband murdered her and then fingered a black male. It would strain credibility to say that the Boston police would have undertaken a door-to-door search of any community had Carol Stuart and her fetus been black, or, on a similar note, that Donald Trump would have taken out a full-page ad in the *New York Times* calling for the reinstatement of the death penalty had that **investment banker raped in Central Park** been a black service worker. Surely the black woman who was gang-raped during that same week, whose pelvis and ankles were shattered when she was thrown down an elevator shaft and left to die, along with the twenty-eight other women who were raped that week and received no outpouring of public concern, would find it impossible to deny that society views the victimization of some women as being less important than that of others.

❖ **Carol Stuart:** murdered by her husband Charles (who said a black man had shot his wife in the head and pregnant abdomen and himself in the leg) in 1989; a raid on Boston housing developments occurred, during which many black "suspects" were forcibly questioned and searched before the police finally considered Charles Stuart a suspect

❖ **investment banker raped in Central Park:** 28-year old white woman beaten and raped while jogging in Central Park in Manhattan in 1989; the story of "the Central Park jogger" was front page news for weeks, and five minority youths were convicted of the brutal attack and served more than five years in jail; in December 2002, convicted rapist Matias Reyes confessed to the rape and assault and was subsequently linked to the scene by DNA evidence, causing a firestorm of controversy over the "confessions" of the boys convicted, and resulting in the initial convictions being vacated by the Manhattan District Attorney; in 2003, Trisha Meili revealed her identity and told her side of the story in *I Am the Central Park Jogger*

Black women experience much of the sexual aggression that the feminist movement has articulated but in a form that represents simultaneously their subordinate racial status. While the fallen-woman imagery that white feminists identify does represent much of black women's experience of gender domination, given their race, black women have in a sense always been within the fallen-woman category. For black women the issue is not the precariousness of holding on to the protection that the madonna image provides or the manner in which the madonna image works to regulate and thereby constrain black women's sexuality. Instead, it is the denial of the presumption of "madonna-hood" that shapes responses to black women's sexual victimization.

15. In Your Journal: How does the "denial of the presumption of 'madonna-hood'" affect the credibility of black women in Crenshaw's opinion?

White feminists have been reluctant to incorporate race into their narratives about gender, sex, and power. Their unwillingness to speak to the race-specific dimensions of black women's sexual disempowerment was compounded by their simultaneous failure to understand the ways that race may have contributed to Anita Hill's silence. Their attempt to explain why she remained silent spoke primarily to her career interests. Yet the other reasons why many black women have been reluctant to reveal experiences of sexual abuse—particularly by African-American men—remained unexamined. In fact, many black women fear that their stories might be used to reinforce stereotypes of black men as sexually threatening. Others who may not share this particular concern may nevertheless remain silent, fearing ostracism from those who do. Black women face these kinds of dilemmas throughout their lives; efforts to tell these stories may have shaped perceptions of Anita Hill differently among black women, perhaps providing some impetus for breaking through the race-versus-gender dichotomy. Content to rest their case on a raceless tale of gender subordination, white feminists missed an opportunity to to span the chasm between feminism and antiracism. Indeed, feminists actually helped maintain the chasm by endorsing the framing of the event as a race versus a gender issue. In the absence of narratives linking race and gender, the prevailing narrative structures continued to organize the Hill and Thomas controversy as either a story about the harassment of a white woman or a story of the harassment of a black man. Identification by race or gender seemed to be an either/or proposition, and when it is experienced in that manner, black people, both men and women, have traditionally chosen race solidarity. Indeed, white feminist acquiescence to the either/or frame worked directly to Thomas's advantage: with Hill thus cast as simply a de-raced—that is, white—woman, Thomas was positioned to claim that he was the victim of racial discrimination with Hill as the perpetrator. However, that many black people associated Hill more than Thomas with the white world is not solely based on the manner in which feminist discourse is perceived as white. As discussed below, the widespread embrace of Thomas is also attributable to

16. In Your Journal: Why do you think black women feel a pressure to make a choice between race and gender discrimination when speaking out in public? Why might some choose to be more vocal about racial discrimination than gender discrimination?

the patriarchal way that racial solidarity has been defined within the black community.

III. ANITA HILL AS VILLIAN: THE LYNCHING TROPE

One of the most stunning moments in the history of American cultural drama occurred when Clarence Thomas angrily denounced the hearings as a "high-tech lynching." Thomas's move to drape himself in a history of black male repression was particularly effective in the all-white male Senate, whose members could not muster the moral authority to challenge Thomas's sensationalist characterization. Not only was Thomas suddenly transformed into a victim of racial discrimination, but Anita Hill was further erased as a black woman. Her racial identity became irrelevant in explaining or understanding her position, while Thomas's play on the lynching metaphor racially empowered him. Of course, the success of this particular reading was not inevitable; there are several competing narratives that could conceivably have countered Thomas's move. Chief among them was the possibility of pointing out that allegations relating to the sexual abuse of black women have had nothing to do with the history of lynching, a tradition based upon white hysteria regarding black male access to white women. Black women's relationship to the lynch mob was not as a perpetrator but as one of its victims, either through their own lynching or the lynching of loved ones. Moreover, one might have plausibly predicted that, given Thomas's persistent denunciation of any effort to link the history of racism to ongoing racial inequalities, the American public would have scornfully characterized this play as a last-ditch effort to pull his troubled nomination out of the fire. African Americans in particular might have easily rejected Thomas's bid for racial solidarity by concluding that a man who has adamantly insisted that blacks be judged on the content of their character rather than the color of their skin should not be supported when he deploys the color of his skin as a defense to judgments of his character. Yet the race play was amazingly successful; Thomas's approval ratings in the black community sky-rocketed from 54 percent to nearly 80 percent immediately following his performance. Indeed, it was probably his solid support in the black community, particularly in the South, that clinched the seat on the Court. Implicit in this response was a rejection, at times frighteningly explicit, of Anita Hill.

The **deification** of Thomas and the **vilification** of Anita Hill were prefigured by practices within the black community that have long subordinated gender domination to the struggle against racism. In the process the particular experiences of black men have often come to represent the

deification: act of raising someone to a divine rank

vilification: act of defaming; denigration

racial domination of the entire community, as is demonstrated by the symbolic currency of the lynching metaphor and the marginalization of representations of black female domination. Cases involving sexual accusations against black men have stood as hallmarks of racial injustice; **Emmett Till,** the **Scottsboro boys,** and others wrongly accused are powerful symbolic figures in our struggle for racial equality. Black women have also experienced sexualized racial violence; the frequent and unpunished rape and mutilation of black women by white men is a manifestation of racial domination. Yet the names and faces of black women whose bodies also bore the scars of racial oppression are lost to history. To the limited extent that sexual victimization of black women is symbolically represented within our collective memory, it is as tragic characters whose vulnerability illustrates the racist **emasculation** of black men. The marginalization of black female narratives of racism and sexuality thus worked directly to Thomas's advantage by providing him with the ready means to galvanize the black community on his behalf. Thomas's angry denunciations of Hill's allegations as a "high-tech lynching" invoked powerful images linking him to a concrete history that resonated deeply within most African Americans. Hill, had she been so inclined, could have invoked only vague and hazy recollections in the African-American memory, half-digested experiences of black female sexual abuse that could not withstand the totalizing power of the lynching metaphor.

emasculation: castration; act of making effeminate

17. In Your Journal: What does Crenshaw mean when she refers to "the symbolic currency of the lynching metaphor"?

18. In Your Journal: Crenshaw calls lynching a "concrete history" that Clarence Thomas successfully attached himself to. Is there a similar concrete history of rape/sexual harassment to which Hill could have attached herself? Explain your answer.

The discourse of racial liberation, traditionally built around the claim of unequal treatment of black and white people, is of course relevant to the Thomas-Hill conflict, but only partially. In one sense the racial narrative of differential treatment based on race partly comprehends the situation that Hill was in. It seems relatively clear that had Hill been white she would have been read differently by most Americans; as a black female, she had to overcome not only the burdens that feminists have so well articulated in the rape-trial trope but the additional obstacles of race. But, like the dominant feminist narrative, it is again only partial; the abstract description of differential subordination based on skin color is crystallized

Emmett Till: fourteen-year-old black boy from Chicago visiting relatives in Mississippi in 1951, who was brutally tortured and killed for speaking flirtatiously to a white woman in a local store; his white killers were found "not guilty" despite the eyewitness testimony of several (black) witnesses; the case, while it garnered national attention, was merely representative of a widespread practice of lynching that endured throughout the pre-Civil Rights period

Scottsboro boys: nine black youths accused of raping two white women in Alabama in 1931; all were sentenced to death or 75–99 years in prison, but all were eventually pardoned or freed on procedural grounds and witness recantations; the last to be freed was released from prison in 1976

into narrative tropes that translate racial inequality into the terms of inequality between men.

The relative potency of male-centered images of sexual racism over female-centered ones is manifested in the contemporary marginalization of black female sexual abuse within black political discourse. Dominant narratives representing the intersections of racism and sexual violence continue to focus on the way that black men accused of raping white women are disproportionately punished relative to black-on-black or white-on-white rape. Within traditional antiracist formulations, this disproportionality has been characterized as racial discrimination against black men. Yet the pattern of punishing black men accused of raping white women more harshly than those accused of raping black women is just as surely an illustration of discrimination against black women. Indeed, some studies suggest that the race of the victim rather than the race of the defendant is the most salient factor determining the disposition of men convicted of rape. Clearly, black women are victims of a racial hierarchy that subordinates their experiences of sexual abuse to those of white women. Yet this intersectional oppression is rarely addressed in antiracist discourses, in part because traditional readings of racism continue to center on power differentials between men. Consequently, there is relatively little emphasis on how racism contributes to the victimization of black women both inside and outside the criminal-justice system. The rape of black women has sometimes found its way to the center of antiracist politics, particularly when the rapist is white. But the more common experience of intraracial rape is often disregarded within antiracist political discourses, perhaps as a consequence of the view that politicizing such rapes conflicts on some level with efforts to eradicate the prevailing stereotype of the black male rapist. While racism may help explain why white victims are more likely to see their assailants punished than are black victims, one must look to gender power within the black community in order to understand why this persistent devaluation of black women is marginalized within the prevailing conceptions of racism.

> ***19. In Your Journal:*** How and why is the racial composition in a rape case significant?

Intraracial rape and other abusive practices have not been fully addressed within the African-American community in part because African Americans have been reluctant to expose any internal conflict that might reflect negatively on the black community. Although abiding by this "code of silence" is experienced by African Americans as a self-imposed gesture of racial solidarity, the maintenance of silence also has coercive dimensions. Coercion becomes most visible when someone—male or female—breaks the code of silence. Elements of this coercive dimension of gender silence is illustrated in part by the coverage of the hearings in the black press. In many such accounts Hill was portrayed as a traitor for coming forward with her story. Many commentators were less interested in exploring

> ***20. In Your Journal:*** "Coercion becomes most visible when someone—male or female—breaks the code of silence." Explain this statement in terms of the Hill/Thomas case.

whether the allegations were true than in speculating why Hill would compromise the upward mobility of a black man and embarrass the African-American community. Anger and resentment toward Hill was reflected in opinions of commentators traversing the political spectrum within black political discourses. Liberal, centrist, and conservative opinion seemed to accept a view of Hill as disloyal and even treasonous.[11] One columnist, a teacher, reported—without criticism—that one of her third-grade students advocated that Hill be taken out and shot. The theme of treachery was also apparent in a column authored by psychologists Nathan and Julia Hare. In an article titled "The Many Faces of Anita Faye Hill,"[12] they linked Hill to other black women who had in some way violated the code by linking gender issues to black women. Along with the almost routine vilification of Alice Walker, Ntozake Shange, and Michelle Wallace was also criticism of Congresswoman Maxine Waters and Faye Wattleton for their prochoice activities and of Margaret Bush Wilson, chair of the NAACP, for opposing Thomas's nomination on the basis of his antiaffirmative-action stand despite the fact that "white women benefit more from affirmative action than blacks." The Hares ended their piece with a remarkably candid warning to other "Anita Hills" in the making: "We'll be watching you."

The rhetorical deployment of race-based themes to ostracize Anita Hill as an outlaw in the black community received an unexpected boost from noted Harvard sociologist Orlando Patterson in a widely circulated opinion piece that appeared in the *New York Times*.[13] While many critics who lambasted Hill for voicing her complaints shied away from offering a direct defense of the behavior of which she complained, Patterson deployed race to normatively embrace such behavior and to ostracize Anita Hill for having been offended by it at all. Themes of treachery and betrayal, so central in Hill's indictment for breaking the code of silence, reemerged as disingenuity and inauthenticity under Patterson's indictment of Hill for acting white. Setting forth what the preconversion Thomas might have pejoratively labeled an affirmative-action defense to sexual harassment, Patterson argued that Thomas's sexual taunting of Professor Hill was defensible as a "down-home style of courting," one that black women are accustomed to and apparently flattered by. According to Patterson, even if Thomas did say the things Anita Hill claimed he said, not only must Thomas's behavior be weighed against a different racial standard, but Thomas's identity as a black man must be taken into account in determining whether he was justified in perjuring himself. Patterson concludes that in this case perjury was a justifiable means toward winning a seat on the highest court of the land because white America could never understand that such sexual **repartee** was in fact common among black men and women.

repartee: swift and witty banter

Patterson's text warrants extensive analysis because it articulates and exemplifies the underlying ways in which certain notions of race and culture function to maintain patriarchy and deny or legitimize gender practices that subordinate the interests of black women. Patterson's argument basically functions as a cultural defense of the harassment Hill complained about. Similar defenses have been articulated in various forms to justify other misogynistic or patriarchal practices perpetuated by some black men. Indeed, were the thesis not so readily available in the rhetorical discourse within the black community, one might follow Senator Hatch's allegation that Hill found Long Dong Silver in a court case and wonder whether Patterson's defense of Thomas was found in the case of *California* v. *Jacinto Rhines.*[14] Mr. Rhines, a black man, appealed his conviction for raping two black women, arguing that his conviction should be overturned because the trial court failed to take into account cultural differences between blacks and whites. This failure, he claimed, transformed an ordinary consensual encounter into an actionable rape. According to Rhines, the victim implicitly consented to having intercourse with him when she agreed to accompany him to his apartment. Rhines also argued that the victim was unreasonable in feeling threatened and coerced by his behavior. Black people are often quite animated and talk loudly to each other all the time, he contended. Because the social meaning of the event in the black community differed dramatically from the way whites would read the event, Rhines concluded that he was wrongly convicted. This "cultural defense," trading on familiar stereotypes of black women as hardier than white women, and more accustomed to aggressive, gritty, even violent sex, essentially amounted to a claim that the complainant was not really a rape victim because she was black.

What caused the downfall of Rhines's argument was that he was unable to explain why the "victims" were apparently unaware of these cultural codes. Whether unreasonable or not, if the women were frightened, the sexual intercourse that occurred was coerced. The court was not only unconvinced that race had any bearing on a woman's reaction to coersion; it also deemed Rhino's argument an "inexcusable slur" designed to "excuse his own conduct by demeaning females of the Black race."

> ***21. In Your Journal:*** Discuss your understanding of the *California* v. *Jacinto Rhines* case and its relation to cultural identity in a general sense.

For Rhines's argument to have worked, he would have had to convince the court that the cultural practice he identified was so pervasive that the victim's claims of fear and nonconsent were implausible. In effect, Rhines had to convince the court that the black woman should be held to a different standard of victimhood because she was black. Patterson's argument picks up where Rhines's argument failed. Through labeling Hill's reaction to Thomas's "flirtations" **disingenuous,** Patterson implies that either Hill was not, in fact, emotionally injured by Thomas's barrage of sexual innuendo or that if she was, she was influenced to reinterpret her experience through the lens of middle-class white feminism. Indeed, he suggests that the harassment may have actually served to affirm their common origins. This pattern of "bonding" is apparently so readily acceptable that any

disingenuous: not straightforward; insincere

black woman who is offended or injured by it must be acting on a white feminist impulse rather than a culturally grounded black female sensibility.

Patterson has subsequently defended his argument as an attempt to counter the failure of white feminists to comprehend the many ways that gender issues differ across race and class lines.[15] There should be, of course, little question that sexism often manifests itself in varying ways within racial contexts. The complexities of racism present black women with many issues that are unfamiliar to white feminists. Yet one of the thorniest issues that black women must confront is represented by Patterson's own descent into cultural relativism. Patterson subtly transformed the quite perceptive claim that black women often have different issues with black men than white women do with white men into a claim that sexual harassment as described in the testimony of Anita Hill is not one of them. He seemed to ground this assertion on a claim that black women have played along with and apparently enjoyed this "sexual repartee." Thus, like Rhines, he argued that attempts to sanction this behavior as abusive or offensive to black women are grounded in a white feminist misreading of black cultural practices.

There are a number of reasons why Patterson's analysis is off the mark in explaining the particularities of black women's sexual subordination, yet it succeeds wonderfully as a discursive illustration of it. Patterson's argument initially rests on a failure to draw any distinction between sexual practices that occur privately and those that occur within the work environment. More fundamentally, the argument reflects a failure to understand the power dynamics that shape those sexual practices in the first place. His argument thus amounts to an uncritical acceptance of sexual practices that he observes in some social settings, an assumption that these practices are characteristic of the whole, and a use of these practices as a normative base to discredit black women who claim to be offended and injured by them.

Patterson's misunderstanding of the nature of sexual harassment is exemplified by his failure to take into account the particular consequences of sexualizing relationships in a highly stratified work environment. In defending Thomas's alleged banter by claiming that such behavior is typical among black men and black women, Patterson constructs the relationship between black men and women as essentially personal and self-contained, no matter what the context. Thus, the rules that prevail in the private social world dictate the terms and conditions of interaction in the more public work world. Setting aside for the moment the power dynamics that shape sexual repartee elsewhere, Patterson overlooks the fact that the highly stratified workplace so thoroughly raises the stakes for black women that engaging in this sexual competition, however skilled at or familiar with the "game" they might be, is a dangerously risky proposition. In a work context, black women are not dealing with a man who, when rebuffed or bested by a woman, will simply move on. Often they are dealing with a supervisor who can wield his superior institutional power over them either to impose sanctions for their response or to pressure them to compromise their sexual autonomy. Patterson's failure to understand these workplace consequences of sexual harassment is actually consistent with the responses of federal judges who initially refused to see sexual harassment as anything other than private sexual banter that routinely occurs between men and women. Because these practices are quite common throughout society, judges saw them as normative and indeed essential to relations between men and women. Women plaintiffs, however, eventually succeeded in forcing courts to recognize that regardless of the currency of sexual game-playing elsewhere, the perpetuation of these practices in the workplace significantly contributes to women's subordination in the work force.

22. In Your Journal: Why is the absence of the workplace context in Patterson's argument so significant?

Black and white women thus share the burden of overcoming assumptions that sexual harassment in the workplace is essentially a "private" issue. Yet race does shape the problem somewhat differently for black women. The racial specificity is grounded in the fact that there is a certain connection between black men and black women born from a common social history of racial exclusion. Often there is a sense of camaraderie between African Americans, a "we're in this together" sensibility. I call this a zone of familiarity, one that creates expectations of support and mutuality that are essential to survival in a work world that is in some ways alien. In fact, this camaraderie is based on a belief that ultimately came to bear on Thomas's behalf—a belief that the interests of African Americans as a whole are advanced by efforts to increase the number of successful and well-placed blacks. However, this zone of familiarity can sometimes be seen as one of privileged sexual access as well. Consequently, one of the workplace dilemmas faced by black women is trying to negotiate between overlapping expectations in this zone, to maintain much-needed relationships but to avoid unwanted intimacy. This camaraderie and the notions of a shared fate make many black women reluctant to complain about or even to decisively reject the harasser. No doubt this silence contributes to some degree of confusion as to exactly where the boundaries between desired camaraderie and unwanted intimacy exist. This confusion, however, does not render sexual harassment a nonissue. Quite the contrary: claims similar to those made by Patterson contribute to the problem by reinforcing attitudes that feminist critiques of sexuality and power are inapplicable to the sexual dynamic between black men and women. This failure to confront and debate the terms of sex and power allows men to continually dismiss the possibility that their actions or advances might be unwelcome.

Even if we acknowledge that confusion about boundaries might sometimes contribute to harassment, this possibility does little to account for occasions when black men intentionally use and abuse power over black women. Indeed, it was this misuse of power that was consistently misinterpreted or intentionally mischaracterized during the hearings. Ironically, Patterson's characterization of Thomas's alleged behavior as "down-home courting" recalls Hatch's disbelief that any man who wanted to date a women would use such an offensive approach. Although Patterson, of course, seems to be saying "Yes, he would, if they were black" while Hatch maintains that such a man would be a pervert, they are actually in agreement that sexual harassment is really about a miscommunicated negotiation over dating. Yet the kind of sexual harassment that women find threatening and harmful is seldom about dating but is, instead, often an expression of hostility or an attempt to control. All women have probably experienced abusive, sexually degrading comments that are almost routinely hurled our way when we initially decline or ignore a solicitation from strangers. Sexual harassment is often no different, particularly in contexts where the harasser believes for whatever reason that the woman needs to be "loosened up," "brought down to size," or "taught a lesson."

Patterson's defense of the kind of behavior Hill described remains troubling even outside a formally stratified work context. Patterson's argument takes as a given the sexual repartee that he believes is simply endemic to the black community "down home." Since he has observed black women responding to such sexual verbal gestures by putting men in their place, he contends that it was somehow "out-of-character" and consequently disingenuous for a black woman to claim that she was repulsed and injured by it. Moreover, such verbal gestures are not only typical but somewhat desirable as down-home courting. Of course, Patterson's failure to specify where "down home" is (it later turns out to be working-class Jamaica) gives uninformed readers the impression that all African Americans are familiar with, participate in, and enjoy this "**Rabelaisian** humor." The fact that many black people—African-American and Afro-Caribbean alike—do not participate in this "down-home" style is actually beside the point. The more troubling issue is how his attempt to defend this mode of sexual repartee by focusing on black women's participation in it so completely overlooks the way in which this sexual discourse reflects a differential power relationship between men and women.

Patterson assumes that simply because black women have responded to such behavior by displacing aggressive sexual overtures onto a plane of humor and wit, they are neither offended nor threatened by it, and that somehow this "style" is defensible as cultural. Yet merely because black women have developed this particular style of self-defense does not mean that they are not defending themselves against unwanted sexual gestures. A description of the particular way in which women participate and re-

---

Rabelaisian: Francois Rabelais was a French humorist in the early sixteenth century, noted for his ribald sense of humor. Eventually Rabelais would become a Benedictine monk spond to this sexual repartee does not suffice as an analysis of its power dimensions or as a reasonable defense of its subordinating characteristics. Patterson's claims do succeed in centering white women's patterns of interactions by implying that since black women respond differently to verbal aggression, then what they experience is not sexual harassment. Yet women of all races, classes, and cultures no doubt respond in different ways, ways that probably reflect to some degree their particular sociocultural position. White middle-class women have a repertoire of responses to deflect verbal aggression as do working-class black women and middle-class black women, and these responses are likely to differ. The humor or verbal competition that typifies the way some black women react to harassment probably results from the dearth of options available to nonelite black women within a society that has demonstrated manifest disregard for their sexual integrity. After all, to what authority can women who have been consistently represented as sexually available appeal? Since they have little access to any rhetorical or social power from which to create a sphere of sexual autonomy, it is not surprising that some women have learned to displace the aggression onto a humorous, discursive plane. The paradox of Patterson's position is that, given the greater exposure of black women to various forms of sexual aggression, many have developed defense mechanisms that Patterson then points to, in effect to confirm the racist stereotypes that black women are tougher than white women and thus not injured by the same practices that would injure white women. Black women's historical lack of protection becomes a basis for saying no protection is necessary.

Finally, it may be that Patterson's argument, while intellectually and politically indefensible, might in fact provide a clue into how someone like Clarence Thomas might differentiate between women. The plausibility of the *People* magazine image of Thomas and his wife together reading the Bible in their home as a counterimage to Hill's charges made sense for a public that would assume that he would in fact treat all women the same.[16] In other words, sexual harassment is read as only implicating a deraced notion of gender power. But like many men, black and white, Patterson perpetuates images that give a ready rationale for different treatment of black and white women. White women could be pure, madonna-like figures needing vigilant protection, but black women can take care of themselves—indeed, they even implicitly consent to aggression by participating in a cultural repartee.

The overall strategy of Patterson's defense seems to rest on an assumption that merely identifying the culturally specific dimensions of some practice or dynamic constitutes a normative shield against any criticism of it. But mere descriptions of the practices do little to engage the conditions of power that created them. This point is not unfamiliar to African-American scholars and activists. Indeed, there was a time when "cultural defense" arguments were made against those who opposed the racial caste system that prevailed in the South. Many white community leaders argued that patterns of interaction between blacks and whites were maintained by mutual consent and that local blacks were content in their subordinate roles. Having portrayed blacks as willing participants in the racial regime, defenders of the southern way of life were able to claim that demands for equality were imposed from without by northern agitators who did not share the cultural mores of the South.

African Americans as a group refused to allow these arguments to deter their quest for equality. Focusing on the coercive conditions under which consent had been maintained and enforced, critics revealed the way that white supremacy was manifest in relationships not only between dominant whites and subordinate blacks but among blacks as well. Most important, critics exposed the role of coercion in creating these "voluntary" racial practices. This critique included a full accounting of the way that dissent and other **counterhegemonic** practices were suppressed.

counterhegemonic: against the preponderant influences

Drawing on this history, the deployment of the cultural defense where gender subordination is alleged requires that we examine not only the way that cultural practices among African-American men and women are an expression of particular power arrangements but also the different means by which these practices are maintained and legitimated. A critical dimension of this examination involves acknowledging the ways that African-American women have contributed to the maintenance of sexist and debilitating gender practices. For example, the Anita Hill controversy and the commentary it has spawned have shed light on how women's own participation in this conspiracy of silence has legitimated sexism within our community. Our failure to break ranks on the issue of misogyny permits writers like Patterson to argue not only that these behaviors are harmless but that they function to affirm our cultural affinity. Our historical silence functions in much the same way that Hill's silence did: we have played along all this time; thus it is far too late in the game for black women to voice offense.

23. In Your Journal: How does Crenshaw suggest that black women have participated in the very conspiracy she criticizes?

Of course, not all black women have silently acquiesced in sexism and misogyny within the African-American community. Indeed, many writers, activists, and other women have voiced their opposition and paid the price: they have been ostracized and branded as either man-haters or pawns of white feminists, two of the more predictable modes of disciplining and discrediting black feminists. Patterson's argument is of course a model illustration of the latter mode.

In the ongoing debates over black feminism, some critics argue that their objective is not to suppress discussions of gender power within the black community but to stem the tide of negative black stereotypes. Yet even this principle, when examined, reveals a pattern of criticism that seems to suggest that the concern over black male stereotypes functions in a specifically gendered way. For example, the black community has sometimes been embroiled in a debate over political and literary representations of black women's experiences of sexism and misogyny.[17] Yet there is a remarkable willingness to accept, virtually without debate, similar images of black men when these images are **valorized** and sometimes politicized. Ranging from political tracts such as Eldridge Cleaver's *Soul on Ice* to movies such as *Boyz 'N the Hood* to rap lyrics such as those of NWA, the Geto Boys, and 2 Live Crew, black men have been depicted in sexist and often violently misogynistic terms. In these "scripts" black women serve simply as the objects of masculine rage or sexuality. Yet when the objects take on the voice and the same male images are re-presented through the eyes of the newly empowered subjects, accusations fly. This suggests that it is not the perpetuation of the images themselves that enrages these writers' harshest critics but rather the implicit critique and complaint that is being lodged against patriarchy in the black community. Take, for example, the aforementioned and highly acclaimed movie *Boyz 'N the Hood*. Had the story been told through the perspective of any of the women in the movie, *Boyz* probably would have been picketed as yet another example of black feminist male-bashing.

valorized: prized

24. In Your Journal: Discuss Crenshaw's analysis of "objects" and "subjects" as they express some gender relations in the black community

The framing of these conflicts, along with Patterson's defense of Clarence Thomas, reveals how politics and culture are frequently deployed to suppress or justify many of the troubling manifestations of patriarchial power within the black community. Of course, cultural integrity and political solidarity are important values in the black community. Yet the ways in which these values have functioned to reinscribe gender power must constantly be interrogated. That black people across a political and class spectrum were willing to condemn Anita Hill for breaking ranks is a telling testament to how deep gender conflicts are tightly contained by the expectation of racial solidarity. But more specifically it is a testament to the greater degree to which differences over gender are suppressed as compared with other political differences. The vilification of Anita Hill and the embracing of Clarence Thomas reveal that a black woman breaking ranks to complain of sexual harassment is seen by many African-Americans as a much greater threat to our group interests than a black man who breaks ranks over race policy. This double standard is apparent in Patterson's rush to defend Thomas's behavior and to assail Professor Hill. Stumbling over the central contradiction in his own argument, Patterson cites as a benefit of the hearings the fact that African Americans don't all think alike and are instead a diverse aggregate of thirty million people "with class differences, subcultural and regional resources, strengths, flaws and ideologies." Unfortunately, Patterson cannot see that African-American women might also differ in their willingness to tolerate a particular "sexual style," that class and subcultural differences might as readily explain why Professor Hill and other black women might take offense at this "down-home courting style" just as these same differences might explain why Thomas and many of his associates reject affirmative action. Yet, in Patterson's world, Anita Hill and other black women are no longer black, while Thomas and other critics of group-based race policies are simply diverse. At the very least Professor Patterson's celebration of diversity should be extended to allow women like Anita Hill the same independence and integrity that he so enthusiastically grants to **neoconservatives** like Clarence Thomas.

neoconservative: "new conservative"; describing persons or politics generally characterized more by socially conservative values than economically conservative

IV. POLITICAL IMPLICATIONS

Now, over a year after one of the most extraordinary public spectacles involving race and gender in this country's history, we are left asking what have we learned. Among the most painful of the lessons to be drawn from the Thomas-Hill affair is that feminism must be recast in order to reach women who do not see gender as relevant to an understanding of their own disempowerment. In an attempt to recast the face of feminism, women organizers have to begin to apply gender analysis to problems that might initially appear to be shaped primarily by exclusively racial or class factors. Nonwhite and working-class women, if they are ever to identify with the organized women's movement, must see their own diverse experiences reflected in the practice and policy statements of these predominantly white middle-class groups.

25. In Your Journal: How must feminism be recast, in Crenshaw's opinion?

The confirmation of Clarence Thomas, one of the most conservative voices to be added to the Court in recent memory, carries a sobering message for the African-American community as well. As he begins to make his mark upon the lives of African Americans, we must acknowledge that his successful nomination is due in no small measure to the support he received from black Americans.[18] On this account, it is clear that we still operate under a reflexive vision of racial solidarity that is problematic on two fronts. First, our failure to readily criticize African Americans, based on a belief that our interests are served whenever a black rises through the ranks of power, will increasingly be used to undermine and dismantle policies that have been responsible for the moderate successes that group politics have brought about. Already, African-American individuals have played key roles in attacking minority scholarships, cutting back on available remedies for civil rights injuries, and lifting sanctions against South Africa. While group-based notions of solidarity insulate these people from serious criticism and scrutiny, it is precisely their willingness to pursue a ruthlessly individualist agenda that renders this strategy effective and ultimately profitable. Yet the Thomas-Hill story is about more than the political ways that racial solidarity must be critically examined. It is also about the way that our failure to address gender power within our community created the conditions under which an ultimately self-destructive political reaction took place. If we are not to continue to be victimized by such understandable but still counter-productive responses, we must achieve a more mature and purposeful vision of the complex ways in which power is allocated and withheld in contemporary American politics. In particular, we must acknowledge the central role that black women's stories play in our coming to grips with how public power is manipulated. If black women continue to be silenced and their stories ignored, we are doomed to have but a limited grasp of the full range of problems we currently face. The empowerment of black women constitutes therefore the empowerment of our entire community.

NOTES

1. See Crenshaw, "Demarginalizing the Intersection of Race and Gender in Antidiscrimination Law, Feminist Theory, and Antiracist Politics," 1989 *Chicago Legal Forum* 139.
2. As recently as 1978, Wigmore's Treatise on Evidence, Section 62, provided that where the nonconsent of a rape complainant is a material element in a rape case, "the character of a woman for chastity is of considerable probative value in judging of the likelihood of that consent." Wigmore went on to say that "the same doctrine should apply . . . in a charge of mere assault with intent to commit rape or of indecent assault, or the like, not because it is logically relevant where consent is not in issues, but because a certain type of feminine character predisposes to imaginary or false charges of this sort." Some states continue to admit such evidence in certain instances.
3. Historically, a woman was required to fight off her attacker until her resistance was overcome. If a woman failed to struggle, or if she gave in before she was subdued, the conclusion drawn was that she was not raped. See Susan Estrich, "Real Rape," 95 *Yale Law Journal* 1087, 1122 (1986): "in effect, the 'utmost resistance' rule required both that the woman resist to the 'utmost' and that such resistance must not have abated during the struggle."
4. See "An Analysis of the Views of Judge Clarence Thomas," NAACP Legal Defense and Education Fund, Inc., August 13, 1991, pointing out the contradiction between Thomas's pre-1986 speeches and writings and the speeches and writings he produced starting in late 1986. His earlier statements explicitly condemned only three Supreme Court decisions—***Dred Scott***, ***Plessy* v. *Ferguson***, and a conservative decision. In contrast, the later statements con-

---

Dred Scott: in 1846, Scott and his wife Harriet filed suit for their freedom in the St. Louis Circuit Court, which began an eleven-year legal fight that ended in the U.S. Supreme Court; a landmark decision declaring that Scott remain a slave was issued; this decision contributed to rising tensions between the free and slave states just before the American Civil War

Plessy* v. *Ferguson: 1896 case in which the Supreme Court upheld state laws segregating people by their race; many believe these "Jim Crow" laws were passed in large part to stop poor whites from a political and economic alliance with blacks, which would have threatened the established order in the South tained "an outburst of denunciations of both the Supreme Court and its civil rights decisions." The Legal Defense Fund position paper also points out Thomas's shift from praising Justices Black, Douglas, Frankfurter, and Warren to praising Scalia and Bork.

5. Thomas's criticism of his sister as a welfare dependent created an image that contrasted starkly with her actual work history, which included both work-force participation and caring for family members. See Joel Handler, "The Judge and His Sister: Growing Up Black," *New York Times,* July 23, 1991.
6. Wright, a former employee of the Equal Employment Opportunity Commission during Thomas's tenure with the commission, is quoted as saying that Judge Thomas pressured her for dates, asked her breast size, and showed up at her apartment uninvited. Peter Applebom, "Common Threads Between the Two Accusing Thomas of Sexual Improprieties," *New York Times,* October 12, 1990.
7. I do not mean to suggest that race is only relevant in the sexual domination of black women. Race is clearly a factor—though a hidden one—in white women's experiences, just as gender also figures in the experiences of black men. However, because white is the default race in feminism and male is the default gender in antiracism, these identity characteristics usually remain unarticulated.
8. Patricia Hill Collins, "The Sexual Politics of Black Womanhood," *Black Feminist Thought: Knowledge, Consciousness, and the Politics of Empowerment* (New York: Unwin Hyman, 1990), p. 168.
9. See Jennifer Wriggins, "Race, Racism and the Law," 6 *Harvard Women's Law Journal* 103 (1983).
10. See Gary LaFree, *Rape and Criminal Justice: The Social Construction of Sexual Assault* (Belmont, Calif.: Wadsworth Publishing, 1991).
11. Hamil R. Harris, "Hill Is Lying, Says EEOC Staffer," *Washington Afro-American,* October 12, 1991, quoting Armstrong Williams, who called Hill "an outrageous liar"; "Betrayal of Friendship," *Bay State Banner,* October 17, 1991, attacking Anita Hill's credibility and stating that the case "demonstrates the vulnerability of all men in important positions to bogus sexual harassment charges as a power play by ambitious women." And in the white press, many of the black women interviewed expressed little or no sympathy for Hill, ignoring the reality of their own experiences with gender-based abuses of power, and placing the responsibility for avoiding harassment squarely on the shoulders of the victim. See Felicity Barringer, "The Drama as Viewed by Women," *New York Times,* October 18, 1991, A12, documenting women's adverse reactions to Hill: "It's unbelievable that a woman couldn't stop something like that at its inception," said one. Another asked, "Wouldn't you haul off and poke a guy in the mouth if he spoke in that manner?" And still another said had this to say: "You have to make sure you get across that you're a professional. If someone isn't willing to accept that, you make sure you're not in a room alone with him."
12. See Nathan Hare and Julia Hare, "The Many Faces of Anita Hill," in *The Final Call,* the newspaper published by The Nation of Islam under Minister Louis Far-

rakhan. The headline on the paper in which the Hares' article appeared read "Thomas Survives High-Tech Lynching."

13. Orlando Patterson's "Race, Gender, and Liberal Fallacies" appeared in the *New York Times* on October 20, 1991, the Sunday following Thomas's confirmation.
14. *People* v. *Jacinto Aniello Rhines,* 131 Cal. App. 3d. 498, May 6, 1982.
15. See "Roundtable: Sexuality in America After Thomas/Hill," *Tikkun,* January/February 1992, p. 25.
16. Virginia Lamp Thomas, "Breaking Silence," *People,* November 11, 1991, p. 111. Virginia Hill tells how she and her husband invited two couples to their home to pray for two to three hours each day. "They brought over prayer tapes, and we would read parts of the Bible," she stated.
17. Mel Watkins, "Sexism, Racism, and Black Women Writers," *New York Times,* June 15, 1986; Donna Britt, "What About the Sisters? With All the Focus on Black Men, Somebody's Getting Left Out," *Washington Post,* February 2, 1992, citing black male objections to Alice Walker's and Ntozake Shange's work, and questioning where those black male voices are when black male violence is being condoned . . . glamorized, ignored; Susan Howard, "Beware of 'Black-lash,'" *Newsday,* February 12, 1992, arguing that there is a blacklash against black women, and citing the communities' unwillingness to forgive Alice Walker and Ntozake Shange for writing *The Color Purple* and *For Colored Girls Who Have Considered Suicide When the Rainbow Is Enuf* to support this proposition.
18. "In Other Words," *USA Today,* March 7, 1992: "Rookie Justice Clarence Thomas already is leaving his mark on America's legal system. Based on the dissent he wrote in a recent case, it's not just a mark—it's more like a welt. Fortunately, all but one other justice on the high court viewed the actions of a Louisiana prison guard—who shackled and beat a prisoner—as the kind of cruel and unusual punishment that the Eighth Amendment forbids. . . . Those who harbored hopes that Justice Thomas might feel a shred of concern for society's victims got a firm sock in the kisser." In another of his more notable contributions, in *Presley* v. *Etowah City Commission,* Thomas paid tribute to his southern roots by denying the voting-rights claims of a newly elected black official who was deprived of decision-making authority. Even the Bush administration agreed that the actions violated the Voting Rights Act.

FOR USE IN DISCUSSION

Questions about Substance

1. In her discussion about "doctrinal exclusion," Crenshaw examines the way the law makes it difficult for black women to be acknowledged by "existing legal categories for recognizing injury." What does she mean by this? Why

do you think the law has so much trouble with social identities defined by "intersectionality"?

2. How significant is it that the "jury" for these hearings was made up almost exclusively of white men?
3. Why would feminist legal scholars use "rape as a framework" (143) for looking at sexual harassment law? How are the two things similar? How are they different?
4. What is Crenshaw getting at by examining the "pursued . . . narratives" (145) in the Hill/Thomas hearings? What does it mean to *pursue* a narrative, ideologically speaking? Why were some narratives in this case pursued and some not?
5. How does Crenshaw see it as the fault of mainstream feminism that Thomas was eventually able to characterize himself as a victim of discrimination? (148)
6. Explain the significance of Thomas's approval rating before and after the "high-tech lynching" statement (149).
7. If the culture at large (and the more specific subculture that Patterson describes) has an implicit disregard for black women's sexual integrity, what effect would black women's refusal to participate in the banter have on the outcome of such interchanges?
8. Is it possible for cultural groups to achieve solidarity without giving up critical privilege? Can feminism and anti-racism ever coexist comfortably, given what you have seen in this illustration of their interaction?

Questions about Structure and Style

1. Crenshaw spends half of her argument examining what she calls the "rape trope" and the other half examining the "lynching trope." How would the essay be different if the sequence of the sections were reversed?
2. The argument of this essay emphasizes role analysis, specifically discussing what roles Anita Hill was *unable to play*. What roles do you think she *did fill*, given what you know now about the case? How would Crenshaw's argument be different if structured around the roles Hill fulfilled rather than those she could not fulfill?
3. There is very little reference to the events of the actual hearings. How much of an effect does this have on the persuasiveness of Crenshaw's argument?
4. There is a heavy use of footnoting in this essay. Examine the contents of the footnotes, and discuss your opinion of their effectiveness.

Multimedia Review

1. Orlando Patterson's article "Race, Gender, and Liberal Fallacies" has been anthologized in a collection called *Sexual Harassment: Issues and Answers*, edited by Linda LeMoncheck and James P. Sterba. If you can locate the article, read it and examine the way that Crenshaw has presented it in her essay. Does she provide a fair account of Patterson's argument? Are there parts of Patterson's

article that you think she should have emphasized but chose not to? What is your overall impression of Patterson now that you have read his original text?

2. In his 1993 book *The Real Anita Hill: The Untold Story,* David Brock portrayed Anita Hill as an ambitious liar out for revenge. In 2001, he published *Blinded by the Right: The Conscience of an Ex-Conservative,* which retracted his condemnation of Hill and explained that he had been pressured to fabricate the allegations about Hill by Clarence Thomas supporters and other conservatives. Listen to or read the interview with Brock at *http://www.npr.org/programs/atc/features/2001/jul/010702.brock.html*, which examines the scandal. How is Crenshaw's account of the Hill-Thomas hearings different in its purpose and effects from Brock's tell-all book?
3. Read Suzan Lori-Parks's play about the Hottentot Venus, *Venus,* which tells the tragic tale of a black South African woman, Sara Baartman. Her exploitation by white European scientists and others who believed that race determined one's sexual characteristics relates directly to Crenshaw's examination of sexual stereotypes. How far have we come in western culture since Sara Baartman's time?
4. View some films representing the African-American experience, which also address gender issues—whether directly or indirectly (Spike Lee's *She's Gotta Have It* (1986), John Singleton's *Boyz 'N the Hood* (1991), Terry McMillan's *Waiting to Exhale* (1995), or Tim Blake Nelson's *O* (2001), for example)—to see how some of the issues Crenshaw discusses play out in the movies.
5. Examine some contemporary rap lyrics featuring negative stereotypes of men and women—by both male and female rappers. Do you notice any illustrations of Orlando Patterson's argument playing out in songs by 2 Live Crew, Eve, Foxy Brown, Ice Cube, Lil Kim, or Wu Tang Clan? Can you provide any counter examples?

SUGGESTIONS FOR WRITING AND RESEARCH

1. Why does Crenshaw spend so much time critiquing Orlando Patterson? She suggests in her critique that Patterson would like cultural identity to be a shield against criticism of individuals. Do you agree? Are there conditions under which you think culture can and should be a defense? Do you see other choices besides some degree of participation for black women in the repartee that Patterson defends (152)? Write an essay that traces and evaluates Crenshaw's engagement with Patterson's claims.
2. Examine the logic of Crenshaw's argument that an intersection causes loss rather than gain. Why aren't black women doubly powerful instead of doubly burdened? Write an essay that substantiates or disagrees with this logic, using passages from the text.

3. Look at another identity based on cultural intersection (e.g., class and gender, religion and race, race and class, sexuality and religion, etc.) and examine the associated tropes. Write an essay modeled after Crenshaw's that looks at a specific case where this intersection is involved (e.g., the Matthew Shepard murder in Wyoming in which class and sexuality played prominent roles).
4. Compare the Hill/Thomas case to another major media story involving race and gender (e.g., the Carol Stuart murder, the Susan Smith case, the O.J. Simpson trial). Demonstrate the way that Crenshaw's concepts apply to the other case, and enumerate any ways in which her paradigm might fall short.
5. Research one of the court cases or other historical references in Crenshaw's footnotes. Explain its relevance to Crenshaw's argument and examine what new insights into the Hill/Thomas hearings you have after completing your research.

WORKING WITH CLUSTERS

Cluster 2: Constructing and Corrupting the Feminine

Cluster 5: The Law and the Public

Cluster 6: The Race for Representation

Discipline: The Social Sciences

Rhetorical Mode: Compare and Contrast

White Noise

by Don DeLillo

Don DeLillo, one of America's most acclaimed novelists, was born in New York City. As a young man, DeLillo quit a brief career in advertising to focus his attention on writing, although the language of advertising has made a profound impression on his fiction. His many novels include Americana; End Zone; Great Jones Street; Players; The Names; White Noise, *which won the National Book Award and is the source of this excerpt;* Libra; Mao II, *winner of the PEN/Faulkner award;* Underworld; *and* The Body Artist. *DeLillo's honors also include the Jerusalem Prize, awarded to an author "whose work expresses the theme of the freedom of the individual in society." He was the first American to receive the honor.*

1

The station wagons arrived at noon, a long shining line that coursed through the west campus. In single file they eased around the orange I-beam sculpture and moved toward the dormitories. The roofs of the station wagons were loaded down with carefully secured suitcases full of light and heavy clothing; with boxes of blankets, boots and shoes, stationery and books, sheets, pillows, quilts; with rolled-up rugs and sleeping bags; with bicycles, skis, rucksacks, English and Western saddles, inflated rafts. As cars slowed to a crawl and stopped, students sprang out and raced to the rear doors to begin removing the objects inside; the stereo sets, radios, personal computers; small refrigerators and table ranges; the cartons of phonograph records and cassettes; the hairdryers and styling irons; the tennis rackets, soccer balls, hockey and lacrosse sticks, bows and arrows; the controlled substances, the birth control pills and devices; the junk food still in shopping bags—onion-and-garlic chips, nacho thins, peanut creme patties, Waffelos and Kabooms, fruit chews and toffee popcorn; the Dum-Dum pops, the Mystic mints.

> ***1. In Your Journal:*** What does the station wagon symbolize for DeLillo? How would the station wagon as a symbol of American culture compare to the SUV or the sports car?

I've witnessed this spectacle every September for twenty-one years. It is a brilliant event, invariably. The students greet each other with comic cries and gestures of **sodden** collapse. Their summer has been bloated with criminal pleasures, as always. The parents stand sundazed near their automobiles, seeing images of themselves in every direction. The conscientious suntans. The well-made faces and wry looks. They feel a sense of renewal, of communal recognition. The women crisp and alert, in diet trim, knowing people's names. Their husbands content to measure out the time, distant but ungrudging, accomplished in parenthood, something about them suggesting massive insurance coverage. This assembly of station wagons, as much as anything they might do in the course of the year, more than formal liturgies or laws, tells the parents they are a collection of the like-minded and the spiritually akin, a people, a nation.

sodden: soaking

> ***2. In Your Journal:*** What does DeLillo mean by the description "conscientious suntans"?

I left my office and walked down the hill and into town. There are houses in town with turrets and two-story porches where people sit in the shade of ancient maples. There are Greek revival and Gothic churches. There is an insane asylum with an elongated **portico,** ornamented **dormers** and a steeply pitched roof topped by a pineapple **finial.** Babette and I and our children by previous marriages live at the end of a quiet

portico: entry

dormer: window set in a gable on a sloping roof

finial: ornament at the top of an arch

street in what was once a wooded area with deep ravines. There is an expressway beyond the backyard now, well below us, and at night as we settle into our brass bed the sparse traffic washes past, a remote and steady murmur around our sleep, as of dead souls babbling at the edge of a dream.

I am chairman of the department of Hitler studies at the College-on-the-Hill. I invented Hitler studies in North America in March of 1968. It was a cold bright day with intermittent winds out of the east. When I suggested to the chancellor that we might build a whole department around Hitler's life and work, he was quick to see the possibilities. It was an immediate and electrifying success. The chancellor went on to serve as adviser to Nixon, Ford and Carter before his death on a ski lift in Austria.

3. In Your Journal: The narrator announces himself as the department chair (and inventor) of "Hitler Studies." What do you think would be the purpose of such a department? How is this department similar to or different from those college departments you are familiar with?

At Fourth and Elm, cars turn left for the supermarket. A policewoman crouched inside a boxlike vehicle patrols the area looking for cars parked illegally, for meter violations, lapsed inspection stickers. On telephone poles all over town there are homemade signs concerning lost dogs and cats, sometimes in the handwriting of a child.

2

Babette is tall and fairly ample; there is a girth and heft to her. Her hair is a fanatical blond mop, a particular tawny hue that used to be called dirty blond. If she were a petite woman, the hair would be too cute, too mischievous and contrived. Size gives her tousled aspect a certain seriousness. Ample women do not plan such things. They lack the **guile** for conspiracies of the body.

guile: cleverness

4. In Your Journal: Respond to the narrator's characterization of "ample women."

"You should have been there," I said to her.

"Where?"

"It's the day of the station wagons."

"Did I miss it again? You're supposed to remind me."

"They stretched all the way down past the music library and onto the interstate. Blue, green, burgundy, brown. They gleamed in the sun like a desert caravan."

"You know I need reminding, Jack."

Babette, disheveled, has the careless dignity of someone too preoccupied with serious matters to know or care what she looks like. Not that she is a gift-bearer of great things as the world generally reckons them. She gathers and tends the children, teaches a course in an adult education program, belongs to a group of volunteers who read to the blind. Once a week she reads to an elderly man named Treadwell who lives on the edge of town. He is known as Old Man Treadwell, as if he were a landmark, a rock formation or brooding swamp. She reads to him from the *National Enquirer*, the *National Examiner*, the *National Express*, the *Globe*, the *World*, the *Star*. The old fellow demands his weekly dose of cult mysteries. Why deny him? The point is that Babette, whatever she is doing, makes me feel sweetly rewarded, bound up with a full-souled woman, a lover of daylight and dense life, the miscellaneous swarming air of families. I watch her all the time doing things in measured sequence, skillfully, with seeming ease, unlike my former wives, who had a tendency to feel estranged from the objective world—a self-absorbed and high-strung bunch, with ties to the intelligence community.

5. In Your Journal: What does the narrator reveal about himself through his description of his wife, Babette?

"It's not the station wagons I wanted to see. What are the people like? Do the women wear plaid skirts, cable-knit sweaters? Are the men in hacking jackets? What's a hacking jacket?"

6. In Your Journal: Why does Babette ask whether the people were wearing hacking jackets when she doesn't know what they are?

"They've grown comfortable with their money," I said. "They genuinely believe they're entitled to it. This conviction gives them a kind of rude health. They glow a little."

"I have trouble imagining death at that income level," she said.

"Maybe there is no death as we know it. Just documents changing hands."

"Not that we don't have a station wagon ourselves."

"It's small, it's metallic gray, it has one whole rusted door."

"Where is Wilder?" she said, routinely panic-stricken, calling out to the child, one of hers, sitting motionless on his tricycle in the backyard.

Babette and I do our talking in the kitchen. The kitchen and the bedroom are the major chambers around here, the power haunts, the sources. She and I are alike in this, that we regard the rest of the house as storage space for furniture, toys, all the unused objects of earlier marriages and different sets of children, the gifts of lost in-laws, the hand-me-downs and rummages. Things, boxes. Why do these possessions carry such sorrowful weight? There is a darkness attached to them, a foreboding. They make me wary not of personal failure and defeat but of something more general, something large in scope and content.

7. In Your Journal: Summarize the narrator's characterization of the objects in rooms other than the bedroom or kitchen. How does this characterization contribute to the overall scene being set in this piece?

She came in with Wilder and seated him on the kitchen counter. Denise and Steffie came downstairs and we talked about the school supplies they would need. Soon it was time for lunch. We entered a period of chaos and noise. We milled about, bickered a little, dropped utensils. Finally we were all satisfied with what we'd been able to snatch from the cupboards and refrigerator or swipe from each other and we began quietly plastering mustard or mayonnaise on our brightly colored food. The mood was one of deadly serious anticipation, a reward hard-won. The table was crowded and Babette and Denise elbowed each other twice, although neither spoke. Wilder was still seated on the counter surrounded by open cartons, crumpled tinfoil, shiny bags of potato chips, bowls of pasty substances covered with plastic wrap, flip-top rings and twist ties, individually wrapped slices of orange cheese. Heinrich came in, studied the scene carefully, my only son, then walked out the back door and disappeared.

8. In Your Journal: Why do you think the narrator refers to the "bright color" of the food the characters are eating for lunch?

"This isn't the lunch I'd planned for myself," Babette said. "I was seriously thinking yogurt and wheat germ."

"Where have we heard that before?" Denise said.

"Probably right here," Steffie said.

"She keeps buying that stuff."

"But she never eats it," Steffie said.

"Because she thinks if she keeps buying it, she'll have to eat it just to get rid of it. It's like she's trying to trick herself."

"It takes up half the kitchen."

"But she throws it away before she eats it because it goes bad," Denise said. "So then she starts the whole thing all over again."

"Wherever you look," Steffie said, "there it is."

"She feels guilty if she doesn't buy it, she feels guilty if she buys it and doesn't eat it, she feels guilty when she sees it in the fridge, she feels guilty when she throws it away."

"It's like she smokes but she doesn't," Steffie said.

Denise was eleven, a hard-nosed kid. She led a more or less daily protest against those of her mother's habits that struck her as wasteful or dangerous. I defended Babette. I told her I was the one who needed to show discipline in matters of diet. I reminded her how much I liked the way she looked. I suggested there was an honesty inherent in bulkiness if it is just the right amount. People trust a certain amount of bulk in others.

But she was not happy with her hips and thighs, walked at a rapid clip, ran up the stadium steps at the **neoclassical** high school. She said I made virtues of her flaws because it was my nature to shelter loved ones from the truth. Something lurked inside the truth, she said.

neoclassical: related to the 17th and 18th century revival of classical aesthetics

The smoke alarm went off in the hallway upstairs, either to let us know the battery had just died or because the house was on fire. We finished our lunch in silence.

3

Department heads wear academic robes at the College-on-the-Hill. Not grand sweeping full-length affairs but sleeveless tunics puckered at the shoulders. I like the idea. I like clearing my arm from the folds of the garment to look at my watch. The simple act of checking the time is transformed by this flourish. Decorative gestures add romance to a life. Idling students may see time itself as a complex embellishment, a romance of human consciousness, as they witness the chairman walking across campus, crook'd arm emerging from his medieval robe, the digital watch blinking in late summer dusk. The robe is black, of course, and goes with almost anything.

9. In Your Journal: Why do you think the narrator is so fond of his academic robe?

There is no Hitler building as such. We are quartered in Centenary Hall, a dark brick structure we share with the popular culture department, known officially as American environments. A curious group. The teaching staff is composed almost solely of New York émigrés, smart, thuggish, movie-mad, trivia-crazed. They are here to decipher the natural language of the culture, to make a formal method of the shiny pleasures they'd known in their Europe-shadowed childhoods—an **Aristotelianism** of bubble gum wrappers and detergent jingles. The department head is Alfonse (Fast Food) **Stompanato,** a broad-chested glowering man whose collection of prewar soda pop bottles is on permanent display in an alcove. All his teachers are male, wear rumpled clothes, need haircuts, cough into their armpits. Together they look like teamster officials assembled to identify the body of a mutilated colleague. The impression is one of pervasive bitterness, suspicion and intrigue.

Aristotelianism: school of thought emphasizing scientific method and thought

An exception to some of the above is Murray Jay Siskind, an exsportswriter who asked me to have lunch with him in the dining room, where the institutional odor of vaguely defined food aroused in me an obscure and gloomy memory. Murray was new to the Hill, a stoop-shouldered man with little round glasses and an Amish beard. He was a visiting lecturer on living icons and seemed embarrassed by what he'd gleaned so far from his colleagues in popular culture.

10. In Your Journal: What do you think Murray's job as "lecturer on living icons" involves? Can you think of what icons he might address in his lecture?

"I understand the music, I understand the movies, I even see how comic books can tell us things. But there are full professors in this place who read nothing but cereal boxes."

"It's the only avant-garde we've got."

"Not that I'm complaining. I like it here. I'm totally enamored of this place. A small-town setting. I want to be free of cities and sexual entanglements. Heat. This is what cities mean to me. You get off the train and walk out of the station and you are hit with the full blast. The heat of air, traffic and people. The heat of food and sex. The heat of tall buildings. The heat that floats out of the subways and the tunnels. It's always fifteen degrees hotter in the cities. Heat rises from the sidewalks and falls from the poisoned sky. The buses breathe heat. Heat emanates from crowds of shoppers and office workers. The entire infrastructure is based on heat, desperately uses up heat, breeds more heat. The eventual heat death of the universe that scientists love to talk about is already well underway and you can feel it happening all around you in any large or medium-sized city. Heat and wetness."

"Where are you living, Murray?"

"In a rooming house. I'm totally captivated and intrigued. It's a gorgeous old crumbling house near the insane asylum. Seven or eight boarders, more or less permanent except for me. A woman who harbors a terrible secret. A man with a haunted look. A man who never comes out of his room. A woman who stands by the letter box for hours, waiting for

---

Stompanato: possibly an allusion to Johnny Stompanato, boyfriend of actress Lana Turner in 1958 (and former mob bodyguard to Mickey Cohen), who was killed by Turner's 14-year-old daughter Cheryl Crane, allegedly because he was threatening Turner something that never seems to arrive. A man with no past. A woman with a past. There is a smell about the place of unhappy lives in the movies that I really respond to."

"Which one are you?" I said.

"I'm the Jew. What else would I be?"

There was something touching about the fact that Murray was dressed almost totally in corduroy. I had the feeling that since the age of eleven in his crowded plot of concrete he'd associated this sturdy fabric with higher learning in some impossibly distant and tree-shaded place.

11. In Your Journal: Why does Murray suggest there's nothing else he could be (in his rooming house) but "the Jew"?

"I can't help being happy in a town called Blacksmith," he said. "I'm here to avoid situations. Cities are full of situations, sexually cunning people. There are parts of my body I no longer encourage women to handle freely. I was in a situation with a woman in Detroit. She needed my semen in a divorce suit. The irony is that I love women. I fall apart at the sight of long legs, striding, briskly, as a breeze carries up from the river, on a weekday, in the play of morning light. The second irony is that it's not the bodies of women that I ultimately crave but their minds. The mind of a woman. The delicate chambering and massive unidirectional flow, like a physics experiment. What fun it is to talk to an intelligent woman wearing stockings as she crosses her legs. That little staticky sound of rustling nylon can make me happy on several levels. The third and related irony is that it's the most complex and neurotic and difficult women that I am invariably drawn to. I like simple men and complicated women."

Murray's hair was tight and heavy-looking. He had dense brows, wisps of hair curling up the sides of his neck. The small stiff beard, confined to his chin and unaccompanied by a mustache, seemed an optional component, to be stuck on or removed as circumstances warranted.

"What kind of lectures do you plan giving?"

"That's exactly what I want to talk to you about," he said. "You've established a wonderful thing here with Hitler. You created it, you nurtured it, you made it your own. Nobody on the faculty of any college or university in this part of the country can so much as utter the word Hitler without a nod in your direction, literally or metaphorically. This is the center, the unquestioned source. He is now your Hitler, Gladney's Hitler. It must be deeply satisfying for you. The college is internationally known as a result of Hitler studies. It has an identity, a sense of achievement. You've evolved an entire system around this figure, a structure with countless substructures and interrelated fields of study, a history within history. I marvel at the effort. It was masterful, shrewd and stunningly preemptive. It's what I want to do with Elvis."

12. In Your Journal: Examine Murray's wish to "do with Elvis" what Jack has done with Hitler. What comment is this meant to make on academia?

Several days later Murray asked me about a tourist attraction known as the most photographed barn in America. We drove twenty-two miles into the country around Farmington. There were meadows and apple orchards. White fences trailed through the rolling fields. Soon the signs started appearing. THE MOST PHOTOGRAPHED BARN IN AMERICA. We counted five signs before we reached the site. There were forty cars and a tour bus in the makeshift lot. We walked along a cowpath to the slightly elevated spot set aside for viewing and photographing. All the people had cameras; some had tripods, telephoto lenses, filter kits. A man in a booth sold postcards and slides—pictures of the barn taken from the elevated spot. We stood near a grove of trees and watched the photographers. Murray maintained a prolonged silence, occasionally scrawling some notes in a little book.

"No one sees the barn," he said finally.

A long silence followed.

"Once you've seen the signs about the barn, it becomes impossible to see the barn."

He fell silent once more. People with cameras left the elevated site, replaced at once by others.

"We're not here to capture an image, we're here to maintain one. Every photograph reinforces the aura. Can you feel it, Jack? An accumulation of nameless energies."

There was an extended silence. The man in the booth sold postcards and slides.

"Being here is a kind of spiritual surrender. We see only what the others see. The thousands who were here in the past, those who will come in the future. We've agreed to be part of a collective perception. This literally colors our vision. A religious experience in a way, like all tourism."

Another silence ensued.

"They are taking pictures of taking pictures," he said.

13. In Your Journal: How does the scene of tourists "taking pictures of taking pictures" compare to the "history within a history" that the Hitler Studies program has created?

He did not speak for a while. We listened to the incessant clicking of shutter release buttons, the rustling crank of levers that advanced the film.

"What was the barn like before it was photographed?" he said. "What did it look like, how was it different from other barns, how was it similar to other barns? We can't answer these questions because we've read the signs, seen the people snapping the pictures. We can't get outside the aura. We're part of the aura. We're here, we're now."

He seemed immensely pleased by this.

4

When times are bad, people feel compelled to overeat. Blacksmith is full of obese adults and children, baggy-pantsed, short-legged, waddling. They struggle to emerge from compact cars; they don sweatsuits and run in families across the landscape; they walk down the street with food in their faces; they eat in stores, cars, parking lots, on bus lines and movie lines, under the stately trees.

Only the elderly seem exempt from the fever of eating. If they are sometimes absent from their own words and gestures, they are also slim and healthy-looking, the women carefully groomed, the men purposeful and well dressed, selecting shopping carts from the line outside the supermarket.

I crossed the high school lawn and walked to the rear of the building and toward the small open stadium. Babette was running up the stadium steps. I sat across the field in the first row of stone seats. The sky was full of streaking clouds. When she reached the top of the stadium she stopped and paused, putting her hands to the high parapet and leaning into it to rest diagonally. Then she turned and walked back down, breasts chugging. The wind rippled her oversized suit. She walked with her hands on her hips, fingers spread. Her face was tilted up, catching the cool air, and she didn't see me. When she reached the bottom step she turned to face the seats and did some kind of neck stretching exercise. Then she started running up the steps.

Three times she ascended the steps, walked slowly down. There was no one around. She worked hard, hair floating, legs and shoulders working. Every time she reached the top she leaned into the wall, head down, upper body throbbing. After the last descent I met her at the edge of the playing field and embraced her, putting my hands inside the sweatband of her gray cotton pants. A small plane appeared over the trees. Babette was moist and warm, emitting a creaturely hum.

She runs, she shovels snow, she caulks the tub and sink. She plays word games with Wilder and reads erotic classics aloud in bed at night. What do I do? I twirl the garbage bags and twist-tie them, swim laps in the college pool. When I go walking, joggers come up soundlessly behind me, appearing at my side, making me jump in idiotic fright. Babette talks to dogs and cats. I see colored spots out of the corner of my right eye. She plans ski trips that we never take, her face bright with excitement. I walk up the hill to school, noting the white-washed stones that line the driveways of newer homes.

14. In Your Journal: Examine and paraphrase the comparison of Babette's and Jack's activities and personalities in this paragraph.

Who will die first?

This question comes up from time to time, like where are the car keys. It ends a sentence, prolongs a glance between us. I wonder if the thought itself is part of the nature of physical love, a reverse Darwinism that awards sadness and fear to the survivor. Or is it some inert element in the air we breathe, a rare thing like neon, with a melting point, an **atomic weight?** I held her in my arms on the cinder track. Kids came running our way, thirty girls in bright shorts, an improbable bobbing mass. The eager breathing, the overlapping rhythms of their footfalls. Sometimes I think our love is inexperienced. The question of dying becomes a wise reminder. It cures us of our innocence of the future. Simple things are doomed, or is that a superstition? We watched the girls come round again. They were strung out now, with faces and particular gaits, almost weightless in their craving, able to land lightly.

15. In Your Journal: What do you think is meant by "reverse Darwinism"?

atomic weight: average weight of an atom of an element

The Airport Marriott, the Downtown Travelodge, the Sheraton Inn and Conference Center.

On our way home I said, "Bee wants to visit at Christmas. We can put her in with Steffie."

"Do they know each other?"

"They met at Disney World. It'll be all right."

"When were you in Los Angeles?"

"You mean Anaheim."

"When were you in Anaheim?"

"You mean Orlando. It's almost three years now."

"Where was I?" she said.

My daughter Bee, from my marriage to Tweedy Browner, was just starting seventh grade in a Washington suburb and was having trouble readjusting to life in the States after two years in South Korea. She took taxis to school, made phone calls to friends in Seoul and Tokyo. Abroad she'd wanted to eat ketchup sandwiches with Trix sticks. Now she cooked fierce sizzling meals of scallion bushes and baby shrimp, monopolizing Tweedy's restaurant-quality range.

16. In Your Journal: Examine the description of Jack's daughter Bee. What does she reveal about Jack?

That night, a Friday, we ordered Chinese food and watched television together, the six of us. Babette had made it a rule. She seemed to think that if kids watched television one night a week with parents or stepparents, the effect would be to de-glamorize the medium in their eyes, make it wholesome domestic sport. Its narcotic undertow and eerie diseased brain-sucking power would be gradually reduced. I felt vaguely slighted by this reasoning. The evening in fact was a subtle form of punishment for us all. Heinrich sat silent over his egg rolls. Steffie became upset every time something shameful or humiliating seemed about to happen to someone on the screen. She had a vast capacity for being embarrassed on other people's behalf. Often she would leave the room until Denise signaled to her that the scene was over. Denise used these occasions to counsel the younger girl on toughness, the need to be mean in the world, thick-skinned.

It was my own formal custom on Fridays, after an evening in front of the TV set, to read deeply in Hitler well into the night.

On one such night I got into bed next to Babette and told her how the chancellor had advised me, back in 1968, to do something about my name and appearance if I wanted to be taken seriously as a Hitler innovator. Jack Gladney would not do, he said, and asked me what other names I might have at my disposal. We finally agreed that I should invent an extra initial and call myself J. A. K. Gladney, a tag I wore like a borrowed suit.

The chancellor warned against what he called my tendency to make a feeble presentation of self. He strongly suggested I gain weight. He wanted me to "grow out" into Hitler. He himself was tall, paunchy, ruddy, jowly, big-footed and dull. A formidable combination. I had the advantages of substantial height, big hands, big feet, but badly needed bulk, or so he believed—an air of unhealthy excess, of padding and exaggeration, hulking massiveness. If I could become more ugly, he seemed to be suggesting, it would help my career enormously.

I am the false character that follows the name around.

17. In Your Journal: Why does the chancellor want Jack to have "an air of unhealthy excess"?

18. In Your Journal: Why does Jack call himself a "false character"?

5

Let's enjoy these aimless days while we can, I told myself, fearing some kind of deft acceleration.

At breakfast, Babette read all our horoscopes aloud, using her storytelling voice. I tried not to listen when she got to mine, although I think I wanted to listen, I think I sought some clues.

After dinner, on my way upstairs, I heard the TV say: "Let's sit half lotus and think about our spines."

That night, seconds after going to sleep, I seemed to fall through myself, a shallow heart-stopping plunge. Jarred awake, I stared into the dark, realizing I'd experienced the more or less normal muscular contraction known as the **myoclonic jerk.** Is this what it's like, abrupt, peremptory? Shouldn't death, I thought, be a swan dive, graceful, white-winged and smooth, leaving the surface undisturbed?

myoclonic jerk: involuntary muscle spasm meant to interrupt the feeling of falling caused by lowered heart rate and slowed breathing that can occur when one is just falling asleep

Blue jeans tumbled in the dryer.

We ran into Murray Jay Siskind at the supermarket. His basket held generic food and drink, nonbrand items in plain white packages with simple labeling. There was a white can labeled CANNED PEACHES. There was a white package of bacon without a plastic window for viewing a representative slice. A jar of roasted nuts had a white wrapper bearing the words IRREGULAR PEANUTS. Murray kept nodding to Babette as I introduced them.

"This is the new austerity," he said. "Flavorless packaging. It appeals to me. I feel I'm not only saving money but contributing to some kind of spiritual consensus. It's like World War III. Everything is white. They'll take our bright colors away and use them in the war effort."

He was staring into Babette's eyes, picking up items from our cart and smelling them.

"I've bought these peanuts before. They're round, cubical, pockmarked, seamed. Broken peanuts. A lot of dust at the bottom of the jar. But they taste good. Most of all I like the packages themselves. You were right, Jack. This is the last avant-garde. Bold new forms. The power to shock."

A woman fell into a rack of paperback books at the front of the store. A heavyset man emerged from the raised cubicle in the far corner and moved warily toward her, head tilted to get a clearer sightline. A checkout girl said, "Leon, parsley," and he answered as he approached the fallen woman, "Seventy-nine." His breast pocket was crammed with felt-tip pens.

"So then you cook at the rooming house," Babette said.

"My room is zoned for a hot plate. I'm happy there. I read the TV listings, I read the ads in *Ufologist Today.* I want to immerse myself in American magic and dread. My seminar is going well. The students are bright and responsive. They ask questions and I answer them. They jot down notes as I speak. It's quite a surprise in my life."

19. In Your Journal: Why do you think Murray is so surprised by the way his seminar is going?

He picked up our bottle of extra-strength pain reliever and sniffed along the rim of the child-proof cap. He smelled our honeydew melons, our bottles of club soda and ginger ale. Babette went down the frozen food aisle, an area my doctor had advised me to stay out of.

"Your wife's hair is a living wonder," Murray said, looking closely into my face as if to communicate a deepening respect for me based on this new information.

"Yes, it is," I said.

"She has important hair."

"I think I know what you mean."

"I hope you appreciate that woman."

"Absolutely."

"Because a woman like that doesn't just happen."

"I know it."

20. In Your Journal: What does Murray mean when he says that Babette's hair is "important"?

"She must be good with children. More than that, I'll bet she's great to have around in a family tragedy. She'd be the type to take control, show strength and affirmation."

"Actually she falls apart. She fell apart when her mother died."

"Who wouldn't?"

"She fell apart when Steffie called from camp with a broken bone in her hand. We had to drive all night. I found myself on a lumber company road. Babette weeping."

"Her daughter, far away, among strangers, in pain. Who wouldn't?"

"Not her daughter. My daughter."

"Not even her own daughter."

"No."

"Extraordinary. I have to love it."

The three of us left together, trying to maneuver our shopping carts between the paperback books scattered across the entrance. Murray wheeled one of our carts into the parking lot and then helped us heave and push all our double-bagged merchandise into the back of the station wagon. Cars entered and exited. The policewoman in her zippered minicab scouted the area for red flags on the parking meters. We added Murray's single lightweight bag of white items to our load and headed across Elm in the direction of his rooming house. It seemed to me that Babette and I, in the mass and variety of our purchases, in the sheer plenitude those crowded bags suggested, the weight and size and number, the familiar package designs and vivid lettering, the giant sizes, the family bargain packs with Day-Glo sale stickers, in the sense of replenishment we felt, the sense of well-being, the security and contentment these products brought to some snug home in our souls—it seemed we had achieved a fullness of being that is not known to people who need less, expect less, who plan their lives around lonely walks in the evening.

21. In Your Journal: Why do Jack and Babette get such a sense of well-being from their groceries?

Murray took Babette's hand on leaving.

"I'd ask you to visit my room but it's too small for two people unless they're prepared to be intimate."

Murray is able to produce a look that is sneaky and frank at the same time. It is a look that gives equal credence to disaster and lecherous success. He says that in the old days of his urban entanglements he believed there was only one way to seduce a woman, with clear and open desire. He took pains to avoid self-depreciation, self-mockery, ambiguity, irony, subtlety, vulnerability, a civilized world-weariness and a tragic sense of history—the very things, he says, that are most natural to him. Of these he has allowed only one element, vulnerability, to insert itself gradually into his program of straightforward lust. He is trying to develop a vulnerability that women will find attractive. He works at it consciously, like a man in a gym with weights and a mirror. But his efforts so far have produced only this half sneaky look, sheepish and wheedling.

He thanked us for the lift. We watched him walk toward the lop-sided porch, propped with cinder blocks, where a man in a rocker stared into space.

6

Heinrich's hairline is beginning to recede. I wonder about this. Did his mother consume some kind of gene-piercing substance when she was pregnant? Am I at fault somehow? Have I raised him, unwittingly, in the vicinity of a chemical dump site, in the path of air currents that carry industrial wastes capable of producing scalp degeneration, glorious sunsets? (People say the sunsets around here were not nearly so stunning thirty or forty years ago.) Man's guilt in history and in the tides of his own blood has been complicated by technology, the daily seeping falsehearted death.

The boy is fourteen, often evasive and moody, at other times disturbingly complaint. I have a sense that his ready yielding to our wishes and demands is a private weapon of reproach. Babette is afraid he will end up in a barricaded room, spraying hundreds of rounds of automatic fire across an empty mall before the **SWAT** teams come for him with their heavy-barreled weapons, their bullhorns and body armor.

SWAT: (Special Weapons and Tactics) responsible for high-risk policing, such as might be involved in hostage or crowd control situations

"It's going to rain tonight."

"It's raining now," I said.

"The radio said tonight."

I drove him to school on his first day back after a sore throat and fever. A woman in a yellow slicker held up traffic to let some children cross. I pictured her in a soup commercial taking off her **oilskin** hat as she entered the cheerful kitchen where her husband stood over a pot of smoky lobster bisque, a smallish man with six weeks to live.

oilskin: cloth treated with oil to make it waterproof

"Look at the windshield," I said. "Is that rain or isn't it?"

"I'm only telling you what they said."

"Just because it's on the radio doesn't mean we have to suspend belief in the evidence of our senses."

"Our senses? Our senses are wrong a lot more often than they're right. This has been proved in the laboratory. Don't you know about all those theorems that say nothing is what it seems? There's no past, present or future outside our own mind. The so-called laws of motion are a big hoax. Even sound can trick the mind. Just because you don't hear a sound doesn't mean it's not out there. Dogs can hear it. Other animals. And I'm sure there are sounds even dogs can't hear. But they exist in the air, in waves. Maybe they never stop. High, high, high-pitched. Coming from somewhere."

"Is it raining," I said, "or isn't it?"

"I wouldn't want to have to say."

"What if someone held a gun to your head?"

"Who, you?"

"Someone. A man in a trenchcoat and smoky glasses. He holds a gun to your head and says, 'Is it raining or isn't it? All you have to do is tell the truth and I'll put away my gun and take the next flight out of here.' "

"What truth does he want? Does he want the truth of someone traveling at almost the speed of light in another galaxy? Does he want the truth of someone in orbit around a neutron star? Maybe if these people could see us through a telescope we might look like we were two feet two inches tall and it might be raining yesterday instead of today."

"He's holding the gun to *your* head. He wants your truth."

"What good is my truth? My truth means nothing. What if this guy with the gun comes from a planet in a whole different solar system? What we call rain he calls soap. What we call apples he calls rain. So what am I supposed to tell him?"

22. In Your Journal: Why do you think Heinrich has so much trouble with "the truth"?

"His name is Frank J. Smalley and he comes from St. Louis."

"He wants to know if it's raining *now,* at this very minute?"

"Here and now. That's right."

"Is there such a thing as now? 'Now' comes and goes as soon as you say it. How can I say it's raining now if your so-called 'now' becomes 'then' as soon as I say it?"

"You said there was no past, present, or future."

"Only in our verbs. That's the only place we find it."

"Rain is a noun. Is there rain here, in this precise locality, at whatever time within the next two minutes that you choose to respond to the question?"

"If you want to talk about this precise locality while you're in a vehicle that's obviously moving, then I think that's the trouble with this discussion."

"Just give me an answer, okay, Heinrich?"

"The best I could do is make a guess."

"Either it's raining or it isn't," I said.

"Exactly. That's my whole point. You'd be guessing. Six of one, half dozen of the other."

"But you *see* it's raining."

"You see the sun moving across the sky. But is the sun moving across the sky or is the earth turning?"

"I don't accept the analogy."

"You're so sure that's rain. How do you know it's not sulfuric acid from factories across the river? How do you know it's not fallout from a war in China? You want an answer here and now. Can you prove, here and now, that this stuff is rain? How do I know that what you call rain is really rain? What *is* rain anyway?"

"It's the stuff that falls from the sky and gets you what is called wet."

"I'm not wet. Are you wet?"

"All right," I said. "Very good."

"No, seriously, are you wet?"

"First-rate," I told him. "A victory for uncertainty, randomness and chaos. Science's finest hour."

"Be sarcastic."

"The **sophists** and the hairsplitters enjoy their finest hour."

"Go ahead, be sarcastic, I don't care."

Heinrich's mother lives in an **ashram** now. She has taken the name Mother Devi and runs the business end of things. The ashram is located on the outskirts of the former copper-smelting town of Tubb, Montana, now called Dharamsalapur. The usual rumors abound of sexual freedom, sexual slavery, drugs, nudity, mind control, poor hygiene, tax evasion, monkey-worship, torture, prolonged and hideous death.

I watched him walk through the downpour to the school entrance. He moved with deliberate slowness, taking off his camouflage cap ten yards from the doorway. At such moments I find I love him with an animal desperation, a need to take him under my coat and crush him to my chest, keep him there, protect him. He seems to bring a danger to him. It collects in the air, follows him from room to room. Babette bakes his favorite cookies. We watch him at his desk, an unpainted table covered with books and magazines. He works well into the night, plotting chess moves in a game he plays by mail with a convicted killer in the penitentiary.

sophist: nitpicking scholar

ashram: Hindu religious retreat

23. In Your Journal: How does Jack describe his feelings for Heinrich? What is significant about these feelings?

It was warm and bright the next day and students on the Hill sat on lawns and in dorm windows, playing their tapes, sunbathing. The air was a reverie of wistful summer things, the last languorous day, a chance to go bare-limbed once more, smell the mown clover. I went into the Arts Duplex, our newest building, a winged affair with a facade of anodized aluminum, sea-green, cloud-catching. On the lower level was the movie theater, a sloped and dark-carpeted space with two hundred plush seats. I sat in shallow light at the end of the first row and waited for my seniors to arrive.

They were all Hitler majors, members of the only class I still taught, Advanced Nazism, three hours a week, restricted to qualified seniors, a course of study designed to cultivate historical perspective, theoretical rigor and mature insight into the continuing mass appeal of fascist tyranny, with special emphasis on parades, rallies and uniforms, three credits, written reports.

Every semester I arranged for a screening of background footage. This consisted of propaganda films, scenes shot at party congresses, outtakes from mystical epics featuring parades of gymnasts and mountaineers—a collection I'd edited into an impressionistic eighty-minute documentary. Crowd scenes predominated. Close-up jostled shots of thousands of people outside a stadium after a **Goebbels** speech, people surging, massing, bursting through the traffic. Halls hung with swastika banners, with mortuary wreaths and death's-head insignia. Ranks of thousands of flagbearers arrayed before columns of frozen light, a hundred and thirty antiaircraft searchlights aimed straight up—a scene that resembled a geometric longing, the formal notation of some powerful mass desire. There was no narrative voice. Only chants, songs, arias, speeches, cries, cheers, accusations, shrieks.

I got to my feet and took up a position at the front of the theater, middle aisle, facing the entranceway.

They came in out of the sun in their poplin walk shorts and limited-edition T-shirts, in their easy-care knits, their polo styling and rugby stripes. I watched them take their seats, noting the subdued and reverent air, the uncertain anticipation. Some had notebooks and pencil lights; some carried lecture material in bright binders. There were whispers, rustling paper, the knocking sound of seats dropping as one by one the students settled in. I leaned against the front of the apron, waiting for the last few to enter, for someone to seal the doors against our voluptuous summer day.

Soon there was a hush. It was time for me to deliver the introductory remarks. I let the silence deepen for a moment, then cleared my arms from the folds of the academic robe in order to gesture freely.

Goebbels: (Paul Joseph) (1897–1945) Nazi propaganda minister who had complete control over all German press, radio, cinema, and theater during World War II; killed himself and his family after Germany's defeat

When the showing ended, someone asked about the plot to kill Hitler. The discussion moved to plots in general. I found myself saying to the assembled heads, "All plots tend to move deathward. This is the nature of plots. Political plots, terrorist plots, lovers' plots, narrative plots, plots that are part of children's games. We edge nearer death every time we plot. It is like a contract that all must sign, the plotters as well as those who are the targets of the plot."

24. In Your Journal: What is Jack trying to say about plots? Do you agree or disagree?

Is this true? Why did I say it? What does it mean?

FOR USE IN DISCUSSION

Questions about Substance

1. "This assembly of station wagons, as much as anything they might do in the course of the year, more than the formal liturgies or laws, tells the parents they are a collection of the like-minded and the spiritually akin, a people, a nation" (168). What comment is this passage making about economic class and privilege?
2. "Something lurked inside the truth," Babette said (171). What does this statement mean? How is it related to the overall message of this excerpt from *White Noise?*
3. The "Hitler Studies" department shares a building with the "popular culture department," which studies such things as "bubble gum wrappers and detergent jingles" (172). Why does DeLillo lump these things together in his fictitious college?
4. Murray tells Jack that Hitler is now "Gladney's Hitler" (173). How is this statement a commentary on Hitler? How is it a commentary on modern academic institutions?
5. Why do you think Jack calls his department and his professional name "inventions"? See pages 169 and 176 for references.
6. Note all of the references to bright colors and crowdedness in this selection from *White Noise.* What is DeLillo suggesting to the reader with all of these references? What do color and space have to do with higher education, Hitler, or contemporary culture?

Questions about Structure and Style

1. The following sentence is also an entire paragraph: "The Airport Marriott, the Downtown Travelodge, the Sheraton Inn and Conference Center" (176). Reread the surrounding passages. What function does the above-referenced paragraph have? How does it complicate or elucidate the scenes and passages around it?
2. DeLillo's writing is largely descriptive. How does he manage to convey so many ideas and theories with only some dialogue and very little plot?

3. The lengthiest conversation in this piece takes place between Heinrich and Jack while they are driving through the rain (179–181). What kind of relationship between the father and son is established in this conversation? What other relationships could this one be meant to represent or evoke?

Multimedia Suggestions

1. There are many films that attempt to take an ironic stance on Nazis or other aspects of the Holocaust: *Shoulder Arms* (1918), *Stalag 17* (1953), *The Producers* (1968), and *Life is Beautiful* are some good examples. Watch one or more of these films and make comparisons to *White Noise*. Which genre seems more effective to you in terms of conveying such delicate ironies?
2. Looking for meaning in a fast-paced, noisy, technological society is a theme throughout DeLillo's novel, but it is also a common contemporary concern. The advertising industry (to which DeLillo once belonged) is particularly good at exploiting this concern. Find some ads that you think speak to consumers' anxieties about contemporary society. Do they "speak" about clothes or food in any manner similar to DeLillo's?
3. The Web site "White Noise on White Noise" presents a series of textual fragments from DeLillo's novel that contain embedded hyperlinks to Web sites that provide context for many of DeLillo's popular culture references. Click around the site briefly. Does it provide any insights you hadn't gotten from reading the excerpt? Does *White Noise* seem to have a special relationship to "fragments" and "links" that is aptly suited to a hypertext Web site? The URL is *http://www.theobvious.com/noise/toc.html*.

SUGGESTIONS FOR WRITING AND RESEARCH

1. On their trip to the "most photographed barn," Murray tells Jack that "Once you've seen the signs about the barn, it becomes impossible to see the barn" (174). What does Murray mean by this? What other objects in this excerpt from *White Noise* are obscured by the "signs" around them? Can you think of other objects or figures in contemporary culture for which/whom this is true? How does this effect relate to the concept of "white noise"?
2. Compare and contrast two of the characters in this piece (e.g., Jack and Murray, Babette and Heinrich, etc.) and then discuss what purpose you think each character serves in DeLillo's overall scheme.
3. Examine Jack's attitude toward his professional interest, Hitler Studies. Why would anyone want to make a career studying Hitler? How does Jack seem to feel about his work? How does this representation of Jack and "his Hitler" comment on the role of the university? Do you see any parallels between the school you attend and the one represented in DeLillo's work?

WORKING WITH CLUSTERS

Cluster 7: Holocausts and Histories

Cluster 11: The Art of Irony

Cluster 16: Imagination and Experience

Discipline: The Humanities

Rhetorical Mode: Description

The Writing Life

by Annie Dillard

Annie Dillard was born in Pittsburgh and attended Hollins College, near Roanoke, Virginia, where she studied English, creative writing, and theology. She won the Pulitzer Prize for general non-fiction in 1975 for Pilgrim at Tinker Creek, *a theological examination of nature and the self. She has also written* Ticket for a Prayer Wheel, An American Childhood, *and* The Living, *among other works. Currently an adjunct professor at Wesleyan University in Connecticut, she is well known for her focus on the divine aspects of daily life, and she has recently begun to write about traveling for a variety of magazines.* The Writing Life, *from which this excerpt is taken, was published in 1989.*

Do not hurry; do not rest.

—Goethe

> ***1. In Your Journal:*** How might "a line of words" be like a "pick," a "gouge," or a "probe"?

> ***2. In Your Journal:*** How can you "follow" your words if you're the one writing them?

epistemological: related to the study of the origin of knowledge

> ***3. In Your Journal:*** What is Dillard saying about writing in this statement: "The new place interests you because it is not clear"?

impunity: exemption from punishment

> ***4. In Your Journal:*** Dillard seems to suggest that throwing away or losing what you've written (even the best parts of it) is a good thing. How can this be true?

jettison: discard; throw overboard

When you write, you lay out a line of words. The line of words is a miner's pick, a woodcarver's gouge, a surgeon's probe. You wield it, and it digs a path you follow. Soon you find yourself deep in new territory. Is it a dead end, or have you located the real subject? You will know tomorrow, or this time next year.

You make the path boldly and follow it fearfully. You go where the path leads. At the end of the path, you find a box canyon. You hammer out reports, dispatch bulletins.

The writing has changed, in your hands, and in a twinkling, from an expression of your notions to an **epistemological** tool. The new place interests you because it is not clear. You attend. In your humility, you lay down the words carefully, watching all the angles. Now the earlier writing looks soft and careless. Process is nothing; erase your tracks. The path is not the work. I hope your tracks have grown over; I hope birds ate the crumbs; I hope you will toss it all and not look back.

The line of words is a hammer. You hammer against the walls of your house. You tap the walls, lightly, everywhere. After giving many years' attention to these things, you know what to listen for. Some of the walls are bearing walls; they have to stay, or everything will fall down. Other walls can go with **impunity;** you can hear the difference. Unfortunately, it is often a bearing wall that has to go. It cannot be helped. There is only one solution, which appalls you, but there it is. Knock it out. Duck.

Courage utterly opposes the bold hope that this is such fine stuff the work needs it, or the world. Courage, exhausted, stands on bare reality: this writing weakens the work. You must demolish the work and start over. You can save some of the sentences, like bricks. It will be a miracle if you can save some of the paragraphs, no matter how excellent in themselves or hard-won. You can waste a year worrying about it, or you can get it over with now. (Are you a woman, or a mouse?)

The part you must **jettison** is not only the best-written part; it is also, oddly, that part which was to have been the very point. It is the original key

---

❖ **Goethe:** (Johann Wolfgang von) (1749–1832) German writer best known for the dramatic poem *Faust* passage; the passage on which the rest was to hang, and from which you yourself drew the courage to begin. **Henry James** knew it well, and said it best. In his preface to *The Spoils of Poynton,* he pities the writer, in a comical pair of sentences that rises to a howl: "Which is the work in which he hasn't surrendered, under dire difficulty, the best thing he meant to have kept? In which indeed, before the dreadful *done,* doesn't he ask himself what has become of the thing all for the sweet sake of which it was to proceed to that extremity?"

So it is that a writer writes many books. In each book, he intended several urgent and vivid points, many of which he sacrificed as the book's form hardened. "The youth gets together his materials to build a bridge to the moon," **Thoreau** noted mournfully, "or perchance a palace or temple on the earth, and at length the middle-aged man concludes to build a wood-shed with them." The writer returns to these materials, these passionate subjects, as to unfinished business, for they are his life's work.

It is the beginning of a work that the writer throws away.

A painting covers its tracks. Painters work from the ground up. The latest version of a painting overlays earlier versions, and obliterates them. Writers, on the other hand, work from left to right. The discardable chapters are on the left. The latest version of a literary work begins somewhere in the work's middle, and hardens toward the end. The earlier version remains lumpishly on the left; the work's beginning greets the reader with the wrong hand. In those early pages and chapters anyone may find bold leaps to nowhere, read the brave beginnings of dropped themes, hear a tone since abandoned, discover blind alleys, track **red herrings,** and laboriously learn a setting now false.

5. *In Your Journal:* Dillard compares writing to painting, in the sense that painters "cover their tracks." What does she mean by this? In what other ways do you think writing and painting are similar?

red herring: distraction

Several delusions weaken the writer's resolve to throw away work. If he has read his pages too often, those pages will have a necessary quality, the ring of the inevitable, like poetry known by heart; they will perfectly answer their own familiar rhythms. He will retain them. He may retain those pages if they possess some virtues, such as power in themselves, though they lack the cardinal virtue, which is pertinence to, and unity with, the book's thrust. Sometimes the writer leaves his early chapters in place from gratitude; he cannot contemplate them or read them without feeling again

6. *In Your Journal:* A writer's "cardinal virtue," according to Dillard, "is pertinence to, and unity with, the book's thrust." What do you think this means? Where does the book's thrust come from?

Henry James: (1843–1916) one of American literature's greatest novelists; his "psychological realism" features concentrated attention to the subtleties of character (particularly among Americans abroad), and called for a highly complex style; his most famous novels include *The Portrait of a Lady* (1881), *Wings of the Dove* (1902), and *The Golden Bowl* (1904)

Thoreau: (Henry David) (1817–1862), an American philosopher and naturalist, was an advocate of transcendentalism (emphasizing modes of being beyond mundane experience) and civil disobedience; author, most famously, of *Walden* (1854)

the blessed relief that exalted him when the words first appeared—relief that he was writing anything at all. That beginning served to get him where he was going, after all; surely the reader needs it, too, as groundwork. But no.

Every year the aspiring photographer brought a stack of his best prints to an old, honored photographer, seeking his judgment. Every year the old man studied the prints and painstakingly ordered them into two piles, bad and good. Every year the old man moved a certain landscape print into the bad stack. At length he turned to the young man: "You submit this same landscape every year, and every year I put it on the bad stack. Why do you like it so much?" The young photographer said, "Because I had to climb a mountain to get it."

A cabdriver sang his songs to me, in New York. Some we sang together. He had turned the meter off; he drove around midtown, singing. One long song he sang twice; it was the only dull one. I said, You already sang that one; let's sing something else. And he said, "You don't know how long it took me to get that one together."

> ***7. In Your Journal:*** Explain what you think Dillard means by the "price tag" on a writer's "gift."

How many books do we read from which the writer lacked courage to tie off the umbilical cord? How many gifts do we open from which the writer neglected to remove the price tag? Is it pertinent, is it courteous, for us to learn what it cost the writer personally?

fiber optic: means of transmitting messages of light and glass fibers, which can carry much more information than traditional wires and cables

You write it all, discovering it at the end of the line of words. The line of words is a **fiber optic,** flexible as wire; it illumines the path just before its fragile tip. You probe with it, delicate as a worm.

Few sights are so absurd as that of an inchworm leading its dimwit life. Inchworms are the caterpillar larvae of several moths or butterflies. The cabbage looper, for example, is an inchworm. I often see an inchworm: it is a skinny bright green thing, pale and thin as a vein, an inch long, and apparently totally unfit for life in this world. It wears out its days in constant panic.

bight: loop in, or slack part of, an extended rope

davening: recitation of Jewish prayers, sometimes accompanied by a rocking motion

Every inchworm I have seen was stuck in long grasses. The wretched inchworm hangs from the side of a grassblade and throws its head around from side to side, seeming to wail. What! No further? Its back pair of nubby feet clasps the grass stem; its front three pairs of nubs rear back and flail in the air, apparently in search of a footing. What! No further? What? It searches everywhere in the wide world for the rest of the grass, which is right under its nose. By dumb luck it touches the grass. Its front legs hang on; it lifts and buckles its green inch, and places its hind legs just behind its front legs. Its body makes a loop, a **bight.** All it has to do now is slide its front legs up the grass stem. Instead it gets lost. It throws up its head and front legs, flings its upper body out into the void, and panics again. What! No further? End of world? And so forth, until it actually reaches the grasshead's tip. By then its wee weight may be bending the grass toward some other grass plant. Its **davening,** apocalyptic prayers sway the grasshead and bump it into something. I have seen it many times. The blind and frantic numbskull makes it off one grassblade and onto another one, which it will climb in virtual hysteria for several hours. Every step brings it to the universe's rim. And now—What! No further? End of world? Ah, here's ground. What! No further? Yike!

"Why don't you just jump?" I tell it, disgusted. "Put yourself out of your misery."

8. In Your Journal: What is the author's point about the inchworm? Why is she so disgusted with it?

I admire those eighteenth-century **Hasids** who understood the risk of prayer. Rabbi Uri of Strelisk took sorrowful leave of his household every morning because he was setting off to his prayers. He told his family how to dispose of his manuscripts if praying should kill him. A ritual slaughterer, similarly, every morning bade goodbye to his wife and children and wept as if he would never see them again. His friend asked him why. Because, he answered, when I begin I call out to the Lord. Then I pray, "Have mercy on us." Who knows what the Lord's power will do to me in that moment after I have invoked it and before I beg for mercy?

Hasids: sect of Jews originating in 18th century Poland who resisted the academic formalism of Talmudists, seeking instead "purity of heart"

When you are stuck in a book; when you are well into writing it, and know what comes next, and yet cannot go on; when every morning for a week or a month you enter its room and turn your back on it; then the trouble is either of two things. Either the structure has forked, so the narrative, or the logic, has developed a hairline fracture that will shortly split it up the middle—or you are approaching a fatal mistake. What you had planned will not do. If you pursue your present course, the book will explode or collapse, and you do not know about it yet, quite.

In Bridgeport, Connecticut, one morning in April 1987, a six-story concrete-slab building under construction collapsed, and killed twenty-eight men. Just before it collapsed, a woman across the street leaned from her window and said to a passerby, "That building is starting to shake." "Lady," he said, according to the Hartford *Courant*, "you got rocks in your head."

9. In Your Journal: How does the structure of a book, according to Dillard, function like the structure of a building?

You notice only this: your worker—your one and only, your prized, coddled, and driven worker—is not going out on that job. Will not budge, not even for you, boss. Has been at it long enough to know when the air smells wrong; can sense a tremor through boot soles. Nonsense, you say; it is perfectly safe. But the worker will not go. Will not even look at the site. Just developed heart trouble. Would rather starve. Sorry.

What do you do? Acknowledge, first, that you cannot do nothing. Lay out the structure you already have, x-ray it for a hairline fracture, find it, and think about it for a week or a year; solve the insoluble problem. Or subject the next part, the part at which the worker balks, to harsh tests. It harbors an unexamined and wrong premise. Something completely necessary is false or fatal. Once you find it, and if you can accept the finding, of course it will mean starting again. This is why many experienced writers urge young men and women to learn a useful trade.

Every morning you climb several flights of stairs, enter your study, open the French doors, and slide your desk and chair out into the middle of the air. The desk and chair float thirty feet from the ground, between the crowns of maple trees. The furniture is in place; you go back for your thermos of coffee. Then, wincing, you step out again through the French doors and sit down on the chair and look over the desktop. You can see clear to the river from here in winter. You pour yourself a cup of coffee.

Birds fly under your chair. In spring, when the leaves open in the maples' crowns, your view stops in the treetops just beyond the desk; yellow warblers hiss and whisper on the high twigs, and catch flies. Get to work. Your work is to keep cranking the flywheel that turns the gears that spin the belt in the engine of belief that keeps you and your desk in midair.

Putting a book together is interesting and exhilarating. It is sufficiently difficult and complex that it engages all your intelligence. It is life at its most free. Your freedom as a writer is not freedom of expression in the sense of wild blurting; you may not let rip. It is life at its most free, if you are fortunate enough to be able to try it, because you select your materials, invent your task, and pace yourself. In the democracies, you may even write and publish anything you please about any governments or institutions, even if what you write is demonstrably false.

obverse: counterpart

The **obverse** of this freedom, of course, is that your work is so meaningless, so fully for yourself alone, and so worthless to the world, that no one except you cares whether you do it well, or ever. You are free to make several thousand close judgment calls a day. Your freedom is a by-product of your days' triviality. A shoe salesman—who is doing others' tasks, who must answer to two or three bosses, who must do his job their way, and must put himself in their hands, at their place, during their hours—is nevertheless working usefully. Further, if the shoe salesman fails to appear one morning, someone will notice and miss him. Your manuscript, on which you lavish such care, has no needs or wishes; it knows you not. Nor does anyone need your manuscript; everyone needs shoes more. There are many manuscripts already—worthy ones, most edifying and moving ones, intelligent and powerful ones. If you believed *Paradise Lost* to be excellent, would you buy it? Why not shoot yourself, actually, rather than finish one more excellent manuscript on which to gag the world?

10. In Your Journal: Dillard says that "everyone needs shoes more" than a writer's work. Do you agree? Is this a fair comparison?

11. In Your Journal: "To find a honey tree, first catch a bee." What does this metaphor describe? What is the honey, and what is the bee?

To find a honey tree, first catch a bee. Catch a bee when its legs are heavy with pollen; then it is ready for home. It is simple enough to catch a bee on a flower: hold a cup or glass above the bee, and when it flies up, cap the cup with a piece of cardboard. Carry the bee to a nearby open spot—best an elevated one—release it, and watch where it goes. Keep your eyes on it as long as you can see it, and **hie** you to that last known place. Wait there until you see another bee; catch it, release it, and watch. Bee after bee will lead toward the honey tree, until you see the final bee enter the tree. Thoreau describes this process in his journals. So a book leads its writer.

hie: hurry

You may wonder how you start, how you catch the first one. What do you use for bait?

You have no choice. One bad winter in the Arctic, and not too long ago, an **Algonquin** woman and her baby were left alone after everyone else in their winter camp had starved. **Ernest Thompson Seton** tells it. The woman walked from the camp where everyone had died, and found at a lake a **cache.** The cache contained one small fishhook. It was simple to rig a line, but she had no bait, and no hope of bait. The baby cried. She took a knife and cut a strip from her own thigh. She fished with the worm of her own flesh and caught a jackfish; she fed the child and herself. Of course she saved the fish gut for bait. She lived alone at the lake, on fish, until spring, when she walked out again and found people. Seton's informant had seen the scar on her thigh.

Algonquin: North American Indian

cache: store of hidden goods

12. In Your Journal: Does it seem extreme that Dillard compares writing to the Algonquin woman's fishing with her own flesh as bait? If so, do you think the extremity is intended?

It takes years to write a book—between two and ten years. Less is so rare as to be statistically insignificant. One American writer has written a dozen major books over six decades. He wrote one of those books, a perfect novel, in three months. He speaks of it, still, with awe, almost whispering. Who wants to offend the spirit that hands out such books?

Faulkner wrote *As I Lay Dying* in six weeks; he claimed he knocked it off in his spare time from a twelve-hour-a-day job performing manual labor. There are other examples from other continents and centuries, just as **albinos,** assassins, saints, big people, and little people show up from time to time in large populations. Out of a human population on earth of four and a half billion, perhaps twenty people can write a book in a year. Some people lift cars, too. Some people enter week-long sled-dog races, go over Niagara Falls in barrels, fly planes through the **Arc de Triomphe.** Some people feel no pain in childbirth. Some people eat cars. There is no call to take human extremes as norms.

albino: organism lacking normal pigmentation

Arc de Triomphe: triumphal arch in Paris commemorating Napoleon Bonaparte

---

Ernest Thompson Seton: (1860–1946) American writer and artist who founded the Woodcraft Indians, precursor to the Boy Scouts

Faulkner: (William) (1897–1962) American novelist who primarily examined the decay of the post-Civil War South, Faulkner employed a highly symbolic and technical style; *The Sound and the Fury* (1929), *As I Lay Dying* (1930), and *Light in August* (1932) are his most widely read novels

Writing a book, full time, takes between two and ten years. The long poem, **John Berryman** said, takes between five and ten years. **Thomas Mann** was a prodigy of production. Working full time, he wrote a page a day. That is 365 pages a year, for he did write every day—a good-sized book a year. At a page a day, he was one of the most prolific writers who ever lived. **Flaubert** wrote steadily, with only the usual, appalling, strains. For twenty-five years he finished a big book every five to seven years. My guess is that full-time writers average a book every five years: seventy-three usable pages a year, or a usable fifth of a page a day. The years that biographers and other nonfiction writers spend amassing and mastering materials are well matched by the years novelists and short-story writers spend fabricating solid worlds that answer to immaterial truths. On plenty of days the writer can write three or four pages, and on plenty of other days he concludes he must throw them away.

Octavio Paz cites the example of "Saint-Pol-Roux, who used to hang the inscription 'The poet is working' from his door while he slept."

13. In Your Journal: Paraphrase Dillard's description of the relationship "between a writer's estimation of a work in progress and its actual quality." How her description compare with your experience of writing? Do you think you know when you have written something better or worse? If so, how?

The notion that one can write better during one season of the year than another **Samuel Johnson** labeled, "Imagination operating upon luxury." Another luxury for an idle imagination is the writer's own feeling about the work. There is neither a proportional relationship, nor an inverse one, between a writer's estimation of a work in progress and its actual quality. The feeling that the work is magnificent, and the feeling that it is abominable, are both mosquitoes to be repelled, ignored, or killed, but not indulged.

bole: tree trunk

The reason to perfect a piece of prose as it progresses—to secure each sentence before building on it—is that original writing fashions a form. It unrolls out into nothingness. It grows cell to cell, **bole** to bough to twig to leaf; any careful word may suggest a route, may begin a strand of metaphor or event out of which much, or all, will develop. Perfecting the work inch by

---

- **John Berryman:** (1914–1972) American writer of complex dramatic poems about the anguish of living in a trivial age; Berryman won a Pulitzer Prize for *77 Dream Songs* in 1964 and committed suicide in 1972
- **Thomas Mann:** (1875–1955) German writer of psychological and mythological novels; most well-known for *The Magic Mountain* (1927) and *Dr. Faustus* (1947)
- **Flaubert:** (Gustave) (1821–1880) French writer whose prose aspires to absolute precision and objectivity; *Madame Bovary* (1856) is his greatest work
- **Octavio Paz:** (1914–) Mexican poet known for his elegant and intelligent writing; winner of the Nobel Prize for Literature in 1990
- **Samuel Johnson:** (1709–1784) English scholar of the "Augustan Age"; poet, satirist, essayist, and biographer, Johnson's influence was profound

inch, writing from the first word toward the last, displays the courage and fear this method induces. The strain, like **Giacometti**'s penciled search for precision and honesty, enlivens the work and impels it toward its truest end. A pile of decent work behind him, no matter how small, fuels the writer's hope, too; his pride emboldens and impels him. One Washington writer—Charlie Butts—so prizes momentum, and so fears self-consciousness, that he writes fiction in a rush of his own devising. He leaves his house on distracting errands, hurries in the door, and without taking off his coat, sits at a typewriter and retypes in a blur of speed all of the story he has written to date. Impetus propels him to add another sentence or two before he notices he is writing and seizes up. Then he leaves the house and repeats the process; he runs in the door and retypes the entire story, hoping to squeeze out another sentence the way some car engines turn over after the ignition is off, or the way Warner Bros.' Wile E. Coyote continues running for several yards beyond the edge of a cliff, until he notices.

14. In Your Journal: When Dillard describes Charlie Butts's writing process, she suggests that it is helpful to be writing somewhat unconsciously. How does this compare to the ways you've been taught to think about writing?

The reason not to perfect a work as it progresses is that, **concomitantly**, original work fashions a form the true shape of which it discovers only as it proceeds, so the early strokes are useless, however fine their sheen. Only when a paragraph's role in the context of the whole work is clear can the envisioning writer direct its complexity of detail to strengthen the work's ends.

concomitantly: concurrently

Fiction writers who toss up their arms helplessly because their characters "take over"—powerful rascals, what is a god to do?—refer, I think, to these structural mysteries that seize any serious work, whether or not it possesses fifth-column characters who wreak havoc from within. Sometimes part of a book simply gets up and walks away. The writer cannot force it back in place. It wanders off to die. It is like the astonishing—and common—starfish called the sea star. A sea star is a starfish with many arms; each arm is called a ray. From time to time a sea star breaks itself, and no one knows why. One of the rays twists itself off and walks away. Dr. S. P. Monks describes one species, which lives on rocky Pacific shores:

"I am inclined to think that *Phataria* . . . always breaks itself, no matter what may be the impulse. They make breaks when conditions are changed, sometimes within a few hours after being placed in jars. . . . Whatever may be the stimulus, the animal can and does break of itself. . . . The ordinary method is for the main portion of the starfish to remain fixed and passive with the tube feet set on the side of the departing ray, and for this ray to walk slowly away at right angles to the body, to change position, twist, and do all the active labor necessary to the breakage." Marine biologist Ed Ricketts comments on this: "It would seem that in an animal that

Giacometti: (Alberto) (1901–1966) Swiss surrealist sculptor and painter known for his elongated figures

acme: peak, summit

deliberately pulls itself apart we have the very **acme** of something or other."

The written word is weak. Many people prefer life to it. Life gets your blood going, and it smells good. Writing is mere writing, literature is mere. It appeals only to the subtlest senses—the imagination's vision, and the imagination's hearing—and the moral sense, and the intellect. This writing that you do, that so thrills you, that so rocks and exhilarates you, as if you were dancing next to the band, is barely audible to anyone else. The reader's ear must adjust down from loud life to the subtle, imaginary sounds of the written word. An ordinary reader picking up a book can't yet hear a thing; it will take half an hour to pick up the writing's modulations, its ups and downs and louds and softs.

15. In Your Journal: What kind of weakness do you think Dillard refers to here? How can this be true when so much of our culture and society depends on and grows out of written language?

entomological: pertaining to the study of insects

An intriguing **entomological** experiment shows that a male butterfly will ignore a living female butterfly of his own species in favor of a painted cardboard one, if the cardboard one is big. If the cardboard one is bigger than he is, bigger than any female butterfly ever could be. He jumps the piece of cardboard. Over and over again, he jumps the piece of cardboard. Nearby, the real, living female butterfly opens and closes her wings in vain.

16. In Your Journal: Why does the male butterfly prefer the cardboard female to the real one? How does this help Dillard describe the purpose of and audience for literature?

Films and television stimulate the body's senses too, in big ways. A nine-foot handsome face, and its three-foot-wide smile, are irresistible. Look at the long legs on that man, as high as a wall, and coming straight toward you. The music builds. The moving, lighted screen fills your brain. You do not like filmed car chases? See if you can turn away. Try not to watch. Even knowing you are manipulated, you are still as helpless as the male butterfly drawn to painted cardboard.

That is the movies. That is their ground. The printed word cannot compete with the movies on their ground, and should not. You can describe beautiful faces, car chases, or valleys full of Indians on horseback until you run out of words, and you will not approach the movies' spectacle. Novels written with film contracts in mind have a faint but unmistakable, and ruinous, odor. I cannot name what, in the text, alerts the reader to suspect the writer of mixed motives; I cannot specify which sentences, in several books, have caused me to read on with increasing dismay, and finally close the books because I smelled a rat. Such books seem uneasy being books; they seem eager to fling off their disguises and jump onto screens.

Why would anyone read a book instead of watching big people move on a screen? Because a book can be literature. It is a subtle thing—a poor thing, but our own. In my view, the more literary the book—the more purely verbal, crafted sentence by sentence, the more imaginative, reasoned, and deep—the more likely people are to read it. The people who read are the people who like literature, after all, whatever that might be. They like, or require, what books alone have. If they want to see films that evening, they will find films. If they do not like to read, they will not. People who read are not too lazy to flip on the television; they prefer books. I cannot imagine a sorrier pursuit than struggling for years to write a book that attempts to appeal to people who do not read in the first place.

You climb a long ladder until you can see over the roof, or over the clouds. You are writing a book. You watch your shod feet step on each round rung, one at a time; you do not hurry and do not rest. Your feet feel the steep ladder's balance; the long muscles in your thighs check its sway. You climb steadily, doing your job in the dark. When you reach the end, there is nothing more to climb. The sun hits you. The bright wideness surprises you; you had forgotten there was an end. You look back at the ladder's two feet on the distant grass, astonished.

The line of words fingers your own heart. It invades arteries, and enters the heart on a flood of breath; it presses the moving rims of thick valves; it palpates the dark muscle strong as horses, feeling for something, it knows not what. A queer picture beds in the muscle like a worm **encysted**—some film of feeling, some song forgotten, a scene in a dark bedroom, a corner of the woodlot, a terrible dining room, that exalting sidewalk; these fragments are heavy with meaning. The line of words peels them back, dissects them out. Will the bared tissue burn? Do you want to expose these scenes to the light? You may locate them and leave them, or poke the spot hard till the sore bleeds on your finger, and write with that blood. If the sore spot is not fatal, if it does not grow and block something, you can use its power for many years, until the heart resorbs it.

encysted: enclosed in a cyst (bodily sac)

The line of words feels for cracks in the **firmament.**

firmament: expansive sky; the heavens

The line of words is heading out past Jupiter this morning. Traveling 150 kilometers a second, it makes no sound. The big yellow planet and its white moons spin. The line of words speeds past Jupiter and its **cumbrous,** dizzying orbit; it looks neither to the right nor to the left. It will be leaving the solar system soon, single-minded, rapt, rushing heaven like a soul. You are in **Houston,** Texas, watching the monitor. You saw a simulation: the line of words waited still, hushed, pointed with longing. The big yellow planet spun toward it like a pitched ball and passed beside it, low and outside. Jupiter was so large, the arc of its edge at the screen's bottom looked flat. The probe twined on; its wild path passed between white suns small as dots; these stars fell away on either side, like the lights on a tunnel's walls.

cumbrous: cumbersome; difficult to manage or handle

Houston: (Texas) National Aeronautics and Space Administration (NASA) headquarters

Now you watch symbols move on your monitor; you stare at the signals the probe sends back, transmits in your own tongue, numbers. Maybe later you can guess at what they mean—what they might mean about space at the edge of the solar system, or about your instruments. Right now, you are flying. Right now, your job is to hold your breath.

FOR USE IN DISCUSSION

Questions about Substance

1. Examine Dillard's epigraph from Goethe: to what extent does it apply to Dillard's prose?
2. This essay has metaphors in almost every paragraph, many of which compare the natural world of plants, animals, and earth to the cerebral world of sentences and paragraphs. Identify some of these metaphors. Why do you think Dillard goes to such lengths to draw this parallel?
3. What do you think Dillard most wants the reader to know about writing?
4. The theme of loss is persistent in this essay (see 188, 189, 191, 193 and 195). How is writing related to loss in Dillard's mind?
5. Dillard compares the writer to a miner, a builder, a painter, and a photographer. Why does she use such concrete endeavors as analogies? Is writing as concrete as mining for coal or building a house?
6. Explain Dillard's definition of a writer's "freedom" (192).
7. Examine Dillard's extended comparison between television and literature (196–197). Do you agree or disagree with her characterization?

Questions about Structure and Style

1. Examine the variety of section lengths and breaks in this essay. Can you find any reason in the apparently inconsistent structure of this essay?
2. Dillard uses many anecdotes: the photographer (190), the praying Hasid (191), the building collapse (191), the Algonquin woman (193), and Charlie Butts's writing process (195). What purpose do these anecdotes serve in helping Dillard explain the writing process?
3. Some of the paragraph-to-paragraph transitions are explicit (you can see the connection between the paragraphs stated directly), and some of them are implicit (the connection is suggested rather than stated). Find some examples of each kind of transition and try to explain the purpose of Dillard's choice in each instance.
4. Why does this essay end with a trip into space? Why do you think Dillard chooses the planet Jupiter as the symbolic destination of this trip?
5. Discuss the reasons why you think Dillard addresses the reader directly throughout this essay, rather than speaking in the third person.

Multimedia Suggestions

1. Watch a movie that tries to represent the creative process [*Julia* (1977), *The Shining* (1980), *Barton Fink* (1991), *Husbands and Wives* (1992), *The Wonder Boys* (2000), *Finding Forrester* (2000), *Adaptation* (2002), or *The Hours* (2002),

for example]. Compare the movie's representation of writing to Dillard's description. What are the similarities? What are the differences?

2. Take an essay that you've written for class and try to represent it in a more physical medium. For example, using pipe cleaners as paragraphs, shape the pieces according to their purpose (e.g., a circle for a main idea and several connected tails for examples or illustrations); alternately, you can use clay, paint, Legos, flowers, or whatever else seems appropriate. Present your creation to the class and compare it to those of other students. What materials do you think Dillard would use to represent her prose?

SUGGESTIONS FOR WRITING AND RESEARCH

1. Write a reflective essay about one of your recent papers and how you wrote it. Describe your attitude toward the assignment, your state of mind while doing the project, and your sense of accomplishment when the assignment was completed. Use some of Dillard's terms and metaphors to describe how you eventually came to produce the paper, and personify or animate as many of the concrete details of the process as possible—e.g., "Sometimes part of a book simply gets up and walks away. The writer cannot force it back into place. It wanders off to die" (195).
2. Read a short work by one of the writers invoked by Annie Dillard in this essay (good choices might be "Beast in the Jungle" by Henry James, "Civil Disobedience" by Henry David Thoreau, or "A Rose for Emily" by William Faulkner). Compare the two authors. Describe the traces of influence on Dillard that you find in the author whose work you've examined.
3. Imitate Dillard's concrete metaphoric style in an essay of your own. Take as your subject another abstract or intellectual practice (solving a math problem, falling in love, or grieving a loss, for instance).

WORKING WITH CLUSTERS

Cluster 1: Sensory Knowledge
Cluster 8: Metaphor and Truth
Discipline: The Humanities
Rhetorical Mode: Description

"Closing the Strength Gap" (from *The Frailty Myth: Women Approaching Physical Equality*)

by Colette Dowling

Colette Dowling is a New York-based, internationally known writer and lecturer whose books have been translated into twenty languages. She is the author of Maxing Out: Why Women Sabotage Their Financial Security, Red Hot Mamas: Coming into Our Own at Fifty, You Mean I Don't Have to Feel This Way?: New Help for Depression, Anxiety, and Addiction, *and* The Cinderella Complex: Women's Hidden Fear of Independence, *which has been in print since it was published in 1981. Her articles have appeared in* The New York Times Magazine, New York, Harper's, *and many other magazines.* The Frailty Myth: Women Approaching Physical Equality, *from which this essay is drawn, was published in 2000.*

I grew up in a house where my mother had the Metropolitan Opera on the radio every Saturday afternoon and my father had on at least two ball games, one on television, one on the radio. For the longest time I hated baseball. Only much later, when suddenly (it seemed) women had become pitchers, and tight ends, and goalies, when they were risking life and limb and rib cage to play in even the most rugged of contact sports, did I begin wondering why women had been excluded from certain sports (baseball among them) to begin with. Who, and what, had interfered with women's sense of their own physical possibility, so that as they came of age, sport had seemed the all-too-unpeaceable kingdom of men? What was the message being given to females of all ages about risk, courage, and the potential—hideous thought—for getting hurt? What was making us so bloody *scared*?

Day after day, when I was a child, I saw the same images on television and in the sports section: male muscle, male aggression, male explosive power. Men in face-slashing fights with gloves and sticks. Men jumping vertically. Men in huge pileups, tackling one another. Men, men, men. How bored I was by men's sports, as a girl growing up in Baltimore. And how I repressed the underlying message: Men are on top. My father wore a tie and a white shirt, always, whether to work, or to dinner, or on weekends. I never saw him do more than throw the occasional ball with my brother in the backyard, even then in his white shirt. But the shirt was a ruse, a kind of genteel drag, for what I really associated with my father was not the primness of his dress. What I associated him with were the loud voices of sportscasters calling the plays. I associated him, and my brother, and the boys I grew up with, with men in boxing rings knocking hell out of one another, men in giant pileups on the football field. I associated them with the lacrosse sticks so popular in Baltimore, invented by Native American men in the early days of our country and slung in such a way that the ball could knock your eye out with the force of its velocity. I associated them with the raucous cheers and stomping that made the stands quake around me on the rare occasions when I was taken to a game. I associated them with screams of "Blood on the ice!" I associated them with raw physical power that seemed only barely contained by the rules of a game. For wasn't there a connection between "Blood on the ice!" and blood on the war fields, blood in the streets? Violence was symbolized, ever present, in the reined-in but eminently unleashable explosive power of the male. There was rage in it. And there were people who got caught in the rage and hurt by it. There was always the possibility of injury, always the possibility of things getting out of control. And so we girls were warned: Don't stay out after dark; avoid narrow streets; keep your eyes down; don't look at them; don't take the chance; if you get hurt, you've only yourself to blame. All of this, from the belief in our own weakness to the excessive fear of male strength and power, is pumped up by the cultural institution of sport.

Sport is more than just the swinging of a bat, the jumping of a hurdle, the sliding, all mud-covered, to a base. It is a male-defined agenda no less powerful than education or even, for that matter, religion (to which it is often compared). Sport has always been an agenda, from the time of the Greek city-states, when, by excluding slaves and women, it contributed to their subjugation, to the nineteenth-century preparation of middle- and upper-class boys for the military. Sport has been used to perpetuate racism and classism, and it is used, still, to dominate women. The body, after all, is an instrument of power. Through sport, the male body signifies "better than," "stronger than," "more than." And this superiority appears to be inevitable—a "natural" result of differences in size, strength, and physical power.

> ***1. In Your Journal:*** Dowling states that sports have been used to "dominate women" and signify males as inevitably and naturally superior. How does she think this has been accomplished?

The more I examined this obvious-seeming but misguided idea, the more disturbed I became. *On average,* males are 10 to 15 percent larger in physical stature than women. There are many women who are larger than men, of course, just as there are many smaller men in relation to large men. How big a power difference could really be legitimated by the fact that *some* men are larger than *some* women? Hasn't a **mystique** been generated here? And what would happen to that mystique if women—more women, *most* women—actually had the knowledge, the training, and the encouragement to make the most of themselves physically? How would things change if women knew how to use their bodies for power, and leverage, and social position, just as men do? If they used their bodies not for surrogate power, through passively pleasing men, but directly, getting what they want in their lives through a sense of their own physical agency and competence?

mystique: aura of mystery or secrecy

> ***2. In Your Journal:*** What does Dowling mean when she suggests that women know how to "use their bodies . . . for surrogate power"?

Women today compete at levels comparable to men. The threat this creates, conscious or not, produces a steady effort on the part of sports officials to slow their advance. It's too late now to keep women out of sports, so the tactics for undermining their accomplishments have had to grow subtler. Today the goal is more one of deflecting attention from just *how* physically similar males and females actually are.

One method has been to divide and conquer: keeping men's games separate from women's. When the chips are down, men don't want to contend with the other sex. The reasons put up against doing so, when they're put up at all, are laughable. In a variation on the "no women in the locker room" theme, bass fishermen excluded females from competition on the

auspicious: favored by fortune; prosperous; fortunate

grounds that women shouldn't watch men urinate over the side of the boat. It took an organization no less **auspicious** than the Army Corps of Engineers to confront male modesty by refusing to allow use of a lake for a bass tournament unless women were admitted. (This was in the early 1990s, still the Dark Ages in the male world of fishing.)

Another tactic has been the creation of minor differences in the rules, which makes it harder to compare men's and women's increasingly similar abilities. In archery, for example, men shoot at 30, 50, 70, and 90 meters, women at 30, 50, 60, and 70 meters. What's the point of such a minimal distinction—a false distinction, some would say. Female athletes began to get the sense that the rules were being changed as soon as it appeared they were catching up. They found it suspicious, for example, when, after Chinese skeet shooter Zhang Shan became the first woman to win a gold medal in a mixed shooting event, in 1992, the IOC immediately decided to separate men and women skeet shooters in the next Games. (This was not an unprecedented move. The International Shooting Federation quickly segregated most of its mixed events when a woman took first place in rifle shooting, in 1976.)

3. In Your Journal: Compare the "divide and conquer method" to the method of rule changing in the world that Dowling describes. Why would both tactics be necessary?

Earlier in the century, women who defeated men simply had their titles taken away. When Helene Mayer beat the men's U.S. fencing champion in 1938, the Fencing Commission not only imposed a ban on male-female competition, it revoked the winner's title. The grounds? Mayer had won in an unfair fight, since men can't go all out when playing against a woman. To continue mixed-sex fencing, the officials decided, would be "almost as bad as punching a girl in the eye."

Since body contact in fencing involves the tip of a foil pressing up against a thickly padded player, there isn't much danger involved. We can only assume the commission didn't want women beating men.

4. In Your Journal: What do the reactions of sports officials, the IOC, and men in general suggest about how men feel about the similarities between men and women?

The fear of female physical power is cross-cultural. When Barbara Mayer Winters became a finalist at the Acapulco cliff-diving championships, she was promptly disqualified from further jumping—for "her own protection," she was told. The men had complained about having to compete against her. "This is a death-defying activity," one male diver protested. "What would be the point if everyone saw that a woman could do the same?"

5. In Your Journal: Was it for Barbara Mayer Winters' protection that she was disqualified, or was it for the protection of something else?

What would be the point indeed? In some cultures the very rites of passage into adulthood require men's being able to scare the hell out of women with their physical daring. Young boys from Bunlap, on the island of Pentecost in the South Pacific, are taught to hurl themselves from absurdly high platforms, making twenty-five-foot dives when they're as young as five, then going on to higher and higher jumping platforms as they grow older. A *National Geographic* reporter watched a sixteen-year-old dive from seventy feet. When his lianas, vines tied to the ankles to break the fall, snapped, the boy remained facedown on the ground, pretending to be dead, until his mother and sisters broke out sobbing, whereupon he leaped up shouting and laughing.

I wonder what this youth would have made of the eighty-three-year-old woman who recently bungee-jumped from a bridge over a gorge in Queenstown, New Zealand, dropping 150 feet and bobbing on her line like a yo-yo. Was she scared? Not really. She said it was exhilarating.

MEN'S FEAR OF WOMEN'S STRENGTH

Historically men have been able to disempower and subordinate women, use their labor, influence their thoughts, and secure their cooperation mainly because of the power they have held over women's bodies. At a conscious level this has manifested itself in actual physical servitude, wherein women have been coerced into performing duties deemed appropriate to their sex. That Tegla Loroupe's fellow male athletes from Kenya expected her to launder their dirty clothes during the Olympics is an example. But there are subtler forms of domination. Most effective of all has been getting women to experience their bodies in ways that make *men* more comfortable. This conspiring of women in their own physical oppression can be seen in female bodybuilding. The sport became serious with the creation of the American Federation of Women Bodybuilders in 1980. But from the beginning women took care to establish their femininity by posing differently from male bodybuilders. They affect dancelike, less static postures that prevent onlookers from being able to see the full extent of their muscular development. This has been encouraged, if not required, by male officials, who have focused entirely on the feminine image as a judging criterion. "First and foremost, the judge must bear in mind that he or she is judging a woman's bodybuilding competition and is looking for an ideal feminine physique," the International Federation of Bodybuilding states unambiguously in its guidelines. "Therefore, the most important aspect is shape, a feminine shape, and controlling the development of muscle—it must not be carried to excess, where it resembles the massive muscularity of the male physique."

6. In Your Journal: What does it mean for men to be "getting women to experience their bodies in ways that make men more comfortable"?

Here at last we see, written out and unvarnished, the message females have been getting since they were girls: *Don't get too muscular. Keep yourself smaller, so as to seem weaker than the boys.* Bodybuilding is a contest that is about being strong. It is about developing oneself physically to the max. But lo and behold, as women got more muscular, the event was redesigned for female competitors so that it has less to do with looking strong and more to do with looking female. The old bottom line was right there in the black and white of the International Federation of Women Bodybuilders' criterion: For females, it's not what you do, it's how you look while doing it. The beauty of the surface is what's relevant for women. In addition to rewarding smaller muscles and more feminine dance poses, judges of female bodybuilding are instructed to *take off points* for typical female wear and tear: stretch marks, surgical scars, cellulite. So get rid of them, girls, if you want to have a chance on the bodybuilding stage.

When it comes to muscle, the question "How much is too much?" is, for women, continually being reassessed and redefined. In female bodybuilding truly muscular women have always been at a disadvantage. The irony was not lost on two filmmakers, who used it to hype the drama in *Pumping Iron II: The Women.* To create a documentary effect, two actual bodybuilders, Bev Francis, a muscular power lifter, and Rachel McLish, who describes herself as a "powder puff," were used as the film's main characters. Bev can deadlift 520 pounds. Here was a woman, as sociologist Ellis Cashmore puts it, "who had not only challenged traditional concepts of femininity, but crushed them like an aluminum beer can in her mighty fist."

Rachel, by comparison, is a lifter of another dimension—someone who poses for magazine photo sessions in superfemme costumes: for example, a zebra-print bikini and feather headdress with gold chains around her belly. In the story, the contest between Bev and Rachel, who are preparing for a staged competition, structures the film's plot. "On one level, the film is about the competition between these two female bodies. But at another level it is a film about ideologies of femininity," says feminist scholar Anne Balsamo.

> ***7. In Your Journal:*** What perspectives are Bev and Rachel meant to represent in *Pumping Iron II?*

Pumping Iron II shows by whom—and for what—women bodybuilders get rewarded, and its message is clear: They *don't* get rewarded for out-and-out strength. Of eight women lifters, Bev finished last—not because she didn't lift great, but because she didn't *look* right. Her last-place finish was used to symbolize her body's "transgressions against the cultural norm," says Balsamo. A judge was shown explaining that "women with 'big grotesque muscles' violate the natural differences between men and women"—just in case the film audience didn't get it.

> ***8. In Your Journal:*** If "big grotesque muscles" are intrinsically vulgar, why are they admired on men? What "natural differences" was the judge referring to?

In the end, Rachel didn't win, either. That would have been too obviously retrograde. To finish off the story, the scriptwriter brought in a third woman, neither too massive nor too feminine. That Carla Dunlap is a black athlete, however, threw a new variable into the mix, so that the initial tension between macho woman and powder-puff girl was never resolved, it was simply dropped. Carla became the way out of a plot dilemma that seemed, to the filmmakers, impossible. Though apparently they were entranced by the drama of women exhibiting great strength, they couldn't find a way to extricate themselves from the very issue they found so dramatic. They couldn't bring themselves to say that a woman capable of deadlifting 520 pounds is a woman like any other.

> ***9. In Your Journal:*** What dilemma did Carla Dunlap solve? Why was it a dilemma in the first place?

> ***10. In Your Journal:*** What fault does Dowling find with the filmmakers of *Pumping Iron II?*

In the real world of female bodybuilding, 1993 was a big year because the federation finally lifted its ban on big muscles. The achievements of Bev Francis were instrumental in the rule change. By the end of the

1990s the bigger and harder shape had become the norm, with women competitors being judged on virtually the same criteria as men. Today women bodybuilding champions can actually make as much money from appearances and endorsements as male body-builders—perhaps the final indignity for many men.

While extreme muscular development in women is still a turnoff to many, there has been, in fact, a growing acceptance of bigger and harder muscles. In the women's sports magazines, showing bodies that are highly developed and even big has become the norm. The fashion magazines trail behind, although today even models show off bodies that are subtly shaped with muscle. Before the 1990s, muscle in models was total **anathema.**

anathema: something detested or loathed

THE MYTH OF THE "MANNISH" WOMAN

No less an authority than Lewis Terman, the creator of the first IQ test, got involved in the pressing issue of masculinity and femininity in sports. He concocted what would become the extremely influential Attitude Interest Analysis Survey. One's attitudes and interests, he believed, were the key to determining where a given individual fell on the masculinity-femininity spectrum. An interest in sport, in Terman's schema, was a major indicator; indeed, he declared that an interest in sport was "the most masculine interest" a woman could have. His tests, he believed, showed that college athletes, male *or* female, were high scorers in "masculinity."

One of Terman's students, E. Lowell Kelly, took all this masculine/feminine insanity to its inevitable conclusion when he came up with a system to tease out "potential homosexuality." Based on a ridiculously small sample, the research results, highly publicized, caught everyone's eye. After analyzing a test group of eighteen lesbians, he had found—oh boy!—that they were "slightly less masculine" than a group of thirty-seven female college athletes. Terman and Kelly's "scales" lent supposedly scientific validity to the idea that women athletes not only lacked femininity but were even more masculine than the much-feared lesbians. This was exciting stuff. Popular magazines published articles on the new studies, articles with titles like "How Masculine or Feminine Are You?," accompanied by clever little male/female surveys that encouraged anxious readers to rate themselves. Football, skating, and tennis were the possibilities from which one was to choose a favorite sport. If one chose football, that was two points. Skating and tennis were gender neutral enough to confer zero points. The higher the total points (there were other scoring categories besides sports), the greater the masculinity. Terman and Kelly's vaunted M/F scales fed into and supported midcentury gender proscriptions. If a girl wanted to play on her school football team, there was clearly something wrong with her. End of story.

11. In Your Journal: Compare Terman's idea that sports are "the most masculine interest" women could have to Kelly's idea of "potential homosexuality" readings. What do their studies suggest to you about statistical data in general?

The threat of seeming masculine has kept a lot of girls and women from entering sports in a serious way—and understandably. Formidable female athletes have been shamelessly ridiculed, reduced to little more than sideshow freaks. The stronger and more athletically brilliant, the freakier their portrayal in the media. The story of Martina Navratilova is *the* classic example. A young defector from Communist Czechoslovakia, Navratilova was sworn in as a U.S. citizen in 1981 and went on to take the world of women's tennis by storm. Over the course of her career she netted eighteen grand slam singles titles and a record 1,438 single match victories. By 1985 she had accumulated $8.5 million in winnings, more than any other player in the history of the sport. This athlete's stunning achievements might have been construed as an example of using natural talent, hard work, and first-rate training to reach a new level of performance. Yet the media took the position that anyone who performed as well as Martina couldn't possibly be a real woman, she could only be some sort of overly aggressive misfit. Navratilova was characterized as a "bionic sci-fi creation," an "Amazon," even "some kind of hulking predator who kept 'beating up on all those innocent girls.' " A writer for *Sports Illustrated* referred to her as "the bleached blonde Czech bisexual defector" who "bludgeoned" and "teased" her hopelessly inferior opponents and suggested she was something other than a "natural" female. *Time* magazine wrote that in order to play so well, Navratilova "must have a chromosomic screw loose somewhere."

12. In Your Journal: Note the description of Martina Navratilova as a "hulking predator who kept beating up on all those innocent girls." Why should Navratilova's competitors be classified as "innocent girls"? Does this language sound like the descriptions of men given by Dowling in the beginning pages of this essay? What do these descriptions suggest about violent behavior and gender?

13. In Your Journal: Do the words "masculine" and "feminine" have equal numbers of positive and negative connotations, in your opinion?

virilism: female "disorder," in which there is development of secondary male sexual characteristics, such as hirsutism and lowered voice, caused by various conditions affecting hormone regulation

Within a few years other women had developed their skills to the point of being able to beat Navratilova, but the smear of **virilism** didn't stop there. Instead of returning talented female athletes to the category of normal as their ranks swelled in all sports, male writers became yet more hostile and suspicious. Even in the 1990s top women athletes were ridiculed as unfeminine. A story in *The Washington Post,* "The (Lesser) Games Women Play," said of female basketball players in the 1992 Barcelona Games, "They walked like men, slapped hands like men."

14. In Your Journal: What is the difference between "behaving like men" and "playing like men"?

They may have behaved like men, but of course they didn't *play* like men. Rather, this sportswriter gibed, "They played like junior high school boys."

Women who are successful as athletes invariably have the experience, at some point in their careers, of being described as masculine. The British golfer Enid Wilson could "punch out an iron with masculine vigor." Tennis players were robotlike, exhibiting "cold, tense, machine-like qualities." Aggressive male players were praised. Aggressive female players were not talented, they were cruelly merciless. When Helen Wills played tennis, it "was almost as though a man with a rapier were sending home his vital thrusts against a foeman unarmed."

15. In Your Journal: Analyze the analogy used for Helen Wills as the "man with a rapier . . . sending home his vital thrusts against a foreman unarmed." What are the connotations of this imagery? How does this compare to the earlier description of Martina Navratilova?

In women's sport the underlying tension has always come from the presumed contradiction between physical intelligence and womanhood.

From the 1930s to the 1950s, Mildred "Babe" Didrikson's fabulous athletic accomplishments were shredded in the journalistic mill. Tabloids were littered with comments about her "mannish" appearance, her "hawkish and hairy" face, and her "unusual amount of male dominance." Reporters were always asking Didrikson if she ever intended to marry. "It gets my goat," she said. "They seem to think I'm a strange, unnatural being summed up in the words Muscle Moll." Poor Babe. It's no wonder she finally took a husband (who knew about her lesbianism). As a career saver, it worked. "Babe Is a Lady Now: The World's Most Amazing Athlete Has Learned to Wear Nylons and Cook for Her Huge Husband," *Life* magazine raved. But with all the **brouhaha** about Didrikson's femininity, her remarkable athletic ability got less attention than it deserved. First starring in basketball, track and field, and baseball, she then, between bouts of cancer, became the top woman golfer in the United States. When she died of the illness in her forties, the press spent less time celebrating Didrikson's athletic accomplishments than her achievement of "femininity."

brouhaha: excited public interest, discussion, or the like, as the clamor attending some sensational event; hullabaloo

Men didn't stop at slapping the label of gender abnormality on female *children* who were good athletes. At a girls' soccer match in Lewisville, Texas, fathers whose daughter's team was defeated charged out onto the field and demanded that the three best players on the winning team be sent to the bathroom to have their sex verified. (This was in 1990!) After the game one of the fathers further humiliated the team's nine-year-old star goalie, calling out to her, "Nice game, boy!" and "Good game, son." Young Natasha Dennis, to her credit, didn't fold but instead remarked that someone should take the men "and check to see if they have anything between their ears."

16. In Your Journal: When faced with a truly exceptional female athlete (like Martina Navratilova or Babe Didrikson), how have some reporters explained (or even explained away) those athletes' accomplishments?

The soccer fathers, of course, were revealing their own insecurities. Historically men have dominated the playing fields, with athletic qualities such as aggression, competitiveness, strength, speed, and power being viewed entirely as masculine. And now not only women but girls, *kids,* were demonstrating those very traits. "Nice game, boy!" meanly and deliberately addressed to a girl of nine is the sound of the world tilting.

17. In Your Journal: Why do the fathers of these young *female* soccer players have such hostile responses to the star players?

Not all girls are as clearheaded as Natasha. The implication of lesbianism is still a fearsome challenge—for young females especially. It was partly a result of homophobic attitudes toward strong, athletic females that girls' participation in high school sports barely increased during the sixties and seventies. Post—**Title IX,** far fewer girls entered sports than progressive educators would have hoped. It was because if you were a girl, you had to have guts if you wanted to play your heart out. Even in the 1990s you could be chewed up and spat out for that transgression.

Title IX: clause in the 1972 Education Act stating that no one shall because of sex be denied the benefits of any educational program or activity that receives direct federal aid

The taint of homosexuality is the modern-day equivalent of the mark of the tar brush. For the woman so marked, it changes everything. It certainly dissuades women from pursuing careers in coaching or athletic administration. A former high school athlete and later a coach, Laura Noah knew when she was young that much of her identity was wrapped up in sports: "My mother says I was an athlete in the womb. I could pick up a basketball before I could walk." Yet she was constantly feeling that she could be successful in sports "only as long as I still looked and acted like a 'girl.'" Laura was a soccer and basketball star in high school and a four-year soccer starter at Division III Kenyon College in Ohio, and she won all-conference and all-regional honors and the North Coast Athletic Conference's scholar-athlete award. But she was also a lesbian. By the time she was a senior in college Laura was "out" to the team captains and dearly wanted to come out to the rest of her team. The team captains didn't think so. They said if she came out, it would be too upsetting and disruptive to the team. To Laura it seemed as if she couldn't be both an open lesbian and an athlete. "I was holding back. I didn't feel whole." When she left coaching at the age of twenty-six, it was because she feared she'd have to remain in the closet if she wanted to succeed in her field.

18. In Your Journal: Although Dowling makes no direct comment about it, can we infer whether gay male athletes receive the same treatment as lesbian athletes?

Some say homophobia has gotten worse as women get stronger. It has always been a big issue for female athletic coaches, whether or not they're lesbian. If they are, they're advised not to "come out." If they're not, they're categorized as lesbian anyway. For some, like Laura, the whole atmosphere is so destructive, they're forced to leave the profession to protect their integrity.

People's confusion about gender and athleticism is nowhere more dramatically revealed than in the story of Richard Raskind, a six-foot-two high-ranking player in the thirty-five and older men's division of the United States Tennis Association (USTA). Richard became a surgically constructed female in 1975, changed his name to Renee Clarke, and in 1976 thrashed the defending champion in the women's division of a local tournament in La Jolla, California. A suspicious reporter looked into the situation—the winner *was* six-two—and discovered that Renee Clarke was actually Renee Richards, the name Richard Raskin had taken after becoming a transsexual. Talk about a media circus. The clamor might eventually have died down had Richards not accepted an invitation to play in a national tournament that was a warm-up for the U.S. Open. That did it. The USTA, the Women's Tennis Association (WTA), and the U.S. Open Committee leaped to the challenge by requiring *all* women competitors to take a sex chromosome test. Richards refused and one year later took the case to the New York Supreme Court, which ruled that "this person is now female" and that requiring Richards to pass a chromosome test was "grossly unfair, discriminatory and inequitable, and violative of her rights." How ironic that the court finally deemed sex tests unlawful in the case of a biological male surgically turned female. The decision opened the way for Richards to play in the women's singles in the 1977 U.S. Open, where she promptly lost in the first round to Virginia Wade. That's right. Husky, six-two Renee lost to a woman. What *had* everyone been so afraid of? "[T]hat the floodgates would be opened," in Richards's words. That through them "would come tumbling an endless stream of made-over Neanderthals who would brutalize Chris Evert and Evonne Goolagong. . . . Some player who was not quite good enough in men's tennis might decide to change only in order to overpower the women players."

19. In Your Journal: Summarize the outcome of the Richard Raskin/Renee Richards affair. What ideas or arguments does it help Dowling begin to develop?

Here, perhaps, is the most peculiar possibility of all. Did Richards lose his game as part of his makeover? Did he subconsciously weaken himself in order to play—in Bob Dylan's famous refrain—"just like a woman"?

NEW WAYS OF ASSESSING PERFORMANCE

The idea that women are unable to achieve the same levels of physical development as men is today under question. The only reason some women don't perform at similar levels, suggest some sport sociologists and even physicians, is that women have been cast as biologically incapable for so long. In the new edition of the *Oxford Textbook of Sports Medicine,* Per-Olof Åstrand, professor emeritus of Sweden's Karolinska Institute, is one who suggests how close women's records may end up coming to men's, despite physiological differences.

Ellis Cashmore, a professor of sociology at Staffordshire University in England, has done a historical analysis of marathon results, comparing changes in men's and women's running times. Over a thirty-year period, between 1964 and 1995, the world record for women improved by 1 hour, 5 minutes, 21 seconds. During that same period the male world record improved by only 5 minutes, 2 seconds. By the last year of the period studied, the glaring ability gap between men and women was no longer so glaring. The difference in the world's bests was down to 12 minutes, 13 seconds—or about 9 percent.

"*Is* the performance of women inferior to that of men?" asks movement analyst Jackie Hudson. "It depends on the terms of comparison: Who, and what, is being compared?" A method developed for comparing male weight lifters is finally being considered a fairer and more accurate way of assessing performance comparisons between males and females. Based on biomechanics, the calculation converts fixed race distances into units of competitor height. An example: Suppose you stand 1.67 meters (5 feet 5¾ inches) tall and run the 10K in 50 minutes, or 3,000 seconds. Convert the length of the race to heights by dividing race length by height. That's 10,000 meters divided by 1.67 meters equals 6,000 heights. Velocity is then computed by dividing heights by time. Using this method, says Hudson, it's possible to get an accurate comparison of male and female world record holders. She used it to make a comparative analysis of Carl Lewis and Florence Griffith Joyner. A runner of the 100-meter dash, Lewis, who stood 6 feet 2 inches tall and held the men's world record of 9.92 seconds, had a relative velocity of 5.36 heights per second. But was he faster than Flo-Jo at the 100 meters? You probably have guessed the biomechanical answer. Joyner, who was 5 feet 6½ inches tall, ran the 100-meter dash in 10.49 seconds and thus had a relative velocity of 5.64 heights per second. "In other words," says Hudson exultantly, "the fastest woman is 5.3 percent faster than the fastest man!"

> ***20. In Your Journal:*** Jackie Hudson poses the question: "Who, and what, is being compared?" What does Hudson suggest **should be** compared? What is actually being compared?

What about men's vaunted upper body strength and relatively wider shoulders? Would they be better equipped for an upper body sport such as swimming? Not necessarily. Hudson compares Janet Evans, a 5-foot-5-inch women's world record holder with 15:52.1 minutes in the 1,500-meter freestyle, with Vladimir Salnikov, the 5-foot-11-inch men's record holder with 14:54.76 minutes. When a biomechanical assessment is made, Hudson shows us, Evans's velocity is .949 heights per second and Salnikov's is .926 heights per second, a difference of 2.5 percent in favor of Evans. (Let's hear it for fancy math.) When measurements are made in absolute terms, the males are faster. However, when these fairer biomechanical measurements, which take into account an individual's size, are made, the physical abilities of elite-level females appear to be equal, and sometimes superior, to those of elite-level males.

> ***21. In Your Journal:*** Hudson poses mathematics and science as weapons to challenge past ideologies. Do you find her research convincing? Why or why not? How does it differ from past methods of comparing male and female athletes?

What happens, skeptics may wonder, when the base of comparison is broadened? When fifty-seven women and seventy men who swam the 100-meter freestyle in the 1988 Olympics were compared inch for inch, the men were 2.1 percent faster. This difference appears to support the hypothesis that swimming, because it's an upper body sport, favors men. However, other characteristics of the contestants are relevant: age is significantly related to velocity, and the men were 2.8 years older. Might the women reduce the velocity differential with 2.8 more years of training? That is an unanswered but tantalizing question.

But surely males have *some* physical advantages. Well, yes, but females have their advantages, too. On average, men can carry and use more oxygen. They tend to be heavier—an advantage in football—and taller: handy in basketball and volleyball. Men have more lean muscle mass, convenient in sports requiring explosive power. Less muscle-bound, women generally have greater flexibility, useful in gymnastics, diving, and skating. Their lower center of gravity helps in hockey, golf, tennis, baseball, and even basketball. Women sweat better (less dripping, therefore better evaporation), which is critical, since bodies need to remain cool to function efficiently. A physiologist at the University of Virginia tested athletes under various conditions of heat, humidity, exercise, and nutritional intake and concluded that women are better able to adjust to environmental changes. "In every case, females were better able to handle the stress," she says.

> ***22. In Your Journal:*** What does the comparison of male and female physical advantages suggest about the way we generally assess "physical ability" in our culture? Do we use balanced enough criteria?

You might be wondering whether closing the strength gap is something only elite female athletes are capable of. Significantly, the difference between elite and ordinary female athletes is greater than it is between elite and ordinary male athletes. As an example, the *average* female eighteen-year-old needs 10 minutes, 51 seconds, to run a mile, whereas the women's world record holder needs just 39 percent of that time (4:15). By contrast, the male champion completes the mile in about half (49 percent) the time taken by the average male eighteen-year-old (7:35). Young women, then, are farther from their athletic potential than young men.

Much of the gap has to do with predictable differences in level of skill. Jackie Hudson's research found that when novice, intermediate/advanced, and elite college women basketball players were compared on free-throw-shooting technique, for example, the novice players were more likely to use restricted—or partially "frozen"—range of motion and to veer off balance. She deduced that the limited range of motion may have been a function of the instability, and that improving balance might be a goal for players in the *novice phase*. At the *intermediate/advanced phase* of skill development, reduced range of motion correlated with missed shots. This led Hudson to speculate that tasks for improving range of motion might be a general goal for players in the intermediate learning phase.

Analyzing jumping in men and women, researchers tested military trainees on the task of maximal vertical jumping while carrying a rifle and wearing an eighty-pound backpack. The women and men differed significantly in three ways: the men jumped higher, took longer to jump, and created greater forces against the ground in preparing to jump. From this the researchers concluded that the men were "better performers" than the women. Yet biomechanics experts like Jackie Hudson will tell you that the differences in jump scores probably would have been insignificant if the trainees' heights had been taken into consideration. And taking longer to jump is a characteristic of poor performance, she points out. Also interesting, the trainees' performance declined when subjects were wearing the eighty-pound pack as opposed to no pack, and the decline was similar for both 135-pound women and 160-pound men.

Most comparisons of male and female strength are crudely determined and misleading, and these are what we're most likely to hear about. We hear, for example, how a woman's hand span is too small for single-hand gripping of a fire hose (the reason given by the New York Fire Department for the small number of female firefighters it hires), but we don't hear that grip strengthening can compensate for the size difference. The New York Fire Department has recently offered a training program for women to strengthen their physical skills before taking the firefighter's test. In the most recent test the women who didn't make the grade were also the women who hadn't taken the training program. Apparently word isn't out yet on the degree of difference two months of three training sessions a week can make.

23. In Your Journal: Why does Dowling discuss the updated training programs for the New York Fire Department? What point is she trying to make?

What does all this mean for women? It's the importance of the training effect again. What biomechanical models do is break down skill problems into precise units with clear-cut techniques for correcting them. As the performance mystique is penetrated by more sophisticated assessment tools, it becomes clearer not only what is required for better performance, but that the potential for improvement has nothing to do with gender and everything to do with know-how.

THE BACKLASH

With women around the world developing physical intelligence, using strength to justify a power difference between genders is on its way to becoming history. Just as we're uncovering historical evidence of women whose physical feats had been lost to us, so, now, are we gaining scientific evidence that women are no more physiologically frail than men. The breaking through of this information, with all its unsettling implications, has brought crashing down the boom of male backlash. As Susan Faludi so solidly nailed it in her Pulitzer Prize–winning book, *Backlash,* the negative reaction to women's progress is a recurring phenomenon. Its chilling effect can be counted on whenever women appear to be making another leap toward equality.

Virtually everyone involved in the forward movement of women's sport has been subjected to male hostility. Sometimes the backlash is personal, sometimes institutional. Sometimes it is ridiculous in its effect, sometimes devastating. But this much can be said without risk of rebuttal: Men don't like women's bold new intrusion into the **insular,** comforting, historically antifemale world of sport. As Faludi wrote, backlash is triggered not by women's achieving full equality but by their demonstrations of an increased possibility of doing so. "It is a **preemptive** strike," she writes, and it "stops women long before they reach the finish line."

insular: detached; standing alone; isolated

preemptive: taken as a measure against something possible, anticipated, or feared; preventive

Even women once removed in the fight for the right to play—not the players themselves but those who write about the players—have been punished for their **temerity,** especially if they were writing about men. Jeannie Roberts, a Florida sportswriter, recalls entering male locker rooms in the early 1970s: "I had things like jockstraps 'accidentally' thrown at me . . . and my fellow reporters would pretend that they didn't see a thing." A male fraternity of sportswriters felt too "embarrassed," Roberts says, "to show any kind of support for female reporters." Empathy was "a sign of weakness." To show any allegiance at all was to become "a traitor to the fraternity."

temerity: reckless boldness; rashness

Only a dozen or so women sportswriters had broken into the coverage of men's sports when Time Inc. sued to allow *Sports Illustrated* reporter Melissa Ludtke to enter the New York Yankees clubhouse—the first time a woman had breached this **hermetically** sealed bubble of masculine sweat and self-aggrandizement. It was 1978. Certainly getting into the clubhouse, or locker room, or any other fortress of male exclusivity had never been pleasant for the women pioneering the break-ins, but in the

hermetically: so as to be airtight

arena of sport, the very physicality of the atmosphere heightened the men's hostility. And the hostility didn't abate with time. In September 1990 Lisa Olson, a sports reporter for the *Boston Herald* whose regular beat was football, was sexually harassed in the New England Patriots locker room. Zeke Mowatt shook his genitals at her while making lewd remarks. Team members watched and cheered. Management took no action.

Supported by her peers, Olson launched a protest. The owner of the team, Victor Kiam, ignored it all until media attention convinced him the public was taking the incident seriously. Eventually, Kiam sent Olson an apology, but the smarm continued. Four months later Kiam found himself in the indefensible position of having to apologize once again—this time for having made a sexist joke about the reporter at a Patriots banquet.

Olson, in the meantime, was receiving threats and harassing phone calls. The incident in the Patriots locker room had apparently touched a chord, and the reaction was widespread and venomous. Inflatable "Lisa" dolls were sold outside Foxboro Stadium, and male fans amused themselves by engaging the dolls in "lewd and suggestive acts." This jolly romp spread to other venues. In Fenway Park the following year, male spectators at a baseball game tossed plastic, life-size female blowup dolls from spectator to spectator. It was a gang-bang atmosphere. "Yeah, yeah, do her!" men yelled, fists punching the air. Reporter Bella English wrote, "They were touching her breasts. . . . They threw her around to each other. These are grown men we're talking about. It was disgusting. It was like an advertisement for rape."

24. In Your Journal: Paraphrase the reaction to the Olson affair. What does the treatment of women sports reporters reveal about general sexism in sports?

Reports of harassment of female sportswriters mounted: a football player running a razor up a woman's leg; another player sending a female sportswriter a rat in a pink box; the hurling of jockstraps and obscenities at women writers as they tried to get the after-game story—as any male sportswriter would do—in the locker room. There were those in the world of sport, like Frank Deford (six times named Sportswriter of the Year), who tried to explain away the hostility toward women. "It's not a matter of . . . breaking into a profession," he said. "It's a matter of breaking down a culture, and that is eminently harder to do. We [men] think we need you for procreation and recreation, but we don't need you for sports."

25. In Your Journal: Do Frank Deford's comments reveal him as critical of or sympathetic towards women in sports?

Nowhere is **misogyny** more blatantly on display than in male rugby culture, where, postgame, men sing songs depicting women as "loathsome creatures with insatiable sexual appetites and dangerous sexual organs." They talk about raping other men's girlfriends and mothers, sociologist-anthropologist Steven P. Schacht informed a meeting of the North American Society for the Sociology of Sport. In a presentation on the misogyny that flourishes in rugby culture, Schacht described witnessing a coach telling a player, "Fuck you, you pussy. Just shut the fuck up, or I'll bend you over [and] fuck ya like a bitch." Code terms for plays included "Fucked your mother"; "Your mother's a cunt"; "Gang-banged your girlfriend"; and "Suck my dick."

misogyny: hatred, dislike, or mistrust of women

26. In Your Journal: Do you agree that the misogyny described in rugby culture is a "reflection of society's attitude in general" about women?

seamy: unpleasant or sordid

"There is a **seamy** side to sport that involves inequality, oppression, discrimination, scandal, deviant behavior, and violence," write the authors of a book on the sociology of sport. "For many years this seamy side of sport remained hidden." The seaminess came out in the open as women's inroads into male sport cut deeper. The misogyny of the sort Schacht describes in rugby culture isn't an encapsulated instance of violence and hatred; it is a reflection of society's attitude in general. Athletic skill *is* masculinity, as far as men are concerned. Nor is it only the strongest, most aggressive female athletes who create a threat. For what they can do, others can obviously do if they put in the training effort. "All of us, collectively, are a threat," wrote basketball coach Mariah Burton Nelson. "A threat to male privilege and to masculinity as defined through manly sports."

THE ESTROGEN EFFECT

In the nineteenth century anatomists believed that one's sex was not limited to one's reproductive organs, but affected every part of the body. The skeleton itself was thought to prove woman's inferiority, particularly her smaller (and thus, presumably, less intellectually capable) cranium. By the end of the nineteenth century female and male bodies were virtually understood as opposites, each having different organs, different functions, and even different feelings.

In the 1920s and 1930s, the discovery of the hormones estrogen and testosterone added a new dimension to medicine's beliefs about sexual differences. The findings of endocrinology seemed profoundly to validate male-female polarity. Estrogen and testosterone (which today are no longer viewed as "sex" hormones, both being necessary to the health and functioning of males *and* females) became the new scientific bedrock of the view of women as soft and weak and men as tough and strong. In the popular imagination hormones almost replaced genitals as the signifiers of sex. This endocrinologic view of male and female persisted all the way to the year 2000.

Women are "the disadvantaged gender." You think no one would have the nerve to say that anymore? Not so. It was the entire point of an article on the glories of testosterone, "The He Hormone," published in *The New York Times Magazine.* Its author, Andrew Sullivan, spelled out with damning certainty the biological deficiencies limiting women from ever making it—in the electorate, in the military, and even in venture capitalism. They just don't have the ***cojones.***

cojones: testicles; in slang, courage

27. In Your Journal: What do the definitions of ***cojones*** suggest about the way society defines men? What do they suggest about the way we define courage?

Since the hormone was discovered in the male testicle in the 1930s (it was subsequently discovered in the female ovary and adrenals), testosterone has been falsely equated with greater male aggression in humans (the literature doesn't support this theory), greater assertiveness, and even clearer thinking. Historically, such luminously "male" qualities have been used as the rationale for job discrimination in every imaginable field, from construction work to firefighting to tenure-track college teaching.

What a stunning throwback to centuries-old, presumably medical, misogyny Sullivan's highly controversial article was! The bandying of testosterone to perpetuate discrimination against women, as we enter the twenty-first century, is no more scientifically justified than was late-nineteenth-century medicine's advice to women to refrain from physical and mental work so that they could preserve their limited energies for childbirth. Female physical frailty is not a reality but a myth with an agenda.

The long-standing perception that women are "the weaker sex" continues to affect women's attitudes toward sport and physical activity. But this is changing as the extraordinary breakthroughs of elite-level women athletes shatter the remnants of the frailty myth. Consider, as one dramatic example, Sweden's Ludmila Engquist, the thirty-two-year-old runner who won the gold medal in the 100-meter hurdles in the 1996 Summer Olympic Games in Atlanta and then, in the spring of 1999, went on to face the greatest trial of her life so far. In March of that year she discovered a lump in her breast. In April she had a mastectomy. In May she began chemotherapy. But then, stunningly, after the fourth of her six scheduled chemo sessions, she was back in action, competing at a track meet! When her name was announced as she stood behind the starting blocks, the other racers clapped. Finishing that race would have been triumph enough, but lo! she won it—won it in 12.68 seconds, shaving 18/100 of a second off her Olympic gold medal time.

Ludmila's physician, Dr. Arne Ljungqvist, vice president of the International Amateur Athletic Federation and head of the cancer foundation in Sweden, explained that the athlete's strength had been a bonus in the healing process. Engquist didn't let enough time pass to lose muscle. Five days after surgery she was using small weights; a month after, she was doing clean-and-jerk exercises with over 120 pounds of weight. She continued training throughout the balance of her chemotherapy.

> ***28. In Your Journal:*** The story of Ludmila Enquist shows that bodily strength is not the only form of strength needed to succeed in sports. How does this example help or hurt Dowling's main claim that women may indeed be capable of the same physical strength as men, if that strength is properly measured?

Farewell to the cult of female invalidism. Yes, many men have more lean muscle mass than women—owing, in part, to their having more testosterone—but women have physical advantages that come from having more estrogen. Recent studies suggest that the hormone long associated with women's reproductive functioning buffers them against muscle soreness after exercise. Soreness results from microtears in muscle tissue. "The animal data are very clear," says Dr. Priscilla Clarkson, an exercise physiologist at the University of Massachusetts at Amherst. Male rats show much more muscle damage, post-exercise, than female rats. "Estrogen seems to explain the difference." When male rats were given estrogen, they sustained less muscle damage. It's not clear yet how estrogen does its protecting, but Clarkson speculates that the hormone "may be able to insert itself into cells, like muscle membranes, and stabilize them, which would protect them from tearing."

The sex difference in muscle soreness may help explain why women can endure longer exercise sessions than men. "Women may accumulate less damage over the course of the long event, which would enable them to perform better," one physiologist suggests.

New hormone research challenges the traditional view of osteoporosis as a "women's" disease linked to menopause. Of the 10 million Americans who have osteoporosis, more than 1.5 million are men, and 1 in 8 men over fifty will suffer an osteoporosis-related fracture. In an ironic reverse of the frailty myth, osteoporosis is actually far more prevalent in men than had previously been thought. Medical textbooks used to describe osteoporosis in men as the result of low testosterone levels caused by hypogonadism; a quite rare phenomenon. But new studies show that estrogen is the more central player in men's osteoporosis. In Framingham, Massachusetts, researchers studied 385 elderly men for eight years, tracking both their bone density and their estrogen levels. The correlation was startling: Men with the best bones had the highest estrogen levels. The connection between **hypogonadism** and low bone density in men was in fact negligible. "This is surprising," said Dr. B. Lawrence Riggs, a professor of medical research at the Mayo Clinic in Rochester, Minnesota, who found that estrogen naturally falls in men after about age sixty-five. "Three years ago none of us would have thought estrogen loss was a factor in male osteoporosis."

hypogonadism: condition of having an underdeveloped reproductive gland

29. In Your Journal: What is ironic about the presence of estrogen in male and female athletes?

Historically, men's reproductive capacity has never been suspected of being compromised by physical exertion, but that idea is being shattered by modern science. (Medicine giveth, and medicine taketh away.) A recent study, for example, found that sperm count was lowered in men following long-distance racing. And as endocrinology advances, we are beginning to find that the precious "sex hormones" sometimes provide advantages for the *opposite* sex. For example, androgen (testosterone) *enhances spatial ability in women but inhibits it in men,* according to a fascinating study published in *Perceptual Motor Skills* in 1998. Researchers tested spatial abilities (visualization and orientation) in 150 men and 150 women collegiate athletes in different varsity sports. Across the board, women scored significantly higher than men in their ability to visualize and orient, but in basketball their superior spatial capacities were off the charts.

It is no coincidence that the great jaws of sex discrimination clamp down at particular moments in history. At the turn of the nineteenth century, changes in work and family, urbanization, and the increasing female domination of public schools created a crisis of masculinity that led to the cults of the "he-man" and the invalided woman. At the turn of the twenty-first century, women's growing physical competence in every conceivable sport from soccer to rock climbing has apparently produced another crisis in masculinity. Now, suddenly, we are hearing about testosterone again, as if it were the magic potion conferring kingship on men.

The "cult of invalidism" dogged women throughout the entire twentieth century as they tried to get into the Olympics, to be allowed to run races longer than 400 meters, to get into contact sports (finally girls by the thousands in this country are playing ice hockey and contact football), and even to get into Little League. Talk about a masculinity crisis. But now women's advances in elite-level athletics are challenging the entire concept of significant strength differences between the genders, wrecking any justification for male dominion. Men are not better equipped to deal with life's slings and arrows because they are stronger. Nor are they required to protect women because women are weaker. The argument for the whole social structure—men stronger, women weaker; men in charge, women their subservient helpmates—collapses as the strength gap between males and females closes. Testosterone, however mistakenly, appears to men to be the final saving grace. This is precisely why "We have more than you do" has once again become men's plaintive schoolyard cry.

30. In Your Journal: What does Dowling mean by the "cult of invalidism"?

THE NEW PHYSICAL WOMAN

In New York City there's an outdoor basketball court on the corner of West Fourth Street and Sixth Avenue that's been there for years. It's called "the Cage." Men slam into one another in the Cage every day of the year. In the summer of 1999 a girl walked into the Cage one day. Natasha Green, a high school basketball star, had taken the subway down from the Bronx to try out her skills against the men and boys. Sixteen years old and five feet nine, Natasha jumped right in. "She stayed with her man as he tried to switch directions and drive to the basket," said a newspaper reporter, Chris Ballard, who happened to catch her act. "Reaching out her hand, she poked the ball loose as he headed by"—"stripping him clean," as the expression goes. She turned, took five hard dribbles, and charged back to the basket for a layup. Hoots and whistles of appreciation came from a couple of fence-hanging spectators who weren't used to seeing a woman hold her own on the blacktop, much less at this particular spot, the most revered of all for pickup basketball in Manhattan.

Guys "playing her like a guy" is the supreme compliment a female player can receive, Natasha told Ballard. It's not because she wants to be like a guy, but because she wants to improve her game. "Coming out here is how I get better," she says. "So if a guy's not going to play me hard, I'd rather he not even play."

Women's attitudes change when they push themselves athletically. Nicola Thost of Germany represents a new breed of female snowboarders, "going bigger" than ever before. At nineteen she brought a gold medal home from the 1998 Olympics in Nagano. She's so extreme in her moves, spectators often mistake her for a boy. "It's a pleasure to see other girls improving so much: like Shannon Dunn with a 720 and so many girls with a good, clean McTwist," she says. "We have to push the limits all the time."

It's a matter of understanding the particular challenges of any given sport. With snowboarding, it's important to get height. You have to be strong, but strong isn't the whole game. As Nicola says, some of the guys who snowboard are "so tiny, so muscular. It's clear it's technique."

Technique and attitude. "You must get in your mind that you can do it." Nicola says she has no "scary feelings." Fear plays no part in it for her. "I just take speed, and don't speed-check, and then just see how high I can go. It's such a good feeling to go big. If you think, Oh, my gosh, I can't fall hard, I'm afraid I'll injure myself, then it's already too late."

Overcoming the fear of falling is a challenge for today's woman, just as overcoming the "fear of flying"—the fear of risk and adventure—was something for Erica Jong's generation of overly protected females to overcome. A best-selling book in the 1970s, *Fear of Flying* celebrated *emotional* risk taking and sexual adventure for women. Today it's fear of *physical* risk taking that women have come to see is holding them back. They want the courage to go the distance, to raise their sights past what they'd thought they were capable of. Modeling this so dramatically are the exploits of elite women athletes, women who started out with ordinary skills but kept pushing. In doing so—although this was rarely if ever the intent—they began seriously challenging the concept of male physical superiority.

GOING THE DISTANCE

"In 1967 people thought women couldn't do long runs. It wasn't supposed to be 'feminine,' " says Katherine Switzer, the woman who opened the gateway to women's phenomenal success in long-distance sports. That year an irate official had tried to pull Switzer out of the then all-male Boston Marathon. She dodged him and kept running, becoming the first woman to officially complete the race. Her run made headlines, the twenty-year-old college student made history, and women's competitive running took off. Switzer would be the one to push women's distance running all the way to the Olympics. In 1974 she won the women's division of the New York Marathon, then went on to launch a series of international races that led to the establishment of the first women's Olympic marathon, in the 1984 Summer Games. Now in her fifties, Switzer brings the message of running to women of all ages via her work promoting the Avon races. She's inspired by her own mother, Ruth Rothfarb, who began walking to recover from heart surgery at age seventy-two and completed her first marathon at eighty-one.

Some of the elite women athletes' most compelling advances have been in swimming. In marathon and long-distance cold-water swims, women usually outswim the men. In 1995 Australian champion Shelley Taylor-Smith set the record for both men and women when she swam around Manhattan in 5 hours, 45 minutes, 26 seconds. In 1998 she did it again, this time pulling ahead to win after she'd dropped half a mile behind two male swimmers. "I call it 'catching up with the boys,' " she said.

31. In Your Journal: Is there any hidden meaning in Shelley Taylor-Smith's phrase, "catching up with the boys"?

Seana Hogan recently cycled the four hundred miles from San Francisco to Los Angeles in 19 hours, 49 minutes, breaking the previous men's record by almost an hour. Helen Klein's world-record distance in a twenty-four-hour race—109.5 miles—exceeds the best distance for an American man in her age group, which was sixty-five to sixty-nine.

The phenomenon of the older woman athlete is one of the more amazing aspects of the shattering of the frailty myth. If women keep training, they can retain endurance capabilities into late life. I am thinking in particular of a woman who looks forward each year to participating in the Avon Running Global Women's Circuit. In the summer of 1998 Mary Hanes was eighty-three and preparing to run in Connecticut, in the Hartford 10K, when I heard her story. She'd started running fifteen years earlier, at the age of sixty-five. "I lost twenty-two pounds when I started and have kept it off," says Hanes, who also plays tennis and basketball and throws javelin. "Once you get going, you'd be amazed at what you can do."

Today, results of medical studies are encouraging to the woman who wants to keep moving no matter what her age. A study in *The New England Journal of Medicine* found that walking/strolling just two miles a day cuts the risk of death almost in half for people in their sixties, seventies, and eighties. A 1995 Harvard Medical School study noted a 40 percent reduction in the risk of heart disease for women who exercise.

As amazing as the marathoning octogenarians, on the other end of the age spectrum are the football-playing girls. Girls began playing football in the late 1980s and by the 1990s had graduated to *tackle* football, all padded up and helmeted, playing on their high school football teams with and against boys their own age. As the century turned, a sixth-grader in New Orleans who'd been playing tackle football for five years became the first girl to play on the all-star team in her parish. Her coach says she's one of the best offensive players he's ever worked with.

32. In Your Journal: Note the attitude of the coach of the New Orleans girl who played on a football all-star team. How does it contrast with those of the soccer fathers and coaches of years back?

It's not just tokenism, either. At Lincoln High School in Los Angeles, four girls play on the football team. One of them, in the fall of 1999, was a finalist for homecoming queen. "The world as we knew it has changed forever," said *Time* magazine, reporting the girl's double accomplishment. In 1998 there were 708 girls playing high school football, according to the National Federation of State High School Associations.

33. In Your Journal: Why does Dowling include the story about the Lincoln High School girl who plays football and is elected homecoming queen?

Efforts are under way to launch a professional tackle football league for women. In December 1999 the New York Sharks played an exhibition game with the Minnesota Vixens. "This is a dream come true for all of us," said lawyer Lyn Lewis, who plays offensive tackle for the Sharks. "I grew up playing football with the guys. Then when you got to a certain age you couldn't play anything organized. . . . Out of all the major sports, this is the last one that brought women to its playground."

Women, there is no doubt about it, are going the distance. America's women's ice hockey team made its Olympic debut in 1998—and won the gold its first time out! "These were warriors, hard-charging competitors who came to win, not just play," said *The New York Times,* describing the 1998 Olympic women's ice hockey team. The social implications of the win were not lost on the sports world. Said Tara Mounsey's hockey coach, "This is the final public knell of the artificial construct of what is masculine and feminine in sports."

It's apparent that no one foresaw the radical changes Title IX would lead to—that girls were not only going to catch up with boys, but in some sports they would even surpass them. That in the process they would flood the gyms and athletic fields. Not only would they enter the competition, they would take on the most challenging and aggressive sports. By the end of the century they would be playing football, ice hockey, and rugby—and would be starting these sports at younger and younger ages. Even preschool girls were learning contact sports—ice hockey, for example—spurred on by fathers and brothers.

By century's end the excitement over competition, team sports, and personal best had become thoroughly contagious. Two million girls were playing soccer. Sixteen million women were playing softball. The breakthroughs of young females were carrying over into the lives of older women—mothers, aunts, grandmothers. As female athletics became huge in the television ratings, the effect on the rest of us was like the blowing of the whistle at the beginning of the game. Suddenly, it seemed, sixty- and seventy-year-olds were in-line skating. The young were rock climbing and challenging themselves with wilderness expeditions. Teenagers—even *pre*teenagers—were excelling at "extreme" sports: aggressive skating, half-pipe snowboarding, skateboarding. Females of all ages had discovered that they no longer had to hold themselves back.

It is now, as we've entered a new millennium, that we are finally seeing the truth: Women don't have to restrict themselves physically because of being mothers. Not only can they handle the rigors of elite-level sport, they can manage their children while they're doing it. Thirteen members of the WNBA are mothers, many taking their children along with them, and nannies and grandmothers to help, as they travel around the world. They were upset, in the spring of 1999, when Pamela McGee, who'd played the previous season for the Los Angeles Sparks, lost custody of her three-year-old daughter after her former husband said she had missed several scheduled visits with her child. In court the husband's lawyer argued that McGee's basketball career interfered with her parenting. Forced to choose between child and career, McGee retired. "Being a professional woman, in the spotlight, making good money, would put a strain on any relationship," she said. "Then with the travel. A lot of people can't handle that."

> ***34. In Your Journal:*** Do you think a male athlete in Pamela McGee's shoes would have to give up his career because of child custody issues? Why or why not?

Fortunately not all husbands squelch their wives' athletic ambitions. Suzie McConnell Serio had four children ranging in age from one to seven when she decided to reenter the competitive world of sport she'd left six years earlier. An Olympic gold medalist in 1988, she had dropped out in 1991 to raise a family. It was her husband, Peter, who looked at her one day in the summer of 1997, while the two were watching women basketball players on TV in their Pittsburgh home, and said, "You're as good as they are." She was nursing her newborn fourth at the time. "You should think about playing next year."

Ten months later she was back in the WNBA, playing for the Cleveland Rockers. It was fun; she was excited; she hadn't realized how much she missed it. In August of 1998 she was the WNBA's player of the week, having played thirty-six minutes in one game, taken five shots, and become her team's most indispensable player. Her husband, a coach of high school girls, was proud. He saw his wife as a leader.

Players for the WNBA are rarely away from home more than several days at a time, so those who are moms can generally manage their time spent as mothers and as athletes. It doesn't work that way for soccer players. Joy Fawcett and Carla Overbeck are basically gone on a six-month road trip, except for a week's break each month, while they prepare for the World Cup. So the kids go with them. "Breast-feeding at halftime, or on the sideline, that can get interesting," Fawcett told a reporter. "It's like, 'I'll be back in a minute.' "

Fawcett has two daughters, three and six, Katey and Carli. When Carli was born in 1997, Fawcett was coaching the USLA women's soccer team, commuting two hours each way from her home in Orange County, California, and also coaching a youth team—all while playing on a national team herself. Overbeck, who is thirty-two, was running stadium steps through her ninth month of pregnancy to stay fit. She lifted weights the day she delivered her son, Jackson, now three.

The women's team travels with a load of equipment, from car seats to strollers and diaper bags. They have a nanny who gets paid $750 a week—by the U.S. Soccer Federation! But soccer-playing women traveling with their kids are still a rarity. Japanese women who came to the U.S. tune-up for the World Cup seemed "wistful" to find that Overbeck and Fawcett could continue their careers after becoming mothers. An American who played professionally in Japan for a year says that Japanese women quit the sport once they marry. "Seeing our players doing it as mothers gives them hope that they may be able to do it, too."

Greg Overbeck, who stays home in Chapel Hill, North Carolina, tries to see his son every two weeks. "It's tough, it's hard, but I understand why we go through it, and I totally support what Carla is doing," he said. "To see how far they've come is amazing. Before the 1991 World Cup, they didn't get paid, there was no insurance, no exposure, no endorsements. Not enough to make a living at it. Carla worked at an elementary school."

> ***35. In Your Journal:*** What are the examples of WNBA and women's soccer players integrating motherhood into their athletic careers meant to illustrate?

Overbeck sees it as a triumph—physical, emotional, professional—for his wife, for her teammates, and for all women. To him the women are heroes: "They had sacrificed relationships and career, put everything on hold, then they reached the pinnacle. . . . It's great for women."

"In the beginning, I questioned whether this [life] was good for the kids," says Fawcett. She'd talked to other moms whose kids eat and sleep on a regular schedule. "My kids eat when they can, sleep in the stroller. But they're adaptable. Things don't bother them too much. I think it's good. They get to see the world, and it allows me to play soccer."

> ***36. In Your Journal:*** Summarize the major changes that have occurred in the treatment of women athletes. Has the strength gap been closed? Why or why not?

> ***37. In Your Journal:*** How does having independence "from" something differ from the independence "to be" something? What does the difference mean in terms of female athletes and non-athletes?

Learning these stories about the personal lives of the World Cup mothers and their husbands and kids, and the even more challenging situation facing the players who are single moms, made me think once again: I never thought I would live to see this. It was exciting to see these women playing, unencumbered and free and beautiful, in the final game against China. But knowing their personal histories, their fight to do what they have done, to get the support they need from husbands and relatives and officials holding the purse strings, and to do it while traveling thousands of miles a year and sleeping in motels with their kids, was even more overwhelming. It brought me to tears.

The independence women are achieving today is not independence *from* anything, it is the independence to *be*. To lift huge loads. To run for miles. To defend themselves, ourselves, whether against sexual discrimination or sexual aggression. This, it turns out, has been the missing link in women's emancipation. Physically they are now able to occupy their full stature, to stand tall, chest open, and face the world.

FOR USE IN DISCUSSION

Questions about Substance

1. What are the requirements given for the "ideal feminine physique" (205) in bodybuilding? Do these requirements make sense in the context of bodybuilding? Is there anything ironic about the fact that females lose points for such things as stretch marks, surgical scars and cellulite?
2. Dowling says fashion magazines lag behind women's sports magazine in terms of representing strong women. What is the goal of a fashion magazine? Should the images of women in a fashion magazine necessarily evoke strength?
3. Why is homophobia a major motivator in attitudes toward women athletes? How do you think this would affect female athletes who are, in fact, lesbians?
4. When Babe Didrikson got married, her "achievement" of femininity" (209) seemed to displace her athletic accomplishments. Do you think the public still wants to see female athletes in love with or married to men before it can feel comfortable with them?

5. Susan Faludi argues that gender backlash happens not when women achieve some kind of equality, but when they are on the verge of that achievement (214). Does this make sense to you? What do you think happens after an actual achievement?
6. Consider the amount of pain and bodily stress involved in pregnancy, and the amount of endurance and strength carrying a child for nine months and then giving birth requires. Many women athletes have given birth more than once, even three or four times. Does it make sense to state that women are not strong enough to participate in sports because they need to save their "limited energies" for childbirth? Why was this idea so apparently convincing in the past?
7. Note the change in the attitude of sportswriters toward female athletes as shown by the article on the United States Women's Olympic hockey team (202). How do you suppose nationalism plays a part in this shift?

Questions about Structure and Style

1. Dowling begins to shift away from the sports-related physical aspects of female athletes to examining more psychological obstacles (214). Do you think this shift in her focus mirrors any historical shifts? How would the essay be different if the issues were presented in reverse order?
2. Why does Dowling describe her upbringing in her introduction to this topic? How does Dowling's anecdotal introduction relate to the thesis she begins to develop thereafter?
3. "Historically men have been able to disempower and subordinate women, use their labor, influence their thoughts, and secure their cooperation mainly because of the power they have over women's bodies" (205). What stylistic effect are the verbs in this first sentence meant to have on the reader?
4. Why would "machine-like" be used as a synonym for masculine (208)? Is it meant to present positive or negative connotation of the word masculine?
5. Why does Dowling include the discussion of "young women being farther from their athletic potential than young men" (213)? Does this help or hinder her argument? How?
6. To Natasha Green, "playing her like a guy" (219) is a compliment. How does this quote complicate Dowling's argument? Why does Dowling include it?

Multimedia Suggestions

1. Compare the Web site of Anna Kournikova (at *http://www.kournikova.com*) to that of the Women's Tennis Association (at *http://www.wtatour.com/*). Describe the kinds of photos, stories, and other links available on each site. Why do you think a professional tennis player with a relatively low ranking has her own official Web site? How many of the top ten players on the women's tour have their own Web sites?
2. In December 2002, *Sports Illustrated for Women* had to fold for financial reasons. The "Swimsuit Edition" of *Sports Illustrated*, however, continues to be a

bestseller (admirers can even get a special DVD supplement now) and *Esquire* features "sexy women athletes" frequently. How do you think sports coverage of women will change in the next five to ten years? Are the current trends indicative of future coverage?

3. Compare and contrast *Pumping Iron* (1976) (largely about Arnold Schwartzenegger) with *Pumping Iron II* (1984), which Dowling discusses in this essay. Discuss the ways the athletes themselves talk about their sport, then examine the ways the filmmakers reveal their opinions about the athletes.

SUGGESTIONS FOR WRITING AND RESEARCH

1. What is Dowling's argument? What do you think she hopes to accomplish by making this argument? Is it persuasive, in your opinion? Does she provide enough evidence to support her claims? Explain your assessment.
2. Recent studies show that neither men nor women sports fans want to read articles about sports that focus on the attractiveness of the athletes more than their skill. So why do you think the media insist on emphasizing the looks of women athletes who are attractive (e.g., Anna Kournikova, Gabrielle Reese, Lisa Leslie, etc.)? Pick up some sports magazines that feature stories about women athletes, and analyze the articles using Dowling's perspective and vocabulary as a lens.
3. According to Dowling, culture clearly affects women athletes. How do you think women athletes affect culture? Write an essay that uses Dowling's discussion as well as examples of famous women athletes in response to this question.

WORKING WITH CLUSTERS

Cluster 2: Constructing and Corrupting the Feminine

Cluster 9: Bodies of Knowledge

Discipline: The Social Sciences

Rhetorical Mode: Compare and Contrast

"Postmodernism and Holocaust Denial"

by Robert Eaglestone

Robert Eaglestone teaches in the English Department at Royal Holloway, University of London. His scholarship spans many disciplines, including ethics, contemporary European philosophy, science, the Holocaust, archaeology and historiography. Eaglestone's publications include Ethical Criticism: Reading after Levinas, Doing English, *the monograph* Postmodernism and Holocaust Denial *(of which this selection is a large part), as well as numerous articles in* THES, Times Literary Supplement, The Independent *and* The Guardian. *He is also the Series Editor of* Routledge Critical Thinkers. *In 2001, he was awarded a Leverhulme Research Fellowship to research the relationship between the Holocaust and Postmodernism.*

INTRODUCTION: TRIALS AND GENRES

> The charges which I have found to be substantially true include the charges that Irving has for his own ideological reasons persistently and deliberately misrepresented and manipulated historical evidence; that for the same reasons he has portrayed Hitler in an unwarrantedly favourable light, principally in relation to his attitude towards and responsibility for the treatment of the Jews; that he is an active Holocaust denier; that he is anti-Semitic and racist and that he associates with right wing extremists who promote neo-Nazism.
>
> (*Judgement,* 13.167)[1]

1. In Your Journal: Eaglestone's essay begins with an excerpt from the final judgment in the libel case with which his essay is concerned. For what discussion does this excerpt prepare the reader?

Accuracy and clarity are important for all intellectual discussions. Discussions about the Holocaust, whether historical or philosophical, are no exception. The constellation of ideas described as **postmodernism** is often accused of being neither accurate nor clear. So, in order to anchor this discussion of postmodernism and Holocaust denial, I am going to concentrate on one particular, concrete, high-profile incident.

postmodernism: broad term with many definitions, but used here to signify a literary movement that questions the assumptions underlying many of the "truths" upon which Western culture has been built—particularly the possibility of pure objectivity

In the spring of 2000, the UK press was full of stories about a court case that ran from 11 January to 11 April: they called it 'The Irving Trial'. This name was inaccurate. Although trying 'to give the impression he was being sued and was the defendant in the case',[2] David Irving himself had brought libel charges against an American academic **Deborah Lipstadt** who had discussed him in her book *Denying the Holocaust: The Growing Assault on Truth and Memory.* If anyone, it was Lipstadt who was on trial. Irving argued that Lipstadt had 'vandalised [his] legitimacy as an historian' and had ruined his reputation by accusing him of being a Nazi apologist who distorted facts and manipulated documents. For Irving—and for the Judge, Mr. Justice Gray—the accusation that he was a bad historian was at the core of the case.

genre: category of artistic, musical, or literary composition characterized by a particular style, form, or content

The misnaming of the trial is one of its lessons: a postmodern lesson about types or, more technically, ***genres*** of writing and their rules. News is a genre—it needs a 'story'. Covering the trial, journalists followed the old

---

Deborah Lipstadt: Director of the Institute for Jewish Studies and Professor of Modern Jewish and Holocaust Studies at Emory University; author of *Denying the Holocaust: The Growing Assault on Truth and Memory*

adage: 'dog bites man, no story: man bites dog, story'. There's no story, no surprise, in 'Jewish American academic attacks anti-Semitic Holocaust deniers'. In contrast, 'non-Jewish English historian denies Holocaust' has 'reader appeal'. Combining this with his skilful milking of press attention—he 'loved being the star of the show he himself had set in motion in **Court 73** and revelled in the newspaper and television coverage'—the anti-Semitic and racist Irving got pages and pages of newsprint and airtime in the UK.[3] Photos of Irving, not Lipstadt, were on the front pages on the day after the judgement. Lipstadt didn't let Irving cross-examine her and turned down requests for interviews. With only a few exceptions, the press didn't bother explaining why she turned down interviews and spent hardly any time covering her arguments. Reading just the first page of *Denying the Holocaust* makes her reasons for both these decisions clear.

In other more important ways, the question of understanding and combating Holocaust denial is intimately tied up with ideas about genre and ideas about what history is. Outside the court, the issue raised questions about the role and scope of historians and the works of history they produce. As the newspapers said, but in a different sense, history was on trial here. And because the history under discussion was about the Holocaust, the event **Elie Wiesel** calls the 'black hole of history', it demanded to be approached seriously and soberly.[4]

Many who fight Holocaust denial, and many historians in general, put postmodernism, **deconstruction** or **'cultural relativism'** together and find them threatening. Some suggest that these sorts of ideas, in fact, lead to Holocaust denial. Sometimes, for example, they point to the fact that the German philosopher Martin Heidegger (1889–1976), an influence on postmodernism, was a Nazi. That Holocaust denial happens at all is often posited as a 'knockdown' argument against postmodernism. The authors of *Telling the Truth about History* argue that 'cultural relativism had reached its limits in the death camps' and so seem to be drawing a parallel between contemporary postmodern thinkers and the Nazis.[5] (Has any group been *less* culturally relativist than the Nazis?) Richard Evans, one of the most significant contemporary historians of Germany and the defence's chief expert at the trial, wrote that postmodernist history 'demeans the dead'.[6] Lipstadt herself, although she acknowledges that postmodernists are not deniers or sympathetic to deniers, argues that:

> [T]he 'climate' these sort[s] of ideas create is of no less importance than the specific truth they attack . . . It is a climate that

2. *In Your Journal:* How does the "man bites dog" adage apply to Eaglestone's subject?

Court 73: room in Britain's high court where the Irving/Lipstadt case took place; one of the high court's biggest rooms, chosen to accommodate the extensive public and media interest in the trial

deconstruction: act of literary analysis based on the view that meaning in language rests not on essential truths but on oppositions (something is one thing only because it is not another), and that there are multiple conflicting interpretations of every text

cultural relativism: view asserting that concepts of good and bad are relative to culture, and that "good" means what is "socially approved" by the majority in a given culture

3. *In Your Journal:* What does the author accomplish by making his point through a rhetorical question? What about the Nazis made them an extremely "culturally relativist" group?

Elie Wiesel: Jewish survivor of the Auschwitz and Buchenwald camps, Wiesel was born in 1928 in Sighet, Transylvania; after the war, he wrote his acclaimed memoir of the camps, *Night,* won the Nobel Peace Prize in 1986, and is now a professor of humanities, religion, and philosophy at Boston University

> fosters deconstructionist history at its worst. No fact, no event, and no aspect of history has any fixed meaning or content. Any truth can be retold. Any fact can be recast. There is no ultimate historical reality . . . Holocaust denial is part of this phenomenon.[7]

I want to argue that these accusations are, in the main, misplaced. Generally, I believe that postmodernism is a response to the Holocaust, questioning to its very core the culture that made it possible. But more than this, I want to argue here that the questions postmodernism asks of history and historians are very strong weapons in the fight against Holocaust denial. These questions are ways we can strip the masks of 'impartiality' and 'historical objectivity' from deniers to reveal denial for what it really is.

4. In Your Journal: How do you think "postmodernism is a response to the Holocaust," as Eaglestone asserts?

WHAT IS DENIAL?

Bluntly, Holocaust denial is the claim that the murder of approximately six million Jews in the Nazi genocide during the Second World War did not happen. Those who study denial attempt to divide deniers into 'hard' and 'soft' categories. 'Hard' deniers claim, for example, that the whole genocide is a hoax, concocted after the war. 'Soft' deniers claim, for example, that Jews were imprisoned in camps but died in limited numbers as a result of illness and other wartime deprivations, or that the genocide was not the result of a systematic Nazi policy, but the work of extremist Nazis elements (the idea of *extremist* Nazis—implying moderate Nazis—is an odd one, of course). However, these distinctions are rarely fixed, as they demand too much consistency from the world of bigotry and false argument that these people inhabit. Deniers find it hard to keep their stories straight and, when challenged, change their approaches, alter their theories and shift their emphasis. David Irving, for example, changed from a 'soft' denier to a 'hard' denier after reading a totally flawed and denier-motivated report on the gas chambers: a report that the distinguished Holocaust historian Robert Jan Van Pelt dismissed during the trial as 'scientific garbage' (see *Judgement,* 7.113–117). Van Pelt discusses and easily demolishes the changing stories and bizarre theories that have been offered by deniers about the **Auschwitz** gas chambers in his short book, *The Science of Holocaust Research and the Art of Holocaust Denial.*

5. In Your Journal: What is Eaglestone's point about "extremist Nazis"?

However, more or less all the deniers in Europe and North America have a number of things in common. First, they are always anti-Semitic. So much so, in fact, that Holocaust denial can most simply and clearly be un-

Auschwitz: Nazi Germany's largest concentration and extermination camp, located in southern Poland, where millions (mostly Jews but also Roma [Gypsies], Slavs, alleged mental "defectives," and others) were gassed to death derstood as a form of anti-Semitism: a post-war version of the forged anti-Semitic key text, ***The Protocols of the Elders of Zion.***[8] Second, these deniers almost always support **neo-fascist** parties or sects. They seem to believe that if the Holocaust is 'removed' from the equation, if the Nazis are acquitted, if fascism is exonerated of these terrible deeds, people will somehow find their murderous and evil creeds of hate convincing. Third, and I will return to this, European and North American deniers are almost always racist, believing in both racist categories (that is, that people are defined in their very being by a pseudoscientific, unhistorical and unhistoricised concept of race) and in the superiority of 'the Aryan race'. Finally, it is very hard to argue with deniers. Like all conspiracy theorists, they always find new ways of explaining away the consensus of historians. For them, denying the Holocaust is not like establishing a historical datum, like how many ships fought at the Battle of Trafalgar or how many women died in childbirth in New York in 1905. For them—the self-selected arch-doubters—the non-existence of the genocide is beyond question, like an article of faith. Denying the Holocaust is a cornerstone for their anti-Semitic, racist and fascist beliefs.

neo-fascist: contemporary supporter of fascist beliefs, supporting dictatorship, severe economic and social regimentation, and forcible governmental suppression of opposition

6. In Your Journal: Rephrase this point in your own words. What does a "pseudoscientific, unhistorical, and unhistoricised concept of race" mean?

In the last twenty years or so, deniers have developed new strategies to convey their message. Analysing the history of denial from its roots in pre-war anti-Semitism to the present day, Lipstadt's book is particularly acute about these changing strategies. Lipstadt explores in detail several of the different approaches deniers have taken. Deniers use tricks to get publicity. Here is one example, not covered by Lipstadt (although she does discuss this particular denier's other approaches). One denier wrote a book claiming that flying saucers were **Axis** secret weapons. In a phone conversation with Frank Miele who was writing a piece on Holocaust denial for *Skeptic* magazine, the denier revealed that this was simply a ruse:

Axis: of or relating to the three powers (Germany, Italy, and Japan) opposing the Allied nations in World War II

> I realised that North Americans were not interested in being educated. They want to be entertained. The book was for fun. With a picture of the Führer on the cover and flying saucers coming out of Antarctica it was a chance to get on radio and TV talk shows. For about 15 minutes of an hour program I'd talk about that **esoteric** stuff. Then . . . that was my chance to talk about what I wanted to talk about.[9]

7. In Your Journal: Describe the tone of the Holocaust denier's comments presented here.

The 'wacky' title gave him the chance to broadcast his anti-Semitic Holocaust denial on Network TV, with the tacit support of Network broadcasters, who might not give airtime to a more 'typical', upfront denier.

esoteric: of or relating to knowledge that is restricted to a small group

However, this sort of pretence is minor, compared to the real threat Lipstadt analyses. She points out that, in recent years, deniers have tried to

***The Protocols of the Elders of Zion*:** forged text, contrived around the turn of the 20th century by the Russian Czarist secret police to stir up anti-Semitism; supposedly documents plans by Jewish leaders to take over the world make their work look and sound like the work of professional historians engaged in an intellectual debate. To combat people like these, who she considers the main danger, Lipstadt writes that '*above all, it is essential to expose the illusion of reasoned inquiry that conceals their extremist view*'.[10] Lipstadt uses two broad 'pincers' to expose them. The first is to point out that the idea of a debate over the existence of the Holocaust is simply a sham. The second is to argue that there is a difference between what historians do and what Holocaust deniers do: between history and denial. These two strategies give the book its **polemical** tone and contentious edge.

polemical: controversial; inherently argumentative

Sham Debates

On the first page of *Denying the Holocaust,* Lipstadt tells a story that serves as a **leitmotif** for her whole book.

leitmotif: dominant recurring theme in a work of art

> The producer was incredulous. She found it hard to believe that I was turning down an opportunity to appear on her nationally televised show: 'But you are writing a book on this topic. It will be great publicity'. I repeatedly explained that I would not participate in a debate with a Holocaust denier. The existence of the Holocaust was not a matter of debate . . . I would not appear with them . . . To do so would give them a legitimacy and a stature they in no way deserve . . . [I]n one last attempt to get me to change my mind, she asked me a question: 'I certainly don't agree with them, but don't you think our viewers should hear the other side?'

8. In Your Journal: Do you agree with Lipstadt's decision not to appear on the show? Why or why not?

The point is that there simply is no debate in any meaningful sense, no 'other side' about the existence of the Holocaust. Reasonable and responsible people don't have this debate, not least because, for the Holocaust, the 'evidence is overwhelming' (*Judgement,* 7.7). An expert on French denial, Pierre Vidal-Naquet, asks if an astronomer would discuss things with an astrologer, 'or with a person who claims that the moon is made of green cheese?'.[11] There are debates about the Holocaust, of course: history is not set in stone. For example, historians debate over how and why the murders took place when they did and how the Nazi hierarchy organised them; philosophers and theologians discuss the implications of the Holocaust; experts in cultural studies discuss questions of memorialisation, and so on. There is no shortage of debates involving the Holocaust. But there is no debate over its *existence.* Those who assert that there is such a debate, like the Nazi UFOs denier, are doing so to get 'airtime' and to make themselves seem more serious. This is why Lipstadt refused to give interviews: talking to them as if they were reasonable people gives credence to deniers.[12]

Imagine: what sort of person would appear on national TV to argue that you and your family are vermin? Why? Would you go on and argue that you weren't? Against a point of view like that, neither unprejudiced nor likely to be convinced by argument, how would you prove you weren't? What would that achieve, apart from a 'contentious' debate? What 'genre' of TV would it be? Serious documentary? Or just high-octane entertainment? Who would benefit? You? The TV company? The people taken seriously enough to go on TV with the original accusation? The audience?

The **penultimate** chapter of *Denying the Holocaust* is a case study of the 'sham debate' strategy. Entitled 'The Battle for the Campus', it describes how, in the early 1990s, a denier placed advertisements or opinion-editorial pieces denying the Holocaust in a number of U.S. university newspapers. From his point of view, this was a win/win situation. If the pieces went in, his **noxious** ideas spread and the claim that this was 'the other side' of the story was made, giving credit to this sham debate. If they were refused, he got to make a fuss, claiming that he was being censored and that his constitutional right to free speech was being silenced by sinister Jewish interests and 'anti-freedom' elements (more anti-Semitism, of course). In fact, Lipstadt argues that this appeal to the U.S. Constitution is a 'failure to understand the true implications of the **First Amendment.**'[13] Some papers refused publication: more did not. Some condemned the ads from their editorials. The series of events left Lipstadt pessimistic: students who had read, or even heard of the 'controversy', 'may have walked away . . . convinced that there are two sides to this debate: the "revisionists" and the "establishment historians" . . . That is the most frightening aspect of this entire matter'.[14]

penultimate: second-to-last

noxious: physically harmful or destructive to living beings

9. In Your Journal: Do you agree with Lipstadt's claim about the First Amendment? Why or why not?

Significantly, these events coincided with what was called 'the culture wars' on American campuses and in American intellectual life. To sum up a complex series of arguments, with rights and wrongs on both sides, the 'culture wars' debates, ostensibly over education, were actually about the whole structure of American society. On one side were more traditional, conservative ideas, described most famously in **Allan Bloom**'s 1987 *The Closing of the American Mind* and echoed by others, such as the journalist Dinesh D'Souza. On the other was a **fissiparous** grouping of those with more radical and often leftist ideas about issues such as race, gender and sexuality. Also on this side, often uneasily, were many 'postmodern' and deconstructive critics and writers. The debates over the mostly meaningless label of 'political correctness' were tied up in this, too.

fissiparous: tending to break up into parts or be divisive

First Amendment: Amendment I of the Constitution states: "Congress shall make no law respecting an establishment of religion, or prohibiting the free exercise thereof; or abridging the freedom of speech, or of the press; or the right of the people peaceably to assemble, and to petition the Government for a redress of grievances."

Allan Bloom: (1930–1992) political philosopher, cultural and literary critic, and professor at the University of Chicago; considered to be one of the first and foremost challengers of the PC movement

These 'campus deniers' used the 'culture wars' and discussions of 'PC' as a way in. Since the 'PC' position was that the Holocaust had happened, they suggested that to attack this belief was daring, challenging and radical, just like the risqué U.S. talk show, 'Politically Incorrect', seemed to be. Anti-Semitism and race hatred, 'correctly cast and properly camouflaged', were trying to claim the pseudo-rebellious kudos of being 'politically incorrect'.[15] Of course, those pilloried for 'being PC' fought these hatreds just as Lipstadt fights them in her book. **Peter Novick** suggests that Lipstadt saw the success of this denial campaign as 'evidence of the strength of postmodernism and deconstructionism in the Universities' and, as a 'front' in the culture war, this was a 'theme picked up by conservative commentators'.[16] In contrast, Novick suggests that the real influences on the editors were the much less contentious liberal thinkers **Thomas Jefferson** and **John Stuart Mill.** The deniers' trick here was to 'piggyback' in on a real debate. Denial was not and is not a symptom of the intellectual substance of the 'culture wars' or debates over 'PC', despite the fact that the conservative side seemed to think it was. It is important to differentiate, as Lipstadt does, between real debates and sham debates. As I will argue below, postmodernism excludes denial as reasonable debate. That said, of course, deniers will use any trick they can to broadcast their views, and presumably enjoy the **dissension** sown amongst all those people of good will opposing them. And posing as conservative historians is one of their strongest tricks.

> ***10. In Your Journal:*** What do Holocaust deniers have to do with political correctness on American college campuses?

> ***11. In Your Journal:*** In what ways might the editors' actions have reflected the influence of Jefferson and Mill?

dissension: partisan and contentious quarreling

Deniers Posing as Historians

The false idea of an 'other side of a debate' relies on there seeming to be 'serious people' involved in this debate. This is the second target of Lipstadt's book. Part of the camouflage that deniers use is the appearance of 'reasoned historical inquiry'. One of the most significant examples is The Institute of Historical Review in California. It sounds like a research centre in an established university: it produces a journal, complete with scholarly footnotes and apparatus, holds conferences and so on. It is, however, an organisation dedicated to Holocaust denial.

But David Irving was much more significant. As one leading professor of Jewish history, David Cesarani, pointed out, and as ***The Guardian***

The Guardian: popular British newspaper

-:- **Peter Novick:** professor of history at The University of Chicago

-:- **Thomas Jefferson:** (1743–1826) author of the Declaration of Independence and the Statute of Virginia for Religious Freedom, and third president of the United States

-:- **John Stuart Mill:** (1806–1873) British philosopher, economist, and moral and political theorist who promoted a liberal view of society and culture, emphasizing the progress of human knowledge and individual freedom; *On Liberty* (1859) is his most famous work declared, he was 'the Holocaust deniers' best shot'.[17] Irving began writing in the early 1960s: his books, generally published by reputable publishers, cover the events of the Second World War and, in part because he didn't talk about Nazi flying saucers, he was seen by many as a serious historian. It was this reputation as a historian that was at the centre of the case. If he was credible as a historian, his findings, however 'controversial', would stand as history to be debated and discussed. If he was not a credible or reasonable historian, his work—and he—would fall. This means that the case was also about what history is and what historians do.

12. In Your Journal: Discuss Eaglestone's claim here that the Irving/Lipstadt case was, in some fundamental way, about "what history is and what historians do."

In 1990, Irving gave a speech to the Institute of Historical Review, called 'Battleship Auschwitz'. It ended, in the pseudo-heroic rhetoric typical of deniers, in a rather creepy parody of British and American naval war films: he commanded 'Sink the Auschwitz!'.[18] Like the deniers who have had high-profile trials in Canada and Germany, Irving was setting out to encounter his enemies on the seas that suited him best. A leading lawyer wrote that 'English **libel** law has notorious **draconian** features reflecting its origins in the seventeenth-century **Court of Star Chamber.** It puts the burden on the publisher to prove the truth of his [*sic*] allegations'.[19] English libel law takes the side of the plaintiff and assumes the libellous allegations to be false until substantially justified. Additionally, in recent high-profile cases in the UK, judgements have usually gone with the plaintiff. Irving was presumably hoping that a debate in a law court would confirm his standing as a historian and so his 'findings'. By doing this he would validate some of the claims of Holocaust deniers. If it didn't, he still had the chance to broadcast his views: another denier's win/win situation. This was why he forced a confrontation by suing Lipstadt and Penguin. Penguin was not 'out for Irving's blood', as some suggested (rather distastefully, given the subject matter).[20] Irving wanted to use a court of law as a tool for Holocaust denial. Both Lipstadt and her publishers deserve to be congratulated for standing up to this. Irving lost spectacularly, leaving his reputation in tatters.

13. In Your Journal: Why did Irving use allusions to British and American naval war films in his rhetoric about Auschwitz?

libel: written or oral defamatory statement or representation that conveys an unjustly unfavorable impression

draconian: cruel or severe

But the court case did more than just finish off Irving's reputation and damage—let's hope irreparably—Holocaust denial. It also raised questions about the nature of history itself.

THE NATURE OF HISTORY

Despite their very great differences, Irving and Lipstadt have something in common. They share one particular understanding of what history actually is: they have what might be called a traditional **empiricist view.** And it is

empiricist view: view based on the belief that all knowledge originates in experience, which relies on observation and experimentation

Court of Star Chamber: in English law, a court that grew out of the medieval king's council as a supplement to the common-law courts

14. In Your Journal: Do you think it's fair of Eaglestone to put both Lipstadt and Irving in the same category of historian (traditional-empiricist)? Is it logical?

15. In Your Journal: How apt do you find Eaglestone's desktop and software analogy?

epistemology: study or theory of the nature and grounds of knowledge, especially with reference to its limits and validity

precisely this view that postmodernism questions. As I have suggested, many historians and cultural commentators are profoundly worried by this, especially in relation to the Holocaust. However, I aim to show that these questions are important and extremely useful tools with which to fight denial.

To adapt a metaphor from Mary Midgley, the British philosopher of science, history is like a computer. Usually we send e-mails, surf the net or word process, without a thought for the software that supports these applications. However, when the computer crashes or becomes infected with a virus, we need to look below the 'desktop' and into the complexities and details of the software. When history 'crashes' or becomes infected, what we take for granted—principally, I suggest, the 'objectivity' of history—has to be closely examined and perhaps 'debugged'. And this is what postmodernism offers to history.

History, as we understand it, has a history. It was constructed as a particular form of knowledge and way of doing things. As there are a number of excellent studies of this, I will only offer here a very short summary.[21] What we generally understand to be 'history' today, a fully established subject separate from other disciplines, stems from the work of Otto Von Ranke, a nineteenth-century German historian. The way of studying the past that he established spread over the Western world and is basically what both Lipstadt and Irving mean by 'history'. From Ranke and his followers, too, comes the discipline's desire to be a 'science of the past': to explain the past by representing it. This has perhaps three key features. First, it aims to recreate the past by representing (re-presenting), in Ranke's famous phrase, *wie es eigentlich gewesen,* 'what actually happened'. (Richard Evans suggests a better translation: 'how it actually was', but the sense remains fairly similar.[22]) Second, it demands that the historian must be objective and ignore his or her location in the world. Third, it demands that the historian follows an empirical method and passive in the face of the facts, simply marshal the evidence.

However, many people—not just postmodernists—have questioned these ideas. These questions can be put into three broad categories: questions about **epistemology** or *how* we know about the past; questions about *who* is creating the history; and questions about the *nature of language and writing* itself. The outcome of these questions seems to disrupt traditional and sometimes naïve notions of history.

How We Study the Past: Knowing and Telling

Epistemology is the branch of philosophy that deals with how we know things. When I ask you not 'if', but '*how*' you know that it is raining outside, this is an epistemological question. In relation to the past, epistemology explores how we can claim to know historical facts. To any historian, this presents a number of substantial, but often unexamined, problems.

First, no historian's account can cover the bulk of the past. The fact that there is so much of it means that anything like a full account is simply impossible. This is the novelistic insight of the English eighteenth-century writer Laurence Sterne's *Tristram Shandy:* no matter how fast Tristram writes he can never describe his whole life. Most—if not nearly all—information is not recorded (what colour socks did your neighbour wear last week? Last year? Did his great grandfather wear?) or is **evanescent,** here then gone (how many people on that street now, this second? Did you take a photo? What do they think about this morning's main news story?).

evanescent: tending to vanish like vapor

Second, the past is not an account, but events, responses and situations that have, well, passed. We can't judge the accuracy of an account of the past by going back to it, the way we might be able to judge the accuracy of a map of a city by walking around the area it is supposed to represent. In fact, most of us judge the accuracy of one historian's accounts by comparing them to another historian's accounts. This is rather like checking yesterday's events by comparing different newspapers from today. Other historians can check archival sources: rather like seeing if, as a journalist reported, the thief's footprint is still there the next morning. But neither of these is the same as checking the account against the actual event, which is impossible, as the past has gone forever.

Third, events happen one way—forwards—but are learnt about and written about in another—backwards. History is retrospective. **David Lowenthal** cites an essay from 1964: 'time is foreshortened, details selected and highlighted, action concentrated, relations simplified not to deliberately alter . . . the events but to . . . give them meaning'.[23] History is made up of 'significant events'. Of course, not all the historical knowledge a historian has is written down, but the events of the past are always seen, explained and represented retrospectively.

So, knowledge about the past is edited, unverifiable by simple comparison, and studied backwards. This means that there is a difference between the past (the events that have now gone, are no longer actually present, however strong our memories of them) and history. History is not the recreation of the past as it actually was. It is the name for the *stories we tell about the past*. It is a type or *genre* of story. This is not to say that any particular account isn't true, but that the 'truth of the past' cannot be established in the same sort of way that the truth of the statement 'it is now

---

David Lowenthal: professor (University College, London) and scholar in the fields of political science, environmental psychology, geography, and landscape architecture; known for his extensive writings about human attitudes toward and relationship to the past raining outside' can be. How we know about the past is not straightforward and all historians know this.

Who is Creating the History?

This is another issue that questions the traditional understanding of history. It is often misunderstood in the following way: people sometimes claim that 'men write different history from women, white people write different history from black people' and so on. This is not necessarily the case. What *is* the case is that historians of different nationalities, races, sexes, sexualities and so on, often have different aims and interests that stem from who they are: these different interests will cause them to look at different things in different ways. Predictably, for example, 'Women's history' and 'Black history' were ignored for much of the twentieth century, as, more or less, white men were interested in the events they took to be centrally important. However, there is nothing in principle to stop a man writing a fascinating and detailed history of women in nineteenth-century America, or a black person writing the history of almost all-white Ireland. Suggesting that the person's identity is the same as their method is a mistake, albeit an easily made one. (This is not to say that the 'location' of a historian isn't important. Like most people, historians and academics in general want to be successful, to have good careers, to be respected and so on, and this affects their interests: in this light Lipstadt's refusal to appear on national TV—with the money and kudos that would entail—is even more principled!) What is crucial is not, as it were, the historian's genes, but *what* the historian chooses to focus on, *how* they choose to do it and finally, in turn, what those choices themselves depend on.

16. In Your Journal: Explain Eaglestone's distinction between "writing like" a particular gender, race, etc. and having perspectives that grow out of one's gender, race, etc.

I have already argued that there is just too much of the past to 'simply' recreate it 'as it happened'. Historians choose what to focus on. For example, in his masterpiece *The Destruction of the European Jews* the great Holocaust historian Raul Hilberg chose to focus on the victims of the Holocaust and, in general, the administrative and bureaucratic means of their murder: the work of 'desk killers' like **Eichmann.** More recently, in his book *Ordinary Men,* Christopher Browning chose to focus on the perpetrators by looking in detail at the day-to-day genocidal activities in occupied Poland of one particular group of Germans—Reserve Police Battalion 101—'who were quite literally saturated in the blood of victims at point-blank range'.[24] (*Pause: writing and reading about the Holocaust is, and ought to be,*

Eichmann: (Adolf) (1906–1962) German high official and bureaucrat who oversaw the transport of Jews to the Nazi death camps and was eventually hanged by the state of Israel for his part in the Holocaust *distressing: however, sometimes, for me at least, it can happen that the nature of the subject is eclipsed for a moment by the heat of writing and debate. This is wrong. So, compare: think about getting blood on your clothes from a nosebleed: think how much, much more blood—the blood of the victims—would 'saturate with blood' a thick military uniform. On one day. And the killings, of all sorts, lasted years. This so-called 'comparison' is not even really a comparison.*) These books, Hilberg's and Browning's, offer different, but linked, histories of the past.

17. In Your Journal: What does Eaglestone intend to get across with this nosebleed analogy?

But these choices are more than just a question of where the camera is pointed. They also rely, to extend this metaphor, on what *sort* of camera is used. Each historian takes for granted some key concepts. These ideas will vary with each approach: for a **Marxist** historian, concepts like 'base and superstructure' or 'class' will structure his or her view and orient his or her historical knowledge; a more conservative historian, believing that the future is dark and the present burdensome, will take for granted the inevitably imperfect make-up of human nature; a historian influenced by the French thinker Michel Foucault (1926–84) will have ideas about 'the body', **'genealogy'** and **'rupture'** at the front of his or her mind; a liberal, believing that '**from the crooked timber of humanity** no straight thing can ever be made' will praise tolerance and look askance at the intolerant; for those of the influential Annalist school, wider issues of geography or economics will be central, and so on. These are enormous differences of perspective and approach and they lead to differences of interpretation and explanation. As a result, history—the genre of stories about the past—is never *just* stories. Implicitly or explicitly, any particular history also embodies a methodology or philosophy of history. More than being about the past, any history is also an example of how that methodology works. Perhaps different ways of writing history might correspond to different 'sub-genres' of history.

Marxist: one who adheres to the political, economic, and social principles of Karl Marx, who established a theory of socialism focusing on class struggle and the rights of the working class

genealogy: process of researching the history, of the discourses or ideas that we use to define ourselves (i.e., asking how history has shaped the stories we use to understand ourselves and our world)

rupture: literally, a breaking apart; in Michel Foucault's theories, an emphasis on historical moments of breaking from traditional ways of understanding notions of truth, representation, and the self

'from the crooked timber of humanity . . .': quote from the German philosopher Immanuel Kant (1724–1804)

An example of this, again drawn from Holocaust history, is the conflict of views between Christopher Browning and Daniel Jonah Goldhagen. Browning aims 'to explain why ordinary men—shaped by a culture that had its own particularities but was nonetheless within the mainstream of Western, Christian and Enlightenment tradition—under specific circumstances willingly carried out the most extreme genocide in human history'.[25] As his title suggests, his study looks at the *Ordinary Men* who murdered Jews. As a basically liberal historian looking at recorded activities, Browning's study reveals how most of these seemingly average men were transformed into killers. He argues that indoctrination, peer pressure, wartime Nazi propaganda and the very nature of the Second World War led to this transformation. While in no way equating these murderous perpetrators with their innocent victims, he points out how they were manipulated by the structure of the Nazi regime. He draws a guarded parallel with the famous 1960s 'obedience to authority'

experiments of Stanley Milgram, in which scientists persuaded volunteers to 'electrocute' fake subjects in a laboratory.

Goldhagen, looking mostly at the same records and archives, had a different approach: his disagreement with Browning and his own conclusion are clearly signified in his title, *Hitler's Willing Executioners: Ordinary Germans and the Holocaust*. Goldhagen wants to answer the question: 'what was the structure of beliefs and values that made a genocidal onslaught against the Jews intelligible and sensible to the ordinary Germans who became perpetrators?'[26] Seemingly unlike Browning, Goldhagen is explicitly interested in the ideas and mindsets that lead to people's actions: not 'structural' reasons, but what he calls the 'ideational causes of social action'.[27] Although he acknowledges that the 'incentive structure' (for example, indoctrination, fear of punishment or hope for official or social reward) is important, he believes that this alone cannot cause people to act but works 'in conjunction with the cognitive and value structures' already in place in an individual.[28] This, he argues, is the difference between his and other explanations of the Holocaust, 'generated either in a laboratory' (a pop at Browning's use of Milgram's results) or 'deduced from some philosophical or theoretical system'.[29] (Goldhagen's approach is 'theoretical' too, of course: he uses, in part, the 'thick description' approach, discussed by the anthropologist Clifford Geertz.) Goldhagen's conclusion? Germany, unlike other European countries, had a 'dominant cultural thread' of 'eliminationist anti-Semitism'.[30] The mindset of ordinary Germans was used to—and supported—the idea of the utter annihilation of the Jews. Thus, unlike Browning's killers, manipulated into genocide, Goldhagen argues that Germans in general and the killers specifically were willing accomplices, motivated by a thoroughgoing and deep-seated hatred of the Jews. As Browning says in his generous but critical account of Goldhagen, it is, of course, not unusual 'for different scholars to ask different questions of, apply different methodologies to, and derive different interpretations from the same sources'.[31] The differences between these two accounts stem from wide differences in perspective and approach; differences, in fact, in their philosophy of history.

18. In Your Journal: In your own words, explain the difference Eaglestone (using Goldhagen's terms) is asserting here between "structural" and "ideational" causes of human action.

However, and even more importantly, differences in perspective, in methodology and in the philosophy of history, such as the differences be-

experiments of Stanley Milgram: Milgram conducted his experiments on obedience to authority partly in response to the Holocaust; the study was conducted at Yale University in 1961–1962 and yielded disturbing results: 65% of the subjects, ordinary residents of New Haven, were willing to give apparently harmful electric shocks of up to 450 volts to a protesting victim, simply because a scientific authority commanded them to, and in spite of the fact that the victim did not do anything to deserve such punishment; the victim was in reality an actor who was not actually being shocked, but the subjects learned this only at the end of the experiment tween Goldhagen and Browning, stem from 'extra-historical' ideas. That is, such differences don't just stem from a historian's belief about the past, but from their wider beliefs about the world—their philosophical 'world-view'—however clearly or indistinctly it is worked out. A Marxist historian is a Marxist because he or she believes that Marxism is the best way to bring about social justice; liberal historians believe that tolerance is the greatest virtue; a conservative believes that traditions can teach us how to live best, and so on. It is because of this that history is always history for a particular reason which supports, without necessarily stating it explicitly, a certain cause or worldview. So, not only is all history shaped by a methodology or philosophy of history, but it is also directed, unavoidably, by an implicit or explicit worldview, too. History is always *history from* a certain worldview.

This is why, in the main, postmodernists argue that 'pure', 'neutral' or 'objective' history is impossible. Not because one can only tell the story of one's own identity (e.g. as a white man), but because each history, each story about the past, evolves from the historian's focus, the historian's methodology and philosophy of history, which is in turn shaped by the historian's ideas, clear or fuzzy, about life and the world: their worldview. And there is no such thing as an objective philosophy or worldview—if there were, everybody would share it, and philosophers would stop arguing. (It was hoped that science would prove to be an 'objective philosophy' and indeed, science tells us a great deal. Carbon dating gives us approximate dates for excavated bodies and so on: but science can't tell us what actions will result in social justice, whether human nature exists or, if it does, whether it can be improved. Science can't tell us what poor women in London in 1789 thought about the French Revolution. Nor can science, I suspect, tell us how to make ethically good decisions.) Of course, some of these points have been raised before. **Herodotus,** often heralded as the 'father of history', knew he was writing from a position. But postmodernism, as I suggest below, makes these points again, in new and urgent ways.

The Nature of Language and Writing

So far, I have argued that history is a genre that writes and learns retrospectively about the past, selecting key meaningful events. I have stated that it is impossible to verify an account about the past by going back to the past (the way you can verify the weather *right now* by stepping outside). Accounts are shaped by the historian's methodology and this, in turn, relies on their worldview. This means that history is not recreation of the past 'as it really was', but the name we give to the genre of stories we

---

Herodotus: (484?–425? BC) Greek author of the first great narrative history produced in the ancient world, the history of the wars between Greece and Persia (499–479 BC)

tell about the past. It is because of this that Hayden White, an influential thinker on the nature of history, argues that a historical work is 'a narrative prose discourse that purports to be a model, or icon, of past structures and processes in the interests of explaining what they were by representing them'.[32] This is absolutely not to say that events didn't happen or are 'made up' (or made to disappear), but that unlike the novelist:

> . . . the historian confronts a veritable chaos of events already constituted, out of which he [*sic*] must choose the elements of the story he [*sic*] would tell. He [*sic*] makes his [*sic*] story by including some events and excluding others, by stressing some and subordinating others. This process . . . is carried out in the interest of constituting a story of a particular kind. That is to say, he [*sic*] 'emplots' his [*sic*] story.[33]

Writing meaningfully about the past is, and can only be, the 'emplotment' of events of the past into certain types of story.

In his major study, *Metahistory,* White outlines the interactions between what he calls the 'model of ideological implication' (roughly, what I called the worldview), the mode of argument (roughly, the sort of 'camera' or methodology used) and 'mode of emplotment'—what sort of story it is. He identifies four 'modes' of story: romantic, tragic, comic and satiric. I am not going to discuss these in detail, but mention them in order to show that, because of the nature of writing and narrating itself, a particular history is not 'objective'. It will always be in a mode of 'emplotment': not necessarily one of the forms from White's list, but in the form of a story of some sort. Even 'chronicle history', made up of simple lists of events, is like this. A king is crowned, fights invaders and dies: a simple story, of course, but a story nonetheless. This also displays the characteristics of history I discussed above, through, for example, the events chosen—the death of a king is chosen over the death of a queen or a shepherd. The very need to keep a chronicle reflects a wider worldview showing the chronicler's desire to impose his or her values, a society that wants or needs to pass down information, and so on.

More than just 'emplotted', each history is also constructed as a narrative *for* an audience. Quite rightly, history books for students at school aged 12 are different from those written with a specialised, highly informed and critical audience in mind, and these in turn differ from books written for the general reader. This too means that works of history cannot be 'objective', as the choices made about level of detail, for example, don't reflect an objective past but **putative** readers: all history is history for an audience. Furthermore, any work of history also has to be written in a certain style. Traditionally, history is written in the third person, in the style favoured by realist novelists. 'The advantage of third person narration',

putative: commonly accepted or supposed

writes the eminent critic Frank Kermode, 'is that it is the mode which best produces the illusion of pure reference. But it is an illusion, the effect of a rhetorical device'.[34] That is, the key feature of this 'realist' style is to give the impression that it is not really a style at all, but a transparent window (or 'reference') to the world beyond—in the past or in fiction. Despite this impression, the 'realist style' is one choice from many different styles of writing, and one chosen with a reason: as the old joke has it, once you can fake sincerity, you can fake anything.

19. In Your Journal: What are the stylistic similarities of a realist novel and a traditional historical account?

The central point of all these arguments is that a history text is not a clear window to the past: it is not really objective at all. Instead, history books are texts about the past: they stand in for, or are perhaps analogous to, the absent and unrecoverable past. 'Pure', 'neutral' or 'objective' history is impossible. Historical knowledge is produced, and history books are written, as a genre. And it is this concept of 'history as genre' that was central to the Lipstadt–Irving case.

THE RULES OF GENRES

Genres of writing and types of knowledge have rules or 'generic conventions'. There are, of course, many genres of text, normally divided by content. In fiction, it's easy to spot genres such as the thriller, romance and science fiction. While novels are divided by content, works of history are almost always divided up chronologically and geographically, although there are sub-genres such as 'Women's history', 'Oral history' and 'Military history'. But more important than where the books go in a bookshop are the generic conventions that structure the works. Generic conventions are parts of plot or style that are special to that genre: all texts, not just novels, have generic rules. These rules are present in the content: you expect a dashing hero in a romantic novel; you expect to read about grain production in economic history, troop movements in military history; we all expect a cookbook to be about cooking food. The conventions are also present in the style: hard-boiled detective stories have a terse style; academic histories have long sentences and lots of footnotes; cookbooks have lists of ingredients. The rules of a particular genre don't just set up the parameters, however: they actually *construct* that text. After all, what is a detective thriller without a detective or a cookbook without recipes? Genres are not pigeonholes into which academics and bookshop owners put books: they are the rules underlying the books themselves. To write anything is to be part of a genre, to follow (and sometimes to bend slightly or to adapt) generic rules. Some of these rules matter very little (it doesn't matter whether the heroic cowboy has a black or a white hat), some of them are absolutely central and vital. The genre of history has a number of central rules. The historian Geoffrey Elton, distinctly unpostmodern and

20. In Your Journal: Why does Eaglestone refer to the generic conventions of so many different kinds of writing?

21. In Your Journal: What does Eaglestone mean by saying that genre rules "*construct*" a text?

pro-Rankean, was aware of this. He argued that the 'conditions of professional competence and integrity' for historical work were only guaranteed by a professional training as a historian.[35] This can be read as arguing that the generic conventions that are central to history are taught implicitly through this arduous, professional training, and only once this has taken place—only once the historian knows the rules—is the history any good.

Generic conventions or rules are, then, extremely important for history. If 'objectivity' is a myth, these conventions offer the idea of the 'reasonable historian' and a way of understanding what the genre of history is.

Much in law depends on assessments of what a 'reasonable person' would expect or think. Exactly what the 'reasonable person' believes in every case is hard to pin down—after all, you'd need a list of everything from aardvarks to zebras to do the concept full justice—but it is part of the reason for 'trial by jury' by one's peers. This 'reasonable person' concept plays a crucial part in professional negligence cases. When deciding whether a defendant has met the standard of care in medical negligence cases, courts apply the 'Bolam test', named for the *Bolam* v. *Friern Hospital Management Committee* case of 1957: a 'doctor is not guilty of negligence if he has acted in accordance with a practice accepted as proper by a responsible body of medical men [*sic*] skilled in that particular art'. Not all doctors have to agree that the practice in question is the only practice, but only that it is a recognised, responsible one. The Bolam test, or versions of it, has been accepted outside medical cases too: anywhere, in fact, that issues of negligence and the duty of care arise. Among those who write history, there is the same sort of idea in a more limited spectrum: the idea of a 'reasonable historian'.

> ***22. In Your Journal:*** Explain how medicine's "Bolam test" relates to the concept of a "reasonable historian". How are medical professionals and historians similar, in Eaglestone's opinion?

The idea of the 'reasonable historian' stems from two things. First, it comes from the tradition that—like scientists—all historians share a huge project, all working to illuminate the past, as nuclear physicists work to illuminate the nature of the atom. Historians (although it might not seem like it) form a community that, like all communities, is constructed and defined by implicit or explicit adherence to certain *conventions* (the word originally means 'coming together'). Second, the idea of a 'reasonable historian' means that each historian has followed a recognised mode of argument, or argued for and defended the way they have chosen to work: thus, they are 'reasonable' in that they have a reasoned method. Both of these can be seen as ways in which historians define and police the genre of history by a circular definition that relies on generic conventions. A 'reasonable historian' is somebody who writes according to the generic conventions that define history: history is written in the light of the generic

---

pro-Rankean: German historian Leopold Von Ranke (1795–1886), known as the father of the modern objective historical school (now called historicism), asserted that the study of history should be objective, scientific, and untainted by the spirit of the present conventions that historians, usually implicitly, decide upon. What makes both a 'reasonable historian' and a work generically 'history' is an adherence to the appropriate generic conventions. (Although this might seem odd, there isn't anything strange about it. After all, a Society of Thriller Writers won't give its annual award to the author of a cookbook, and cookbooks don't usually contain white-knuckle car chases.) For reasons I have discussed above, a 'reasonable historian' is often, wrongly, thought of as being an 'objective historian'. And again, let me stress that this doesn't mean history isn't true: it just means that history texts are not transparent or objective and can't establish the truth in the same way as you can check the weather.

23. In Your Journal: What is the difference between a "reasonable historian" and an "objective historian," in Eaglestone's terms?

This concept of the 'reasonable historian' explains why controversies between historians are rarely about 'particular facts' and are so fierce. A historian seldom attacks another's knowledge of an archive: more often they attack the way they have chosen to approach history. Controversies are about the way history is done and what is 'reasonable'. As I have argued, this in turn relies on worldviews. So with Irving, the attack was not basically about what archives he had used, but *how* he had used them and so about his worldview. A reasonable historian is at least one that other historians can 'reason' with, even if there could be no final agreement. Of course, what defines 'reasonable' can change as new ideas and methods sweep across the historical community, just as new sub-genres of writing are created. But this takes time, happens slowly and with great debate. Feminist historians had to fight hard, and for a long time, before their different ways of being 'reasonable historians' became accepted, for example.

Despite changes, there are some conventions that have remained fairly stable. One of the most significant of these is the use of evidence. The support of argument from evidence is perhaps the central convention of the genre of history, and differentiates it most clearly from fiction. Just as scientists undertake experiments, historians use traces of the past in the present—for example, documents and oral statements—to support their arguments. Crudely, this is the demand that historical texts have sources: more technically, as Frank Kermode puts it, the genre of history needs 'metatextual announcements [that is, references to texts apart from itself], references to sources and authorities, assurance to the credibility of witnesses'.[36] People who don't follow this convention—say, by discussing UFOs without evidence—are simply not doing history.

24. In Your Journal: Can you infer the meaning of "metatext" based on Kermode's description of the "metatextual announcements" required by the genre of history?

But the 'evidence convention' is even stronger. Evidence has to be 'reliable' or 'testable'. This is best thought about as an analogue to 'scientific repeatability'. Basically, when a historian makes 'metatextual reference' by citing a piece of evidence (a letter, say), another historian needs to be able to find it and check it, just as scientists need to be able to repeat their colleague's experiments. The Lipstadt trial has an example of this. Studying Himmler's phone log, Irving argued that on 1 December 1941 Himmler telephoned an SS General to tell him that Jews were to 'stay where they are', thus portraying Himmler as saving Jews. Irving read 'Verwaltungsfuhrer der SS haben zu bleiben' (Administrative leaders of the SS have to stay) and mistook 'haben' for 'Juden' (thus: 'Administrative leaders of the SS. Jews to stay'). He ignored the lack of a full stop and the fact that 'Administrative leaders of the SS. Jews to stay' doesn't actually make sense. As the chief defence witness, Richard Evans checked the documents ('repeated the experiment') and found Irving's error. Evans argued that it was 'deliberately a perverse misreading' and it does seem an odd mistake for a man so keen on factual detail to make. Irving now admits that he misread 'haben'. This insistence on 'testability' is a central convention of the genre of history.

25. In Your Journal: How does Irving's mistranslation of the word "haben" call his "historical" work into question?

Another convention linked to this is the use of sources. An example: Irving wanted to claim that Hitler didn't know about the extermination of the Jews in Eastern Europe (a typical 'soft' denier claim). In his accounts, he cites a particular passage from Goebbels's diary: the 'Jews must get out of Europe. If need be, we must resort to the most brutal methods'. However, in addition to ignoring an array of other sources and documents, Irving has edited out a great deal of the passage. Crucial, according to Evans, is Irving's omission of Goebbels's description of Hitler as 'the persistent pioneer and spokesman of a radical solution' which, Evans argued, 'must indicate that Hitler was aware what was going on in the extermination camps in the East' (*Judgement,* 5.174, 5.175). The issue here is more complicated because it is obviously impossible for any historian to cite every source completely, and because each historian uses sources in the light of their own methodology and worldview. However, relying on the 'testability' of evidence and the idea of the 'reasonable historian', it is possible to see how far the generic conventions have been followed. A 'reasonable historian' doesn't make unreasonable edits from quotations.

Historical writing must also be consistent. Where a novelist, like Norman Mailer in the 'factional' *The Executioner's Song,* can mix evidence with speculation and invented ideas, a work of history must be consistent in the way it follows genre conventions. Where it doesn't (where more is speculation, for example), this has to be clearly signalled.

Another convention, as I have already suggested, is that historians generally write in the third person in a style recognised as 'realist'. Not writing in this style is frowned upon. Those who don't choose this style are not seen as historians. An example: Gitta Sereny has written a number of historical books, complete with scholarly apparatus, archival research and interviews. However, because her books are in the first person and are mostly concerned with what Goldhagen might call 'ideational causes of social action', she is described in Mr. Justice Gray's report, and in other places, as a 'journalist' (*Judgement,* 6.104). She uses the wrong style for the generic conventions.

In conclusion then, being a 'reasonable historian' and producing history means following the rules of the genre. I have discussed a handful of these above. These rules can be followed more or less well. Following these rules does not make texts more or less objective: objectivity is a fondly cherished myth. What it does is to make the works more or less historical, more or less of that genre of knowledge and of writing. Holocaust denial doesn't obey the rules of the genre. Therefore, Holocaust denial isn't part of the genre of history, but another genre, the genre of politics or of 'hate-speech'. What Irving was desperate to do was show that he was a valid historian, that he had followed the generic conventions and that his conclusions were, as a consequence, part of 'history'. In fact, he showed that he didn't follow the conventions and so his work was simply anti-Semitism.

26. In Your Journal: How can Eaglestone claim to define the genre of history if he believes that "objectivity is a fondly cherished myth"? Doesn't definition involve some type of objectivity?

POSTMODERNISM, HISTORY AND THE TRIAL

To return to the 'computer' metaphor: we can only deal with the virus of Irving's claim to be a reasonable and objective historian, by looking deep into the software of history. The issues I have discussed are 'postmodern' for two reasons. One, because they are to do with the fact that history (separate from memory) is not the past objectively reconstructed, but texts constituted by generic rules that claim to represent the past. Two, and as a consequence of the first, because it is by thinking about and admitting that historical writing evolves from specific methodologies and worldviews, and is not 'objective work', that the link between denial and anti-Semitism, fascism and racism is made utterly explicit. As I suggested earlier, postmodernism has been much criticised because it can seem antithetical to history. Some writers, categorised as postmodern, have indeed written rather foolishly on history and no one should defend bad scholarship or lack of thought. However, I have suggested that postmodern questions are, in fact, neither 'pro' nor 'con' history as such. Rather, they seek to open up the processes by which history is done and the claims made for historical work. When the computer of history has become infected with a virus, it is no good just pressing the same keys that used to make it work: it has to be looked into in depth. If objectivity as an idea for history has broken down, it is no good repeatedly stating that history should be objective: the ideas that underlie history must be re-examined. Even Richard Evans, no friend of postmodernism, argues that it 'is right and proper that postmodernist theories and critics should force historians to rethink the categories and assumptions by which they work, and to justify the manner in which they pursue their discipline'.[37]

My argument has been very influenced by the work of the French philosopher Jean-François Lyotard.[38] Lyotard is a key figure for postmodernism and summarising his thought in detail is impossible in a book of this genre. As the author of *The Postmodern Condition,* he suggested that what made us 'postmodern' was the fact that we were 'incredulous about metanarratives'.

27. In Your Journal: Describe how Lyotard's concept of the "metanarrative" complicates the generally perceived function of history.

For Lyotard, a metanarrative was a huge story that helped orient us in the world, that gave us direction and explained all the other narratives around us. Marxism is an example of a metanarrative. For a Marxist, the dynamic of 'class struggle' and the materialist theory of Marx explain every event and human action. Another metanarrative would be 'Whig' liberalism or progress: the idea that the human race is getting better with each passing moment and will eventually become perfect. However, after all the changes in the last third of the twentieth century, he suggests that we are no longer able to trust any of these stories. We no longer believe them or that any one theory seems to explain everything. This is the 'climate' that Lipstadt thinks aids Holocaust denial.

Lyotard, like Lipstadt, was well aware that this sort of 'climate' raised problems for ethical and historical discussion. But rather than passing over it, and because, as a philosopher, he thought deeply about the Holocaust, he wrote *The Differend: Phrases in Dispute.* The book begins with an account of Holocaust denial and aims to show how the postmodern condition repudiates denial. The book is very complex, drawing on the history of philosophy, law, ethics, epistemology and history. One result of this complexity is that the different readings of it stress different aspects of the argument: usually the ethical argument is seen as most important. However, one of the key parts of the book is about precisely how, in postmodernity, after 'objectivity' has been revealed to be a comforting myth, facts and events in the past can be found to be truly represented.

Lyotard writes that reality 'is not "given" . . . it is the state of the referent (that about which one speaks) which results from the effectuation of establishment procedures defined by a unanimously agreed upon protocol, and from the possibility offered to anyone to recommence this effectuation as often as he or she wants'.[39] He spends much of the book working out in detail how to establish reality. He argues that we work in 'phrases': by this he means something like 'language-games', ways of talking and understanding or, significantly, genres. Each type of phrase has different 'rules' and blind spots. For example, the phrase of naming gives a relationship to other phrases ('London' is in 'Britain', 'Hamlet' is 'Claudius's nephew'), but no actual location or solidity (where are they both? There was and is no 'actual' Hamlet). He argues that reality is established only when three sorts of phrases, three sorts of definition coincide: when reality is 'able to be signified, to be shown and to be named'.[40] With any item, to be signified is to be given a context in which it makes sense; to be shown is literally to be shown it; to be named is to be given a designation and identity that fixes it. To give an example: 'an agricultural implement, here, a spade' (signified, shown, named). Or 'a telephone log entry relevant to the murder of Jews, here is the text, made by Himmler' (signified, shown, named). None of these phrases can validate itself by itself: just being shown an object that you really couldn't identify several times wouldn't help you know what it is. Just being shown the diary entry isn't enough: it needs a name, context and meaning to become a 'historical fact'. All this means that, in order to establish the sort of 'historical reality' that Lipstadt wants, it is vitally important to know what sort of phrases or genre you are using, or are being used. Holocaust deniers, Lyotard argues, do not 'have a stake in establishing reality', do not 'accept the rules for forming and validating' statements: 'his [*sic*] goal is not to convince. The historian need not convince [a denier] if [the denier] is "playing" another genre of discourse, one in which conviction, or, obtaining a consensus over a defined reality is not at stake. Should the historian persist along this path, he [*sic*] will end up in the position of victim'.[41] Lipstadt was, indeed, the defendant in the case.

28. *In Your Journal:* Summarize this discussion of "establishing reality" in your own words.

But what genres was Irving using? Not the genre of history. David Irving failed the generic conventions of history in many ways. The court found the following long list of accusations substantially justified: Irving 'distorts accurate historical evidence and information; misstates; misconstrues; misquotes; falsifies statistics; falsely attributes conclusions to reliable sources; manipulates documents; wrongfully quotes from books that directly contradict his arguments in such a manner as completely to distort their authors' objectives and while counting on the ignorance or indolence of the majority of readers not to realise this . . . wears blinkers and skews documents and misrepresents data in order to reach historically untenable conclusions specifically those that exonerate Hitler' (*Judgement*, 2.10). But more than this, his worldview was an unreasonable one. He was judged to be an anti-Semite and a racist. These things prevented him doing 'reasonable history'. (This is the significance to the case of the poem, much discussed in the press, that he often sang to his daughter—'I am a Baby Aryan/Not Jewish or Sectarian/I have no plans to marry an/Ape or Rastafarian' (*Judgement*, 9.6). Irving is a racist through and through and that worldview affects his historical writing.) The details of his 'history' showed that his methodology was wrong, which in turn showed that his worldview was and is profoundly flawed.

This means that, counter-intuitively, the point of all the historical testimony was *not* really to prove Irving *wrong* as a historian. It was to show that most of the time he wasn't really a historian at all, he was writing a different genre altogether, an anti-Semitic fascist diatribe. *Holocaust denial isn't bad history: it isn't any sort of history at all, and simply can't be discussed as if it is.*

29. *In Your Journal:* What is the important difference between proving Irving's history "wrong" and proving Irving not to be an historian at all?

This was the position argued by Richard Rampton, defending Lipstadt and Penguin (who is more aware of genre than lawyers?). He began his speech, echoing Richard Evan's report, by arguing 'Mr. Irving calls himself an historian. The truth is, however, that he is not an historian at all'. The defence's winning case rested on providing substantial examples of where Irving had failed the genre requirements of history. The judge, too, was aware of the utmost significance of 'genre' too. Throughout the judgement,

Mr. Justice Gray is at pains to point out that a law court is not the 'court of history'. He states that his job is to 'evaluate the criticisms' of Irving's 'conduct as an historian in the light of the available historical evidence':

> But it is not for me to form, still less to express, a judgement about what happened. That is a task for historians. It is important that those reading this judgement should bear well in mind the distinction between my judicial role in resolving the issues arising between these parties and the role of the historian seeking to provide an accurate narrative of past events.
> (*Judgement,* 1.3)

And again,

> The question . . . is whether the Defendants have discharged the burden of establishing the substantial truth of their claim that Irving has falsified the historical record . . . the issue with which I am concerned is Irving's treatment of the available evidence. It is no part of my function to attempt to make findings as to what actually happened during the Nazi regime. The distinction may be a fine one but it is important to bear it in mind.
> (*Judgement,* 13.3)

30. In Your Journal: What does Justice Gray perceive his role to be?

The question is whether 'the available evidence, considered in its totality, would convince any objective and reasonable historian' (*Judgement,* 7.5), that is, whether the evidence would be enough to fit the generic conventions. The judgement compares Irving's work to the conventions of history and finds it wanting. Instead of a 'Bolam test', we could, perhaps rather fancifully, imagine an 'Irving test': a historian is guilty of negligence if he or she has not acted in accordance with a practice or genre requirement accepted as proper by a responsible body of historians skilled in that particular art. Negligent doctors are struck off, no longer doctors. It's worse for negligent historians: they only had the illusion of being historians in the first place. Irving was condemned not because of his relation to the past, which is, as the judge makes clear, beyond the remit of the courts, but because much of his writing wasn't history.

This conclusion also raises an interesting point about Lipstadt's book. Her argument against deniers is that they are not objective and that they are anti-Semitic. However, I have shown that historical 'objectivity' is a myth: historical writing depends on methodology, which in turn relies on the historian's worldview. An anti-Semite world-view will, clearly, produce anti-Semitism. Thus, Lipstadt's arguments show that denial is simply anti-Semitism, which is what she maintained all along. By her own logic, Lipstadt simply didn't need the flawed idea of 'objective' history to make her point. Holocaust denial is not history.

SELECT BIBLIOGRAPHY

Joyce Appleby, Lynn Hunt and Margaret Jacob, *Telling the Truth about History*, London: W.W. Norton and Company, 1994.

Neal Ascherson, 'The battle may be over—but the war goes on', in *The Observer*, 16 April 2000, p. 19.

Christopher Browning, *Ordinary Men: Reserve Police Battalion 101 and the Final Solution*, 2nd edn, London: HarperCollins, 1998.

David Cesarani, 'History on trial', in *The Guardian*, 18 January 2000.

David Cesarani, 'Holocaust on the right side of kitsch', in *Times Higher Education Supplement*, 7 July 2000, p. 20.

Geoffrey Elton, *The Practice of History*, London: Fontana, 1969.

Richard Evans, *In Defence of History*, London: Granta, 1997.

Richard Evans, 'Truth lost in vain views', in *Times Higher Education Supplement*, 12 September 1997, p. 18.

Patrick Finney, 'Ethics, historical relativism and Holocaust denial', in *Rethinking History*, 1998, vol. 2, no. 3, pp. 359–70.

Saul Friedlander (ed.), *Probing the Limits of Representation: Nazism and the 'Final Solution'*. London: Harvard University Press, 1992.

Paul Gilroy, *Between Camps: Nations, Culture and the Allure of Race*, London: Penguin, 2000.

Daniel Jonah Goldhagen, *Hitler's Willing Executioners: Ordinary Germans and the Holocaust*, London: Abacus, 1997.

Keith Jenkins, *On 'What is History?'*, London: Routledge, 1995.

Frank Kermode, *The Genesis of Secrecy: On the Interpretation of Narrative*, London: Harvard University Press, 1979.

Lord Lester of Herne Hill, QC, 'Finding a common purpose', in *The Observer*, 23 July 2000, p. 28.

Deborah Lipstadt, *Denying the Holocaust: The Growing Assault on Truth and Memory*, London: Penguin, 1994.

David Lowenthal, *The Past is a Different Country*, Cambridge, UK: Cambridge University Press, 1985.

Jean-François Lyotard, *The Differend: Phrases in Dispute*, trans. Georges Van Den Abbeele, Manchester, UK: Manchester University Press, 1988.

Frank Miele, 'Giving the Devil his due: Holocaust revisionism as a test case for free speech and the Sceptical Ethic', in *Skeptic*, 1994, vol. 2, no. 4, pp. 58–70.

Peter Novick, *The Holocaust and Collective Memory: The American Experience*, London: Bloomsbury, 2000. Published in US as *The Holocaust in American Life*.

Robert Jan Van Pelt, *The Science of Holocaust Research and the Art of Holocaust Denial*, Ontario: Department of Geography, University of Waterloo, 1999.

Gill Seidel, *The Holocaust Denial: Antisemitism, Racism and the New Right*, Leeds, UK: Beyond the Pale Collective, 1986.

Pierre Vidal-Naquet, *Les Assassins de Mémoire,* Paris: Éditions de la Découverte, 1987.

Pierre Vidal-Naquet and Limar Yagil, *Holocaust Denial in France,* Tel Aviv Faculty of Humanities, Project for the Study of Anti-Semitism, 1996.

Hayden White, *Metahistory: The Historical Imagination in Nineteenth Century Europe,* Baltimore: Johns Hopkins University Press, 1973.

Elie Wiesel, *All Rivers Run to the Sea,* London: HarperCollins, 1996.

NOTES

1. The *Judgement* refers to that handed down on Tuesday 11 April 2000 by The Hon. Mr. Justice Gray. At the time of writing, it is available at *http://www.guardianunlimited.co.uk/irving* and at *http://www.nizkor.org/hweb/people/i/irving-david/judgment-00-00.html*. It is also available as a book, *The Irving Judgement,* London: Penguin, 2000. It is very accessible and well worth reading.
2. Michael Lee, 'A witness in court', in *Perspective: Journal of the Holocaust Centre,* 2000, vol. 3, no. 2, p. 8.
3. Dan Jacobson, 'The downfall of David Irving', in *Times Literary Supplement,* 21 April 2000, p. 12.
4. Elie Wiesel, *All Rivers Run to the Sea,* London: HarperCollins, 1996, p. 79.
5. Joyce Appleby, Lynn Hunt and Margaret Jacob, *Telling the Truth about History,* London: W. W. Norton and Company, 1994, p. 7.
6. Richard Evans, 'Truth lost in vain views', in *Times Higher Education Supplement,* 12 September 1997, p. 18.
7. Deborah Lipstadt, *Denying the Holocaust: The Growing Assault on Truth and Memory,* London: Penguin, 1994, pp. 18, 19.
8. Gill Seidel argues this in *The Holocaust Denial: Antisemitism, Racism and the New Right,* Leeds: Beyond the Pale Collective, 1986. Dan Jacobson makes this point, too.
9. Frank Miele, 'Giving the Devil his due: Holocaust revisionism as a test case for free speech and the Sceptical Ethic', in *Skeptic,* 1994, vol. 2, no. 4, pp. 58–70.
10. Lipstadt, *Denying the Holocaust,* p. 28, original italics.
11. Pierre Vidal-Naquet and Limar Yagil, *Holocaust Denial in France,* Tel Aviv Faculty of Humanities, Project for the Study of Anti-Semitism, 1996, p. 14. Pierre Vidal-Naquet also wrote several articles opposing denial, compiled in *Les Assassins de Mémoire,* Paris: Éditions de la Découverte, 1987, a strong influence and precursor to Lipstadt's work. In English as *Assassins of Memory,* trans. Jeffery Mehlman, New York: Columbia University Press, 1993.
12. This is why, with the exception of Irving, I have not named any of the deniers in this book. This is not a book rebutting denial, as there are much better qualified people than me to do that: this is a book about denial, postmodernism and history. The books and articles cited in this bibliography are sources for information on rebutting deniers.
13. Lipstadt, *Denying the Holocaust,* p. 207.
14. Ibid., p. 208.

15. Ibid., p. 208.
16. Peter Novick, *The Holocaust and Collective Memory: The American Experience*, London: Bloomsbury, 2000, p. 271. Published in the USA as *The Holocaust in American Life.*
17. *The Guardian*, 12 April 2000, p. 22.
18. See Robert Jan Van Pelt, *The Science of Holocaust Research and the Art of Holocaust Denial*, Ontario: Department of Geography, University of Waterloo, 1999, p. 17.
19. Lord Lester of Herne Hill, QC, 'Finding a common purpose', in *The Observer*, 23 July 2000, p. 28.
20. Neal Ascherson discusses (and also dismisses) this view in 'The battle may be over—but the war goes on', in *The Observer*, 16 April 2000, p. 19.
21. See, for example, Keith Jenkins, *Rethinking History*, London: Routledge, 1991, for an excellent, highly accessible introduction. See also: Keith Jenkins, *On 'what is history?'*, London: Routledge, 1995, and Keith Jenkins (ed.), *The Postmodern History Reader*, London: Routledge, 1997; Alun Munslow, *Deconstructing History*, London: Routledge, 1997. Hayden White, *Metahistory: The Historical Imagination in Nineteenth Century Europe*, Baltimore: Johns Hopkins University Press, 1973 is the origin of much of this discussion. For a complete (and useful) contrast see Richard Evans, *In Defence of History*, London: Granta, 1997 and for the classic Rankean statement see Geoffrey Elton, *The Practice of History*, London: Fontana, 1969.
22. Evans, *In Defence of History*, p. 17.
23. David Lowenthal, *The Past is a Different Country*, Cambridge, UK: Cambridge University Press, 1985, p. 218.
24. Christopher Browning, *Ordinary Men: Reserve Police Battalion 101 and the Final Solution*, 2nd edn, London: HarperCollins, 1998, p. 162.
25. Ibid., p. 222.
26. Daniel Jonah Goldhagen, *Hitler's Willing Executioners: Ordinary Germans and the Holocaust*, London: Abacus, 1997, p. 24.
27. Ibid., p. 8.
28. Ibid., p. 21.
29. Ibid., p. 24.
30. Ibid., p. 47.
31. Browning, *Ordinary Men*, p. 191.
32. White, *Metahistory*, p. 2.
33. Ibid., p. 6.
34. Frank Kermode, *The Genesis of Secrecy*, London: Harvard University Press, 1979, p. 117.
35. Elton, *The Practice of History*, p. 68.
36. Kermode, *The Genesis of Secrecy*, p. 116.
37. Evans, *In Defence of History*, p. 252.
38. Another excellent discussion of postmodernism and denial, less influenced by Lyotard, is by Patrick Finney, 'Ethics, historical relativism and Holocaust denial', in *Rethinking History*, 1998, vol. 2, no. 3, pp. 359–70.

39. Jean-François Lyotard, *The Differend: Phrases in Dispute,* trans. Georges Van Den Abbeele, Manchester, UK: Manchester University Press, 1988, p. 4.
40. Ibid., p. 50.
41. Ibid., p. 19 (translation slightly modified).

FOR USE IN DISCUSSION

Questions about Substance

1. Discuss Lipstadt's view, described on page 233, that "the most frightening aspect" of the events described in "The Battle for the Campus" is that students who had "even heard of the 'controversy' may have walked away convinced that there are two sides" to the debate over the existence of the Holocaust. Why does Lipstadt suggest that, in some respects, this would be even more disturbing than the existence of the deniers themselves?
2. Discuss Eaglestone's point that "history has a history" (236). What does he mean by this? How is this view different from the one he mentions next, that history should be a "science of the past"?
3. Eaglestone prompts us (in his "*pause*") to think beyond simplistic semantics to a more profound level of meaning, when he claims that, "*this so-called 'comparison' is not even really a comparison*" (239). How does his insistence on the difference between semantics and literal meaning reflect Eaglestone's questioning of the relationship between postmodernism and Holocaust denial?
4. How is Eaglestone's claim that " 'Pure,' 'neutral,' or 'objective' history is impossible" (243) different from the claim that there is no such thing as a "true" history or an accurate "emplottment" of events (242)? Do you agree that there's a difference between these two descriptions (i.e., between pure, neutral, or objective, and true or accurate)? If so, is it a meaningful difference?
5. Compare and contrast Eaglestone's reliance on scholars Francois Lyotard and Hayden White. How does he use each of their theories? Do Lyotard and White's ideas seem fully compatible, or are there any distinctions you would point out?
6. Given what one learns about Deborah Lipstadt during the course of this essay how do you suppose she would respond to Eaglestone's analysis?

Questions about Structure and Style

1. From the bottom of page 232 to the top of 233, what does Eaglestone accomplish by directing these questions directly at his reader? Why should he shift his style here from narration in the third person to inquiry in the second person?

2. Why might Eaglestone have neglected to provide the name of the person responsible for putting denial-based pieces in various university papers? What does Eaglestone accomplish by referring to this person as simply "a denier," without giving his or her proper name (233)?
3. What does the author imply by repeatedly putting the terms "culture wars" and "PC" in quotes (234)?
4. From the bottom of page 238 through the middle of 239, Eaglestone directly addresses the reader. Why provide this "pause" here? What effect does it have, especially coming so abruptly in the middle of his descriptions of two authors' books?
5. Eaglestone inserts the qualifier "[sic]" after every use of "he" or "his," throughout the entire quoted passage from Hayden White (242). What point is he implicitly making here, and which "worldview" is he challenging when he uses this rhetorical technique?
6. Examine Eaglestone's use of italics throughout this essay. When does he use them, and why?
7. In the final paragraph, does Eaglestone distinguish his point of view from Lipstadt's, or concur with her (250–251)?

Multimedia Suggestions

1. View Errol Morris's documentary *Mr. Death* (1999), about Fred A. Leuchter, Jr., an electric chair designer who was sought out by Holocaust deniers to provide "scientific evidence" that Jews had *not* been incinerated in concentration camps. How do the deniers present themselves in this film? According to the film, does it seem that the deniers distort the conventions of "science" in the same manner they distort the conventions of history?
2. David Irving has put together what he perceives to be the relevant documents of his libel trial, including lots of personal information about Deborah Lipstadt (see *http://www.fpp.co.uk/Legal/Penguin/*). How does this Web site, like Irving's brand of "history," attempt to masquerade as something it's not?
3. Check out the Holocaust History Project at *http://www.holocaust-history.org/*, which provides a free archive of information that answers to the baseless claims of Holocaust denial. How do the articles and documents on this site fit with Eaglestone's definition of "history"?
4. The film *The Producers* (1968) and the book *Maus* experiment with genre conventions in order to make specific points about the Holocaust. Using Eaglestone's definition of genre, explain how these texts fit into, as well as subvert, the genres of comedy and comic books. How—and why—do these texts use and subvert generic conventions in order to make their points more powerful, their messages more evocative?

SUGGESTIONS FOR WRITING AND RESEARCH

1. In what genre would you put Eaglestone's essay? From its title, to its use of research, to its various uses of point-of-view, to Eaglestone's writing style, how do you think this essay's conventions compare to those listed by Eaglestone as the conventions of history?
2. Research existing examples of Nazi propaganda from the WWII era. How does the genre of propaganda differ from other kinds of artistic production? Can propaganda even be called art? Using Eaglestone's method of distinguishing between history and denial—a method that relies on ideas about genre—discuss how the author might argue for the difference between art and propaganda.
3. Research Adolph Eichmann, whom Eaglestone mentions on page 238, and the Eichmann trial. What was Eichmann's defense? In what ways did his defense rely on the definition of a war criminal, or on the conventions people have used to define what a war criminal is? Are you convinced by Eichmann's argument that he should not be considered a criminal? Why or why not? A useful book to start with is German American political theorist Hannah Arendt's *Eichmann in Jerusalem* (1963).

WORKING WITH CLUSTERS

Cluster 7: Holocausts and Histories
Cluster 10: Interpretation and/as Ideology
Discipline: The Humanities
Rhetorical Mode: Definition

A Heartbreaking Work of Staggering Genius

by Dave Eggers

David Eggers was a founding editor of Might *magazine. He is a contributor to many periodicals and an editor of* McSweeney's *journal. He also founded a non-profit writing and tutoring program for city youth in San Francisco called 826 Valencia. His memoir,* A Heartbreaking Work of Staggering Genius, *from which this material is drawn, was published in 1999. Eggers published a novel,* They Shall Know Our Velocity, *in 2002.*

THIS WAS
UNCALLED FOR.

Simon & Schuster
Rockefeller Center
1230 Avenue of the Americas
New York, NY 10020

Copyright © 2000 David ("Dave") Eggers
All rights reserved, including the right of reproduction in whole or in part in any form.

All rights reserved under International and Pan-American Copyright Conventions. Published in the United States by Simon & Schuster, a division of a larger and more powerful company called Viacom Inc., which is wealthier and more populous than eighteen of the fifty states of America, all of Central America, and all of the former Soviet Republics combined and tripled. That said, no matter how big such companies are, and how many things they own, or how much money they have or make or control, their influence over the daily lives and hearts of individuals, and thus, like ninety-nine percent of what is done by official people in cities like Washington, or Moscow, or São Paulo or Auckland, their effect on the short, fraught lives of human beings who limp around and sleep and dream of flying through bloodstreams, who love the smell of rubber cement and think of space travel while having intercourse, is very very small, and so hardly worth worrying about.

SIMON & SCHUSTER and colophon are registered trademarks of Simon & Schuster, Inc.
First published in the United States by Simon & Schuster, 2000.

A portion of this book appeared in *The New Yorker* in a somewhat different form.

Manufactured in the United States of America
3 5 7 9 10 8 6 4 2
Library of Congress Cataloging-in-Publication Data
Eggers, Dave.
A heartbreaking work of staggering genius / by Dave Eggers.
p. cm.
1. Eggers, Dave. 2. Parents—Death—Psychological aspects. 3. Brothers—Biography. I. Title.
CT275.E37 A3 2000
973.92'092—dc21
[B] 99-053475
ISBN: 0-684-86347-2

Height: 5'11"; Weight: 170; Eyes: blue; Hair: brown; Hands: chubbier than one would expect; Allergies: only to dander; Place on the sexual-orientation scale, with 1 being perfectly straight, and 10 being perfectly gay:

1 2 3 4 5 6 7 8 9 10

NOTE: This is a work of fiction, only in that in many cases, the author could not remember the exact words said by certain people, and exact descriptions of certain things, so had to fill in gaps as best he could. Otherwise, all characters and incidents and dialogue are real, are not products of the author's imagination, because at the time of this writing, the author had no imagination whatsoever for those sorts of things, and could not conceive of ***making up*** a story or characters—it felt like driving a car in a clown suit—especially when there was so much to say about his own, true, sorry, and inspirational story, the actual people that he has known, and of course the many twists and turns of his own thrilling and complex mind. Any resemblance to persons living or dead should be plainly apparent to them and those who know them, especially if the author has been kind enough to have provided their real names and, in some cases, their phone numbers. All events described herein actually happened, though on occasion the author has taken certain, very small, liberties with chronology, because that is his right as an American.

1. In Your Journal: Carefully read Eggers's description of Simon & Schuster, his publisher. What attitude does Eggers have about the business of publishing? How does this attitude affect your understanding of his publishing a novel?

2. In Your Journal: In Eggers's note about the identities of his characters, are you able to discern whether or not the characters are real or indeed fictional?

A HEARTBREAKING WORK OF STAGGERING GENIUS.

BY DAVE EGGERS

SIMON & SCHUSTER
New York London Sydney Singapore

First of all:

I am tired.
I am true of heart!

And also:

You are tired.
You are true of heart!

3. In Your Journal: How is Eggers's dedication different from others you've read?

4. In Your Journal: Why would Eggers provide "rules" for reading—or more specifically "enjoying"—his book? How do these rules compare with the usual function of a preface, which Eggers is here telling the reader not to read?

RULES AND SUGGESTIONS FOR ENJOYMENT OF THIS BOOK:

1. There is no overwhelming need to read the preface. Really. It exists mostly for the author, and those who, after finishing the rest of the book, have for some reason found themselves stuck with nothing else to read. If you have already read the preface, and wish you had not, we apologize. We should have told you sooner.

2. There is also no overarching need to read the acknowledgments section. Many early readers of this book (see p. xxxix) suggested its curtailment or removal, but they were defied. Still, it is not necessary to the plot in any major way, so, as with the preface, if you have already read the acknowledgments section, and wish you had not, again, we apologize. We should have said something.

3. You can also skip the table of contents, if you're short of time.

4. Actually, many of you might want to skip much of the middle, namely pages 209–301, which concern the lives of people in their early twenties, and those lives are very difficult to make interesting, even when they seemed interesting to those living them at the time.

5. Matter of fact, the first three or four chapters are all some of you might want to bother with. That gets you to page 109 or so, which is a nice length, a nice novella sort of length. Those first four chapters stick to one general subject, something manageable, which is more than what can be said for the book thereafter.

6. The book thereafter is kind of uneven.

PREFACE TO THIS EDITION

For all the author's bluster elsewhere, this is not, actually, a work of pure nonfiction. Many parts have been fictionalized in varying degrees, for various purposes.

DIALOGUE: This has of course been almost entirely reconstructed. The dialogue, though all essentially true—except that which is obviously not true, as when people break out of their narrative time-space continuum to cloyingly talk about the book itself—has been written from memory, and reflects both the author's memory's limitations and his imagination's nudgings. All the individual words and sentences have been run through a conveyor, manufactured like: 1) they are remembered; 2) they are written; 3) they are rewritten, to sound more accurate; 4) they are edited to fit within the narrative (though keeping with their essential truth); 5) they are rewritten again, to spare the author and the other characters the shame of sounding as stupid as they invariably do, or would, if their sentences, almost invariably begun with the word "Dude"—as in, for example, "Dude, she died"—were merely transcribed. It should be noted, however, that what's remarkable is that the book's most surreal dialogue, like that with the Mexican teenagers and that with the beleaguered Deirdre, is that which is most true to life.

CHARACTERS, AND THEIR CHARACTERISTICS: The author, though he was loath to do it, had to change a few names, and further disguise these name-changed characters. The primary example is the character named John, whose real-life name is not actually John, because John's real-life counterpart justifiably did not want some of the dark portions of his life chronicled—though after reading the manuscript, he did not object to his deeds and words being spoken by another. Especially if the character were less a direct facsimile, and more of an amalgam. Which he is, in fact. Now, to make John work, and create a manageable narrative, his alteration had a sort of domino effect, making necessary a few other fictions. Among them:

5. In Your Journal: How can dialogue be both "entirely reconstructed" and "essentially true"?

cloyingly: in a syrupy manner

6. In Your Journal: When Eggers says that the "book's most surreal dialogue" is "the most true to life," what is he saying about the relationship between fiction and reality?

facsimile: exact copy

amalgam: combination

> *7. In Your Journal:* Why would Eggers include omitted material in the preface? What context does this omitted material provide for the reader *before* she has begun to read the actual novel?

In real life, Meredith Weiss, who is real, does not know John all that well. The person who in real life acted as intermediary was not Meredith, but another person, whose presence would give away the connection, indeed, would give away poor John, and we could not have that. Thus, the author called Meredith:

"Hey."

"Hey."

"So, do you mind doing [such and such] and saying [such and such], which in real life you did not actually do and say?"

"No, not at all."

So that was that. It should be noted, though, that Meredith's main scene, in Chapter V, contains no fabrications. You can ask her. She lives in Southern California.

Otherwise, name changes are addressed in the body of the text. Hoo-ha.

LOCATIONS AND TIME: First, there have been a few instances of location-switching. In Chapter V, there were two in particular. The conversation with Deirdre, wherein the narrator tells her that Toph has fired a gun at his school and then disappeared, did not happen that night in that location, but instead happened in the backseat of a car, traveling from one party to the next, on New Year's Eve, 1996. Later in the same chapter, the narrator, with the same Meredith mentioned above, encounters some youths on a San Francisco beach. This episode, though otherwise entirely factual, actually occurred in Los Angeles. Also, in this chapter, as in a few other chapters, there has been compression of time. It is, for the most part, referenced in the text, but we will reiterate here that in the latter third of the book, much happens in what seems to be a short period of time. Though most of the events rendered did in fact happen within a very close span of time, a few did not. It should be noted, however, that the following chapters feature no time-compression: I, II, IV, VII.

A NOTE ABOUT COLUMBINE: This book was written, and the dialogue it recounts was spoken, many years before the events at that school and elsewhere. No levity is being attached to such things, intentionally or not.

OMISSIONS: Some really great sex scenes were omitted, at the request of those who are now married or *involved.* Also removed was a fantastic scene—100 percent true—featuring most of the book's primary characters, and a whale. Further, this edition reflects the omission of a number of sentences, paragraphs, and passages.

Among them:

> p. 34: As we lie on the bed, there are only a few long hours when Beth is asleep and Toph is asleep and my mother is asleep. I am awake for much of that time. I prefer the dark part of the night, after midnight and before four-thirty, when it's more bare, more hollow. Then I can breathe, and can think while others are

sleeping, in a way can stop time, can have it so—this has always been my dream—so that while everyone else is frozen, I can work busily about them, doing whatever it is that needs to be done, like the elves who make the shoes while the children sleep.

As I lay, drenched in the amber room, I wonder if I will nap in the morning. I think I can, believe I can sleep from maybe five until ten, before the nurses start coming in, adjusting and wiping, and so am content to stay up.

But this hideabed is killing me, the flimsiness of the mattress, the way that bar is digging into my back, bisecting my spine, grinding into it. Toph turning, kicking. And on the other side of the room, her uneven breathing.

p. 109: How do you handle this? Bill is up visiting, and he and Toph and I are driving over the Bay Bridge, and we are talking about stockbrokering. We are talking about how, after Toph spent a weekend in Manhattan Beach with Bill and Bill's two stockbroker roommates, Toph now wants to be a stockbroker, too. Bill is so excited about it all he can hardly stand it, wants to buy him a pair of suspenders, a starter-sized ticker...

"We were thinking that, with Toph so good with numbers and all, that something like that would be a perfect career—"

I almost drive the car over the bridge.

p. 181: Alcoholism and death make you omnivorous, amoral, desperate.

Do you really believe that?

Sometimes. Sure. No. Yes.

p. 190: ...But see, in high school, I did a series of paintings of members of my family. The first was of Toph, from a photograph I had taken. Because for the assignment we were required to grid the picture out for accuracy, the painting, in tempera, was dead-on; it looked just like him. Not so with the rest of them. I did one of Bill, but his face came out too rigid, his eyes too dark, and his hair looked matted, Caesar-like, which was not at all the case in real life. The painting of Beth, from a photograph of her dressed for the prom, was off too—I abandoned it right away. The one of my mom and dad, from an old slide, showed them on a boat together on a gray day. My mother takes up most of the frame, facing the camera, while my dad is over her shoulder, at the front of the boat, looking off to the side, unaware a picture is being taken. I screwed that one up, too—couldn't get the likenesses. When they saw the paintings, they loathed them. Bill was incensed when the one of him was shown at the public library. "Is that legal?" he asked my father. "Can he even do that? I look like a monster!" He was right. He did. So when Ricky Wolfgram asked me to do a portrait of his father, I hesitated, because I had been so repeatedly frustrated by my limits, by my inability to render someone without distorting them, clumsily, horribly. But to Ricky I said yes, out of respect, thrilled in a way that he had bestowed the honor on me with the painting of a memorial. He provided a formal black-and-white photograph, and I worked at it for weeks, with tiny brushes. When I was done, the likeness, to me, was unassailable. I told Ricky to come to the school's art room, that it was ready. He finished his lunch early one day and came down. I turned it around, with a flourish, with great pride, ready for us both to glow in its presence.

But he said:

"Oh. Oh. That's not what I expected. That's not...what I expected."

He left the room and the painting with me.

unassailable: indisputable

p. 172: ***Why the scaffolding?***

See, I like the scaffolding. I like the scaffolding as much as I like the building. Especially if that scaffolding is beautiful, in its way.

p. 190: When we would drive past a cemetery we would click our tongues and marvel, unbelieving. Especially the big ones, the crowded one, obscene places, so few trees, all that gray, like some sort of monstrous ashtray. When we went by Toph could not look, and I looked only to know, to reconfirm my own promise, that I would never be in such a place, would never bury anyone in such a place—who were these graves for? Who did they comfort?—would never allow myself to be buried in such a place, that I would either disappear completely—

I have visions of my demise: When I know I have only so much more time left—for example if I do in fact have AIDS as I believe I probably do, if anyone does, it's me, why not—when the time comes, I will just leave, say goodbye and leave, and then throw myself into a volcano.

Not that there seems to be any appropriate place to bury someone, but these municipal cemeteries, or any cemetery at all for that matter, like the ones by the highway, or the ones in the middle of town, with all these bodies with their corresponding rocks—oh it's just too primitive and vulgar, isn't it? The hole, and the box, and the rock on the grass? And we glamorize this process, feel it fitting and dramatic, austerely beautiful, standing there by the hole as we lower the box. It's incredible. Barbaric and base.

Though I should say I once saw a place that seemed fitting. I was walking—I would say "hiking," if we were doing anything but walking, but since we were just walking, I will not use the word "hiking," which everyone feels compelled to use anytime they're outside and there's a slight incline—in a forest above the Carapa, a tributary of the Amazon. I was on a junket, with a few other journalists—two from *Reptile* magazine—and a group of herpetologists, a bunch of chubby American snake experts with cameras, and we had been brought through this forest, on an upward-meandering path, looking for boa

herpetologist: zoologist specializing in reptiles and amphibians constrictors and lizards. After maybe forty-five minutes under this dappled dark forest, suddenly the trees broke, and we were at the top of the trail, in a clearing, over the river, and at that point you could see for honestly a hundred miles. The sun was setting, and in that huge Amazonian sky there were washes of blue and orange, thick swashes of each, mixed loosely, like paint pushed with fingers. The river was moving slowly below, the color of caramel, and beyond it was the forest, the jungle, green broccoli chaos as far as you could see. And immediately before us there were about twenty simple white crosses, without anything in the way of markings. A burial ground for local villagers.

And it occurred to me that I could stay there, that if I had to be buried, my rotting corpse heaped on with dirt, I could stand to have it done there. With the view and all.

It was odd timing, too, because earlier that day, I was almost sure I was leaving this world, via piranha.

We had anchored our boat, a three-story riverboat, in a small river cul-de-sac, and the guides had begun fishing for piranha, using only sticks and string, chicken as bait.

The piranhas took to it immediately. It was a cinch—they were jumping onto the boat, flopping around with their furious little faces.

And then, on the other side of the boat, our American guide, a bearded Bill, was swimming. The water, like tea, made his underwater limbs appear red, making all the more disconcerting the fact that he was swimming amid a school of piranhas.

"Come in!" he said.

Oh god no way.

Then everyone else was in, the chubby herpetologists were in, all their limbs in the bloodred tea. I had been told that piranha attacks were extremely rare (though not unheard of), that there was nothing to fear, and so soon enough I jumped from the boat and was swimming, too, relatively content that, even if there was some feeding frenzy, at least my odds were better than if I were in the water alone—while the fish were gorging on someone else, I'd have time to swim to safety. I actually did the math, the math of how long it would take the fish to eat the other four people vis-à-vis how long I'd have to get to the riverbank. After about three or four minutes, each one panic-stricken, trying not to touch my feet to the muddy ground, keeping my movements minimal so as not to attract attention, I got out.

Later, I tried out one of the guides' dugout canoes. After a few of the herpetologists had failed to stay afloat in it, I was convinced that I, being so very svelte and agile, could paddle and keep it afloat. I got in the tiny canoe, steadied myself, and paddled away. And for a while I did it. I set off from the main boat, downriver, alternating sides with the small paddle, the very picture of skill and grace.

But about two hundred yards down the river, the canoe began to sink. I was too heavy. It was taking in water.

I looked back to the boat. The Peruvian guides were all watching, were hysterical. I was sinking into the brown water, the current taking me farther downstream, and they were laughing, doubled over. They were loving it.

The canoe tipped, and I fell in, at this point in the middle of the river, where it was much deeper, a darker shade of brown. I could not see my limbs. I climbed onto the capsized canoe, desperate.

I was sure I was gone. Yes, the piranhas over there by the main boat had not touched us, but how could you be sure that out here, that they wouldn't take a nip from a finger? They often nipped fingers and toes, and that would draw blood and from there...

Oh God Toph.

I was there, and the canoe was sinking again, capsized but sinking under my weight, and soon I would be wholly in this river again, the river infested with piranhas, and my thrashing would draw them to me—I was trying, trying to keep it to a minimum, just kicking my legs, staying afloat—and then I would be picked at slowly, chunks from my calves and stomach, then, once the flesh was torn, and blood ribboning out, there would be the flurry, a hundred at once, I would look down and see my extremities overcome by a terrible blur of teeth and blood, and I would be picked clean, to the bone, and why? Because I had to show the entourage that I could do whatever any Peruvian river guide could do—

And I thought of poor Toph, this poor boy, three thousand miles away, staying with my sister—

How could I leave him?

p. 191: [M]y mother read a horror novel every night. She had read every one in the library. When birthdays and Christmas would come, I would consider buying her a new one, the latest Dean R. Koontz or Stephen King or whatever, but I couldn't. I didn't want to encourage her. I couldn't touch my father's cigarettes, couldn't look at the Pall Mall cartons in the pantry. I was the sort of child who couldn't even watch *commercials* for horror movies—the ad for *Magic*, the movie where the marionette kills people, sent me into a six-month nightmare frenzy. So I couldn't look at her books, would turn them over so their covers wouldn't show, the raised lettering and splotches of blood—especially the V. C. Andrews oeuvre, those turgid pictures of those terrible kids, standing so still, all lit in blue.

p. 355: Bill and Beth and Toph and I are watching the news. There is a small item about George Bush's grandmother. It is apparently her birthday.

We debate about how old the grandmother of a man in his late sixties must be. It seems almost impossible that she's still breathing.

Beth changes the channel.

"That's disgusting," she says.

p. 367: [S]he was living in a sort of perpetual present. Always she had to be told of her context, what brought her here, the origins and parameters of her current situation. Dozens of times each day she had to be told everything again—What made me? Whose fault am I? How did I get here? Who are these people?—the accident recounted, sketched in broad strokes, her continuously reminded but always forgetting—

Not forgetting. Having, actually, no capacity to grip the information—

But who does? Fuck it, she was alive and she knew it. Her voice sang the same way it always did, her eyes bulged with amazement over the smallest things, anything, my haircut. Yes, she still knew and had access to those things that had been with her for years—that part of her memory was there, intact—and while I wanted to punish those responsible, would relish it and presumed that I would never tire of it, being with her, so close to her skin and the blood rushing beneath it, drains me of hatred.

The music from the pool changed.

"Ooh, I like this song," she said, doing a zig-zag with her neck.

Finally, this edition reflects the author's request that all previous epigraphs—including "The heart's immortal thirst to be completely known and all forgiven." *(H. Van Dyke)*; "[My poems] may hurt the dead, but the dead belong to me." *(A. Sexton)*; "Not every boy thrown to the wolves becomes a hero." *(J. Barth)*; "Everything will be forgotten and nothing will be redressed." *(M. Kundera)*; "Why not just write what happened?" *(R. Lowell)*; "Ooh, look at me, I'm Dave, I'm writing a book! With all my thoughts in it! La la la!" *(Christopher Eggers)*—be removed, as he never really saw himself as the type of person who would use epigraphs.

—AUGUST 1999

8. In Your Journal: What is Eggers's opinion of epigraphs?

> ***9. In Your Journal:*** How do the table of contents' headings and sub-headings compare to others you've seen? Why are there so many "Etc.'s"? What do you expect from this novel given the sub-heading descriptions?

CONTENTS

Rules and Suggestions for Enjoyment of This Book vii
Preface to This Edition ix
Contents xvii
Acknowledgments xix
Incomplete Guide to Symbols and Metaphors xxxviii

PART I.

THROUGH THE SMALL TALL BATHROOM WINDOW, ETC. 1

Scatology—video games—blood—"blind leaders of the blind" [Bible]—some violence—turtles—embarrassment, naked men—mapping

PART II.

PLEASE LOOK. CAN YOU SEE US, ETC. 43

California—ocean plunging, frothing—Little League, black mothers—rotation and substitution—hills, views, roofs, toothpicks—numbing and sensation—Johnny Bench—motion

PART III.

THE ENEMIES LIST, ETC. 63

Demotion—teachers driven before us—menu—plane crash—light—knife—Barry Gifford—State of the Family Room Address—half-cantaloupes—so like a fragile girl—old model, new model—Bob Fosse Presents

PART IV.

OH I COULD BE GOING OUT, SURE 93

But no. No no!—the weight—seven years one's senior, how fitting—potential sagging—John Doe—decay v. preservation—burgundy, bolts

PART V.

OUTSIDE IT'S BLUE-BLACK AND GETTING DARKER, ETC. 109

Stephen, murderer, surely—The Bridge—Jon and Pontius Pilate—John, Moodie, et al.—Merchant Marine—lies—a stolen wallet—the 99th percentile—Mexican kids—lineups, lights—a trail of blood, and then silence, and then Russia

PART VI.

WHEN WE HEAR THE NEWS AT FIRST 147

What's In, What's Out—mailing lists—daughter of Charles Bronson, stunning—[some mild nudity]—Randy Stickrod—all the hope of history to date—an interview—death and suicide—mistakes—keg beer—Mr. T—Steve the Black Guy—a death faked, perhaps (the gray car)—a possible escape, via rope, of sheets—a broken door—betrayal justified

¡ Les saludo, muchachos!: Greetings, boys!

10. In Your Journal: What kind of help do you suspect Eggers got from NASA and the United States Marine Corps? Why does he acknowledge them here?

ACKNOWLEDGMENTS

The author wishes first and foremost to acknowledge his friends at NASA and the United States Marine Corps, for their great support and unquantifiable help with the technical aspects of this story. *¡Les saludo, muchachos!* He wishes also to acknowledge the many people who have stretched the meaning of generosity by allowing their real names and actions to appear in this book. This goes doubly for the author's siblings, especially his sister Beth, whose memories were in most places more vivid, and triply for Toph (pronounced "Tofe"), for obvious reasons. His older brother Bill is not being singled out because he is a Republican. The author would like to acknowledge that he does not look good in red. Or pink, or orange, or even yellow—he is not a spring. And until last year he thought Evelyn Waugh was a woman, and that George Eliot was a man. Further, the author, and those behind the making of this book, wish to acknowledge that yes, there are perhaps too many memoir-sorts of books being written at this juncture, and that such books, about real things and real people, as opposed to kind-of made up things and people, are inherently vile and corrupt and wrong and evil and bad, but would like to remind everyone that we could all do worse, as readers and as writers. ANECDOTE: midway through the writing of this...this...*memoir*, an acquaintance of the author's accosted him at a Western-themed restaurant/bar, while the author was eating a hearty plate of ribs and potatoes served fried in the French style. The accoster

xix

Evelyn Waugh: (1903–1966) English novelist and journalist, most well known for *Brideshead Revisited* (1945), a novel critical of many traditional English social conventions

George Eliot: (1857–1876) English Victorian novelist, most well known for *Middlemarch* (1872), a novel primarily concerned with the subtleties of English social class and manners sat down opposite, asking what was new, what was *up*, what was he working on, etc. The author said Oh, well, that he was kind of working on a book, kind of mumble mumble. Oh great, said the acquaintance, who was wearing a sport coat made from what seemed to be (but it might have been the light) purple velour. What kind of book? asked the acquaintance. (Let's call him, oh, "Oswald.") What's it about? asked Oswald. Well, uh, said the author, again with the silver tongue, it's kind of hard to explain, I guess it's kind of a memoir-y kind of thing— *Oh no!* said Oswald, interrupting him, loudly. (Oswald's hair, you might want to know, was feathered.) *Don't tell me you've fallen into that trap!* (It tumbled down his shoulders, Dungeons & Dragons–style.) *Memoir! C'mon, don't pull that old trick, man!* He went on like this for a while, using the colloquial language of the day, until, well, the author felt sort of bad. After all, maybe Oswald, with the purple velour and the brown corduroys, was right—maybe memoirs were *Bad*. Maybe writing about actual events, in the first person, if not from Ireland and before you turned seventy, was *Bad*. He had a point! Hoping to change the subject, the author asked Oswald, who shares a surname with the man who killed a president, what it was that *he* was working on. (Oswald was some sort of professional writer.) The author, of course, was both expecting and dreading that Oswald's project would be of grave importance and grand scope—a renunciation of Keynesian economics, a reworking of *Grendel* (this time from the point of view of nearby conifers), whatever. But do you know what he said, he of the feathered hair and purple velour? What he said was: a screenplay. He didn't italicize it

Grendel: monster slain by *Beowulf* in the classic Old English epic

conifer: evergreen tree

xx

"Oswald": possible allusion to Lee Harvey Oswald, the man officially responsible for the murder of John F. Kennedy; many consider Oswald a mere "fall guy" for a much larger conspiracy plot, possibly involving organized crime, the CIA, and/or the Cuban government

Keynesian: refers to the economic theories of John Maynard Keynes (1883–1946); Keynes's theories were related to unemployment and advocated active government intervention to ensure stability and growth

> *11. In Your Journal:* Why does Eggers think that "screenplay" should be italicized?

> *12. In Your Journal:* What is Eggers's attitude toward the genre of memoir? Why does he write one given that attitude?

> *13. In Your Journal:* How does Eggers's advice "PRETEND IT'S FICTION" relate to the notes on the copyright page about what's true and what's made up?

then but we will here: ***a screenplay.*** What sort of screenplay? the author asked, having no overarching problem with screenplays, liking movies enormously and all, how they held a mirror to our violent society and all, but suddenly feeling slightly better all the same. The answer: A screenplay "about William S. Burroughs, and the drug culture." Well, suddenly the clouds broke, the sun shone, and once again, the author knew this: that even if the idea of relating a true story is a bad idea, and even if the idea of writing about deaths in the family and delusions as a result is unappealing to everyone but the author's high school classmates and a few creative writing students in New Mexico, there are still ideas that are ***much, much worse.*** Besides, if you are bothered by the idea of this being real, you are invited to do what the author should have done, and what authors and readers have been doing since the beginning of time:

PRETEND IT'S FICTION.

As a matter of fact, the author would like to make an offer. For those of you on the side of Oswald, he will do this: if you send in your copy of this book, in hardcover or paperback, he will send you, in exchange, a 3.5" floppy disk, on which will be a complete digital manuscript of this work, albeit with all names and locations changed, in such a way that the only people who will know who is who are those whose lives have been included, though thinly disguised. *Voila!* Fiction! Further, the digital version will be interactive, as we expect our digital things to be (hey, have you heard of these new molecule-sized microchips? The ones that can do, like all the functions ever

William S. Burroughs: (1914–1997) Beat novelist primarily known for chronicling his drug addiction in *Naked Lunch* (1959)

performed by all computers since the beginning of time, in one second, in a grain of salt? Can you believe that? Well, it's as true now as ever: technology is changing the way we live). About the digital version, for starters, you'll have the option of choosing the protagonist's name. We'll provide dozens of suggestions, including "the Writer," "the Author," "the journalist," and "Paul Theroux"—or you can go it alone and make up your own! Matter of fact, using the search-and-replace function your computer surely features, readers should be able to change all the names within, from the main characters down to the smallest cameos. (This can be about *you*! You and *your* pals!) Those interested in this fictional version of this book should send their books to A.H.W.O.S.G. Special Offer for Fiction-Preferrers, c/o Simon & Schuster, 1230 Avenue of the Americas, New York, NY 10020. NOTE: This offer is real. ALTHOUGH: Books sent in, unfortunately, cannot be returned. INSTEAD: They will be remaindered with the rest. Moving on: The author wishes to acknowledge the existence of a planet just beyond Pluto, and further, wishes, on the basis of his own casual research and faith, to reassert Pluto's planethood. *Why did we do that to Pluto?* We had it good with Pluto. The author wishes to acknowledge that because this book is occasionally haha, you are permitted to dismiss it. The author wishes to acknowledge your problems with the title. He too has reservations. The title you see on the cover was the winner of a round-robin sort of title tourney, held outside Phoenix, Arizona, over a long weekend in December 1998. The other contenders, with reasons for failure: *A Heartbreaking Work of Death and Embarrassment* (kind of too-sad); *An Astounding*

xxii

Paul Theroux: contemporary U.S. novelist and travel writer, best known for *Mosquito Coast* (1981), about a family that moves to Honduras ostensibly to live a utopian life

Pluto: controversy began in 1994 and accelerated in 1998 over the planet status of Pluto; some scientists have begun to refer to Pluto as a comet while others have circulated a petition to defend Pluto's planet status

risqué bordering on improper; suggestive of impropriety

titular: so-called

Work of Courage and Strength (sounded like Stephen Ambrose); *Memories of a Catholic Boyhood* (also taken, pretty much); and *Old and Black in America* (risque, some say). We preferred the last one, alluding as it does to both aging and an American sort of *otherness*, but it was dismissed out of hand by the publisher, leaving us with *A Heartbreaking Work of Staggering Genius*. Yes, it caught your eye. First you took it at face value, and picked it up immediately. "This is just the sort of book for which I have been looking!" Many of you, particularly those among you who seek out the maudlin and melodramatic, were struck by the "Heartbreaking" part. Others thought the "Staggering Genius" element seemed like a pretty good recommendation. But then you thought, Hey, can these two elements work together? Or might they be like peanut butter and chocolate, plaid and paisley—never to peacefully coexist? Like, if this book is, indeed, heartbreaking, then why spoil the mood with the puffery? Or, if the title is some elaborate joke, then why make an attempt at sentiment? Which is to say nothing of the faux (real? No, you beg, please no) boastfulness of the whole title put together. In the end, one's only logical interpretation of the title's intent is as a) a cheap kind of joke b) buttressed by an interest in lamely executed titular innovation (employed, one suspects, only to shock) which is c) undermined of course by the cheap joke aspect, and d) confused by the creeping feeling one gets that the author is dead serious in his feeling that the title is an accurate description of the content, intent, and quality of the book. Oh, pshaw—does it even matter now? Hells no. You're here, you're in, we're havin' a party! The author would like to

---

Memories of a Catholic Boyhood: allusion to Mary McCarthy's *Memories of a Catholic Girlhood* (1972), a memoir about the author losing her parents as a young girl acknowledge that he did, indeed, vote for Ross Perot in 1996, and is not the least ashamed about it, because he is an ardent fan of the rich and insane, particularly when their hearts bleed, which Mr. Perot's does, it really does. On a different note, the author feels obligated to acknowledge that yes, the success of a memoir—of any book, really—has a lot to do with how appealing its narrator is. To address this, the author offers the following:

a) That he is like you.
b) That, like you, he falls asleep shortly after he becomes drunk.
c) That he sometimes has sex without condoms.
d) That he sometimes falls asleep when he is drunk having sex without condoms.
e) That he never gave his parents a proper burial.
f) That he never finished college.
g) That he expects to die young.
h) That, because his father smoked and drank and died as a result, he is afraid of food.
i) That he smiles when he sees young black men holding babies.

One word: appealing. And that's just the beginning!

Now, the author also wishes to acknowledge the major themes of this book. They are:

14. *In Your Journal:* How is this list intended to paint an "appealing" portrait of the narrator?

A) The Unspoken Magic of Parental Disappearance

It is every child's and teen's dream. Sometimes it is borne of bitterness. Sometimes it is borne of self-pity. Sometimes one wants attention. Usually all three factors play a part. The

15. *In Your Journal:* What does Eggers mean by the "UNSPOKEN MAGIC OF PARENTAL DISAPPEARANCE"?

point is that everyone at one point or another daydreams about their parents dying, and about what it would be like to be an orphan, like Annie or Pippi Longstocking or, more recently, the beautiful, tragic naifs of ***Party of Five***. One pictures, in place of the love perhaps unpredictably given and more often withheld by one's parents, that, in their absence, that love and attention would be lavished upon them, that the townspeople, one's relatives, one's friends and teachers, the world around, would suddenly be swept up in sympathy and fascination for the orphaned child, that his or her life would be one of celebrity mixed with pathos, fame sprung from tragedy—the best kind, by far. Most daydream it, some live it, and this aspect of the book will intimate that just as it was in Pippi, it is in real life. Thus, an incomparable loss begets both constant struggle and heart-hardening, but also some unimpeachable rewards, starting with absolute freedom, interpretable and of use in a number of ways. And though it seems inconceivable to lose both parents in the space of 32 days—there was that line from ***The Imp. of Being Earnest***: "To have lost one parent, Mr. Worthing, might be considered a misfortune. To have lost both smacks of carelessness"—and to lose them to completely different diseases (cancer, sure, but different enough, in terms of location, duration, and provenance), that loss is accompanied by an undeniable but then of course guilt-inducing sense of mobility, of infinite possibility, having suddenly found oneself in a world with neither floor nor ceiling.

unimpeachable: impeccable; perfect

provenance: origin; derivation

xxv

Party of Five: popular 1990's television drama about five orphaned siblings

The Imp.[ortance] of Being Earnest: Oscar Wilde play (1895) about a man who invents a brother to use as a convenient social excuse symbiosis: relationship (usually in biology) between two or more organisms that may benefit each other in some way

B) THE BROTHERLY LOVE / WEIRD SYMBIOSIS FACTOR

This thread will be going throughout, and was as a matter of fact supposed to be the surprise conclusion reached at the end of the book, the big pay-off, as it were, that, while the author searches for love—there will be some episodes involving that—and his brother searches for, you know, whatever little kids search for (gum and pennies?) and together they try to be normal and happy, they actually will probably always be unsuccessful in any and every extracurricular relationship, given that the only people who they truly admire and love and find perfect are each other.

C) THE PAINFULLY, ENDLESSLY SELF-CONSCIOUS BOOK ASPECT

This is probably obvious enough already. The point is, the author doesn't have the energy or, more importantly, skill, to fib about this being anything other than him telling you about things, and is not a good enough liar to do it in any competently sublimated narrative way. At the same time, he will be clear and up-front about this being a self-conscious memoir, which you may come to appreciate, and which is the next theme:

16. In Your Journal: What does Eggers mean by "self-conscious" here?

C.2) THE KNOWINGNESS ABOUT THE BOOK'S SELF-CONSCIOUSNESS ASPECT

While the author is self-conscious about being self-referential, he is also knowing about that self-conscious self-referentiality. Further, and if you're one of those people who can tell what's going to happen before it actually happens, you've predicted the next element here: he also plans to be clearly, obviously aware of his knowingness about his self-consciousness of self-referentiality. Further, he is fully cognizant, way ahead of you, in terms of knowing about and fully admitting the gimmickry inherent in all this, and will preempt your claim of the book's irrelevance due to said gimmickry by saying that the gimmickry is simply a device, a defense, to obscure the black, blinding, murderous rage and sorrow at the core of this whole story, which is both too black and blinding to look at—*avert...your...eyes!*—but nevertheless useful, at least to the author, even in caricatured or condensed form, because telling as many people as possible about it helps, he thinks, to dilute the pain and bitterness and thus facilitate its flushing from his soul, the pursuit of which is the basis of the next cluster of themes:

D) THE TELLING THE WORLD OF SUFFERING AS MEANS OF FLUSHING OR AT LEAST DILUTING OF PAIN ASPECT

For example, the author spends some time later relating his unsuccessful, though just barely unsuccessful, attempt to become a cast member of *The Real World* in 1994, when the show's third season was being filmed in San Francisco. At that point, the author sought to do two related things: 1) to purge himself of his past by trumpeting his recent life's events to the world, and thus, by spreading his pain, his heartbreaking story, to the show's thousands or millions of watchers, he would receive in return a thousand tidal waves of sympathy and support, and never be lonely again; and 2) To become well known for his sorrows, or at least to let his suffering facilitate his becoming well known, while at the same time not shrinking from the admission of such manipulations of his pain for profit, because the admission of such motivations, at least in his opinion, immediately absolves him of responsibility for such manipulations' implications or consequences, because being aware of and open about one's motives at least means one is not lying, and no one, except an electorate, likes a liar. We all like full disclosure, particularly if it includes the admission of one's 1) mortality and 2) propensity to fail. (Related, but not the same.)

17. In Your Journal: How could "mortality" and "propensity to fail" be "related"?

E) THE PUTTING THIS ALL DOWN AS TOOL FOR STOPPING TIME GIVEN THE OVERLAP WITH FEAR OF DEATH ASPECT

and E)'s self-explanatory corollary,

E.2) IN ADDITION TO PUTTING THIS DOWN AS TOOL FOR STOPPING TIME, THE SEXUAL RENDEZVOUS WITH OLD FRIENDS OR GRADE SCHOOL CRUSHES AS TOOL FOR COLLAPSING OF TIME AND VINDICATION OF SELF-WORTH

F) THE PART WHERE THE AUTHOR EITHER EXPLOITS OR EXALTS HIS PARENTS, DEPENDING ON YOUR POINT OF VIEW

G) THE UNMISTAKABLE FEELING ONE GETS, AFTER SOMETHING TRULY WEIRD OR EXTRAORDINARY, OR EXTRAORDINARILY WEIRD, OR WEIRDLY TERRIBLE, HAPPENS TO THEM, THAT IN A WAY THEY HAVE BEEN *CHOSEN* ASPECT

This of course happened to the author. After the double-deaths, and his guardianship, he felt suddenly *watched*—he could not help but think, in much the same way someone

18. *In Your Journal:* What kind of memoir does this language (i.e., "that . . . *he had been chosen . . . to lead!*") seem to allude to? Is the allusion sincere?

who had been struck by lightning might, that he had somehow been singled out, and that his life was thereafter charged with purpose, with the gravest importance, that he could not be wasting time, that he must act in accordance with his destiny, that it was so plainly obvious that...that...*he had been chosen...to lead!*

H) The Aspect Having to Do with (Perhaps) Inherited Fatalism

This part concerns the unshakable feeling one gets, one thinks, after the unthinkable and unexplainable happens—the feeling that, if this person can die, and that person can die, and this can happen and that can happen...well, then, what exactly is preventing everything from happening to this person, he around whom everything else happened? If people are dying, why won't he? If people are shooting people from cars, if people are tossing rocks down from overpasses, surely he will be the next victim. If people are contracting AIDS, odds are he will, too. Same with fires in homes, car accidents, plane crashes, random knifings, stray gunfire, aneurysms, spider bites, snipers, piranhas, zoo animals. It's the confluence of the self-centeredness discussed in G), and a black sort of outlook one is handed when all rules of impossibility and propriety are thrown out. Thus, one starts to feeling that death is literally around each and every corner—and more specifically, in every elevator; even more literally, that, each and every time an elevator door opens, there will be standing, in a trenchcoat, a man, with a gun, who will fire one bullet, straight into him, killing him instantly, and deservedly, both

confluence: convergence; coming together

in keeping with his role as the object of so much wrath in general, and for his innumerable sins, both Catholic and karmic. Just as some police—particularly those they dramatize on television—might be familiar with death, and might expect it at any instant—not necessarily their own, but death generally—so does the author, possessing a naturally paranoid disposition, compounded by environmental factors that make it seem not only possible but ***probable*** that whatever there might be out there that snuffs out life is probably sniffing around for him, that his number is perennially, eternally, up, that his draft number is low, that his bingo card is hot, that he has a bull's-eye on his chest and target on his back. It's fun. You'll see.

karmic: relating to one's fate with respect to the consequence of one's actions throughout successive stages of existence

perennially: lasting or active over many years

And finally:

1) THE MEMOIR AS ACT OF SELF-DESTRUCTION ASPECT
It can and should be the shedding of a skin, which is something one should do, as necessary and invigorating as the occasional facial, or colonic. Revelation is everything, not for its own sake, because most self-revelation is just garbage—*oop!*—yes, but we have to purge the garbage, toss it out, throw it into a bunker and burn it, because it is fuel. It's fossil fuel. And what do we do with fossil fuel? Why, we dump it into a bunker and burn it, of course. No, we don't do that. But you get my meaning. It's endlessly renewable, usable without diminishing one's capacity to create more. The author falls asleep shortly after he becomes drunk. The author has sex without condoms. The author falls asleep when he's

colonic: type of enema; cleansing of the colon

19. In Your Journal: Why does Eggers repeat these confessions about falling asleep when drunk and having sex without condoms, which already appear as part of the list on page twenty-four (277)? What point does he use the repetition to illustrate?

drunk having sex without condoms. There. That's something. You have something. But what do you *have*?

I.2) THE EASY AND UNCONVINCING NIHILISTIC POSEURISM RE: FULL DISCLOSURE OF ONE'S SECRETS AND PAIN, PASSING IT OFF UNDER A SEMI-HIGH-MINDED GUISE WHEN IN FACT THE AUTHOR IS HIMSELF VERY PRIVATE ABOUT MANY OR MOST MATTERS, THOUGH HE SEES THE USE IN MAKING CERTAIN FACTS AND HAPPENINGS PUBLIC

I.3) THE FACT THAT, BELOW, OR MAYBE NEXT TO, THE SELF-RIGHTEOUSNESS, AND THE SELF-HATRED, IS A CERTAIN HOPE, INSTILLED FAR BEFORE ANY OF THIS HAPPENED.

There will also be these threads, which are all more or less self-explanatory:

J) THE FLOUTING OF SUBLIMATION AS EVIDENCE OF ENFORCED SOLIPSISM ASPECT

K) THE SOLIPSISM AS LIKELY RESULT OF ECONOMIC, HISTORICAL AND GEOPOLITICAL PRIVILEGE ASPECT

L) THE TOPH DIALECTIC: HE SERVING AS BOTH INSPIRATION FOR AND IMPEDIMENT TO WRITING OF MEMOIR

M) THE TOPH DIALECTIC II: HE SERVING AS BOTH MAGNET AND, WHEN THE NEED ARISES, WEDGE VIS-À-VIS RELATIONS WITH WOMEN

20. In Your Journal: How does this list appear to be, as Eggers says, *"self-explanatory"*?

solipsism: theory that the self is the only reality

dialectic: process of arriving at the truth by overcoming opposition

Similarly:

N) THE PARENTAL LOSS DIALECTIC: IN TERMS OF THAT FACTOR LENDING ITSELF WELL TO SITUATIONS NECESSITATING THE GARNERING OF SYMPATHY AND ALSO TO THOSE REQUIRING A QUICK EXIT

Not to mention:

O) THE ASPECT CONCERNING THE UNAVOIDABILITY, GIVEN THE SITUATION WITH BROTHER, OF NEAR-CONSTANT POIGNANCE

P) THE SELF-AGGRANDIZEMENT AS ART FORM ASPECT

Q) THE SELF-FLAGELLATION AS ART FORM ASPECT

R) THE SELF-AGGRANDIZEMENT DISGUISED AS SELF-FLAGELLATION AS EVEN HIGHER ART FORM ASPECT

S) THE SELF-CANONIZATION DISGUISED AS SELF-DESTRUCTION MASQUERADING AS SELF-AGGRANDIZEMENT DISGUISED AS SELF-FLAGELLATION AS HIGHEST ART FORM OF ALL ASPECT

T) THE SEARCH FOR SUPPORT, A SENSE OF COMMUNITY, IF YOU WILL, IN ONE'S PEERS, IN THOSE ONE'S AGE, AFTER ONE LOOKS AROUND AND REALIZES THAT ALL OTHERS, ALL THOSE OLDER, ARE EITHER DEAD OR PERHAPS SHOULD BE ASPECT

U) THE FACT THAT T) DOVETAILS QUITE NICELY WITH G) ASPECT

Or, in graph form (opposite):

xxxii

21. In Your Journal: How does this discussion of "art form" relate to the earlier defense of the memoir as a genre?

22. *In Your Journal:* As with the Table of Contents, "The Deaths" chart makes frequent use of the abbreviation "Etc." What things do you think Eggers believes so obvious that he need only to refer to them as "Etc."? How does this practice comment on the themes with which he is working?

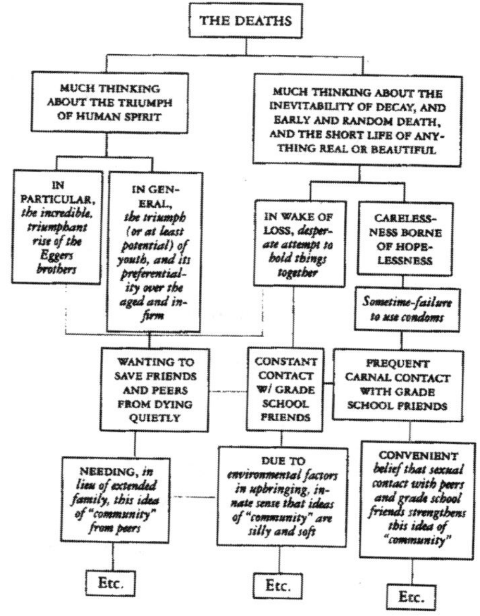

NOTE: The above is actually part of a much larger chart, 18" × 24" (though not to scale), which maps out the entire book, mostly in type too small to read. It was supposed to be included with your purchase, but you know how these publishing companies are. It is instead available through the mail, at the address listed elsewhere in this section. The cost is $5. You will not be disappointed. Unless you are usually disappointed, in which case this will be yet another disappointment.

xxxiii

The author would also like to acknowledge what he was paid to write this book:

TOTAL (GROSS)	\$100,000.00
DEDUCTIONS	
Agent's fee (15%)	\$15,000.00
Taxes (after agent's fee)	\$23,800.00
EXPENSES RELATED TO PRODUCTION OF BOOK	
Portion of rent, two years (btw \$600 & \$1,500/mo)	approx. \$12,000.00
Trip to Chicago (research)	\$850.00
Trip to San Francisco (research)	\$620.00
Food (consumed while ostensibly writing)	\$5,800.00
Sundries	\$1,200.00
Laser printer	\$600.00
Paper	\$242.00
Postage (to send manuscript, for approval, to siblings Beth (somewhere in No. California), and Bill (an advisor to the Comptroller of Texas, in Austin), Kirsten (San Francisco, married), Shalini (living at home in L.A., doing well), Meredith Weiss (freelance wardrobe stylist, San Diego), Jamie Carrick (in L.A., part of management team for Hanson, a popular music outfit), Rick Wolfgram (San Francisco, investment banker—high tech IPOs), etc. etc.)	\$231.00
Copy of *Xanadu* Original Movie Soundtrack	\$14.32
Information retrieval service (unsuccessful attempt to retrieve two years' worth of journal entries from external hard drive, expired)	\$75.00
NET TOTAL	\$39,567.68

Which still isn't so bad, come to think of it—more than the author, who is not a pet owner, can spend. Therefore, he

23. In Your Journal: Describe the tone of Eggers's offer for $5 to the first 200 readers of his book. What is Eggers's intention here? How does he increase, decrease, or otherwise affect the level of his credibility or reliability as a narrator?

pledges some of it to you, or at least some of you. The first 200 readers of this book who write with proof that they have read and absorbed the many lessons herein will each receive a check, from the author, for $5, drawn from a U.S. bank, probably Chase Manhattan, which is not a good bank—do not open an account there. Now: how to prove that you have bought and read the book? Let's say we do this: Take the book, which you are required to have purchased*—enclose your receipt, or a copy of the receipt—and have someone take a picture of you reading the book, or maybe putting it to better use. Special consideration for a) the inclusion in the picture of a baby (or babies), as everyone knows that babies are nice; b) the inclusion in the picture of a baby with an exceptionally large tongue; c) pictures taken in exotic locales (with the book, remember); d) pictures of the book being rubbed against by a red panda, a small bear + raccoon-looking mammal, also known as the "lesser panda," native of central China and frequent-rubber-againster of things for marking of territory. DO NOT FORGET TO: center yourself, or whatever your subject, in the picture. If you're using an auto-focus camera with a 35mm lens, get closer than you feel you should; the lens, because it's convex, has the effect of backing you up 5–8 feet. ALSO: Keep your clothes on, please. Those readers who are savvy enough to have picked up a copy of one quarterly

* It should go without saying that if you've checked this book out from the library, or are reading it in paperback, you are much, much too late. Come to think of it, you may be reading this far, far in the future—it's probably being taught in all the schools! Do tell: What's it like in the future? Is everyone wearing robes? Are the cars rounder, or less round? Is there a women's soccer league yet?

publication in particular will already know the most expeditious address to receive this free-ish money (though that address is only good until maybe August, 2000), and will therefore be at an advantage, timewise. Otherwise, send your tasteful photographs to:

A.H.O.St.G. Offer, c/o Geoff Kloske
Simon & Schuster
1230 Avenue of the Americas
New York, NY 10020

If, by the time the author receives your letter, he has already distributed the 200 checks, good fortune may yet strike. If your picture is amusing or your name or hometown unfortunate-sounding, and you include a self-addressed stamped envelope, he will put something (not money) inside the envelope and will send it back, because he does not have cable, and needs diversion.

Now.* The author would like to acknowledge your desire to get started with the plot, the body of the book, the *story*. He will do that, and, contrary to what was said in D), he will be giving you, for a good 100 pages or so, uninterrupted, unself-conscious prose, which will entertain and make sad and, here and there, hearten. He will get on with that story any moment now, because he

*Interesting story: My father once related how he and his friend Les had come up with a way, when stalling for time in a meeting or deposition (he and Les were lawyers [Les, alive and well, still is a lawyer]), instead of saying "Um...," or "Uh...," one could say "Now...," a word which accomplishes two things: it serves the same stalling purpose as "Um...," or "Uh...," but instead of being dumb-sounding offputting, it creates suspense for what is coming next, whatever that might be, that which the speaker doesn't yet know.

24. In Your Journal: How do Eggers's stalling tactics compare to his father's use of "Now" in meetings and depositions? Do you feel irritation with his stalling? Do you think Eggers intends you to feel irritation?

recognizes when the time has come, when the time is right, when the getting's good. He acknowledges the needs and feelings of a reader, the fact that a reader only has so much time, so much patience—that seemingly endless screwing about, interminable clearing of one's throat, can very easily look like, or even ***become***, a sort of contemptuous stalling, a putting-off of one's readers, and no one wants that. (Or do they?) So we will move on, because the author, like you, wants to move on, into the meat of it, dive right in and revisit this stuff, because it's a story that ought to be told, involving, as it does, death and redemption, bile, and betrayal. So dive in we will, after a few more acknowledgments. The author would like to acknowledge the brave men and women serving in the United States Armed Forces. He wishes them well, and hopes they come home soon. That is, if they want to. If they like it where they are, he hopes they stay there. At least until such time as they want to come home. Then they should come straight home, on the very next plane. The author would also like to acknowledge the makers of comic book villains and superheroes, those who invented, or at least popularized, the notion of the normal, mild-mannered person transformed into mutant by freak accident, with the mutant thereafter driven by a strange hybrid of the most rancid bitterness and the most outrageous hope to do very, very odd and silly things, many times in the name of Good. The makers of comic books seemed to be onto something there. Now, in a spirit of interpretive *glasnost*, the author would like to save you some trouble by laying out a rough guide to a little over half of the metaphors in the book. (Next page)

glasnost: Soviet policy permitting open discussion of political and social issues

INCOMPLETE GUIDE TO SYMBOLS AND METAPHORS

Sun	=	Mother
Moon	=	Father
Family room	=	Past
Nosebleed	=	Decay
Tumor	=	Portent
Sky	=	Emancipation
Ocean	=	Mortality
Bridge	=	Bridge
Wallet	=	Security
		Father
		Past
		Class
Lattice	=	Transcendental-equivalent
White bed	=	Womb
Furniture, rugs, etc.	=	Past
Tiny stuffed bear	=	Mother
Toph	=	Mother
Dolls	=	Mother
Lake Michigan	=	Mother
		Past
		Peace
		Chaos
		Unknown
Mother	=	Mortality
Mother	=	Love
Mother	=	Rage
Mother	=	Cancer
Betsy	=	Past
John	=	Father
Shalini	=	Promise
Skye	=	Promise
Me	=	Mother

Note: No symbolism is meant by the use of Journey's "Any Way You Want It."

xxxviii

25. In Your Journal: Is Eggers's symbol and metaphor guide meant to help or confuse you? How does it recall the way you have been taught to read literature in school? What comment does it make on the way one is expected to read and interpret a book?

The author would also like to acknowledge his propensity to exaggerate. And his propensity to fib in order to make himself look better, or worse, whichever serves his purposes at the time. He would also like to acknowledge that no, he is not the only person to ever lose his parents, and that he is also not the only person ever to lose his parents and inherit a youngster. But he would like to point out that he is currently the only such person with a book contract. He would like to acknowledge the distinguished senator from Massachusetts. And Palestinian statehood. And the implicit logic of the instant replay rule. And that he too is well aware of all of the book's flaws and shortcomings, whatever you consider them to be, and that he tips his hat to you for noticing them. And come to think of it, he would actually like to acknowledge his brother Bill after all; his brother Bill is such a good man. And this book's editor, Geoff Kloske, and Mr. Kloske's assistant, Nicole Graev, who has her vowels transposed but is otherwise very nice. And of course Elyse Cheney, who was, too bad for her, there from the beginning of all this. Also C. Leyshon, A. Quinn, J. Lethem, and V. Vida, for the assuaging of fears, not to mention Adrienne Miller, John Warner, Marny Requa and Sarah Vowell, whose readings of this book before it was readable were much appreciated (even though, come to think of it, the author did toss Warner $100, which makes his acknowledgment kind of unnecessary). And once again, all the people who star in this story, especially Mr. C.M.E., who knows who he is. Finally, the author would also like to acknowledge the men and women of the United States Postal Service, for performing a sometimes thankless task with great aplomb and, given the scale and scope of the endeavor, with stunning efficiency.

26. In Your Journal: This drawing of a stapler marks the end of the front matter of Eggers's book; on the next page of the book, the story does begin in earnest. What do you suppose the stapler is meant to indicate in this regard?

Here is a drawing of a stapler:

xxxix

distinguished Senator from Massachusetts: refers to Senator Edward Kennedy; and to the practice of Senators addressing each other in this manner immediately preceding a major disagreement or criticism

the instant replay rule: currently in use in the National Football League, and recently approved by the National Basketball Association; where referees use taped replay to confirm difficult (usually scoring-related) calls

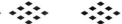

FOR USE IN DISCUSSION

Questions about Substance

1. Does this excerpt of Eggers's book compare to anything else you have read—either in the realm of traditional literature or popular prose? Based on the material you have here, how would you characterize Eggers's writing?
2. Review the Acknowledgments (272–292). Can you tell which of these acknowledgments are sincere and which are ironic? How does Eggers comment on the general role of Acknowledgments in book publishing by presenting such strange and varied examples?
3. Does the note about Eggers's "The Deaths" chart (286) or the special offer for a $5 check from the author (288) bear any resemblance to other types of merchandising gimmicks you're familiar with? What is Eggers's point in making these offers?
4. Why do you think Eggers shares his expense budget with the reader (521)?

Questions about Structure and Style

1. Eggers calls into question just about every standard convention in book publishing, as well as the major conventions of memoir. Do his questions and commentaries about convention have an effect on your ability to read these excerpts conventionally?
2. Eggers's style could be characterized as highly "parenthetical," in that he frequently interrupts himself often to go on a tangent, provide additional information, or qualify what he has just written. For example: "2. There is also no overarching need to read the acknowledgments section. Many early readers of this book (see 526) suggested its curtailment or removal, but they were defied. Still, it is not necessary to the plot in any major way, so as with the preface, if you have already read the acknowledgments section, and wish you had not, again, we apologize. We should have said something" (262). Is this style meant to be irritating, humorous, or both? Does this style seem appropriate to Eggers's highly personal story?
3. While this material is in fact just Eggers's *introduction* to a somewhat more conventionally written memoir, does it somehow tell a story all by itself? If so, what is that story?
4. How do you think Eggers's style reflects the characteristics or values of his generation? He was in his twenties in the late 1990's when he wrote this book. Are there cultural or popular contexts or trends that you would refer to in attempting to place this writing within the era of the 1990's?

Multimedia Suggestions

1. *Orphans* (1987) and *In Country* (1989), two films about orphans, both have a more reverent and linear narrative style than Dave Eggers's *A Heartbreaking*

Work of Staggering Genius. Watch one or both of these films and compare them in terms of tone and point-of-view as they relate to the theme of the orphan.

2. Dave Eggers edits McSweeney's, an alternative magazine (available at *www.mcsweeneys.net*) and is also a founder of 826 Valencia, a non-profit tutoring and writing center in San Francisco's Mission District (information available at *www.826valencia.org).* Check out one or both of these Web sites and describe the way this new information affects your impression of Eggers's writing.
3. *The Onion* is a satirical news source, which pokes fun at the conventions of journalism and popular print culture. Compare Eggers's work to the writing you find in *The Onion* (available at: *http://www.theonion.com/ onion3908/index.html*).

SUGGESTIONS FOR WRITING AND RESEARCH

1. Examine the introductory material for several other memoirs (some you have read and some you have not read). Compare and contrast those prefaces, acknowledgements, and any other notes with what you have read of Eggers's book. Describe the implicit critique Eggers's material makes of the other memoirs you have examined.
2. Write an essay about Dave Eggers's memoir introduction in the same kind of self-conscious, parenthetical, and ironic style he uses. Determine which essay-writing conventions (e.g., titling, subtitling, thesis statement and topic sentences, paragraph transitions, use of evidence, citation, etc.) you would like to call into question, and draw attention to those conventions by over-emphasizing, inverting, or otherwise "playing" with them.
3. Eggers prefers his books to be sold only through independently-owned bookstores rather than large chains. Do you have any sense, based on your reading here, of why that might be true? Write an essay about the role of publisher's and booksellers in a writer's career. Do some of your research by visiting different kinds of bookstores and evaluating the variety and originality of their stock.

WORKING WITH CLUSTERS

Cluster 4: Conceiving Death

Cluster 11: The Art of Irony

Cluster 19: Structuring Chaos

Discipline: The Humanities

Rhetorical Mode: Description

"Saudi Arabia 1997"

by Wendy Ewald

Wendy Ewald was born in Detroit, Michigan. She has photographed and taught photography to young people and women around the world, encouraging her students to turn their experiences and dreams into poetic images. Ewald is creator and Project Director of the Literacy through Photography programs in Houston, Texas and Durham, North Carolina. She is a Senior Research Associate at the Center for Documentary Studies and Artist-in-Residence at the John Hope Franklin Center, and Senior Associate of the Vera List Center for Art and Politics at the New School University at Duke University. She has also received many awards, including a MacArthur Fellowship, several National Endowment for the Arts grants, and the Lila Wallace Reader's Digest *Visual Arts Fellowship for South Africa. Much of her work, including this excerpted series, appears in* Secret Games: Collaborative Works with Children *1969–1999.*

In **Morocco** I had begun to understand some of the subtleties of Islam and to experience its comforting effect on the town I was living in. Never before had I lived in a place that felt so safe; I imagined the **medina** as a womb surrounding me. But I still wanted to see what life might be like in a more strictly religious Islamic country. So far, as a Westerner, I had been able to avoid many of the restrictions placed on the people I worked with. To really understand such rules, I would have to live with and experience them personally.

medina: the old section of a city in Arab North Africa (e.g., Morocco); usually characterized by enclosing walls and winding streets

graven image: (sacrilegious) idols, usually carved in stone or wood, which signify a serious betrayal to one's god(s)

1. In Your Journal: Ewald says that the "culture of the city is traditional . . . but . . . open to new ideas." What do you suppose Ewald wants her Western audience to perceive in these photographs, given this dichotomy?

2. In Your Journal: What do you think it means to "look for metaphors" to explain who one is? Can you think of any metaphors that would explain who you are?

Jeddah, on the west coast of the Kingdom of Saudi Arabia, is the port of entry for millions of pilgrims who travel to **Mecca** every year. The culture of the city is traditional, but perhaps because of its interaction with the entire Muslim world, it is open to new ideas. Still, photography is considered controversial; in much of the Muslim world, representational graphics can be construed as **graven images.** In Jeddah, people rarely take pictures in public, though many families do so at home. In addition to these considerations, there is a strict taboo against any mingling of the sexes and against public exposure of any part of a woman's body except for her hands and eyes.

Every morning and evening for two weeks, chauffeurs dropped off my students—professional women, housewives and schoolgirls—wrapped in *abayas* (shroud-like gowns) at the girls' school where my photography workshop was being held. (The women couldn't drive themselves because women are not allowed to drive in Saudi Arabia.) We decided that the most challenging subject we could explore was self-representation. I wanted to find ways in which the women could do this in a public arena. Many of the women chose to make pictures of themselves unveiled, photographs they knew could never be shown publicly. Others looked for metaphors to ex-

Morocco: Ewald taught photography to children in Asilah, Morocco in 1995

Mecca: the birthplace of Muhammad the prophet (founder of Islam), located in Hejaz, (west) Saudi Arabia; considered the holiest site in the Muslim world; one of the greatest goals for every Muslim is to make a pilgrimage to Mecca (during the annual hajj) plain who they were, like **Raja Alem,** a writer, who used two shells to represent herself and her sister Shadia, a painter.

Finally I asked the women if they would work with me to make collaborative portraits that could be exhibited and published. After some discussion, it was agreed that they would need to cover themselves, or represent themselves in indirect ways.

Nadine chose her veiled daughter as her stand-in. At my suggestion she added her own hands. Anoud, because she was a young girl, was able to pose in Western clothes, without her *abaya*. Another young girl named Johainah chose a more traditional route: She pictured herself wearing her *abaya,* and holding her little sister. Later she asked if I would add more, lines to the negative and further obscure her face.

3. In Your Journal: Ewald explains how she suggested that Nadine add her own hands to the photograph of her daughter. What value is this piece of information to the viewer of the photograph?

Eventually an exhibition of these portraits, self-portraits, and dream pictures was mounted at Jeddah's House of Photography. The women decided that they wanted their work seen by an integrated audience; that is, by men and women. This meant that the images had to be carefully edited to get by the censors. Parts of some photographs had to be blocked out with Magic Markers to erase areas that revealed women's faces or bodies. Raja's portrait, which made use of an ancient Arabic text called *The Book of Dreams,* was **culled** by censors wary of controversial symbolism.

cull: select; pick out

The exhibition opened with great fanfare. The opening night, which was for ladies only, was presided over by a princess of the Saudi royal family. The second night was for men only, and the third was for husbands and wives together.

Raja Alem: contemporary Saudi Arabian author of six novels; published *Fatma: A Novel of Arabia* in English in 2003 with co-author Tom McDonough (novelist and husband of Wendy Ewald); her style blends magical realism, fairy tale, and mythology

4. *In Your Journal:* In what ways is this portrait traditional? In what ways is it modern?

Nadine holding her daughter

5. *In Your Journal:* The writing on this photograph reads: "When I were a lady." To whom do you think this caption refers—Nadine or her daughter? What does it mean?

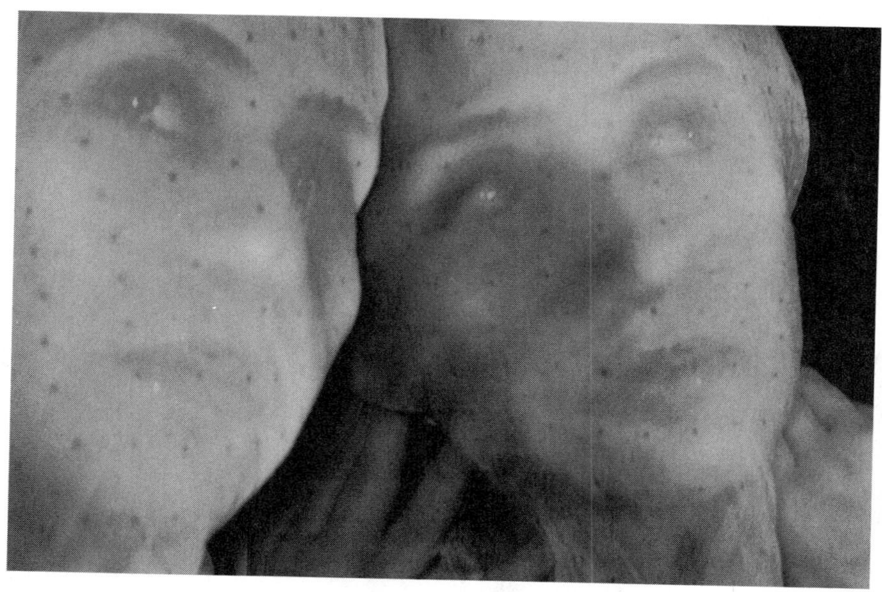

Self-portrait—Raja Alem

> ***6. In Your Journal:*** How does the Saudi view of taking someone's photograph compare to the Western view, in your opinion?

> ***7. In Your Journal:*** How do you think photographers compare to hunters in this author's understanding?

> ***8. In Your Journal:*** Why do you suppose Raja Alem chooses to feature two images of herself in this self-portrait?

ALL KINDS OF VEILS

High in the mountains of Saudi Arabia, carved and painted on cliffs, there are many prehistoric pictures of horses and human beings. Since the beginning of time, these images have had no respite from prying idolizing eyes. For those of us who live in a culture as ancient as Saudi Arabia's, the historical and spiritual weight of these images suggests that making portraits is no light matter. Taking someone's photograph is equivalent to capturing his twin self, his spirit; it is a way of taking complete control of the person whose picture is taken. Photography is a glimpse into the soul, stolen for the sake of illuminating a dark, impersonal sheet of paper.

In this case photography turned out to be something more. It began when we allowed an outsider to see behind the veil. Then, assuming the role of hunters put us in another realm and gave us a place to stand that was powerful enough to alter the male-controlled orbits we move in. When we took our cameras into the street, people reacted with sincerity and entertained new possibilities. The bodies they had lived in so long opened to whatever experiences they might encounter. They seemed oblivious to the dangers of intrusion or captivity. They opened up and posed happily, smiling at the camera's charm and at our courage in openly pursuing stories in circumstances that are ordinarily closed. By posing, they allowed us to steal their souls. And in the very act of announcing our power, we women gained power over the men.

—Raja Alem

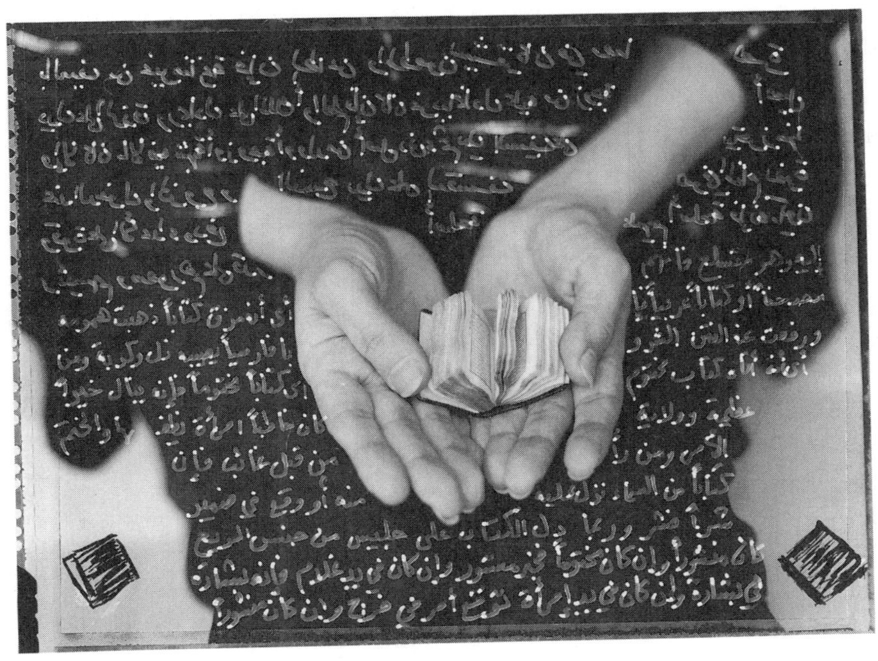

The Queen of all queens in the kingdom of keys. . . .
Each key controls thousands and thousands of spirits,
And each spirit has thousands of followers.
Each spirit rules thousands and thousands of giants.
This is written in ink made of **alum.**

I own the keys of creation.
This is written in ink made of alum.

Foreheads and fingers are merely doors to the invisible world.

The letter A is the king of the alphabet,
But it is silenced by **Ibn Sereen's** *Book of Dreams.*

—Raja Alem (translation of inscription on photograph)

alum: kind of metal

9. In Your Journal: Why do you think there is writing on the body in this photograph, but not on the hands?

⁘ **Ibn Sereen:** (Allama Muhammad Ibn Sireen) Islamic writer and interpreter of dreams

10 In Your Journal: What does Shadia Alem mean when she claims here that her painting "dreamt" her?

Shadia Alem

Johainah holding her little sister

FOR USE IN DISCUSSION

Questions about Substance

1. In her introduction, Ewald makes several references to her influence on the composition of these photographs: in addition to taking most of the photographs, she encouraged the eventual exhibition of the works, she changed the pose in one photograph, and she altered the negative of another. Whose vision is presented here? Why does Ewald make her involvement in the creation of these images so clear?
2. Examine the ways that eyes figure in the images in many of these photographs. Many of them look directly at the viewer, despite the apparent general modesty of the subjects. Is this a contradiction of sorts? Why or why not?
3. Raja Alem's short essay that introduces her multimedia work "All Kinds of Veils" presents a view of Saudi Arabia that is both very ancient and very modern (300). What aspects of this viewpoint surprise you? How does the symbol of the veil relate to both the ancient traditions of Islam and the modern preoccupation with self-representation?
4. In the inscription/poem to Raja Alem's photograph featuring the *Book of Dreams*, the author uses the word "thousands" five times, and she also emphasizes "keys" and "ink" (301). What inferences can you draw about the *Book of Dreams* based on this combination of imagery? How do these images relate to any religion with which you are familiar?
5. Why do you think both Nadine and Johainah put young girls in the foreground of their portraits (209 and 303)? What are the major similarities and differences between these two photographs?

Questions about Structure and Style

1. In all of these photographs, the subjects' faces are partially or fully obscured, and yet the goal of the photographs—as stated by Ewald—is self-representation. Do you think it is possible to represent the self without presenting one's face? How important is the face in the process of self-representation? Can you imagine how you might properly represent yourself without using your face in any way?
2. The negatives of many of these photographs have been manually altered. What does this say about Ewald's opinion of her art form? What does it say about the subjects' attitude toward self-representation? How is Ewald's opinion similar to or different from the Saudi Arabian women's attitudes?
3. There is almost no "setting" or context for these portraits. While the negatives are altered or decorated in some cases, most of the images feature only the female subjects, albeit in an obscured form. How do you interpret this combination of directness (the simple portraiture) and indirectness (the physical alteration or obscuring of the subjects in the portraits)?

Multimedia Suggestions

1. A number of Web sites feature Wendy Ewald's work. Go to *http://globetrotter.berkeley.edu/Ewald/weblinks.html*, and view some of her other projects by clicking on the links there. How does the "Saudi Arabia 1997" project compare to Ewald's other projects?
2. Because Saudi Arabia is a somewhat conservative Muslim country, there are no bars, nightclubs, or movie theatres. There are, however, a number of shopping malls that have become very popular with young people. Because of the Saudi laws related to not fraternizing with the opposite sex unless they are family members, the malls have had to make a number of accommodations that would seem strange to Western sensibilities. See the following articles to learn more about the ways that Saudi Arabia stays traditional while embracing modern convenience:

   http://www.time.com/time/magazine/1998/int/980727/middle_east.our_veils_ou11.html

   http://www.sptimes.com/2002/webspecials02/saudiarabia/day4/story2.shtml

   http://www.library.cornell.edu/colldev/mideast/saudmll.htm

   http://news.bbc.co.uk/1/hi/world/middle_east/451374.stm

SUGGESTIONS FOR WRITING AND RESEARCH

1. Ewald explains in her introduction to these photographs that "photography is considered controversial; in much of the Muslim world, representational graphics can be construed as graven images" (296). Do some research about Islamic perspectives on representation and photography, as well as some reading on the role of women in Saudi Arabia. How does Ewald's work (and the work of her students) in this selection make a comment on both of those issues? Why is the graphic representation of women particularly problematic in Saudi Arabia? How is this problem similar to or different from the graphic representation of women in the United States?
2. Portraiture, especially in photographs, has religious and/or mythological implications in many cultures and traditions. Research this subject in general or in relation to a specific religious tradition, and write an essay that explains the connection between photography and the soul.
3. Raja Alem's essay alludes to the "power" inherent in taking pictures, in being behind the camera (300). Compare and contrast Wendy Ewald's photography with the photographs of Susan Meiselas, Rosalind Solomon, Annie Liebowitz, or another contemporary woman photographer of your choice. How do the two artists' works compare in terms of content, composition, and cultural contexts? What do critics say about the "power" of the camera from a woman's perspective?
4. Write an essay that addresses Ewald's perspective as a white Western woman working with these Saudi Arabian Muslim women. Does she reveal any biases? Does she force her own values onto their work, or does she seem to have a

"hands off approach"? How would this project have turned out differently if organized by another Saudi woman?

WORKING WITH CLUSTERS

Cluster 2: Constructing and Corrupting the Feminine
Cluster 12: Visual Language
Discipline: The Humanities
Rhetorical Mode: Illustration

"Tourist with an Attitude" (from *The Lexus and the Olive Tree: Understanding Globalization*)

by Thomas Friedman

Thomas L. Friedman is one of America's most prominent interpreters of world affairs. He was born in Minneapolis and educated at Brandeis University and St. Antony's College, Oxford. His first book, From Beirut to Jerusalem, *won the National Book Award in 1988. Friedman has also won two Pulitzer Prizes for his reporting as bureau chief in Beirut and Jerusalem for* The New York Times. The Lexus and the Olive Tree: Understanding Globalization, *from which this selection is drawn, was published in 1999. His latest book is* Longitudes and Attitudes: Exploring the World after September 11th *(2002).*

At the wonderful science museum in Barcelona, I saw an exhibit that beautifully illustrated "chaos." A nonlinear version of a pendulum was set up so that the visitor could hold the bob and start out in a chosen position and with a chosen velocity. One could then watch the subsequent motion, which was also recorded with a pen on a sheet of paper. The visitor was then invited to seize the bob again and try to imitate exactly the previous initial position and velocity. No matter how carefully that was done, the subsequent motion was quite different from what it was the first time . . . I asked the museum director what the two men were doing who were standing in a corner watching us. He replied, "Oh, those are two Dutchmen waiting to take away the 'chaos.'" Apparently, the exhibit was about to be dismantled and taken to Amsterdam. But I have wondered ever since whether the services of those two Dutchmen would not be in great demand across the globe, by organizations that wanted their chaos taken away.

—Murray Gell-Mann, author of *The Quark and the Jaguar*

inveterate: seasoned; habitual

What was it that Forrest Gump's mama liked to say? Life is like a box of chocolates: you never know what you're going to get inside. For me, an **inveterate** traveler and foreign correspondent, life is like room service—you never know what you're going to find outside your door.

Take for instance the evening of December 31, 1994, when I began my assignment as the foreign affairs columnist for *The New York Times*. I started the column by writing from Tokyo, and when I arrived at the Okura Hotel after a long transpacific flight, I called room service with one simple request: "Could you please send me up four oranges." I am addicted to citrus and I needed a fix. It seemed to me a simple enough order when I telephoned it in, and the person on the other end seemed to understand. About twenty minutes later there was a knock at my door. A room service waiter was standing there in his perfectly creased uniform. In front of him was a cart covered by a starched white tablecloth. On the tablecloth were four tall glasses of fresh-squeezed orange juice, each glass set regally in a small silver bowl of ice.

"No, no," I said to the waiter, "I want oranges, oranges—not orange juice." I then pretended to bite into something like an orange.

"Ahhhh," the waiter said, nodding his head. "O-ranges, o-ranges."

I retreated into my room and went back to work. Twenty minutes later there was another knock at my door. Same waiter. Same linen-covered room service trolley. But this time, on it were four plates and on each plate was an orange that had been peeled and diced into perfect little sections that were fanned out on a plate like sushi, as only the Japanese can do.

"No, no," I said, shaking my head again. "I want the whole orange." I made a ball shape with my hands. "I want to keep them in my room and eat them for snacks. I can't eat four oranges all cut up like that. I can't store them in my mini-bar. I want the whole orange."

Again, I did my best exaggerated imitation of someone eating an orange.

"Ahhhh," the water said, nodding his head. "O-range, o-range. You want whole o-range."

Another twenty minutes went by. Again there was a knock on my door. Same waiter. Same trolley, only this time he had four bright oranges, each one on its own dinner plate, with a fork, knife and linen napkin next to it. That was progress.

1. *In Your Journal:* When Friedman says "That was progress," do you think he is sincere or facetious?

"That's right," I said, signing the bill. "That's just what I wanted."

As he left the room, I looked down at the room service bill. The four oranges were $22. How am I going to explain that to my publisher?

But my citrus adventures were not over. Two weeks later I was in **Hanoi,** having dinner by myself in the dining room of the Metropole Hotel. It was the tangerine season in Vietnam, and vendors were selling pyramids of the most delicious, bright orange tangerines on every street corner. Each morning I had a few tangerines for breakfast. When the waiter came to get my dessert order I told him all I wanted was a tangerine.

He went away and came back a few minutes later.

"Sorry," he said, "no tangerines."

"But how can that be?" I asked in exasperation. "You have a table full of them at breakfast every morning! Surely there must be a tangerine somewhere back in the kitchen?"

"Sorry." He shook his head. "Maybe you like watermelon?"

"O.K.," I said, "bring me some watermelon."

Five minutes later the waiter returned with a plate bearing three peeled tangerines on it.

"I found the tangerines," he said. "No watermelon."

2. *In Your Journal:* Why do you think Friedman spends so much time telling the reader about his difficulties finding the fruit he wants in foreign countries?

Had I known then what I know now I would have taken it all as a **harbinger.** For I too would find a lot of things on my plate and outside my door that I wasn't planning to find as I traveled the globe for the *Times.*

harbinger: omen; indication

Being the foreign affairs columnist for *The New York Times* is actually the best job in the world. I mean, someone has to have the best job, right? Well, I've got it. The reason it is such a great job is that I get to be a tourist with an attitude. I get to go anywhere, anytime, and have attitudes about what I see and

---

Hanoi: capital of Vietnam; noted for European style buildings and tree-lined streets

3. *In Your Journal:* Why can't every tourist have an "attitude"? What does Friedman mean by "tourist with an attitude"?

opine: preach

hear. But the question for me as I embarked on this odyssey was: Which attitudes? What would be the lens, the perspective, the organizing system—the superstory—through which I would look at the world, make sense of events, prioritize them, **opine** upon them and help readers understand them?

In some ways my predecessors had it a little easier. They each had a very obvious superstory and international system in place when they were writing. I am the fifth foreign affairs columnist in the history of the *Times.* "Foreign Affairs" is actually the paper's oldest column. It was begun in 1937 by a remarkable woman, Anne O'Hare McCormick, and was originally called "In Europe," because in those days, "in Europe" was foreign affairs for most Americans, and it seemed perfectly natural that the paper's one overseas columnist would be located on the European continent. Mrs. McCormick's 1954 obituary in the *Times* said she got her start in foreign reporting "as the wife of Mr. McCormick, a Dayton engineer whom she accompanied on frequent buying trips to Europe." (*New York Times* obits have become considerably more politically correct since then.) The international system which she covered was the disintegration of balance-of-power **Versailles** Europe and the beginnings of World War II.

4. *In Your Journal:* Why does Friedman include a description of McCormick's obituary in the context of discussing the job of a foreign correspondent?

As America emerged from World War II, standing astride the world as the preeminent superpower, with global responsibilities and engaged in a global power struggle with the Soviet Union, the title of the column changed in 1954 to "Foreign Affairs." Suddenly the whole world was America's playing field and the whole world mattered, because **every corner** was being contested with the Soviet Union. The **Cold War** international system, with its competition for influence and supremacy between the capitalist West and the communist East, between Washington, Moscow and Beijing, became the superstory within which the next three foreign affairs columnists organized their opinions.

every corner: Friedman alludes especially to China and Southeast Asia, Hungary, and Cuba

By the time I started the column at the beginning of 1995, though, the Cold War was over. The **Berlin Wall** had crumbled and the Soviet Union was history. I had the good fortune to witness, in the **Kremlin,** one of the last gasps of the Soviet Union. The day was December 16, 1991.

Versailles: French site of elaborate palaces and grounds built for Louis XIV; site of several significant treaty signings, most notably the 1919 Treaty of Versailles, which facilitated the end of World War I

Cold War: refers to the post–World War II struggle between western capitalist democratic powers and the communist bloc; entered a relaxed "détente" period in the 1960's

Berlin Wall: barrier between East and West Germany, erected in 1961 and dismantled in 1989

Kremlin: 90-acre walled-in center of Moscow; political and administrative center of the U.S.S.R.

Secretary of State James A. Baker III was visiting Moscow, just as Boris Yeltsin was easing Mikhail Gorbachev out of power. Whenever Baker had met Gorbachev previously, they had held their talks in the Kremlin's gold-gilded St. Catherine Hall. There was always a very orchestrated entry scene for the press. Mr. Baker and his entourage would wait behind two huge wooden double doors on one end of the long Kremlin hall, with Gorbachev and his team behind the doors on the other end. And then, by some signal, the doors would simultaneously open and each man would stride out and they would shake hands in front of the cameras in the middle of the room. Well, on this day Baker arrived for his meeting at the appointed hour, the doors swung open and Boris Yeltsin walked out, instead of Gorbachev. Guess who's coming to dinner! "Welcome to Russian soil and this Russian building," Yeltsin said to Baker. Baker did meet Gorbachev later in the day, but it was clear that power had shifted. We State Department reporters who were there to chronicle the event ended up spending that whole day in the Kremlin. It snowed heavily while we were inside, and when we finally walked out after sunset we found the Kremlin grounds covered in a white snow blanket. As we trudged to the Kremlin's Spassky Gate, our shoes crunching fresh tracks in the snow, I noticed that the red Soviet **hammer and sickle** was still flying atop the Kremlin flagpole, illuminated by a spotlight as it had been for some seventy years. I said to myself, "That is probably the last time I'll ever see that flag flying there." And, indeed, in a few weeks it was gone, and with it went the Cold War system and superstory.

5. In Your Journal: What is significant about Boris Yeltsin's welcome of James Baker? Why does Friedman quote what seems like a fairly standard greeting?

But what wasn't clear to me as I embarked upon my column assignment a few years later was what had replaced the Cold War system as the dominant organizing framework for international affairs. So I actually began my column as a tourist without an attitude—just an open mind. For several years, I, like everyone else, just referred to "the post-Cold War world." We knew some new system was **aborning** that constituted a different framework for international relations, but we couldn't define what it was, so we defined it by what it wasn't. It wasn't the Cold War. So we called it the post-Cold War world.

aborning: getting underway

The more I traveled, though, the more it became apparent to me that this system had its own logic and deserved its own name: "globalization." Globalization is not a phenomenon. It is not just some passing trend. Today it is the overarching international system shaping the domestic politics and foreign relations of virtually every country, and we need to understand it as such.

6. In Your Journal: It takes Friedman a long time to begin articulating his argument. Why is he just now beginning to do so?

---

hammer and sickle: flag of the Soviet Union beginning in 1918; now international symbol of communism; hammer represents industrial workers, sickle represents agricultural workers, red color represents the blood of the working classes

When I speak of the "the Cold War system" and "the globalization system," what do I mean?

I mean that, as an international system, the Cold War had its own structure of power: the balance between the United States and the U.S.S.R. The Cold War had its own rules: in foreign affairs, neither superpower would encroach on the other's sphere of influence; in economics, less developed countries would focus on nurturing their own national industries, developing countries on export-led growth, communist countries on **autarky** and Western economies on regulated trade. The Cold War had its own dominant ideas: the clash between communism and capitalism, as well as **detente, nonalignment** and **perestroika.** The Cold War had its own demographic trends: the movement of peoples from east to west was largely frozen by the **Iron Curtain,** but the movement from south to north was a more steady flow. The Cold War had its own perspective on the globe: the world was a space divided into the communist camp, the Western camp, and the neutral camp, and everyone's country was in one of them. The Cold War had its own defining technologies: nuclear weapons and the second Industrial Revolution were dominant, but for many people in developing countries the hammer and sickle were still relevant tools. The Cold War had its own defining measurement: the **throw weight** of nuclear missiles. And lastly, the Cold War had its own defining anxiety: nuclear annihilation. When taken all together the elements of this Cold War system influenced the domestic politics and foreign relations of virtually every country in the world. The Cold War system didn't shape everything, but it shaped many things.

autarky: policy of national self-sufficiency, without reliance on foreign aid or imports

détente: (French) easing of tensions between nations

nonalignment: condition of not being aligned with any power bloc; neutral

perestroika: restructuring period in the 1980's in the USSR

throw weight: total weight of a warhead

Today's era of globalization, which replaced the Cold War, is a similar international system, with its own unique attributes.

To begin with, the globalization system, unlike the Cold War system, is not static, but a dynamic ongoing process: globalization involves the inexorable integration of markets, nation-states and technologies to a degree never witnessed before—in a way that is enabling individuals, corporations and nation-states to reach around the world farther, faster, deeper and cheaper than ever before, and in a way that is also producing a powerful backlash from those brutalized or left behind by this new system.

7. In Your Journal: What is the difference between something "static" and something "dynamic"? How do these two terms relate to Friedman's argument?

The driving idea behind globalization is free-market capitalism—the more you let market forces rule and the more you open your economy to free trade and competition, the more efficient and flourishing your economy will be. Globalization means the spread of free-market capitalism to virtually every country in the world. Globalization also has its own set of

❖ **Iron Curtain:** Soviet bloc and Eastern Europe from 1945 to 1990, so named because of restricted travel and trade economic rules—rules that revolve around opening, **deregulating** and **privatizing** your economy.

deregulate: remove controlling mechanisms; allow self-regulation

privatize: remove from public or government ownership; transfer to private ownership

Unlike the Cold War system, globalization has its own dominant culture, which is why it tends to be homogenizing. In previous eras this sort of cultural homogenization happened on a regional scale—the Hellenization of the Near East and the Mediterranean world under the Greeks, the Turkification of Central Asia, North Africa, Europe and the Middle East by the Ottomans, or the Russification of Eastern and Central Europe and parts of Eurasia under the Soviets. Culturally speaking, globalization is largely, though not entirely, the spread of Americanization—from Big Macs to iMacs to Mickey Mouse—on a global scale.

8. In Your Journal: Why is the "homogenization" of globalization different from the previous cultural homogenizations Friedman lists?

Globalization has its own defining technologies: computerization, miniaturization, digitization, satellite communications, fiber optics and the Internet. And these technologies helped to create the defining perspective of globalization. If the defining perspective of the Cold War world was "division," the defining perspective of globalization is "integration." The symbol of the Cold War system was a wall, which divided everyone. The symbol of the globalization system is a World Wide Web, which unites everyone. The defining document of the Cold War system was "The Treaty." The defining document of the globalization system is "The Deal."

9. In Your Journal: Why is this system called "globalization" if it is "largely," as Friedman says, "the spread of Americanization"?

Once a country makes the leap into the system of globalization, its elites begin to internalize this perspective of integration, and always try to locate themselves in a global context. I was visiting Amman, Jordan, in the summer of 1998 and having coffee at the Inter-Continental Hotel with my friend Rami Khouri, the leading political columnist in Jordan. We sat down and I asked him what was new. The first thing he said to me was: "Jordan was just added to CNN's worldwide weather highlights." What Rami was saying was that it is important for Jordan to know that those institutions which think globally believe it is now worth knowing what the weather is like in Amman. It makes Jordanians feel more important and holds out the hope that they will be enriched by having more tourists or global investors visiting. The day after seeing Rami I happened to go to Israel and meet with Jacob Frenkel, governor of Israel's Central Bank and a University of Chicago–trained economist. Frenkel remarked that he too was going through a perspective change: "Before, when we talked about **macroeconomics,** we started by looking at the local markets, local financial system and the interrelationship between them, and then, as an afterthought, we looked at the international economy. There was a feeling that what we do is primarily our own business and then there are some outlets where we will sell abroad. Now we reverse the perspective. Let's not ask what markets we should export to, after having decided what to produce; rather let's first study the global framework within which we operate and then decide what to produce. It changes your whole perspective."

10. In Your Journal: What do the CNN weather highlights have to do with globalization?

macroeconomics: study of large-scale economics

silicon chips: kind of semi-conductor material

While the defining measurement of the Cold War was weight—particularly the throw weight of missiles—the defining measurement of the globalization system is speed—speed of commerce, travel, communication and innovation. The Cold War was about Einstein's mass-energy equation, **$e = mc^2$.** Globalization is about **Moore's law,** which states that the computing power of **silicon chips** will double every eighteen to twenty-four months. In the Cold War, the most frequently asked question was: "How big is your missile?" In globalization, the most frequently asked question is: "How fast is your modem?"

11. In Your Journal: According to Friedman, what is the difference between Einstein's equation and Moore's law?

If the defining economists of the Cold War system were **Karl Marx** and **John Maynard Keynes,** who each in his own way wanted to tame capitalism, the defining economists of the globalization system are Joseph Schumpeter and **Intel** chairman Andy Grove, who prefer to unleash capitalism. Schumpeter, a former Austrian Minister of Finance and Harvard Business School professor, expressed the view in his classic work *Capitalism, Socialism and Democracy* that the essence of capitalism is the process of "creative destruction"—the perpetual cycle of destroying the old and less efficient product or service and replacing it with new, more efficient ones. Andy Grove took Schumpeter's insight that "only the paranoid survive" for the title of his book on life in Silicon Valley, and made it in many ways the business model of globalization capitalism. Grove helped to popularize the view that dramatic, industry-transforming innovations are taking place today faster and faster. Thanks to these technological breakthroughs, the speed by which your latest invention can be made obsolete or turned into a commodity is now lightning quick. Therefore, only the paranoid, only those who are constantly looking over their shoulders to see who is creating something new that will destroy them and then staying just one step ahead of them, will survive. Those countries that are most willing to let capitalism quickly destroy inefficient companies, so that money can be freed up and directed to more innovative ones, will thrive in the era of globalization. Those which rely on their governments to protect them from such creative destruction will fall behind in this era.

12. In Your Journal: What do you think the phrase "'creative destruction'" means?

- **$e = mc^2$:** states that a measured quantity of energy is equivalent to a measured quantity of mass
- **Moore's law:** named for Gordon Moore, co-founder of Intel; 1965 prediction about exponential growth in transistor density
- **Karl Marx:** (1818–1883) German social philosopher, economist, and revolutionary theorist who wrote works about communism and modern socialism, such as *Communist Manifesto* (1848)
- **John Maynard Keynes:** (1883–1946) English economist who advocated government spending to increase business activity
- **Intel:** large producer of computer "microprocessors," the "brains" of personal computers

James Surowiecki, the business columnist for *Slate* magazine, reviewing Grove's book, neatly summarized what Schumpeter and Grove have in common, which is the essence of globalization economics. It is the notion that: "Innovation replaces tradition. The present—or perhaps the future—replaces the past. Nothing matters so much as what will come next, and what will come next can only arrive if what is here now gets overturned. While this makes the system a terrific place for innovation, it makes it a difficult place to live, since most people prefer some measure of security about the future to a life lived in almost constant uncertainty . . . We are not forced to re-create our relationships with those closest to us on a regular basis. And yet that's precisely what Schumpeter, and Grove after him, suggest is necessary to prosper [today]."

Indeed, if the Cold War were a sport, it would be sumo wrestling, says Johns Hopkins University foreign affairs professor Michael Mandelbaum. "It would be two big fat guys in a ring, with all sorts of posturing and rituals and stomping of feet, but actually very little contact, until the end of the match, when there is a brief moment of shoving and the loser gets pushed out of the ring, but nobody gets killed."

By contrast, if globalization were a sport, it would be the 100-meter dash, over and over and over. And no matter how many times you win, you have to race again the next day. And if you lose by just one-hundredth of a second it can be as if you lost by an hour. (Just ask French multinationals. In 1999, French labor laws were changed, requiring—*requiring*—every employer to implement a four-hour reduction in the legal workweek, from 39 hours to 35 hours, with no cut in pay. Many French firms were fighting the move because of the impact it would have on their productivity in a global market. Henri Thierry, human resources director for Thomson—CSF Communications, a high-tech firm in the suburbs of Paris, told *The Washington Post:* "We are in a worldwide competition. If we lose one point of productivity, we lose orders. If we're obliged to go to 35 hours it would be like requiring French athletes to run the 100 meters wearing flippers. They wouldn't have much of a chance winning a medal.")

> ***13. In Your Journal:*** Why do you think the French government would require a four-hour work reduction for all employers? Do you think this policy is related to globalization?

To paraphrase German political theorist Carl Schmitt, the Cold War was a world of "friends" and "enemies." The globalization world, by contrast, tends to turn all friends and enemies into "competitors."

> ***14. In Your Journal:*** Can't "friends and enemies" be considered "competitors"? What difference is Carl Schmitt getting at here?

If the defining anxiety of the Cold War was fear of annihilation from an enemy you knew all too well in a world struggle that was fixed and stable, the defining anxiety in globalization is fear of rapid change from an enemy you can't see, touch or feel—a sense that your job, community or workplace can be changed at any moment by anonymous economic and technological forces that are anything but stable.

In the Cold War we reached for the hot line between the White House and the Kremlin—a symbol that we were all divided but at least someone, the two superpowers, was in charge. In the era of globalization we reach for the Internet—a symbol that we are all connected but nobody is in charge. The defining defense system of the Cold War was radar—to expose the threats coming from the other side of the wall. The defining defense system of the globalization era is the X-ray machine—to expose the threats coming from within.

demographic: relating to the statistical features of a population

Globalization also has its own **demographic** pattern—a rapid acceleration of the movement of people from rural areas and agricultural lifestyles to urban areas and urban lifestyles more intimately linked with global fashion, food, markets and entertainment trends.

Last, and most important, globalization has its own defining structure of power, which is much more complex than the Cold War structure. The Cold War system was built exclusively around nation-states, and it was balanced at the center by two superpowers: the United States and the Soviet Union.

The globalization system, by contrast, is built around three balances, which overlap and affect one another. The first is the traditional balance between nation-states. In the globalization system, the United States is now the sole and dominant superpower and all other nations are subordinate to it to one degree or another. The balance of power between the United States and the other states still matters for the stability of this system. And it can still explain a lot of the news you read on the front page of the papers, whether it is the containment of Iraq in the Middle East or the expansion of **NATO** against Russia in Central Europe.

The second balance in the globalization system is between nation-states and global markets. These global markets are made up of millions of investors moving money around the world with the click of a mouse. I call them "the Electronic Herd," and this herd gathers in key global financial centers, such as Wall Street, Hong Kong, London and Frankfurt, which I call "the Supermarkets." The attitudes and actions of the Electronic Herd and the Supermarkets can have a huge impact on nation-states today, even to the point of triggering the downfall of governments. You will not understand the front page of newspapers today—whether it is the story of the toppling of Suharto in Indonesia, the internal collapse in Russia or the monetary policy of the United States—unless you bring the Supermarkets into your analysis.

The United States can destroy you by dropping bombs and the Supermarkets can destroy you by downgrading your bonds. The United States is the dominant player in maintaining the globalization gameboard, but it is

---

NATO: National Atlantic Treaty Organization (now including Belgium, Canada, Denmark, France, Great Britain, Iceland, Italy, Luxembourg, the Netherlands, Norway, Portugal, the United States, Greece, Turkey, Germany, Spain, the Czech Republic, Hungary, and Poland), established in 1949 to safeguard the freedoms of its members not alone in influencing the moves on that gameboard. This globalization gameboard today is a lot like a **Ouija board**—sometimes pieces are moved around by the obvious hand of the superpower, and sometimes they are moved around by hidden hands of the Supermarkets.

Ouija board: (pronounced "weejee") board game in which players ask questions of the board that will predict their futures

The third balance that you have to pay attention to in the globalization system—the one that is really the newest of all—is the balance between individuals and nation-states. Because globalization has brought down many of the walls that limited the movement and reach of people, and because it has simultaneously wired the world into networks, it gives more power to individuals to influence both markets and nation-states than at any time in history. So you have today not only a superpower, not only Supermarkets, but, as I will also demonstrate later in the book, you have Super-empowered individuals. Some of these Super-empowered individuals are quite angry, some of them quite wonderful—but all of them are now able to act directly on the world stage without the traditional mediation of governments, corporations or any other public or private institutions.

15. In Your Journal: How do you suppose an individual can have a relationship with a nation-state?

Without the knowledge of the U.S. government, Long-Term Capital Management—a few guys in Greenwich, Connecticut—amassed more financial bets around the world than all the foreign reserves of China. Osama bin Laden, a Saudi millionaire with his own global network, declared war on the United States in the late 1990s, and the U.S. Air Force had to launch a cruise missile attack on him as though he were another nation-state. **We fired cruise missiles** at an individual! Jody Williams won the Nobel Peace Prize in 1997 for her contribution to the international ban on landmines. She achieved that ban not only without much government help, but in the face of opposition from the Big Five major powers. And what did she say was her secret weapon for organizing 1,000 different human rights and arms control groups on six continents? "E-mail."

Nation-states, and the American superpower in particular, are still hugely important today, but so too now are Supermarkets and Super-empowered individuals. You will never understand the globalization system, or the front page of the morning paper, unless you see it as a complex interaction between all three of these actors: states bumping up against states, states bumping up against Supermarkets, and Supermarkets and states bumping up against Super-empowered individuals.

It has taken all of us a long time to bring this globalization system into clear focus and to appreciate its implications. Like everyone else trying to adjust to it, I literally had to retrain myself and develop new lenses to see it. In order to explain how, let me start with a confession that I have wanted

---

We fired cruise missiles . . . !: bin Laden was not, at the time, formally so affiliated with Afghanistan, so the missile firing was unique in that sense to unburden myself of for a long, long time. Are you ready? Here it is: I used to make up the weather reports from Beirut.

Well, actually, I didn't make them up. That would be wrong. I "estimated" them. It was 1979 and I was working as a cub reporter in Beirut for United Press International. I often had to work the late-night shift, and one of the responsibilities of the late person was to file the weather report from Beirut, which would be included in UPI's worldwide weather roundup that went out to newspapers each day, with the highs and lows. The only problem was that there was no weatherman in Beirut, or at least none I was aware of. The country was in the midst of a civil war. Who cared what the temperature was? People were just glad to be alive. The only temperature you cared about in Beirut in those days was your own—98.6 degrees. So I estimated what the temperature was, often by **ad hoc** polling. Gathering the weather report basically involved my shouting down the hall or across the room: "Hey, Ahmed, how does it feel out there today?"

16. In Your Journal: Why would 98.6 be the only temperature a person cared about in Beirut in 1979?

And Ahmed or Sonia or Daoud would shout back, "Ya'ani, it feels hot."

ad hoc: (Latin) "toward this"; for a specific purpose

"About 90 degrees?" I would ask. "Sure, Mr. Thomas, whatever you say," the answer would come back. "Something like that." So I would write, "High 90 degrees." Then I would ask later, "Kinda cool out there now?" "Sure, Mr. Thomas," the answer would come back. "About 72 degrees, would you say?" "Sure, Mr. Thomas, whatever you say," the answer would come back. And so I would write, "Low 72 degrees." And thus was the weather report filed from Beirut.

17. In Your Journal: How does this "weather story" compare to Friedman's reference to the CNN weather highlights in Jordan?

Years later I would recall those moments when I found myself working in the Business Day section of *The New York Times*. I was occasionally assigned to write the daily dollar or stock market stories and had to call around to brokers after the markets closed to find out where the dollar finished against other major currencies, or to ascertain why the Dow Jones Industrial Average moved up or down. I was always amazed that whichever way the markets moved, whether the dollar fell or rose, some analyst always had a **pithy** one-liner explaining why $1.2 trillion in transactions on six different continents across twenty-four different time zones resulted in the dollar falling or rising against the Japanese yen by half a penny. And we all believed this explanation. But somewhere in the back of my mind I used to wonder whether these commentators weren't just pulling my leg. Somewhere in the back of my mind I used to wonder whether this wasn't just the Wall Street version of the weather report from Beirut, with someone shouting down the hall at the offices of Merrill Lynch or PaineWebber the equivalent of "Hey, Ahmed, why did the dollar go down today?" And whatever the stock boy or the secretary or the first broker to walk by his desk happened to answer ended up in the next day's newspaper as the global explanation for the behavior of thousands of different traders around the world.

pithy: to the point

In 1994 I was the *New York Times* international trade and finance correspondent, covering the United States–Japan trade talks. I was sitting, scrolling through the news wires on my computer one afternoon, when I noticed two items move on Reuters, one right after the other:

> **Dollar Ends Higher on Optimism over Trade Talks**
> NEW YORK (Reuters)—The dollar finished higher against most leading currencies Friday as optimism grew that Washington and Tokyo would reach a trade agreement.
>
> **Blue Chip Stocks End Lower on Uncertainty over Trade Talks**
> NEW YORK (Reuters)—Blue chip stocks closed lower Friday amid uncertainty over U.S.-Japan trade talks ahead of a midnight deadline for possible sanctions.

"Hey, Ahmed, what do you think of the U.S.–Japan talks?"

What I was doing back in those days filing the weather report from Beirut, and what Reuters was doing with its stock and currency stories, was trying to order the chaos—without much success in either of our cases. I knew when I began my foreign affairs column in 1995 that I would not survive very long if all I was doing to order the chaos was the political equivalent of just guessing the temperature in Beirut. So what to do? How to understand and explain this incredibly complex system of globalization?

> ***18. In Your Journal:*** How would you describe Friedman's tone when he recounts the coverage of United States–Japan trade talks?

> ***19. In Your Journal:*** How does Friedman's analysis about "trying to order the chaos" play off of the epigraph at the beginning of this essay?

The short answer is that I learned you need to do two things at once—look at the world through a multidimensional, multilens perspective and, at the same time, convey that complexity to readers through simple stories, not grand theories. That's why when people ask me how I cover the world these days, I answer that I use two techniques: I "do information arbitrage" in order to understand the world, and I "tell stories" in order to explain it.

Let's look at each of these methods. What is information arbitrage? Arbitrage is a market term. Technically speaking, it refers to the simultaneous buying and selling of the same securities, commodities or foreign exchange in different markets to profit from unequal prices and unequal information. The successful arbitrageur is a trader who knows that pork bellies are selling for $1 per pound in Chicago and for $1.50 in New York and so he buys them in Chicago and sells them in New York. One can do arbitrage in markets. One can do it in literature. It was said of the great Spanish writer José Ortega y Gasset that he "bought information cheap in London and sold it expensive in Spain." That is, he frequented all the great salons of London and then translated the insights he gained there into Spanish for Spanish readers back home. But whether you are selling pork bellies or insights, the key to being a successful arbitrageur is having a wide net of informants and information and then knowing how to synthesize it in a way that will produce a profit.

If you want to be an effective reporter or columnist trying to make sense of global affairs today, you have to be able to do something similar. Because today, more than ever, the traditional boundaries between politics, culture, technology, finance, national security and ecology are disappearing. You often cannot explain one without referring to the others, and you cannot explain the whole without reference to them all. Therefore, to be an effective foreign affairs columnist or reporter, you have to learn how to arbitrage information from these disparate perspectives and then weave it all together to produce a picture of the world that you would never have if you looked at it from only one perspective. That is the essence of information arbitrage. In a world where we are all so much more interconnected, the ability to read the connections, and to connect the dots, is the real value added provided by a journalist. If you don't see the connections, you won't see the world.

20. In Your Journal: How do the "traditional boundaries" that Friedman refers to compare to the boundaries in academia?

I came to this approach entirely by accident, as successive changes in my career kept forcing me to add one more lens on top of another, just to survive. Here's what happened:

21. In Your Journal: Why does Friedman criticize himself as "the most narrow of reporters"?

I began my journalistic life as the most narrow of reporters. For the first decade of my career I covered the "Mother of All Tribal Wars"—the Arab-Israeli conflict, first from Beirut and then from Jerusalem. In those days, journalism for me was basically a two-dimensional business. It was about politics and culture, because in the Middle East your culture pretty much defined your politics. To put it another way, the world for me was all about watching people clinging to their own roots and uprooting their neighbors' roots.

Then in 1988 I left Jerusalem, after a decade in the Middle East, and came to Washington, where I became the *New York Times* diplomatic correspondent. The first story I was assigned to cover was Secretary of State–designate James A. Baker III's confirmation hearing before the Senate. I am embarrassed to say that since both my B.A. and M.A. were in Arabic and Middle Eastern Studies, and since I had spent almost my entire journalistic career up to that point covering the Middle East, I really did not know very much about any other parts of the world, and I certainly did not know anything about most of the issues the senators were quizzing Mr. Baker about, such as the **START treaty,** the **Contras, Angola,** the CFE (Conventional

---

START treaty: between the United States and the Soviet Union, on the reduction and limitation of strategic offensive arms; negotiations began in 1982, and in 1992 the United States, Russia, Belarus, Kazakhstan and Ukraine (Soviet successor states) signed a protocol to limit strategic arms

---

Contras: Nicaraguan guerillas; in the early 1980's the "Iran-Contra Affair" revealed a secret arrangement whereby the United States provided (prohibited) military aid to the Contras with money received from secret arms

Forces in Europe) arms control negotiations and NATO. My head was swimming as I came out of the hearing. I had no idea what the lead was. I didn't even know what half the **acronyms** stood for. I couldn't keep straight whether the Contras were our guys or their guys, and I thought CFE was a typo and was actually "cafe" without the "a." As I took a taxi back to the *Times* bureau, all I could see in my head was a banner headline in *The Washington Post* the next morning about something Baker had said that I would not even have mentioned in my story. Only thanks to help from the *Times*'s Pentagon reporter, Michael Gordon, did I manage to pull a story together that day. But I knew then and there that two dimensions weren't going to cut it anymore. Fortunately, thanks to four years of covering diplomacy, including some 500,000 miles on the road with Baker, I managed to add a new dimension to politics and culture—the national security, balance-of-power dimension. This comprises the whole nexus of issues revolving around arms control, superpower competition, Cold War alliance management and power geopolitics. As I added this new dimension, my old two-dimensional view of the world was transformed. I remember once flying with Baker to Israel, and his plane got diverted briefly over the Tel Aviv airport and was sent on a big, wide arc over the **West Bank** before coming in for its landing. I found myself looking out the window of the Secretary of State's airplane, down at the West Bank, and thinking, "You know, in raw power terms, this place really isn't very important anymore. Interesting, yes. But geopolitically important, no."

acronym: abbreviation derived from combining the first letters of several words

22. In Your Journal: Why doesn't Friedman consider the West Bank to have geopolitical importance?

Following my tour at the State Department, and then a mercifully brief stint as a White House correspondent (none dare call that journalism), I added another lens in 1994 when the *Times* asked me to start a new beat that would cover the intersection between foreign policy and international finance. It was becoming apparent that with the end of the Cold War and the collapse of the Soviet Union, finance and trade were clearly taking on a bigger role in shaping international relations. Having a beat that was at the intersection of economics and national security policymaking was something of an experiment for me and the *Times*. I was technically assigned to be the Treasury-trade correspondent, but given my

sales to Iran, which was supposed to encourage the release of Iranian-held U.S. hostages in Lebanon

Angola: troubled by the growing Soviet and Cuban presence in Angola, the United States sought to reduce this influence by becoming directly involved in negotiations for a withdrawal of Cuban troops from Angola and for Namibian independence

West Bank: area between Syria, Jordan, and Israel, occupied by Israel after the 1967 war; an elected Palestinian Authority now exercises jurisdiction over portions of the West Bank background covering the State Department and the White House, I was asked to integrate it all. We described the beat variously as "Commercial Diplomacy" or "Foreign Affairs and Finance." What I discovered when I stood at that intersection were two things. First was that with the end of the Cold War system, this intersection was going to produce a huge amount of news. The other thing I discovered was that nobody else was there. Instead, there were a lot of trade reporters who didn't cover diplomacy. There were a lot of finance reporters who didn't cover national security affairs. There were a lot of diplomatic reporters who didn't cover finance. And there were White House reporters who didn't cover trade, finance or foreign affairs, but only what the President said or did.

For me, adding the financial markets dimension to politics, culture and national security was like putting on a new pair of glasses and suddenly looking at the world in 4-D. I saw news stories that I would never have recognized as news stories before. I saw causal chains of events that I never could have identified before. I saw invisible hands and handcuffs impeding leaders and nations from doing things that I never imagined before.

But it was not long before I discovered that four dimensions were not enough. Once I was assigned to be the foreign affairs columnist, I gradually realized that what was driving the rise and power of markets, what was reshaping how nations and individuals interacted with one another, and what was really at the heart of globalization, was the recent advances in technology—from the Internet to satellite telecommunications. I realized that I could not explain to myself, let alone to readers, the forces that were shaping global politics unless I better understood these technologies that were empowering people, companies and governments in all sorts of new ways. Who controls the guns in a society is always critical. But who controls the phones and how they work also matters. How many troops and nukes your country possesses is always critical. But how much bandwidth you have for your Internet also matters. So I had to add yet another dimension—technology—and become a 5-D reporter. It meant adding **Silicon Valley** to the list of world capitals—Moscow, Beijing, London, Jerusalem—that I felt I had to visit once a year just to stay abreast of what was going on.

23. In Your Journal: Respond to Friedman's claim that Silicon Valley has become a "world capital." Does this concern you or comfort you? Explain why.

Finally, the more I observed the system of globalization at work, the more obvious it was that it had unleashed forest-crushing forces of development and Disney-round-the-clock homogenization, which, if left unchecked, had the potential to destroy the environment and uproot cultures, at a pace never before seen in human history. I gradually realized that if I didn't bring this environmental perspective into my analysis, I would be

Silicon Valley: industrial region of central California; home to many large technology companies leaving out one of the major forces that could limit development and trigger a backlash against globalization. So I added the sixth dimension to my arbitrage—educating myself in environmentalism—and began adding environmental side trips to my travels to understand how ecosystems were being affected by globalization and how their degradation was affecting globalization.

Now that I am up to six D's, I don't know what's next. But if and when a new dimension becomes apparent, I will add it. Because I am a "globalist." That is the school of thought to which I belong. That means I am not a realist, who thinks everything in foreign affairs can be explained by the quest for power and geopolitical advantage—and markets don't matter. I am not an environmentalist, who looks at the fate of the world only through the prism of the environment and what must be done to save it—and development doesn't matter. I am not a technologist—one of those Silicon Valley techno-nerds who believe that history began with the invention of the microprocessor and that the Internet will determine mine the future of international relations—and geopolitics doesn't matter. I am not an **essentialist** who believes that people's behavior can be explained by some essential cultural or DNA trait—and technology doesn't matter. And I am not an economist who believes that you can explain the world with reference only to markets—and power politics and culture don't matter.

24. In Your Journal: Why isn't Friedman a realist? How do you think he defines the term? Do you think his definition is conventional?

essentialist: one who espouses a theory of identity based on *essence* rather than social construction (e.g., an essentialist would argue that there is an essence of Germanness that all Germans innately possess, whereas a social constructivist would argue that Germans are taught by society how to be German)

I believe that this new system of globalization constitutes a fundamentally new state of affairs, and the only way to see it, understand it and explain it is by arbitraging all six dimensions I have laid out above—assigning different weights to different perspectives at different times in different situations, but always understanding that it is the interaction of all of them together that is really the defining feature of international relations today. And therefore being a globalist is the only way to systematically connect the dots, see the system of globalization and thereby order the chaos.

If I am wrong about this world, that will be apparent soon enough. But if I am not wrong, there are a lot of people who are going to have to go back to school. I believe it is particularly important for both journalists, who are charged with explaining the world, and strategists, who are responsible for shaping it, to think like globalists. There is increasingly a seamless web between all of these different worlds and institutions, and reporters and strategists need to be as seamless as that web. Unfortunately, in both journalism and academe, there is a deeply ingrained tendency to think in terms of highly segmented, narrow areas of expertise, which ignores the fact that the real world is not divided up into such neat little beats and that the boundaries between domestic, international, political and technological affairs are all collapsing.

sanction: restriction; injunction

Let me offer just one example. For years, the Clinton Administration kept threatening to impose trade **sanctions** on Japan unless it eliminated certain official and hidden tariffs on a variety of goods. But every time the savvy U.S. Trade Representative Mickey Kantor would seem to have won the argument inside the Administration for taking action, and the President was about to lower the boom on Japan, at the last minute Clinton would back off. Here is what I imagine was going on inside the Oval Office at the time:

Kantor would walk into the Oval Office, pull up a chair next to the President and say, "Mr. President, those damn Japanese are stonewalling, they are sticking it to us again. They are not allowing our exports in. It's time we really lowered the boom. Sanctions, Mr. President. Big-time sanctions. This is the time for them. This is the place for them, and, by the way, Mr. President, the unions will love us for it."

"Mickey, you are dead right," the President would say. "Go for it." But just as Kantor was about to leave to lower the boom on Tokyo, Treasury Secretary Robert Rubin would come in the side door of the Oval Office.

"Ah, Mr. President," Rubin would say, "you realize that if we impose trade sanctions on Japan the dollar is going to nosedive and the Japanese could start selling all the U.S. Treasury bills they hold, and domestic U.S. interest rates will rise."

The President would then motion to Kantor, who was halfway out the door. "Yo, Mickey, Mickey, Mickey. Come back here for a second. We've got to think this over."

A few days later, Kantor would be back. He would make the same arguments. This time the President would be really convinced. He would tell Kantor: "I am not going to take it from those Japanese anymore, Mickey. Sanctions. Lower the boom."

Just as Kantor would be about to leave to lower the boom on Tokyo, Defense Secretary William Perry would come in the side door of the Oval Office.

"Ah, Mr. President," Perry would say, "you realize that if we impose trade sanctions on Japan, the Japanese will not renegotiate our base agreement at Okinawa, or pay for that North Korean nuclear reactor we're counting on."

The President would then frantically motion to Kantor, who was trying to get out the door. "Yo, Mickey, Mickey, Mickey. Come back here for a second. We've got to think this over."

This is an imaginary scene, but I would bet a lot of money it bears a close resemblance to what was actually going on, and the reporter who will capture it properly for readers will not be the trade reporter, Treasury reporter or Pentagon reporter, but the one who is moving back and forth, arbitraging all three beats at the same time.

The Yale international relations historians Paul Kennedy and John Lewis Gaddis see one of their jobs as training the next generation of American strategists. To their great credit, they have been exploring how to broaden their curriculum in order to produce a new generation of strategists who can think as globalists and not just particularists. In an essay they jointly authored, Gaddis and Kennedy bemoaned the fact that particularists are too often, in too many countries, the ones still making and analyzing foreign policy.

"These people," the two Yale historians wrote, "are perfectly competent at taking in parts of the picture, but they have difficulty seeing the entire thing. They pigeonhole priorities, pursuing them separately and simultaneously, with little thought to how each might undercut the other. They proceed confidently enough from tree to tree, but seem astonished to find themselves lost in the forest. The great strategists of the past kept forests as well as the trees in view. They were generalists, and they operated from an ecological perspective. They understood that the world is a web, in which adjustments made here are bound to have effects over there—that everything is interconnected. Where, though, might one find generalists today? . . . The dominant trend within universities and the think tanks is toward ever-narrower specialization: a higher premium is placed on functioning deeply within a single field than broadly across several. And yet without some awareness of the whole—without some sense of how means converge to accomplish or to frustrate ends—there can be no strategy. And without strategy, there is only drift."

Some people are starting to catch on. That's why in the late 1990s the super-secret National Security Agency (NSA), which eavesdrops all over the globe, vacuuming up huge amounts of intelligence, decided it had to shift its internal way of handling information from the Cold War motto of "need to know," meaning you only got to see information if you had a need to know it, to "need to share," meaning we'll never understand the big picture unless we all share our little ones.

Maybe that explains why I gradually found that some (but by no means all) of my best intellectual sources these days were neither professors of international relations nor State Department diplomats, but rather the only real thriving school of globalists in the world today—hedge fund managers. I found myself drawn more and more to smart hedge fund managers—as opposed to diplomats or professors—because the best of them tended to be extremely well informed about global affairs and had a natural ability and willingness to arbitrage and **interpolate** information from all six dimensions before drawing their conclusions. One of the best of this group is Robert Johnson, who used to be a partner of George Soros. Johnson and I often remarked, after one of our conversations analyzing the world, that we were both basically doing the same thing—the only difference was that at the end of the day he was making a bet on a stock or bond and I was writing an opinion about some aspect of international relations. But we both had to go through the same arbitrage process to get there.

interpolate: interpose; interject

While six-dimensional information arbitrage is the best way to see the system of globalization, the best way to explain it often is through simple stories—and that's why the reader will find this book full of stories. Globalization is too complex a system to be explained by grand theories alone. It's too hard to grasp. I mentioned that one afternoon to Robert Hormats, the vice-chairman of Goldman Sachs International, and he deftly articulated what I meant: "To understand and then to explain globalization it is useful to think of yourself as an intellectual **nomad.** In the world of the nomad, there is no carefully defined turf. That's why the nomads were the ones who developed the monotheistic religions of Judaism and Islam. If you were sedentary you could develop all sorts of mythologies about this rock or that tree, and think that God was in that rock or that tree, alone. But the nomads always saw more of the world. They knew that God was not in that rock. He was everywhere. And the nomads, sitting around their campfires or walking from oasis to oasis, then conveyed that complex truth through simple stories."

nomad: wanderer; itinerant

In the old days a reporter, columnist or statesman could get away with thinking of his "market" as City Hall, or the Statehouse, or the White House, or the Pentagon, or the Treasury Department, or the State Department. But the relevant market today is the planet Earth and the global integration of technology, finance, trade and information in a way that is influencing wages, interest rates, living standards, culture, job opportunities, wars and weather patterns all over the world. It is not that the system of globalization explains everything happening in the world today. It is simply that to the extent that one system is influencing more people in more ways at the same time, it is globalization.

Unfortunately, for reasons I will explain later, the system of globalization has come upon us far faster than our ability to retrain ourselves to see and comprehend it. Think about just this one fact: Most people had never even heard of the Internet in 1990, and very few people had an E-mail address then. That was just nine years ago! But today the Internet, cell phones and E-mail have become essential tools that many people, and not only in developed countries, cannot imagine living without. It was no different, I am sure, at the start of the Cold War, with the first appearance of nuclear arsenals and deterrence theories. It took a long time for leaders and analysts of that era to fully grasp the real nature and dimensions of the Cold War system. They emerged from World War II thinking that this great war had produced a certain kind of world, but they soon discovered it had laid the foundations for a world very different from the one they anticipated. Much of what came to be seen as great Cold War architecture and strategizing were responses on the fly to changing events and evolving threats. Bit by bit, the Cold War strategists built the institutions, the perceptions, and the reflexes that came to be known as the Cold War system.

It will be no different with the globalization system, except that it may take us even longer to get our minds around it, because it requires so much retraining just to see this system and because it is built not just around superpowers but also around Supermarkets and Super-empowered individuals. I would say that in 1999 we understand as much about how today's system of globalization is going to work as we understood about how the Cold War system was going to work in 1946—the year **Winston Churchill** gave his speech warning that an "Iron Curtain" was coming down, cutting off the Soviet zone of influence from Western Europe. If you want to appreciate how few people understand exactly how this system works, think about one amusing fact. The two key economists who were advising Long-Term Capital Management, Robert C. Merton and Myron S. Scholes, shared the Nobel Prize for economics in 1997, roughly one year before Long-Term Capital Management so misunderstood the nature of risk in today's highly integrated global marketplace that it racked up the biggest losses in hedge fund history. And what did LTCM's two economists win their Nobel Prize for? For their studies on how complex financial instruments, known as derivatives, can be used by global investors to offset risk! In 1997 they won the Nobel Prize for managing risk. In 1998 they won the booby prize for creating risk—same guys, same market, new world.

25. In Your Journal: Previously, Friedman called Long-Term Capital Management a group of "super-empowered individuals." Is this label inconsistent with their company's failure?

Murray Gell-Mann, the Nobel laureate, former professor of theoretical physics at **Caltech** and one of the founders of the **Santa Fe Institute,** once argued in a series of lectures that what I call information arbitrage is not much different from the approach taken by scientists trying to make sense of **complex systems.** He is right. And there is no more complex political system today than globalization, and understanding it requires the journalist and strategist to be equally complex.

complex systems: study of the relationship between equilibrium and chaos

"Here on earth, once it was formed, systems of increasing complexity have arisen as a consequence of the physical evolution of the planet, biological evolution and human cultural evolution," said Gell-Mann. "The process has gone so far that we human beings are now confronted with immensely complex ecological, political, economic and social problems. When we attempt to tackle such difficult problems, we naturally tend to break them up into more manageable pieces. That is a useful practice, but it has serious limitations. When dealing with any non-linear system, especially a complex one, you can't just think in terms of parts or aspects and just add things up and say that the behavior of this and the behavior of

Winston Churchill: (Sir Winston Leonard Spenser Churchill) (1874–1965) Prime Minister of England during World War II

Caltech: California Institute of Technology

Santa Fe Institute: private, non-profit research and education center emphasizing interdisciplinary studies of complex systems that, added together, makes the whole thing. With a complex non-linear system you have to break it up into pieces and then study each aspect, and then study the very strong interaction between them all. Only this way can you describe the whole system."

That to me is the essence of what I consider the globalist school in international relations. But to have a globalist school, we need more students, professors, diplomats, journalists, spies and social scientists trained as globalists.

crude: rudimentary

"We need a corpus of people who consider that it is important to take a serious and professional **crude** look at the whole system," says Gell-Mann. "It has to be a crude look, because you will never master every part or every interconnection. You would think most journalists would do this. But they don't. Unfortunately, in a great many places in our society, including academia and most bureaucracies, prestige accrues principally to those who study carefully some [narrow] aspect of a problem, a trade, a technology, or a culture, while discussion of the big picture is relegated to cocktail party conversation. That is crazy. We have to learn not only to have specialists but also people whose specialty is to spot the strong interactions and the entanglements of the different dimensions, and then take a crude look at the whole. What we once considered the cocktail party stuff—that's a crucial part of the real story."

So, on to my cocktail party.

FOR USE IN DISCUSSION

Questions about Substance

1. Friedman wondered, when he became the foreign affairs columnist for *The New York Times,* what would be his "lens," his "organizing system," his "superstory"—the thing that would help him make sense of the world for his readers. Why do you think Friedman was so anxious about this? Why do journalists have to have a "superstory"?
2. What does it say about the American world view during the 40's and 50's that foreign affairs was known as "in Europe"?
3. What is the relationship between "free-market capitalism" (312) and "globalization capitalism" (314)?
4. What can James Surowiecki mean when he says that "the present—or perhaps the future—replaces the past" in globalization economics (315)?
5. What "three balances" is the globalization "built around" (316–317)? Which of those balances is the most recent?

6. Friedman refers to a "superstory, "superpowers," "supermarkets," and "super-empowered" individuals. What is the literal meaning of the prefix "super-"? Why is this concept so prominent in Friedman's thinking?
7. Friedman describes the new lens he sees the world through since he began adapting to the system of globalization in this manner: "I saw news stories that I would never have recognized as news stories before. I saw casual chains of events that I never could have identified before. I saw invisible hands and handcuffs impeding leaders and nations from doing things that I never imagined before" (322). Do you think the things he sees are more "true" than what he used to see, or are they just the result of a changing perspective?

Questions about Structure and Style

1. How does opening with a line from the movie *Forrest Gump* set the tone for this essay? Why do you think Friedman chooses such a popular symbol to introduce this essay about such a complex topic?
2. After a long discussion about the differences between the Cold War and globalization, Friedman returns to personal anecdotes confessing that he made up weather reports when he worked in Beirut. What effect is this intended to have on the reader?
3. How does Friedman's essay illustrate his theory that he should use "information arbitrage" and "storytelling" to cover the system of globalization?
4. Friedman asserts: "I am not a realist . . . I am not an environmentalist . . . I am not a technologist . . . I am not an essentialist . . . I am not an economist". (323). Why does he provide such a long list of what he is *not?* Why wouldn't he just describe what he *is?*

Multimedia Suggestions

1. Read the transcript for the PBS program *Globalization and Human Rights* at *http://www.pbs.org/globalization/transcript.html*. How do you think Friedman would respond to the issues presented here?
2. Listen to the September 2001, May 2002, and March 2003 interviews with Thomas Friedman at *http://freshair.npr.org/guest_info_fa.jhtml?name=thomasfriedman*. Do you notice Friedman's thinking beginning to develop or change over the course of the three interviews?

SUGGESTIONS FOR WRITING AND RESEARCH

1. In the past, a foreign correspondent probably would not have compared himself to a tourist for fear of seeming conspicuous or out of touch with the local culture. How has globalization most likely changed the image of tourists? Are foreign correspondents and tourists closer to being in the same category now? Do tourists, like Friedman, have "an attitude" related to the process of globalization?

2. Friedman tells personal anecdotes and confesses secrets at different points throughout this essay. He opens with an anecdote about ordering room service, he confesses to making up the weather reports, and he relates his embarrassment at being out of touch with Washington DC when he started as diplomatic correspondent for *The New York Times.* Why does Friedman use such personal information in an essay that is basically about everything in the world but him? What effect are these personal details meant to have on the reader? What is the difference between Thomas Friedman the essayist and Thomas Friedman the subject of this essay?
3. Based on your reading of Friedman's essay and whatever you may have read elsewhere on globalization (see Arundhati Roy's essay in this anthology), write an essay in support of or opposition to globalization. Analyze Friedman's reasoning in the course of your essay, and note whether his essay was instrumental in the forming of your opinion.

WORKING WITH CLUSTERS

Cluster 13: Global Knowledge

Cluster 15: Spatial Realities

Cluster 19: Structuring Chaos

Discipline: Social Sciences

Rhetorical Mode: Compare and Contrast

"Final Cut" (from *Complications: A Surgeon's Notes on an Imperfect Science*)

by Atul Gawande

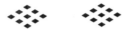

Atul Gawande has been a surgical resident at Brigham and Women's Hospital in Boston since he finished his medical degree from Harvard University in 1995. He also has degrees in politics, philosophy and economics, he is a staff writer for the New Yorker *magazine, and he has written speeches for former President Clinton. His books are* Good Medicine *and* Complications: A Surgeon's Notes on an Imperfect Science *(from which this essay is drawn), which both display a focused interest in the human aspects of medical science and its practitioners.* Complications *was a finalist for the National Book Award for Nonfiction in 2002.*

Your patient is dead; the family is gathered. And there is one last thing that you have to ask about: the autopsy. How should you go about it? You could do it offhandedly, as if it were the most ordinary thing in the world: "Shall we do an autopsy, then?" Or you could be firm, use your **Sergeant Joe Friday** voice: "Unless you have strong objections, we will need to do an autopsy, ma'am." Or you could take yourself out of it: "I am sorry, but they require me to ask, Do you want an autopsy done?"

Sergeant Joe Friday: main character on *Dragnet*, a popular 1950's television crime show set in Los Angeles,

mealymouthed: unwilling to state opinions directly

What you can't be nowadays is **mealymouthed** about it. I once took care of a woman in her eighties who had given up her driver's license only to get hit by a car—driven by someone even older—while she was walking to a bus stop. She sustained a depressed skull fracture and cerebral bleeding, and, despite surgery, she died a few days later. So, on the spring afternoon after the patient took her last breath, I stood beside her and bowed my head with the tearful family. Then, as delicately as I could—not even using the awful word—I said, "If it's all right, we'd like to do an examination to confirm the cause of death."

1. In Your Journal: Gawande's patient responds to the autopsy request by asking "Hasn't she been through enough?" Why does it seem like such a violation to cut a dead body open? Who does it violate?

"An *autopsy*?" a nephew said, horrified. He looked at me as if I were a buzzard circling his aunt's body. "Hasn't she been through enough?"

The autopsy is in a **precarious** state these days. A generation ago, it was routine; now it has become a rarity. Human beings have never quite become comfortable with the idea of having their bodies cut open after they die. Even for a surgeon, the sense of violation is inescapable.

precarious: unstable

Not long ago, I went to observe the dissection of a thirty-eight-year-old woman I had taken care of who had died after a long struggle with heart disease. The dissecting room was in the sub-basement, past the laundry and a loading dock, behind an unmarked metal door. It had high ceilings, peeling paint, and a brown tiled floor that sloped down to a central drain. There was a Bunsen burner on a countertop, and an old-style grocer's hanging scale, with a big clock-face red-arrow gauge and a pan underneath, for weighing organs. On shelves all around the room there were gray portions of brain, bowel, and other organs soaking in **formalin** in Tupperware-like containers. The facility seemed run-down, chintzy, low-tech. On a rickety gurney in the corner was my patient, sprawled out, completely naked. The autopsy team was just beginning its work.

formalin: preservative and disinfectant

2. In Your Journal: How would you characterize Gawande's description of the dissection room? What effect do you think this description is meant to have?

Surgical procedures can be grisly, but dissections are somehow worse. In even the most gruesome operations—skin grafting, amputations—surgeons maintain some tenderness and **aestheticism** toward their work. We

aestheticism: pursuit of beauty and good taste

know that the bodies we cut still pulse with life, and that these are people who will wake again. But in the dissecting room, where the person is gone and only the shell remains, you naturally find little delicacy, and the difference is visible in the smallest details. There is, for example, the simple matter of how a body is moved from gurney to table. In the operating room, we follow a careful, elaborate procedure for the unconscious patient, involving a canvas-sleeved rolling board and several gentle movements. We don't want so much as a bruise. Down here, by contrast, someone grabbed my patient's arm, another person a leg, and they just yanked. When her skin stuck to the stainless-steel dissecting table, they had to wet her and the table down with a hose before they could pull her the rest of the way.

The young **pathologist** for the case stood on the sidelines and let a pathology assistant take the knife. Like many of her colleagues, the pathologist had not been drawn to her field by autopsies but by the high-tech detective work that she got to do on tissue from living patients. She was happy to leave the dissection to the assistant, who had more experience at it anyway.

pathologist: one who studies the nature and cause of disease

The assistant was a tall, slender woman of around thirty with straight sandy-brown hair. She was wearing the full protective garb of mask, face shield, gloves, and blue plastic gown. Once the body was on the table, she placed a six-inch metal block under the back, between the shoulder blades, so that the head fell back and the chest arched up. Then she took a scalpel in her hand, a big No. 6 blade, and made a huge Y-shaped incision that came down diagonally from each shoulder, curving slightly around each breast before reaching the midline, and then continued down the abdomen to the pubis.

Surgeons get used to the opening of bodies. It is easy to detach yourself from the person on the table and become absorbed by the details of method and anatomy. Nevertheless, I couldn't help wincing as she did her work: she was holding the scalpel like a pen, which forced her to cut slowly and jaggedly with the tip of the blade. Surgeons are taught to stand straight and parallel to their incision, hold the knife between the thumb and four fingers, like a violin bow, and draw the belly of the blade through the skin in a single, smooth slice to the exact depth desired. The assistant was practically sawing her way through my patient.

3. In Your Journal: Why does the scalpel grip of the PA matter so much to Gawande?

From there, the **evisceration** was swift. The assistant flayed back the skin flaps. With an electric saw, she cut through the exposed ribs along both sides. Then she lifted the rib cage as if it were the hood of a car, opened the abdomen, and removed all the major organs—including the heart, the lungs, the liver, the bowels, and the kidneys. Then the skull was sawed open, and the brain, too, was removed. Meanwhile, the pathologist was at a back table, weighing and examining everything, and preparing samples for microscopy and thorough testing.

evisceration: removal of organs

For all this, however, I had to admit: the patient came out looking remarkably undisturbed. The assistant had followed the usual procedure and kept the skull incision behind the woman's ears, where it was completely hidden by her hair. She had also taken care to close the chest and abdomen neatly, sewing the incision tight with weaved seven-cord thread. My patient seemed much the same as before, except now a little collapsed in the middle. (The standard consent allows the hospital to keep the organs for testing and research. This common and long-established practice has caused huge controversy in Britain—the media have branded it "organ stripping"—but in America it remains generally accepted.) Most families, in fact, still have open-casket funerals after autopsies. Morticians employ fillers to restore a corpse's shape, and when they're done you cannot tell that an autopsy has been performed.

> ***4. In Your Journal:*** If the work of an autopsy is practically undetectable once it's over, why does it seem to matter to people so much whether one is done or not?

Still, when it is time to ask for a family's permission to do such a thing, the images weigh on everyone's mind—not least the doctor's. You strive to achieve a cool, dispassionate attitude toward these matters. But doubts nevertheless creep in.

> ***5. In Your Journal:*** Why are images so important in this process? And why would they matter so much to the doctor?

One of the first patients for whom I was expected to request an autopsy was a seventy-five-year-old retired New England doctor who died one winter night while I was with him. Herodotus Sykes (not his real name, but not unlike it, either) had been rushed to the hospital with an infected, rupturing abdominal **aortic aneurysm** and taken to emergency surgery. He survived it, and recovered steadily until, eighteen days later, his blood pressure dropped alarmingly and blood began to pour from a drainage tube in his abdomen. "The aortic stump must have blown out," his surgeon said. Residual infection must have weakened the suture line where the infected aorta had been removed. We could have operated again, but the patient's chances were poor, and his surgeon didn't think he would be willing to take any more.

aortic aneurysm: blood-filled expansion in artery

He was right. No more surgery, Sykes told me. He'd been through enough. We called Mrs. Sykes, who was staying with a friend about two hours away, and she set out for the hospital.

It was about midnight. I sat with him as he lay silent and bleeding, his arms slack at his sides, his eyes without fear. I imagined his wife out on the **Mass Pike,** frantic, helpless, with six lanes, virtually empty at that hour, stretching far ahead.

Sykes held on, and at 2:15 A.M. his wife arrived. She turned **ashen** at the sight of him, but she steadied herself. She gently took his hand in hers. She squeezed, and he squeezed back. I left them to themselves.

ashen: pale, gray-colored

At 2:45, the nurse called me in. I listened with my stethoscope, then turned to Mrs. Sykes and told her that he was gone. She had her husband's Yankee reserve, but she broke into quiet tears, weeping into her hands, and seemed suddenly frail and small. A friend who had come with her soon appeared, took her by the arm, and led her out of the room.

Mass Pike: Interstate highway 90, which runs horizontally across Massachusetts

We are instructed to request an autopsy on everyone as a means of confirming the cause of death and catching our mistakes. And this was the moment I was supposed to ask—with the wife despondent and reeling with shock. But surely, I began to think, here was a case in which an autopsy would be pointless. We knew what had happened—a persistent infection, a rupture. We were sure of it. What would cutting the man apart accomplish?

And so I let Mrs. Sykes go. I could have caught her as she walked through the ICU's double doors. Or even called her on the phone later. But I never did.

Such reasoning, it appears, has become commonplace in medicine. Doctors are seeking so few autopsies that in recent years the *Journal of the American Medical Association* has twice felt the need to declare "war on the nonautopsy." According to the most recent statistics available, autopsies have been done in fewer than 10 percent of deaths; many hospitals do none. This is a dramatic turnabout. Through much of the twentieth century, doctors diligently obtained autopsies in the majority of all deaths—and it had taken centuries to reach this point. As Kenneth Iserson recounts in his fascinating almanac, *Death to Dust,* physicians have performed autopsies for more than two thousand years. But for most of history they were rarely performed. If religions permitted them at all—Islam, Shinto, orthodox Judaism, and the Greek Orthodox Church still frown on them—it was generally only for legal purposes. The Roman physician Antistius performed one of the earliest forensic examinations on record, in 44 B.C., on Julius Caesar, documenting twenty-three wounds, including a final, fatal stab to the chest. In 1410, the Catholic Church itself ordered an autopsy—on Pope Alexander V, to determine whether his successor had poisoned him. No evidence of this was apparently found.

The first documented postmortem examination in the New World was actually done for religious reasons, though. It was performed on July 19, 1533, on the island of Española (now the Dominican Republic), upon conjoined female twins connected at the lower chest, to determine if they had one soul or two. The twins had been born alive, and a priest had baptized them as two separate souls. A disagreement subsequently ensued about whether he was right to have done so, and when the "double monster" died at eight days of age an autopsy was ordered to settle the issue. A surgeon, one Johan Camacho, found two virtually complete sets of internal organs, and it was decided that two souls had lived and died.

Even in the nineteenth century, however, long after church strictures had loosened, people in the West seldom allowed doctors to autopsy their family members for medical purposes. As a result, the practice was largely **clandestine.** Some doctors went ahead and autopsied hospital patients immediately after death, before relatives could turn up to object. Others waited until burial and then robbed the graves, either personally or through accomplices, an activity that continued into the twentieth century. To deter

clandestine: concealed or secret

such autopsies, some families would post nighttime guards at the grave site—hence the term "graveyard shift." Others placed heavy stones on the coffins. In 1878, one company in Columbus, Ohio, even sold "torpedo coffins," equipped with pipe bombs rigged to blow up if they were tampered with. Yet doctors remained undeterred. **Ambrose Bierce**'s *The Devil's Dictionary,* published in 1906, defined "grave" as "a place in which the dead are laid to await the coming of the medical student."

By the turn of the twentieth century, however, prominent physicians such as Rudolf Virchow in Berlin, Karl Rokitansky in Vienna, and William Osler in Baltimore began to win popular support for the practice of autopsy. They defended it as a tool of discovery, one that had already been used to identify the cause of tuberculosis, reveal how to treat appendicitis, and establish the existence of Alzheimer's disease. They also showed that autopsies prevented errors—that without them doctors could not know when their diagnoses were incorrect. Moreover, most deaths were a mystery then, and perhaps what clinched the argument was the notion that autopsies could provide families with answers—give the story of a loved one's life a comprehensible ending. Once doctors had insured a dignified and respectful dissection at the hospital, public opinion turned. With time, doctors who did *not* obtain autopsies were viewed with suspicion. By the end of the Second World War, the autopsy was firmly established as a routine part of death in Europe and North America.

6. In Your Journal: The author explains that autopsies have helped in important discoveries related to tuberculosis, appendicitis, and Alzheimer's disease. What is his motive in listing these contributions?

7. In Your Journal: Autopsies can "provide families with answers." What role can answers play in the grief of those who have lost someone?

So what accounts for its decline? In truth, it's not because families refuse—to judge from recent studies, they still grant that permission up to 80 percent of the time. Instead, doctors, once so eager to perform autopsies that they stole bodies, have simply stopped asking. Some people ascribe this to shady motives. It has been said that hospitals are trying to save money by avoiding autopsies, since insurers don't pay for them, or that doctors avoid them in order to cover up evidence of malpractice. And yet autopsies lost money and uncovered malpractice when they were popular, too.

Instead, I suspect, what discourages autopsies is medicine's twenty-first-century, tall-in-the-saddle confidence. When I failed to ask Mrs. Sykes whether we could autopsy her husband, it was not because of the expense, or because I feared that the autopsy would uncover an error. It was the opposite: I didn't see much likelihood that an error would be found. Today, we have MRI scans, ultrasound, nuclear medicine, molecular testing, and much more. When somebody dies, we already know why. We don't need an autopsy to find out.

Or so I thought. Then I had a patient who changed my mind.

⁖ **Ambrose Bierce:** (1849–1914) American writer/journalist whose most well-known work, *The Devil's Dictionary,* a sardonic reference book of mock definitions

He was in his sixties, whiskered and cheerful, a former engineer who had found success in retirement as an artist. I will call him Mr. Jolly, because that's what he was. He was also what we call a vasculopath—he did not seem to have an undiseased artery in him. Whether because of his diet or his genes or the fact that he used to smoke, he had had, in the previous decade, one heart attack, two abdominal aortic aneurysm repairs, four bypass operations to keep blood flowing past blockages in his leg arteries, and several balloon procedures to keep hardened arteries open. Still, I never knew him to take a dark view of his lot. "Well, you can't get miserable about it," he'd say. He had wonderful children. He had beautiful grandchildren. "But, aargh, the wife," he'd go on. She would be sitting right there at the bedside and would roll her eyes, and he'd break into a grin.

Mr. Jolly had come into the hospital for treatment of a wound infection in his legs. But he soon developed congestive heart failure, causing fluid to back up into his lungs. Breathing became steadily harder for him, until we had to put him in the ICU, **intubate** him, and place him on a ventilator. A two-day admission turned into two weeks. With a regimen of **diuretics** and a change in heart medications, however, his heart failure reversed, and his lungs recovered. And one bright Sunday morning he was reclining in bed, breathing on his own, watching the morning shows on the TV set that hung from the ceiling. "You're doing marvelously," I said. I told him we would transfer him out of intensive care by the afternoon. He would probably be home in a couple of days.

intubate: insert tube into a passage or organ, usually to help flow

diuretic: substance that encourages or increases urination

Two hours later, a code-blue emergency call went out on the overhead speakers. When I got to the ICU and saw the nurse hunched over Mr. Jolly, doing chest compressions, I blurted out an angry curse. He'd been fine, the nurse explained, just watching TV, when suddenly he sat upright with a look of shock and then fell back, unresponsive. At first, he was asystolic—no heart rhythm on the monitor—and then the rhythm came back, but he had no pulse. A crowd of staffers set to work. I had him intubated, gave him fluids and **epinephrine,** had someone call the attending surgeon at home, someone else check the morning lab test results. An X-ray technician shot a portable chest film.

epinephrine: adrenalin-like heart stimulant

I mentally ran through possible causes. There were not many. A collapsed lung, but I heard good breath sounds with my stethoscope, and when his X ray came back the lungs looked fine. A massive blood loss, but his abdomen wasn't swelling, and his decline happened so quickly that bleeding just didn't make sense. Extreme acidity of the blood could do it, but his lab tests were fine. Then there was cardiac tamponade—bleeding into the sac that contains the heart. I took a six-inch spinal needle on a syringe, pushed it through the skin below the breastbone, and advanced it to the heart sac. I found no bleeding. That left only one possibility: a pulmonary embolism—a blood clot that flips into the lung and instantly wedges off all blood flow. And nothing could be done about that.

I went out and spoke to the attending surgeon by phone and then to the chief resident, who had just arrived. An embolism was the only logical explanation, they agreed. I went back into the room and stopped the code. "Time of death: 10:23 A.M.," I announced. I phoned his wife at home, told her that things had taken a turn for the worse, and asked her to come in.

This shouldn't have happened; I was sure of it. I scanned the records for clues. Then I found one. In a lab test done the day before, the patient's clotting had seemed slow, which wasn't serious, but an ICU physician had decided to correct it with vitamin K. A frequent side effect of vitamin K is blood clots. I was furious. Giving the vitamin was completely unnecessary—just fixing a number on a lab test. Both the chief resident and I lit into the physician. We all but accused him of killing the patient.

> ***8. In Your Journal:*** Gawande criticizes the ICU doctor for merely "fixing a number on a lab test." How do you think the doctor himself perceived his prescription of Vitamin K?

When Mrs. Jolly arrived, we took her to a family room where it was quiet and calm. I could see from her face that she'd already surmised the worst. His heart had stopped suddenly, we told her, because of a pulmonary embolism. We said the medicines we gave him may have contributed to it. I took her in to see him and left her with him. After a while, she came out, her hands trembling and her face stained with tears. Then, remarkably, she thanked us. We had kept him for her all these years, she said. Maybe so, but neither of us felt any pride about what had just happened.

I asked her the required question. I told her that we wanted to perform an autopsy and needed her permission. We thought we already knew what had happened, but an autopsy would confirm it, I said. She considered my request for a moment. If an autopsy would help us, she finally said, then we could do it. I said, as I was supposed to, that it would. I wasn't sure I believed it.

I wasn't assigned to the operating room the following morning, so I went down to observe the autopsy. When I arrived, Mr. Jolly was already laid out on the dissecting table, his arms splayed, skin flayed back, chest exposed, abdomen open. I put on a gown, gloves, and a mask, and went up close. The assistant began buzzing through the ribs on the left side with the electric saw, and immediately blood started seeping out, as dark and **viscous** as crankcase oil. Puzzled, I helped him lift open the rib cage. The left side of the chest was full of blood. I felt along the pulmonary arteries for a hardened, embolized clot, but there was none. He hadn't had an embolism after all. We suctioned out three liters of blood, lifted the left lung, and the answer appeared before our eyes. The thoracic aorta was almost three times larger than it should have been, and there was a half-inch hole in it. The man had ruptured an aortic aneurysm and had bled to death almost instantly.

> **viscous:** thick; having high resistance to flow

> ***9. In Your Journal:*** How is Mr. Jolly's cause of death related to the disease of Herodotus Sykes, who Gawande declined to autopsy?

In the days afterward, I apologized to the physician I'd reamed out over the vitamin, and pondered how we had managed to miss the diagnosis. I looked through the patient's old X rays and now saw a shadowy outline of what must have been his aneurysm. But none of us, not even the radiologists, had caught it. Even if we had caught it, we wouldn't have dared to do anything about it until weeks after treating his infection and heart failure, and that would have been too late. It disturbed me, however, to have felt so confident about what had happened that day and to have been so wrong.

10. In Your Journal: Gawande is most disturbed by his thorough confidence in his faulty judgment. But isn't confidence the attitude we want from doctors?

The most perplexing thing was his final chest X ray, the one we had taken during the code blue. With all that blood filling the chest, I should have seen at least a haze over the left side. But when I pulled the film out to look again, there was nothing.

How often do autopsies turn up a major misdiagnosis in the cause of death? I would have guessed this happened rarely, in 1 or 2 percent of cases at most. According to three studies done in 1998 and 1999, however, the figure is about 40 percent. A large review of autopsy studies concluded that in about a third of the misdiagnoses the patients would have been expected to live if proper treatment had been administered. George Lundberg, a pathologist and former editor of the *Journal of the American Medical Association,* has done more than anyone to call attention to these figures. He points out the most surprising fact of all: the rates at which misdiagnosis is detected in autopsy studies have not improved since at least 1938.

11. In Your Journal: What is so disturbing about these statistics?

12. In Your Journal: If the rates of misdiagnosis haven't changed since 1938, what does this say about our confidence in medical progress?

With all the recent advances in imaging and diagnostics, it's hard to accept that we not only get the diagnosis wrong in two out of five of our patients who die but that we have also failed to improve over time. To see if this could really be true, doctors at Harvard put together a simple study. They went back into their hospital records to see how often autopsies picked up missed diagnoses in 1960 and 1970, before the advent of CT, ultrasound, nuclear scanning, and other technologies, and then in 1980, after those technologies became widely used. The researchers found no improvement. Regardless of the decade, physicians missed a quarter of fatal infections, a third of heart attacks, and almost two-thirds of pulmonary emboli in their patients who died.

In most cases, it wasn't technology that failed. Rather, the physicians did not consider the correct diagnosis in the first place. The perfect test or scan may have been available, but the physicians never ordered it.

13. In Your Journal: Which do you think is worse: physician misdiagnosis or technical failure? Why? Do you think either is more preventable than the other?

In a 1976 essay, the philosophers Samuel Gorovitz and Alasdair MacIntyre explored the nature of fallibility. Why would a meteorologist, say, fail to correctly predict where a hurricane was going to make landfall? They saw three possible reasons. One was ignorance: perhaps science affords only a limited understanding of how hurricanes behave. A second reason was ineptitude: the knowledge is available, but the weatherman fails to apply it correctly. Both of these are sur-mountable sources of error. We believe that science will overcome ignorance, and that training and technology will overcome ineptitude. The third possible cause of error the philosophers posited, however, was an insurmountable kind, one they termed "necessary fallibility."

> ***14. In Your Journal:*** What does the term "necessary fallibility" mean? Why does it seem strange to associate this with the scientific methodology of modern medicine?

There may be some kinds of knowledge that science and technology will never deliver, Gorovitz and MacIntyre argued. When we ask science to move beyond explaining how things (say, hurricanes) generally behave to predicting exactly how a particular thing (say, Thursday's storm off the South Carolina coast) will behave, we may be asking it to do more than it can. No hurricane is quite like any other hurricane. Although all hurricanes follow predictable laws of behavior, each one is continuously shaped by **myriad** uncontrollable, accidental factors in the environment. To say precisely how one specific hurricane will behave would require a complete understanding of the world in all its particulars—in other words, **omniscience.**

myriad: incalculably numerous

omniscience: total knowledge of everything

It's not that it's impossible to predict anything; plenty of things are completely predictable. Gorovitz and MacIntyre give the example of a random ice cube in a fire. Ice cubes are so simple and so alike that you can predict with complete assurance that an ice cube will melt. But when it comes to inferring exactly what is going on in a particular person, are people more like ice cubes or like hurricanes?

Right now, at about midnight, I am seeing a patient in the emergency room, and I want to say that she is an ice cube. That is, I believe I can understand what's going on with her, that I can discern all her relevant properties. I believe I can help her.

Charlotte Duveen, as we will call her, is forty-nine years old, and for two days she has had abdominal pain. I begin observing her from the moment I walk through the curtains into her room. She is sitting cross-legged in the chair next to her stretcher and greets me with a cheerful, tobacco-beaten voice. She does not look sick. No clutching the belly. No gasping for words. Her color is good—neither flushed nor pale. Her shoulder-length brown hair has been brushed, her red lipstick neatly applied.

She tells me the pain started out crampy, like a gas pain. But then, during the course of the day, it became sharp and focused, and as she says this she points to a spot in the lower right part of her abdomen. She has developed diarrhea. She constantly feels as if she has to urinate. She doesn't have a fever. She is not nauseated. Actually, she is hungry. She tells me that she ate a hot dog at Fenway Park two days ago and visited the exotic birds at the zoo a few days before that, and she asks if either might have anything to do with this. She has two grown children. Her last period was three months ago. She smokes half a pack a day. She used to use heroin but says she's clean now. She once had hepatitis. She has never had surgery.

I feel her abdomen. It could be anything, I think: food poisoning, a virus, appendicitis, a urinary-tract infection, an ovarian cyst, a pregnancy.

Her abdomen is soft, without distension, and there is an area of particular tenderness in the lower right quadrant. When I press there, I feel her muscles harden reflexively beneath my fingers. On the pelvic exam, her ovaries feel normal. I order some lab tests. Her white blood cell count comes back elevated. Her urinalysis is normal. A pregnancy test is negative. I order an abdominal CT scan.

I am sure I can figure out what's wrong with her, but, if you think about it, that's a curious faith. I have never seen this woman before in my life, and yet I presume that she is like the others I've examined. Is it true? None of my other patients, admittedly, were forty-nine-year-old women who had had hepatitis and a drug habit, had recently been to the zoo and eaten a Fenway frank, and had come in with two days of mild lower-right-quadrant pain. Yet I still believe. Every day, we take people to surgery and open their abdomens, and, broadly speaking, we know what we will find: not eels or tiny chattering machines or a pool of blue liquid but coils of bowel, a liver to one side, a stomach to the other, a bladder down below. There are, of course, differences—an adhesion in one patient, an infection in another—but we have catalogued and sorted them by the thousands, making a statistical profile of mankind.

I am leaning toward appendicitis. The pain is in the right place. The timing of her symptoms, her exam, and her white blood cell count all fit with what I've seen before. She's hungry, however; she's walking around, not looking sick, and this seems unusual. I go to the radiology reading room and stand in the dark, looking over the radiologist's shoulder at the images of Duveen's abdomen flashing up on the monitor. He points to the appendix, wormlike, thick, surrounded by gray, streaky fat. It's appendicitis, he says confidently. I call the attending surgeon on duty and tell him what we've found. "Book the OR," he says. We're going to do an appendectomy.

This one is as sure as we get. Yet I've worked on similar cases in which we opened the patient up and found a normal appendix. Surgery itself is a kind of autopsy. "Autopsy" literally means "to see for oneself," and, despite our knowledge and technology, when we look we're often unprepared for what we find. Sometimes it turns out that we had missed a clue along the way, made a genuine mistake. Sometimes we turn out wrong despite doing everything right.

> ***15. In Your Journal:*** What does Gawande mean when he says that, "Surgery itself is a kind of autopsy"?

Whether with living patients or dead, however, we cannot know until we look. Even in the case of Mr. Sykes, I now wonder whether we put our stitches in correctly, or whether the bleeding had come from somewhere else entirely. Doctors are no longer asking such questions. Equally troubling, people seem happy to let us off the hook. In 1995, the United States National Center for Health Statistics stopped collecting autopsy statistics altogether. We can no longer even say how rare autopsies have become.

From what I've learned looking inside people, I've decided human beings are somewhere between a hurricane and an ice cube: in some respects, permanently mysterious, but in others—with enough science and careful probing—entirely scrutable. It would be as foolish to think we have reached the limits of human knowledge as it is to think we could ever know everything. There is still room enough to get better, to ask questions of even the dead, to learn from knowing when our simple certainties are wrong.

FOR USE IN DISCUSSION

Questions about Substance

1. Autopsy means "see for yourself" (341). How does this literal definition relate to Gawande's main ideas?
2. Gawande says that "humans have never quite been comfortable" (332) with the autopsy. Why do you think this is true?
3. Why is the description of the autopsy in Gawande's introduction so graphic? Isn't the author trying to convince us of the value of the autopsy?
4. Gawande hopes for his patient to be an easy-to-predict melting ice cube rather than a highly unpredictable hurricane (340). Why does he use such extreme analogies here? Is there no middle ground?
5. Toward the end of the essay, Gawande says that "there may be some kinds of knowledge that science and technology will never deliver" (340). Is his conclusion meant to leave the reader with an uneasy feeling? Is it antithetical to the goals of science?

Questions about Structure and Style

1. The first sentence of this essay reads, "Your patient is dead." Analyze the tone, point of view, and sentence structure. What is the immediate effect of this sentence?
2. In the first paragraph, three potential choices of how to request an autopsy are provided. Do any of them seem reasonable or appealing? If not, what could be the purpose for including them?
3. A lot of time is spent describing the actual autopsy practice (332–334) without much attempt to be flattering to the process. If Gawande ultimately wants to advocate the autopsy, why does he paint such a bleak picture so early in his essay?
4. Look at the various cases addressed here—there are a fair number of them. How does each case illustrate a different part of Gawande's argument?
5. Why does Gawande present the theory that hospitals have cut down on autopsies to save money only to discredit it (336)?

6. This essay is achronological—it does not only move forward; it begins in the present and flashes back several times. Why do you think Gawande uses this structure?
7. The author provides a very lengthy list of symptoms for Charlotte Duveen, the last patient discussed in this article. What is the point of all this detail?

Multimedia Suggestions

1. Many recent popular television shows center around the results of autopsies (*Law and Order* and *CSI*, for example). Why are we so fascinated with this theme? Are we less squeamish about autopsies than Gawande thinks?
2. Leicester University in England has created a "Virtual Autopsy" Web site (see *www.le.ec.uk/pathology/teach/va/welcome.html*). The Web site functions almost like a game, where users choose from a list of potential diagnoses after reading charts and pathology reports for an individual cadaver. Does this bear any similarities to the cases in Gawande's essay? What do you think of the Web site's playful approach?

SUGGESTIONS FOR WRITING AND RESEARCH

1. Write an essay that compares and contrasts Gawande's decisions about and reactions to the different patients he loses. Why does he include so many examples in this essay?
2. Respond to Gawande's argument about the decline of the autopsy from the point of view of a hospital administrator or the family of a deceased patient. Answer each of Gawande's criticisms of this decline, quoting from Gawande's text as necessary.
3. There are many types of investigations that require retrospective thinking other than the autopsy. Using the autopsy as a metaphor, describe another kind of inquiry (e.g., historical analysis, crime scene analysis, or even the college admissions process). Compare and contrast the two types of "autopsy." in terms of purpose and outcomes—both intended and unintended.
4. Go to the library and find *The Journal of the American Medical Association*'s articles (especially in 1988) that have declared "war on the non-autopsy." Analyze the claims and evidence the articles present. Is there any additional information—statistical, anecdotal, or other—which Gawande has omitted from his article that you find useful?

WORKING WITH CLUSTERS

Cluster 4: Conceiving Death
Cluster 9: Bodies of Knowledge
Cluster 14: Epistemologies
Discipline: The Natural Sciences
Rhetorical Mode: Argument

"A Tale of Two Work Sites" (from *The Lying Stones of Marrakech: Penultimate Reflections in Natural History*)

by Stephen Jay Gould

Stephen Jay Gould, a renowned paleontologist whose work is known both within academia and popular culture, received an A.B. from Antioch College in geology and a doctorate from Columbia University. As the Alexander Agassiz Professor of Zoology and curator of invertebrate paleontology at Harvard University, Gould received many honors, including more than 40 honorary degrees from institutions such as Rutgers University, the University of St. Andrews in Scotland, and Antioch College. He was named the "Scientist of the Year" by Discover Magazine, *received the Medal of Excellence from Columbia University, the Silver Medal from the Zoological Society of London, the Gold Medal for Service to Zoology from the Linnean Society of London, and the Distinguished Scientist Award from The Center for the Study of Evolution and the Origin of Life at University of California, Los Angeles. In addition, Gould published twenty-four books (two posthumously) and hundreds of essays in national newspapers and magazines. He received the National Book Award for* The Panda's Thumb, *the National Book Critics Circle Award for* The Mismeasure of Man, *and the Phi Beta Kappa Book Award in Science for both* Hen's Teeth and Horse's Toes *and* Wonderful Life. *For the latter, he also received the Rhone-Poulenc Prize and the Golden Trilobite Award for excellence in paleontological writing from The Paleontological Society. Gould died of cancer in 2002.*

sarcophagus: stone coffin

1. *In Your Journal:* What does Gould suggest about gravesites—specifically, tombstones?

vicarious: feeling as if one were having the experiences of another

2. *In Your Journal:* What does Gould think of "legends"?

Christopher Wren, the leading architect of London's reconstruction after the great fire of 1666, lies buried beneath the floor of his most famous building, **St. Paul's Cathedral.** No elaborate **sarcophagus** adorns the site. Instead, we find only the famous epitaph written by his son and now inscribed into the floor: "*si monumentum requiris, circumspice*"—if you are searching for his monument, look around. A tad grandiose perhaps, but I have never read a finer testimony to the central importance—one might even say sacredness—of actual places, rather than replicas, symbols, or other forms of **vicarious** resemblance.

An odd coincidence of professional life turned my thoughts to this most celebrated epitaph when, for the second time, I received an office in a spot laden with history, a place still redolent of ghosts of past events both central to our common culture and especially meaningful for my own life and choices.

In 1971, I spent an academic term as a visiting researcher at Oxford University. I received a cranny of office space on the upper floor of the University Museum. As I set up my books, fossil snails, and microscope, I noticed a metal plaque affixed to the wall, informing me that this reconfigured space of shelves and cubicles had been, originally, the site of the most famous public confrontation in the early history of **Darwinism.** On this very spot, in 1860, just a few months after Darwin published ***The Origin of Species,*** T. H. Huxley had drawn his rhetorical sword, and soundly skewered the slick but superficial champion of creationism, Bishop "Soapy Sam" Wilberforce.

(As with most legends, the official version ranks as mere cardboard before a much more complicated and multifaceted truth. Wilberforce and Huxley did put on a splendid, and largely spontaneous, show—but no clear

---

·:·· **St. Paul's Cathedral:** towering 305-year-old cathedral in London where, in addition to regular Christian worship services, major royal events and important lectures are held

·:·· **Darwinism:** theory of biological evolution developed by Charles Darwin; states that small, inherited variations improve an individual organism's ability to survive and reproduce

·:·· ***The Origin of Species:*** Charles Darwin's 1859 work, which outlines his theory of evolution victor emerged from the scuffle, and Joseph **Hooker,** Darwin's other champion, made a much more effective reply to the bishop, however forgotten by history. See my essay on this debate, entitled "Knight Takes Bishop?" and published in an earlier volume of this series, *Bully for Brontosaurus.*)

I can't claim that the lingering presence of these Victorian giants increased my resolve or improved my work, but I loved the sense of continuity **vouchsafed** to me by this happy circumstance. I even treasured the **etymology**—for *circumstance* means "standing around" (as Wren's *circumspice* means "looking around"), and here I stood, perhaps in the very spot where Huxley had said, at least according to legend, that he preferred an honest ape for an ancestor to a bishop who would distort a known truth for **rhetorical** advantage.

vouchsafe: verify as safe

etymology: historical development of a word or other linguistic element

rhetorical: for stylistic purposes

Not so long ago, I received a part-time appointment as visiting research professor of biology at New York University. I was given an office on the tenth floor of the Brown building on Washington Place, a nondescript early-twentieth-century structure now filled with laboratories and other academic spaces. As the dean took me on a casual tour of my new digs, he made a passing remark, intended as little more than "tour-guide patter," but producing an electric effect upon his new tenant. Did I know, he asked, that this building had been the site of the infamous Triangle Shirtwaist fire of 1911, and that my office occupied a corner location on one of the affected floors—in fact, as I later discovered, right near the escape route used by many workers to safety on the roof above. The dean also told me that, each year on the March 25 anniversary of the fire, the International Ladies' Garment Workers Union still holds a ceremony at the site and lays wreaths to memorialize the 146 workers killed in the blaze.

If the debate between Huxley and Wilberforce defines a primary legend of my chosen profession, the Triangle Shirtwaist fire occupies an even more central place in my larger view of life. I grew up in a family of Jewish immigrant garment workers, and this holocaust (in the literal meaning of a thorough sacrifice by burning) had set their views and helped to define their futures.

3. In Your Journal: What do Gould's two worksites have in common?

The shirtwaist—a collared blouse designed on the model of a man's shirt and worn above a separate skirt—had become the fashionable symbol of more independent women. The Triangle Shirtwaist Company, New York City's largest manufacturer of shirtwaists, occupied three floors (eighth through tenth) of the Asch Building (later bought by New York University and rechristened Brown, partly to blot out the infamy of association with the fire). The company employed some five hundred workers, nearly all young women who had recently arrived either as Jewish immigrants from eastern Europe or as Catholics from Italy. Exits from the building, in

Hooker: (Joseph Dalton) (1817–1911) English botanist; colleague, friend, and defender of Darwin addition to elevators, included only two small stairways and one absurdly inadequate fire escape. But the owners had violated no codes, both because general standards of regulation were then so weak, and because the structure was supposedly fireproof—as the framework proved to be (for the building, with my office, still stands), though inflammable walls and ceilings could not prevent an internal blaze on floors crammed full of garments and cuttings. The Triangle company was, in fact, a deathtrap—for fire hoses of the day could not pump above the sixth floor, while nets and blankets could not sustain the force of a human body jumping from greater heights.

The fire broke out at quitting time. Most workers managed to escape by the elevators, down one staircase (we shall come to the other staircase later), or by running up to the roof. But the flames trapped 146 employees, nearly all young women. About fifty workers met a hideous, if dramatic, end by jumping in terror from the ninth-floor windows, as a wall of fire advanced from behind. Firemen and bystanders begged them not to jump, and then tried to hold improvised nets of sheets and blankets. But these professionals and good Samaritans could not hold the nets against the force of fall, and many bodies plunged right through the flimsy fabrics onto the pavement below, or even through the "hollow sidewalks" made of **opaque** glass circles designed to transmit daylight to basements below, and still a major (and attractive) feature of my **SoHo** neighborhood. (These sidewalks carry prominent signs warning delivery trucks not to back in.) Not a single jumper survived, and the memory of these forced leaps to death remains the most searing image of America's prototypical sweatshop tragedy.

opaque: not clear

4. In Your Journal: Why, according to Gould, do "all defining events of history develop simplified legends"?

All defining events of history develop simplified legends as official versions—primarily, I suppose, because we commandeer such events for shorthand moral instruction, and the complex messiness of actual truth always blurs the clarity of a pithy **epigram.** Thus, Huxley, representing the righteousness of scientific objectivity, must slay the dragon of ancient and unthinking **dogma.** The equally oversimplified legend of the Triangle fire holds that workers became trapped because management had locked all the exit doors to prevent pilfering, unscheduled breaks, or access to union organizers—leaving only the fire escape as a mode of exit. All five of my guidebooks to New York architecture tell this "official" version. My favorite book, for example, states: "Although the building was equipped with fire exits, the terrified workers discovered to their horror that the ninth-floor doors had been locked by supervisors. A single fire-escape was wholly inadequate for the crush of panic-stricken employees."

epigram: witty saying; axiom

dogma: creed; belief

These traditional (indeed, virtually "official") legends may exaggerate for moral punch, but such interpretations emerge from a factual basis of

---

SoHo: ("South of Houston") district in southwest New York City, now noted for art galleries and studios greater ambiguity—and this reality, as we shall see in the Triangle case, often embodies a deeper and more important lesson. Huxley did argue with Wilberforce, after all, even if he secured no decisive victory, and Huxley did represent the side of the angels—the true angels of light and justice. And although many Triangle workers escaped by elevators and one staircase, another staircase (that might have saved nearly everyone else) was almost surely locked.

If Wilberforce and his **minions** had won, I might be a laborer, a linguist, or a lawyer today. But the Triangle fire might have blotted me out entirely. My grandmother arrived in America in 1910. On that fatal March day in 1911, she was working as a sixteen-year-old seamstress in a sweatshop—but, thank God, not for the Triangle Shirtwaist Company. My grandfather, at the same moment, was cutting cloth in yet another nearby factory.

minion: follower

5. In Your Journal: Why does Gould think he would have entered a different profession if Wilberforce and Huxley's debate had turned out differently?

These two utterly disparate stories—half a century and an ocean apart, and with maximal contrast between an industrial tragedy and an academic debate—might seem to embody the most unrelatable of items: the apples and oranges, or chalk and cheese (the British version), of our mottoes. Yet I feel that an intimate bond ties these two stories together in illustrating opposite poles of a central issue in the history of evolutionary theory: the application of Darwinian thought to the life and times of our own troubled species. I claim nothing beyond personal meaning—and certainly no rationale for boring anyone else—in the accidental location of my two offices in such sacred spots of history. But the emotion of a personal prod often dislodges a general theme well worth sharing.

The application of evolutionary theory to ***Homo sapiens*** has always troubled Western culture deeply—not for any reason that might be called scientific (for humans are biological objects, and must therefore take their place with all other living creatures on the genealogical tree of life), but only as a consequence of ancient prejudices about human distinctiveness and unbridgeable superiority. Even Darwin tiptoed lightly across this subject when he wrote *The Origin of Species* in 1859 (though he plunged in later, in 1871, by publishing *The Descent of Man*). The first edition of the *Origin* says little about *Homo sapiens* beyond a **cryptic** promise that "light will be thrown on the origin of man and his history." (Darwin became a bit bolder in later editions and ventured the following emendation: "Much light will be thrown . . .")

Homo sapiens: (Latin) "man of reason"; modern species of humans

cryptic: mysterious; obscure

6. In Your Journal: Why does Gould mention the subtle difference between the original and the emended sentence that describes Darwin's "cryptic promise" to connect humans to evolutionary theory?

Troubling issues of this sort often find their unsurprising resolution in a bit of wisdom that has permeated our traditions from such sublime sources as **Aristotle's** *aurea mediocritas* (or **golden mean**) to the **vernacular** sensibility of Goldilocks's decisions to split the difference between two extremes, and find a solution "just right" in the middle. Similarly, one can ask either too little or too much of Darwinism in trying to understand "the origin of man and his history." As usual, a proper solution

Aristotle's golden mean: course between two extremes; compromise

vernacular: relating to a dialect or lingo

lies in the intermediary position of "a great deal, but not everything." Soapy Sam Wilberforce and the Triangle Shirtwaist fire gain their odd but sensible conjunction as illustrations of the two extremes that must be avoided—for Wilberforce denied evolution altogether and absolutely, while the major social theory that hindered industrial reform (and permitted conditions that led to such disasters as the Triangle Shirtwaist fire) followed the most overextended application of biological evolution to patterns of human history—the theory of "Social Darwinism." By understanding the **fallacies** of Wilberforce's denial and social Darwinism's uncritical and total embrace, we may find the proper balance between.

7. In Your Journal: Does the "intermediary position" Gould alludes to here seem a particularly scientific one? Why or why not?

fallacy: erroneous belief

They didn't call him Soapy Sam for nothing. The **orotund** bishop of Oxford saved his finest **invective** for Darwin's attempt to apply his **heresies** to human origins. In his review of *The Origin of Species* (published in the *Quarterly Review,* England's leading literary journal, in 1860), Wilberforce complained above all "First, then, he not obscurely declares that he applies his scheme of the action of the principle of natural selection to Man himself, as well as to the animals around him." Wilberforce then uncorked a passionate argument for a human uniqueness that could only have been divinely ordained:

orotund: pompous; exhibiting undeserved confidence or unnecessary length in speaking

invective: tirade; attack

heresy: sacrilege; blasphemy

> Man's derived supremacy over the earth; man's power of articulate speech; man's gift of reason; man's free-will and responsibility; man's fall and man's redemption; the incarnation of the Eternal Son; the indwelling of the Eternal Spirit,—all are equally and utterly irreconcilable with the degrading notion of the brute origin of him who was created in the image of God, and redeemed by the Eternal Son.

But the tide of history quickly engulfed the good bishop. When Wilberforce died in 1873, from a head injury after a fall from his horse, Huxley **acerbically** remarked that, for once, the bishop's brains had come into contact with reality—and the result had been fatal. Darwinism became the reigning intellectual novelty of the late nineteenth century. The potential domain of natural selection, Darwin's chief explanatory principle, seemed nearly endless to his devotees (though not, interestingly, to the master himself, as Darwin remained cautious about extensions beyond the realm of biological evolution). If a "struggle for existence" regulated the evolution of organisms, wouldn't a similar principle also explain the history of just about anything—from the cosmology of the universe, to the languages, economics, technologies, and cultural histories of human groups?

acerbically: sarcastically; harshly

8. In Your Journal: Respond to Huxley's joke about Wilberforce's accidental death.

Even the greatest of truths can be overextended by zealous and uncritical acolytes. Natural selection may be one of the most powerful ideas ever developed in science, but only certain kinds of systems can be regulated by such a process, and Darwin's principle cannot explain all natural sequences that develop historically. For example, we may talk about the "evolution" of a star through a predictable series of phases over many billion years from birth to explosion, but natural selection—a process driven by the differential survival and reproductive success of some individuals in a variable population—cannot be the cause of stellar development. We must look, instead, to the inherent physics and chemistry of light elements in such large masses.

Similarly, although Darwinism surely explains many universal features of human form and behavior, we cannot invoke natural selection as the controlling cause of our cultural changes since the dawn of agriculture—if only because such a limited time of some ten thousand years provides so little scope for any general biological evolution at all. Moreover, and most importantly, human cultural change operates in a manner that precludes a controlling role for natural selection. To mention the two most obvious differences: first, biological evolution proceeds by continuous division of species into independent lineages that must remain forever separated on the branching tree of life. Human cultural change works by the opposite process of borrowing and amalgamation. One good look at another culture's wheel or alphabet may alter the course of a civilization forever. If we wish to identify a biological **analog** for cultural change, I suspect that infection will work much better than evolution.

> ***9. In Your Journal:*** What is the main reason that biological evolution is an inappropriate model for measuring cultural change?

> ***10. In Your Journal:*** Why is infection a better analog for cultural development than evolution? Why might this be a less attractive model for some social theorists to embrace?

analog: comparison; synonym

Second, human cultural change runs by the powerful mechanism of **Lamarckian** inheritance of acquired characters. Anything useful (or alas, destructive) that our generation invents can be passed directly to our offspring by direct education. Change in this rapid Lamarckian mode easily overwhelms the much slower process of Darwinian natural selection, which requires a **Mendelian** form of inheritance based on small-scale and undirected variation that can then be sifted and sorted through a struggle for existence. Genetic variation is Mendelian, so Darwinism rules biological evolution. But cultural variation is largely Lamarckian, and natural selection cannot determine the recent history of our technological societies.

Nonetheless, the first blush of high Victorian enthusiasm for Darwinism inspired a rush of attempted extensions to other fields, at least by analogy. Some efforts proved fruitful, including the decision of James Murray, editor of *The Oxford English Dictionary* (first volume published in 1884, but under way for twenty years before then), to work strictly by historical principles and to treat the changing definitions of words not by current preferences in use (as in a truly normative dictionary), but by the chronology and

> ***11. In Your Journal:*** How is the *Oxford English Dictionary* a "fruitful application" of Darwinist principles?

Lamarckian: in the spirit of Jean Baptiste Pierre Antoine de Monet Chevalier de Lamarck (1744–1829); relating to the French naturalist who theorized about the modification of species by inheritance of traits acquired or modified by use or disuse of body parts

Mendelian: in the spirit of Gregor Johann Mendel (1822–1884); relating to the Austrian botanist and founder of genetics branching evolution of recorded meanings (making the text more an encyclopedia about the history of words than a true dictionary).

But other extensions proved both invalid in theory, and also (or so most of us would judge by modern moral sensibilities) harmful, if not tragic, in application. As the chief offender in this category, we must cite a highly influential theory that acquired the inappropriate name of "Social Darwinism." (As many historians have noted, this theory should really be called "social Spencerism," since **Herbert Spencer,** chief Victorian pundit of nearly everything, laid out all the basic postulates in his *Social Statics* of 1850, nearly a decade before Darwin published *The Origin of Species.* Darwinism did add the mechanism of natural selection as a harsher version of the struggle for existence, long recognized by Spencer. Moreover, Darwin himself maintained a highly ambivalent relationship to this movement that borrowed his name. He felt the pride of any creator toward useful extensions of his theory—and he did hope for an evolutionary account of human origins and historical patterns. But he also understood only too well why the mechanism of natural selection applied poorly to the causes of social change in humans.)

12. In Your Journal: Why does Darwin get credited with a theory originated by Herbert Spencer?

Social Darwinism often serves as a blanket term for any genetic or biological claim made about the inevitability (or at least the "naturalness") of social inequalities among classes and sexes, or military conquests of one group by another. But such a broad definition distorts the history of this important subject—although pseudo-Darwinian arguments have long been advanced prominently and forcefully, to cover all these sins. Classical Social Darwinism operated as a more specific theory about the nature and origin of social classes in the modern industrial world. The *Encyclopaedia Britannica* article on this subject correctly emphasizes this restriction by first citing the broadest range of potential meaning, and then properly narrowing the scope of actual usage:

> *Social Darwinism:* the theory that persons, groups, and races are subject to the same laws of natural selection as Charles Darwin had perceived in plants and animals in nature. . . . The theory was used to support **laissez-faire** capitalism and political conservatism. Class stratification was justified on the basis of "natural" inequalities among individuals, for the control of property was said to be a correlate of superior and inherent moral attributes such as industriousness, **temperance,** and frugality. Attempts to reform society through state intervention or other means would, therefore, interfere with natural processes; unrestricted competition and defense of the status quo were in accord with biological selection. The poor were the "unfit" and

laissez-faire: (French) "allow to do"; economic principle that advocates a minimum of intervention or interference

temperance: restraint; control, especially as pertains to drinking alcohol

Herbert Spencer: (1820–1903) British philosopher who espoused the belief that evolution moves from the simple to the complex should not be aided; in the struggle for existence, wealth was a sign of success.

Spencer believed that we must permit and welcome such harshness to unleash the progressive development that all "evolutionary" systems undergo if allowed to follow their natural course in an unimpeded manner. As a central principle of his system, Spencer believed that progress—defined by him as movement from a simple undifferentiated homogeneity, as in a bacterium or a "primitive" human society without social classes, to complex and structured heterogeneity, as in "advanced" organisms or industrial societies—did not arise as an inevitable property of matter in motion, but only through interaction between evolving systems and their environments. These interactions must therefore not be obstructed.

The relationship of Spencer's general vision to Darwin's particular theory has often been misconstrued or overemphasized. As stated above, Spencer had published the outline (and most of the details) of his system nearly ten years before Darwin presented his evolutionary theory. Spencer certainly did welcome the principle of natural selection as an even more ruthless and efficient mechanism for driving evolution forward. (Ironically, the word *evolution,* as a description for the genealogical history of life, entered our language through Spencer's urgings, not from Darwin. Spencer favored the term for its vernacular English meaning of "progress," in the original Latin sense of *evolutio,* or "unfolding." At first, Darwin resisted the term—he originally called his process "descent with modification"—because his theory included no mechanism or rationale for general progress in the history of life. But Spencer prevailed, largely because no society has ever been more committed to progress as a central notion or goal than **Victorian Britain** at the height of its colonial and industrial expansion.)

13. In Your Journal: Why does Darwin initially resist the term "evolution," which he is now so wholly identified with?

Spencer certainly used Darwin's mechanism of natural selection to buttress his system. Few people recognize the following historical irony: Spencer, not Darwin, coined the term "survival of the fittest," now our conventional catchphrase for Darwin's mechanism. Darwin himself paid proper tribute in a statement added to later editions of *The Origin of Species:* "I have called this principle, by which each slight variation, if useful, is preserved, by the term Natural Selection. . . . But the expression often used by Mr. Herbert Spencer of the Survival of the Fittest is more accurate, and is sometimes equally convenient."

14. In Your Journal: How does Darwin's term "Natural Selection" compare to Spencer's phrase "survival of the fittest"?

As a mechanism for driving his universal "evolution" (of stars, species, languages, economics, technologies, and nearly anything else)

Victorian Britain: Britain under the reign of Queen Victoria (1837–1901), who was highly imperialistic and immensely popular in the later years of her rule; the period was marked by the development of conservative politics and a growing middle class toward progress, Spencer preferred the direct and mechanistic "root, hog, or die" of natural selection (as William Graham Sumner, the leading American social Darwinian, epitomized the process), to the vaguer and largely Lamarckian drive toward organic self-improvement that Spencer had originally favored as a primary cause. (In this colorful image, Sumner cited a quintessential American metaphor of self-sufficiency that my dictionary of catchphrases traces to a speech by Davy Crockett in 1834.) In a post-Darwinian edition of his *Social Statics,* Spencer wrote:

15. In Your Journal: Why does Spencer prefer Darwin's specific interpretation to the Lamarckian view?

> The lapse of a third of a century since these passages were published, has brought me no reason for retreating from the position taken up in them. Contrariwise, it has brought a vast amount of evidence strengthening that position. The beneficial results of the survival of the fittest, prove to be immeasurably greater than [I formerly recognized]. The process of "natural selection," as Mr. Darwin called it . . . has shown to be a chief cause . . . of that evolution through which all living things, beginning with the lower, and diverging and re-diverging as they evolved, have reached their present degrees of organization and adaptation to their modes of life.

But putting aside the question of Darwin's particular influence, the more important, underlying point remains firm: the theory of Social Darwinism (or social Spencerism) rests upon a set of analogies between the causes of change and stability in biological and social systems—and on the supposedly direct applicability of these biological principles to the social realm. In his founding document, the *Social Statics* of 1850, Spencer rests his case upon two elaborate analogies to biological systems.

1. The struggle for existence as purification in biology and society. Darwin recognized the "struggle for existence" as metaphorical shorthand for any strategy that promotes increased reproductive success, whether by outright battle, cooperation, or just simple prowess in copulation under the old principle of "early and often." But many contemporaries, including Spencer, read "survival of the fittest" only as overt struggle to the death—what T. H. Huxley later dismissed as the "gladiatorial" school, or the incarnation of **Hobbes's** *bellum omnium contra omnes* (the war of all against all). Spencer presented this stark and limited view of nature in his *Social Statics:*

16. In Your Journal: How does Spencer misinterpret Darwin's view of the "struggle for existence"?

> Pervading all Nature we may see at work a stern discipline which is a little cruel that it may be very kind. That state of universal warfare maintained throughout the lower creation, to the

Hobbes: (Thomas) (1588–1679) English philosopher and political theorist whose most well-known work is *Leviathan* (1651), which suggests the only way to a civilized society is by forcing all citizens to submit to absolute authority of a sovereign

> great perplexity of many worthy people, is at bottom the most merciful provision which the circumstances admit of. . . . Note that carnivorous enemies, not only remove from herbivorous herds individuals past their prime, but also weed out the sickly, the malformed, and the least fleet or powerful. By the aid of which purifying process . . . all vitiation of the race through the multiplication of its inferior samples is prevented; and the maintenance of a constitution completely adapted to surrounding conditions, and therefore most productive of happiness, is ensured.

Spencer then compounds this error by applying the same argument to human social history, without ever questioning the validity of such analogical transfer. Railing against all governmental programs for social **amelioration**—Spencer opposed state-supported education, postal services, regulation of housing conditions, and even public construction of sanitary systems—he castigated such efforts as born of good intentions but doomed to dire consequences by enhancing the survival of social dregs who should be allowed to perish for the good of all. (Spencer insisted, however, that he did not oppose private charity, primarily for the salutary effect of such giving upon the moral development of donors. Does this discourse remind you of arguments now advanced as reformatory and spanking-new by our "modern" ultraconservatives? Shall we not profit from **Santayana's** famous dictum that those ignorant of history must be condemned to repeat it?) In his chapter on poor laws (which he, of course, opposed), Spencer wrote in the *Social Statics:*

amelioration: improvement

17. In Your Journal: How does Spencer justify charity but not state-supported welfare for the poor?

> We must call those **spurious** philanthropists who, to prevent present misery, would entail greater misery on future generations. That rigorous necessity which, when allowed to operate, becomes so sharp a spur to the lazy and so strong a bridle to the random, these paupers' friends would repeal, because of the wailings it here and there produces. Blind to the fact that under the natural order of things society is constantly excreting its unhealthy, imbecile, slow, vacillating, faithless members, these unthinking, though well-meaning, men advocate an interference which not only stops the purifying process, but even increases the **vitiation**—absolutely encouraging the multiplication of the reckless and incompetent by offering them an unfailing provision. . . . Thus, in their eagerness to prevent the salutary

spurious: bogus; sham

vitiation: reduction in or impairment of quality, morality, or validity

---

Santayana: (George) (1863–1952), a Spanish-American philosopher and poet

> sufferings that surround us, these sigh-wise and groan-foolish people bequeath to posterity a continually increasing curse.

2. The stable body and the stable society. In the universal and progressive "evolution" of all systems, organization becomes increasingly more complex by division of labor among the growing number of differentiating parts. All parts must "know their place" and play their appointed role, lest the entire system collapse. A primitive **hydra,** constructed of simple "all purpose" modules, can regrow any lost part, but nature gives a man only one head, and one chance. Spencer recognized the basic inconsistency in validating social stability by analogy to the integrated needs of a single organic body—for he recognized the contrary rationales of the two systems: the parts of a body serve the totality, but the social totality (the state) supposedly exists only to serve the parts (individual people). But Spencer never allowed himself to be fazed by logical or **empirical** difficulties when pursuing such a lovely generality. (Huxley was speaking about Spencer's penchant for building grandiose systems when he made his famous remark about "a beautiful theory, killed by a nasty, ugly little fact.") So Spencer barged right through the numerous absurdities of such a comparison, and even claimed that he had found a virtue in the differences. In his famous 1860 article, "The Social Organism," Spencer described the comparison between a human body and a human society: "Such, then, are the points of analogy and the points of difference. May we not say that the points of difference serve but to bring into clearer light the points of analogy."

hydra: a freshwater genus with a cylindrical body and many tentacles; in Greek mythology, a many-headed monster that would grow back two heads for each one cut off

empirical: observed; practical

18. In Your Journal: In Spencer's view, does the individual serve society or does society serve the individual?

19. In Your Journal: Comment on Huxley's tone when he cites Spencer's "beautiful theory, killed by a nasty, ugly little fact."

Spencer's article then lists the supposed points of valid comparison, including such far-fetched analogies as the historical origin of a middle class to the development, in complex animals, of the **mesoderm,** or third body layer between the original **ectoderm** and **endoderm;** the likening of the ectoderm itself to the upper classes, for sensory organs that direct an animal arise in ectoderm, while organs of production, for such activities as digesting food, emerge from the lower layer, or endoderm; the comparison of blood and money; the parallel courses of nerve and blood vessels in higher animals with the side-by-side construction of railways and telegraph wires; and finally, in a comparison that even Spencer regarded as forced, the likening of a primitive all-powerful monarchy with a simple brain, and an advanced parliamentary system with a complex brain composed of several lobes. Spencer wrote: "Strange as this assertion will be thought, our Houses of Parliament discharge in the social economy, functions that are in **sundry** respects comparable to those discharged by the cerebral masses in a vertebrate animal."

mesoderm, ectoderm, and endoderm: three primary germ layers of an animal embryo

20. In Your Journal: Why is Spencer so set on comparing society to the human body? What do his analogies reveal about his ideology?

sundry: various; assorted

Spencer surely forced his analogies, but his social intent could not have been more clear: a stable society requires that all roles be filled and well executed—and government must not interfere with a natural process of sorting out and allocation of appropriate rewards. A humble worker must toil, and may remain indigent forever, but the industrious poor, as an organ of the social body, must always be with us:

> Let the factory hands be put on short time, and immediately the colonial produce markets of London and Liverpool are depressed. The shopkeeper is busy or otherwise, according to the amount of the wheat crop. And a potato-blight may ruin dealers in consols. . . . This union of many men into one community—this increasing mutual dependence of units which were originally independent—this gradual segregation of citizens into separate bodies with reciprocally-subservient functions—this formation of a whole consisting of unlike parts—this growth of an organism, of which one portion cannot be injured without the rest feeling it—may all be generalized under the law of individuation.

Social Darwinism grew into a major movement, with political, academic, and journalistic advocates for a wide array of particular causes. But as historian Richard Hofstadter stated in the most famous book ever written on this subject—*Social Darwinism in American Thought,* first published in 1944, in press ever since, and still full of insight despite some inevitable **archaisms**—the primary impact of this doctrine lay in its buttressing of conservative political philosophies, particularly through the central (and highly effective) argument against state support of social services and governmental regulation of industry and housing:

archaism: out-of-date word, phrase, or idiom

> One might, like William Graham Sumner, take a pessimistic view of the import of Darwinism, and conclude that Darwinism could serve only to cause men to face up to the inherent hardship of the battle of life; or one might, like Herbert Spencer, promise that, whatever the immediate hardships for a large portion of mankind, evolution meant progress and thus assured that the whole process of life was tending toward some very remote but altogether glorious consummation. But in either case the conclusions to which Darwinism was at first put were conservative conclusions. They suggested that all attempts to reform social processes were efforts to remedy the irremediable, that they interfered with the wisdom of nature, that they could lead only to degeneration.

The industrial **magnates** of America's gilded age ("**robber barons,**" in a terminology favored by many people) adored and promoted this argument against regulation, evidently for self-serving reasons, and however frequently they mixed their lines about nature's cruel inevitability with

magnate: industrialist; tycoon

robber baron: American industrial or financial magnate of the late 19th century who gained wealth by unethical means standard Christian piety. **John D. Rockefeller** stated in a Sunday school address:

> **21. *In Your Journal:*** How does Rockefeller's analogy compare to Spencer's thinking?

> The growth of a large business is merely a survival of the fittest. . . . The American Beauty rose can be produced in the splendor and fragrance which bring cheer to its beholder only by sacrificing the early buds which grow up around it. This is not an evil tendency in business. It is merely the working-out of a law of nature and a law of God.

And **Andrew Carnegie,** who had been sorely distressed by the apparent failure of Christian values, found his solution in Spencer's writings, and then sought out the English philosopher for friendship and substantial favors. Carnegie wrote about his discovery of Spencer's work: "I remember that light came as in a flood and all was clear. Not only had I got rid of theology and the supernatural, but I had found the truth of evolution. 'All is well since all grows better' became my motto, and true source of comfort." Carnegie's philanthropy, primarily to libraries and universities, ranks as one of the great charitable acts of American history, but we should not forget his ruthlessness and resistance to reforms for his own workers (particularly his violent breakup of the **Homestead strike** of 1892) in building his empire of steel—a harshness that he defended with the usual Spencerian line that any state regulation must derail an inexorable natural process eventually leading to progress for all. In his most famous essay (entitled "Wealth," and published in *North American Review* for 1889), Carnegie stated:

> While the law may be sometimes hard for the individual, it is best for the race, because it insures the survival of the fittest in every department. We accept and welcome, therefore, as conditions to which we must accommodate ourselves, great inequality of environment, the concentration of wealth, business, industrial and commercial, in the hands of a few, and the law of competition between these, as being not only beneficial, but essential for the future progress of the race.

John D. Rockefeller: (1839–1937) American oil magnate who amassed great wealth with his Standard Oil Company, and spent half of his fortune on philanthropic causes

Andrew Carnegie: (1835–1919) Scottish-born American industrialist and philanthropist who amassed a fortune in the steel industry

Homestead strike: (1892) bitterly fought labor dispute between the Amalgamated Association of Iron and Steel Workers and the Carnegie Steel Company over wage cuts; violence and state intervention, as well as nonunion substitute workers, brought an end to the strike, weakening the steel workers' union for years to come

I don't want to advocate a foolishly grandiose view about the social and political influence of academic arguments—and I also wish to avoid the common fallacy of inferring a causal connection from a correlation. Of course I do not believe that the claims of Social Darwinism directly caused the ills of unrestrained industrial capitalism and the suppression of workers' rights. I know that most of these Spencerian lines functioned as mere window dressing for social forces well in place, and largely unmovable by any academic argument.

On the other hand, academic arguments should not be regarded as entirely impotent either—for why else would people in power invoke such claims so forcefully? The general thrust of social change unfolded in its own complex manner without much impact from purely intellectual rationales, but many particular issues—especially the actual rates and styles of changes that would have eventually occurred in any case—could be substantially affected by academic discourse. Millions of people suffered when a given reform experienced years of legislative delay, and then became vitiated in legal battles and compromises. The Social Darwinian argument of the superrich and the highly conservative did stem, weaken, and slow the tides of amelioration, particularly for workers' rights.

Most historians would agree that the single most effective doctrine of Social Darwinism lay in Spencer's own centerpiece—the argument against state-enforced standards for industry, education, medicine, housing, public sanitation, and so on. Few Americans, even the robber barons, would go so far, but Spencerian dogma did become a powerful bludgeon against the regulation of industry to ensure better working conditions for laborers. On this particular point—the central recommendation of Spencer's system from the beginning—we may argue for a substantial effect of academic writing upon the actual path of history.

Armed with this perspective, we may return to the Triangle Shirtwaist fire, the deaths of 146 young workers, and the palpable influence of a doctrine that applied too much of the wrong version of Darwinism to human history. The battle for increased safety of workplaces, and healthier environments for workers, had been waged with intensity for several decades. The trade union movement put substantial priority upon these issues, and management had often reacted with **intransigence,** or even violence, citing their Spencerian rationale for the perpetuation of apparent cruelty. Government regulation of industry had become a major struggle of American political life—and the cause of benevolent state oversight had advanced from the **Sherman Anti-Trust Act** of 1890 to the numerous and crusading

intransigence: stubbornness; obstinacy

Sherman Anti-Trust Act: named for John Sherman (1823–1900), Senator from Ohio; declared illegal any contract or conspiracy to limit interstate or foreign trade reforms of **Theodore Roosevelt's presidency** (1901–9). When the Triangle fire broke out in 1911, regulations for the health and safety of workers were so weak, and so unenforceable by tiny and underpaid staffs, that the company's managers—cynically and technically "up to code" in their firetrap building—could pretty much impose whatever the weak and **nascent** labor union movement couldn't prevent.

nascent: budding; emerging

If the standard legend were true—and the Triangle workers died because all the doors had been locked by cruel owners—then this heart-wrenching story might convey no moral beyond the personal guilt of management. But the loss of 146 lives occurred for much more complicated reasons, all united by the pathetic weakness of legal regulations for the health and safety of workers. And I do not doubt that the central thrust of Social Darwinism—the argument that governmental regulation can only forestall a necessary and natural process—exerted a major impact in slowing the passage of laws that almost everyone today, even our archconservatives, regard as beneficial and humane. I accept that these regulations would eventually have been instituted even if Spencer had never been born—but life or death for the Triangle workers rode upon the "detail" that forces of pure laissez-faire, buttressed by their Spencerian centerpiece, managed to delay some implementations to the 1920s rather than acceding to the just demands of unions and social reformers in 1910.

One of the two Triangle stairways almost surely had been locked on that fateful day—although lawyers for company owners won acquittal of their clients on this issue, largely by using legal **legerdemain** to confuse, intimidate, and draw inconsistencies from young witnesses with poor command of English. Two years earlier, an important strike had begun at the Triangle company, and had spread to shirtwaist manufacturers throughout the city. The union won in most factories but not, ironically, at Triangle—where management held out, and compelled the return of workers without anything gained. Tensions remained high at Triangle in 1911, and management had become particularly suspicious, even paranoid, about thefts. Therefore, at quitting time (when the fire erupted, and against weakly enforced laws for maintaining multiple active exits), managers had locked one of the doors to force all the women to exit by the Greene Street stairwell, where a supervisor could inspect every handbag to guard against thefts of shirtwaists.

legerdemain: agility; tricks

But if the bosses broke a weak and unenforceable law in this instance, all other causes of death can be traced to managerial compliance with absurdly inadequate standards, largely kept so weak by active political

---

Theodore Roosevelt's presidency: Roosevelt (1858–1919) was the 26th president, after McKinley's assassination; the presidency was known primarily for trust regulation and the establishment of the Panama Canal; Roosevelt was a hero of the Spanish-American War and originated the motto, "speak softly and carry a big stick" resistance to legal regulation of work sites, buttressed by the argument of Social Darwinism. Fire hoses could not pump above the sixth floor, but no law prevented the massing of workers into crowded floors above. No statute required fire drills or other forms of training for safety. In other cases, weak regulations were risibly inadequate, easy to flaunt, and basically unenforced in any case. For example, by law, each worker required 250 cubic feet of air space—a good rule to prevent crowding. But companies had managed to circumvent the intent of this law, and maintain their traditional (and dangerous) density of workers, by moving into large loft buildings with high ceilings and substantial irrelevant space that could be included in calculating the 250-cubic-foot minimum.

22. In Your Journal: What inadequacy seems apparent in the air space regulation law?

When the Asch Building opened in 1900, an inspector for the Buildings Department informed the architect that a third staircase should be provided. But the architect sought and received a **variance,** arguing that the single fire escape could count as the missing staircase required by law for structures with more than ten thousand square feet per floor. Moreover, the single fire escape—which buckled and fell during the fire, as a result of poor maintenance and the weight of too many workers trying to escape—led only to a glass skylight in a closed courtyard. The building inspector had also complained about this arrangement, and the architect had promised to make the necessary alterations. But no changes had been made, and the falling fire escape plunged right through the skylight, greatly increasing the death toll.

variance: in law, the license to act contrary to usual rule

Two final quotations highlight the case for inadequate legal protection as a primary cause for the unconscionable death toll in the Triangle Shirtwaist fire (Leon Stein's excellent book, *The Triangle Fire,* J. B. Lippincott Company, 1962, served as my chief source for information about this event). Rose Safran, a survivor of the fire and supporter of the 1909 strike, said. "If the union had won we would have been safe. Two of our demands were for adequate fire escapes and for open doors from the factories to the street. But the bosses defeated us and we didn't get the open doors or the better fire escapes. So our friends are dead." A building inspector who had actually written to the Triangle management just a few months before, asking for an appointment to discuss the initiation of fire drills, commented after the blaze: "There are only two or three factories in the city where fire drills are in use. In some of them where I have installed the system myself, the owners have discontinued it. The neglect of factory owners in the matter of safety of their employees is absolutely criminal. One man whom I advised to install a fire drill replied to me: 'Let 'em burn. They're a lot of cattle, anyway.' "

The Triangle tire galvanized the workers' reform movement as never before. An empowered force, now irresistible, of labor organizers, social reformers, and liberal legislators pressed for stronger regulation under the theme of "never again." Hundreds of laws passed as a direct result of this belated agitation. But nothing could wash the blood of 146 workers from the sidewalks of New York.

This tale of two work sites—of a desk situated where Huxley debated Wilberforce, and an office built on a floor that burned during the Triangle Shirtwaist fire—has no end, for the story illustrates a theme of human intellectual life that must always be with us, however imbued with an obvious and uncontroversial solution. Extremes must usually be regarded as **untenable,** even dangerous places on complex and subtle continua. For the application of Darwinian theory to human history, Wilberforce's "none" marks an error of equal magnitude with the "all" of an extreme Social Darwinism. In a larger sense, the evolution of a species like *Homo sapiens* should fill us with notions of glory for our odd mental uniqueness, and of deep humility for our status as a tiny and accidental twig on such a sturdy and luxuriantly branching tree of life. Glory *and* humility! Since we can't abandon either feeling for a unitary stance in the middle, we had best make sure that both attitudes *always* walk together, hand in hand, and secure in the wisdom of **Ruth's promise to Naomi:** "Whither thou goest, I will go; and where thou lodgest, I will lodge."

untenable: invalid

Ruth's promise to Naomi: from the book of Ruth; after Naomi loses her husband and two sons (one of whom was Ruth's husband), Ruth promises to stay with Naomi forever rather than returning to her own family

FOR USE IN DISCUSSION

Questions about Substance

1. Evaluate the use of religious terminology in the description of scientific endeavor, for example: "righteousness" (348), "dogma" (348), "angels" (349) and "acolytes" (350).
2. How did the "most overextended application of biological evolution to patterns of human history" lead to disasters like the Triangle Shirtwaist fire? Why is this combination of theory and outcome so ironic (350)?
3. Why does it seem so easy to apply evolutionary theory to everything (350)? Why was Darwin, himself the father of evolutionary theory, so uncomfortable with the extensions of it?
4. Spencer encouraged the use of the word "evolution" and the phrase "survival of the fittest" (353), though these are generally attributed to Darwin. Why do you think this misattribution persists?
5. How are Spencer's theories different from Darwin's? Summarize the two "analogies to biological systems" (354) that Spencer employs in his analysis.

6. Explain what Spencer's means by the following statement: "Such, then, are the points of analogy and the points of difference. May we not say that the points of difference serve but to bring into clearer light the points of analogy" (356)?
7. Gould wishes to avoid the "common fallacy of inferring a causal connection from a correlation" (359). What does he mean by this?
8. Compare Gould's literal use of the term "holocaust" (347) with his allusion to the "never again" slogan (361) of the post-Holocaust world. How much of a distinction does Gould make between a generic holocaust and the specific Holocaust of the 20th century?

Questions about Structure and Style

1. What is the reality that Gould announces will embody a "deeper and more important lesson" (349)? Why does Gould emphasize the ways that the "true angels of light and justice" overexaggerate?
2. Why does Gould claim "nothing beyond personal meaning" (349)? And why does he do so only to articulate its "general theme well worth sharing" (349)?
3. Why does Gould quote Darwin on "the origin of man" twice on page (349)?

Multimedia Review

1. A number of movies reveal society's anxiety about social evolution and species survival. View one or two of the following films and see if you can locate the allusions to or misuses of Darwinism (e.g., social Darwinism) or applications of "the survival of the fittest" theme: *The Birth of a Nation* (1915), *Greed* (1924), *Inherit the Wind* (1960), *Planet of the Apes* (1968), *Trading Places* (1983), *Gattaca* (1997), and *AI* (2001). Be sure to mention others you know of during class discussion.
2. Go to *http://www.ilr.cornell.edu/trianglefire/*, a resource developed by Cornell University, to read more about the Triangle Shirtwaist factory fire. The site includes original newspaper articles, photos, and testimonials, among other resources.

SUGGESTIONS FOR WRITING AND RESEARCH

1. As Gould emphasizes, evolutionary theory is a very specific scientific concept. However, related concepts such as "survival of the fittest" and "natural selection" are often used metaphorically. Write an essay about why you think evolutionary theory is so easy to make metaphoric use of, referring to Gould's examples in the text, as well as any additional examples of evolutionary metaphors you have heard used.
2. Today's creationists call themselves believers in "Intelligent Design," and they, too, have problems with evolutionary theory. Go to the library to research this new area of study, looking for journal and magazine articles that outline the major beliefs. How would Gould perceive these efforts to take a more "scien-

tific" approach to the goals of creationism? While in the library, you might also look for materials related to social Darwinism or creationism. How do the various schools of thought compare?

3. Gould's title is a reference to Charles Dickens's novel *A Tale of Two Cities*, which is a story set during the French Revolution involving themes of fate, violence, honor, and redemption. Read Dickens's novel, and compare its themes to those of Gould's essay here. How does Gould's argument play off of the themes of the novel?

WORKING WITH CLUSTERS

Cluster 10: Interpretation and/as Ideology

Cluster 15: Spatial Realities

Discipline: The Natural Sciences

Rhetorical Mode: Cause and Effect

We Wish To Inform You That Tomorrow We Will Be Killed with Our Families

by Philip Gourevitch

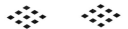

Philip Gourevitch earned a B.A. from Cornell and an M.F.A. from Columbia, and has written two books: We Wish To Inform You That Tomorrow We Will Be Killed with Our Families: Stories from Rwanda *and the novel* A Cold Case. *He is a contributing editor at* The Forward *and a staff writer at the* New Yorker, *and he has also written for* Harper's, Granta, *and the* New York Review of Books. We Wish To Inform You, *from which this excerpt is drawn, won a National Book Critics Circle Award for non-fiction.*

Leontius, the son of Aglaion, was coming up from the Peiraeus, close to the outer side of the north wall, when he saw some dead bodies lying near the executioner, and he felt a desire to look at them, and at the same time felt disgust at the thought, and tried to turn aside. For some time he fought with himself and put his hand over his eyes, but in the end the desire got the better of him, and opening his eyes wide with his fingers he ran forward to the bodies, saying, "There you are, curse you, have your fill of the lovely spectacle."

—Plato, ***The Republic***

1

In the province of Kibungo, in eastern Rwanda, in the swamp- and pastureland near the Tanzanian border, there's a rocky hill called Nyarubuye with a church where many Tutsis were slaughtered in mid-April of 1994. A year after the killing I went to Nyarubuye with two Canadian military officers. We flew in a United Nations helicopter, traveling low over the hills in the morning mists, with the banana trees like green starbursts dense over the slopes. The uncut grass blew back as we dropped into the center of the parish schoolyard. A lone soldier materialized with his **Kalashnikov,** and shook our hands with stiff, shy formality. The Canadians presented the paperwork for our visit, and I stepped up into the open doorway of a classroom.

1. In Your Journal: How does the author's tone contribute to his initial description of the dead bodies?

At least fifty mostly decomposed cadavers covered the floor, wadded in clothing, their belongings strewn about and smashed. Macheted skulls had rolled here and there.

The dead looked like pictures of the dead. They did not smell. They did not buzz with flies. They had been killed thirteen months earlier, and they hadn't been moved. Skin stuck here and there over the bones, many of which lay scattered away from the bodies, dismembered by the killers, or by scavengers—birds, dogs, bugs. The more complete figures looked a lot like people, which they were once. A woman in a cloth wrap printed with flowers lay near the door. Her fleshless hip bones were high and her legs slightly spread, and a child's skeleton extended between them. Her

2. In Your Journal: What does the author mean by the sentence: "The dead looked like pictures of the dead"?

The Republic: one of Plato's works on the relationship between the soul and the state and the cosmos

Kalashnikov: Soviet-made assault rifle

torso was hollowed out. Her ribs and spinal column poked through the rotting cloth. Her head was tipped back and her mouth was open: a strange image—half agony, half repose.

I had never been among the dead before. What to do? Look? Yes. I wanted to see them, I suppose; I had come to see them—the dead had been left unburied at Nyarubuye for memorial purposes—and there they were, so intimately exposed. I didn't need to see them. I already knew, and believed, what had happened in Rwanda. Yet, looking at the buildings and the bodies, and hearing the silence of the place, with the grand Italianate **basilica** standing there deserted, and beds of exquisite, decadent, death-fertilized flowers blooming over the corpses, it was still strangely unimaginable. I mean one still had to imagine it.

basilica: ancient Roman-style cathedral

Those dead Rwandans will be with me forever, I expect. That was why I had felt compelled to come to Nyarubuye: to be stuck with them—not with their experience, but with the experience of looking at them. They had been killed there, and they were dead there. What else could you really see at first? The Bible bloated with rain lying on top of one corpse or, littered about, the little woven wreaths of thatch which Rwandan women wear as crowns to balance the enormous loads they carry on their heads, and the water gourds, and the Converse tennis sneaker stuck somehow in a pelvis.

3. In Your Journal: Why does Gourevitch find the massacre at Nyarubuye, which he already knows about and believes, "strangely unimaginable" when he is confronted with the actual sight of it? Shouldn't the sight of it confirm his belief?

The soldier with the Kalashnikov—Sergeant Francis of the Rwandese Patriotic Army, a Tutsi whose parents had fled to Uganda with him when he was a boy, after similar but less extensive massacres in the early 1960s, and who had fought his way home in 1994 and found it like this—said that the dead in this room were mostly women who had been raped before being murdered. Sergeant Francis had high, rolling girlish hips, and he walked and stood with his butt stuck out behind him, an oddly purposeful posture, tipped forward, driven. He was, at once, candid and briskly official. His English had the punctilious clip of military drill, and after he told me what I was looking at I looked instead at my feet. The rusty head of a hatchet lay beside them in the dirt.

4. In Your Journal: What do the diverse details of Gourevitch's description (i.e., the bloated Bible, the thatch wreaths, the Converse sneaker) convey about the scene and his reaction to it?

A few weeks earlier, in Bukavu, Zaire, in the giant market of a refugee camp that was home to many Rwandan Hutu militiamen, I had watched a man butchering a cow with a machete. He was quite expert at his work, taking big precise strokes that made a sharp hacking noise. The rallying cry to the killers during the genocide was "Do your work!" And I saw that it *was* work, this butchery; hard work. It took many hacks—two, three, four, five hard hacks—to chop through the cow's leg. How many hacks to dismember a person?

5. In Your Journal: Why does Gourevitch emphasize the physical work it took for the Hutus to kill so many Tutsis during this massacre?

Considering the enormity of the task, it is tempting to play with theories of collective madness, mob mania, a fever of hatred erupted into a mass crime of passion, and to imagine the blind orgy of the mob, with each member killing one or two people. But at Nyarubuye, and at thousands of other sites in this tiny country, on the same days of a few months in 1994, hundreds of thousands of Hutus had worked as killers in regular shifts. There was always the next victim, and the next. What sustained them, beyond the frenzy of the first attack, through the plain physical exhaustion and mess of it?

A pygmy I met in Gikongoro said that humanity is part of nature and that we must go against nature to get along and have peace. But mass violence, too, must be organized; it does not occur aimlessly. Even mobs and riots have a design, and great and sustained destruction requires great ambition. It must be conceived as the means toward achieving a new order, and although the idea behind that new order may be criminal and objectively very stupid, it must also be compellingly simple and at the same time absolute. The **ideology** of genocide is all of those things, and in Rwanda it went by the bald name of Hutu Power. For those who set about systematically exterminating an entire people—even a fairly small and unresisting subpopulation of perhaps a million and a quarter men, women, and children, like the Tutsis in Rwanda—blood lust surely helps. But the engineers and perpetrators of a slaughter like the one just inside the door where I stood need not enjoy killing, and they may even find it unpleasant. What is required above all is that they want their victims dead. They have to want it so badly that they consider it a necessity.

ideology: philosophy that reflects self-interest

6. In Your Journal: Why does the author distinguish between enjoyment and desire when discussing the motivation for the Rwandan genocide? Why does it matter whether the Hutus enjoyed killing the Tutsis or not?

So I still had much to imagine as I entered the classroom and stepped carefully between the remains. These dead and their killers had been neighbors, schoolmates, colleagues, sometimes friends, even in-laws. The dead had seen their killers training as militias in the weeks before the end, and it was well known that they were training to kill Tutsis; it was announced on the radio, it was in the newspapers, people spoke of it openly. The week before the massacre at Nyarubuye, the killing began in Rwanda's capital, Kigali. Hutus who opposed the Hutu Power ideology were publicly denounced as "accomplices" of the Tutsis and were among the first to be killed as the extermination got under way. In Nyarubuye, when Tutsis asked the Hutu Power mayor how they might be spared, he suggested that they seek sanctuary at the church. They did, and a few days later the mayor came to kill them. He came at the head of a pack of soldiers, policemen, militiamen, and villagers; he gave out arms and orders to complete the job well. No more was required of the mayor, but he also was said to have killed a few Tutsis himself.

The killers killed all day at Nyarubuye. At night they cut the Achilles tendons of survivors and went off to feast behind the church, roasting cattle looted from their victims in big fires, and drinking beer. (Bottled beer, banana beer—Rwandans may not drink more beer than other Africans, but they drink **prodigious** quantities of it around the clock.) And, in the morning, still drunk after whatever sleep they could find beneath the cries of their prey, the killers at Nyarubuye went back and killed again. Day after

prodigious: impressively huge

day, minute to minute, Tutsi by Tutsi: all across Rwanda, they worked like that. "It was a process," Sergeant Francis said. I can see that it happened, I can be told how, and after nearly three years of looking around Rwanda and listening to Rwandans, I can tell you how, and I will. But the horror of it—the idiocy, the waste, the sheer wrongness—remains uncircumscribable.

7. In Your Journal: Gourevitch uses a lot of repetition in his description of the killing. What effect do you think this repetition is meant to have?

Like Leontius, the young Athenian in Plato, I presume that you are reading this because you desire a closer look, and that you, too, are properly disturbed by your curiosity. Perhaps, in examining this extremity with me, you hope for some understanding, some insight, some flicker of self-knowledge—a moral, or a lesson, or a clue about how to behave in this world: some such information. I don't discount the possibility, but when it comes to genocide, you already know right from wrong. The best reason I have come up with for looking closely into Rwanda's stories is that ignoring them makes me even more uncomfortable about existence and my place in it. The horror, as horror, interests me only insofar as a precise memory of the offense is necessary to understand its legacy.

8. In Your Journal: The reader is addressed personally in this section. Why do you think Gourevitch turns to the reader this way in between his initial description and his lengthy elaboration on what he saw in Rwanda?

The dead at Nyarubuye were, I'm afraid, beautiful. There was no getting around it. The skeleton is a beautiful thing. The randomness of the fallen forms, the strange tranquillity of their rude exposure, the skull here, the arm bent in some uninterpretable gesture there—these things were beautiful, and their beauty only added to the affront of the place. I couldn't settle on any meaningful response: revulsion, alarm, sorrow, grief, shame, incomprehension, sure, but nothing truly meaningful. I just looked, and I took photographs, because I wondered whether I could really see what I was seeing while I saw it, and I wanted also an excuse to look a bit more closely.

We went on through the first room and out the far side. There was another room and another and another and another. They were all full of bodies, and more bodies were scattered in the grass, and there were stray skulls in the grass, which was thick and wonderfully green. Standing outside, I heard a crunch. The old Canadian colonel stumbled in front of me, and I saw, though he did not notice, that his foot had rolled on a skull and broken it. For the first time at Nyarubuye my feelings focused, and what I felt was a small but keen anger at this man. Then I heard another crunch, and felt a vibration underfoot. I had stepped on one, too.

Rwanda is spectacular to behold. Throughout its center, a winding succession of steep, tightly terraced slopes radiates out from small roadside settlements and solitary compounds. Gashes of red clay and black **loam** mark fresh hoe work; eucalyptus trees flash silver against brilliant green tea plantations; banana trees are everywhere. On the theme of hills, Rwanda produces countless variations: jagged rain forests, round-shouldered **buttes,** undulating **moors,** broad swells of **savanna,** volcanic peaks sharp as filed teeth. During the rainy season, the clouds are huge and low and fast, mists cling in highland hollows, lightning flickers through the nights, and by day

loam: organic sand and clay mixture

butte: abrupt hill with sloping sides and flat top

moor: poorly drained, broad tract of open land

savanna: flat treeless grassland

9. In Your Journal: Describe your response to Gourevitch's juxtaposition of the beautiful Rwandan countryside and the endless scattering of the dead bodies.

10. In Your Journal: Joseph rejects Gourevitch's appreciation of Rwanda's beauty. How is "empty" the opposite of "beauty" in Joseph's logic?

the land is lustrous. After the rains, the skies lift, the terrain takes on a ragged look beneath the flat unvarying haze of the dry season, and in the savannas of the Akagera Park wildfire blackens the hills.

One day, when I was returning to Kigali from the south, the car mounted a rise between two winding valleys, the windshield filled with purple-bellied clouds, and I asked Joseph, the man who was giving me a ride, whether Rwandans realize what a beautiful country they have. "Beautiful?" he said. "You think so? After the things that happened here? The people aren't good. If the people were good, the country might be OK." Joseph told me that his brother and sister had been killed, and he made a soft hissing click with his tongue against his teeth. "The country is empty," he said. "Empty!"

It was not just the dead who were missing. The genocide had been brought to a halt by the Rwandese Patriotic Front, a rebel army led by Tutsi refugees from past persecutions, and as the RPF advanced through the country in the summer of 1994, some two million Hutus had fled into exile at the behest of the same leaders who had urged them to kill. Yet except in some rural areas in the south, where the desertion of Hutus had left nothing but bush to reclaim the fields around crumbling adobe houses, I, as a newcomer, could not see the emptiness that blinded Joseph to Rwanda's beauty. Yes, there were grenade-flattened buildings, burnt homesteads, shot-up facades, and mortar-pitted roads. But these were the ravages of war, not of genocide, and by the summer of 1995, most of the dead had been buried. Fifteen months earlier, Rwanda had been the most densely populated country in Africa. Now the work of the killers looked just as they had intended: invisible.

From time to time, mass graves were discovered and excavated, and the remains would be transferred to new, properly consecrated mass graves. Yet even the occasionally exposed bones, the conspicuous number of amputees and people with deforming scars, and the superabundance of packed orphanages could not be taken as evidence that what had happened to Rwanda was an attempt to eliminate a people. There were only people's stories.

"Every survivor wonders why he is alive," Abbé Modeste, a priest at the cathedral in Butare, Rwanda's second-largest city, told me. Abbé Modeste had hidden for weeks in his **sacristy,** eating communion wafers, before moving under the desk in his study, and finally into the rafters at the home of some neighboring nuns. The obvious explanation of his survival was that the RPF had come to the rescue. But the RPF didn't reach Butare till early July, and roughly seventy-five percent of the Tutsis in Rwanda had been killed by early May. In this regard, at least, the genocide had been entirely successful: to those who were targeted, it was not death but life that seemed an accident of fate.

sacristy: place in a church where sacred objects are stored

"I had eighteen people killed at my house," said Etienne Niyonzima, a former businessman who had become a deputy in the National Assembly. "Everything was totally destroyed—a place of fifty-five meters by fifty meters. In my neighborhood they killed six hundred and forty-seven people. They tortured them, too. You had to see how they killed them. They had the number of everyone's house, and they went through with red paint and marked the homes of all the Tutsis and of the Hutu moderates. My wife was at a friend's, shot with two bullets. She is still alive, only"—he fell quiet for a moment—"she has no arms. The others with her were killed. The militia left her for dead. Her whole family of sixty-five in Gitarama were killed." Niyonzima was in hiding at the time. Only after he had been separated from his wife for three months did he learn that she and four of their children had survived. "Well," he said, "one son was cut in the head with a machete. I don't know where he went." His voice weakened, and caught. "He disappeared." Niyonzima clicked his tongue, and said, "But the others are still alive. Quite honestly, I don't understand at all how I was saved."

Laurent Nkongoli attributed his survival to "**Providence,** and also good neighbors, an old woman who said, 'Run away, we don't want to see your corpse.' " Nkongoli, a lawyer, who had become the vice president of the National Assembly after the genocide, was a robust man, with a taste for double-breasted suit jackets and lively ties, and he moved, as he spoke, with a brisk determination. But before taking his neighbor's advice, and fleeing Kigali in late April of 1994, he said, "I had accepted death. At a certain moment this happens. One hopes not to die cruelly, but one expects to die anyway. Not death by machete, one hopes, but with a bullet. If you were willing to pay for it, you could often ask for a bullet. Death was more or less normal, a resignation. You lose the will to fight. There were four thousand Tutsis killed here at Kacyiru"—a neighborhood of Kigali. "The soldiers brought them here, and told them to sit down because they were going to throw grenades. And they sat.

Providence: control exercised by a supreme deity

"Rwandan culture is a culture of fear," Nkongoli went on. "I remember what people said." He adopted a pipey voice, and his face took on a look of disgust: " 'Just let us pray, then kill us,' or 'I don't want to die in the street, I want to die at home.' " He resumed his normal voice. "When you're that resigned and oppressed you're already dead. It shows the genocide was prepared for too long. I detest this fear. These victims of genocide had been psychologically prepared to expect death just for being Tutsi. They were being killed for so long that they were already dead."

11. In Your Journal: How is the theme of resignation among the Tutsis conveyed by Laurent Nkongoli's description? Are you surprised by the way the victims responded to their immanent deaths?

I reminded Nkongoli that, for all his hatred of fear, he had himself accepted death before his neighbor urged him to run away. "Yes," he said. "I got tired in the genocide. You struggle so long, then you get tired."

12. In Your Journal: Nkongoli tries to explain the connections between fear, resignation, and fatigue in his discussion about the genocide. Can you paraphrase what he means here?

Every Rwandan I spoke with seemed to have a favorite, unanswerable question. For Nkongoli, it was how so many Tutsis had allowed themselves to be killed. For François Xavier Nkurunziza, a Kigali lawyer, whose father was Hutu and whose mother and wife were Tutsi, the question was how so many Hutus had allowed themselves to kill. Nkurunziza had escaped death only by chance as he moved around the country from one hiding place to another, and he had lost many family members. "Conformity is very deep, very developed here," he told me. "In Rwandan history, everyone obeys authority. People revere power, and there isn't enough education. You take a poor, ignorant population, and give them arms, and say, 'It's yours. Kill.' They'll obey. The peasants, who were paid or forced to kill, were looking up to people of higher socio-economic standing to see how to behave. So the people of influence, or the big financiers, are often the big men in the genocide. They may think that they didn't kill because they didn't take life with their own hands, but the people were looking to them for their orders. And, in Rwanda, an order can be given very quietly."

As I traveled around the country, collecting accounts of the killing, it almost seemed as if, with the machete, the *masu*—a club studded with nails—a few well-placed grenades, and a few bursts of automatic-rifle fire, the quiet orders of Hutu Power had made the neutron bomb obsolete.

13. In Your Journal: What does Gourevitch mean when he says that "the quiet orders of Hutu Power had made the neutron bomb obsolete"?

"Everyone was called to hunt the enemy," said Theodore Nyilinkwaya, a survivor of the massacres in his home village of Kimbogo, in the southwestern province of Cyangugu. "But let's say someone is reluctant. Say that guy comes with a stick. They tell him, 'No, get a *masu*.' So, OK, he does, and he runs along with the rest, but he doesn't kill. They say, 'Hey, he might denounce us later. He must kill. Everyone must help to kill at least one person.' So this person who is not a killer is made to do it. And the next day it's become a game for him. You don't need to keep pushing him."

votive: dedicated to or expressing a vow or prayer

At Nyarubuye, even the little terracotta **votive** statues in the sacristy had been methodically decapitated. "They were associated with Tutsis," Sergeant Francis explained.

2

If you could walk due west from the massacre memorial at Nyarubuye, straight across Rwanda from one end to the other, over the hills and through the marshes, lakes, and rivers to the province of Kibuye, then, just before you fell into the great inland sea of Lake Kivu, you would come to another hilltop village. This hill is called Mugonero, and it, too, is crowned by a big church. While Rwanda is overwhelmingly Catholic, Protestants **evangelized** much of Kibuye, and Mugonero is the headquarters of the Seventh-Day Adventist mission. The place resembles the brick campus of an American community college more than an African village; tidy tree-lined footpaths connect the big church with a smaller chapel, a nursing school, an infirmary, and a hospital complex that enjoyed a reputation for giving excellent medical care. It was in the hospital that Samuel Ndagijimana sought refuge during the killings, and although one of the first things

evangelize: convert to Christianity

he said to me was "I forget bit by bit," it quickly became clear that he hadn't forgotten as much as he might have liked.

Samuel worked as a medical orderly in the hospital. He had landed the job in 1991, when he was twenty-five. I asked him about his life in that time that Rwandans call "Before." He said, "We were simple Christians." That was all. I might have been asking about someone else, whom he had met only in passing, and who didn't interest him. It was as if his first real memory was of the early days in April of 1994 when he saw Hutu militiamen conducting public exercises outside the government offices in Mugonero. "We watched young people going out every night, and people spoke of it on the radio," Samuel said. "It was only members of Hutu Power parties who went out, and those who weren't participants were called 'enemies.' "

14. *In Your Journal:* "I forget bit by bit," Samuel says. Does Gourevitch believe him? Why or why not?

15. *In Your Journal:* Why is Gourevitch surprised by Samuel's statement, "We were simple Christians"?

On April 6, a few nights after this activity began, Rwanda's longstanding Hutu dictator, President Juvénal Habyarimana, was assassinated in Kigali, and a clique of Hutu Power leaders from the military high command seized power. "The radio announced that people shouldn't move," Samuel said. "We began to see groups of people gathering that same night, and when we went to work in the morning, we saw these groups with the local leaders of Hutu Power organizing the population. You didn't know exactly what was happening, just that there was something coming."

At work, Samuel observed "a change of climate." He said that "one didn't talk to anyone anymore," and many of his co-workers spent all their time in meetings with a certain Dr. Gerard, who made no secret of his support for Hutu Power. Samuel found this shocking, because Dr. Gerard had been trained in the United States, and he was the son of the president of the Adventist church in Kibuye, so he was seen as a figure of great authority, a community leader—one who sets the example.

After a few days, when Samuel looked south across the valley from Mugonero, he saw houses burning in villages along the lake-front. He decided to stay in the church hospital until the troubles were over, and Tutsi families from Mugonero and surrounding areas soon began arriving with the same idea. This was a tradition in Rwanda. "When there were problems, people always went to the church," Samuel said. "The pastors were Christians. One trusted that nothing would happen at their place." In fact, many people at Mugonero told me that Dr. Gerard's father, the church president, Pastor Elizaphan Ntakirutimana, was personally instructing Tutsis to gather at the Adventist complex.

Wounded Tutsis converged on Mugonero from up and down the lake. They came through the bush, trying to avoid the countless militia checkpoints along the road, and they brought stories. Some told how a few miles to the north, in Gishyita, the mayor had been so frantic in his impatience to kill Tutsis that thousands had been slaughtered even as he herded them to the church, where the remainder were massacred. Others told how a few miles to the south, in Rwamatamu, more than ten thousand Tutsis had taken refuge in the town hall, and the mayor had brought in truckloads of policemen and soldiers and militia with guns and grenades to surround the place; behind them he had arranged villagers with machetes in case anyone escaped when the shooting began—and, in fact, there had been very few escapees from Rwamatamu. An Adventist pastor and his son were said to have worked closely with the mayor in organizing the slaughter at Rwamatamu. But perhaps Samuel did not hear about that from the wounded he met, who came "having been shot at, and had grenades thrown, missing an arm, or a leg." He still imagined that Mugonero could be spared.

By April 12, the hospital was packed with as many as two thousand refugees, and the water lines were cut. Nobody could leave; militiamen and members of the Presidential Guard had cordoned off the complex. But when Dr. Gerard learned that several dozen Hutus were among the refugees, he arranged for them to be evacuated. He also locked up the pharmacy, refusing treatment to the wounded and sick—"because they were Tutsi," Samuel said. Peering out from their confines, the refugees at the hospital watched Dr. Gerard and his father, Pastor Ntakirutimana, driving around with militiamen and members of the Presidential Guard. The refugees wondered whether these men had forgotten their God.

> ***16. In Your Journal:*** How do Dr. Gerard and Pastor Ntakirutimana's professions make their actions ironic?

Among the Tutsis at the Mugonero church and hospital complex were seven Adventist pastors who quickly assumed their accustomed role as leaders of the flock. When two policemen turned up at the hospital, and announced that their job was to protect the refugees, the Tutsi pastors took up a collection, and raised almost four hundred dollars for the policemen. For several days, all was calm. Then, toward evening on April 15, the policemen said they had to leave because the hospital was to be attacked the next morning. They drove away in a car with Dr. Gerard, and the seven pastors in the hospital advised their fellow refugees to expect the end. Then the pastors sat down together and wrote letters to the mayor and to their boss, Pastor Elizaphan Ntakirutimana, Dr. Gerard's father, asking them in the name of the Lord to intercede on their behalf.

"And the response came," Samuel said. "It was Dr. Gerard who announced it: 'Saturday, the sixteenth, at exactly nine o'clock in the morning, you will be attacked.'" But it was Pastor Ntakirutimana's response that crushed Samuel's spirit, and he repeated the church president's words twice over, slowly: "Your problem has already found a solution. You must die." One of Samuel's colleagues, Manase Bimenyimana, remembered Ntakirutimana's response slightly differently. He told me that the pastor's words were "You must be eliminated. God no longer wants you."

> ***17. In Your Journal:*** Examine the grammar of Ntakirutimana's statement that, "Your problem has already found a solution." Why is "problem" an active subject here, doing all of the work ("being found") in this sentence?

In his capacity as a hospital orderly, Manase served as the household domestic for one of the doctors, and he had remained at the doctor's house after installing his wife and children—for safety—among the refugees at the hospital. Around nine o'clock on the morning of Saturday, April 16, he was feeding the doctor's dogs. He saw Dr. Gerard drive toward the hospital with a carload of armed men. Then he heard shooting and grenades exploding. "When the dogs heard the cries of the people," he told me, "they too began to howl."

Manase managed to make his way to the hospital—foolishly, perhaps, but he felt exposed and wanted to be with his family. He found the Tutsi pastors instructing the refugees to prepare for death. "I was very disappointed," Manase said. "I expected to die, and we started looking for anything to defend ourselves with—stones, broken bricks, sticks. But they were useless. The people were weak. They had nothing to eat. The shooting started, and people were falling down and dying."

There were many attackers, Samuel recalled, and they came from all sides—"from the church, from behind, from the north and south. We heard shots and cries and they chanted the slogan 'Eliminate the Tutsis.' They began shooting at us, and we threw stones at them because we had nothing else, not even a machete. We were hungry, tired, we hadn't had water for more than a day. There were people who had their arms cut off. There were dead. They killed the people at the chapel and the school and then the hospital. I saw Dr. Gerard, and I saw his father's car pass the hospital and stop near his office. Around noon, we went into a basement. I was with some family members. Others had been killed already. The attackers began to break down the doors and to kill, shooting and throwing grenades. The two policemen who had been our protectors were now attackers. The local citizenry also helped. Those who had no guns had machetes or *masus*. In the evening, around eight or nine o'clock, they began firing tear gas. People who were still alive cried. That way the attackers knew where people were, and they could kill them directly."

On the national average, Tutsis made up a bit less than fifteen percent of Rwanda's population, but in the province of Kibuye, Tutsis counted for a much higher proportion of the citizenry. It is estimated that on April 6, 1994, at least one out of three people in Kibuye was Tutsi. A month later most of them had been killed. In many of Kibuye's villages, no Tutsis survived.

Manase told me that he was surprised when he heard that "only a million people" were killed in Rwanda. "Look at how many died just here, and how many were eaten by birds," he said. It was true that the dead of the genocide had been a great boon to Rwanda's birds, but the birds had also been helpful to the living. Just as birds of prey and carrion will form a front in the air before the advancing wall of a forest fire to feast on the parade of animals fleeing the inferno, so in Rwanda during the months of extermination the kettles of buzzards, kites, and crows that boiled over massacre sites marked a national map against the sky, flagging the "no-go" zones for people like Samuel and Manase, who took to the bush to survive.

> ***18. In Your Journal:*** What role did Rwanda's birds play during the period of the genocide?

Sometime before midnight on April 16, the killers at the Mugonero Adventist complex, unable to discover anybody left there to kill, went off to loot the homes of the dead, and Samuel in his basement, and Manase hiding with his murdered wife and children, found themselves unaccountably alive. Manase left immediately. He made his way to the nearby village of Murambi, where he joined up with a small band of survivors from other massacres who had once more taken shelter in an Adventist church. For nearly twenty-four hours, he said, they had peace. Then Dr. Gerard came with a convoy of militia. Again there was shooting, and Manase escaped. This time, he fled high up into the mountains, to a place called Bisesero, where the rock is steep and craggy, full of caves and often swaddled in cloud. Bisesero was the only place in Rwanda where thousands of Tutsi civilians mounted a defense against the Hutus who were trying to kill them. "Looking at how many people there were in Bisesero, we were convinced we could not die," Manase told me. And at first, he said, "only women and children were killed, because the men were fighting." But in time tens of thousands of men fell there, too.

Down in the corpse-crowded villages of Kibuye, live Tutsis had become extremely hard to find. But the killers never gave up. The hunt was in Bisesero, and the hunters came by truck and bus. "When they saw how strong the resistance was, they called militias from far away," Manase said. "And they did not kill simply. When we were weak, they saved bullets and killed us with bamboo spears. They cut Achilles tendons and necks, but not completely, and then they left the victims to spend a long time crying until they died. Cats and dogs were there, just eating people."

Samuel, too, had found his way to Bisesero. He had lingered in the Mugonero hospital, "full of dead," until one in the morning. Then he crept out of the basement and, carrying "one who had lost his feet," he proceeded slowly into the mountains. Samuel's account of his ordeal following the slaughter at his workplace was as telegraphic as his description of life in Mugonero before the genocide. Unlike Manase, he found little comfort at Bisesero, where the defenders' only advantage was the terrain. He had concluded that to be a Tutsi in Rwanda meant death. "After a month," he said, "I went to Zaire." To get there he had to descend through settled areas to Lake Kivu, and to cross the water at night in a pirogue—an outrageously risky journey, but Samuel didn't mention it.

Manase remained in Bisesero. During the fighting, he told me, "we got so used to running that when one wasn't running one didn't feel right." Fighting and running gave Manase spirit, a sense of belonging to a purpose greater than his own existence. Then he got shot in the thigh, and life once again became about little more than staying alive. He found a cavern, "a rock where a stream went underground, and came out below," and made it his home. "By day, I was alone," he said. "There were only dead people. The bodies fell down in the stream, and I used those bodies as a bridge to cross the water and join the other people in the evenings." In this way, Manase survived.

> ***19. In Your Journal:*** What is ironic about how Manase manages to cross the water to join other survivors?

3

Rwanda has good roads—the best in central Africa. But even the roads tell a story of Rwanda's affliction. The network of proper two-lane **tarmac** that spokes out from Kigali, stitching a tidy web among nine of the country's ten provincial capitals, excludes Kibuye. The road to Kibuye is an unpaved mess, a slalom course of steep hairpin switchbacks, whose surface alternates between bone-rattling rocks and red dirt that turns to deep, slurping clay in the rain, then bakes to stone-hard ruts and ridges in the sun. That the Kibuye road is in this condition is no accident. In the old order—"Before"—Tutsis were known in Rwanda as *inyenzi,* which means cockroaches, and, as you know, Kibuye was teeming with them. In the 1980s, when the government hired road builders from China, the Kibuye road was last on the list for a makeover, and when its turn finally came, the millions of dollars set aside for the job had vanished. So beautiful Kibuye, pinned east and west between mountains and lake, hemmed in north and south by swaths of **primeval** forest, remained (with a hotel full of idle Chinese road builders) a sort of equatorial **Siberia.**

tarmac: paved area

20. In Your Journal: How do Rwanda's roads reveal the ideology of the Hutu Power?

primeval: original; belonging to the earliest of ages

The seventy-mile trip from Kigali to Kibuye town could normally be accomplished in three to four hours, but it took my convoy of four-wheel-drives twelve. A downpour began just after we started, around three in the afternoon, and by six, when the slick, shin-deep mud of a mountain pass sucked the first of our vehicles into the ditch, we had made only half the journey. Night fell and clouds of rippling mist closed in, amplifying the darkness. We didn't see the soldiers—a dozen men with Kalashnikovs, in slouch hats, trench coats, and rubber Wellington boots, picking their way through the mud with long wooden staffs—until they tapped on our windows. So it was no comfort when they informed us that we should shut off our lights, gather in one vehicle, and keep quiet, while we waited for rescue. This was in early September of 1996, more than two years after the genocide, and Hutu militiamen were still terrorizing Kibuye almost nightly.

On one side of the road, the mountain formed a wall, and on the other side, it plunged into an apparently vertical banana plantation. The rain dwindled to a beady mist, and I stood outside the designated vehicle, listening to the arrhythmic plink and plonk of water globules bouncing among the banana leaves. Unseen birds clucked fitfully. The night was a sort of **xylophone,** and I stood keenly alert. "You make a nice target," one of the soldiers had told us. But, so long as our periphery held, I was glad to be out there, on an impassable road in an often impossible-seeming country, hearing and smelling—and feeling my skin tighten against—the sort of

xylophone: musical percussion instrument

Siberia: sparsely populated area near Russia and China; site of many exile and penal colonies dank, drifting midnight that every Rwandan must know and I had never experienced so unprotectedly.

An hour passed. Then a woman down in the valley began to scream. It was a wild and terrible sound, like the war whoop of a Hollywood Indian flapping his hand over his mouth. Silence followed for as long as it takes to fill lungs with air, and the **ululating** alarm rang out again, higher now and faster, more frantic. This time, before the woman's breath broke, other voices joined in. The whooping radiated out through the nether darkness. I took it that we were under attack, and did nothing because I had no idea what to do.

ululate: howl; lament loudly

Within moments, three or four soldiers materialized on the road, and went over the shoulder, pitching down through the banana trees. The continuous whooping knotted around a focal point, reached a peak of volume, and began to subside into shouting, in which the voice of the original woman stood out with magnificently adamant fury. Soon the valley fell quiet, except for the old plink and plonk among the banana leaves. Another hour elapsed. Then, just as cars arrived from Kibuye to escort my halted party to our predawn beds, the soldiers climbed back onto the road, leading a half dozen ragged peasants who carried sticks and machetes. In their midst walked a roughed-up, hang-dog-looking prisoner.

A Rwandan in my convoy made inquiries and announced, "This fellow was wanting to rape the woman who cried." He explained that the whooping we'd heard was a conventional distress signal and that it carried an obligation. "You hear it, you do it, too. And you come running," he said. "No choice. You must. If you ignored this crying, you would have questions to answer. This is how Rwandans live in the hills." He held his hands up flat, and tipped them against each other this way and that, shuffling them around to indicate a patchwork, which is the way the land is parceled up, plot by plot, each household well set off from the next within its patch. "The people are living separately together," he said. "So there is responsibility. I cry, you cry. You cry, I cry. We all come running, and the one that stays quiet, the one that stays home, must explain. Is he in league with the criminals? Is he a coward? And what would he expect when he cries? This is simple. This is normal. This is community."

It struck me as an enviable arrangement. If you cry out, where you live, can you expect to be heard? If you hear a cry of alarm, do you add your voice and come running? Are rapes often averted, and rapists captured, in this way in your place? I was deeply impressed. But what if this system of communal obligation is turned on its head, so that murder and rape become the rule? What if innocence becomes a crime and the person who protects his neighbor is counted as an "accomplice"? Does it then become normal for tear gas to be used to make people in dark hiding places cry so that they can be killed? Later, when I visited Mugonero, and Samuel told me about the tear gas, I remembered the woman's cry in the valley.

21. In Your Journal: What is surprising about the woman crying out during this attempted rape? What other crying does Gourevitch compare it to?

In mid-July of 1994, three months after the massacre at the Mugonero Adventist complex, the church president, Pastor Elizaphan Ntakirutimana, fled with his wife to Zaire, then to Zambia, and from there to Laredo, Texas. It wasn't easy for Rwandans to get American visas after the genocide, but the Ntakirutimanas had a son named Eliel in Laredo, a cardiac anesthesiologist who had been a naturalized United States citizen for more than a decade. So the pastor and his wife were granted green cards—"permanent resident alien" status—and settled in Laredo. Shortly after they arrived, a group of Tutsis who lived in the Midwest sent a letter to the White House, asking that Pastor Ntakirutimana be brought to justice for his conduct during the Mugonero massacre. "After several months," one of the letter's signers told me, "an answer came from Thomas E. Donilon, Assistant Secretary of State for Public Affairs, expressing sympathy for what happened and then just stating the terms of all the foreign aid America was giving to Rwanda. We were saying, here are one million people killed, and here's one man—so we were kind of upset."

On the second anniversary of the Mugonero massacre, a small group of Tutsis descended on Laredo to march and wave signs outside the Ntakirutimanas' residence. They hoped to attract press coverage, and the story *was* sensational: a preacher accused of presiding over the slaughter of hundreds in his congregation. Serbs suspected of much less extensive crimes in the former Yugoslavia—men with no hope of American green cards—were receiving daily international coverage, but aside from a few scattered news briefs, the pastor had been spared such unpleasantness.

Yet, when I returned to New York in September of 1996, a week after my visit to Mugonero, I learned that the FBI was preparing to arrest Elizaphan Ntakirutimana in Laredo. The United Nations' International Criminal Tribunal for Rwanda, sitting in Arusha, Tanzania, had issued an indictment against him, charging him with three counts of genocide and three counts of crimes against humanity. The indictment, which made the same charges against Dr. Gerard Ntakirutimana, as well as the mayor, Charles Sikubwabo, and a local businessman, told the same story that survivors had told me: the pastor had "instructed" Tutsis to take refuge at the Adventist complex; Dr. Gerard had helped to extricate "non-Tutsis" from among the refugees; father and son had arrived at the complex on the morning of April 16, 1994, in a convoy of attackers; and "during the months that followed" both men were held to have "searched for and attacked Tutsi survivors and others, killing or causing serious bodily or mental harm to them."

The indictment was a secret, as were the FBI's plans for an arrest. Laredo, a hot, flat town, tucked into one of the southern-most bends of the Rio Grande, overlooks Mexico, and the pastor had a record of flight.

The address I had for Dr. Eliel Ntakirutimana in Laredo was 313 Potrero Court—a suburban brick ranch house at the end of a drab cul-de-sac. A dog growled when I rang the bell, but nobody answered. I found a pay phone and called the local Adventist church, but I don't speak Spanish, and the man who answered didn't speak English. I had a tip that Pastor Ntakirutimana was working at a health-food store, but after making the rounds of a few places with names like Casa Ginseng and Fiesta Natural that seemed to specialize in herbal remedies for constipation and impotence, I went back to Potrero Court. There was still nobody at 313. Down the street I found a man spraying his driveway with a garden hose. I told him I was looking for a family of Rwandans, and indicated the house. He said, "I don't know about that. I only know the people next door here a little." I thanked him, and he said, "Where'd you say these people were from?" Rwanda, I said. He hesitated a moment, then said, "Colored people?" I said, "They're from Africa." He pointed to 313, and told me, "That's the house. Fancy cars they drive. They moved out about a month ago."

22. *In Your Journal:* Why do you think Gourevitch quotes the Laredo neighbor of Ntakirutimana about where his neighbors were from?

Eliel Ntakirutimana's new phone number was unlisted, but late at night I got hold of an operator who gave me his address, and in the morning I drove there. The house was on Estate Drive, in an expensive-looking new private community, designed, as in Rwanda, with each home set within a walled compound. An electronic gate controlled access to the subdivision, where most of the plots were still empty prairie. The few houses were wild, vaguely Mediterranean fantasias, whose only common attribute was immensity. The Ntakirutimanas' stood at the end of the road behind another electronic security fence. A barefoot Rwandan maid led me past an open garage that housed a white Corvette convertible and into a vast kitchen area. She phoned Dr. Ntaki—he had chopped down his name as a professional courtesy to American tongues—and I told him I was hoping to meet his father. He asked how I'd found the house. I told him that, too, and he gave me an appointment in the afternoon at a hospital called Mercy.

While I was still on the phone, the doctor's wife, Genny, a handsome woman with an easy manner, came home from taking her kids to school. She offered me a cup of coffee—"From Rwanda," she said proudly. We sat on huge leather couches beside a gigantic television in an alcove of the kitchen, with a view over a patio, a barbecue pavilion, and, on the far shore of a tiled swimming pool, a patch of garden. The distant voices of the Rwandan maid and a Mexican nanny echoed off the marble floors and lofty ceilings of further rooms; and Genny said, "With my father-in-law, we were the last ones to hear anything. He was in Zaire, he was in Zambia, a refugee, and an old man—more than seventy years old. His one great wish was retirement and old age in Rwanda. Then he comes here and suddenly they say he killed people. You know Rwandans. Rwandans go crazy with jealousy. Rwandans don't like if you are rich or in good health."

23. *In Your Journal:* Describe Genny's assessment of her father-in-law's predicament.

Genny's own father was a Hutu who had been involved in politics and was killed by rivals in 1973. Her mother was a Tutsi who was saved by chance on the brink of being killed in 1994, and who still lived in Rwanda.

"We mixed people don't hate Tutsi or Hutu," Genny said. This was an inaccurate generalization—many people of mixed parentage had killed as Hutus, or been killed as Tutsis—but Genny had been living in exile, and she explained, "Most Rwandans who are here in America like my husband have been here so long that they all take positions according to their families. If they say your brother killed, then you take his side." She did not seem to have her own mind entirely made up about her father-in-law, the pastor. She said, "This is a man who can't stand to see blood even when you kill a chicken. But anything is possible."

Just before noon, Dr. Ntaki called with a new plan: we would lunch at the Laredo Country Club. Then the family lawyer, Lazaro Gorza-Gongora, showed up. He was dapper and mild-mannered and very direct. He said that he wasn't prepared to let the pastor speak to me. "The accusations are outrageous, monstrous, and completely destructive," he said with disarming tranquillity. "People say whatever they want, and an old man's last years are in jeopardy."

Dr. Ntaki was a round, **loquacious** man with strikingly bulging eyes. He wore a malachite-faced Rolex watch and a white dress shirt with a boldly hand-stitched collar. As he drove Gorza-Gongora and me to the country club in a Chevrolet Suburban that had been customized to feel like a living room, complete with a television set, he spoke with great interest about Russian President Boris Yeltsin's preparations for open-heart surgery. Dr. Ntaki himself presided over the intravenous drips of open-heart patients, and he shared his wife's view that any charges against his father were the product of typical Rwandan class envy and spite. "They see us as rich and well educated," he said. "They can't take it." He told me that his family owned a spread of five hundred acres in Kibuye—kingly proportions in Rwanda—with coffee and banana plantations, many cattle, "and all those good Rwandan things." He said, "Here's a father with three sons who are doctors and two other children who work in international finance. This is in a country that didn't have a single person with a bachelor's degree in 1960. Of course everyone resents him and wants to destroy him."

loquacious: very talkative

We ate overlooking the golf course. Dr. Ntaki held forth on Rwandan politics. He didn't use the word "genocide"; he spoke of "chaos, chaos, chaos," with every man for himself just trying to save his own skin. And Tutsis had started it, he said, by killing the President. I reminded him that there was no evidence linking Tutsis to the assassination; that, in fact, the genocide had been meticulously planned by the Hutu extremists who set it in motion within an hour of the President's death. Dr. Ntaki ignored me. "If President Kennedy had been assassinated in this country by a black man," he said, "the American population would have most certainly killed all the blacks."

24. In Your Journal: What is the logic behind Ntaki's invocation of the assassination of John F. Kennedy?

Gorza-Gongora watched me writing this absurd statement in my notebook and broke his silence. "You say 'extermination,' you say 'systematic,' you say 'genocide,' " he said to me. "That's just a theory, and I think you've come all the way to Laredo to hold up my client as a clever proof of this theory."

No, I said, I had come because a man of God was accused of having ordained the murder of half his flock, co-religionists, simply because they had been born as something called Tutsi.

25. In Your Journal: Why is this statement by Gorza-Gongora chilling?

"What's the evidence?" Gorza-Gongora said. "Eyewitnesses?" He chuckled. "Anybody can say they saw anything."

Dr. Ntaki went further; he detected a conspiracy: "The witnesses are all government tools. If they don't say what the new government wants, they'll be killed."

Still, Dr. Ntaki said that despite his lawyer's counsel, his father was concerned for his honor and wished to speak to me.

"The pastor thinks silence looks like guilt," Gorza-Gongora said. "Silence is peace."

Leaving the country club, I asked Dr. Ntaki if he ever had doubts about his father's innocence. He said, "Of course, but—"and, after a second, "Do you have a father? I will defend him with everything I have."

Pastor Elizaphan Ntakirutimana was a man of stern composure. He sat in a wing chair in the doctor's parlor, clutching a manila folder in his lap, and wearing a gray cap over his gray hair, a gray shirt, black suspenders, black pants, black square-toed shoes, and squarish wire-rimmed glasses. He spoke in Kinyarwanda, the language of his country, and his son translated. He said, "They are saying I killed people. Eight thousand people." The number was about four times higher than any I had previously heard. The pastor's voice was full of angry disbelief. "It is all one hundred percent pure lies. I did not kill any people. I never told anybody to kill any people. I could not do such things."

When the "chaos" began in Kigali, the pastor explained, he didn't think it would reach Mugonero, and when Tutsis began going to the hospital, he claimed he had to ask them why. After about a week, he said, there were so many refugees that "things started turning a little weird." So the pastor and his son Gerard held a meeting to address the question "What are we going to do?" But at that moment two policemen showed up to guard the hospital, and he said, "We didn't have the meeting, because they had done it without our asking."

Then, on Saturday, April 16, at seven in the morning, the two policemen from the hospital came to Pastor Ntakirutimana's house. "They gave me letters from the Tutsi pastors there," he said. "One was addressed to me, another to the mayor. I read mine. The letter they gave me said, 'You understand they are plotting, they are trying to kill us, can you go to the mayor and ask him to protect us?" Ntakirutimana read this, then went to the mayor, Charles Sikubwabo. "I told him what my message from the

Tutsi pastors said, and gave him his letter. The mayor told me, 'Pastor, there's no government. I have no power. I can do nothing.'

"I was surprised," Ntakirutimana went on. "I returned to Mugonero, and I told the policemen to go with a message to the pastors to tell them, 'Nothing can be done, and the mayor, too, said he can do nothing.' " Then Pastor Ntakirutimana took his wife and some others who "wanted to hide" and drove out of town—to Gishyita, which is where Mayor Sikubwabo lived, and where many of the injured refugees at Mugonero had received their wounds. "Gishyita," he explained, "had killed its people already, so there was peace."

Pastor Ntakirutimana said that he hadn't returned to Mugonero until April 27. "Everybody was buried," he told me, "I never saw anything." After that, he said, "I never went anywhere. I stayed at my office. Only, one day I went to Rwamatamu because I heard that pastors had also died there, and I wanted to see if I could find even a kid of theirs to save. But I found nothing to save. They were Tutsis."

The pastor made himself out as a great patron of Tutsis. He said he had given them jobs and shelter, and promoted them within the Adventist hierarchy. He lifted his chin and said, "As long as I live, in my whole life, there is nobody I tried to help more than Tutsis." He could not understand how Tutsis could be so ungrateful as to make accusations against him. "It looks as if there is no justice anymore," he said.

The name Ntakirutimana means "nothing is greater than God," and the pastor told me, "I think I'm closer to God than I have ever been in my life." He said, "When I see what happened in Rwanda, I'm very sad about it because politics is bad. A lot of people died." He didn't sound sad; he sounded tired, harassed, indignant. "Hatred is the result of sin, and when Jesus Christ comes, he's the only one who's going to take it away," he said, and once more, he added, "Everything was chaos."

"They say you organized it," I reminded him.

He said, "Never, never, never, never."

I asked him whether he remembered the precise language of the letter addressed to him by the seven Tutsi pastors who were killed at Mugonero. He opened the folder in his lap. "Here," he said, and held out the handwritten original and a translation. His daughter-in-law, Genny, took the documents to make me copies on the fax machine. Dr. Ntaki wanted a drink, and fetched a bottle of scotch. The lawyer, Gorza-Gongora, told me, "I was always against this meeting with you." Genny brought me the letter. It was dated April 15, 1994.

Our dear leader, Pastor Elizaphan Ntakirutimana,

How are you! We wish you to be strong in all these problems we are facing. We wish to inform you that we have heard that tomorrow we will be killed with our families. We therefore request you to intervene on our behalf and talk

26. *In Your Journal:* Describe the relationship between the tone and content of the letter Pastor Ntakirutimana received from the Tutsi pastors.

with the Mayor. We believe that, with the help of God who entrusted you the leadership of this flock, which is going to be destroyed, your intervention will be highly appreciated, the same way as the Jews were saved by Esther.

We give honor to you.

The letter was signed by Pastors Ezekiel Semugeshi, Isaka Rucondo, Seth Rwanyabuto, Eliezer Seromba, Seth Sebihe, Jerome Gakwaya, and Ezekias Zigirinshuti.

Dr. Ntaki walked me out to my car. In the driveway, he stopped and said, "If my father committed crimes, even though I am his son, I say he should be prosecuted. But I don't believe any of it."

27. *In Your Journal:* Why does Gourevitch take so much time to present Ntakirutimana's U.S. story?

Twenty-four hours after we met, Pastor Elizaphan Ntakirutimana was in his car, driving south on Interstate 35 toward Mexico. To the FBI agents who were tailing him, his driving appeared erratic—he would speed up, slow down, change lanes, and again accelerate abruptly. A few miles from the border, they pulled him over and took him into custody. The arrest went almost entirely unnoticed in the American press. A few days later, in the Ivory Coast, the pastor's son Dr. Gerard was also arrested, and he was quickly transferred to the UN tribunal. But the pastor had a United States green card and the rights that came with it, and he retained Ramsey Clark, a former Attorney General, who specialized in defending politically repugnant cases, to fight his extradition. Clark argued, **speciously,** that it would be unconstitutional for the United States to surrender the pastor—or anybody else—to the tribunal, and Judge Marcel Notzon, who presided over the case in federal district court, agreed. On December 17, 1997, after fourteen months in a Laredo jail, Pastor Ntakirutimana was released unconditionally, and he remained a free man for nine weeks before FBI agents arrested him a second time, pending an appeal of Judge Notzon's decision.

speciously: fallaciously, though possessing a ring of truth

When I heard that Pastor Ntakirutimana had been returned to his family in time for Christmas, I went back through my notes from Mugonero. I had forgotten that after my meetings with survivors, my translator, Arcene, asked me to go with him to the hospital chapel, where there had been a lot of killing; he wanted to pay homage to the dead, who were buried nearby in mass graves. We stood in silence in the empty chapel with its cement pews. On the floor below the altar sat four memorial coffins, draped in white sheets, painted with black crosses. "The people who did this," Arcene said, "didn't understand the idea of a country. What is a country? What is a human being? They had no understanding."

28. *In Your Journal:* Respond to the final sentence of this essay: "They had no understanding." How does it encapsulate many of Gourevitch's thoughts and feelings throughout his experiences in Rwanda?

FOR USE IN DISCUSSION

Questions about Substance

1. Describe your response to the title of this work. What effect does it have before reading? What effect does it have after?
2. "The dead at Nyarubuye were, I'm afraid, beautiful" (369). Is this statement shocking to you? Does Gourevitch do enough to explain what he means by this?
3. Why is Gourevitch so incredulous about whether he "can really see" what's right in front of him? Does this incredulity begin to suggest an argument within this highly descriptive personal narrative about the author's own reaction to the events?
4. Compare the passivity of the Tutsis to the aggression of the Hutus. Which is more disturbing?
5. Why do you think Dr. Ntaki and his father both use the word "chaos" so emphatically to describe what happened in Kibuye (381, 383)? Does this word seem especially inappropriate after Gourevitch's description of the events there? How is their description different from that of the witnesses?
6. Does Gourevitch pass judgment on the American press by noting what it does not discuss in relation to the events in Rwanda (384)?

Questions about Structure and Style

1. How does the epigraph from Plato function in this context? Why do you think the author chooses such an ancient classical work to excerpt at the beginning of this modern piece of journalism?
2. Why do you think that the author works achronologically—in other words, why does he describe the massacre first and the events that led up to the massacre next?
3. Examine the repeated juxtaposition of beauty and death. How does this theme contribute to Gourevitch's main point?
4. At times, Gourevitch paraphrases what he's seen and heard, and at times, he uses direct quotation. What are the different effects of these techniques?
5. Why does this essay end with a focus on the culpability of the Ntakis? Why doesn't it end where it began: with the dead bodies?

Multimedia Suggestions

1. Hollywood has a clear fascination with war and the aftermath of battle. Movies like *Braveheart* (1995), *Gladiator* (2000), *Saving Private Ryan* (1998) *Platoon* (1978) and *The Deer Hunter* (1978), for example, present grisly battle scenes with vivid details. Compare and contrast the battle scenes in one or more of

these films with the description of the scenes of genocide in Gourevitch's work. Are any of the representations too gratuitous in their violence?

2. Find out what has been happening with the war crimes trials in Rwanda since the genocide. You can see the Human Rights Watch World Report 2002 on Rwanda at *www.hrw.org/wr2k/africa9.html.*
3. Read the interview with Philip Gourevitch at *http://globetrotter.berkeley.edu/people/Gourevitch/gourevitch-con0.html.* How do his responses to the questions fulfill your expectations of what he would be like? What new insights do you have about his reporting and writing after reading this interview?
4. See if your school carries the documentary *Triumph of Evil,* a documentary about the Rwanda genocide. If not, you can access the transcripts of the film at *http://www.pbs.org/wgbh/pages/frontline/shows/evil/.* How does the documentary's portrayal compare to Gourevitch's?

SUGGESTIONS FOR WRITING AND RESEARCH

1. Write an essay about the use of objective prose in Gourevitch's work. Does it make his point-of-view objective? How do you think a journalist makes choices about what details to include and what ones to exclude? Does this affect the level of objectivity in a work? Does it affect the level of objectivity in Gourevitch's writing?
2. Examine the role of death in another context (an accident, a terminal illness, or at the end of a long life, for example). Compare the context of your choice with the Rwanda story in terms of the meaning, emotion, and aftermath of death. Can Gourevitch's ideas be applied outside of their specific context?
3. It is difficult to read about an event like the genocide in Rwanda without comparing it to other events, such as the Holocaust, the war in Bosnia, the "killing fields" of Cambodia, and other such events. Are such comparisons even useful to think about? Do they inevitably lead to a kind of ranking of suffering that suggests some massacres are "worse" or, by comparison, "better" than others? What do you think of such comparisons? Does it help historicize individual events and trace global trends, or does it only lead to chauvinism?

WORKING WITH CLUSTERS

Cluster 4: Conceiving Death

Cluster 7: Holocausts and Histories

Cluster 13: Global Knowledge

Cluster 18: Ethnicity and Conflict

Discipline: The Humanities

Rhetorical Mode: Narration

"Inside Out or Outside In: Who Says You're Married?" (from *What Is Marriage For?*)

by E. J. Graff

E. J. Graff is an author and journalist who has an M.F.A. in writing from Warren Wilson College. Her work explores American identity via personal stories, journalistic reporting, and social history to expose the intersection of society and self. Much of Graff's writing has focused on lesbian, gay, bisexual, and transgender issues, especially same-sex marriage. She is author of the book What Is Marriage For? The Strange Social History of Our Most Intimate Institution, *from which this excerpt is taken. Her journalism, essays, and short stories have appeared in* The New York Times Magazine, The Boston Globe, Ms., The American Prospect, The Nation, Out, The Village Voice, Salon.com, The Women's Review of Books, The Iowa Review, The Kenyon Review, *and more than a dozen anthologies. She has also served as an expert witness and has spoken widely at conventions, universities, churches, synagogues, public forums, and on public and commercial TV and radio shows across the country. Graff has been a Visiting Scholar at the Radcliffe Schlesinger Library and a Liberal Arts Fellow at Harvard Law School. She has received the Astraea Foundation's Emerging Writers Award, the Margolis Award for political essay and journalism, and the Massachusetts Cultural Council Award for Fiction. She also serves on the advisory board for the Massachusetts Freedom to Marry Foundation and the steering committee of the Massachusetts Freedom to Marry Coalition, and is a contributing editor to* The American Prospect *and* Out *magazine.*

Everywhere a distinction exists between marriage, i.e., a legal group-sanctioned bond . . . and the type of permanent or temporary union resulting from violence or consent alone. This group intervention may be a notable or a slight one, it does not matter. The important thing is that every society has some way to operate a distinction between free unions and legitimate ones. . . . it remains true that marriage is not, is never, and cannot be a private business.

—**Claude Lévi-Strauss,** "The Family" (1956)

1. In Your Journal: Claude Levi-Strauss asserts that marriage "can never be a private affair." Do you agree?

Nothing is more gratifying to the mind of man than power or dominion, and this I think myself amply possessed of, as I am the father of a family . . . I look upon my family as a patriarchal sovereignty in which I am myself, both king and priest.

—*The Spectator* (1712)

I desire you would Remember the ladies . . . Do not put such unlimited power into the hands of the Husbands. Remember all Men would be tyrants if they could.

—Abigail Adams, letter to John Adams (1776)

Marriage is a coming together for better or for worse, hopefully enduring, and intimate to the degree of being sacred.

—U.S. Supreme Court, *Griswold* v. *Connecticut* (1965)

To marry, in the public sense, means to expect the world to treat your life as shared—to announce that your sexual partner has first claim on you and your efforts. For the couple to fulfill the wedding vows that make mothers and strangers weep, that claim must be honored by others in things large and small, from holiday invitations to burial instructions. From conversation to finance, the couple's bond can never entirely be severed from the *polis*, the collective, the society in which they live.

❖ **Claude Lévi-Strauss:** (1908–) French anthropologist; founder of structural anthropology, which is heavily influenced by linguistics, which suggests that culture is largely a communication system

Usually those claims are made and honored day to day, in the private social circle: for instance, everyone at the office understands and pitches in when a particular employee is preoccupied and less than productive during his wife's months of chemo. But now and then the larger institutional machinery is invoked to enforce a claim. You may go to court to insist that your parents were legitimately married and that you therefore count as an Athenian citizen—a status you get only because both your grandfathers fully intended to send money, power, and status your way. Or you may insist that you really *were* married and therefore should, after he dies, get to keep not only your two dresses and one cookpot, but also one-third of the land in his name. Or eight years after you moved out and left him to raise the kids, you may go back to court insisting that he's unfit because he's now living—unmarried—with another man, while you're properly and heterosexually remarried, not just in your heart but in the eyes of the law. Society has a stake in seeing that each of those disputes are settled justly, based on some larger social consensus—partly because everyone else's property, or citizenship, or relationship to their offspring may be redefined depending on how *your* dispute is resolved.

Given, in other words, that human beings are flawed—that we do not always treat each other as we should, and worse, that we disagree over what it means to "treat each other as we should"—marriage is not merely an inner experience but also a political institution, an accretion of decisions about how to order a couple's promises and obligations. Whenever two parties disagree—a father wants to marry off a daughter who refuses; a wife says she was raped by a husband who insists her body is his property; a couple demands health insurance from an employer who says they're not married—society must make some reasoned judgment about their dispute. And so marriage's borders are always critical political territory, roiling with such questions as: Which sexual bonds or private promises create publicly policed commitments? On what grounds do we decide what's just? When can society intervene to right private wrongs? Who adjudicates when those involved disagree? Most politically significant, whose interests define marriage, how, and why?

> ***2. In Your Journal:*** Summarize the types of disputes that Graff demonstrates all have "a stake" in the definition of marriage.

> ***3. In Your Journal:*** Why are the "borders" of marriage so important?

One of the most basic tensions in the history of marriage is between those two interlocking sides of marriage: marriage as a publicly policed institution and marriage as an inner experience. Which one turns your bond into a marriage: a public authority or your heart? Are you married when the two of you decide to care for each other for life, a decision you live out day to day, a decision only afterwards recognized by your community? Or is it the other way around: does the family, or church, or state pronounce some words over your head, write your names side by side in a registry, and bestow upon you a marriage, a license and legal obligation to carry out the responsibilities of affection and care? This may sound like one of those faces/vases illusions, and for good reason: marriage doesn't exist unless both parts happen—two human beings behave as married, and everyone else treats them as such. But it *does* matter which side you think counts more: the decisions made about individual marriages will be quite different if you think marriage is a publicly conferred status or an immanent state. And each position's internal contradictions can—and have—caused social havoc when unchecked.

inextricable: incapable of being disentangled, undone, loosed, or solved

In history, this debate is almost **inextricable** from the debate over which authority rules marriage. *Who* decides where the enforceable marriage is made—in your heart, or in a registry—and why? That decision might be less complex if the only people who have to recognize your marriage live within twenty-five miles, when the people who see you two behaving as married are also the ones who oversee the granting of the **widow's dower.** And it might be *more* complex in our world, in which each of our daily lives goes beyond our circle of acquaintances to touch dozens of strangers and anonymous entities, from the motor vehicles registry to our children's schools. The story of the public/private marriage line is therefore also a story of how marriage has shifted, in comparative legal scholar Mary Ann Glendon's words, from custom to law.

widow's dower: money or real estate allotted to a widow after her husband dies

4. In Your Journal: Graff provides examples of marriages in different historical, cultural settings over the next few paragraphs. As you read these, note in your journal whether each is more social/political or more intimate, and why.

Roman marriage was the immanent kind: when challenged in court (over, say, whether a widow inherits or whether a child is legitimate), a marriage could not be proved by anything so simple as a public registry. A judge had to investigate whether the two lived together with *affectio maritalis,* "the intention of being married." To be married, all a couple had to do was "regard each other as man and wife and behave accordingly." What does that mean, "behave accordingly"? The Romans may never have defined it, but (like Americans and pornography) they knew it when they saw it. A judge sized up the couple's "marital intentions" by such signals as whether she'd brought a dowry, or whether he openly called her his wife. Augustine and his concubine, for instance, were living together without *affectio maritalis,* since he was intending a later power-marriage. But had the same pair *intended* to be married—with no change in their behavior—they would have been. Marriage was a private affair: the state could police only the consequences, not the act.

5. In Your Journal: Do you think it is odd that Graff would use such an analogy as "Americans and pornography" to discuss marriage? Do you think it is an effective analogy?

While the Jewish configuration changed over the millennia, what remained central is marriage as a private act: only bride and groom could say the magic words that turned them into husband and wife. After many centuries the rabbis inserted themselves and their seven blessings into the ceremony, before the big feast, but even they knew they were not essential: the pair made the marriage within themselves. Which is why, in Jewish law, a court could neither "grant" nor refuse a divorce. If a husband's inner willingness to be married evaporated (sometimes hers counted but often it did not), then the marriage *itself* had evaporated: the rabbinical court or *bet din* could merely decide questions of fault and finances.

Christianity, as we know, wanted nothing to do with marriage for centuries. When asked, some priests might come by and say a blessing as a favor, just as they'd say a blessing over a child's first haircut. No one considered marriage sacred, as celibacy was: marriage was one of those secular and earthbound forms rendered unto Caesar. But as centuries rolled by, an increasingly powerful Church saw that marriage was central to ordering Europe's civil and political life—not so much those few called to sainthood, sacrifice, and martyrdom, but the many ordinary folk who needed to be told how to behave.

6. In Your Journal: Are you surprised by the history of Christian marriage? How has it changed?

And so the Church launched a battle for power over marriage's rules, a battle that lasted roughly a thousand years. Today we have the peculiar impression that Catholicism has always had one vision of marriage, but for every marriage rule eventually imposed on Europe, the Church's own debates were abundant. It first formally ruled on marriage in 774, when one pope handed **Charlemagne** a set of writings that defined legitimate marriage and condemned all deviations. After another five hundred years of struggle, the Church came up with a marriage liturgy and imposed its new and radical rules—the ballooning incest rules, the one-man-one-marriage rule, and most controversial, the girl-must-consent rule—on the powerful clans. "It is clear," writes one historian, "that this attempt to impose order on matrimonial practice was part of a more ambitious plan to reform the entire social order. . . . regulating the framework of lay society, from baptisms to funerals," the most intimate acts of most people's lives. The Church's push to rule marriage was slow and uneven but very determined. Here and there it would issue a decree and struggle with local nobles over whether it would be observed; now it would retract a bit to permit a lord to marry his dead wife's sister or annul his existing marriage; then it would push forward again.

7. In Your Journal: How could the Church "reform the entire social order" by imposing order on marriage practices?

It was not until 1215 that the Church finally decreed marriage a **sacrament**—the least important one, but a sacrament nonetheless—*and* set up a systematic canon law of marriage, with a system of ecclesiastical courts to enforce it—*and* had a fair amount of people willing to observe those rules. By 1215, the year that the Fourth Lateran Council issued its

Charlemagne: "Charles the Great" (A.D. 742–814), king of the Franks 768–814; as Charles I, emperor of the Holy Roman Empire 800–814

sacrament: in the Catholic Church, an outward sign instituted by Jesus Christ to give grace; the Seven Sacraments of the Catholic Church are Baptism, Penance, Holy Eucharist, Confirmation, Marriage, Holy Orders and Extreme Unction matrimonial decrees, the Church had "broke[n] the back of aristocratic resistance . . . after lengthy individual battles with the nobility, kings included."

And according to the Church, what turned two individuals into a married couple? It was—drumroll, please—the couple's private vows.

> ***8. In Your Journal:*** Does Graff find the Catholic Church's declaration that marriage is mostly about human feelings an improvement over the more politically oriented ideas of marriage set forth by other cultures? Why or why not?

Why a drumroll? Because the Church insisted that a private promise was an unbreakable sacrament—that marriage was an *immanent* experience, a spiritual reality created by the *pair's* free and equal consent. That was practically a declaration of war against the upper classes, a radical and subversive idea emphasizing the sacredness of the individual spirit. Marriage, the Church insisted, was not just about land and power and wombs, but about human feelings.

Unfortunately, saying that *consent* makes a marriage can leave courts in as awkward a position as saying that *affectio maritalis* makes a marriage. How do you define consent? At precisely what point does marriage become "What God has joined, let no man put asunder"—an indissoluble sacrament? This second question was especially important, since—bucking all human precedent, and even going against the example of the Church's own early decisions—the Church started to insist that consent once given could *never* be revoked. After a great many theological volleys and debates, theologians decided that a marriage was made and permanently sealed at the moment that the pair knowingly and willingly said "I marry you." Even if they said their vows in absolute secrecy, with no witnesses. Even if they never actually consummated their union (how could a Church based on a virgin birth elevate sex to the marriage sacrament?). *Words* made the marriage—not family agreements or contracts, and not sex. It was a dramatic break with custom. The Church divided these words into two complex formulas—*verba de praesenti* and *verba de futuro*—that no one but theologians and lawyers fully understood. The basic principle, however, was clear, at least to the Church itself: did you two say you are married? Then poof! You are.

> ***9. In Your Journal:*** Why should Graff think it incredulous that the Church made marriage an indissoluble sacrament?

That principle caused social havoc. For the upper classes, there were three problems: disobedience, disobedience, and murkiness. Disobedience 1: a balky adolescent could thwart carefully planned mergers and acquisitions, although locking her up and beating her usually brought her around. Disobedience 2: from age twelve and fourteen respectively, a girl and boy could simply meet in a back hall and say those foolish *verba* to each other—and be irrevocably married. (Romeo and Juliet, are you listening?) In one fifteenth-century British landed family, the Pastons, a seventeen-year-old daughter pledged herself to the family bailiff. For three years Margery's parents shut her up in her house, until her fiancé somehow got a hearing with the local bishop. The bishop flatly commanded the young woman's parents to bring her in—and after talking to her, ruled that Margery was married. (The Pastons disinherited her and her children and never spoke to her again—although they didn't fire her husband the bailiff.)

The third upper-class *verba* problem was murkiness. Since not sex but *words* made a marriage, you couldn't always tell when you were merely betrothed and when you were actually married. The Pastons' eldest son John met a woman with whom he exchanged vows. But what kind? *Verba de praesenti,* meaning they'd already married each other, or *verba de futuro,* meaning they were engaged? Neither was sure. After that meeting the pair never spent a night under the same roof, rarely saw each other, and treated each other so coolly that he had trouble getting an appointment to see her—and yet when he finally decided to break things off, her "conscience required an annulment from Rome." *That* took six years and a thousand ducats. If private consent makes a marriage, and if you're not sure whether you consented, who but God—or God's representatives in Rome—can say whether or not you're married?

10. In Your Journal: List the three problems with the verbal marriage of the Church that created "social havoc" and explain one.

For the working classes, those *verba* could be just as problematic—but for more personal reasons. Individuals exchanged vows "under an ash tree, in a bed, in a garden, in a small storehouse, in a field, in a blacksmith's shop, in a kitchen, at a tavern, and in the king's highway"—to use some examples that got into English ecclesiastical court records—and then wound up in court having violent "he said/she said" arguments. Had they gotten married after all, or was one fabricating? Most female readers will grasp immediately how much men will promise (and later deny) to get a woman into bed—and most men can testify how women's memories can expand vague sentiments into definite commitments. But women could also be the ones who changed their minds, as when a certain John was about to travel overseas and Agnes begged him to marry her first. They said their vows in front of witnesses. On his trip John lost most of his money, however, and Agnes broke things off. He took her to the ecclesiastical court, saying they were already married—but she countered that, since they hadn't had sex, they'd been only engaged. Which was, the Church notwithstanding, how most people saw things: *verba* put you under contract, but only sex transformed words into marriage.

11. In Your Journal: What do the problems with verbal contracts say about the relationship between human words and actions?

12. In Your Journal: How did sex compare to consent as an indicator of marriage in the 13th century? Do any of the distinctions still stand?

The *verba*'s murkiness overflowed the court dockets. What happened when a man promised himself to one woman but then promised *and* bedded another: Was his first promise a marriage, making his second tryst adultery, or did the second's consummation make *it* the marriage, eclipsing the first? What happened when a family lured another (wealthy) family's adolescent son on a weekend outing that ended with the girl's parents putting the two young people into a single bed for the evening, by candlelight "witnessing" the boy's "vows." Was he sacramentally bound by his sexual temptation, or could his parents have their tryst annulled? The questions stacked up for centuries; when it comes to marriage, it seems, there is no escape from lawyers.

How was such a mess to be cleaned up? While the working folk stumbled in and out of secret "precontracts," the aristocracy and nobles constantly attacked the Church's idea of marriage-by-consent. By the time it was instituted into canon law, the Church had already run into trouble with its concept that consent-makes-a-marriage—and so at the same time, the Church tried to control the damage by issuing requirements for a *licit* marriage. You had to post the banns, an announcement that a given couple was to be married, three weeks in a row—thus giving plenty of time for someone to come forward and object that, for instance, she was already contracted to John. You had to say vows *in faciem Ecclesiae,* before priest and people, either in front of or even *inside* a church. Both innovations were so disliked that they took centuries to be accepted, and their acceptance was uneven at that. The English middle and upper classes went to church fairly early; the Italians shrugged the demand off entirely, keeping their traditional family wedding procession from bride's to groom's house without so much as a wink at the priest. Everywhere folks kept the bawdy custom (strongly discouraged by the Church) of seeing the couple to bed, where they stood by with a raucous celebration and suggestive toasts, and then checked in a few hours later to see how the sex had gone. Sex, not the priest, was what married you.

13. In Your Journal: Why would the requirement of being married by a priest in front of witnesses be distasteful to some people?

The Church got very little cooperation in its attempts to turn marriage into a soberly witnessed event—in part because its decrees were toothless. Not just in the eyes of the community but even in the eyes of the Church, your marriage was still *valid* even when *illicit*—even if you hadn't met marriage requirements like banns or public vows. Despite itself, the Church had created a new in-between marriage category: illicit but indissoluble marriages.

14. In Your Journal: What does Graff mean by "its decrees were toothless"?

Most were no problem. One historian notes that in one fourteenth-century English town, "of 101 unions mentioned in the register, 89 were of this 'irregular' kind," meaning private rather than public promises: few wound up in court. According to various records, up to one-third or one-half of European adults in the sixteenth century were officially unmarried. Yes, many of these were young unmarrieds, widows, or widowers—but others were cohabitants who believed that *they,* not any outside authority, made their companionship into a marriage. Writes one historian, "The real hurdle for the courts was the persistent idea that people could regulate marriage for themselves."

But while most people might be quite content with their private vows, 70 percent of ecclesiastical court cases were over the *verba* problem: private marriage created public mess. And so what started as the Church's championing of the individual spirit in defiance of clan control became an international scandal. Across Europe people didn't know whether they were married or un-, what with engagements or annulments tied up in court for years; secret vows and seductions that might or might not be binding for life; priests paying annual fees for concubines who were not wives; and of course the proliferation of marriage taxes for dispensations, pronouncements, annulments, and what have you. And so in swept the Protestants, with their ferocious appetite for sexual order.

15. In Your Journal: What effect is the "ferocious appetite" metaphor meant to have?

The reasons that on October 31, 1517 **Luther** pounded his theses in Wittenberg's church door—and the reasons his protest caught fire across Europe, turning into wars both theological and bloody—are far beyond the scope of this book. But reforming the marriage rules was high up on the Protestant agenda. The Protestants considered their marriage reform to be urgent in part because marriage is both an intimate and a politically urgent act, framing most homes and lives: the religion that won the battle to define marriage had closer control of Europe's souls—not to mention its finances. Unlike the old peasant or aristocratic societies, the rising merchant class needed order across families, borders, and seas. More and more people were trading (and marrying) beyond their old ten-mile radius. How could you run a family business if some pretender suddenly showed up, insisted he was your daughter's husband and therefore had a **lien** on your possessions? Marriage had to be governed by something larger than one village's communal memory—and something less costly than endless suits in ecclesiastical courts. The Protestants were sick of marriage ideals that—however spiritual in theory—caused nightmares in practice. Besides, they had ceased to believe that private consent was sacred. As one Protestant reformer wrote, "when two young people secretly and without the knowledge of their parents, in the disobedience and ignorance of youth, as if intoxicated, **wantonly** and deceitfully . . . join themselves together in marriage, who would not agree that such a union has been brought about by Satan and not by the Lord God?" The result: the Protestants ushered in a revolution in the very *definition* of marriage—from announced to pronounced, from privately made to publicly bestowed.

lien: legal claim of one person upon the property of another person to secure the payment of a debt or the satisfaction of an obligation

wantonly: deliberately and without restraint

Depending on the region and jurisdiction, what the Protestants usually required were a priest, several witnesses, a public ceremony, parental consent up to age twenty-one or twenty-five or so, even a register of all births, deaths, and marriages. Yes, the Protestants still believed that the *moment* of marriage was when the two said their vows. But that moment was no longer a mystical sacrament, a concept the Protestants ridiculed openly. Rather, the Protestants insisted, marriage was—by definition—a secular status conferred by an outside authority. No Protestant group had the power to control that public recognition, or was prepared to spend a thousand years building that power. So they handed off marriage to their running mates for power, the rising nation-states. In 1525 **Zurich** flatly denied that private vows were valid, instead insisting that a marriage legally

16. In Your Journal: How do the changes in marriage laws and practices in the Protestant Church compare to those of the Catholic Church?

Luther: (Martin) (1483–1546) German theologian and leader of the Reformation; Luther opposed the wealth and corruption in the Catholic papacy, and he believed that faith alone would lead to salvation

Zurich: largest city in (northeast) Switzerland

required at least "two pious, honorable, and incontestable witnesses." In 1537 **Augsburg and Nuremberg** started fining or jailing those who "mingled themselves sexually" before the church ceremony, while clergy living with concubines had to marry or separate. By 1563, stung by Protestant criticism, even the **Catholic Council of Trent** caught the wave—and declared that any marriage that had *not* been performed publicly, in front of the parish priest, was invalid. So there!

Small and sensible as those rules may now sound, the change was revolutionary. For the first time in history, individuals and families no longer had the power to say who was married. And the real winners in this marriage battle—the nation-states—didn't hold back as much as religious authorities might have in using their power over marriage. Rather, they quite enthusiastically took up marriage regulation, control, and even surveillance. The French king, outraged that the Catholic Church did not invalidate **clandestine** marriages, in 1579 set the *legal* age of marriage without parental consent at twenty-five for women and thirty for men. The longer the states had power over marriage, the more widely they were tempted to use that power. In 1739, Prussian states forbade noblemen to marry peasants, artisans to marry before completing apprenticeships, students to marry before graduation, and cripples or blind persons to marry at all. The French revolutionaries, like all revolutionaries, saw changing marriage as a way to break down the old order, made mandatory a civil ceremony and registration, and officially decreed that the State married you—not you yourselves, and certainly not God. Private power was banished, replaced by the state. As historian Nancy Cott writes, "one of the principal means that the state can use to prove its social existence—to announce its sovereignty and its hold on the populace—is its authority over marriage."

clandestine: characterized by or executed with secrecy or concealment, for purposes of subversion or deception

> ***17. In Your Journal:*** Note the ages the French king set for legal marriage without parental consent. Are you surprised? Why might the king have chosen these ages?

> ***18. In Your Journal:*** Why does having control of marriage give power to the state, as stated by Nancy Cott?

The marriage revolution took a lot longer in the English-speaking countries. England's established church had merely fired the pope without much changing Catholic marriage theology. Unlike the Continental Protestants, the **Anglicans** kept the idea that private vows were the sacrament that created a marriage: if you said you were married, married you were. Writes historian Lawrence Stone, "England was full of people like Robert Davies of Northwich and Elizabeth Madson of Whitegate 'who say they are married together, but 'tis not known whether nor how nor when they were married.'" Of course, people had been marrying for millennia without official recognition—but not in the brave, mobile, urbanizing new world of **capitalism.** Now that the village and ecclesiastical systems had collapsed, the newly organizing state had to pick up the business of tracking con-

Anglican: member of the Church of England

capitalism: economic system in which ownership of the means of production, distribution, and exchange of wealth is largely private rather than public

---

Augsburg and Nuremberg: cities in southern Germany

Catholic Council of Trent: 1545–47, 1551–52, 1562–63; 19th ecumenical council of the Roman Catholic Church, convened to meet the crisis of the Protestant Reformation tracts, fiscal or marital. With neither local community supervision nor proper bureaucratic records, British marriage was a disaster zone. Comments Stone, "The judges were exasperated by having to deal with cases of inheritance, bigamy, incest, etc. in which the evidence was nothing better than a grubby private marriage register kept by some down-at-heel clerk or shifty woman in an alehouse in the Fleet, and full of false erasures, insertions, and back-dating."

Why couldn't Britain just pass a law that regularized marriage? Easy to say, but not so easy to do in a democratic system. Trying to change civil laws about marriage—that institution that touches everybody's family, spiritual, emotional, financial, and public lives—gets everybody pretty darn touchy. There were some **venal** concerns, such as who got to keep all those licensing fees, and whether there would still be enough marriage **litigation** to keep certain **barristers** in business. But the really controversial questions had to do with the definition of marriage—such as whether it was a public and secular institution that the state had the right to regulate, or whether it was a sacrament privately administered and acknowledged only afterwards. The Anglican bishops who sat in the **House of Lords** were particularly worried about whether it could possibly be moral for the secular state to invalidate a marriage that two people—and presumably therefore God—had brought into being. The various bills that attempted to order the public institution of marriage "aroused strong passions" and "debates were extremely long and bitter; one of the debates in the Commons . . . lasted until half past three in the morning."

venal: open to bribery; mercenary

litigation: process of litigating; a lawsuit

barrister: (in England) a lawyer who is a member of one of the Inns of Court and who has the privilege of pleading in the higher courts

After a century or so, they managed it. In 1753, the powerful Lord Hardwicke forced members to sit through endless sessions during **fetid** August heat until they agreed on and passed some basic marriage regulations: licensing, public and daylight ceremonies, registries signed and dated by spouses and witnesses, parental consent up to age twenty-one. Anything else was to be annulled and ferociously punished; ministers who performed clandestine marriages or falsified marriage registries could be transported to the colonies or executed. (The Quakers, who refused to take public vows, and the Jews, those resident foreigners with their own peculiar laws, were exempted and allowed to run their own marriages.) Finally, in England as on the Continent, the definition of marriage had been transformed from a private sacrament to a publicly authorized contract.

fetid: having an offensive odor; stinking

19. In Your Journal: Summarize the transformation of marriage from a "private sacrament to a publicly authorized contract."

Things were a little less simple on the other side of the Atlantic, in the British colonies, where the definition of marriage varied from region to region. The Puritan colonies had, like their Protestant brethren, outlawed the

House of Lords: one body of the English Parliament, historically populated by hereditary peers, who were not elected, unlike those representatives in the House of Commons; in the 20th century the House of Lords was largely redefined and restructured to reflect the modernization of Great Britain scandal of clandestine marriages, while the Southern colonies had marriage laws as messy and uncertain as mother England's. But by the nineteenth century, the courts decided that private marriage was a necessity, not a scandal, and invented an entirely new form, "common-law marriage," even when they had to overrule existing statutes to do so. According to influential nineteenth-century judges, Americans were so mobile and scattered around the frontier that if you acted as if you were married, or said that you were married, then you *were* married—in life and in court. Faced with the dilemma of widows who said they had been married but could show no proof, one judge in 1809 ruled that times had changed and that upholding private promises would be better than defying them. A host of judges followed, using the new "common-law" invention. Some legislatures joined in, as when an 1843 Indiana statute insisted that "no particular form of ceremony shall be necessary, except that the parties shall declare . . . that they take each other as husband and wife." Cohabitation, anyone?

> ***20. In Your Journal:*** What factors enabled the legitimization of "common law marriage"?

> ***21. In Your Journal:*** What is the tone and suggestion of Graff's sentence, "Cohabitation anyone?"

Early nineteenth-century American marriage, in other words, was made by the couple themselves, and recognized only afterward by law. Not vows, not registration, but behavior made a marriage: as one South Carolina chancellor insisted, "it is the agreement itself, not the form in which it is couched which constitutes the contract." When one woman tried to deprive her dead brother's widow of his estate because there'd been no wedding or registration, a New York court ruled for the widow: "Society would not be safe for a moment, in this, the most sacred of its relations, if an open and public cohabitation as man and wife for ten years, continued with all the conventional usages of married life, and followed by the procreation of children, could be overturned." The judge's wording is entertaining, since this is precisely the view that today makes the family-values people shudder: *cohabitation* is sacred, and gets all the legal benefits of marriage, simply because you *treat* each other as married.

> ***22. In Your Journal:*** Do you see any historical patterns emerging through the course of this essay?

> ***23. In Your Journal:*** Why is the judge's ruling in the New York case of the widow striking to Graff?

And the family-values folks of the era *did* shudder. By the 1870s a marriage reform movement erupted, part of what one historian has called a "moral panic." Publicity, formal ceremonies, registration—all the things made unnecessary by the very existence of common-law marriage—were demanded by organizations such as the National League for the Protection of the Family. Common-law marriage, one writer thought, was "suspiciously near the borderland of illicit intercourse." Some courts kept honoring the claims of long established couples even if they had no formalities behind them. But by the nineteenth century's end, for the most part marriage in the United States had also become a public, state-regulated status—bestowed by a central authority, hedged by registries, licenses, fees, and witnesses.

So had the Protestants and the nation-states won a complete triumph over the marriage rules, sweeping all competitors off the field? Perhaps—for a while. But just as state power over marriage peaked in the nineteenth century, there came an upswelling of civil disobedience against externally imposed marriage rules. Just when every civilized Victorian had come to believe that the regulation of marriage and family life was not merely essential to State order but had always and would always exist, that publicly bestowed marriage was the *only* kind of marriage, there arose a romantically rebellious movement insisting that individual spirits, and *not* the family, church, or state, are what create and legitimate each marriage. "Free love"—the idea that the heart made its own marriages, that any law enforcing or policing it was a spiritual travesty—swept not just the poor folks who had long ducked church or state marriage regulation, but the educated classes.

One needn't be a **Marxist** to see how easily "free love" could bubble up from the contradictions within the industrializing democracies. On the one hand, the capitalist states needed and glorified the individual and his (yes, his) imagination and conscience, freed from parental control to run the new economy. On the other hand, as a kind of seatbelt against the new economy's rollercoaster of social change—as if controlling marriage were more important than controlling ***laissez faire*** robber barons—those states were strapping people more tightly into marriage than ever before. Some couldn't stand the contradiction.

laissez faire: (French) "to allow to do"; theory or system believing that government should intervene as little as possible in economic or other affairs

The Victorian free-lovers were fierce moralists, taking seriously the romantic rhetoric on which they'd been raised. Because they believed that the heart makes and unmakes marriages, they insisted that marriage law actually worsened and coarsened spouses, enforcing sin by keeping them legally bound once they disliked each other—and, not coincidentally, legally turning women into helpless maidservants and men into tyrants. Their fervent theories often came from painful conflict with state-enforced marriage. In the 1840s, for instance, when Mary Gove Nichols fled a husband who beat her, she also lost the legal battle to contact her children, as was common for wives who rebelled against the vow to obey. And so when she and her new "husband" Thomas Nichols—husband in life, though not in law—described the situation of a modern wife, their list of legal facts was illumined by her experience:

> Married, she becomes his property, and may become his victim, his slave. She must live where he wishes her to live; she must submit to his embraces, however loathsome; she must bear his children, whether she wish to do so, or not; her property, her liberty, her comfort, her person, her life, are all in his power. He will probably be punished for an outright murder by poison or steel, but there are many ways of killing, which she has no power to resist. The subject of his caprices, the victim of

24. In Your Journal: Explain the concept of "free love" and its use of "romantic rhetoric."

Marxist: in the spirit of Karl Marx (1818–1883), German philosopher, economist, and revolutionary who believed that class struggle is central to understanding society

> his lusts, starved in her sympathies . . . this human being has but one duty, and that is *obedience.*

25. In Your Journal: What did Mary Gove and Thomas Nichols mean by "there are many ways of killing . . ."?

26. In Your Journal: How was the "free love" doctrine similar to that of the early Catholic Church?

The free-lovers took the radical idea at the heart of Catholic marriage theology—the idea that mutual consent is the sacrament—to its logical limit, insisting that "what the law calls fornication, when it is the union of mutual love, may be the holiest action two human beings can engage in . . . as it is sanctified by a mutual sentiment and attraction to which no law or ceremony can impart any additional sanction." And they went farther, insisting, "It is marriage, and the license which it gives, which debauches, enervates, degrades, and pollutes society!"

You can imagine the socially shocking consequences. As the notorious free-lover, feminist, spiritualist, and general hell-raiser Victoria Woodhull thundered from her pulpits, "Who will dare say that love should not be a precedent to marriage? But when this is affirmed, the legitimate **corollary** is not seen: that, since marriage should not begin without love it should cease when love is gone." Wives should be able to say no when their husbands wanted sex; marriages should dissolve when affection failed; husbands and wives should be equal in private and in law; and no **imprimatur** should be needed for sexual relations beside the heart and God. In other words, once the pendulum had swung so sharply toward an understanding of marriage as a *publicly* bestowed status, the free-lovers wanted to define it again as an internal state. And now, back to the *verba!*

corollary: easily drawn conclusion that follows from a previous proposition

imprimatur: sanction or approval; support

apotheosize: deify; glorify

The orderly Victorians, with their newly **apotheosized** family, were appalled: common-law marriage was one thing; open *defiance* of marriage was quite another. Leo Miller was arrested and jailed when he left his wife and openly moved in with his lover, declaring their opposition to marriage in a local free-love paper. Mary Gove Nichols was stripped of her children when she fled her abusive husband and ended up among the free-lovers. "Free love" was an **imprecation** hurled (often accurately) at all sorts of radicals, from **Margaret Sanger** to **Emma Goldman,** as a hint that clean-minded Americans should recoil from the sexual filth that lurked beneath any **putatively** high-minded movement.

imprecation: curse; malediction

putatively: commonly regarded as such; reputed; supposed

And of course, "free love" won.

Yes, it won. The nineteenth-century free-lovers' agenda now runs Western codes of sexuality and marriage (that is, if you leave out the item on the agenda that calls for the institution's complete destruction). The ability to dissolve marriage when love dissolves; the freedom to form sexual relationships based on affection, without state sanction or intervention; equality between spouses in everything from property ownership to di-

27. In Your Journal: Do you agree that free love won?

Margaret Sanger: (1883–1966) American leader of the birth control movement

Emma Goldman: (1869–1940) Russian immigrant to America and activist for anarchy vorce; the idea that affection and companionship are marriage's main goals: the free-lovers' demands have been absorbed into our laws. Or to put it differently, although the nation-states are still registering and tracking marriage, our society has begun moving back to the old and honorable idea that marriage is something made by the couple, not by any outside authority—and has integrated some radically modern ideas about sexual equality and individualism.

The free-love triumph has happened in daily life, in marriage statutes, and in court. In the 1960s, the Western nation-states, which had launched their control over marriage with such comprehensive absolutism, started pulling out of the business of regulating intimate life—freeing love from law, and in very dramatic language striking down such restrictions on marriage as race, debt, imprisonment, and employer approval. "The right to marry is an individual right *d'ordre public* which cannot be restricted or alienated; . . . the freedom to marry should in principle be safeguarded," wrote the highest French court in 1968, deciding—in a radical break with historical precedent—that an employer could not terminate an employee for marrying. In the United States, *Loving* v. *Virginia* was written up in similarly freedom-touting language, saying, "The freedom to marry has long been recognized as one of the vital personal rights essential to the orderly pursuit of happiness . . . one of the 'basic civil rights of man' . . . and cannot be infringed by the State." Or as comparative legal scholar Mary Ann Glendon writes, in the middle of the twentieth century Western courts—all at once—started "sloganizing" about marriage. As if out of nowhere, "the idea of a basic individual right to marry has emerged. . . . a banner has been raised over the slowly shifting **minutiae** of marriage law. The banner is one of the gaily-colored pennants of the pursuit of happiness, and the words inscribed on it are 'Freedom to Marry' and 'Marriage—A Basic Human Right.'"

minutiae: precise details; small or trifling matters

It is firmly within the main current of this triumphing marriage ideology that [my partner] Madeline and I stand. We say we are married—and so we are, in all but law. If the inner life is what makes a marriage, who could have the **hubris** to judge the quality and commitment of mine? When the state has been sweeping away all shackles on marriage except the heart's bond, how can it, in justice, refuse to recognize ours?

hubris: excessive pride; arrogance

28. In Your Journal: What do you deduce as the author's stance on the issue of marriage? Which notions does Graff reject and which does she embrace?

To which definition do you subscribe? Do you believe you are married when you pledge yourself to your spouse, or when the state writes you into its registries? For most people the public vows and the state's acknowledgment are simultaneous—although that's not always so, as when Richard and Mildred Loving were refused recognition by Virginia. If you define marriage as the inner, immanent state, then perhaps you recognize that Madeline and I already *are* married. If you accept the more recent definition of marriage as something conferred by public authority, then perhaps you'll recognize that it has been changing since it first gained the field, and that we belong under its widening twentieth-century "Freedom to Marry" banner.

29. In Your Journal: Answer the questions that Graff poses at the end of the essay. Do you feel that your opinions on the matter have changed by reading this essay or have they remained intact? Why or why not?

FOR USE IN DISCUSSION

Questions about Substance

1. Graff says marriage "doesn't exist" unless both partners in the union "behave as married" and society "treats them as such" (390). What would exist if either of those conditions were removed? Can't someone be legally married without "behaving as such"? Would they be more "married" than a couple who behaves as such but cannot be legally recognized as such?
2. Examine Graff's discussion about the legal concept of "consent" (394). What do you think it means to "consent" to marriage? Is this consent similar to or different from "consent" to have a medical surgery or "consent" to be interviewed by the police about a crime? And how do religious gods play a role in the activity of human "consent" when it comes to marriage? Can "consent" be both a legal and a religious concept?
3. Does it surprise you that Graff wants to be a part of an institution with such a sordid history, as she presents it? None of the "versions" of marriage presented are particularly attractive in an objective sense, yet even the author of this critique seems, on some level, to want to marry.

Questions about Structure and Style

1. There are four epigraphs to this essay. What do they collectively suggest about the subject of marriage? What order is there to their arrangement?
2. Graff's essay is largely chronological in structure. How would the essay be different if it were organized according to themes or issues (e.g., love, money, religion, community, etc.), and just brought the historical examples in for comparison? Do you think the chronological structure helps or hurts Graff's argument?
3. How does Graff's rather personal conclusion tie up her broad sweeping examination of the huge historical institution of marriage?

Multimedia Suggestions

1. Watch Michael Apted's documentary *Married in America* (2002) and see the companion Web site, *http://www.aetv.com/tv/shows/married/ index.html*, for contextual information. What view is presented of the contemporary marriage? How do any of Graff's analyses apply to Apted's subjects?
2. Read the interview with E. J. Graff at *http://www.uua.org/world/0399feat3.html* by a member of the Unitarian Universalist Association, which explores the ramifications of Graff's analysis on the issue of same-sex marriage. What are your thoughts about this issue? If marriage is about love and commitment, then should gay and lesbian couples be able to marry? If marriage is about a law requiring one man and one woman to marry, then is love really a requirement?

Finally, if marriage is a religious rite, then why do marriages have to be recognized by the state to be valid?

SUGGESTIONS FOR WRITING AND RESEARCH

1. What is your personal view of marriage? Do you find it a romantic ideal? Is it a practical contract? Do you think it's outdated? Compare your perspective to Graff's, citing personal examples or anecdotes as well as passages from Graff's text to make your point.
2. What is in store for this institution that has gone through so many radically different stages? What are the state and the fate of contemporary marriage? Compare your speculations to the different historical developments Graff presents. Feel free to do outside research on current marriage trends to expand on your theory.
3. A number of new "reality shows" end with the event of a marriage proposal. How does this new trend fit into Graff's critique of marriage as a public institution? How real are these marriages?
4. Marriage the institution (whether religious or legal) seems to have become eclipsed by the multimillion-dollar wedding industry. Research the language and symbols of a traditional wedding ceremony (whether Christian, Jewish, Hindu, secular, or other), and compare the traditions to any weddings you have recently attended or seen in film or on television. How do you suppose Graff feels about the wedding industry, given her argument here? Make references to the text wherever possible.

WORKING WITH CLUSTERS

Cluster 5: The Law and the Public
Cluster 14: Epistemologies
Discipline: The Social Sciences
Rhetorical Mode: Definition

"The Next Brainiacs" (from *Wired*, August 2001)

by John Hockenberry

Most widely known as a Dateline NBC *correspondent, John Hockenberry was also a longtime foreign correspondent and reporter for National Public Radio and ABC. He has been a paraplegic since the age of 19, when he was in an automobile accident. He wrote a memoir about his experiences called* Moving Violations: War Zones, Wheelchairs, and Declarations of Independence, *which he later performed as the one-man off-Broadway show,* Spokeman. *He has received two Peabody awards and an Emmy award. His second book is* River out of Eden, *a novel set in the Pacific Northwest. This essay was first published in* Wired *magazine in 2001.*

zeitgeist: spirit of the time

specs: abbreviation for specifications for workmanship

1. In Your Journal: Why does the author claim that the "disabled have a serious advantage in this conversation"?

2. In Your Journal: What tone is conveyed by the author's word choice (e.g. "sob-story crap")?

interface: shared boundary between surfaces, regions, or two systems exchanging data

platform: foundational staging for activity (including computer activity)

3. In Your Journal: Does it surprise you to hear the author describe the disabled as "puppets"?

4. In Your Journal: What picture does the condition "locked-in syndrome" conjure in your mind?

When you think disability, think **zeitgeist.** I'm serious. We live at a time when the disabled are on the leading edge of a broader societal trend toward the use of assistive technology. With the advent of miniature wireless tech, electronic gadgets have stepped up their invasion of the body, and our concept of what it means and even looks like to be human is wide open to debate. Humanity's **specs** are back on the drawing board, thanks to some unlikely designers, and the disabled have a serious advantage in this conversation. They've been using technology in collaborative, intimate ways for years—to move, to communicate, to interact with the world.

When you think disability, free yourself from the sob-story crap, all the oversize shrieking about people praying for miracles and walking again, or triumphing against the odds. Instead, think puppets. At a basic level, physical disability is really just a form of puppetry. If you've ever marveled at how someone can bring a smudged sock puppet to life or talked back to Elmo and Grover, then intellectually you're nearly there. Puppetry is the original brain-machine **interface.** It entertains because it shows you how this interface can be ported to different **platforms.**

If puppetry is the clever mapping of human characteristics onto a nonhuman object, then disability is the same mapping onto a still-human object. Making the body work regardless of physical deficit is not a challenge I would wish on anyone, but getting good at being disabled is like discovering an alternative platform. It's closer to puppetry than anything else I can think of. I should know: I've been at it for 25 years. I have lots of moving parts. Two of them are not my legs. When you think John Hockenberry, think wheelchair. Think alternative platform. Think puppet.

Within each class of disability, there are different forms of puppetry, different people and technologies interacting to solve various movement or communication problems. The goal, always, is to project a whole human being, to see the puppet as a character rather than a sock or a collection of marionette strings.

When you meet Johnny Ray, it's a challenge to see the former drywall contractor and amateur musician trapped inside his body, but he's there. Ray, a 63-year-old from Carrollton, Georgia, suffered a brain-stem stroke in 1997, which produced what doctors call "locked-in syndrome": He has virtually no moving parts. Cognitively he's intact, but he can't make a motion to deliver that message or any other to the world.

Getting a puppet with no moving parts to work sounds like a task worthy of the **Buddha,** but a pioneering group of neuroscientists affiliated with Emory University in Atlanta has taken a credible stab at it. In a series of animal and human experiments dating back to 1990, Philip Kennedy, Roy Bakay, and a team of researchers have created a basic but completely functional alternative interface using electrodes surgically implanted in the brain. In 1996, their success with primates convinced the FDA to allow two human tests. The first subject, whose name was withheld to protect her privacy, was a woman in the terminal stages of ALS (Lou Gehrig's disease); she died two months after the procedure. The second was Johnny Ray.

Kennedy, who invented the subcranial cortical implant used in these operations, wanted to create a device that could acquire a signal from inside the brain—a signal robust enough to travel through wires and manipulate objects in the physical world. Making this happen involved creating new access points for the brain, in addition to the natural ones (defunct in Ray's case) that produce muscle motion. Bakay has since moved to Rush-Presbyterian-St. Luke's Medical Center in Chicago, where he's part of an institute devoted entirely to alternative brain-body interfaces. The soft-spoken doctor wouldn't describe anything he does as show business, but to me the results of his work sound like a real-world version of the nifty plug Neo/Keanu sported in *The Matrix.*

5. In Your Journal: Why does the author make reference to the science fiction film *The Matrix* here?

"We simply make a hole in the skull right above the ear, near the back end of the motor cortex, secure our electrodes and other hardware to the bone so they don't migrate, and wait for a signal," Bakay says. The implant is an intriguing hybrid of electronics and biology—it physically melds with brain tissue.

"We use a small piece of glass shaped like two narrow cones into which a gold electrical contact has been glued," Bakay says. "The space in the cones is filled with a special tissue culture, and the whole thing is placed inside the motor cortex." The tissue culture is designed to "attract" brain cells to grow toward the contact. When brain cells meet gold, the electrical activity of individual cells is detectable across the electrode. Gold wires carry signals back out of the skull, where they are amplified. This produces a far more sensitive and usable signal than you get from surface technology like the taped-on electrodes used in EEGs.

To get a broad sense of what the patient's brain is doing, neurologists perform magnetic resonance imaging and compare changes in the motor cortex with voltages monitored through the electrodes. Then the doctors get really clever. The patient is encouraged to think simple thoughts that correspond to distinct conditions and movements, like hot/cold or

---

Buddha: (Siddhartha Gautama) (563?–483? B.C.) Indian philosopher and founder of Buddhism, which specifies that suffering is inseparable from existence

codify: systematize

up/down. Gradually, the doctors extract and **codify** electrical patterns that change as a patient's thoughts change. If a patient can reproduce and trigger the signal using the same thought patterns, that signal can be identified and used to control, say, a cursor on a computer screen. The technique is very crude, but what Bakay and his colleagues have demonstrated is a truly alternative brain-body interface platform.

Ray's implant was installed in 1998, and he survived to start working with the signals, which were amplified and converted to **USB input** for a Dell Pentium box. In the tests that followed, Ray was asked to think about specific physical motions—moving his arms, for example. Kennedy and Bakay took the corresponding signal and programmed it to move the cursor. By reproducing the same brain pattern, Ray eventually was able to move the cursor at will to choose screen icons, spell, even generate musical tones.

That this was in fact an alternative platform, a true brain-machine interface, was demonstrated after months of tests, when Ray reported that the thoughts he used to trigger the electrode—imagined arm motions—were changing. He was now activating the electrode by thinking about facial movements, and as he manipulated the cursor, doctors could see his cheeks move and his eyes flutter. Kennedy and Bakay had predicted that Ray's focused mental activity might result in neurological changes, but to see actual facial movements was a surprise. It didn't mean that his paralysis was receding, rather that his brain had tapped into capabilities rendered dormant by the stroke. The results showed that Ray's thoughts about motion were triggering clusters of motor neurons.

How? Kennedy and Bakay presumed the implant had put various motion centers in Ray's brain back into play. Disconnected from the body/hardware they once controlled, these neurons now had a crude way to interact. Adapting to the new platform, Ray's brain was demonstrating a flexibility standard worthy of **Java or Linux.**

As the brain cells in and around Ray's implant did what he asked them to do, the imagined sensation of moving his body parts gradually disappeared altogether. One day when his skill at moving the cursor seemed particularly adept, the doctors asked Ray what he was feeling. Slowly, he typed "nothing."

Ray was interacting directly with the cursor in a way similar to how he might once have interacted with his hand. "People don't think, 'move hand' to move their hands unless they are small children just learning," Bakay explains. "Eventually the brain just eliminates these intermediate

---

USB input: (Universal Serial Bus) protocol for connecting external devices to computers

---

Java or Linux: open source code (for software engineering); allows the user access to the code behind a program, and therefore more control over it steps until the hand feels like a part of the brain." The description reminds me of how I've heard **Isaac Stern** describe his violin as an extension of his body. I think of my wheelchair the same way.

The fact that Ray's cursor is indistinguishable from almost any other **prosthesis** raises an important philosophical question: Because of the implant, is a Dell Pentium cursor now more a part of Johnny Ray than one of his own paralyzed arms?

prosthesis: artificial limb or body part

6. In Your Journal: How would you answer the question the author poses here about Johnny Ray's cursor? What does the question suggest about the human body in general?

The National Institutes of Health is interested enough in this technology to have provided $1.1 million in seed funding for an additional eight human tests that will continue over the coming year. Bakay hopes the next patients won't be as profoundly disabled as the first two. "The more kinds of applications we find for this," Bakay says, "the more we learn about it."

From my perspective as a wheelchair puppet, life is a question of optimizing the brain-machine interface. In the beginning, this was far from obvious to me. My spinal cord was injured in a car accident when I was 19—an utterly random occurrence in which a woman picked me up while I was hitchhiking and later fell asleep at the wheel. She died. But I emerged from her crumpled car, then from a hospital, and resumed my life. I looked for a way to describe what I was doing: Rehabilitation was a word for it. Courage was a word for it. Coping was a word for it. But none of those labels even approached the reality of what relearning physical life was all about.

7. In Your Journal: According to the author, the labels "rehabilitation," "courage," and "coping" all fall short in describing his effort to relearn his physical life. What does he mean by this?

Since then I've been improvising motion by merging available body functionality (arms, hands, torso, neck, head) with a small arsenal of customized machines (wheelchairs, grabbers, cordless phones, remote controls, broomsticks with a bent nail pounded into the end). At times I've seen my own quest for new physical ability in odd places—a musician seeking virtuosity, an athlete seeking perfection. I've become convinced that the process of fine-tuning one's mobility through practice and the use of tools is as old as humanity itself. I've come to believe it is identical to an infant's task of developing coordination while facing near-zero available functionality of legs, arms, and muscles.

There is no better puppet show than watching your own children teach themselves to walk. In my case, it involved watching Zoë and Olivia, my twin daughters. Their strategies were complicated improvisations that proceeded from observing the world around them. Olivia made especially good use of her hands and arms, grabbing tables, drawer handles, and the spokes on my wheelchair to pull herself upright, where she would stand in place for long periods of time, feeling the potential in her chubby little legs.

Zoë spent weeks on her stomach flapping like a seal, hoping somehow to launch spontaneously onto her feet. She did not see her legs as helpful, and to her credit, in our house walking was merely one of two

Isaac Stern: (1920–) American virtuoso violinist

major models for locomotion. One morning, well before she was 2 years old and long before she walked, I placed Zoë in my wheelchair and watched as she immediately grabbed the wheels and began to push herself forward as though she'd been doing it for years. She had even figured out how to use the different rotation rates of the rear wheels to steer herself. Zoë had grasped that the wheelchair was the most accessible motion platform for someone—in this case, an infant—who couldn't use her legs. She smiled as she looked at me, with an expression that said something like, "Give up the wheels, Mr. Chairhog."

> ***8. In Your Journal:*** What does Hockenberry find so interesting about the way his twin daughters learned to walk?

Zoë and Olivia walk perfectly now, but their choices in those formative weeks were startlingly different. In both, the same brain-machine transaction was at work creating functionality from what was available. Engineers and designers have discovered that this is a process as distinctive as fingerprints. Every person solves problems in his or her own way, with a mix of technology and body improvisation. The variables are cultural and psychological, and precise outcomes are difficult to predict—but they determine what technology will work for which person. Think puppetry as a universal metaphor for the design of machines.

cyborg: robot with human qualities

Jim Jatich has been a **cyborg** puppet for years now and is proud of it. A 53-year-old former engineering technician and draftsman from Akron, Ohio, Jatich is a quadriplegic who first donated his body to science back in 1978. A near-fatal diving accident the year before left him without use of his legs and hands, and with limited use of muscles in his arms and shoulders.

expansion port: connector for adding more memory, processing power, or special purpose interfaces such as networks

local area network: network of computers sharing information

The computer term **expansion port** was unknown back in the late '70s, but Jatich's doctors at Case Western Reserve University in Cleveland arrived at the same idea. They imagined building an alternative path around Jatich's injured spinal cord to restore a **local area network** that could be controlled by his brain.

In a series of operations and therapies starting in 1986, Jatich became the first human to receive surgically implanted electrodes in his hands to mimic nerves by stimulating the muscles with tiny bursts of electricity. The process is known as functional electrical stimulation, or FES. By using a shoulder-mounted joystick to trigger patterns of electrical impulses, Jatich was able to open and close his hands. Others have since used the technology to move leg muscles and allow the exercise of paralyzed limbs.

Two years ago, a research assistant named Rich Lauer came to Jatich with the suggestion that he think about tapping into his brain directly. "This one sounded real crazy," Jatich says. "He claimed he had a way to see if I could control first a computer cursor and then maybe the muscles of my hand, just by thinking. I thought it was BS," he says with a wink. "You know, brain science."

Researchers placed a skullcap containing 64 electrodes on Jatich's head. These produced a waveform of his brain activity, though the signal was much weaker than the one obtained from Johnny Ray's cortical implants. Like Ray's doctors, the researchers asked Jatich to concentrate on simple but opposite concepts like up and down. They carefully observed the EEG for readable changes in brain patterns. They used software to measure the maximums and minimums in his overall brain wave and to calculate the moving averages in exactly the same way stock analysts try to pull signals from the jagged data noise of the stock market. A pattern was identified and fashioned as a switch: Above the average equaled on; below the average, off. With this switch they could control a cursor's direction and, as a **hacker** might say, they were "in."

9. In Your Journal: Hockenberry compares Jim Jatich's doctors to computer hackers: How apt is this comparison?

hacker: someone who "breaks in" to a remote computer, server, or Web site without permission

While Jatich's doctors worked to optimize the software, he concentrated on a wall-size computer screen. Monitoring changes in his EEG and modifying the programming accordingly produced a kind of **biofeedback.** Gradually, like Johnny Ray, Jatich was able to move a flashing cursor to the middle of a projected line. The goal was to have the computer search for distinct, recallable brain-wave patterns that could be used to control any number of devices that could be connected to a chip.

biofeedback: conscious attempt to regulate an involuntary bodily function

Jatich says there was nothing portable about the equipment—he found the electrode skullcap cumbersome and the whole system a bit rickety. "Cell phones down the hall at the hospital would cause the thing to go blank every once in a while." But the enterprise did deliver a breakthrough he hadn't anticipated.

"When I got downstairs after the first couple of experiments," he says, "I was sitting outside, waiting for my ride, and it hit me. I had caused something to move just by using my mind alone. The tears streamed down my face, because it was the first time I had done that since I got injured." Jatich says he felt like "a kid being handed keys to a car for the first time."

10. In Your Journal: Jatich describes a breakthrough in his treatment as making him feel like "a kid being handed keys to a car for the first time." What do you think he means by this?

Going from manually controlled FES to brain implants that bypass the spinal cord to produce muscle movement would represent a significant leap. But Ron Triolo, a professor of orthopedics and biomedical engineering at Case Western and a clinician at the Cleveland FES Center, thinks this is possible. He sees this leap as the possible fulfillment of FES's many, often **outsize,** promises for people with disabilities. The challenge is immense, but, as Triolo puts it, "Failure is closer to success than doing nothing. I've seen some of the preliminary work on cortical control and it's impressive. Clearly, it's going to pay off eventually."

outsize: unusually large

11. In Your Journal: "Failure is closer to success than doing nothing." Do you agree with this statement? What does it mean?

Since Jatich's first implantable hand device was installed, the technology for nerve stimulation has advanced to the point where the reliable, long-lasting electrodes in both of his hands are barely visible, require practically zero maintenance, and have become more or less permanent parts of his body. For the last 15 years, he's used a shoulder joystick controller to move his right hand. Controlling his left hand is an IJAT, or implantable joint angle transducer, which employs a magnet and sensor attached to the bones of the wrist. Slight movements trigger complex hand-grasping motions. The computer mounted on the back of Jatich's wheelchair stores the software that helps produce as many as five different motions, which he can specify depending on whether he wants to hold a pencil and write or grasp a utensil and feed himself—capabilities he would not otherwise have at all.

Over the years, Jatich has gone from being a person completely dependent on others to having some degree of autonomy. His grasping ability means he can use a computer and feed himself, among other simple tasks. In the past few years, Jatich has been able to do some mechanical drawing, using his hand devices along with commercially available computer-aided design systems.

Thinking about taking the next step—an implant that might allow him to connect his brain, via computer, to his electrode-filled hands—excites him. "You could sure get a hell of a signal from the surface of the brain as compared to the electrodes in that ugly skullcap," Jatich says. He speaks as though he's talking about a science fair project and not the tissue under his own cranium. "I would have to think hard about it, but if they could deliver on their promises, it would be great. I would do it in a minute."

Suddenly, million-dollar grants are being thrown around to investigate the possibilities of direct interaction with the brain. While much of the study is geared toward finding ways to reopen avenues closed by massive paralysis, it also raises the possibility of creating alternative brain outlets to the world in addition to the ones we were born with. The FDA won't allow it yet, but there's no scientific barrier preventing some brave pioneer from adding a new ability—for instance, a brain-controlled wireless device to regulate climate and lighting in one's home. In November, British **cybernetics** professor Kevin Warwick plans to have a chip implanted next to his arm's central nerve bundle so he can experiment with sending and receiving digital signals (see "*Cyborg 1.0*," *Wired* 8.02, page 144).

cybernetics: study of information flow between machines and biology

Deep brain stimulation is the overarching term for the therapies in development, and specific projects are under way to address severe nervous system disorders like Parkinson's disease, TBI (traumatic brain injury), and other locked-in syndromes. The NIH has embarked on an aggressive program to develop cortical control devices as the first truly practical neuroprostheses. This is a kind of **low-bandwidth** alternative to the field of spinal cord research focused on repairing injured spinal tissue and restoring the original brain-muscle connection.

low-bandwidth: capable of transmitting low quantities of data per second

Dubbed "the Cure" by its passionate supporters, savvy marketers, and fundraisers, this vision of spinal cord repair has a much higher profile and is far better financed than FES and other alternative-interface explorations. The Cure has Christopher Reeve as its cash-gushing poster boy. FES has Jim Jatich. Cortical implant technology has Johnny Ray. Certainly, anyone who wakes up with a spinal cord injury is inclined to hope for a cure above all other options. But one would expect medical research strategies to be more detached from the emotional trauma of disability. As someone who has lived in a wheelchair comfortably for a quarter century, it is hard to justify why the Cure would be so favored over its alternatives.

12. In Your Journal: How is "the Cure" different from the neuro-prostheses that Hockenberry reports on? Why do you think the Cure offers more hope and attraction than its apparently more "successful" alternatives?

Rush-Presbyterian's Roy Bakay expresses some frustration that his efforts directly compete with the Cure movement for funding. "We can do things for people now, whereas spinal cord research isn't going to pay off for a very long time, if at all. I'm not saying that spinal cord research shouldn't be conducted, just that [deep-brain stimulation] may be a more immediate solution for getting the brain to interact with the outside world." Others report that Reeve's visibility has made it more difficult to find people willing to try new technology involving surgery or implants. "They say they want to keep their bodies in good shape for when the Cure happens," says Jatich, who often counsels people considering FES.

Reeve was injured in a 1995 horse-riding accident; he can't move anything below his neck and needs assistance to breathe. Despite declaring shortly after the accident that he would someday walk again, Reeve is not pro-Cure to the exclusion of all other options. He has carefully maintained that he supports any endeavor that might help people with disabilities. He has muted his personal predictions about walking again, though he is still dedicated to the Cure. The movement Reeve helped create represents those who believe the body is the brain's best interface to the outside world. Certainly, there's nothing on the market to give the fully functioning body any serious competition. Yet for people without one, supplementing bodies with onboard technology to increase functionality is a way around the wait for a full cure.

It's a familiar trade-off: As every technology develops, there is the tension of using the interesting but cumbersome first-wave device versus waiting until the tech is small enough, convenient enough, or integrated enough with the body to bother with it. This trade-off has been debated within the disabled community for generations, and it is just starting to be reflected in the broader culture.

The field with perhaps the best track record in dealing with complicated brain-machine interfaces is communications technology for the sensory- and voice-impaired. It's also the area in which the trade-offs between functionality and ease of use are most critical. With computers, turning text into voice is considerably easier than making a device that operates with the ease and speed of speech.

"There is a real issue of gadget tolerance, and people have finite limits," says Frank DeRuyter, chief of speech pathology at Duke University Medical Center and a leader in the field of augmented communication. "Our smart systems need to be environmentally sensitive or they don't get used." DeRuyter has worked with all kinds of communications devices, from primitive boards—little more than alphabets and pictures used by

13. In Your Journal: What does "gadget tolerance" mean? How does it compete with the functionality of new designs?

noncommunicators to slowly construct sentences by pointing—to more sophisticated electronic speech-synthesis devices. All have their own advantages and disadvantages, which are ignored at a designer's peril.

DeRuyter describes how designers can be locked into narrow functionality traps that keep them from seeing the world the way the disabled do. "Talking is a portable communications system that enhances every other activity. We used to put some of our noncommunicators into the pool each day, and we could never figure out why they hated it. Then we realized that by removing electronic communications boards that couldn't tolerate water, their pool time was the equivalent of being gagged. We designed some simple, waterproof alphabet boards and the problem went away. Pool time became fun."

Michael B. Williams is an augmented communications technology user and a disability rights activist from Berkeley, California. He relies on three devices to communicate: two VOCAs (voice output communication aids, basically chip-controlled text-to-voice synthesizers) and a low-tech waterproof alphabet board. The board, he told me in an email, is there "for when California's power goes out," and for "private thoughts in the shower." Williams' smaller VOCA is a spell-and-speak device that is handy enough for dinner table conversations. His largest and most advanced VOCA is "heavy and hard on the knees," but has rapid word access that enables Williams to give public speeches in a kind of partial-playback mode, which he has been doing for years now.

Diagnosed with cerebral palsy as a young child, Williams struggled with the speech therapy recommended by medical and educational professionals to enable him to control his mouth and use his own voice. His eventual rejection of this mode of communication was a simple technology decision; the brain-machine interface called speech is, in his case, seriously flawed. He describes his voice as being "like used oatmeal," and he has instead acquired the tech to live on his own terms, according to his personal specifications. When Williams gives speeches, his advanced VOCA offers the choice of 10 different programmed voices (he prefers the one called Huge Harry for himself). When he quotes someone, he uses a different voice, and it sounds like two people are on stage.

14. In Your Journal: Michael Williams prefers using "VOCAs" to trying to improve his natural but "seriously flawed" speech. Given his description of what his VOCAs can do, does he seem to sacrifice anything fundamentally human in making this choice?

"This bit of electronic tomfoolery seems to wow audiences," he says in an email, his sly showman's confidence coming through. So when you think about Williams, don't think courageous crippled guy giving a speech. Think puppetry, ventriloquism, **Stephen Hawking.**

Williams says it's impossible to evaluate any technology on function alone. For instance, he says the value of his ability to communicate is di-

---

Stephen Hawking: (1942–) British theoretical physicist (specializing in gravitational collapse) who suffers from Lou Gehrig's disease and speaks via a computer-generated voice rectly related to his mobility. "Someone recently asked me, 'If you were given a choice of having a voice or a power wheelchair, which would you choose?' This is a no-brainer for me. I would choose the power wheelchair. What would I do with only a voice—sit at home and talk to the TV? Another thing I wouldn't give up is my computer. With a computer and a modem I can get my thoughts, such as they are, out to the world."

Frank DeRuyter says designers need to think in the broadest possible terms when they approach human-interface technology. "We're just beginning to realize the importance of integrating movement technology with communications tech. We see that a GPS device can powerfully increase the functionality of a communications board. When people roll their wheelchairs into a grocery store, the GPS will automatically change the board's stored phrases and icons into ones relevant to shopping. Shifting context as you move—that's what the brain does. Now we can do it, too."

15. In Your Journal: "Shifting context as you move—that's what the brain does." Can you explain what it means to for the brain to "shift context"?

This idea of optimizing a personal brain-machine interface is as much an issue for engineers at Nokia, Motorola, and other manufacturers of wireless technology as it is for people designing for the disabled. Companies need people to actually buy and use their devices, not just gawk at them in glossy trade magazines. On a street in Manhattan last fall, it hit me: four people, one intersection. One man with a cell phone and headset was talking calmly and loudly, oblivious to the rest of the world. Another had a cell phone handset pressed to his head and was attempting to get a scrap of paper, one-handed, from his briefcase. A woman was at the pay phone looking for a quarter. The fourth person stood waiting for the light to change, looking at his wristwatch. If the four were frozen at that intersection, how would future **paleontologists** construe their fossilized differences? Four people, four different capabilities, four distinct species. Five, if you count me. Man with wheelchair . . . no cell phone.

16. In Your Journal: What purpose does Hockenberry's traffic light anecdote serve in the context of his larger argument? How does it relate to assistive technology for the disabled?

paleontologist: someone who studies life in prehistoric times

"There is a calculus in this field that we have come to know from decades of experience," says Ron Triolo of the Cleveland FES Center. "People don't want to lose anything they already have, and that includes wasted time, as well as an arm or a leg. But if they can increase functionality without losing anything, they want to do that.

"How we thought people would benefit from FES is different from what actual users have told us," he continues. "For instance, we imagined that FES would be of no value unless it was nearly invisible and provided a level of function comparable to the pre-injured state. We discovered we were talking from an ivory tower. People enjoy the ability to make even the most rudimentary physical motions and don't particularly care if those motions don't lead to jobs or activities associated with their life pre-injury."

Triolo describes novel ways in which disabled people have taken off-the-shelf equipment and used it in sometimes alarming ways, well beyond the designer's imagination. A man who uses his FES system to stand has improvised a way to clumsily hop up and down stairs. A female FES user recently sent Triolo a picture of herself standing, à la *Titanic,* on the bow of a boat under full sail. "If she had gone into the water . . ." He pauses to find words to convey both his fear (of massive product liability, perhaps) and his admiration for the woman's guts. In the end he can only say, "Well, you know."

17. In Your Journal: Can you think of any ways you use a piece of technology in an "alarming" manner—in other words, in a way that was not intended by the designer?

In my case, projecting my independence as a collaboration between machine, body, and brain is an important message, if difficult to convey. I can coast flat out and slalom effortlessly around pedestrians, and produce equal measures of awe and terror. No matter how skilled I am in my chair, people often wonder why I don't use a motorized one. I love using a machine I never have to read a manual to operate. Why can't they see the value of my ragged optimizing strategies? Think Xtreme sports, hot-dogging.

18. In Your Journal: Despite all of his praise of technological advancements, Hockenberry prefers a non-motorized wheelchair. Is this consistent or inconsistent with the general argument of this essay?

There are also deep cultural factors that sometimes surprise and frustrate designers of technology for the disabled. One of the first machine-to-brain devices, the cochlear implant, was heralded as a miracle cure for some forms of deafness when it was fully introduced in the 1990s. The electronic device, mounted inside the ear, works like FES on muscle tissue. In this case, the electrodes, responding to sound, stimulate different regions of the cochlea at a rate equivalent to a 91K modem. The cochlea, in turn, sends signals to the brain that can be processed as sound. The device requires training the brain to decipher the implant's stimulus and does not replace or completely restore hearing. Many deaf people view the implant as a form of ethnic cleansing and physical mutilation. The cochlear implant, according to opponents, is a direct confrontation to the shared experience of deafness, the language of signing, and all of the hot-dogging improvisations deaf people have developed over many generations to function without hearing.

19. In Your Journal: Why do you think, "Many deaf people view the [cochlear] implant as a form of ethnic cleansing and physical mutilation"?

Brenda Battat is the deputy executive director of Self-Help for Hard of Hearing People, a national organization in Bethesda, Maryland, that counsels people who are considering traditional hearing aids and cochlear implants. She believes opposition to the cochlear implant is moderating. Still, she says, technology requires an investment of time and emotion that engineers and users often aren't aware of. "Whatever technology you use, you're still a person with a hearing loss. When the battery breaks down, there is a moment of absolute panic. It's a very scary feeling." That feeling of dependence relates as much to the type A technoid having seizures over the dead batteries in his **BlackBerry** as it does to Johnny Ray adjusting to the imperfections of his brain implant. Anyone using an assistive technology system expects it will work every time, under a wide variety of conditions, without degrading any of their existing capabilities.

BlackBerry: handheld computer device for organizing personal information

Perhaps the best example of a technology solution that interacts directly with the brain is the Ibot wheelchair, now in the final stage of prelaunch testing by Johnson & Johnson and the FDA. Designer Dean Kamen wanted to create a transportation device that would have the equivalent functionality of walking, climbing stairs, standing upright, and all-terrain motion. To operate in upright, two-wheel stand-up mode, the Ibot uses an onboard computer and a system of miniaturized aviation-grade **gyros** to assess the center of gravity and deliver a signal to high-speed motors. These turn the wheels accordingly to compensate and keep the user from falling over.

gyro: spinning mass

My first impression of the machine was not positive. The Ibot is a cumbersome, complicated thing that makes you dread being stuck somewhere without a tool kit. But watch the Ibot balancing, making little rocking motions to keep it upright, and you feel as though you're in the presence of some humanoid intelligence.

When Kamen began testing his chair with disabled users, he discovered an eerie and unanticipated brain-machine interface. "Each person we took up the stairs said, 'Great.' They said great when we took them through the sand and the gravel and up the curb and down the curb. But when we stood them up and made them eye level with another person, and they could feel what it was like to balance, every single one of them started crying."

20. In Your Journal: Why did the Ibot testers start crying when they were balancing at eye level with another person?

Kamen believes that people who use the Ibot in its two-wheel balancing mode are literally feeling the experience of walking, even though the machine is doing the work. "If you could get an MRI picture of the balance center of the brain of some person in a wheelchair who goes up on the Ibot's two wheels, I bet you'd see some lights go on," he says. "I'm convinced the brain remembers balancing, and that's why people feel so much emotion."

I felt exactly that when I used the Ibot for the first time and stood upright. The chip was making the wheels move, but my brain's own sense of balance seemed to instantly merge with the machine. Its decisions seemed to be mine. No implants. No wires. It was truly extraordinary. Think **FDR** on a skateboard.

This raises a fairly revolutionary point about brains and the physical world. Bodies are perhaps a somewhat arbitrary evolutionary solution to issues of mobility and communication. By this argument, the brain has no particular preference for any physical configuration as long as functionality can be preserved.

FDR: (Franklin Delano Roosevelt) (1882–1945) 26th president responsible for the "New Deal" relief programs, meant to help the United States recover from the Depression and World War II; FDR suffered from polio, and famously stated, "the only thing we have to fear is fear itself"

Michael Williams believes that the disabled have helped humanity figure this out in terms of technology. He thinks people are rapidly losing their fear of gadgets. "The greatest thing people with disabilities have done for the general population is to make it safe to look weird. It's certainly true that the general population has glommed onto some principles of assistive tech. Just roll down the street and observe the folks with wires dangling from their ears. Look at the TV commercials featuring guys with computerized eyewear."

The history of assistive technology for the disabled shows that people will sacrifice traditional body image if they can have equivalent capabilities. It's a profound lesson for designers and people who irrationally fear brain implants. It perhaps has even more practical implications for people who are waiting for a cure to restore their functions. The brain-body-machine interface doesn't seem to need the body as much as we believe it does.

Think many different puppets . . . same show.

For those open to the possibility, the definition of human includes a whole range of biological-machine hybrids, of which I am only one. The ultimate promise of brain-machine technology is to add functionality—enhanced vision, hearing, strength—to people without disabilities. There is nothing of a technological nature to suggest that this can't happen, and in small but significant ways it has already begun. The organic merging of machine and body is a theme of human adaptation that predates the digital age.

> ***21. In Your Journal:*** How can the merging of machine and body be "organic"?

As I think about the quarter century I've spent in a wheelchair, there are almost no traditional concepts to describe the experience. As I weave around the obstructions of the world's low-bandwidth architecture, with its narrow doors and badly placed steps, I find my journey to be less and less some sentimental, stoic "go on with your life, brave boy" kind of thing and more part of a universal redrafting of the human design specification. I am drawn back to Michael Williams and his disarming motto: "The disabled have made it OK to look weird." There is such wisdom and promise in that statement.

People with disabilities—who for much of human history died or were left to die—are now, due to medical technology, living full lives. As they do, the definition of humanness has begun to widen. I remember encountering, on a street corner in Kinshasa in the former Zaire, a young man with the very same spinal cord injury as my own, rolling around in a fabulous, canopied hand-pedaled bike/wheelchair/street **RV.** He came up to me with a gleam of admiration for my chair and invited me to appreciate his solution to the brain-body interface problem. We shared no common language, but he immediately recognized how seamlessly my body and chair merged. That machine-body integrity is largely invisible to the people who notice only the medical/tragedy aspect of my experience. I could see

> **RV:** recreational vehicle equipped to function as a home away from home

how he had melded even more completely with his chair—in fact, it was almost impossible to see where his body left off and his welded-tube contraption began. It was clear he was grateful for my admiration.

> *22. In Your Journal:* Why is the young man in Kinshasa "grateful" for Hockenberry's "admiration"?

As time has passed, I am conscious of how little I miss specific functions of my pre-accident body, how little I even remember them in any concrete way. I used to think this was some psychological salve to keep me from being depressed over what has been a so-far irreversible injury. I have come to believe that what is really going on is a much more interesting phenomenon. My brain has remapped my physical functions onto the physical world by using my remaining nonparalyzed body, a variety of new muscle skills, tools, reconfigured strategies for movement and other functions, and by making the most of unforeseen advantages (good parking spaces, for instance). This is something that has taken me years to learn.

My daughters have never known any other way of looking at me. As they grow older, they will no doubt be introduced by people around them to the more conventional way of thinking about their poor, injured, incapacitated daddy. I suspect they will see the flaws in this old way of thinking far more quickly than their little friends who come though our house warily regarding the man in the purple chair with wheels.

In a straightforward way that needs no psychological jargon to explain, my former body simply doesn't exist anymore. Like Isaac Stern and his violin, I am now part chair, with some capabilities that exceed my original specifications.

> *23. In Your Journal:* Hockenberry calls himself "part chair." For Hockenberry, do you think this is like being "part French" or "part Native American"?

There's a very old story about a puppet that worked so hard to live in the real world, it eventually stopped being a puppet. The experience of interacting in the world connected this wooden puppet to the humans around him to the point where he was indistinguishable from them. An unstated corollary of the fable is that the humans were equally indistinguishable from the wooden puppet. I'm not lying.

> *24. In Your Journal:* For what purpose does the author invoke the story of Pinocchio?

Think Pinocchio. Think real boy.

FOR USE IN DISCUSSION

Questions about Substance

1. Throughout this essay, the body is represented as just another machine. In what ways is this analogy accurate? In what ways is it inaccurate?
2. When Hockenberry's daughters are learning to walk, he is amused by their different strategies (409–410). What is significant about the two examples? How do their methods compare to the uses of "assistive technology" that this piece is about?

3. Christopher Reeve (a.k.a. "Superman") is the spokesperson for "the Cure," which hopes to return those with spinal cord injuries to their pre-injury state (412–413). Why is Reeve such an appropriate spokesperson? How do you think his celebrity is both a help and a hindrance to the cause he represents?
4. The most explicit references to emotion in this story are when Jim Jatich first moves the cursor by thinking about it (411), and when the Ibot testers see eye-to-eye with others for the first time since their injuries (417). Why do you think references to emotion are kept to a minimum in this article?
5. "Michael Williams believes the disabled have helped humanity" figure out that the brain has "no preference for any physical configuration" (418). Does this theory have any implications beyond those for the disabled?

Questions about Structure and Style

1. The author discloses his own paralysis at the end of his introduction. What effect does this placement have?
2. The tone of the first two paragraphs could be described as "in your face." Why would Hockenberry take this approach with what could be perceived by many as a sensitive topic?
3. The author uses many different examples of disabled users of assistive technology (Johnny Ray, Michael Williams, Jim Jatich, and even himself). Do all of the examples serve the same purpose? How does each example contribute to Hockenberry's argument?
4. Note the number of times the author begins a sentence with the imperative "Think." What effect do you think he means to have on the reader by repeating this word in this tone?

Multimedia Suggestions

1. Check out the Web sites for Kevin Warwick (412), the cybernetics professor conducting ongoing experiments involving technological implants into his nervous system. What do you think of his experiments from an intellectual point of view? From an ethical point of view? Would you ever want to be involved in this type of experiment? Why or why not? See *http://www.kevinwarwick.org/* or *http://www.kevinwarwick.ork.uk/*.
2. View a movie that features "cyborg" characters (e.g., *AI* (2001), *The Matrix* (1999), the *Terminator* (1984), series, or any of the *Star Trek* films). Are the characters more human or more machine? Explain your answer.
3. View the art of some artists who must use some kind of "assistive technology" to do their artwork, at Eric Mohn: *http://www.ericmohn.com/index_ie.htm*; National Disability Arts Forum: *http://www.ndaf.org/artists.html*; and Very Special Arts: *http://www.vsarts.org/gallery/exhibits/disability/index.html*. Is this artwork suggestive of disability in any way? If so, does the suggestion strengthen the works? How do you think Hockenberry would perceive the combination of body and machine in this context?

SUGGESTIONS FOR WRITING AND RESEARCH

1. Research the movement for "the Cure," now called the "Christopher Reeve Paralysis Foundation," for which Christopher Reeve is the Chairman of the Board and primary spokesperson (see *http://www.christopherreeve.org/index.cfm*). What avenues of research on spinal cord injuries are they advocating? Are these ambitious long-term solutions in direct conflict with the more immediate benefits of assistive technology discussed by Hockenberry? Do you think that one approach should be prioritized? Write an essay about long-term versus short-term benefits in medical research, especially in relation to spinal cord injuries, using Hockenberry as support or as an adversary in the context of your argument.
2. Write an essay about someone with a disability who has exceeded expectations in some way or become a role model for others (with or without a disability). Ludwig von Beethoven, Helen Keller, Franklin Delano Roosevelt, Stephen Hawking, or Larry Flynt might be useful choices. How does the person you chose use his or her disability as a strength? Use Hockenberry for support, but also do outside research (look at biographies, autobiographies, news articles, etc.) so that you can include specific details about your subject.
3. The emerging science of digital biology posits not only that technology "evolves" in a manner similar to biology, but also that biology often behaves like a computer. See *http://www.biota.org/* or read Peter J. Bentley's book *Digital Biology*. Write an essay agreeing or disagreeing with this theory, and relating it to Hockenberry's argument.
4. In addition to the disabled being assisted by technology, many of us benefit from such advances in science. Often people are kept alive in the hospital by the use of technology (which we sometimes refer to as "artificial means") and many pregnancies and births are achieved by use of technological innovation (in some cases producing "test tube babies"). Is it "unnatural" to be assisted these ways? What is the difference between natural and unnatural assistance (e.g., an infant needing to be carried by a parent versus a paraplegic needing to be transported by a wheelchair)? Why does society see the unassisted body as the most "natural" and therefore the ideal?

WORKING WITH CLUSTERS

Cluster 9: Bodies of Knowledge
Cluster 17: Dis-Ability and Dis-Ease
Discipline: The Natural Sciences
Rhetorical Mode: Argument

"Occidentalism" (from *The New York Review of Books*, January 17, 2002)

by Avishai Margalit and Ian Buruma

Avishai Margalit

Born in Jerusalem where he still lives, Avishai Margalit is Schulman Professor of Philosophy at the Hebrew University in Jerusalem and lecturer at the Israeli Air Force Officer's School. He writes regularly for the New York Review of Books *and is a Peace Now activist. His books include* The Ethics of Memory, The Decent Society, *and* Idolatry.

Ian Buruma

Ian Buruma was born in the Netherlands to a Dutch father and English mother. Educated in both Holland and Japan, Buruma has also spent a great portion of his life in Asia. He is the author of the nonfiction works God's Dust: A Modern Asian Journey, Behind the Mask, *and* The Wages of Guilt: Memories of War in Germany and Japan, *as well as the fictional biography of an Indian prince in Britain, entitled* Playing the Game. *Buruma has also been a fellow at the Woodrow Wilson Institute for the Humanities in Washington, DC.*

In 1942, not long after the attack on **Pearl Harbor,** a group of Japanese philosophers got together in Kyoto to discuss Japan's role in the world. The project of this ultra-nationalist gathering was, as they put it, to find a way to "overcome modern civilization." Since modern civilization was another term for Western civilization, the conference might just as well have been entitled "Overcoming the West." In a complete reversal of the late-nineteenth-century goal of "leaving Asia and joining the West," Japan was now fighting a "holy war" to liberate Asia from the West and purify Asian minds of Western ideas. Part of the holy war was, as it were, an exercise in philosophical cleansing.

The cleansing agent was a mystical mishmash of German-inspired ethnic nationalism and **Zen**- and **Shinto**-based nativism. The Japanese were a "world-historical race" descended from the gods, whose divine task it was to lead all Asians into a new age of Great Harmony, and so on. But what was "the West" which had to be purged? What needed to be "overcome"? The question has gained currency, since the chief characteristics of this Western enemy would have sounded familiar to Osama bin Laden, and other Islamic extremists. They are, not in any particular order, materialism, liberalism, capitalism, individualism, humanism, rationalism, socialism, decadence, and moral laxity. These ills would be overcome by a show of Japanese force, not just military force, but force of will, of spirit, of soul. The key characteristics of the Japanese or "Asian" spirit were self-sacrifice, discipline, austerity, individual submission to the collective good, worship of divine leadership, and a deep faith in the superiority of instinct over reason.

1. In Your Journal: Compare the lists of characteristics of the Western and "Asian" culture. How would you summarize the differences?

There was of course more at stake in Japan's war with the West, but these were the philosophical underpinnings of Japanese wartime propaganda. The central document of Japan's claim to national divinity was entitled *Cardinal Principles of the National Polity* (*Kokutai no Hongi*). Issued in 1937 by the ministry of education, this document claimed that the Japan-

Pearl Harbor: attack by Japanese on U.S. Pacific naval fleet in Oahu, Hawaii on December 7, 1941, which launched the U.S. into World War II

Zen: school of Buddhism that asserts that Enlightenment can be attained through meditation and self-contemplation rather than faith and devotion

Shinto: ancient Japanese religion that combines elements of Buddhism and Confucianism ese were "intrinsically quite different from so-called citizens of Western nations," because the divine imperial bloodlines had remained unbroken, and "we always seek in the emperor the source of our lives and activities." The Japanese spirit was "pure" and "unclouded," whereas the influence of Western culture led to mental confusion and spiritual corruption.

Western, especially German, ideas inspired some of this. A famous right-wing professor, Dr. Uesugi Shinkichi, began his spiritual life as a Christian, studied statecraft in Wilhelminian Germany, and returned home to write (in 1919): "Subjects have no mind apart from the will of the Emperor. Their individual selves are merged with the Emperor. If they act according to the mind of the Emperor, they can realize their true nature and attain the moral ideal."[1] Of such stuff are holy warriors made.

2. In Your Journal: How do you think Westerners and/or Americans would define "realizing their true nature"?

Similar language—though without the neo-Shintoist associations—was used by German National Socialists and other European **fascists.** They, too, fought against that list of "soulless" characteristics commonly associated with liberal societies. One of the early critical books about Nazi thinking, by Aurel Kolnai, a Hungarian refugee, was actually entitled *The War Against the West.*[2] Nazi ideologues and Japanese militarist propagandists were fighting the same Western ideas. The West they loathed was a multinational, multicultural place, but the main symbols of hate were **republican** France, capitalist America, liberal England, and, in Germany more than Japan, the rootless **cosmopolitan** Jews. Japanese propaganda focused on the "Anglo-American beasts," represented in cartoons of **Roosevelt** and **Churchill** wearing **plutocratic** top hats. To the Nazis "the eternal Jew" represented everything that was hateful about liberalism.

fascist: advocate of government marked by dictatorship, stringent economic controls, suppression of opposition, nationalism, and often racism

republican: favoring a republic where citizens vote for their leaders

cosmopolitan: related or common to the whole world; sophisticated

plutocratic: of or relating to a government where the wealthy rule

War against the West is partly a war against a particular concept of citizenship and community. Decades before the coming of Hitler, the spiritual godfather of Nazism, Houston Stewart Chamberlain, described France, Britain, and America as hopelessly "Jewified" countries. Citizenship in these places had degenerated into a "purely political concept."[3] In England, he said, "every **Basuto** nigger" could get a passport. Later he complained that the country had "fallen utterly into the hands of Jews and Americans."[4] Germany in his view, and that of his friend Kaiser Wilhelm II, was the only nation with enough national spirit and racial solidarity to save

Roosevelt: (Franklin Delano) (1882–1945) 26th president responsible for the "New Deal" relief programs, meant to help the U.S. recover from the Depression and World War II; FDR suffered from polio, and famously remarked, "the only thing we have to fear is fear itself"

Churchill: (Sir Winston Leonard Spenser) (1874–1965) Prime Minister of England during World War II, famous for rousing speeches and refusal to make peace with Hitler

Basuto: (now Lesotho) a South African country that became a British protectorate in 1868 and gained independence in 1966

the West from going under in a sea of decadence and corruption. His "West" was not based on citizenship but on blood and soil.

> ***3. In Your Journal:*** What is the "particular concept of citizenship and community" anti-Western factions object to so strongly?

Oswald Spengler warned in **1933** (of all years) that the main threats to the Occident came from "colored peoples" (*Farbigen*).[5] He prophesied, not entirely without reason, huge uprisings of enraged peoples in the European colonies. He also claimed that after **1918** the Russians had become "Asiatic" again, and that the Japanese **Yellow Peril** was about to engulf the civilized world. More interesting, however, was Spengler's view that the ruling white races (*Herrenvölker*) were losing their position in Europe. Soon, he said, true Frenchmen would no longer rule France, which was already awash with black soldiers, Polish businessmen, and Spanish farmers. The West, he concluded, would go under because white people had become soft, decadent, addicted to safety and comfort. As he put it: "Jazz music and nigger dances are the death march of a great civilization."

If criticism of the West was influenced by half-baked ideas from Germany, more positive views of the West were also influenced by German ideas. The **Slavophiles** and the Westernizers, who offered opposing views of the West in nineteenth-century Russia, were both equally inspired by German intellectual currents. Ideas for or against the West are in fact to be found everywhere. The East does not begin at the river **Elbe,** as **Konrad Adenauer** believed, nor does the West start in **Prague,** as **Milan Kundera** once suggested. East and West are not necessarily geographical territories. Rather, Occidentalism, which played such a large part in the attacks of September 11, is a cluster of images and ideas of the West in the minds of its haters. Four features of Occidentalism can be seen in most versions of it; we can call them the City, the **Bourgeois,** Reason, and Feminism. Each contains a set of attributes, such as arrogance, feebleness, greed, depravity,

---

- **1933:** year the Nazis came to power
- **1918:** year World War I ended
- **Yellow Peril:** slur to describe the threat of Asian expansion in the minds of Westerners
- **Slavophile:** admiring of or advocating for Slavic cultures
- **Elbe:** river that flows through the Czech Republic and Germany
- **Konrad Adenauer:** (1876–1967) First chancellor of West Germany; began post-war economic reconstruction and was leader when the country became a member of NATO
- **Prague:** capital of the Czech Republic
- **Milan Kundera:** (b. 1929) Czech novelist known for extreme and comical skepticism, as illustrated in *The Book of Laughter and Forgetting* (tr. 1980) and *The Unbearable Lightness of Being* (tr. 1984)
- **Bourgeois:** middle-class

and decadence, which are invoked as typically Western, or even American, characteristics.

> ***4. In Your Journal:*** Why is the West so closely associated with America?

The things Occidentalists hate about the West are not always the ones that inspire hatred of the US. The two issues should not be conflated. A friend once asked in astonishment: "Why does he hate me? I didn't even help him." Some people hate the US because they were helped by the US, and some because they were not. Some resent the way the US helped their own hateful governments gain or stay in power. Some feel humiliated by the very existence of the US, and some by US foreign policy. With some on the left, hatred of the US is all that remains of their leftism; anti-Americanism is part of their identity. The same goes for right-wing cultural **Gaullists.** Anti-Americanism is an important political issue, related to Occidentalism but not quite the same thing.

> ***5. In Your Journal:*** What is "leftism"? Is it different from "liberalism"?

Anti-liberal revolts almost invariably contain a deep hatred of the City, that is to say, everything represented by urban civilization: commerce, mixed populations, artistic freedom, sexual license, scientific pursuits, leisure, personal safety, wealth, and its usual concomitant, power. **Mao Zedong, Pol Pot,** Hitler, Japanese agrarian fascists, and of course Islamists all extolled the simple life of the pious peasant, pure at heart, uncorrupted by city pleasures, used to hard work and self-denial, tied to the soil, and obedient to authority. Behind the idyll of rural simplicity lies the desire to control masses of people, but also an old religious rage, which goes back at least as far as the ancient superpower **Babylon.**

The "holy men" of the three monotheistic religions—Christianity, Judaism, and Islam—denounced Babylon as the sinful city-state whose politics, military might, and very urban civilization posed an arrogant challenge to God. The fabled tower of Babylon was a symbol of hubris and idolatry: "Let us build a city and a tower, whose top may reach unto

---

Gaullists: supporters of Charles de Gaulle (1890–1970), advocate of strong executive power, after World War II; de Gaulle (French undersecretary of war) had opposed the Franco-German armistice in 1940 and had to flee to London, where he started the Free French forces; after the war, he became provisional president of France (1954), and then started a political party "Rally of the French People," which lasted until 1953; he was president again from 1959 to 1969

Mao Zedong: (or Tse-tung) (1893–1976) founder of the People's Republic of China; Communist theorist famous for launching "The Great Leap Forward" and the "Cultural Revolution" in China, which both had disastrous effects on the Chinese people

Pol Pot: (1925–1998) Cambodian Communist political leader of the Khmer Rouge, responsible for systematic murders and forced labor in the "killing fields"

Babylon: ancient Mesopotamian city on the Euphrates River, known in its later period for commercial wealth and sensual living heaven; and let us make us a name" (Genesis 11:4). Indeed, God took it as a challenge to Himself: "And now nothing will be restrained from them, which they imagined to do" (Genesis 11:6). That is, the citizens of this urban superpower will act out their fantasies to become God.

"He loveth not the arrogant," the Koran (16:23) tells us, and goes on to say: "Allah took their structures from their foundation, and the roof fell down on them from above; and the Wrath seized them from directions they did not perceive" (16:26). The prophet Isaiah already prophesied that Babylon, "the glory of all kingdoms," would end up as "Sodom and Gomorrah" (Isaiah 13:19), and that the arrogant would be overthrown so that even an "Arabian pitch tent" would not inhabit the place (13:20). The Book of Revelation goes on to say about Babylon the great, "the mother of harlots and of the abominations of the earth" (17:5), that it "is fallen, is fallen" (18:2).

There is a recurring theme in movies from poor countries in which a young person from a remote village goes to the big city, forced by circumstances or eager to seek a new life in a wider, more affluent world. Things quickly go wrong. The young man or woman is lonely, adrift, and falls into poverty, crime, or prostitution. Usually, the story ends in a gesture of terrible violence, a vengeful attempt to bring down the pillars of the arrogant, indifferent, alien city. There are echoes of this story in Hitler's life in Vienna, Pol Pot's in Paris, Mao's in Beijing, or indeed of many a Muslim youth in Cairo, Haifa, Manchester, or Hamburg.

6. In Your Journal: What "advertising, television, pop music, and videos" can you list that convey the "constant presence" of the city?

In our world you don't even have to move to the city to feel its constant presence, through advertising, television, pop music, and videos. The modern city, representing all that shimmers just out of our reach, all the glittering arrogance and harlotry of the West, has found its icon in the Manhattan skyline, reproduced in millions of posters, photographs, and images, plastered all over the world. You cannot escape it. You find it on dusty jukeboxes in **Burma,** in discothèques in **Urumqi,** in student dorms in **Addis Ababa.** It excites longing, envy, and sometimes blinding rage. The Taliban, like the Nazi provincials horrified by "nigger dancing," like Pol Pot, like Mao, have tried to create a world of purity where visions of Babylon can no longer disturb them.

The Taliban, to be sure, have very little idea what the fleshpots of the West are really like. For them even Kabul sparkled with Occidental sinfulness, exemplified by girls in school and women with uncovered faces pop-

---

Burma: (or Myanmar) country in Southeast Asia, where people struggle against an abusive government in pursuit of democracy

Urumqi: capital of Xinjiang in Northwest China; an administrative and commercial hub

Addis Ababa: capital of Ethiopia

ulating and defiling the public domain. But the Taliban, like other purists, are much concerned with the private domain too. In big, anonymous cities, separation between the private and the public makes hypocrisy possible. Indeed, in Occidentalist eyes, the image of the West, populated by city-dwellers, is marked by artificiality and hypocrisy, in contrast to the honesty and purity of a **Bedouin** shepherd's life. **Riyadh,** and its grandiose Arabian palaces, is the epitome of hypocrisy. Its typical denizens behave like puritanical **Wahhabites** in public and greedy Westerners at home. To an Islamic radical, then, urban hypocrisy is like keeping the West inside one like a worm rotting the apple from within.

7. In Your Journal: How do "big, anonymous cities . . . make hypocrisy possible"?

Most great cities are also great marketplaces. **Voltaire** saw much of what he admired about England in the Royal Exchange, "where the Jew, the Mahometan, and the Christian transact together as tho' they all profess'd the same religion, and give the name of Infidel to none but bankrupts."[6] Those who hate what Voltaire respected, who see the marketplace as the source of greed, selfishness, and foreign corruption, also hate those who are thought to benefit from it most: immigrants and minorities who can only better their fortunes by trade. When purity must be restored, and foreign blood removed from the native soil, it is these people who must be purged: the Chinese from Pol Pot's Phnom Penh, the Indians from **Rangoon** or **Kampala,** and the Jews from everywhere.

Sometimes such impurities can extend to nations, or even great powers. In their professed aim to bring back true Asian values to the East, Japanese wartime leaders promised to kick out the white imperialists as one way to "overcome unrestrained market competition."[7] Whatever Israel does, it will remain the alien grit in the eyes of Muslim purists. And the US will always be intolerable to its enemies. In bin Laden's terms, "the crusader-Jewish alliance, led by the US and Israel," cannot do right. The hatred is unconditional. As he observed in a 1998 interview for al-Jazeera TV: "Every grown-up Muslim hates Americans, Jews, and Christians. It is our belief and religion. Since I was a boy I have been at war with and harboring hatred towards the Americans." The September angels of vengeance

Bedouin: nomad Arab people in the Middle East, known for hospitality and emphasis on swift justice

Riyadh: capital of Saudia Arabia

Wahhabite: follower of a strict Muslim theology originating in Saudi Arabia in the 18th century

Voltaire: (Francois Marie Arouet de) (1694–1778) French philosopher and contributor to the Enlightenment; his *Candide* (1759) exemplifies the common-sense philosophy for which Voltaire came to be known

Rangoon: city in Burma

Kampala: city in Uganda

picked their target carefully. Since the Manhattan skyline is seen as a provocation, its Babylonian towers had to come down.

What did Hitler mean by "Jewish science"? For that matter, what explains the deep loathing of **Darwin** among Christian fundamentalists? Nazi propagandists argued that scientific truth could not be established by such "Jewish" methods as empirical inquiry or subjecting hypotheses to the experimental test; natural science had to be "spiritual," rooted in the natural spirit of the ***Volk***. Jews, it was proposed, approached the natural world through reason, but true Germans reached a higher understanding through creative instinct and a love of nature.

Chairman Mao coined the slogan "Science is simply acting daringly." He purged trained scientists in the 1950s and encouraged Party zealots to embark on crazy experiments, inspired by the equally zany theories of Stalin's pseudoscientist T.D. Lysenko. "There is nothing special," Mao said, "about making nuclear reactors, cyclotrons or rockets. . . . You need to have spirit to feel superior to everyone, as if there was no one beside you."[8] All the sense of envious inferiority that Mao and his fellow Party provincials felt toward people of higher education is contained in these words. Instinct, spirit, daring. . . . In 1942, a Japanese professor at Tokyo University argued that a Japanese victory over Anglo-American materialism was assured because the former embodied the "spiritual culture" of the East.

> ***8. In Your Journal:*** There is no mention of religion in this discussion of mind versus spirit. What kind of "spirit" do you think Mao and the WWII Japanese referred to?

Like those towers of Babel in New York, the "Jewish" idea that "science is international" and human reason, regardless of bloodlines, is the best instrument for scientific inquiry is regarded by enemies of liberal, urban civilization as a form of hubris. Science, like everything else, must be infused with a higher ideal: the German *Volk,* God, Allah, or whatnot. But there may also be something else, something even more primitive, behind this. Worshipers of tribal gods, or even of allegedly universal ones, including Christians, Muslims, and Orthodox Jews, sometimes have a tendency to believe that infidels either have corrupt souls or have no souls at all. It is not for nothing that Christian missionaries speak of saving souls. In extreme cases, this can furnish enough justification to kill unbelievers with impunity.

Soul is a recurring theme of Occidentalism. The nineteenth-century Slavophiles pitted the "big" Russian soul against the mechanical, soulless West. They claimed to stand for deep feelings and profound understanding of suffering. Westerners, on the other hand, were deemed to be mechani-

---

❖ **Darwin:** (Charles Robert) (1809–1882) English naturalist who established a theory of evolution in *Origin of the Species* (1859), which explains, among other things, how the human animal evolved from more primitive organisms

---

❖ ***Volk* (German):** romantic, nationalistic notion of "the people"; *"Volkism"* suggests that society is organically connected through language and shared ancestry cally efficient, and to have nothing but an uncanny sense for calculating what is useful. The skeptical intellect, to promoters of soul, is always viewed with suspicion. Occidentalists extol soul or spirit but despise intellectuals and intellectual life. They regard the intellectual life as fragmented, indeed as a higher form of idiocy, with no sense of "totality," the "absolute," and what is truly important in life.

> *9. In Your Journal:* What do you think is so threatening to anti-Westerners about a "skeptical intellect"?

It is a fairly common belief among all peoples that "others" don't have the same feelings that we do. The notion that life is cheap in the Orient, or that coolies feel no pain, is a variation of this, but so is the idea we have heard expressed many times in China, India, Japan, and Egypt that Westerners are dry, rational, cold, and lacking in warm human feelings. It is a mark of **parochial** ignorance, of course, but it also reflects a way of ordering society. The post-**Enlightenment** Anglo-Franco-Judeo-American West sees itself as governed by secular political institutions and the behavior of all citizens as bound by secular laws. Religious belief and other matters of the spirit are private. Our politics are not totally divorced from shared values or moral assumptions, and some of our current leaders would like to see more religion brought into our public life; but still the West is not governed by spiritual leaders who seek to mediate between us and the divine world above. Our laws do not come from divine revelation, but are drawn up by jurists.

parochial: narrow-minded, local, or insular

> *10. In Your Journal:* Do you find it surprising that Westerners are thought of as dry, rational, cold, and lacking in warm human feelings by many non-Westerners? Why or why not?

Societies in which Caesars are also high priests, or act as idols of worship, whether they be Stalinist, monarchical, or Islamist, use a different political language. Again, an example from World War II might be useful. Whereas the Allies, led by the US, fought the Japanese in the name of freedom, the Japanese holy war in Asia was fought in the name of divine justice and peace. "The basic aim of Japan's national policy lies in the firm establishment of world peace in accordance with the lofty spirit of All the World Under One Roof, in which the country was founded." Thus spoke Prime Minister Konoe in 1940. Islamists, too, aim to unite the world under one peaceful roof, once the infidels and their towers have been destroyed.

> *11. In Your Journal:* Is it strange that for some Islamists and anti-Western groups that the way to peace ("divine justice") is through war? How does that rationale compare to the United States' and its allies' use of war to achieve "freedom"?

When politics and religion merge, collective aims, often promoted in the name of love and justice, tend to encompass the whole world, or at least large chunks of it. The state is a secular construct. The Brotherhood of Islam, the Church of Rome, All the World Under One Japanese Roof, world communism, all in their different ways have had religious or **millenarian** goals. Such goals are not unknown in the supposedly secular states of the West either. Especially in the US, right-wing Christian organizations and other religious pressure groups have sought to inject their religious values

millenarian: of or related to the millenium

Enlightenment: scientific and intellectual movement of the 17th century that fostered the belief in natural law, and universal order, and the confidence in human reason that spread to influence all of 18th-century society, contributing to a secular view of the world and a general sense of progress and perfectibility; also known as the Age of Reason and agendas into national politics in ways that would have shocked the Founding Fathers. That **Reverend Jerry Falwell** described the terrorist attacks on New York and Washington as a kind of punishment for our worldly sins showed that his thinking was not so far removed from that of the Islamists.

But ideally, the US and other Western democracies are examples of what **Ferdinand Toennies** termed a *Gesellschaft,* whose members are bound by a social contract. The other kind of community, the *Gemeinschaft,* is based on a common faith, or racial kinship, or on deep feelings of one kind or another. Typically, one German thinker, Edgar Jung, described World War I as a clash between the Intellect (the West) and the Soul (Germany).

12. In Your Journal: What do you make of the phrase "heroic violence"?

Enemies of the West usually aspire to be heroes. As **Mussolini** exhorted his new Romans: "Never cease to be daring!" Islamism, Nazism, fascism, communism are all heroic creeds. Mao's ideal of permanent revolution was a blueprint for continually stirring things up, for a society invigorated by constant heroic violence. The common enemy of revolutionary heroes is the settled bourgeois, the city dweller, the petty clerk, the plump stockbroker, going about his business, the kind of person, in short, who might have been working in an office in the World Trade Center. It is a peculiar trait of the bourgeoisie, perhaps the most successful class in history, at least so far, according to **Karl Marx,** to be hated so intensely by some of its most formidable sons and daughters, including Marx himself. Lack of heroism in the bourgeois ethos, of committing great deeds, has a great

---

Reverend Jerry Falwell: Two days after the September 11th attacks, Falwell commented on the television program "The 700 Club": "I know that I'll hear from them for this. But, throwing God out successfully with the help of the federal court system, throwing God out of the public square, out of the schools. The abortionists have got to bear some burden for this because God will not be mocked. And when we destroy 40 million little innocent babies, we make God mad. I really believe that the pagans, and the abortionists, and the feminists, and the gays and the lesbians who are actively trying to make that an alternative lifestyle, the ACLU, People For the American Way—all of them who have tried to secularize America—I point the finger in their face and say "you helped this happen." The next day on CNN, Falwell apologized: "I would never blame any human being except the terrorists, and if I left that impression with gays or lesbians or anyone else, I apologize."

Ferdinand Toennies: (1855–1936) German sociologist

Mussolini: (Benito) (1883–1945) Italian dictator and Fascist who colluded with Hitler during World War II, after which he was caught, tried, and executed

Karl Marx: (1818–1883) German social philosopher, economist, and revolutionary theorist who wrote works about communism and modern socialism, such as the *Communist Manifesto* (1848)

deal to do with this peculiarity. The hero courts death. The bourgeois is addicted to personal safety. The hero counts death tolls, the bourgeois counts money. Bin Laden was asked by his interviewer in 1998 whether he ever feared betrayal from within his own entourage. He replied: "These men left worldly affairs, and came here for jihad."

Intellectuals, themselves only rarely heroic, have often displayed a hatred of the bourgeois and an infatuation with heroism—heroic leaders, heroic creeds. Artists in Mussolini's Italy celebrated speed, youth, energy, instinct, and death-defying derring-do. German social scientists before World War II were fascinated by the juxtaposition of the hero and the bourgeois: Werner Sombart's *Händler und Helden (Merchants and Heroes)* and Bogislav von Selchow's *Der bürgerliche und der heldische Mensch (The Civil and the Heroic Man)* are but two examples of the genre. Von Selchow was one, among many others, by no means all German, who argued that bourgeois liberal society had become cold, fragmented, decadent, mediocre, lifeless. The bourgeois, he wrote, is forever hiding himself in a life without peril. The bourgeois, he said, is anxious to eliminate "fighting against Life, as he lacks the strength necessary to master it in its very nakedness and hardness in a manly fashion."[9]

To the likes of von Selchow or Ernst Jünger, World War I showed a different, more heroic side of man. That is why the Battle of Langemarck, a particularly horrific episode in 1914, in which Jünger himself took part, became such a subject for hero worship. Some 145,000 men died in a sequence of utterly futile attacks. But the young heroes, many of them from elite universities like the Japanese kamikaze pilots thirty years later, were supposed to have rushed to their early graves singing the *Deutschlandlied.* The famous words of Theodor Körner, written a century before, were often evoked in remembrance: "Happiness lies only in sacrificial death." In the first week of the current war in Afghanistan, a young Afghan warrior was quoted in a British newspaper. "The Americans," he said "love Pepsi Cola, but we love death." The sentiments of the Langemarck cult exactly.

> ***13. In Your Journal:*** How would you characterize the "young Afghan warrior's" assertion that "Americans love Pepsi Cola, but we love death"?

Even those who sympathize with the democratic West, such as **Alexis de Tocqueville,** have pointed out the lack of grandeur, the intellectual conformity, and the cultural mediocrity that is supposed to be inherent in our systems of government. Democracy, de Tocqueville warned, could easily become the tyranny of the majority. He noted that there were no great writers in America, or indeed anything that might be described as great. It is a common but somewhat questionable complaint. For it is not at all clear that art and culture in New York is any more mediocre than it is in **Damascus** or Beijing.

Alexis de Tocqueville: (1805–1859) French politician and writer; author of *Democracy in America* (1835–1840), a study of American politics and culture

---

Damascus: capital of Syria

Much in our affluent, market-driven societies is indeed mediocre, and there is nothing admirable about luxury per se, but when contempt for bourgeois creature comforts becomes contempt for life you know the West is under attack. This contempt can come from many sources, but it appeals to those who feel impotent, marginalized, excluded, or denigrated: the intellectual who feels unrecognized, the talentless art student in a city filled with brilliance, the time-serving everyman who disappears into any crowd, the young man from a third-world country who feels mocked by the indifference of a superior West; the list of possible recruits to a cult of death is potentially endless.

14. In Your Journal: Respond to Bruk's definition of "liberty."

Liberalism, wrote an early Nazi theorist, A. Moeller v.d. Bruck, is the "liberty for everybody to be a mediocre man." The way out of mediocrity, say the sirens of the death cult, is to submerge one's petty ego into a mass movement, whose awesome energies will be unleashed to create greatness in the name of the Führer, the Emperor, God, or Allah. The Leader personifies all one's yearnings for grandeur. What is the mere life of one, two, or a thousand men, if higher things are at stake? This is a license for great violence against others: Jews, infidels, bourgeois liberals, Sikhs, Muslims, or whoever must be purged to make way for a greater, grander world. An American chaplain named Francis P. Scott tried to explain to the Tokyo War Crimes Tribunal the extraordinary brutality of Japanese soldiers during the war. After many interviews with former combatants, he concluded that "they had a belief that any enemy of the emperor could not be right, so the more brutally they treated their prisoners, the more loyal to the emperor they were being."[10]

15. In Your Journal: Why do you think that youth are "the most capable of sacrificial acts"? Don't young people have the most to live for?

The truest holy warrior, however, is not the torturer but the kamikaze pilot. Self-sacrifice is the highest honor in the war against the West. It is the absolute opposite of the bourgeois fear for his life. And youth is the most capable of sacrificial acts. Most kamikazes were barely out of high school. As bin Laden has said, "The sector between fifteen and twenty-five is the one with ability for jihad and sacrifice."

Aurel Kolnai argued in 1938 in his *War Against the West* that "the trend towards the emancipation of women [is] keenly distinctive of the West." This somewhat sweeping claim seems to be born out by the sentiments of Kolnai's enemies. Here is Alfred Rosenberg, the Nazi propagandist: "Emancipation of woman from the women's emancipation movement is the first demand of a generation of women which would like to save the Volk and the race, the Eternal-Unconscious, the foundation of all culture, from decline and fall."[11] Leaving aside what this woolly-headed thinker could have meant by the Eternal-Unconscious, the meaning is clear enough. Female emancipation leads to bourgeois decadence. The proper role for women is to be breeders of heroic men. One reason the Germans imported such huge numbers of workers from Poland and other countries under Nazi occupation was the dogmatic insistence that German women should stay at home.

16. In Your Journal: Why is emancipation of women such a symbol of decadence for the Occidentalists?

Bin Laden is equally obsessed with manliness and women. It is indeed one of his most cherished Occidentalist creeds. "The rulers of that region [the Gulf States] have been deprived of their manhood," he said in 1998. "And they think the people are women. By God, Muslim women refuse to be defended by these American and Jewish prostitutes." The West, in his account, is determined "to deprive us of our manhood. We believe we are men."

Few modern societies were as dominated by males as wartime Japan, and the brutal policy of forcing Korean, Chinese, and Filipina, as well as Japanese, girls to serve in military brothels was a sign of the low status of women in the Japanese empire. And yet, the war itself had the peculiar effect of emancipating Japanese women to a degree that cannot possibly have been intended. Because most able-bodied men were needed on the battlefronts, women had to take care of their families, trade in the black markets, and work in the factories. Unlike the men, who experienced defeat as a deep humiliation, many Japanese women regarded the Allied victory as a step toward their liberation. One of the most important changes in postwar Japan was that women got the right to vote. They did so in large numbers as early as 1946. A new constitution was drawn up mostly by American jurists, but the articles concerning women's rights were largely the work of a remarkable person called Beate Sirota, who represented most things enemies of the West would have loathed. She was European, educated, a woman, and a Jew.

To all those who see military discipline, self-sacrifice, austerity, and worship of the Leader as the highest social ideals, the power of female sexuality will be seen as a dire threat. From ancient times women are the givers and the guardians of life. Women's freedom is incompatible with a death cult. Indeed, open displays of female sexuality are a provocation, not only to holy men, but to all repressed people whose only way to exaltation is death for a higher cause. Pictures of partly naked Western women advertising Hollywood movies, or soft drinks, or whatever, by suggesting sexual acts, are as ubiquitous in the world as those images of the Manhattan skyline. They are just as frustrating, confusing, and sometimes enraging. For again they promise a sinful, libidinous world of infinite pleasure beyond most people's reach.

17. In Your Journal: Why are the life-giving powers of women seen by some as incompatible with expressions of female sexuality?

There is no clash of civilizations. Most religions, especially monotheistic ones, have the capacity to harbor the anti-Western poison. And varieties of secular fascism can occur in all cultures. The current conflict, therefore, is not between East and West, Anglo-America and the rest, or Judeo-Christianity and Islam. The death cult is a deadly virus which now thrives, for all manner of historical and political reasons, in extreme forms of Islam.

Occidentalism is the creed of Islamist revolutionaries. Their aim is to create one Islamic world guided by the *sharia* (Islamic law), as interpreted by trusted scholars who have proved themselves in jihad (read "revolution").

This is a call to purify the Islamic world of the idolatrous West, exemplified by America. The aim is to strike at American heathen shrines, and show, in the most spectacular fashion, that the US is vulnerable, a "paper tiger" in revolutionary jargon. Through such "propaganda by action" against the arrogant US, the forces of jihad will unite and then impose their revolution on the Islamic world.

Ayatollah Khomeini was a "Stalinist" in the sense that he wanted to stage a revolution in one significant country, Iran, before worrying about exporting it. Bin Laden, by contrast, is a "**Trotskyite,**" who views Afghanistan as a base from which to export revolution right away. There is a tension between the "Stalinists" and the "Trotskyites" within the Islamist movement. September 11 gave the "Trotskyites" an advantage.

Al-Qaeda is making a serious bid to stage an Islamist revolution that would bring down governments from Indonesia to Tunisia. It has not succeeded yet. We can expect more "propaganda by action" against the US and US installations, accompanied by crude Occidentalist propaganda. The West, and not just the geographical West, should counter this intelligently with the full force of calculating bourgeois anti-heroism. Accountants mulling over shady bank accounts and undercover agents bribing their way will be more useful in the long-term struggle than special macho units blasting their way into the caves of Afghanistan. But if one thing is clear in this murky war, it is that we should not counter Occidentalism with a nasty form of Orientalism. Once we fall for that temptation, the virus has infected us too.

18. In Your Journal: What do you think would be involved in "a nasty form of Orientalism"?

NOTES

1. D.C. Holtom, *Modern Japan and Shinto Nationalism* (University of Chicago, 1943), p. 10.
2. Viking, 1938.
3. *Briefe 1882–1924* (Munich: Bruckmann, 1928).
4. *England und Deutschland* (Munich: Bruckmann, 1915).
5. *Jahr der Entscheidung* (Munich: C.H. Beck, 1933).
6. *Letters Concerning the English Nation* (Oxford University Press, 1994), p. 30.
7. Akira Iriye, *Power and Culture: The Japanese-American War 1941–1945* (Harvard University Press, 1981).
8. Jasper Becker, *Hungry Ghosts: Mao's Secret Famine* (Free Press, 1996), p. 62.
9. Quoted in Kolnai, *The War Against the West,* p. 215.
10. Arnold C. Brackman, *The Other Nuremberg: The Untold Story of the Tokyo War Crimes Tribunals* (Morrow, 1987), p. 251.
11. Quoted in George L. Mosse, *Nazi Culture: Intellectual, Cultural and Social Life in the Third Reich* (Grosset and Dunlap, 1966), p. 40.

Trotsky: (Leon) (1879–1940) Russian Communist revolutionary; one of the principal leaders of the movement to found the U.S.S.R.

FOR USE IN DISCUSSION

Questions about Substance

1. The Japanese philosophers in Kyoto were brainstorming ways to "'overcome modern civilization'" (424) or the West. Examine the word "overcome." What do the philosophers mean by this? What do you think the West was trying to "overcome" during World War II?
2. In the sentence "Of such stuff are holy warriors made" (425), what is the "stuff" alluded to here?
3. Voltaire characterizes the (Western) marketplace as a place where all types can come together with a kind of equal status (429). Why is this effect so objectionable to anti-Western groups?
4. Why do Occidentalists "despise intellectuals and intellectual life" (431)? How are intellectuals regarded in the U.S.?
5. The authors of this essay tell us that in the West, "Religious belief and other matters of the spirit are private" (431). Do you think this is an accurate characterization? Explain.
6. The "West is not governed by spiritual leaders who seek to mediate between us and the divine world above" (431), as are Occidentalists, this essay tells us. Do you think this culture gap is bigger than those created by race, ethnicity, or language?
7. "The hero courts death. The bourgeois is addicted to personal safety" (433). How does this description of heroism compare and/or contrast with your understanding of the concept? Who are some of the U.S.'s most prominent heroes, in history or the present? What definition of heroism applies to them?
8. The "Manhattan skyline" and "naked Western women" are compared (435) in order to tie together what parts of the Occidentalist ideology? Are there other ways you think the symbols of naked women and urban skylines might be similar?

Questions about Structure and Style

1. Margalit and Buruma characterize Occidentalism as having four features: "the City, the Bourgeois, Reason, and Feminism" (426). How do they use these features in the context of their essay?
2. World War II comes up many times in this essay, and serves as a kind of measuring stick for the current international political crisis. Trace the instances of comparison throughout the essay, and explain why you think World War II figures so prominently.
3. Towards the end of this essay, Margalit and Buruma assert that "the current conflict, therefore, is not between East and West" (435). Have you been prepared for this claim? How would it have a different effect if it appeared in the introduction?

4. The authors argue that "accountants and undercover agents" (436) would be more useful in the conflict with Afghanistan than the military or their weapons. Have they laid enough of a foundation for this claim? If so, how? If not, what do they need to expand on?

Multimedia Suggestions

1. Margalit and Buruma refer to "movies from poor countries in which a young person from a remote village goes to the big city" and encounters disaster (428). One good example of this is the film *Salaam Bombay!* (1988), which traces the difficulties of a poor child trying to survive on his own in a city struggling between traditional and modern values. View the film and identify the objects of its critique.
2. One excellent illustration of how religious extremism can oppose science is the Christian fundamentalist objection to evolution (alluded to on page 734). To find out more about this debate, view the film *Inherit the Wind* (1960), and examine the recent debates over science education at *http://www.ncseweb.org/* (The National Center for Science Education Web site).
3. Read the article about Occidentalism by Victor Davis Hanson of the *National Review Online* magazine (*http://www.nationalreview.com/hanson/hanson051002.asp*). It presents a very different picture of the kinds of issues Margalit and Buruma are interested in. How do you think Margalit and Buruma would respond to this argument?

SUGGESTIONS FOR WRITING AND RESEARCH

1. On pages 429–431, Margalit and Avishai begin a discussion on the difference between those who would deny or reject knowledge, and those who seek to transcend knowledge. What is the distinction? Are both versions of ignorance, or does transcendence just suggest deference for something more mysterious than the known? Write an essay about the nature of knowledge in the context of religious or other fundamentalism.
2. Is Occidentalism synonymous with anti-U.S. ideology? Examine the definition of Occidentalism that Margalit and Buruma present, and explain its relationship to anti-Americanism.
3. How has the history of Occidentalism come to bear on the present crisis involving the United States and Iraq? Think also about the highly varied responses from western allies in the United Nations Security Council, some of whom supported war as an option from the beginning (Great Britain and Spain, for example), and some of whom expressed vehement opposition (especially the French, Russia, and China). Is the term Occidentalism even relevant anymore? What do you think it means to be an Occidentalist in the twenty-first century?

WORKING WITH CLUSTERS

Cluster 10: Interpretation and/as Ideology
Cluster 13: Global Knowledge
Cluster 18: Ethnicity and Conflict
Discipline: The Social Sciences
Rhetorical Mode: Cause and Effect

"Media, Testing, and Safe Sex Education: Controlling the Landscape of AIDS Information" (from *Inventing AIDS*)

by Cindy Patton

Cynthia K. Patton is an Associate Professor at the Graduate Institute of the Liberal Arts at Emory University who writes primarily about the interaction between modern science, media coverage, and local activism. She has a Ph.D. in Communications from the University of Massachusetts, and she is the author of many books, including: Sex and Germs: The Politics of AIDS *(1985),* Last Served: Gendering the HIV Pandemic *(1994),* Fatal Advice: How Safe Sex Education Went Wrong *(1995), and* Inventing AIDS *(1990), from which this excerpt is drawn. Her most recent book is* Globalizing AIDS *(2002).*

Between 1981–1985, efforts to care for the sick and educate those most immediately at risk for AIDS happened at a distance from the public view. The epidemic gained its social meaning in relation to deep prejudices about race, class, gender, sexuality, and "addiction;" public ignorance about AIDS and community response to the epidemic fueled discrimination and thwarted education about risk. However, the onslaught of "lifestyle" stories about the epidemic following **Rock Hudson's death in 1985** created new problems by *publicly* reinforcing a range of stereotypes which were also at the core of the emerging AIDS service industry. The persistent depictions of people living with AIDS as isolated and the erasure of the social realities which shaped the epidemic within communities of color paralleled both groups' growing alienation from the **ASO**s.

ASO: AIDS Service Organization

Aimed at a compassionate society (and *not* aimed at people living with AIDS or anyone "at risk"), lifestyle journalism constructed the person living with AIDS as a figure with a unique vantage point on both death and on the post-modern era. The questions put to the person living with AIDS became so much a part of the psychic unconscious that they were answered even when they were not directly asked. Lifestyle journalists were (with important exceptions) concerned not with the experience of this illness, but with reproducing the calculus of conservative morality in a deeply puritanical culture. Reporters interrogated gay men living with AIDS about their lives; the unspoken clauses rendered the answers ambiguous enough to erase anything positive an individual might try to say. "How do you feel now (read: that your "lifestyle" has betrayed you)?" "Was it (sex) worth it (death)?" In human interest journalism, aimed at a "general public" that wanted to feel compassionate but safe, the person living with AIDS stands in for Anglo-American culture which, at the edge of the twenty-first century, is still unable to separate its fear of sexuality from the **vicissitudes** of a little understood virus. And of course, the virus itself becomes a character—the little hunk of protein that refuses to give up its secrets. "Perhaps the virus is trying to tell us something," both new right doomsday prophets and scientists have said. The virus is itself overlayed with communications

> *1. In Your Journal:* What does Patton mean by the phrase "reproducing the calculus of conservative morality"?

> *2. In Your Journal:* Can you paraphrase what Patton says that the "general public" wanted when reading "human interest journalism"?

vicissitudes: changes or variations

Rock Hudson's death in 1985: this event helped bring mainstream awareness to the AIDS crisis, as Hudson had been such a heterosexual icon in American culture language—**messenger RNA,** codes, evasion, changing its surface, transcription, long terminal repeats.

messenger RNA: biochemical mechanism for transferring genetic information

Newspapers and magazines usually depicted volunteers as earnest gay men, perky white women, or grandmothers. Scientists and physicians were frequently represented as serious white men, who sometimes appeared to be gay if they were from hard-hit cities like San Francisco, New York, or Houston. Drug use was represented as the cause of AIDS in prostitutes and in the African American and Latin communities. These media efforts to "put a face on AIDS" converged with and created new expectations for the AIDS service organizations. As "gay" organizations, the groups had largely been political outsiders: after about 1985, the media began to suggest AIDS work as a form of middle-class volunteerism, an image that fit nicely with the attempts of many ASOs to mainstream in order to gain power and broader funding.

3. In Your Journal: How accurate does Patton appear to think are the media representations of volunteers and scientists?

REWRITING MYTHS

Between 1985 and 1989 control of AIDS information was simultaneously professionalized and democratized through a series of inter-related processes, including the appearance of media AIDS experts and the institution of alternative HIV antibody test sites (ATS). While the AIDS service organizations were shaped by their roots in the gay community, and by four years of experience coping with the HIV epidemic, the information institutions were relative latecomers who imposed their own techniques of analyzing problems. Establishing control of AIDS information was accomplished through organizing and absorbing the disjunct issues of the HIV epidemic into pre-existing academic and professional disciplines.

Systematic scientific coverage of the epidemic, dating from about the First International AIDS Conference in Atlanta in 1985, quickly informed people that AIDS existed; however, the emergence of a core of media experts increased the gap between producers and consumers of scientific knowledge. In their efforts to translate science, reporters fell prey to **elisions** and simplifications. Terms like "the AIDS test,"[1] "promiscuity," "AIDS carrier," and "inevitably fatal" distorted the scientific "facts" and their social implications.[2] Media science frequently articulated pre-existing stereotypes in a new, objective-sounding language. Science reporters often accused gay activists and right-wing commentators of "politicizing" AIDS, but did not acknowledge the cultural politics underlying the popular and scientific media's descriptions of the epidemic.

elisions: intentional omissions

Media reports on the vast new research industry devoted almost entirely to Human Immunodeficiency Virus (HIV) narrativized the "progress" being made in the "fight against AIDS."[3] Media accounts of the breakthroughs and "forward march" of research are largely an uncritical reproduction of science's own self-narrative; other than identification of a

4. In Your Journal: For what audience do you think these "uncritical" accounts of AIDS research were produced?

probable virus in 1983,[4] progress has been incremental and tentative, at least from the perspective of people hoping for treatments. The scientific gains with practical results of saving or improving lives have come not from experimental new drugs but from perfecting already known drugs for use in treating secondary infections associated with AIDS. While the media have been instrumental in raising social and medical awareness about AIDS, the reportage has consistently misrepresented the basic concepts of HIV, sensationalized faulty research, and selectively reported on conflicting data. Despite coverage of particular events by many excellent journalists (especially those who have covered AIDS for years in spite of the alternating cache and stigma of the "AIDS beat"), the media have comprised a bleak and complex backdrop of AIDS (dis)information.[5]

5. In Your Journal: What does Patton mean by "(dis)information"?

The consistent confusion of a positive antibody test with an AIDS diagnosis and the failure to distinguish anti-viral treatments from treatments for opportunistic infections create an unnecessarily pessimistic interpretation of the idea that there is "no cure for AIDS." Coupled with images of **PLWAs** in extreme pain or as romantically sick figures, the media obscure the reality that many PLWAs continue to lead full, "normal" lives.[6] Anecdotal reports in the U.S. and studies in Europe suggest that there is a increased rate of suicide among people learning they are HIV-Ab+, especially among injecting drug users and homosexually active men not connected with supportive, informed communities.[7]

PWLAs: people living with AIDS

GAY VISIBILITY AND AIDS EPIDEMIOLOGY

In one sense, AIDS constitutes a revolution in concepts of diagnosis and disease, since the symptoms of AIDS are in fact other diseases. AIDS is historically specific, arising (presumably) at the moment when advanced technology could relate a primary causative agent to a set of extremely diverse symptoms. Had AIDS occurred fifty years ago, it would probably have been considered inexplicably untreatable forms of a dozen different diseases rather than as symptoms of an underlying immune disorder. From a sociopolitical viewpoint, AIDS was recognized by epidemiologists because gay men, by the late 1970s, were a visible community. In order to perceive a possible epidemic in the apparently unrelated deaths from *Pneumocistis carinii* pneumonia (PCP) in 1980–81, doctors had first to recognize that the men shared a demographic trait in common. But their homosexuality was not sufficient: it now appears that injecting drug users had already experienced an epidemic of HIV-related pneumonia deaths in the late 1970s.[8] The epidemic, noted at the time as "junky pneumonia," did not trigger public health investigators' interest because it was not considered remarkable that injecting drug users should get sick and die from any number of illnesses, as users were considered intrinsically unhealthy. The emerging syndrome was defined as immune malfunction in "previously healthy" people; the rapid and unexplained decline in health which set the Centers for Disease Control into motion was noticeable only because the gay men affected had previously been considered "healthy." That gay men were seen as "healthy" despite having a variety of treatable sexually transmitted diseases attested to the acceptance and positive valuation of gay men and their sexuality in the urban settings where these early cases were under study. Had these cases appeared fifty years ago, and had the homosexuality of the patients been recognized, doctors would probably have viewed homosexuals *per se* as constitutionally weaker and explained their immune system breakdown on this fact alone.

6. In Your Journal: What does Patton suggest about the particular stage in scientific progress during which the AIDS crisis arose?

MEDIA EVENTS AND LIFE IN THE HIV LANDSCAPE

The sheer volume of AIDS research and the real need to share as much data as possible resulted in a loosening up of **peer-review** standards for publishing new studies.[9] With a flood of preliminary and often conflicting studies, mainstream reporters with more desire for a breaking story than knowledge of AIDS research reported on whatever data caught their fancy. For example, in 1987–88, the mainstream press was filled with particularly sensational—and erroneous—reports that HIV-Ab+ people might develop neurological and cognitive symptoms long before seeing any of the classic diagnostic symptoms of **ARC** or AIDS. These reports rationalized screening certain "sensitive" employees; SAS, the Swedish airline, seemed to have been influenced by these reports when they initiated HIV antibody screening of pilots in early 1988.[10]

peer review: process of critical review by professional colleagues

ARC: AIDS-related complex; older term for the diagnosis of certain illnesses that precede full-blown AIDS

Naturally, gay men around the world panicked; already distressed by lurid reporting on shattered lives and untimely death, gay men were now told they might go quietly mad before they even realized they were ill. More complete reports showed that this early data was wrong: a controlled study of 1543 HIV-Ab+ gay and bisexual men did not even find a trend toward early development of cognitive problems.[11] Researchers tried to dispel the myth of early cognitive symptoms, but the damage had already been done. The idea of "AIDS madness" provided the popular imagination with a pseudoscientific basis for the longstanding fears of the psychologically impaired homosexual or the crazed junky.

TESTING: THE DATA IS IN, BUT POLICY MAKERS PLAN ON

Mandatory HIV antibody testing (originally developed and based on standards for screening blood donations) for insurance, jobs, immigration, and as a focus of risk reduction education has been criticized by activists, lawyers, and even by the **World Health Organization.** Nevertheless, testing continues to be used widely in Europe and in the U.S., which requires proof of HIV-Ab-status for immigration and increasingly centers risk reduction education on the testing event.

Many health educators, including people from the gay groups and injecting drug serving agencies, have asserted that knowledge of HIV antibody status is important in promoting behavior change. The apparent self-evidence of a relationship between behavior and knowledge of antibody status rests on the assumption that drug use and sexuality are most importantly individual behaviors, ignoring the social norms and symbolic meanings that determine *how* sex is practiced or drugs are used. In fact, widespread testing only creates sexual apartheid and a two-tiered medical care system. Sweden, often praised as having the world's most progressive AIDS prevention policy, instituted a complicated set of laws to encourage "voluntary" testing and prevent people of unlike antibody status from engaging in sex with each other, regardless of whether "safe sex" were practiced. Under Swedish policy, HIV infection is categorized as a venereal disease, requiring anyone who believes they have been exposed to report for testing.[12] Although it is impossible to enforce this law widely, it has been used to coerce people who have been named as sexual partners of HIV-Ab + people. Several prostitutes were "medically detained" in a special HIV facility just days before the beginning of the International AIDS Conference in Stockholm in 1988.

7. In Your Journal: How might "antibody status" promote behavior change?

8. In Your Journal: Why does Patton include this point about the arrest of prostitutes?

There is now general scientific consensus that there is no predictable relationship between knowledge of HIV anti-body status and subsequent behavior change, although policy makers continue to place testing programs at the center of their education and prevention campaigns. The large studies of testing and behavior conducted by the U.S. Multi-center AIDS Cohort Studies (MACS), funded largely by the National Institutes of Health and the Centers for Disease Control, showed no predictable relationship between knowledge of test result and subsequent behavior, attitudes, or psychological stress in year three of the prospective study.[13] Despite its own data, the CDC continues to fund primarily educational projects that focus on test taking. The insistence that there is a relationship between test result knowledge and behavior change means millions of dollars are spent on testing individuals (and studying them after they are tested) instead of spending the money on educational campaigns located within and designed by communities.[14]

9. In Your Journal: Why do you think the CDC might continue to primarily fund test-related education initiatives when its data suggests that test status has little bearing on the behavior of individuals?

The media *have* reported on small, poorly designed studies which showed correlations between test result knowledge and sexual behavior

---

World Health Organization: agency created by the United Nations in 1948 and charged with the goal of promoting positive health throughout the world change as proof that widespread testing in itself will result in behavior change.[15] Popular views of the test as a motivator of sexual behavior change, and the conflation of HIV-Ab + and AIDS, combined with the potential of incorrect self-diagnosis (i.e., deciding one "actually" has AIDS upon receiving test results), have turned a test of limited diagnostic use into an appealing but dangerous quick-information stop. This unthoughtful faith in testing legitimates things like HIV home test kits. Even if they were user-proof, analogous kits would never be released for similarly complex illnesses like cancer, multiple sclerosis, or arthritis because professional interpretation and sensitive counselling would be considered essential.

10. In Your Journal: What is Patton's point about HIV home test kits?

Reporters largely ignored studies of community-based educational projects in gay communities in the U.S. The CDC-funded Community Demonstration Projects indicate that the greatest changes toward safer sex practices occured in cities where gay men perceive their community to be changing toward the new "safer sex" norm. A dozen-city comparative study analyzed factors like pre-existing gay community institutions, gay media, and the role of specific community education projects. Cities with strong gay communities and positive images of gay men showed greater trends toward safer sex behavior. According to Community Demonstration Projects director Kevin O'Reilly, the "perception of the community's attitude and a belief that men in your community can and are making changes were the strongest factors in individual men's changing." O'Reilly said projects "aimed at individual beliefs are not as effective as programs aimed at community beliefs and norms."[16]

These studies suggest the importance of the women's, Black, and gay health movements' focus on empowering groups to take a role in advocating for their own health.

MEDIA AND THE INTERPRETIVE PROCESS

Media must do more than present information which seems accurate, clear, and accessible because popular understandings of information are constantly in flux. Media consumers' interpretive processes are complex and even the most straightforward media effort can result in many unanticipated interpretations. Clear-cut relationships between media consumption and individual or social attitudes or behaviors are difficult to **quantify** because media use and interpretation are embedded in complex social networks. Thus it is critical to understand the individual and group interpretive practices of the people to whom media "information" is directed. No media message is interpretation-proof because consumers already have ritualized ways of using media, which serve as interpretation contexts. Media criticism must evaluate "factual" accounting and assess the reception of information campaigns, as well as examine the historical uses of media by people in interpretive subgroups. A range of evolving practices

quantify: determine; measure

and expectations (on individual, social, and national levels) may influence interpretation.

The perceived relevance of new information about HIV/AIDS will be affected by whether HIV/AIDS is initially viewed as of concern to individuals, communities, nations, or a mix of these. For example, a risk reduction campaign in the U.S. might be viewed as appropriately directed toward individuals, whereas in Zambia, where AIDS among young men would seriously affect the mining industry, risk reduction would be considered a national economic concern. A nationally oriented safer sex campaign like "Have safe sex and keep America strong," would seem absurd, while a campaign of that variety might be quite meaningful in Zambia.

Consumers also have expectations of what *type* of media is likely to supply particular types of information about HIV/AIDS. If HIV is perceived as an personal behavioral concern, individuals may be more likely to trust a local or oppositional media source for advice or sympathetic portrayals of PLWAs. On the other hand, the same individuals might look to national news media for scientific information. Gay men in the U.S. may view local gay papers as ideal sources of information about social support but seek information on scientific breakthroughs from national or scientific journals.

The form of messages—advertisements, public service announcements, news items, human interest features, editorials—each has different meanings to the media user. In capitalist media, advertising campaigns may be quite effective precisely because readers know that they "cost." Alternatively, editorials in community papers may be more effective because they signal leadership and unity.

Established patterns of group and individual media use and secondary discussions may be the strongest context of interpretation. If people regularly talk in groups about what they read/hear in the media, interpretations are more likely to be thoughtful, uniform, and relevant to local concerns. If media are publicly used, as might be the case with television or radio in poor rural communities, sensitive topics may become legitimated for conversation. The act of passing on print media may be a source of small group discussions; in Western gay communities, gay-produced newspapers are widely passed around providing word-of-mouth reinforcement and reinterpretation of important developments in AIDS research or treatment. However, differing patterns of media circulation may reinforce or contradict particular ideas; for example, small communities in West African countries often first heard about AIDS in sensationalist Francophone or Anglophone radio broadcasts from Europe. These were variously dismissed as a European plot and a catalyst for concern that the government was not taking appropriate steps. For some countries, international broadcasting contains a set of ideas that contradict more carefully created local or national media campaigns. Likewise, conflicts in local and national media, with their differing political investments, shape the interpretive practices of individuals and groups.

The complexity of how, why, and what is communicated about AIDS suggests why apparently neutral information is subject to radically different interpretations. Understanding the field of AIDS information and interpretation as highly contingent on social practices, rather than on individuals' **intransigence** or ignorance, requires designers of information campaigns to coordinate media on many levels and include participants from communities and micro-groups in order to reflect their interpretive practices.

intransigence: unwillingness to compromise

THE EPISTEMOLOGY OF ELISA

epistemology: study of the nature, origin, and validity of knowledge

Group and individual understandings of antibody testing are also contingent on interpretive practices and on the structure and purpose of testing programs. Testing is used in a range of settings: research, diagnosis, education, counselling, job screening, insurance screening, blood screening. Far from constituting objective meanings, test results take on a range of contradictory individual and collective meanings. Historically specific forms of medical practice, changing sexual and affectional norms, and, especially in the U.S., how antibody status is incorporated into identity politics—all these pull the simple test result into larger discursive and institutional formations.

Most people seem to believe that, barring occasional testing errors, medical testing in general produces infallible evidence. Outside the highly AIDS-informed core of the gay community, the HIV antibody test is misunderstood as diagnostic for AIDS. Many people interpret the test result as a guideline about whether to practice safe sex. Most media coverage and many popular advice books about AIDS and antibody testing promote the idea that a negative test gives you a "clean bill of health" and means you do not need to practice safe sex. Some people understand the negative test as a signal of immunity, others simply do not think about the possibilities of future exposure to HIV.

11. In Your Journal: What was your understanding of HIV testing before reading this essay?

The mainstream media and many doctors use the term "the AIDS test." They argue that this term is accurate enough for popular consumption, that it was hard enough to raise awareness about AIDS, and thus introducing the term HIV would merely confuse. The test is however more properly called the "HIV antibody test"; this is the term used by most AIDS educators and involved clinicians. But even this term rests on a model of medical knowledge that creates confusion. The test doesn't actually look for the "antibody" to HIV but detects—reacts with—certain proteins which, in **sero-epidemiological** studies of North Americans and Northern Europeans, appear in the blood of people who have mounted an immunologic reponse to HIV. The two procedures commonly used to detect these proteins are called **ELISA** and Western Blot. ELISA and Western blot are not tests in the popular sense of absolute diagnostic value, but rather are chemical reactions that indicate that a particular biochemical process has

sero-epidemiological: related to the study of factors pertaining to blood-transmitted diseases

ELISA: (Enzyme-Linked Immunosorbant Assay) blood test for antibodies commonly used to detect infection with HIV occurred in the blood of the subject. This reaction of blood chemistry is not specific to HIV (the proteins which are considered representative of HIV antibody are *also* characteristic of antibody to malaria), and even in the presence of HIV, it varies in strength. This is nothing new to scientists; all assays are statistically-based procedures which take the presence of a particular compound to be indicative of the presence of a whole substance. This is how the biochemical disciplines work: they rarely "see" what they are studying, but experiment with purified elements.[17] Thus, laboratory scientists must interpret the strength of reaction in order to decide whether a particular blotter strip is to be considered reactive or non-reactive. ELISA interpretation is now done by computer, but Western Blot is still generally done visually—it requires considerable skill and practice to interpret "correctly" a reactive versus a non-reactive strip.

What is important to understand, then, is not that the test may be "wrong," but that it is not one hundred percent *specific*. However statistically insignificant these cross-reactions (with malaria antibody and other unknown factors) are, they mean that there is a margin of error in every individual test. There is an important difference here between scientific and popular understandings of the test: the laboratory scientist simply establishes whether, in a situation which meets the required laboratory standards (though these may vary somewhat—there are also errors caused by poor lab controls) the assay performed reacts or does not react, or produces a partial reaction that is inconclusive. It is in the counselling process that the categories "positive" or "negative" are assigned to the test, supposedly after the counselor has determined whether the person tested has any traits (exposure to malaria, recent pregnancy) that could potentially cause test reactivity in the absence of HIV. In practice, such assessment is usually omitted, except when people who deny any exposure possibilities actually return reactive tests. In this case, CDC guidelines direct the counselor to advise the person that the test may be inaccurate and to suggest that she/he retest at a later time.[18]

12. In Your Journal: Why does Patton emphasize that counselors rather than lab technicians assign the labels " 'positive' or 'negative' "?

Although there are several forms of antibody testing now in use, I prefer to call the reaction by its proper name, ELISA or Western Blot, to highlight the procedural nature of "testing." The "test" is a series of events, not a moment of **transcendentally** assessing truth; there are important differences between a reactive ELISA/Western Blot (what happens in the lab) and a positive test (the interpretation made in the counselling setting and modified in the subsequent social interactions of the person who has tested). Numerous studies attempt to link behavior change directly to knowledge of test results, or examine these same links as they are made in the sequence of counselling, testing, and ongoing therapy. What such studies fail to understand is the interplay between specific interpretations of ELISA; the ongoing social production of meanings about "the test" in the media and in daily conversations; and the disciplinary effects of using

transcendentally: in a fashion that minimizes physical reality in favor of the mystical or supernatural; in a way that rises above concrete reality

ELISA in marriage licensing, job or insurance screening. This does not mean the ELISA and associated counselling are never useful; some people clearly construct those experiences in a way that helps them start or maintain behavioral changes and renegotiate the meaning of their lives in the context of this epidemic.[19] But this is never a simple effect of either **serostatus** knowledge or counselling. Individual changes only occur *and take on meaning* in the context of complex interaction among shifting community demographics, changing relationship patterns, individual interactions between sexual partners, friends, and counsellors, and as a result of the haphazard assimilation of information gleaned from a variety of news and educational sources. A mixture of community and individual changes have continually shifted the context of test-taking—for example, the heavily debated change from testing to enhance sexual behavior change to testing as a route to early treatment. It is impossible to separate the effect of debates about the value of test taking from any direct effect of either serostatus knowledge or counselling; ELISA literally means substantially different things at different times and within different interpretive communities. The issues raised by testing are located, then, not so much at the level of possible inaccuracies or legal problems, but at the level of the organization, disruption, or reinforcement of the processes of meaning production which take place as individuals and groups make sense of their relationship to the AIDS epidemic.

serostatus: presence or absence of antibodies in the serum portion of blood

13. In Your Journal: What does this discussion about ELISA's status in both social and legal contexts imply about the way society transforms scientific data into socially meaningful information?

INSTITUTING WIDESPREAD TESTING

In 1984, the U.S. announced the development of a test for the antibody to the then recently identified HTLV-III (now called HIV)—the putative AIDS agent. Testing, with its counselling component and apparent objectivity and simplicity, appeared to democratize AIDS education in the face of impenetrable facts about exotic viruses and an ever-changing cast of amazing new drugs. CDC and NIH (National Institutes of Health) officials early advocated widespread testing, even before the test was through its clinical trials, and despite the fact that it had less diagnostic value than research value. It did not show who would get AIDS or ARC and who would not, who was infectious and who was not. The test had been designed to accept a high false positive rate as a trade-off for decreasing the number of false negatives, as is typical in calibrating tests for screening blood products. Early estimates of the test placed the false positive rate at as much as 10 to 30 percent. However, false positivity rates in actual use are a statistical function contingent on the probable **seroprevalence** within a particular group. Thus, statistically speaking, in groups of heterosexual non-injecting drug users, the false positive rate would be higher because the likelihood of infection would be quite low.[20] On the other hand, in a group of highly

seroprevalence: tendency toward the presence of antibodies in the serum of the blood sexually active gay men in a large urban area, again statistically speaking, the rates of false positivity would be relatively low. Counselling protocols are based on these statistical functions, so that positive results among people reporting risk behaviors go unquestioned, even though a number of gay men and injecting drug users are among the false positives.[21]

Subsequent testing protocols began to remedy the problem of false positives in the commonly used ELISA by adding follow-up testing with Western Blot, a technique which had a somewhat higher false negative rate and was thus unacceptable for blood banking purposes. Additional research over the past four years has refined test technology and created a range of testing procedures which assess different aspects of antibody response. But whatever the accuracy of testing now, it is important to recall that the early calls for mass and mandatory testing were made at a time when the test had inordinately high false positive rates, at a time when no one knew the incubation period of the virus (from infection to symptoms—indeed the assessment of symptoms and thus of diagnostic criteria for AIDS was still in considerable flux), and when no one knew the length of time between infection and production of antibodies. Initial calls for mass testing, and the administrative system that developed around testing, were expanding in a context of considerable ambiguity over test accuracy, counselling procedures, and over the relationship between knowledge of test results and behavior or attitudes. There were no **prophylactic** treatments and no civil rights guarantees specifically for people with HIV or AIDS. Though in retrospect these fears seem paranoid, in 1985, the calls for mass testing seemed to point in the direction of quarantine and detention.

prophylactic: preventative

14. In Your Journal: As calls for "mass testing" increased, the "ambiguity over test accuracy" was largely ignored, Patton suggests. What do you think precipitated this informational conflict?

Certainly, the wish to prevent any infected blood from entering the blood supply prompted quick government and drug company action—a reasonably good test was available within a year of identifying the virus. Research and technological development to improve the test moved *much* more quickly than research on pentamadine, which early proved highly successful in combatting *Pneumocystis carinii* pneumonia (PCP) even in highly immune-compromised patients. However, intravenously administered pentamadine caused severe side effects in many people. It was immediately clear that another means of administering the lifesaving drug was needed, but it was nearly two years before a simple aerosolizer was developed and released. In other words, the research trend was toward improving the surveillance capacity of the test rather than providing a prophylactic treatment for the number one killer of people living with HIV.

15. In Your Journal: What does Patton mean by the "surveillance capacity" of the HIV antibody test?

It is important to remember that, in 1985, when testing became feasible, CDC and NIH officials widely believed that transfusion and blood products were the chief route of transmission from the gay and injecting drug user populations into the general population. The idea hardly crossed their minds that there might be significant numbers of non-gay-identified men who had sex with other men, or that there might be substantial recreational drug injection occurring among "nice" suburbanites. In addition, when the tests first went into use, little was known about the epidemiology of HIV, especially outside the original, hardest hit communities. Indeed, some scientists still believed that HIV might be **endemic** in certain populations, perhaps in society at large, and that gay men and injecting drug users were experiencing a newly fatal version of a formerly benign virus.[22]

endemic: prevalent

GAY COMMUNITY REACTIONS TO TESTING

AIDS activists and gay leaders in the mid-1980s moved quickly to discredit the testing programs. In advising public health officials before the testing programs were established, gay leaders expressed concern that widespread, non-anonymous testing might drive underground those who would most benefit from this knowledge. If testing demanded an admission of homosexual sex or drug use, then individuals who were not already comfortable with their sexuality or who feared legal consequences for revealing drug use would simply avoid testing. Public health officials agreed that a poorly designed testing and counselling program would only make things worse. At the same time, the gay press launched an effective campaign to educate the core of the gay community about AIDS and about cautions on testing. The gay community had been coping with AIDS for three years before testing became available as a mechanism for making social and personal adjustments to AIDS, and in the absence of treatment, testing was initially of mixed benefit. Sharing concerns about testing did however create informed gay consumers, though this broader debate about testing did not extend to people outside the gay community.

Activists did not only criticize the test on grounds of potential inaccuracy, or of the psychological impact on those tested; they also argued that those testing positive would be at risk of losing jobs, housing, insurance (insurers had already tried to claim AIDS was a pre-existing condition, and in some cases, an "elective" illness). Some feared that positive test lists would leak from agencies and might be used to round up people for quarantine, to legitimate the harassment of sex workers, or as a pretext for accusing those seeking the test of being gays or drug users, statuses not protected under most civil rights laws.

The government countered these concerns by offering to fund anonymous sites, called, in true government doublespeak, "alternative test sites."[23] This was made to seem like a concession to gay activists, but in fact, the use of the traditional STD clinic as a model for the new test sites, coupled with financial stringency on the basis of government cost/benefit analysis, severely curtailed the counselling activities of ATS. It would only

16. In Your Journal: Why does Patton think the term "alternative test sites" is an example of "government doublespeak"?

take another year before demand for testing was so high that a substantial number of people would be tested by private doctors who were not trained in counselling and often knew very little about AIDS and HIV infection. These demands for testing legitimized testing over counselling, education, or community awareness—though all of these had been proven to influence the meaning and consequences of test taking.

17. In Your Journal: Why would some parts of the gay community mobilize *against* AIDS testing? Are you surprised by this response?

Between 1984 through 1985, most gay-based AIDS groups—the overwhelming majority of non-profit and volunteer groups—advised gay community members against test taking. At best, they saw alternative test sites as a means of getting the government to pay for counselling gay men about AIDS. Groups in Chicago and New York produced material for wide public distribution that admonished "don't take the test," and emphasized the importance of practicing safe sex regardless of serostatus. But by the spring of 1985, gay activists in San Francisco had begun to argue that test taking would promote behavior change. They accused East Coast gay communities of paranoia, saying that properly designed record systems could assure the confidentiality of those taking the test—even though there were already four documented cases of government agencies accidently releasing test lists. Some went as far as to accuse anti-test activists of irresponsibility for counselling against taking the test. There are some important epidemiological features which may account for some of this difference in attitude toward testing: in San Francisco, and to a lesser extent in Los Angeles, the overwhelming majority of people living with AIDS and HIV were gay. In Chicago, Boston, Philadelphia, Atlanta, Washington D.C., and Miami, a large number of PLWAs and HIV-Ab+ people were non-gay IV drug users, women and children, and the epidemic was increasing in the Black and Latin communities. The politically powerful San Francisco gay community was able to control the image of and responses to the epidemic in a more uniform way than could gay communities in other cities who were grappling with the different effects of and responses to AIDS in other communities. It is also important to remember that there was in San Francisco a cohort of some 8,000 men who were already socialized to be study subjects, having participated since 1978 in hepatitis B vaccine trials. Confidentiality structures, perceptions of trust and control, and willingness to frame experience in terms of scientific tests thus seem likely to have been already well established in San Francisco's gay community. In addition, some sexual behavior change may have already begun in response to education about protecting men from hepatitis B, a sometimes fatal illness and a debilitating epidemic in some gay communities.

18. In Your Journal: Why did the San Francisco community have such a unique experience of the AIDS epidemic in terms of controlling transmission and gathering data?

The debate about testing eventually coalesced into the consensus that the pros and cons of testing be listed, and the decision left up to the individual. Lost was the recognition that people sought testing based on erroneous information gleaned from media accounts, and on the expectation of learning t[illegible] which the test could not tell them. Nationally, AIDS hotlines still sp[illegible] huge amount of time answering test-related questions.[24]

EXPANDED TESTING: GAY PEOPLE AND HETEROSEXUAL AIDS

Until there was wide discussion of AIDS among heterosexuals, gay and AIDS activists held the line against widespread testing. There were dissenters, including those who believed that knowledge of test results facilitated behavior change, a position that is now disputed. From about 1985 until late 1986, gay activists, civil libertarians, and AIDS activists were quite successful in controlling how and when the test was used. But social concern about the "innocent victims" of AIDS increased and began to focus on pregnant women, and women who unknowingly married an HIV-infected person. In the critical two years after testing began, but before it came to dominate AIDS policy, feminists failed to take up AIDS or HIV testing as an issue, while gay men failed to recognize that arguments for testing women would become pivotal in a process that dragged testing down the slippery slope toward isolating those infected with HIV. Social stereotypes about women—especially African American women—and sensational reporting about sick babies made policy-makers irrational and contradictory in formulating AIDS policy. Their notions about individual responsibility in sexual behavior, and about women's capacity (or supposed lack of it) to make reasonable decisions about childrearing, were based on social stereotypes rather than on careful analysis of the decision-making options, life priorities, and information available to women at risk. Educational strategies, therefore, were based on stereotypical notions of risk perception and behavioral ethics among those thought to be at highest risk.

> *19. In Your Journal:* How did feminists play a role in the development of HIV testing programs, according to Patton?

In 1985, Army researchers at the Walter Reed Hospital in Maryland announced that they had men with AIDS whose only risk contact had been with female sex workers in other countries. Women, especially sex workers, immediately came to be viewed as the "vector" moving HIV from the sex and drug underworld to heterosexual men, who then passed it to their wives, the "vessels" of procreation. Only privately did anyone challenge the Army data, suggesting that claiming to have visited an out-of-country (and therefore untraceable) sex worker was more acceptable than admitting to homosexual sex or drug use. Thus, while for both good reasons (the resistance to testing programs among gay activists) and bad reasons (the perception that gay men infected only each other) gay men were largely left to decide for themselves whether to be tested. Women who were potential mothers were pressured to be tested. The mandatory or aggressive "volunteer" testing programs for pregnant women and marriage applicants

> *20. In Your Journal:* Why does Patton put the terms "vector" and "vessels" in quotation marks? What comment is she making about language used by the Army in the context of AIDS research?

> *21. In Your Journal:* Patton suggests that it was more acceptable for an Army member to admit to visiting a prostitute than being gay or using IV drugs. Do you think this would have been any less true in civilian society? Why or why not?

dereliction: neglect

were established in several states in the spring of 1987; unwillingness to be tested became a sign of moral **dereliction.** Calls for mandatory testing of certain groups (usually prisoners, hospital admittees, and pregnant women) gathered momentum; the Army soon began testing all recruits, and in 1988, the U.S. began requiring antibody tests of all immigrants.

The expansion of testing has taken two forms: forced testing of those who might infect "the innocent," however that is socially defined, and voluntary programs for those under pressure to identify themselves as and organize their life around the idea of being a "positive" or a "negative." Few heterosexuals agonize about test taking, though the test may at some point strike them as a mechanism for displacing or relieving anxiety. For gay men by contrast, at least in cities with identifiable gay communities, life now requires them to take a stand on testing; serostatus has become part of the identity of gay men involved in urban gay communities.

Complicating the meaning and role of HIV testing is the persistent confusion over "heterosexual AIDS." Testing and counselling centers report great upsurges in appointments from heterosexuals in the wake of any extensive news coverage of heterosexual AIDS. To further complicate the issue, in the mid-1980s policy seemed to change monthly on whether all heterosexuals or heterosexuals *per se* or only heterosexual partners of IV drug users and bisexuals were at risk and should be tested. There is indeed still ongoing discussion about the cost efficiency of testing people with no probable exposure in order to catch the minute number who fail to recognize that they may have been exposed. While gay men who do not know the serostatus of all past partners simply assume there is a good chance they have been exposed to HIV, heterosexuals have difficulty accurately assessing their potential risk. Counselors are told to discuss the test taker's past behavior, making the counselling strategy and decision to test contingent on the counselors' skill at eliciting sex histories, on their perception of the probability of the individual's exposure to HIV, and on their willingness to take responsibility for influencing the decision of the person seeking the test.

SOCIALIZING INDIVIDUALS TO THE AIDS REALITY

The alternative test sites have emerged as the center for socializing individuals (as opposed to communities) to the new reality of HIV. The media and the government-funded AIDS education programs promote HIV antibody testing as the centerpiece of their efforts to stop AIDS. The belief of many policy makers that it is widespread testing and not community organizing that has slowed the spread of HIV among gay men makes plausible legislation like the Helms Amendment in the U.S. (1987) and Section 28 of the Local Government Act (1988) in Britain. The Helms Amendment forbids AIDS funding to projects which "promote homosexuality," which has been construed to include any gay-positive material. In Great Britain, local governments have been prohibited since 1988 from funding any activity (exclusive of AIDS education) which promotes homosexuality or "pretended family relationship." The passage of these ultra-homophobic laws stems directly from denying the role played in risk assessment and reduction by positive gay identity, or by measures to decrease prejudice against homosexual behavior for those not "gay-identified." The public health debate in the U.S. pretends that "neutral" testing can solve the problem, although nearly every other country in the world rejects widespread testing programs as expensive, ineffective, and misleading as an educational strategy.[25]

22. In Your Journal: How do the Helms Amendment and Section 28 of the Local Government Act stem from the media's decision to ignore the effect of "positive gay identity" on risk reduction?

Non-diagnostic uses of the HIV antibody test promote the construction of sexual identities based on perceived risk and test result. Although it is often argued that testtaking reinforces or stimulates behavior change, identifying as a "high-risk person" is not in fact synonymous with thinking through the exact practices which create risk and non-risk in their social locations of sex and drug use. In the early years of the epidemic, we fought to get people to talk about "risk behavior" rather than "risk groups," the latter category being defined at the time by social identity labels such as homosexual, IV drug user, prostitute, or partner of any of the above. Testing simply revises the categories to "positive" and "negative"—with no regard for significant mislabelling as a result of testing error—while pretending to ignore race, class, and sexual bias. The implicit association between positivity and high risk behaviors, negativity and purity serves further to reinforce the stigma and patterns of discrimination already insinuated into AIDS risk logic: the "risky behaviors" for which testing is essentially a confirmatory exercise are already connected in the public mind with gay men, prostitutes, drug users, and people of color.

23. In Your Journal: What does Patton mean by "the construction of sexual identities"? Who does the constructing? How or by what means does the constructing happen?

PROFESSIONAL SAFE SEX

Finally, the introduction in around 1985 of health education professionals to a pre-existing HIV and safe sex education framework brought a further shift in attitudes toward reducing the incidence of AIDS. Traditional health educators demanded **empirical** proof that particular strategies worked; their **behaviorist** orientation blinded them to the symbolic meanings and social organization of both sex and IV drug use. They failed to recognize that the people they sought to educate pursued their pleasures in communities and subcultures that operated by rules different from those of mainstream society (which itself, of course, fails to adhere to the rules it has itself asserted). Health education professionals trained in the **"scared straight"**

empirical: observed; practical

behaviorist: of the school of thought that observable behavior is indicative of psychological state, and that all behavior is dependent upon positive and negative incentives in an organism's environment

"scared straight": refers to a documentary called *Scared Straight* (1978) that follows teenagers who have broken the law as they are confronted by "lifers" in a maximum security prison for various violent crimes; the prisoners attempt to scare the teens into leading better lives so that they will not wind up "lifers" themselves style of education manipulated existing fears, making it difficult to separate false, pedagogically inspired panic from justifiable alarm. Overly individualistic in their approach, the traditional professionals never realized that gay men and IV drug users had coped with the fear and reality of AIDS long before the traditional professionals began *en masse* to confront this "new" phenomenon of AIDS. Both subcultures—though in different ways and to different degrees—had already begun to adapt to new group mores promoting safer practices and to mount a defense against the new repression accompanying the AIDS epidemic. Especially for IV drug users, safer practices brought increased social attack: getting one's own needles meant risking arrest for carrying. For gay men, promoting condom use meant publicly highlighting the practice of anal sex, a great social taboo in the U.S. Nevertheless, major sexual risk reduction among gay men had occurred by 1985, well before professional educators exerted influence in the burgeoning AIDS industry. These shifts in mores—enough to reduce seroconversion in San Francisco to less than 2% per year in 1987[26]—were the result of efforts by activists who had little knowledge of traditional health education theory or strategy.

24. In Your Journal: What does Patton see as problematic about the " 'scared straight' style of education" practiced by mainstream health professionals? What method of education does she suggest was more effective in preventing transmission of HIV?

SAFE SEX: WHY DO MEN DO IT?

Safe sex organizing efforts before about 1985 grew out of the gay community's understanding of the social organization of sexuality and from extrapolations of information hidden in poorly constructed epidemiological studies. Reliant on a self-help model indebted to the women's health movement critique of health care and to the gay liberation discussion of sexuality, safe sex was viewed by early AIDS activists, not as a practice to be imposed on the reluctant, but as a form of political resistance and community building that achieves both sexual liberation and sexual health. It is this liberatory subtext that seems to have most raised the ire of the far right, and it was the first premise of safe sex organizing lost when professionals unveiled their plans for safe sex education.

The first safe sex advice was put into circulation by gay men, and was constructed in opposition to the insulting dictates of doctors. By 1983 enough safe sex information was available for a group of gay men, including men with AIDS, to write a forty page booklet called "How to Have Sex in an Epidemic." It still stands as the single most comprehensive guide to safe sex, including explanations of theories of transmission, sexual techniques, and the psycho/social problems of coping with the change to safe sex and with the fear of AIDS. It is important to realize that this booklet was written before a retrovirus was associated with AIDS: men understood and made major, effective changes without the benefit of HIV antibody testing. The lines which divide safety from unsafety have not changed since the first safe sex guidelines; yet the professionalization of safe sex education in 1985–86 led people to believe they could not come up with a personal safe sex plan based on a few facts and a lot of common sense. Professionalized health education displaced authority for understanding and enforcing safe sex standards from the people who engage in sex, and placed that authority instead in the hands of medical experts.

25. In Your Journal: What point does Patton make here about the "displacement of authority"?

Despite the existence of several community organizing projects promoting risk reduction, and despite the active role of local gay organizations and the local gay press in safe sex education, professionalized health education—especially testing—was credited with the dramatic community-wide shifts in mores represented by the San Francisco seroconversion statistics. The national news played a key role in promoting the idea that professionalized education and testing were responsible for this success, although to a lesser extent, "San Francisco" is held up as a model gay community against other cities where behavior change seems less dramatic. As indicated above, however, San Francisco is hardly the best case study from which to draw conclusions about risk reduction nationally. The opinions about testing, studies of the role of testing in behavior change, and fears about abuse of testing are quite different in San Francisco from elsewhere in the U.S. While small scale studies from the densely gay areas of San Francisco indicate that test knowledge seems to reinforce behavior change, virtually identical studies conducted among gay men in Baltimore and Chicago, and differently structured studies in New York City among gay men and IV drug users, do not show a correlation between test knowledge and shifts toward safer sex techniques.[27] As noted above, in San Francisco about 95% of cases are among gay men, whereas the other cities have sizable clusters of cases around IV drug use, within communities of color, and within linguistic subgroups. The conflicting social concerns of those groups fragment those engaging in high risk activities into multiple communities, making targetted education more complex and normative shifts difficult to identify.

There are, in sum, serious questions to be raised about the effect of differing demographics on the use of testing programs to promote behavior change. It may well be that the apparent correlation between test knowledge and behavior change in the San Francisco studies is an effect of the community's general agreement that such a correlation might exist—an assertion widely publicized even before studies were conducted. San Francisco has a longstanding and highly articulated sexual culture with extensive political clout, a culture that was easily formed into an extensive social support structure for people living with AIDS or testing HIV-Ab+ (at least, for white gay men, the largest subject group in the behavioral studies). It may indeed not be test knowledge *per se* that promotes safe sex, but subsequently being referred to tailored support groups which function as places to meet partners who will carry out safe sex commitments.

Anecdotally, counselors and psychotherapists who run safe sex rap/education groups remark that for some men, groups have replaced bars as a place to find sexual partners who can be assumed to be willing to practice safe sex.

grassroots: originating with people far removed from the political center

26. In Your Journal: Why would bartenders have been trained as educators or "leather-clad hunks" have "raided bars to pass out condoms and AIDS literature" during the early days of the epidemic?

27. In Your Journal: Why was there "increasing pressure for standardized, clonable, and statistically evaluable short-range projects"?

Professionalized education programs ignored or let atrophy the more innovative **grassroots** programs because they did not fit traditional models and because they could not be evaluated by traditional pencil and paper tests or statistical methods. Gone were programs that trained bartenders as educators, or community involvement projects where leather-clad hunks raided bars to pass out condoms and AIDS literature.[28] Although the late 1980s saw more innovative programming, especially for "hard-to-reach populations" (the rationale being that you might as well try anything), traditional evaluation measures are poorly equipped to show the rich changes occurring as a result of such programming. Under increasing pressure for standardized, clonable, and statistically evaluable short-range projects, even gay health educators became reluctant to take social risks in order to promote sexual safety.

This traditional pedagogy also sets up a system of categories which make those who do not "hear the message" subject to special emergency measures and laws. Professionalized AIDS education tends to direct programs at good learners, not at the people who most need concrete, nonjudgmental information and support for making changes in their lives and social groups. Professionalized education which emphasizes clonable programs loses sight of the needs of local groups and overlooks the long-term value of participatory projects in which groups generate their own strategies. Even among gay educators, homosexual subcultures outside the urban gay male community are viewed as aberrant variations on groups targetted in tried and true urban projects. Evaluation techniques like pre- and post-testing of fact-based information and charting sero-conversion levels within communities do not adequately reflect the forms and degree of long-term change in groups that are subject to the pressures of poverty and policing, or which have differing conceptions of risk, safety, and the value of the community. The Centers for Disease Control (CDC) require a testing component in most educational programs they fund, not only because they believe testing reinforces behavior change, but because it enables them to monitor seroprevalence in communities where consent for testing would otherwise be difficult to obtain.

28. In Your Journal: What point is Patton trying to make about the "*process* of AIDS education"?

There are, despite all this, some very exciting projects underway in communities disenfranchised by the white middle-class AIDS industry—in communities of color, among IV drug users, among sex workers, in communities in post-colonial and post-revolutionary nations. These projects rely on community involvement, are open-ended, and view the *process* of AIDS education as important in determining how AIDS will be perceived and how well behavior changes will succeed. But these programs are under funded and in danger of the absorption which homogenized the early projects by and for the gay male community.

THE RETURN OF UNNATURAL ACTS: NOTES FOR A GENEALOGY OF SAFE SEX

It is now commonly believed—among gay men as much as in society at large—that gay male sexual culture before AIDS was chaotic, amoral, and thoughtless. Randy Shilts' epic *And the Band Played On* has been particularly influential in confirming just this view. Shilts argues that gay men used doublespeak to avoid the "truth" of the epidemic, which in Shilts' view is that the community's sexual heyday was over once the epidemic set in, and that it was time to adopt relationships like those of the heterosexual mainstream. Describing the ethos of gay culture of June 1983, Shilts says:

> "The linguistic roots of AIDSpeak sprouted not so much from the truth as from what was politically facile and psychologically reassuring . . . The new **vernacular** allowed virtually everyone to avoid challenging the encroaching epidemic in medical terms."

vernacular: dialect; lingo

In marked contrast are the many gay periodicals and gay-produced advice pamphlets. The May 1983 News from the Front publication, *How to Have Sex in an Epidemic,* advises:

> ". . . limit what sex acts you choose to perform to ones which interrupt disease transmission. The advantage of this approach is that if you avoid taking in your partner(s)' body fluids, you will better protect yourself not only from most serious diseases but also from many of the merely inconvenient ones. The key to this approach is modifying what you do—not how often you do it nor with how many different partners . . . As you read on, we hope we make at least one point clear: Sex doesn't make you sick—diseases do . . . Once you understand how diseases are transmitted, you can begin to explore medically safe sex.
>
> Our challenge is to figure out how we can have gay, life-affirming sex, satisfy our emotional needs, and stay alive!"

AIDS words—the linguistic constructs used to talk about AIDS—are never simply "facts" or "truths" but take on particular meanings at particular times, and are understood differently by different people.[29] The challenge to AIDS organizers is to understand how much information and how much disinformation is conveyed by each term at any given point. For example, "body fluids" is a useful term—it highlights the importance of biological transportation, the *active* movement of infected fluid from one body to another. While it is less specific than "semen and blood," its use avoids the difficulties of dealing with the heavy moral baggage carried by both semen and blood in this culture—both are already constructed as venal, fatal fluids. Juxtaposing "body fluids" and "blood and semen" in a single safe sex pamphlet conveys two sets of ideas, each of which has particular symbolic resonances, but which together may convey a more useful understanding about the biology of safe sex.

29. In Your Journal: What is Patton's interest in the term "bodily fluids"?

Even "safe sex" has had different meanings. The term emerged in about 1983 and rang as a radical slogan within the urban gay male community. In its originating moments, it suggested that sex could indeed be safe. As the slogan made its way through scientific meetings, the media, and into heterosexual parlance, it took on new meanings and became fixed as if it were an absolute practice which had only one interpretation. Reconstructing the history of the shifts in the context for understanding safe sex provides some guidelines for devising a "medically safe sex" that is also powerfully liberatory.

30. In Your Journal: Patton says the term "safe sex . . . took on new meanings and became fixed" by "heterosexual parlance." What had the term meant before? Had it been "fixed" previously?

THE PRE-HISTORY OF SAFE SEX

In the highly articulated urban gay male culture of the late 1970s and early 1980s, there were intersecting discourses about sex. There was sexual identity, which meant "gay" for most of these men, though other identities were included, such as leather man, clone, or disco queen. This rich plethora of sexual possibilities was included within the category "gay." There was also sexual practice (the acts men engaged in) and sexual location (the places where men engaged in such acts—sex bars and clubs, bathhouses, outdoor cruising areas, at home). Oral sex, for example, might mean something different and be conducted according to different rules in a bar or in the bushes, when done by/with a leather man or when done by/with a disco queen. There were also **affective** constructs around sexuality: monogamy, open relationships, casual relationships, anonymous sex. Each of these carried varying meanings and rules depending on practice and location. For example, an open relationship might include anal sex at home, and jerking off with anonymous partners at a cinema. This was the fantastic world of possibilities open to urban gay men, the economy of pleasures and representations in which their sex was negotiated.

affective: pertaining to emotion rather than thought

31. In Your Journal: What does Patton mean by the phrase "economy of pleasure"?

These gay men knew a lot about sex. One of the most interesting products of this culture was the hanky code, the expanding **semiotic** use of bandanas of different colors indicating the specific preferences of individual men. While this has been viewed as a **commodification** of sex, it was also the embodiment of a sexual ethic. On a practical level, use of the code avoided the problem of getting home with a person of non-compatible practices. But even more, the hanky code rested on the assumption that sex was to be negotiated between rough equals. Choosing a hanky or hankies drew identity and practice together in an articulation of who one was

semiotic: of or relating to the connection between signs and symbols and what they represent

commodification: practice of turning something into a commercial object sexually and how one expected to enact sex. In **Foucaultian** terms, the hanky code was a discourse about the care of the self. By contrast, heterosexuals in the late 1970s had little sense of themselves as "heterosexual" and functioned under an implied ethical code in which vaginal intercourse was the paradigmatic practice and in which women negotiated from a position of lesser power. Given these different sexual ethics, it is no surprise that it is heterosexuals—the amorphous general public—who have such profound difficulty accepting safe sex.

This was the sexual symbolic terrain onto which the first information about safe sex entered. In the days before "The Test," the urban gay male ethic derived its principles from the possibility that anyone could be infected, and thus required everyone to protect others and themselves from further infection, or infection with possible co-factors. The first safe sex pamphlets—*How to Have Sex in an Epidemic* and others—tried to reinforce the broad range of practices traditional to urban gay male culture, while at the same time getting men to make specific, transmission-interrupting modifications in those practices. In symbolic terms, the strategy was to keep the hanky code and the negotiation structure it represented, but make some changes in the conduct of particular practices (largely in the navy blue hanky of anal intercourse) to prevent transmission of the postulated virus.

In 1984, the safe sex hanky was invented by a group in Texas. This reversed the previous understanding of the relationship between safety and a multiplicity of practices. The black and white checked hanky constructed safe sex as a single practice or set of practices, under which might fall variations. This formed a new logical structure for thinking safe sex. Now, safe sex was a category unto itself—there was safe sex and all other sex, rather than a broad range of existing practices which might require modification to make them safer. The safe sex hanky did, however, make safe sex a positive choice rather than a limitation, and laid the groundwork for constructing a notion of self—an identity—around safe sex: "I demand (am) safe sex."

At about the same time doctors began equating safe sex with reduction in the number of partners. "Number of partners" had not existed before as a preferential category, although doing often and with many people the various sexual acts one enjoyed was celebrated as part of this open sexual economy. Promiscuity was always a loose concept among gay men—often as much a symbolic badge of belonging as it was a numerical reality. The advice to reduce partners was based on a probability model and erased the notion that some *practices* were risky, others safe. What

---

⁘ **Foucaultian:** in the spirit of Michel Foucault (1926–1984), French philosopher and cultural critic interested in the effects of morally disturbing power relations as well as the self's ethical relationship to itself was actually achieved by the shift to an emphasis on reducing the number of partners was not so much behavior change, as a change in the mythology of promiscuity. Men in long-term relationships who had always had multiple partners, and who had formerly projected an image of themselves as promiscuous, now talked more publicly of their long-term relationship, while often retaining the same number of actual partners.

Then in late 1984 came the Heterosexual AIDS Panic, Phase One. The appearance of a half dozen or so "heterosexual" cases (these were heterosexuals who did not fit the previous categories of gay, IV drug user, prostitute, hemophiliac, or partners of the above) recast the notion of safe sex in two ways: first, it strongly promoted the idea that there are safe people (true heterosexuals) and dangerous people (closeted gay men, bisexuals, IV drug users, prostitutes); and second, since among heterosexuals, or at least in the public culture of heterosexual men, penile-vaginal intercourse is the **hegemonic** and identity-creating act, the meaning of safe sex shifted toward abstinence, monogamy, or the use of condoms. On the rare occasions when non-penetrative means to heterosexual orgasm were discussed, they were posed as alternatives to the real thing, in much the same way that teenagers learn that petting is their alternative to intercourse. Adults who develop their sexual practice around non-penetrative activities are thought to be either kinky, or doing it for some medical reason.

hegemonic: of or related to the preponderant power

This insistence that intercourse is the real sex soon spilled over into gay safe sex literature. Condom advertisement controversies in 1986/87 created the first, if limited, public discourse about safe sex that actually made reference to genital sex rather than number of partners or body fluids. Yet they also contributed to a situation in which safe sex discussions inevitably began with a discussion of the importance of condoms, and only then discussed the range of other possibilities for a fulfilling sex life.

When the so-called "AIDS test" arrived on the scene in 1985, it was widely interpreted to be a means of determining whether one needed to practice safe sex. The widespread implementation of sexual counselling around ELISA and ATS further reinforced this new understanding of safe sex. Implicit in the testing process and explicit in some health advice and nearly all media accounts was the idea that any act between ELISA negative people was safe, and any sexual contact with ELISA positive people was unsafe. From now on, people rather than acts defined what was safe sex. This totally disrupted the negotiation logic of organized gay male sexual cultures. Under the regime of ELISA, paradoxically, any discussion of safe sex carries with it a presumption of danger—if you demand safe sex practices, you must either believe yourself to be infected, or you must fear your partner is infected.

32. In Your Journal: What does it mean for "people rather than acts" to define "safe sex"?

The discourse of safe sex has become involved in constructing identities around infection or presumption of infection, instead of focusing—as in the early years—on the biology of transmission, and on the technology and practice of safe sex. For those confronted with the possibility of testing, safe sex becomes a symbol of danger, with ELISA as an indicator of safe versus dangerous persons. Safe sex ceases to be a practice of sexual pleasure, and becomes an avoidance of sexual danger. Thus, for example, Masters and Johnson's 1988 *Crisis: Heterosexual Behavior in the Age of AIDS* articulates a bizarre idea of safe versus "natural" sex. The authors are particularly disgusted by the implications of using latex accoutrements, and never seriously consider non-intercourse practices. Their attitude projects a deep-seated fear of the cultural danger of safe sex:

> "sex partners of uncertain [HIV antibody] testing status [could] . . . wear disposable plastic gloves during all intimate moments. These gloves, after all, aren't too different from condoms. Yet we are unwilling to seriously entertain such an outlandish notion—right now, it seems so unnatural and artificial as to violate the essential dignity of humanity."

Masters and Johnson willfully ignore the difference between creating "intimate moments" and the practical realities of transmission; the point is not to wrap oneself in a latex barrier at the moment of sexual transcendence, but to don appropriate protection before a potentially transmission-enabling moment. They assume a seamless, natural sexual narrative with a beginning, middle, and end, and the premeditated disruption of this story with techniques of safe sex is not seen to restore health to sex, but rather to dehumanize it. The old hanky code, and the wide range of identities, sites, and practices of sex it implied, constructed sex as perverse and fragmented, a montage of inchoate desires, objects charged with symbolism, and unexpected orderings of the sexual drama. Masters and Johnson imply that safe sex is unnatural, and that "natural sex," which in their view is intercourse between ELISA negatives, is safe. Lost is any notion that acts, not people or transcendence, create the condition that allows HIV to move from point A to point B. This safe sex discourse neatly reinscribes normal and abnormal sexuality along the lines of heterosexual intercourse without condoms, versus all forms of safe sex; "safe people" (as determined by ELISA) can have sex naturally, while everyone else—those who "fail" or simply refuse to take the test—is punished with unnatural, dehumanized (that is, "safe") sex.

NOTES

1. The widely offered ELISA and Western Blot "tests" detect antibodies to Human Immunodefiency Virus (HIV), the virus generally believed to render the immune system incapable of fighting the relatively common opportunistic infections which become fatal in AIDS. Although research has demonstrated a high

correlation between presence of HIV and presence of antibodies, ELISA and Western Blot do not test for the virus, do not tell who will progress to clinical AIDS, and do not predict appearance of symptoms. The correlation between antibody status and an individual's ability to infect others is unknown. The "window" time between infection with virus and production of antibodies varies from six weeks to eighteen months, and in some cases lasts years. The effective knowledge gained from the test is quite small and qualified.

Thus, HIV and AIDS are *not* synonymous: HIV is a virus with a wide range of possible outcomes—from no health-altering changes to AIDS. Researchers do not know why some people show no symptoms with HIV infection, others show some chronic, mild, or moderate symptoms, and others die as a result of immune system collapse. The media's persistent collapsing of HIV and AIDS (for example, by using the incorrect term "AIDS virus" instead of HIV) works together with the common belief that "testing positive" on the HIV antibody test (HIV-Ab +) means you will soon "die of AIDS," an unnecessarily pessimistic landscape in which to negotiate health decisions and make sense of what is at stake in unsafe sex and sharing of needles. Simon Watney's *Policing Desire* (Minnesota, 1987) provides an excellent case study of the British media's confusing coverage of AIDS, especially the conflation of HIV and AIDS. On test takers' perceptions of test meaning, see M. Gold et al. "Counselling Seropositives," in *What to Do About AIDS: Physicians and Health Care Professionals Discuss the Issues,* ed. L. McKusick, Los Angeles: University of California Press, 1986.

2. Acquired Immune Deficiency Syndrome is, as the name says, a *syndrome,* not a single disease. AIDS is a definition: it describes an advanced state of immune system breakdown in which a person is progressively less able to fight off common, treatable infections, and can no longer keep in balance the bacteria and yeasts that are normally a part of the body's ecosystem. AIDS is widely believed to be the result of infection with a newly identified virus—in fact, a newly identified *form* of virus—Human Immunodeficiency Virus (HIV, a so-called RNA or retro-virus). "AIDS" and most of the opportunisitic infections which are its symptoms are *not* communicable. Strictly speaking, most of the opportunistic infections are not communicable to people who do not have suppressed immune systems. However, other immune suppressed people may be more susceptible to each others' infections.

HIV is communicable through specific routes, but is not contagious (i.e., it is not easily "caught"). HIV has most commonly been transmitted through receiving infected semen into the vagina or anus, through injecting infected blood, or perinatally. AIDS is diagnosed when one of a set of twenty or so unusual opportunistic infections becomes uncombattable by the person with HIV infection. Many of these OI are treatable until very late stages of immune system breakdown. Although there is not yet a way to completely halt HIV replication once a person shows severe immune system breakdown, the idea that there is "no cure for AIDS" is somewhat tautological: if the definition of AIDS is, in essence, irreversible immune system failure, and thus, death, then "AIDS" precludes the idea of "cure" in the traditional sense. Given that untreated HIV infection extends as many as ten years from infection to "AIDS" diagnosis, and two to five years or more from AIDS diagnosis to "death" (depending on the OI—people with kaposi's sarcoma have a better prognosis than people with PCP, although pentamadine and bactrim prophalaxis are changing these projections), then HIV might better be viewed as a chronic, but manageable disorder, which may decrease lifespan, but is not rapidly and immediately fatal. AZT and other experimental drugs may further slow viral progress, suspending or extending immune system breakdown for many more years. With improved early treatment, the entire course of HIV illness, if fatal, may extend to twenty or thirty or more years from time of infection. In addition, a variety of known drug therapies, holistic measures, and nutritional supplements dramatically improve the quality of life. Increasing general access to health care, especially in poor and disenfranchised communities, and better coordination of HIV care will also improve the overall prognosis for those currently infected. *The New England Journal of Public Policy* Winter/Spring 1988 issue contains several excellent overviews of the medical aspects of HIV.

3. Nearly 6,000 scientific papers were presented in full or in abstracts at the Fifth International AIDS Conference in Montreal, June 1989, but this was the first year that newspaper accounts admitted that there was little "new" among the scientific reports.
4. F. Barre-Sinoussi, J. C. Chermann, F. Rey, et al. "Isolation of a T-lymphotropic retrovirus from a patient at risk for AIDS." *Science,* 1983, 220: 868–871. R. C. Gallo, S. Z. Salahuddin, M. Popovic, et al. "Frequent detection and isolation of cytopathic retroviruses (HTLV-III) from patients with AIDS and at risk for AIDS." *Science,* 1984, 224: 500–501.
5. The "effects" of media coverage are complex, fragmented, and contingent, as decades of media-effects research demonstrate. While specific correlations between particular stories or kinds of representations can sometimes be demonstrated, surveys, "exposure" to media in experimental situations, self-reports on the importance or use of media, and even the broadest trend surveys of general attitudes in relation to media content are all problematic research methods, especially if a "postmodern" critique of information is taken seriously. I cannot rehearse the exhaustive debates on media effects or on postmodernity here; however, my own position is that media are more like a landscape of potential "information" units which are interpreted in contexts which are partly socially interactive (something like interpretive micro-networks or interpretive communities) and partly idiosyncratically reproduced and incorporated or "owned" as knowledge. Thus, some parts of media reports become "meanings" to be circulated and reinterpreted in social contexts, while some parts are simply ignored or incorporated into "knowledge" as if they were not subject to interpretation. The latter are what are "known" as "facts." My discussion of the media here and later is intended to trace convergences between popular mediations of science presented as "new" and older cultural notions. Events in which policy or attitudes seem directly correlated with media reports are not to be interpreted as "media effects," but rather as symptoms of the convergences between two or more discursive formations.

6. In a course on representations of AIDS, taught at Amherst College in the fall of 1989, I assigned extensive readings from self-help books by people living with AIDS. The students remarked that these had challenged their perception of AIDS as rapidly fatal. In addition, many said they could relate the life skills advice of the PLWAs to their own experience in other areas—dealing with sensitive issues with their families, disappointing their friends, coping with physical differences and fears. The "ordinariness" of the lives described by PLWAs was the most striking difference between the view of AIDS the students had formed from media accounts and the sensibility they discovered in the PLWA literature. Certainly, the social context of "reading for school" affected their interpretive and incorporative processes.
7. See especially B. Henricksson, "Social Democracy or Societal Control: A Critical Analysis of Swedish AIDS Policy," Institute for Social Policy, June 1988, also presented at the Fourth International AIDS Conference in Stockholm, 13–16 June 1988.
8. Don Des Jarlais and Samuel Friedman, "HIV infection among intravenous drug users: Epidemiology and risk reduction," *AIDS,* No. 1, 1987.
9. Dr. Edward Brandt, head of the National Institutes of Health until late 1984, pressured medical journals to speed up their review processes so that AIDS-related research could be more quickly available and critiqued. This decision—though controversial—was considered important because of the severity of the new epidemic and because no research paradigm against which to evaluate projects had stabilized. This freeing up of the market place of ideas, while probably necessary at the time, was only the first of many changes in the long-standing internal checks on the quality and reliability of research. Brandt discussed his decision at the First International AIDS Conference in Atlanta, 15 April 1985, in a plenary paper, "Health Policy Implications of AIDS" and again at the Public Responsibility in Medicine and Research Conference on legal and ethical aspects of AIDS, held in Boston, 24–25 April 1985.
10. Henricksson, op. cit.
11. Olna A. Selnes, presenting data from a multi-cohort study conducted by the Centers for Disease Control in the U.S., at the Fourth International AIDS Conference in Stockholm, June 1988.
12. Henricksson, op. cit.
13. David Ostrow, et al. "Drug use and sexual behavior change in a cohort of homosexual men," at the Third International AIDS Conference, Washington, D.C., 1987, and David Ostrow, "Antibody testing won't cut risky behavior," *American Medical Association News,* 5 June 1987.
14. For example, of the $542 million spent on AIDS by the U.S. federal government in 1986, 6% went to education, 45% to research, and the rest to blood screening and testing programs.
15. The 1988 MAC data was not picked up by the mainstream media until April of 1989, and then the study was reported as a preview of the Fifth International AIDS Conference, as if this data had not previously been available.
16. Presented at the Fourth International AIDS Conference in Stockholm, June 1988. See similar Australian data: Gary Dowsett. "Reaching men who have sex

with men in Australia," plenary paper at the Second International AIDS Information and Education Conference, Yaounde, Cameroon, October 1989.

17. Steve Wolgar and Bruno Latour's *Laboratory Life,* Princeton: Princeton University Press, 1986, provides an excellent case study of the process of identifying and creating technologies to study biochemical substances.
18. Centers for Disease Control cost assessment and new counselling protocols for HIV-antibody testing, 30 April 1987.
19. David Silverman, "Making Sense of a Precipice: Constituting Identity in a HIV Clinic," in *AIDS: Social Representations, Social Practices,* ed. Peter Aggleton, Graham Hart, and Peter Davies, Philadelphia: Falmer Press, 1989.
20. See Michael Gross, "HIV Antibody Testing: Performance and Counselling Issues," *New England Journal of Public Policy,* Vol. 4, No. 1, Winter/Spring 1988.
21. The statistical projections for false positives and false negatives are useless caveats for individual test seekers. A deep irony is embedded in the test interpretation process—many individuals simultaneously claim (or are told by counselors) that they are not at risk or low at risk based on their reported behaviors, and yet they demand to be tested anyway. Clearly, the deep ambivalence about sexuality in our culture and the ambiguity about terms like "safe" and "sex" creates an intense anxiety that renders many people unable to believe that the particular sexual activities in which they have engaged have not placed them at risk, even though they feel guilty about engaging in any sex at all. Alternatively, whatever gay men, prostitutes, drug users, and people of color do or don't do is immediately suspect because they are already inscribed as "risky people."
22. This view stemmed from data suggesting that HIV was endemic but non-fatal in Rwanda and from unwillingness to abandon the earlier hypothesis that gay men and injecting drug users were suffering from immune depletion caused by sexual and drug practices which left them prey to various illnesses ordinarily benign. There are still a minority of practitioners and some people living with AIDS who do not believe HIV to be sufficiently or at all causal. I will not detail these debates here, as they have been well-rehearsed in the *New York Native* and in several books on alternative theories of AIDS. What is important to recognize here is that at the time of instituting Alternative Test Sites, the scientific community was considerably more divided than it is today about the prevalence and significance of HIV. Many viewed HIV as requiring co-factors, either environmental or pathological. Only with the compilation of test data on Army recruits did it appear that HIV was indeed a rare virus.
23. The alternative testing sites, funded and supervised through state and federal programs, were set in place in late 1985 after the antibody test became available in spring of that year. The test was designed for screening blood donations. Before a virus was identified and a screening test was available, blood banks asked donors at high risk to refrain from donating. A check list and pamphlet were given to donors, who were expected to self-assess their risk or ask questions. Blood banks agreed that voluntary donor deferral was highly successful and screening would further reduce donation of blood by people who didn't realize or understand their risk. Gay activists argued that blood

testing positive—which included a large number of false positive units—should be destroyed but that donors should not be put on any kind of register which might open them up to discrimination. Blood banks finally rejected this idea and decided that they had a moral obligation and legal liability to notify those whose blood was rejected that they had tested positive for HIV antibody and should seek additional counselling or medical advice. The blood banks feared that if it became widely known that testing was available at donation sites, high risk people might come in for testing and some HIV infected units might slip by undetected, since there is also a small but significant number of false negative tests. Thus, the decision to notify donors of their test result meant that donating might be used for self-testing, necessitating, apparently, the creation of sites where anonymous testing could take place. These were called alternative test sites—alternative not in the leftist or progressive sense, but alternative to seeking HIV antibody status knowledge through blood donations.

24. In conversations with AIDS Action Committee Hotline Coordinator Ken Smith, one of the longest tenured hotline people in the U.S., it became clear that asking for the test is the most common route to obtaining other kinds of information, especially risk reduction information. Most hotlines now seem to pursue with the caller why they want to be tested and urge the caller to begin practicing safe sex and needle hygiene whether or not they pursue testing.
25. The strange-bedfellow exceptions which do test are West Germany, Japan, Cuba, and South Africa. Sweden is considering limited testing proposals and the gutter press in Britain as well as the fascist National Front advocate mass testing.
26. Since it takes six weeks to 18 months from infection to production of antibody—seroconversion—a 2% rate in early 1987 means that significant changes had already taken place in the years before. The seroconversion rates for HIV must be considered in this long-term perspective, unlike rates for syphilis or gonorrhea, which reflect infections occuring in previous weeks to months.
27. Gerald Soucy et al., "Two key studies: 'Comparison of recreational drug and alcohol use among homosexual and bisexual men who are HIV antibody seropositive, and subsequent PWAs,' and 'Effects of HIV antibody disclosure upon sexual behavior and recreational drug and alcohol consumption by homosexual and bisexual men,'" paper presented at the 1987 National Lesbian and Gay Health Conference and the Fifth Annual National AIDS Forum, Los Angeles, 26–29 March 1987.
28. Mr. Leather, a gay man chosen through regional and later national "leather" contests, is nonetheless still mandated by the organizations that support him to spend his year doing safe sex education.
29. See also Paula Treichler, "AIDS, Homophobia, and Biomedical Discourse: An Epidemic of Signification," in *AIDS: Cultural Analysis, Cultural Activism,* ed. Douglas Crimp, Cambridge: MIT Press, 1988.

FOR USE IN DISCUSSION

Questions about Substance

1. Patton describes the way that IV drug users with AIDS were initially overlooked because of presumptions about their general health, whereas gay men were considered generally healthy and therefore apparently stricken by an emerging syndrome. How does this allow her to speculate about the direction the research would have taken fifty years earlier? What is she saying about the larger relationship between social values and medical diagnosis?
2. While many health educators initially thought that knowledge of one's antibody status would cause behavior change, this assumption turned out to be erroneous. Patton says that "social norms and symbolic meanings determine *how* sex is practiced or drugs are used" (446). To what do you think she alludes here? How could behavior not be affected by knowledge of one's antibody status?
3. Patton writes that "Cities with strong gay communities and positive images of gay men showed greater trends towards safer sex behavior" and explains that community projects that focus on "'community beliefs and norms'" have a greater effect on individual behavior than do projects focused on "'individual beliefs'" (447). What is the logic that underlies these effects?
4. Biochemists "rarely 'see' what they are studying" (450), Patton explains. How do you think the "invisible" nature of HIV and AIDS has affected the way that society has responded to the epidemic?
5. Patton makes clear that the decision to test a heterosexual for HIV antibody status was made very differently from the decision to test a homosexual. How did the test site counselor's conversation skills affect the likelihood of testing in the case of heterosexuals? What determined the decision to test in the case of homosexuals? How might these practices come to bear on the social definitions of heterosexuality and homosexuality?
6. How did the term "safe sex" change in meaning over the course of the epidemic? How do the changes reflect the overall development of our response to AIDS?
7. What is Patton's interpretation of the "hanky code"? How does this ethic contrast, in Patton's opinion, with the sexual ethics of heterosexuals? How did the "safe sex hanky" (463) invented in Texas complicate the code's original meaning?

Questions about Structure and Style

1. At the end of the section titled "Media and the Interpretive Process" Patton argues, "Understanding the field of AIDS information and interpretation as highly contingent on social practices, rather than on individuals' intransigence or ignorance, requires designers of information campaigns to coordinate media on

many levels and include participants from communities and micro-groups in order to reflect their interpretive practices" (449). How does this statement sum up what Patton has outlined in this section? Is it a re-statement, a conclusion, or an expansion on the points she has made throughout the section. Explain your answer by quoting from other parts of the section.

2. Trace Patton's references to the pamphlet *How to Have Sex in an Epidemic*. How are the references organized? What contrast does she use this pamphlet to illustrate?
3. While the science of this issue may not be overly complicated, Patton's language and analysis are at times very difficult to follow. What do you think this difficulty reveals about Patton's relationship to the subject matter?

Multimedia Review

1. Patton refers to Randy Shilts's book *And the Band Played On* when she discusses perceptions of the pre-AIDS gay male culture. View the film version (1993) of this book and examine the representations of gay male culture as portrayed in the film. Does the film, as Patton asserts of the book, present gay male culture as "chaotic, amoral, and thoughtless" (461)?
2. Check out the Public Service Announcements (PSAs) at *http://www.unaids.org/wac/2001/psa.htm* and *http://www.cablepositive.org/programspsas.html*. How effective are these efforts to educate young people about the need to have "safe sex"? How do you think Patton would rate these ads?

SUGGESTIONS FOR WRITING AND RESEARCH

1. "No media message is interpretation-proof because consumers already have ritualized ways of using media, which serve as interpretation contexts" (447), Patton writes. She illustrates this point by comparing the way a safe sex media campaign would be framed in two different countries (the United States and Zambia). Given the information Patton provides throughout the text about the injecting drug user community and the gay men's community (both in the United States), design media campaigns that you think would be appropriate for each of those "interpretation contexts." What kind of media should be used? What would the "message" be? How would the message be delivered? Using support from Patton's text, explain your choices for each of the campaigns.
2. When Patton explains the inaccuracy of the label "AIDS test," she shows the mainstream media thought the term appropriate for "popular consumption" despite the inaccuracy, whereas "HIV antibody test" was thought too confusing for the general public (449). Write an essay about the ramification of this "dumbing down" of AIDS research for public consumption. How does Patton think the simpler but less accurate terminology has affected the public's general understanding of, and reaction to, AIDS? Has the mainstream media

changed its terminology since the time this essay was written? Does the public have a better understanding of the science of AIDS, in your opinion?

3. "The discourse of safe sex has become involved in constructing identities around infection or presumption of infection, instead of focusing—as in the early years—on the biology of transmission, and on the technology and the practice of safe sex" (464–465). What identities, according to Patton's essay, are constructed by safe sex discourse? How would those constructions be different if biology and technology remained at the center of social understandings of HIV and AIDS? What does Patton's critique of media representations of HIV and AIDS say about the apparent relationship between social discourse and scientific discourse?

WORKING WITH CLUSTERS

Cluster 9: Bodies of Knowledge
Cluster 10: Interpretation and/as Ideology
Cluster 14: Epistemologies
Cluster 17: Dis-Ability and Dis-Ease
Discipline: The Natural Sciences
Rhetorical Mode: Analysis

"Avoiding the World" (from *For Common Things: Irony, Trust, and Commitment in America Today*)

by Jedediah Purdy

Jedediah Purdy was born and raised in West Virginia, where he was home- and self-schooled until the age of 14. He then attended Phillips Exeter Academy, after which he returned to West Virginia to work as a carpenter and become involved in environmental politics. He was selected as a Truman Scholar and as West Virginia's nominee for the Rhodes Scholarship, graduating summa cum laude from Harvard University with a degree in social studies. Purdy is now a senior correspondent of The American Prospect *and a second-year student at Yale Law School. He has written many articles about culture, technology and ethics, politics, and the environment. He has also served as a faculty member at the Century Institute Summer Program on America's liberal and progressive political traditions. His first book,* For Common Things: Irony, Trust, and Commitment in America Today, *from which this essay is taken, was published in September 1999. His most recent book is* Being America *(2003).*

All things are full of weariness; a man cannot utter it; the eye is not satisfied with seeing, nor the ear filled with hearing. What has been is what will be, and what has been done is what will be done; and there is nothing new under the sun.

—***Ecclesiastes*** *1:8–9*

1. *In Your Journal:* What is the main point of this epigraph? What does it announce the main topic or theme of this essay to be?

Certain personalities bring together the convictions, aspirations, and misgivings that are ambient in an era. Today the attitude that we all encounter and must come to terms with is the ironist's. This is the stance of comedian Jerry Seinfeld, whose departure from the airwaves in 1998 made the front page of the *New York Times*. The end of the show seemed curiously insignificant, not because *Seinfeld* didn't matter, but because the program so perfectly echoed the tone of the culture that its new half-hour each week had triumphed by achieving redundancy. Like **William Butler Yeats in W. H. Auden's elegy**, Seinfeld became his admirers. There is some of him in all of us.

irony: figure of speech in which what is stated is the opposite of what is meant

For he is **irony** incarnate. Autonomous by virtue of his detachment, disloyal in a manner too vague to be mistaken for treachery, he is matchless in discerning the surfaces whose creature he is. The point of irony is a quiet refusal to believe in the depth of relationships, the sincerity of motivation, or the truth of speech—especially earnest speech. In place of the romantic idea that each of us harbors a true self struggling for expression, the ironist offers the suspicion that we are just **quantum** selves—all **spin**, all the way down.

2. *In Your Journal:* What is the relationship between irony and "depth of relationships"?

quantum: something that can be counted or measured

spin: shaped and manufactured explanation; rhetorically manipulative statement

The ironic response to these uncertain currents is eager acquiescence. This distinguishes the ironist from that more somber and familiar beast, the cynic. The cynic, harboring at least a residual sense of his own superiority, stays home and denounces callow and frivolous party-goers. The ironist goes to the party and, while refusing to be quite *of* it, gets off the best line of the evening. An endless joke runs through the culture of

Ecclesiastes: book from the Old Testament which asserts that wickedness is everywhere and life bears no inherent order

William Butler Yeats in W.H. Auden's elegy: refers to W.H. Auden's poem "In Memory of W.B. Yeats," an elegy for the dead poet, whose voice only remains in the mouths of his admirers left behind irony, not exactly at anyone's expense, but rather at the expense of the idea that anyone might take the whole affair seriously.

Irony does not reign everywhere; it cannot be properly said to reign at all. It is most pronounced among media-savvy young people. The more time one has spent in school, and the more expensive the school, the greater the propensity to irony. This is not least among the reasons that New York and Hollywood, well populated with Ivy League–educated scriptwriters, produce a popular culture drenched in irony. Even where the attitude is most prevalent, most people move between irony and seriousness as they shift from the workplace to their apartments to conversations with parents or romantic partners. Still, the idiom is recognizable everywhere, and it is a rare person under thirty-five who does not participate in it.

> ***3. In Your Journal:*** What is the difference between the "ironist" and the "cynic"?

> ***4. In Your Journal:*** How is class status related to irony?

The ironic attitude is most pervasive in popular culture, when **Karl Marx**'s dictum that historic events occur twice—"the first time as tragedy, the second as farce"—which had never before been much use except as an insult to alleged second-timers, has found a new vitality. In a movement exemplified by the *Saturday Night Live*–derived movie *Wayne's World*, programmers and screenwriters have turned their own archives into a satiric resource. *Wayne's World* was a pastiche of pop culture, mostly of 1970s vintage, in which heavy metal lyrics blended with stock characters and catchphrases from sitcoms and cartoons. Several years later, MTV presented *Beavis and Butt-head*, a cartoon whose **eponymous** antiheroes spend their time watching MTV—and subtly mocking its melodramatic, oversexed videos. Now, from comedies to commercials, viewers are invited to join TV programmers in celebrating just how much more clever they are than TV programmers.

eponymous: giving one's name to something

Irony is not just something we watch; it is something we do. Although there is nothing so simple as a culture, or even a subculture, of irony, the attitude pervades our thought and behavior. The ironic individual is a bit like Seinfeld without a script: at ease in banter, versed in allusion, and almost debilitatingly self-aware. The implications of his words are always present to him. Like the characters in *Wayne's World*, we find ourselves using phrases that are caught up in webs we did not weave, from their history on *The Brady Bunch* to President Clinton's recent use of them to their role in the latest book of pop spirituality. In our most important moments, we inhabit a cultural echo chamber. The combined effect of **ubiquitous** television personalities, **sanctimonious** political pronouncements, and popular spiritualism has been to render cliché nearly anything that anyone would feel it important to say.

ubiquitous: being seen everywhere at once, omnipresent

sanctimonious: hypocritically devout

> ***5. In Your Journal:*** What does Purdy mean by "a cultural echo chamber"?

Karl Marx: (1818–1883) German social philosopher, economist, and revolutionary theorist who wrote works about communism and modern socialism, such as the *Communist Manifesto* (1848)

Not only our speech, but also our actions and perceptions have undergone the same transformation. We suspect that our feelings, even those we would like to think most intimate, are somehow trite before we express them, sometimes even before we experience them. In romance, we all know picture-perfect courtship from ***Love Story,*** send-ups of the same suit from satires on romantic comedy, and ironic recastings of the original perfection in which perfection itself is the joke. Walking hand in hand, we cast a shadow before the film projector. Echoing the words of screenwriters and the rhythms of perfume advertisements, we mime a thousand carefully set images of spontaneous delight. We know this, but we cannot escape it.

Even as unique moments come to seem impossible, uniqueness itself has been made trivial. The recent apex of this movement is the proliferation of billboards adorned by Apple Computer with black-and-white, pensive facial shots of anointed geniuses, urging each and every one of us to "think different." The exhortation to imitate genius, which properly names only original, nonderivative, and inimitable thought or creation, would mystify anyone who had not been well prepared to accept it.

parasitic: having the nature or habits of a parasite or leech; living off another

6. In Your Journal: Who or what is the "parasite" in this "parasitic relationship"?

7. In Your Journal: Why would we be "urged to imitate genius" [by the media] if "we do not quite believe in it"?

We have been so prepared by years of exposure to idealized portrayals of the moments that make each person's life unique in his own thought: falling in love, marrying, making love, reuniting with an estranged father, saying good-bye to an aged grandparent. The aim of these portrayals, in movies, television, and advertisements, is to draw on the power of intimate moments. But the relationship is **parasitic.** As we become more sophisticated viewers of these portrayals, we also become more sophisticated observers of our own words and acts. Instead of seeing unique significance in the artificial moments of the public world, we begin to doubt the significance of our private words and lives. We can be urged to imitate genius only because we do not quite believe in it. We know too much to think of ourselves, or anybody else, as original or unique.

platitude: trite, unoriginal remark

This is not a conclusion. It is a nagging suspicion, always present to accuse us of triteness in every word or feeling. Faced with a choice between **platitude** and silence, the ironist in more earnest moments offers strings of disclaimers, sometimes explicit, more often conveyed in gesture or tone, insisting on the inadequacy of her sentences even as she relies on them. In lighter moments she revels in cliché, creating the oft-reported impression that today's youthful conversation is little more than an amalgam of pop-culture references, snatches of old song lyrics, and bursts of laughter at what would otherwise seem the most solemn moments.

Love Story: (1970) romantic tearjerker about a young couple who overcome all obstacles and make great sacrifices in the name of love

Jedediah Purdy

GROWING UP IRONIC

Irony is powered by a suspicion that everything is **derivative.** It generates a way of passing judgment—or placing bets—on what kinds of hope the world will support. Jerry Seinfeld's stance resists disappointment or failure by refusing to identify strongly with any project, relationship, or aspiration. An ironic attitude to politics and public life never invites disappointment by a movement's decline or a leader's **philandering.** There is a kind of security here, but it is the negative security of perpetual suspicion.

derivative: copied or adapted from others

philander: engage in love affairs, especially with a casual attitude

> ***8. In Your Journal:*** How is there "security" in the "ironist's stance"?

What do we find so untrustworthy that we dare put such scant weight on it? We surely mistrust our own capacity to bear disappointment. So far as we are ironists, we are determined not to be made suckers. The great fear of the ironist is being caught out having staked a good part of his all on a false hope—personal, political, or both.

Some of this is a reaction against the perceived excesses of the previous generation. People under thirty-five are routinely invited to view their parents' contemporaries as a bit naive, a bit irresponsible, and often blameworthy for those **foibles**. **Douglas Coupland,** the author who popularized the term "**Generation X,**" presents his protagonists' parents as clueless at best, wild-eyed and acid-wasted at worst—all victims of an innocence that our ironists are determined not to revisit. Recent polls showing that college freshmen have fewer grand hopes and more commitment to making money than ever in memory reveal less the grand **avidity** of the movie ***Wall Street*'s Gordon Gecko** than a suspicion that nothing else is quite worth the risk.

foible: weakness of character

> ***9. In Your Journal:*** What does the phrase "victims of innocence" mean?

avidity: desire, craving, eagerness

Some of that suspicion is grounded in the changing currents of history and culture. One of the defining features of the current generation's experience is the disappearance of credible public crusades, of the belief that politics can bring about an elementally different and better world. Instead of inspiration, contemporary irony finds in public life a proliferation of cant that reinforces ironic skepticism. Emotions have attracted relentless and often **vapid** attention in recent decades, abetted by the confessional culture of talk shows and choreographed political repentance that makes such concern unabashedly public. The young ironist rightly feels that *that* species of sincerity is more honored in the breach than in the observance. Today's irony also reacts to a curious conjunction in public life between the rhetoric of **evangelical** revival and the behavior of low **vaudeville;**

vapid: dull, lifeless

evangelical: relating to the Christian gospel; believing that the Christian gospel is the only authority

vaudeville: of or related to a comedic variety show, especially popular in the early 20th century

Douglas Coupland's "Generation X": novel examining the generation following the post-World War II baby boom (those generally born in the 1960's)

***Wall Street*'s Gordon Gecko:** movie character who famously asserted that "greed is good," because it inspires individuals to rise to their potential

Jim and Tammy Faye Baker sometimes seem to have formed the mold for the public figures of the past decade.

10. In Your Journal: What does Purdy mean that talk show confessionals and political repentances are "more honored in the breach than in the observance" (see previous page)?

A deeper commonality brings both public and private life within the ironic **ambit.** It is a truism that the credibility of what we say depends as much on who we are as on our words themselves. When a person declares a moral commitment, in order to take him seriously we must believe that he might lead a life at least partly oriented by that commitment. Exhortations to chastity don't mean much from a philanderer, nor does praise of patriotism from a **quisling.** Realizing this, we have long walked a crooked and not entirely fair line between skepticism and obtuseness. The moral authority that **John F. Kennedy and Martin Luther King, Jr.,** exercised rested partly on the public's not knowing the details of their **private lives,** and most people will grant that ignorance did the country some good.

ambit: circuit; scope

quisling: traitor who serves as the puppet of the enemy

11. In Your Journal: Purdy says that it is a "truism that the credibility of what we say depends as much on who we are as on our words themselves." How does this relate to the "ironist's stance" previously discussed?

Somewhere along the line, though, we adopted two ideas that together make it difficult to take anyone's seriousness very seriously. Self-aware in the extreme, we are permeated by **Sigmund Freud**'s view that "we are all ill," that everyone's motivations are in some measure selfish, ignoble, or neurotic. From Shakespeare to **James Joyce,** good minds have always been able to perceive the base in the trappings of nobility; but more and more, the debunker's language is our vocabulary of first resort. Today's young people are adept with phrases that reduce personality to symptoms, among them "passive-aggressive," "repressed," and "depressive." It is revealing that anyone who regards his own standards a little too reverently is likely to be labeled not proud—hardly a compliment for most of our history—but "anal." We all have it in the back of our minds that our behavior is subject to psychologizing interpretation, and that we, creatures of multiple and obscure motives that we are, cannot protest our integrity in response.

12. In Your Journal: Why is Purdy interested in the contrast between the labels "proud" and "anal"?

This idea has combined with a mainly unspoken presumption that "values" are not unchanging, impersonal standards. Instead they are in-

---

Jim and Tammy Faye Baker: couple who ran and starred in the "PTL (Praise the Lord) Club" evangelical television show; Jim Baker was arrested in 1989 for fraud, and his extramarital affairs were widely publicized

private lives of JFK and MLK: though neither was exposed by the press during his lifetime, both of the charismatic leaders had a number of extramarital affairs, while fulfilling their social roles as moral leaders

Sigmund Freud: (1856–1939) founder of psychoanalysis who profoundly influenced 20th century thought with his work on sexual development and dream interpretation

James Joyce: (1882–1941) Ireland's most famous and renowned novelist whose works include *Portrait of the Artist as a Young Man* (1916) and *Ulysses* (1922); high modernist known for his non-linear portrayal of the interior complexities of identity tensely personal guideposts, selected because they help us to shape our lives at particular times, then replaced as we grow and move on. This is surely one of the reasons that divorce has become so frequent and accepted, and it is one that many see cause to acknowledge, if not exactly to celebrate. We are more inclined than ever before to say that "people's values change," and that new projects discovered in midlife may carry people onto irreconcilable paths. According to this view, professing a value does not so much acknowledge an objective commandment as say something about the shape one has given one's own life.

13. In Your Journal: With what definition of "values" does Purdy seem to be working? How does this contrast with the "ironist's" definition of values to which he alludes here?

It is now common even to hear religion discussed in these terms. If there is a meaningful distinction between religion and the fashionably vague "spirituality," it is that the shape and content of spirituality are almost exclusively personal. All of this means that "values" describe more than they prescribe. Just as economists take our choices to be "preference-revealing," showing what we really want, so we more and more take our actions to reveal what we really value.

14. In Your Journal: How do religion and spirituality differ? Why would the ironist prefer spirituality to religion?

In this climate, someone who professes loyalty to a principle is perceived to be expressing his own character, not describing the strictures that he is subject to as a Christian, a Jew, or just (his view of) a human being. When a gap develops between his expression and his behavior, he is not just another fallen creature or "all too human," but a hypocrite. Hypocrisy, unlike other flaws, can be resolved by redefinition—by professing a set of values closer to one's actions. So we increasingly take high principle to be a source of unnecessary discomfort or unearned self-importance, rather than an acknowledgment that we are called to be better than we are. We are all ill, and to aspire to wellness is to invite debunking. Our being human has become a strong argument against **cleaving** to demanding values, or respecting them in others. In a curious way, we consider ourselves too honest for that.

cleave: cling to; be faithful to

One ironic response to all this skepticism concludes that, if surfaces are all we have to work with, we had better make our surfaces as compelling as possible. Management guru Tom Peters urges the young and ambitious to "brand" themselves, to shape others' perceptions to their own advantage just as they would market a new product. "We are," Peters writes, "CEOs of our own companies: Me, Inc. To be in business today, our most important job is to be head marketer for the brand called You." Marketing becomes a form of life.

Peters's doctrine chimes unsettlingly with a widespread suspicion that marketing is not a bad metaphor for what most of us do most of the time. An inevitable consequence of sophistication about the received significance of words, tones, and gestures is keen awareness of self-presentation as a production. This sophistication adds a new edge to the old question, "What does she mean by that?" The answer will seldom appear at face value. From the utterly self-conscious conventionalism of the

15. In Your Journal: How does marketing function as "a metaphor for what most of us do" in our interactions with others?

book of strategic dating etiquette ***The Rules*** to the contrived anti-conventionalism of shock-jock celebrities and their imitators, we have reason to be less attentive to what people say and do than to what they might be trying to get by it. When speech and action are marketing, what they reveal is not personality but ambition, not an individual one could know, but a bundle of aims and desires that may or may not coincide with one's own.

Yet just as we are too savvy to take commercials seriously, so we can take only a wary pleasure in people whom we know to be peddling themselves, and whose campaigns may shift with their target audience. For all its ready laughter, the ironic mood is secretly sad. Tom Peters has rather grand predecessors, notably **Oscar Wilde,** who declared, "The first duty in life is to be as artificial as possible. What the second duty is no one has yet discovered." But Wilde drew from wells that are now mostly dry. Despite his talk of artificiality, he was in some measure a romantic who believed that he displayed his true identity by **flouting** convention; he was not exactly a quantum self. Moreover, his eccentricities had the charge and thrill of dramatic dissent in a conventional era. Now, the fashions of dissent are on sale at specialty boutiques, and between the prematernal Madonna and the merrily depraved cartoon *South Park* there is less and less left in convention whose flouting can elicit shock.

flouting: showing contempt, scorning

The ironic stance invites us to be self-absorbed, but in selves that we cannot believe to be especially interesting or significant. Its sophistication is sapping, a way of cultivating suspicion of ourselves and others. Refusing to place its trust in the world, irony helps to make a world that is the more likely to be worthy of despair. And so, despite our **assiduous** efforts to defend ourselves from it, disappointment and a quiet, pervasive sadness have crept into our lives.

assiduous: persistent

THE HUNGER FOR HOME

16. In Your Journal: What is the relationship between irony and isolation, according to Purdy?

Irony is only half of a picture with two symmetrical portions. In the ironic view, each individual is essentially alone. The superficiality of relationships and the ambivalent obligation to "brand" one's own personality set up sharp and mainly insurmountable differences among people. At the same time, the ironic reluctance to identify with a larger ambition—say, a political party or a community project—means that the ironist does not have the reassuring experience of finding his own commitments reaffirmed by others. A par-

The Rules: popular 1995 self-help book by Ellen Fein and Sherrie Schneider striving to teach women how to catch "Mr. Perfect" through small deceptions and myriad manipulations

Oscar Wilde: (1854–1900) satirist author of *The Picture of Dorian Gray* (1891) and *The Importance of Being Earnest* (1895), among other works tisan, or just a partner, takes sustenance from relationships that are shaped by a common project and infused with the values that underlie the project. Some sorts of religious believers and political devotees even find their convictions reinforced as they perceive God's plan or the Progress of History fulfilling itself in the world around them. In all of these experiences there is an intimacy with one's setting, a sense of being connected rather than alone, **consonant** rather than **idiosyncratic.** The ironist has none of this.

consonant: being in agreement

idiosyncratic: characteristic peculiar to an individual or group

Partly in response to that privation, our age of irony is also an age of belief—ambivalent, often frustrated belief, which bears the marks of its ironic competitor, but belief nonetheless. Even in the midst of irony, there is a widespread hunger to feel oneself made whole, connected with true values that are also the values of one's community and, in some cases, of the world itself.

Thus we inhabit a culture in which *Seinfeld*'s popularity was recently rivaled by the second-ranked television drama, ***Touched by an Angel,*** part of a flood of material on the benign, winged creatures. The contemporary angel is not the agent of a jealous or even particularly zealous God, but is rather a kind of therapist-cum-advocate and celestial valet. Bestiaries and user's guides have crowded onto best-seller lists in the 1990s, among them Sophy Burnham's *A Book of Angels* and Karen Goldman's *Angel Voices.* In 1994, the *New York Times* best-seller list included eight books on the topic at various times. According to these accounts, angels not only help us to keep our emotions steady, make sound judgments about relationships, and advance our careers, but also provide small incidents of divine intervention, often on the order of retrieving lost keys or starting a **recalcitrant** engine. Angels, that is, tell us that the universe is not indifferent to our existence.

recalcitrant: resistant

The meaningfulness of things is fundamental to a tradition that begins on the one hand in Plato's and Aristotle's discourses on the intelligibility of reality, on the other in the declaration that "In the beginning was the Word." We are inheritors of the idea that intelligence and at least partly comprehensible order lie at the root of all that is. However, the experience of the past hundred-odd years has been marked by the growth of the idea that the world's order can neither guide nor nurture us, that any significance it may have is essentially inhuman. In the phrase of the German thinker **Max Weber,** the world has become "disenchanted."

Perhaps the greatest evocation of this experience comes from the nineteenth-century English poet **Matthew Arnold,** who in "Dover Beach"

❖ ***Touched by an Angel:*** popular late 1990's television drama in which angels offer messages of hope and bring remedies to the characters' problems

❖ **Max Weber:** (1864–1920) German economist and social historian whose works primarily concern the rise of capitalism

❖ **Matthew Arnold:** (1822–1888) English Victorian poet and literary critic known for attention to symmetry and a restrained style describes the withdrawal of "the Sea of Faith." As it passes, there remains before him only "Its melancholy, long, withdrawing roar, / Retreating, to the breath / Of the night wind, down the vast edges drear / And naked shingles of the world." The naked world is, we insistently feel, not ours. We are native to a world clothed in moral significance, one in which our aspirations are recognized and our hopes, whether fulfilled or not, at least registered, recognized, understood. But now, the world naked, deaf, and mute often seems all that remains to us.

17. In Your Journal: Summarize the sentiments presented in the quoted portion of "Dover Beach."

Angels answer this awful apprehension. Ministering to our sadness and loneliness, they assure us that we are not unloved. Our feelings matter to another being—our guardian angel—as much as they do to us. By interceding in the course of events, angels propose that this celestial concern is not subjective—not just the kind of sympathy that another person might feel for us—but tied up with the natural processes that stall an engine or carry a dropped key through a grate. In other words, the very fabric of things can respond to our desires, even our small and transient ones. If the world does not revolve around us, it does at least wobble our way on occasion. Angels tell us that it is all right to do just what the ironist will not: place the gambler's burden of hope on the world.

18. In Your Journal: What does Purdy mean by the "gambler's burden of hope"? What do angels and gamblers have in common?

Irony, it must be said, raises the bar for anyone who would maintain conviction. The belief in angels, indeed the whole mass of loose-knit spirituality, only partly clears that bar. By and large, "belief" in these things is really a diffuse hope; few people believe in angels, at least of the popular variety, with the confidence of a true religious believer, let alone the belief of a scientist who trusts in the reliable behavior of chemical reactions. Instead, belief of this sort is an on-again, off-again affair, a way of giving cosmological significance to pleasing events and good luck, and a source of some comfort in misfortune.

In all of these ways, obsession with angels is a peculiarly expansive form of self-involvement, the **apotheosis** of psychic needs. Angels not only minister to us as isolated, needy bundles of wishes and fears, but paradoxically help us to stay that way. They provide a species of reassurance that we can have alone, in the privacy of our apartments and offices. Being at home in the world does not have to mean changing or reaching beyond ourselves, adjusting our habits and desires to our places and communities; instead, the world answers our wishes, just because they are ours.

apotheosis: exaltation to divine rank

19. In Your Journal: Why does Purdy say that belief in angels is an "expansive form of self-involvement"? What internal cycle does he suggest they create?

Angelic spirituality is also a way of defying the weariness of an ironic culture. By announcing their hope with an almost pointed naivete, the new spiritualists take a stand against ironic skepticism. It is worth noting, however trivial it may seem, that the same cars whose bumpers announce "Magic Happens" are likely to sport the slogan "Mean People Suck." On their face, the first is metaphysical, the second attitudinal. On closer inspection, both are mainly attitudes. Together they form what might be called the anti-Seinfeld position.

20. *In Your Journal:* What is the "anti-Seinfeld" position?

The same hope for a responsive universe, attuned to something other than physical fact, appears in the new, **syncretic** spiritualism of figures such as **Thomas Moore** and works like the ostensibly "scribed," or channeled, *A Course in Miracles*. Even the titles of their prominent works present a rebuke to the relentless banality of the ironist. *A Course in Miracles* declares above all that there are such things, that our tired world regularly admits the magical. Moore's *Re-Enchantment of Everyday Life* makes exactly the same proposal: a sense that some things are sacred, and hold a special moral meaning in contrast to merely worldly things, is still available to us; the prefix that begins the book's title, though, accepts that the sacred has been lost, or at least obscured, and must be won back. Similarly, Moore's *Care of the Soul,* the first in a slew of popular uses of a word that for many years was scarcely whispered in the culture of network TV and respectable publishing, declares foremost that we *have* souls, that we are not quantum selves.

syncretic: fusing differing systems of belief, as in philosophy or religion

Here again, notably in the *Course*'s idiosyncratic borrowing from Christian and other traditions—for instance, keeping salvation while **jettisoning** sin, which raises the question of what exactly we need to be saved from—spirituality is a matter of reassurance. Its sources are emotional need, and its standards and aims are therapeutic. It consoles more than it challenges, and offers much more than it demands. It is a great comfort. On the whole, it, too, can be had alone.

jettison: discard

These are the conflicting moods of the time. We are skeptical, ironic, and inclined to an impoverished self-reliance. At the same time, we want to give up the ironist's jaded independence and believe that we are not alone, that we can find moral communities, clear obligations, and even miracles. We doubt the possibility of being at home in the world, yet we desire that home above all else. We are certain only of ourselves—if in a somewhat precarious way—and we work toward the certainty of something larger. We are fragmentary, even masters of fragmentation, and we hunger for wholeness.

THE FAST LANE HOME

There is another, more heroic attempt to cross the barriers that irony sets against belief. One way of grasping irony's significance is to consider that the ironic attitude pronounces the impossibility of achieving

---

Thomas Moore: contemporary psychotherapist and spiritualist whose books include *The Care of the Soul* (1992) and *Soul Mates* (1994), which offer guidance to readers on the subject of bringing spirituality into their everyday lives

putative: generally regarded or understood

banal: predictable, trite

21. In Your Journal: Why has there been a shift in the way business and information technologies are perceived and marketed (i.e., why is what was once banal now revolutionary)?

22. In Your Journal: What does Purdy mean when he says "the future consumes the past at an unprecedented rate" and that we have "no stable place to stand"?

obtuseness: lack of intelligence or sensitivity

prosaic: straightforward; lacking in imagination

mercenary: motivation driven by a monetary or material gain

Thoreau's "original relation to the universe." Where wishing for angels means lightly retouching the world to make it more responsive to our **putative** originality, the heroic attitude calls on individuals to rework themselves radically enough to become original again. Today this aim finds expression mainly in the walks of life that are widely perceived as the most dynamic, the most transformatory, and the most likely to produce heroes. They are, intriguingly, realms that a few decades ago seemed positively **banal:** the business world and information technology. Their defining vehicles are a pair of lifestyle magazines, *Fast Company* and *Wired.*

The interest of these magazines is that they speak to a pair of transformations that other media have approached with an **obtuseness** verging on physical inaptitude. Changes in technology have left the childhood educations of young adults already obsolete, while changes in the economy make their prospects, even if heady, basically uncertain. Today the future consumes the past at an unprecedented rate, and the present provides no stable place to stand. *Fast Company* and *Wired* promise an understanding of the quaking landscape and perhaps even a place to live in it. Their appeal to puzzlement, more than their pretense to heroics, is the key to their attraction. Their failure is that they answer an unsettling reality with unsatisfying fantasy.

Fast Company, the leading vehicle of the business-person-as-hero idea, is one of the most successful of the wave of start-up magazines from recent years. *Fast Company* presents business as a way of life that leaves behind the **prosaic** stuff of ordinary existence. The magazine's refrain is the idea of "free agency": the contemporary economy has cut people loose from traditional, lifelong corporate jobs and spun each of us centrifugally into total freedom and self-reliance. Now everyone is a freelancer.

Fast Company styles the **mercenary** life a good one. Free agency is not an eviction, but an escape from the constraints of traditional careers, into a new ideal of self-creation as a profit-making exercise. The magazine's definitive discussion of free agency includes the declaration "I declare my independence" from the bonds of job, place, and nation. "Companies do not exist. Countries do not exist. Boundaries are an illusion." Everything that keeps us where we are, weary, flat, and dull, is whisked away as if by the power of a wish. Freedom is born in the pronouncement of freedom.

However, the essential movement of *Fast Company* is less departure than homecoming. The magazine rebels rhetorically against a stereotyped "corporate culture," one of the constraints that the Free Agent is most eager to escape. The villains of its pages are "toxic companies," where bosses are overbearing, employees are alienated, and creativity is stifled. As a representative Free Agent recalls of attending large companies' re-

---

⁂ **Henry David Thoreau:** (1817–1862) American naturalist and literary transcendentalist, author of *Walden* (1854) and "Civil Disobedience" (1849)

cruiting sessions: "They were fake, they were plastic." In contrast to all that, "She was looking for authenticity."

"Fake" and "plastic" are conventional ways of abhorring the **patina** of convention, the all-encompassing triteness that dogs the ironist. They capture the sense that everyone is pretending—and rather inelegantly, at that—to fill out roles that no one can really believe in. Against this, *authenticity* is the real selling point of free agency. This complicated and elusive idea is essential to the "original relation to the universe": we want not just something new, but something that is really *us*. The problem with a world where everything is derivative is the suspicion that we are patched-together remnants of someone else's imagination, unreal, not our own. That is what makes us fear that we are farce rather than tragedy.

patina: sheen produced by age and use

23. In Your Journal: How is the business world's conception of "free agency" ultimately an ironic endeavor?

The fear of losing authenticity is an old one. The wish for clarity about what we are and are not, a decisive repudiation of artificiality, is Thoreau's hope on going to the woods "to live deliberately, to front only the essential facts of life . . . and not, when I came to die, discover that I had not lived at all." It is the source of Hamlet's fear that, as self-doubt stays his determination from becoming action, he fades into a living ghost before the world. To express oneself whole and unadulterated is the aspiration of a long line of dissenters from convention, from **Percy Bysshe Shelley's Romantics** and the **Surrealists** to stream-of-consciousness beat poets.

What is new is that the latest seekers after authenticity are not **bohemians,** but boardroom Romantics. The spreadsheet has replaced the canvas, the stanza, and the journal. For the first time, the way out of convention is by the superior command of conventional achievements. The way home is through the home office.

bohemian: person with artistic or literary interests who disregards conventional standards of behavior

The businessperson is an artist, a genius by turns solitary and collaborative. Accordingly, *Fast Company*'s next-favorite fetish after authenticity is "creativity." The magazine's regular "Unit of One" feature, offering quick lessons from exemplary Free Agents, devotes more than a third of its profiles to this idea. The profiled entrepreneurs offer such slogans as "The key to creativity is clarity," "You can't force-feed creativity," "Creativity is a two-step process," and, with a symmetry that is almost elegant, "There's no creativity without authenticity." Art is good, business is art, and there is no good business without art.

Percy Bysshe Shelley: (1792–1822) influential English romantic poet who had radical views on love, marriage, revolution, politics and religion; Shelley's great masterpiece is *Prometheus Unbound* (1820)

Romantic: movement of art and literature in the 18th and 19th centuries, promoting nature and the individual expression of emotion

Surrealist: early 20th century art and literature movement concerned with evoking and representing the subconscious

Business is also a domesticated form of political commitment. A delighted profile of Chinese entrepreneur Li Lu, who confronted the Beijing regime's tanks at Tiananmen Square in 1989, details his discovery that "business has become the ultimate expression of individuality." "The spirit of Tiananmen," *Fast Company* proclaims, has moved from the streets to the offices of a new breed of Chinese Free Agent. In the less dramatic politics of the United States, the magazine casts a rare approving glance at Mayor John Norquist of Minneapolis because "He certainly doesn't sound like a politician—least of all, like a Democrat. When John Norquist talks, he sounds exactly like a change agent." In the same spirit, tucked between an item on the virtues of bourbon and another on low-cost PCs, is a piece praising an innovative judge as a "Change Agent in a Black Robe." Change agents are the storm troopers of creativity and authenticity, the innovative entrepreneurs and management consultants who make over companies and careers. Politics, in short, is worth attention when it most resembles the heroic version of business. Nothing less can hold the Free Agent's **capricious** attention.

24. In Your Journal: Purdy finds the quote from Tiananmen Square rebel Li Lu a particularly good example of the power of contemporary business rhetoric. Why?

25. In Your Journal: What is a "change agent"?

capricious: impulsive or unpredictable

Thus the artistic heroism of authenticity and the political heroism of declaring principles in the face of power both belong to the business world. This is an extraordinary coup, like Microsoft purchasing Liberty Hall, the Louvre, and perhaps the Vatican. However, it is hardly credible. Business, after all, is neither art nor politics, but only itself. Nor is it a way of remaking oneself, of achieving the elusive original relation to the universe.

Attempts to achieve those aims through money-making and marketing fall back into the unhappy muddle of irony. One of *Fast Company*'s heroes is the same Tom Peters who urges each of us to become something called "brand You." Peters informed readers in a cover article in 1998, "You're every bit as much a brand as Nike, Coke, Pepsi, or the Body Shop. . . . When you're promoting brand You, everything you do—and everything you choose not to do—communicates the value and character of the brand." In other words, life is a hustle.

26. In Your Journal: How might "brand You" fall into the trap of sincerity or cliché that the ironist wishes to avoid?

A hustle, though, is no way to authenticity. With this move we are back to irony, to contrivance, manipulation, and thinness of personality. Surely brand You is no less suspect than the derivative words and phrases that first make the ironist suspect that everything might be more or less reluctant marketing. Yet *Fast Company* manages to be altogether cheerful about this difficulty, overcoming the distastefulness of the hustle by omitting to notice that it is hustling at all. The implausible interconnectedness of art, politics, business, and authenticity is presented with a smile that is much more naive than knowing. The effort is well intended and delivered with enthusiasm. For all that, though, it is not believable.

This implausibility is not incidental; it is tied up with the fantastic character of the whole *Fast Company* scheme. The magazine offers a vision of being at home in the world while being essentially uprooted: the Free

Agent is bound nowhere, but is at ease everywhere. He is comfortable because he is creative and authentic wherever he goes. His creativity shows itself in "working smarter" and "playing the game differently," his authenticity in "strong values." These, though, are not a personality or a form of life; they are catchphrases, like "change agent," notable for signifying nothing in particular. They are phrases that substitute for thought.

27. In Your Journal: Why does Purdy think that the language of the Free Agent is really just a bunch of "catchphrases . . . signifying nothing in particular"?

The Free Agent is advertised as being in harmony with what is best in the world: he is creation, change, and truthfulness. But in fact, as described in his own lifestyle magazine, he is a strikingly thin creature. There is little sense of what his "strong values" are, of *how* he "plays the game," let alone why he chose to play this particular game rather than any other, or no game at all. What he means by *creativity* and *authenticity* is obscure, and probably could not survive clarity. His rebellion is not a movement, not even a statement, but a gesture. He is the fifteen-second clip of personal contentment that one sees in a nonironic commercial. He is, in other words, brand You.

Fast Company ends by being unconvincing because its fantasy is vague, diffuse, made up mainly of gauzy images and pleasant sounds. The Free Agent, though, has more exotic cousins whose fantasies are more adamant. The most outlandish of these is the tribe of the Digerati, the elite of the new information economy celebrated by *Wired* magazine. *Wired,* which a few years ago enjoyed the kind of launch that has hurried *Fast Company* into prominence, tries to do for computer technology what the younger magazine does for business: make it into a way of life that saves its participants from banality. The magazine's first issue announced, "*Wired* is about the most powerful people on the planet today—the Digital Generation." Despite that grand claim, its most tantalizing promise is not that its **lionized** audience will rule the world, but that the Digerati, like the Free Agent, can approach the world originally.

lionized: treated as a celebrity

Where *Fast Company* follows tepidly in the steps of the Romantics, *Wired* inherits a cartoonish version of the thought of **Friedrich Nietzsche,** the nineteenth-century German **iconoclast** whose ideas have become a touchstone for generations of rebels against received morality. Nietzsche believed, like many of our contemporaries, that all myths, magic, and certainty had gone out of the world. The progress of science and rational skepticism had exhausted the plausibility of Europe's great religious tradition, Christianity, and its secular **avatar,** liberal democracy. This process, what Weber would later call disenchantment, was psychologically devastating, but it also presented a heady opportunity. Christianity and democracy

iconoclast: one who seeks to overthrow popular ideas or institutions

avatar: embodiment

Friedrich Nietzsche: (1844–1900) German philosopher who promoted the idea of the *Übermensch*, or superman, and argued that Christianity's emphasis on the afterlife resulted in a sense of decadence; author of *Thus Spake Zarathustra* (1883–1892) had thrived on repression, training the strong, intelligent, and beautiful in the enervating habits of humility, self-reproach, and egalitarianism. This was a painful distortion of the higher human capacities, the power of free expression and, above all, the power to create liberating, sustaining, and strengthening myths. The end of religious belief meant a new freedom for these powers. Those who possessed strong enough imagination, will, and intellect could celebrate their new liberty in freely chosen communities of similarly extraordinary individuals.

> ***28. In Your Journal:*** How is the *Wired* ethos similar to the ideas of Nietzsche? How do they draw from the work of Weber?

Wired adds a twist to this idea. For the magazine, the key to realizing Nietzsche's promise is technology. "No ambition, however extravagant, no fantasy, however outlandish, can any longer be dismissed as crazy or impossible. This is the age when you can finally do it all. . . . Suddenly technology has given us powers with which we can manipulate not only external reality—the physical world—but also, and much more portentously, ourselves. You can become whatever you want to be." The bold invitation stretches across the first few pages of one issue of the magazine, emblazoned over a computer-generated, **Daliesque** landscape populated by transparent human forms whose brains, muscles, and entrails are tangles of silicon chips and fiber-optic cable. The phrases echo one of *Wired* editor Kevin Kelly's favorite slogans, "We are as gods, and we might as well get good at it."

> ***29. In Your Journal:*** Why is a parallel being drawn here between religion and technology?

> ***30. In Your Journal:*** How does Kevin Kelley's quote illustrate Purdy's conception of contemporary attitudes toward religion?

The magazine's writers revel in fantastic descriptions of expensive biological and electronic advances that offer people the capacity to remake themselves. One set of recurring *Wired* heroes is the Extropians, a kind of freewheeling cult committed to becoming supermen through technology. They espouse "a philosophy of freedom from limitations of any kind." On the Extropians' account, those who can afford it will eventually be able to overcome mortality by "down-loading" consciousness into computers, where they will survive forever as disembodied mind, perhaps helped along by robotic accessories and virtual-reality experiences. They are equally committed to pharmaceutical, surgical, and other ways of concentrating and expanding the powers of the mind.

The self-invention that *Wired* imagines is not, though, completely individual. Instead, the magazine invites its readers to mark themselves as members of a tribe, or several tribes, in which an original relation to the world becomes possible.

In this spirit, *Wired* adopts a digital-pagan tone. A 1996 cover story celebrated Burning Man, a weekend gathering in the Nevada desert where high technology and counterculture meet in a festival of body paint, drumming, and electronically enhanced mayhem, culminating in the burning of

---

Daliesque: (related to or in the style of Salvador Dali [1904–1989]) Spanish surrealist artist known for his unique interpretations of the human unconscious; his most famous work is *Persistence of Memory* (1931)

a huge human figure, a custom adopted from Europe's ancient Celts. The magazine has adopted as its muse the late **Marshall McLuhan,** prophet of technological tribalism. In an admiring interview with the successor to McLuhan's professorial chair, Derrick de Kerckhove, *Wired* reports his conviction that Internet users have reattained "a tribal world, [where] the cosmos has a presence. It's alive. The tribe shares in this huge, organic reality." If there is no magic in even the oddest corners of the merely physical world, there can be magic in the artificial worlds of computer-generated virtual reality. There, invented selves can play in invented fields, cultivating an original relation to a thoroughly original universe.

31. In Your Journal: Does de Kerckhove's point about tribalism in any way challenge Purdy's argument about the isolationism of the ironist's stance?

Still, the way to that originality is essentially a consumer's. From the beginning, regular features have announced which ideas and products are "wired" and which "tired"; kept up a "jargon watch"; pointed out the gear and style that bring "street cred," as in credibility; and held forth on "fetishes," the super-products of the super-wired. The magazine's wired/tired and "fetish" features describe the latest symbols of tribal membership, which require constant updating. This tribe is all about being on the move, and about buying. The magazine's ideal reader, when something looks good to him, will do it, buy it, create it, or become it without delay. The Digerati seek comradeship among perceived equals in self-invention and world-making; rather than scorn the less exalted, they are likely to forget their existence altogether. This is an adolescent doctrine, a wish for a fantasy shopping trip without end.

Yet at the same time there is something **plaintive** in *Wired,* a disappointment in the dull business of the world, the sense of **ennui** that occasions irony. In place of **pabulum** and tedium, the magazine offers its readers a glimpse of real community—life in the tribe, where everyone is clever like you, enthusiastic about the same things that delight you, and looking for the same kind of good time that you're after. Kelly's cosmological musings even provide a quasi-religious sense of the meaning of computer work—nature worship rendered in silicon.

plaintive: melancholy

ennui: dissatisfaction as a result of boredom

pabulum: lacking intellectual sustenance

What the Digerati have in common with the Free Agent is that, by and large, neither exists. The magazines' readers are not mainly Free Agents, let alone aspiring Extropians. They are curious, concerned about shaping their futures and understanding the present. As angel-watching involves more attitude than metaphysics, so this readership bears more puzzlement than the conviction and self-congratulation that pervade the magazines' tone. *Fast Company,* although a more serious affair than *Wired,*

Marshall McLuhan: (1911–1980) Canadian cultural theorist and scholar who argued that "the medium *is* the message" (i.e., the method of communicating information has more influence on the public than the information itself) (1964)

> ***32. In Your Journal:*** When Purdy asserts, "We do not, really, ever declare and keep our independence. In the end, we would not wish to," for whom is he speaking?

describes the real lives of very few people. We do not, really, ever declare and keep our independence. In the end, we would not wish to. *Wired,* meanwhile, is a testament to the power of artfully rendered fantasy to distract its participants from reality. The magazine's icons are men and women who can take fantasy in full seriousness—at the cost of being taken seriously themselves.

The Digerati and the Free Agent express the poverty of our resources for thinking of our lives as guided by some purpose, filled by some power, or touched by some loveliness outside what we have learned to call banality. Their eminent unreality bespeaks a weakly held hope for the potency of fantasy. Whether in virtual communities or in self-marketing authenticity, we would like to compose stories about ourselves and see those stories come true. We are looking for words and ways of living that will help us make sense of an increasingly complex and elusive world.

We do not especially want the irony that sometimes seems our lot, and do not find the wholeness that we continue to desire. Our attempts to resolve the dilemma seem to draw on the worst in us. It is little wonder that many of us settle into irony as mildly discontented residents, or into one of the competing versions of wholeness as secretly half-doubting partisans. Our fantasies do not hold together, and reality does not hold us. Of the things that we do try to believe in, moreover, politics is no longer one. It is worthwhile to ask why this should be so.

FOR USE IN DISCUSSION

Questions about Substance

1. Examine the religious and spiritual references scattered throughout the text. Is Purdy putting forward a particular kind of theology, or is he simply trying to differentiate between the material and the philosophical?
2. "The moral authority that John F. Kennedy and Martin Luther King, Jr. exercised rested partly on the public's not knowing the details of their private lives, and most people will grant that ignorance did the country some good (480). How did "good" come from "ignorance" in the cases of JFK and MLK? If both figures were vocally dedicated to eradicating ignorance, does it make sense for the nation to have been so ignorant of the moral leaders' immoral acts?
3. Purdy describes what he perceives as a trend toward fitting values to behavior rather than behavior to values as a way of avoiding hypocrisy or "unearned self-importance." Thus, according to this logic, "We are all ill, and to aspire to wellness is to invite debunking" (481). What does he mean by this? How are

irony and illness related in this theory? Finally, where does "honesty" figure into the equation?

4. "The experience of the past hundred-odd years has been marked by the growth of the idea that the world's order can neither guide nor nurture us, that any significance it may have is essentially inhuman" (483). What kinds of events of the past century do you suppose Purdy is alluding to here?
5. What does Purdy mean by the following statement: "For the first time the way out of convention is by the superior command of conventional achievements. The way home is through the home office" (487)?
6. Purdy notes that recent attempts to bring enchantment and notions of "the soul" into mainstream culture depart from traditional religions because they keep "salvation while jettisoning sin" and they "[console] more than" they "challenge" (485). How is this idea connected to the isolation of the ironist's stance discussed elsewhere in this essay?
7. Are the "branding" that Tom Peters touts and the quest for "authenticity" that *Fast Company* promotes compatible concepts?

Questions about Structure and Style

1. How does "Hunger for Home" mark a shift in Purdy's focus? How is the reader prepared for this shift?
2. Purdy uses the concept/theme of "being at home in the world" several times in this essay. How is this theme used to tie together his points about irony, spirituality, and community? How does it echo or complicate the essay and/or section titles? Is the concept of "home" ever addressed directly? If so, how?
3. There are many categories of people established throughout this essay: ironists, angel watchers, heroes, Free Agents, Change Agents, Digerati, and Extropians are the main examples. Why is Purdy so intent on putting people into labeled categories? How does this organizing principle contribute to the goals of the essay?

Multimedia Suggestions

1. View the movie *Wayne's World* (1992), and try to identify the examples of "phrases that are caught up in webs we did not weave" (477). What is ironic about these phrases? In what other ways do you find the movie ironic?
2. Skim through some mainstream magazines and examine the ads. Recent Apple computer ads have presented "unique" figures or thinkers (478) in order to sell consumers one specific kind of computer. Many Gap ads have used the same idea (featuring iconoclastic personalities to sell very conventional and popular clothing). See if you can find other examples of this type of advertising message—where "unique-ness" is a commodity that can be sold to millions.
3. Look at the lyrics for Alanis Morisette's popular song "Ironic" (*http://www.time.com/time/covers/1101010924/esroger.html*). Can you find any examples of irony in this song? Would Purdy find any?

SUGGESTIONS FOR WRITING AND RESEARCH

1. If you are familiar with both *Seinfeld* and *Touched by an Angel,* try to write an episode where the characters of one show appear on the other. For example, what would happen if the *Touched* angels went to New York City to solve the problems of Jerry, Elaine, George, and Kramer? Then explain—using Purdy's argument—how it is or is not possible to integrate the ironist and the angel-watcher.
2. Purdy's book was widely criticized as too sweeping and imprecise, too smug, too immature, and as presenting far too little evidence to back up the claims it makes. Do any of these criticisms seem accurate to you? Write an essay that looks at this chapter of Purdy's book for examples of immaturity, smugness, and unsubstantiated argument or, if you prefer, examples of maturity, humility, and well-supported claim. Write your own review of Purdy with respect to these criticisms.
3. After the events of September 11th, 2001, *Time* magazine published an article called "The Age of Irony Comes to an End" by Roger Rosenblatt (see: *http://www.time.com/time/covers/1101010924/esroger.html* or get the issue off of microfiche in your library—issue date September 24, 2001). Examine the article for connections to Purdy's argument. How would Purdy's conception of irony fit well into Roger Rosenblatt's scheme of the ironic and our need to move past it? Do they seem to be working with the same definition of irony, or do they have different understandings? Write a compare and contrast essay on these two analyses of irony in contemporary culture.

WORKING WITH CLUSTERS

Cluster 11: The Art of Irony

Cluster 20: The Burdens of Modernity

Discipline: The Humanities

Rhetorical Mode: Argument

The French Collection

by Faith Ringgold

Artist Faith Ringgold is best known for her painted story quilts. She has exhibited in major museums in the United States, Europe, South America, Asia, Africa, and the Middle East. Her work appears in the permanent collection of many museums, including the Studio Museum in Harlem, the Solomon R. Guggenheim Museum, The Metropolitan Museum of Art, and The Museum of Modern Art. Her first book, Tar Beach, *was a Caldecott Honor Book and winner of the Coretta Scott King Award for Illustration. Ringgold has also written and illustrated eleven children's books. She has received more than 75 awards, fellowships, citations and honors, including the Solomon R. Guggenheim Fellowship for painting, two National Endowment for the Arts Awards and seventeen honorary doctorates, including one from her alma mater, The City College of New York. Ringgold is currently a professor of art at the University of California in San Diego. These works are part of a larger collection that can be seen in its entirety in* Dancing at the Louvre: The French Collection and Other Story Quilts.

Note: These quilts and the anecdotes they tell are a part of a larger collection which tells the story of Willia Marie Simone, a fictional black woman from Georgia who travels to Paris to be a part of the 1930's modernist art movement, joining many other American expatriates seeking a more liberating and integrated culture than existed in the United States at that time. Black American writers such as Richard Wright and James Baldwin became fixtures there, as did artists and entertainers such as Josephine Baker. By most accounts, white France was more open to and enthusiastic about black American artists than white America. The scenes Ringgold invents have been painted onto the quilts and the framing panels contain the text provided herein.

DANCING AT THE LOUVRE (1991)

1. In Your Journal: Describe the visual interplay between the figure of Mona Lisa and the figures of Marcia, Willia Marie, and the children.

Dear Aunt Melissa,

Marcia and her three little girls took me dancing at **the Louvre.** I thought I was taking them to see the Mona Lisa. You've never seen anything like this. Well, the French hadn't either. Never mind Leonardo da Vinci and Mona Lisa, Marcia and her three girls were the show.

They ran me ragged. Marcia wanted to go one way and the children another. The baby girl wanted to jump. The other two wanted to run, and did. Then they all just broke into a dance when we finally found the Mona Lisa.

Pierre used to say "Cherchez le fauteuil roulant, just get a wheelchair at the door of the Louvre, 'cause if you don't you're gonna need one going home." I've been to the Louvre a hundred times, but never have I seen it like this. It was like looking at all the pictures upside down from a racing car going 100 kilomètres à l'heure.

Now that Marcia is married to Maurice, and they have moved to Paris, she and her children are determined to speak le bon Français parfaitement by morning. I had to put her straight about me and the children. You know how it is with friends, they all want to tell you whom they think you are and how to live your life, and why.

Well I told her straight out, "Marcia, you know damn good and well your papa never went past the third grade." And that was good in those days, 'cause he wasn't supposed to do that. But my papa was a school prin-

---

The Louvre: most significant French museum, located in Paris; home to the Mona Lisa, the Venus de Milo, and many classic works of French and Italian masters

cipal. He finished Lincoln Academy in Lynnsville. And I got the diploma to prove it.

Papa taught in Florida, South Carolina, and Georgia. I got all his licenses and test scores. Papa and Mama was both teachers. We didn't come up like no weeds. Not saying she did either. But I resent her telling me that my children belong in France. And that I should be raising them, not you.

2. *In Your Journal:* How do class and race intersect in this anecdote about Marcia's view of child raising?

Papa never allowed those Campbell boys in our yard. Chauncey, Buba, and Percy, none of Marcia's brothers was allowed in our yard. Now I'm not saying he was right 'cause Papa était un snob. But I remember Papa, in that little pinstriped coat he used to wear and his glasses on the end of his nose.

Papa was something. "No, young man, you go out of this yard. The Simone girls are doing their chores and they have their studies, supper and to bed. **Allez vous en!** Then he'd hit that tail at the back of his coat like a period and turn at the same time. And those Campbell boys would fly out of our yard.

Allez vous en!: Go in!

Papa wasn't too keen on Marcia either, but she always had a little way about her, like she thought she was très chic. Marcia doesn't remember any thing about growing up poor in Atlanta. As far as she is concerned she was born in a first class cabin on the S.S. Liberté on her way to Paris, sipping **Möet** and smoking a **Gauloise.**

Moët: French champagne

Gauloise: French cigarettes

You should hear the story she told us about how she used to set the table for dinner with silver service and crystal every night 'cause her father would get upset if he came home and the table wasn't formally set for supper. We were at a Paris party and her husband, Maurice, was present so I just "uh-uh'd" her.

3. In Your Journal: What comment is Ringgold making about the fixed nature of personal identity? How are Marcia and Willia Marie different in terms of their histories? How are they similar?

But I remember the time we saw those Campbell boys coming out of Miss Baker's back door carrying food. They said they were cleaning out her ice box and the food was spoiled. Then Miss Baker came over crying to Papa that all the food in her ice box was gone. Papa sat Miss Baker down to our supper table and went straight over to Marcia's house.

And there was Mr. and Mrs. Campbell, and their three sons sitting at their kitchen table in the dark eating Miss Baker's food. When Papa came in they started coughing and gagging. They almost choked. But not Mademoiselle Marcia. Papa said she was on the back porch nursing **un cristal de limonade** and reading ***Madame Bovary.***

un cristal de lemonade: iced lemonade

THE PICNIC AT GIVERNY (1991)

4. In Your Journal: What imagery in this work seems familiar? What aspects are unfamiliar?

Dear Aunt Melissa,

Today I was invited to paint in the garden of the celebrated painter, **Claude Monet** at **Giverny.** There, in an area of the garden composed of water-lily ponds, with weeping willow trees and beautiful flowers everywhere, was a group of American women artists and writers having a picnic and discussing the role of women in art.

I strolled through the beautiful **jardins,** taking in the fantastic, beautiful flower beds and trees, passing over the matrix of Japanese bridges that connect the wildly wooded areas of the jardins with the fields of flowers near Monet's house. Then I settled on the same area near the water-lily ponds flanked by weeping willow trees near the American women who were picnicking.

jardins: gardens

Madame Bovary: masterpiece of Gustave Flaubert (1856); novel chronicling the frustration and love affairs of a romantic woman married to a dull husband, written in a highly controlled style

Claude Monet: (1840–1926) French landscape painter and founder of impressionism, most famous for his fascination with the changes to atmosphere invoked by light and season

Giverny: home of Monet

Figures: Front row, left to right: Picasso, Moira Roth, Ellie Flomenhaft, Lowrey Sims, Judith Lieber, Thalia Gouma-Peterson, Emma Amos, Bernice Steinbaum, Michele Wallace, Willia Marie Simone; back row, left to right: Ofelia Garcia, Johnetta Cole

I kept seeing Manet's ***Le Déjeuner Sur L'Herbe,*** the painting that caused such a scandal in Paris. It was not allowed at the salon because it showed Manet's brother-in-law and a male friend having a picnic with two nude women, all of whom were recognizable. I kept thinking: Why not replace the traditional nude woman at the picnic with Picasso in the nude, and the 10 American women fully clothed?

5. In Your Journal: Why is it so pleasing to Willia Marie that a nude Picasso is featured in the context of "American women fully clothed"?

That would be crossing **Monet's** beautiful ***Nymphéas*** with Manet's scandal, and a reaction to the conversation of the American women about the rôle of women artists to show powerful images of women. They were discussing female nudes in the company of fully clothed men in paintings

Manet's *Le Déjeuner Sur L'Herbe*: ("Lunch on the Grass," 1863) painting featuring a nude female and a half-dressed woman having lunch with two fully clothed men

Monet's *Nymphéas*: large water lily murals painted by Claude Monet at the end of his life when he was almost blind

ma nouvelle conscience: my new conscience/consciousness

like Manet's *The Picnic*. Seeing it and wondering what to paint, this seemed a good idea to begin **ma nouvelle conscience.**

What to paint has always been my greatest problem as an artist. And then how to paint it? These were the questions I looked hard for answers to. Now there is the rôle of women artists? Some special niche we can occupy, like a power station? A woman artist can assume the rights of men in art? And be seen? I am very excited to meet these women. This may be the very first day of my life.

6. In Your Journal: What does Willia Marie mean when she says this may be the "first day of [her] life"?

They are speaking of la libération et la liberté for women. Sometime we think we are free, until we spread our wings and are cut down in mid air. But who can know a slave by the mere look in her eye? Ordinarily I would just paint the jardin and include in it some of these women at a picnic. That was before the question of freedom came up. Is it just the beauty of nature I am after?

Monet painted his most wonderful masterpiece, *Décorations des Nymphéas,* of the garden and the water-lily ponds. Those paintings hang in the circular galleries of the Musée de l'Orangerie in the Tuileries Gardens in Paris. That must be wonderful, to have your work so approved and revered by people to have it hanging in a space specially made for it. What does that amount of respect feel like?

7. In Your Journal: Why would Willia Marie be especially impressed that spaces were specifically designed to display Monet's work? How does this relate to her visit to Paris in general?

Can a woman of my color ever achieve that amount of eminence in art in America? Here or anywhere in the world? Is it just raw talent alone that makes an artist's work appreciated to the fullest? Or is it a combination of things, la magie par une example, le sexe par une autre, et la couleur est encore une autre, magic, sex, and color.

8. In Your Journal: Why does Willia Marie contrast "raw talent" with "magic, sex, and color" in her definition of artistic "eminence"?

One has to get the attention one needs to feed the magic. There is no magic in the dark. It is only when we see it that we know a transformation has taken place, a wonderful idea has been created into art. If we never see it we never know, and it didn't happen. Isn't that why I and so many other negro artists have come to Paris—to get a chance to make magic, and find an audience for our art?

Should I paint some of the great and tragic issues of our world? A **black man toting a heavy load** that has pinned him to the ground? Or a **black woman nursing** the world's population of children? Or the two of them together as slaves, building a beautiful world for others to live free? Non! I want to paint something that will inspire—liberate. I want to do some of this WOMEN ART Magnifique!

What will people think of my work? Will they just ignore it or will they give it some consideration? Maybe tear it apart and say that it is the worst ever and this artist should have her brushes burned and her hands, too. And isolate me as a woman artist because I am no longer trying to

---

black man toting a heavy load and **black woman nursing:** reference to works in Faith Ringgold's "American Collection" paint like, or to be like a man. Paris is full of these women artists who have no first names, wear men's trousers and deny they are married or have children.

I paint like a woman. I always paint wearing a white dress. Now I have a subject that speaks out for women. I can no more hide the fact that I am a woman than that I am a Negro. It is a waste of time to entertain such subterfuge any longer.

> ***9. In Your Journal:*** Why does Willia Marie always wear white dresses and refuse the "subterfuge" of some other women artists in Paris?

There are enough beautiful paintings of nude women in the world. I now want to see nude men painted by women, or nude men in the company of fully clothed women. C'est de la fantaisie pure. The men are expressing their power over women. But I am not interested in having power over anyone. I just want to see nude men in the company of fully clothed women for a change.

> ***10. In Your Journal:*** Why do you think Willia Marie asserts she isn't "interested in power" when she says that she says wants to see nude men in the company of fully clothed women? What "power" is she referring to?

I am deeply inspired by these American women and their conversations about art and women in America. It makes me homesick for my country. And for their women's movement, I have created this painting *Picnic at Giverny* par le tribut. They have given me something new to ponder, a challenge to confront in my art, a new direction. And pride in being a Negro woman.

THE SUNFLOWERS QUILTING BEE AT ARLES (1991)

The National Sunflower Quilters Society of America are having quilting bees in sunflower fields around the world to spread the cause of freedom. Aunt Melissa has written to inform me of this and say: "Go with them to the sunflower fields in **Arles.** And please take good care of them in that foreign country, Willia Marie. These women are our freedom," she wrote.

Today the women arrived in Arles. They are Madame Walker, Sojourner Truth, Ida Wells, Fannie Lou Hamer, Harriet Tubman, Rosa Parks, Mary McLeod Bethune and Ella Baker, a fortress of African American women's courage, with enough energy to transform a nation piece by piece.

Look what they've done in spite of their oppression: Madame Walker invented the hair straightening comb and became the first self-made American-born woman millionaire. She employed over 3,000 people. Sojourner Truth spoke up brilliantly for women's rights during slavery, and could neither read nor write. Ida Wells made an exposé of the horror of lynching in the South.

> ***11. In Your Journal:*** How are Madame Walker's accomplishments ironic (para. 3)?

⁂ **Arles (and Vincent Van Gogh [502]):** Van Gogh (1853-1890) retreated from Paris to Arles when his health began to fail and he thought himself too much a burden on his brother, Theo; in Arles, Van Gogh painted his famous sunflower series; Arles is also where Van Gogh mutilated his ear during a fit of dementia

Figures: Left to right: Madame C.J. Walker, Sojourner Truth, Ida B. Wells, Fannie Lou Hamer, Harriet Tubman, Rosa Parks, Mary McLeod Bethune, Ella Baker, Vincent Van Gogh

12. In Your Journal: What does Van Gogh appear to be doing in this image? Do the quilters seem to notice or recognize him?

13. In Your Journal: The women in this image are not contemporaries. Why does Ringgold treat them as if they are?

Fannie Lou Hamer braved police dogs, water hoses, brutal beatings, and jail in order to register thousands of people to vote. Harriet Tubman brought over 300 slaves to freedom in 19 trips from the South on the Underground Railroad during slavery and never lost a passenger. Rosa Parks became the mother of the Civil Rights Movement when she sat down in the front of a segregated bus and refused to move to the back.

Mary McLeod Bethune founded Bethune Cookman College and was special advisor to Presidents Harry Truman and Franklin Delano Roosevelt. Ella Baker organized thousands of people to improve the condition of poor housing, jobs and consumer education. Their trip to Arles was to complete *The Sunflower Quilt,* an international symbol of their dedication to change the world.

The Dutch painter **Vincent Van Gogh** came to see the black women sewing in the sunflower fields. "Who is this strange looking man?" they asked. "He is un grand peintre," I told them, "though he is greatly troubled in his mind." He held a vase of sunflowers, no doubt une nature morte, a still life, for one of his paintings.

"He's the image of the man hit me in the head with a rock when I was a girl," Harriet said "Make him leave. He reminds me of slavers." But he was not about to be moved. Like one of the sunflowers, he appeared to be growing out of the ground. Sojourner wept into the stitches of her quilting for the loss of her thirteen children mostly all sold into slavery.

One of Sojourner's children, a girl, was sold to a Dutch slaver in the West Indies who then took her to Holland. "Was that something this Dutch man might know something about? He should pay for all the pain his people have given us. I am concerned about you, Willia Marie. Is this a natural setting for a black woman?" Sojourner asked.

"I came to France to seek opportunity," I said. "It is not possible for me to be an artist in the States." "We are all artists. Piecing is our art. We brought it straight from Africa," they said. "That was what we did after a hard day's work in the fields to keep our sanity and our beds warm and bring beauty into our lives. That was not being an artist. That was being alive."

When the sun went down and it was time for us to leave, the tormented little man just settled inside himself and took on the look of the sunflowers in the field as if he were one of them. The women were finished piecing now. "We need to stop and smell the flowers sometimes," they said. "Now we can do our real quilting, our real art: making this world piece up right."

"I got to get back to that railroad," Harriet said. "Ain't all us free yet, no matter how many them laws they pass. Sojourner fighting for women's rights. Fannie for voter registration. Ella and Rosa working on civil rights. Ida looking out for mens getting lynch. Mary Bethune getting our young-uns education, and Madame making money fixing hair and giving us jobs. Lord, we is sure busy."

"I am so thankful to my Aunt Melissa for sending you wonderful women to me," I said. "Art can never change anything the way you have. But it can make a picture so everyone can see and know our true history and culture, from the art. Someday I will make you women proud of me, too. Just wait, you'll see." "We see, Willia Marie," they said. "We see."

> ***14. In Your Journal:*** What do you make of the comparison between Van Gogh and the sunflowers "growing out of the ground"? Why is his presence so upsetting to the quilters? Why does Ringgold portray the women as unable they make him leave?

> ***15. In Your Journal:*** Why is Sojourner Truth worried about Willia Marie? How can Willia Marie's setting be any less "natural for a black woman" than the one Sojourner Truth experienced?

> ***16. In Your Journal:*** Why do you think that quilting is such a significant symbol for black women artists?

> ***17. In Your Journal:*** What does Willia Marie think is the role of art in history and on culture? Do you think this definition applies to everyone or only to black women?

MATISSE'S MODEL (1991)

Every little girl wants to be une **danseuse.** I still do. Matisse's paintings always make me think of dancing, beauty and love. They make me want to strip off my clothes and join hands with a circle of friends to dance till both my body and my soul are so tired I fall asleep on a beautiful chaise longue and say Ahhhhhh. Matisse's *La Danse* did that.

danseuse: female ballet dancer

> **18. In Your Journal:** How does this quilt make more use of quilting technique than some of Ringgold's other works? Why do you think this image is more "quilt-like" than some of the others?

I have always wanted to be beautiful, not like an anonymous beautiful woman but like une belle peinture, beautiful painting. Something that pleases not only the eye but the soul. Here in Matisse's studio I am that beauty. I can't be sure of what HE thinks, but I have known for a long time that a woman has to think for herself. And a black woman has to be sure.

When I was growing up in Atlanta there was a boy living in the next house to ours who used to call me Smokey. He was referring to my skin color which he thought looked like smoke. He was very dark himself but somehow he felt that his color was **indelible.** I never could figure out why, but now I know. It was because he was a man, or would be one day.

indelible: impossible to remove

And when he did, he would not be "courting or marrying no smoke," black as he was. Even though men commonly do the choosing I knew when I got married, black as I was, I wasn't going to marry no fool. Some girls liked fools, not saying that favoring light skin and being a fool go together but sometime they did. To the contrary, there were light skinned boys who didn't waste no time on no light girl.

And there were boys like Preston Wilson, noir comme le charbon, coal black, who used to say, "All a yaller woman could do for me is show me where that little black beauty went." But still, dark skinned girls at school knew we were not the top priority. So we looked for the Preston Wilsons, 'cause most boys favored peaches-and-cream over smoke. That was a natural fact.

Maybe in another life I was white with blonde hair and blue eyes, thin nose and lips; in this life I am black with all that entails. That was hard to accept sometimes when I realized that the Negro man would like me a lot better if I looked more like the *master's woman*. I would have thought the rape of our mothers during slavery would color his thinking.

> ***19. In Your Journal:*** Paraphrase Willia Marie's logic when she says, "I would have thought the rape of our mothers during slavery would color his thinking".

Men are so competitive. They always want what other men have. That is why they have so many wars. They believe they should take what they want. I wonder what men think when they are thinking of women. How can they betray them with deception about loving them? They know that many women live pour l'amour. Without love some women are only half a person, that half which hates itself for being alone.

Do they despise that in us? Or do they just simply use it to their own advantage? We fall in and out of love. Then we watch our daughters and our daughters' daughters, knowing there's no way to share anything to dull the pain. We watch our sons and our sons' sons play the same love games with women. Et personne n'apprend rien d'amour, nobody learns a thing about love.

Right now I feel as strong as all the women who have ever lived, reclining as I am on the women's bed evoking all kinds of illusions. But this is a job: modeling for money. Though I do it to see the magic I bring to the artist's art. There is a certain power I keep in the translation of my image from me to canvas. I enjoy seeing that in the finished work.

> ***20. In Your Journal:*** How does Willia Marie think of her modeling as a source of "power"?

I love playing the beautiful woman, knowing that I am steeped in painting history: **Ingres' *The 'grande odalisque',* Manet's *Olympia,*** and the Egyptian godess Cleopatra before that. It is an extremely thought-provoking position to be in. I ask the question. Why am I here posing like this, and what would HE think if I took out my glasses and started to read a first edition of Tolstoy's *War and Peace* or Richard Wright's *Black Boy?*

> ***21. In Your Journal:*** Why does Willia Marie want to take out a "first edition" of Tolstoy or Wright while she is modeling for Matisse?

Ingres's *Le Grande Odalisque*: (Jean Auguste Dominique) (1780-1867); *Le Grande Odalisque* (1814) features a bathing nude

Manet's *Olympia*: (Edouard) (1832-1883); *Olympia* (1863) was a suggestive painting of a nude that encountered great criticism

22. In Your Journal: How does the couch equalize, according to Willia Marie?

23. In Your Journal: Why would it be "belle aussi" (also beautiful) to see a woman reclining to rest rather than waiting for love?

There is no special couch made for only proper or improper women to lie on. All of us at one time or other have lain on a chaise longue. It may not be so fancy as the ones in Ingres' *The 'grande odalisque'* or in Matisse's many pictures of reclining nudes, though it may be. I think men see these things with dreamy eyes. They see beauty in la vulnerabilité, la passivité, et la soumission.

It wouldn't inspire fantasy to see a woman tired—too tired to be waiting for love? We don't have to have a man lay us out on the couch to accommodate his special love fantasy. We can just lie down there ourselves to just rest after a hard day's work. Ça c'est belle aussi. That is beautiful, too.

PICASSO'S STUDIO (1991)

Dear Aunt Melissa,

24. In Your Journal: Aside from the difference in skin tone, how does the image of Willia Marie compare to the other female images in this piece?

I really think modeling is boring. Standing, sitting or laying down. Peu importe! Doesn't matter. You may know what to do with your hands, your feet, the look on your face. But what do you do with your mind, with your misplaced or mistaken identité? What do you do with time? Et l'artiste, what do you feel about him?

I started hearing voices from the masks and paintings in Picasso's studio but your voice, Aunt Melissa, was the clearest. "You was an artist's model years before you was ever born, thousands of miles from here in Africa somewhere. Only you'all wasn't called artist and model. It was natural that your beauty would be reproduced on walls and plates and sculptures made of your beautiful black face and body."

25. In Your Journal: What do Aunt Melissa's words mean to Willia Marie in the context of modeling for Picasso? What is Aunt Melissa saying about the role of respect for one's subject in the act of representation?

"Europeans discovered your image as art at the same time they discovered Africa's potential for slavery and colonization. They dug up centuries of our civilizations, and then called us savages and made us slaves. First they take the body, then the soul. Or maybe it is the soul, then the body. The sequence doesn't matter, when one goes the other usually follows close behind."

You asked me once why I wanted to become an artist and I said I didn't know. Well I know now. It is because it's the only way I know of feeling free. My art is my freedom to say what I please. N'importe what color you are, you can do what you want avec ton art. They may not like it, or buy it, or even let you show it; but they can't stop you from doing it.

Picasso's first cubist painting was called barbaric, la mort, the death of art! But that didn't stop him. In fact, it started le mouvement moderne

Picasso's first cubist painting: *Les Demoiselles d'Avignon* (1907), a painting of prostitutes characterized by distorted figures and sharp angles

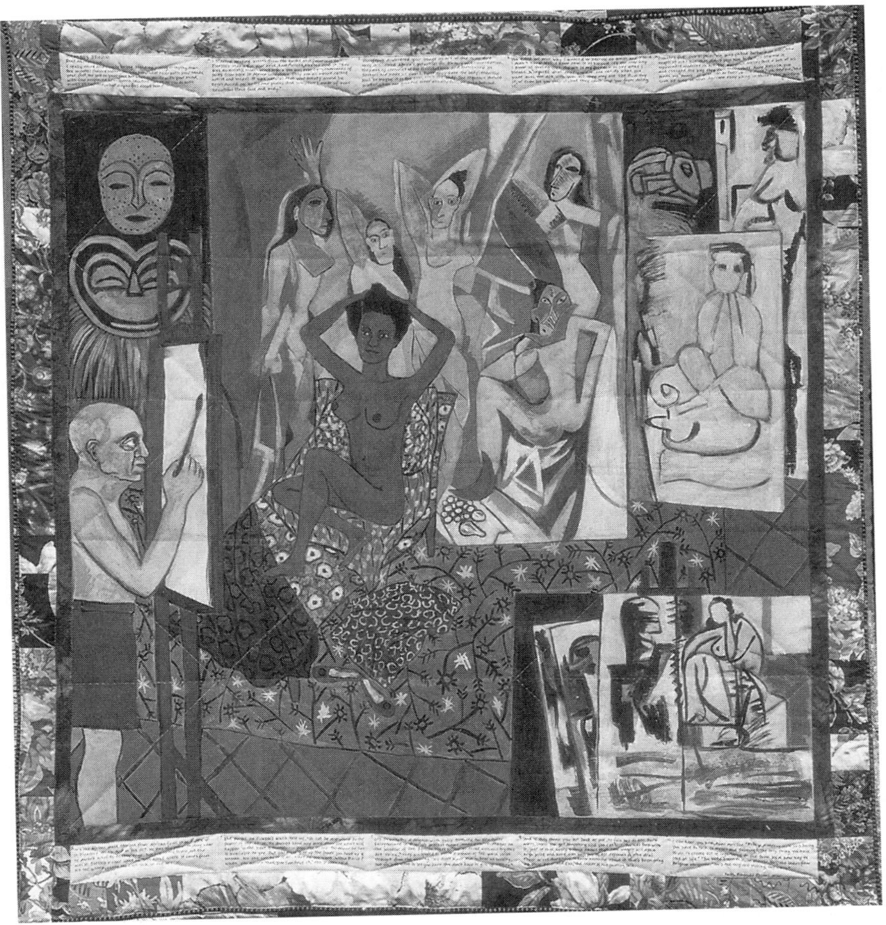

du art. The European artists took a look at us and changed the way they saw themselves. Aunt Melissa, you made me aware of that. "Go to Paris, Willia Marie," you told me, "and soak up some of that Africana they using in those cube paintings."

It's the African mask straight from African faces that I look at in Picasso's studio and in his art. He has the power to deny what he doesn't want to acknowledge. But art is the truth, not the artist. Doesn't matter what he says about where it comes from. We see where, every time we look in the mirror.

26. In Your Journal: What does Willia Marie mean when she says "art is the truth, not the artist"? How does this statement apply to Picasso?

The masks on Picasso's walls told me, "Do not be disturbed by the power of the artist. He doesn't know any more than you what will happen in the next 5 seconds—in your life or his. The power he has is available to you. But you must give up the power you have as a woman. No one can have it all. What do you want, Willia Marie? When you decide that, you can have it," the masks said.

Les Demoiselles d'Avignon, with their tortured twisted faces Europeanized in Picasso's brothel theme, made a contre-attaque on the wisdom of the African masks. "You go ahead, girl, and try this art thing," they whispered to me in a women-of-the-world voice straight from the evening. "We don't want HIM to hear us talking, but we just want to let you know you don't have to give up nothing."

te fais pas de bile: you don't throw a fit

"And if they throw your art back at you, **te fais pas de bile.** Don't worry, 'cause you got something else you can sell. You was born with it, just in case. Every woman knows that. Some women will ask a high price and some men will pay it, all depends on the deal. Their wives don't have to know anything about it. That's been going on since Adam and Eve," the ladies of the painting said.

> ***27. In Your Journal:*** How does this allusion to prostitution relate to the theme of women in art?

I can hear you now, Aunt Melissa. "Willia Marie, modeling ain't so-o boring you have to talk to masks and paintings. The only thing you have to do is create art of importance to YOU. Show us a new way to look at life." "You betta listen to Aunt Melissa, girl," the ladies from Avignon whispered. "She's the only one making any sense."

> ***28. In Your Journal:*** Why do the ladies advise Willia Marie to listen to her Aunt Melissa, as opposed to other artists?

DINNER AT GERTRUDE STEIN'S (1991)

> ***29. In Your Journal:*** Why do you think only Willia Marie is standing in this picture? How does her posture compare with that of the other women in the picture?

Dear Aunt Mel

Last night I had dinner at **Gertrude Stein's.** She is a genius Auntie, not just because she said she is, or because she wrote "A rose is a rose is a rose" or "There is no there, there" about Oakland, California or "Pigeons on the grass, Alas." She is a genius because she has us all repeating her words and wondering—Is it is, or is it art?

Les Demoiselles d'Avignon: painting by Picasso (1907) of prostitutes, notable for the angular facial distortions; an example of cubism, a revolt against the scientific quality of previous artistic movements

Gertrude Stein: (1874-1946) American writer whose work emphasized sound and rhythm more than plot or theme; her most famous works include the poetry volume *Tender Buttons* (1914) and the short story collection *Three Lives* (1909)

Figures: Left to right: Leo Stein, Willia Marie Simone, Zora Neale Hurston, James Baldwin, Alice B. Toklas, Gertrude Stein, Pablo Picasso, Richard Wright, Ernest Hemingway, Langston Hughes

There were 10 of us for dinner at Gertrude Stein's. **Six were being men** and four were being women. One of the four women being Gertrude another one being **Alice.** Both living and being women, though one (Gertrude) smokes a cigar, and has a wife being Alice. Alice was always living and working for Gertrude and cooking and typing "the daily miracle" which is being what Gertrude calls her daily unedited manuscript.

⁘ **Six were being men . . . :** Ringgold parodies Stein's use of language throughout this section; the use of gerunds (e.g., "being" and "knowing") is one of the hallmarks of Stein's style

---

⁘ **Alice (B. Toklas):** longtime companion of Gertrude Stein; the *Autobiography of Alice B. Toklas* was really the autobiography of Gertrude Stein written as though the eyes of Alice

Of the six men being and talking with Gertrude, three of them (**Richard Wright, James Baldwin** and **Langston Hughes**) were being colored, and three of them were not. The three colored men were all being and knowing they were great writers and poets who were geniuses and thinkers of great thoughts about being and living and dying as colored men in America.

Of the three men who were not colored (Pablo Picasso, **Ernest Hemingway** and Leo Stein) one was a great painter, and one was a great writer and journalist but not quite as great as the great painter who was a great genius as well. The other one was being a brother of a genius who was living and being Gertrude Stein.

Two of the four women were colored (**Zora Neale Hurston** and myself, Willia Marie Simone) and two were not. Of the two colored women one was a great writer-genius and was being colored; the other was listening and learning. The other two women (Gertrude Stein and Alice B. Toklas) were always being together. One was always knowing and being an American but living and being in Paris. The other one just being listening and quiet.

The colored writers read from their books and challenged each others points of view on issues concerning race and politics. The others were being quiet and sometimes saying a word or two but mostly being listening and not saying. I was being listening and quiet and standing so that I would not miss anything from being sitting. I was living in deep thoughts and being listening and silent.

- **Richard Wright:** (1908-1960) African American author of *Native Son* (1940) and *Black Boy* (1945); Wright's works are generally interested in the way social constraints determine identity

- **James Baldwin:** (1924-1987) African American author of *Go Tell It on the Mountain* (1953), *Notes of a Native Son* (1955) and *Giovanni's Room* (1956); Baldwin's works concern black identity and relations between the races, and he was significantly influenced by Richard Wright and Langston Hughes

- **Langston Hughes:** (1902–1967) African American poet and prominent figure in the Harlem Renaissance; his work makes frequent use of dialect and jazz rhythms in an efforts to represent the feel of African American experience

- **Ernest Hemingway:** (1899–1961) American novelist and one of the leading spokesmen of the "lost generation" of ex-patriots in post-World War I Paris; known for a direct "muscular" style in works such as *A Farewell to Arms* (1929) and *Old Man and the Sea* (1952, Pulitzer)

- **Zora Neale Hurston:** (1901–1960) African American anthropologist and novelist, famous for her use of black dialect and folk tales in *Mules and Men* (1935) and *Their Eyes Were Watching God* (1937)

One of the colored men was being and reading an essay he wrote about the other one. In it he describes the other one as living and being a "Mississippi **pickaninny.**" A pickaninny that was being so threatening that no one could see that he was really living and being "a fantastic jewel buried in high grass."

"pickaninny": disparaging term for a small black child, often depicted naked with bulging eyes and a large red mouth

I wanted to speaking and explaining what was being a pickaninny. But I was more listening than speaking. So I just thought about knowing that a pickaninny from Mississippi or any other place is a very sad but young colored person who no one loves enough to comb their "picky" hair or feed them. So they are always being needing loving and caring and feeling hungry for nursing their mama's "tittie."

The pickaninny who was being "a fantastic jewel buried in high grass" in Mississippi was now being a pickaninny who was being in Paris out of the grass and wanting and being angry enough to be doing what a pickaninny can do so well to the other one who was really very small. It was then that dinner was served and the men went to being in separate corners of the room.

My favorite event of the evening was Zora Neale Hurston reading from her comedic play, Mule Bone. Zora is being and making a classic of the black folk culture and language we are always being so ashamed of. It is the way we be being talking when there are no white people being around. W.E.B. Du Bois said, "Zora's Mule Bone speaks in a . . . lyrical language that is as far removed from **minstrelsy** as a **margaux** is from **ripple.**"

minstrelsy: entertainment involving extreme "blackface" caricature of slaves (as eternally happy and ignorant), performed by both white and black entertainers

margaux: French wine

ripple: home made alcohol

Zora was being and telling the story of the "bama Nigger" who struck his rival with the hock bone of an ole yaller mule. **De man was arrested.** De case went to trial in de Macademia Baptist Church. De argument was "Can a mule bone be a criminal weapon? If so de man is guilty if not innocent. De donkey is de father of a mule. **Samson** slew 3,000 **Philistines** with the jawbone of an ass. Now what kin be more dangerous dan uh mule bone?"

There was being no time that evening that I was not being there. Not speaking but laughing and thinking and liking and then wanting to speak but not speaking. Then speaking to myself only saying "I leave here with this thinking—A bama Nigger is a Mississippi pickaninny, is a jewel, is a hock bone, is an ole yaller mule—and a man is a man is a woman, and there is no there, here!"

De man was arrested: Ringgold parodies Hurston's use of southern black dialect throughout this paragraph

Samson: biblical figure of great physical strength whose hair symbolized his covenant with God

Philistines: rivals of Israel; often characterized as materialistic and uncultured

Figures: Front row, left to right: William H. Johnson, Archibald Motley, Willia Marie Simone, Elizabeth Catlett, Lois Mailou Jones, Mata Vaux Warrick Fuller, Edmonia Louis, Faith Ringgold; middle row, left to right: Sargent Johnson, Romare Bearden, Aaron Douglas, Henry O. Tanner, Paul Gauguin, Vincent Van Gogh, Augusta Savage; back row, left to right: Ed Clark, Raymond Saunders, Jacob Lawrence, Henri de Toulouse-Lautrec, Maurice Utrillo

LE CAFÉ DES ARTiSTES (1994)

30. In Your Journal: Why do you think Faith Ringgold includes herself in this particular scene?

Dear Aunt Melissa,

Pierre left me as the owner of a Paris cafe, Le Café des Artistes, le rendezvous des arts et des lettres. It is located on the Boulevard des Saint Germain de Prés across from the church in the heart of the artists' quartier.

I am here every day now. We are a very popular café. Every Saturday nite we have **le dancing le plus gai et le plus curieux de Paris**. Today the tables are humming with the usual clientele of artists and writers nursing a cafe crème and making art history right before our eyes.

le dancing le plus gai et le plus curieux de Paris: the most merry/drunken and outlandish dancing in Paris

Pierre would be proud of my associations with the artists and writers. But still I have mixed feelings. Sometimes I feel as though I am one of them; at other times I feel like **"The Spook That Sat By the Door."** I feel that I now have words to say that simply will not wait.

Today I will issue the Colored Woman's Manifesto of Art and Politics. What would Pierre have to say about that? His timid wife all of 20 years old and addressing the greatest artists and writers of the century. I doubt that I would be doing this if Pierre were alive. But he is not and I am.

Madames and Monsieurs, I said, may I have your attention? This is a momentous time in the history of modern art and I am excited to be in Paris, the center of cultural change and exchange. "It is a pleasure to have one so beautiful among us Madame Willia Marie. Bon chère noire."

Like the **symbolists, dadaists, surrealists** and **cubists** I have a proclamation to make for which I beg your indulgence. It is the Colored Woman's Manifesto of Art and Politics. "Women should stay home and make children not art." **"Soulard,** alcoolique." "*You* should go home!" "Silence! Taisez-vous!"

31. In Your Journal: What is the crowd's initial response to Willia Marie's address?

soulard: drunkard

I am an international colored woman. My African ancestry dates back to the beginnings of human origins, 9 million years ago in Ethiopia. The art and culture of Africa has been stolen by western Europeans and my people have been colonized, enslaved and forgotten.

What is very old has become new. And what was black has become white. "**We Wear the Mask**" but it has a new use as cubist art. "But you are influenced by the French Impressionists." "No the German Expressionists." Modern art is not yours, or mine. It is ours.

32. In Your Journal: Why does the crowd want to locate Willia Marie's influences in European traditions?

There is as much of the African masks of my ancestors as there is of the Greek statuary of yours in the art of modern times. "No it is the Fauve that has influenced you Madame Willia Marie." And who made the first art . . . a doll maybe for an unborn child? A woman of course.

33. In Your Journal: What work does Willia Marie's manifesto assert was (possibly) the first "work of art"?

"You are a primitive but very pretty." Paris artists are shaping the culture of the world with their ideas. But modern art is much bigger than Western Europe or Paris. I am here (in Paris). I am there (in Africa) too. That is why I am issuing a Colored Woman's Manifesto of Art and Politics.

"The Spook That Sat by the Door": refers to Sam Greenlee's award-winning novel *The Spook Who Sat by the Door* (1969): a satire of the civil rights problems in the United States in the late 1960s; Dan Freeman, the "spook who sat by the door," is enlisted in the CIA, but upon mastering agency tactics, he drops out to train young Chicago blacks as "Freedom Fighters"; also made into a radical "blaxpoitation" film that was inexplicably pulled out of circulation shortly after release in 1972

symbolists, dadaists, surrealists, cubists: all of these genres of modernist art resisted objective or straightforward representation, in favor of more metaphorical non-linear techniques

"We Wear the Mask": (1896) poem by Paul Lawrence Dunbar (1872–1906), which examines the dichotomy between internal experience and external projection

"You should learn French cooking. It will help you to blend your couleurs." "No she is a natural with couleur. Very Primitive." I will call a congress of African American women artists to Paris to propose that two issues be discussed: What is the image of the Colored Woman in art? And what is our purpose as modern artists?

34. In Your Journal: Willia Marie poses two issues to be discussed at her congress: "the image of the Colored Woman in art" and the "purpose [of Colored Women] as modern artists." How are these issues related?

No important change of a modernist nature can go on without the colored woman. "Her palette is too harsh, she needs to develop a subtle range of greys." Today I became a woman with ideas of my own. Ideas are my freedom. And freedom is why I became an artist.

The important thing for the colored woman to remember is we must speak, or our ideas and ourselves will remain unheard and unknown. The cafe is my academie, my gallery, my home. The artists and writers are my teachers, and my friends. But Africa is my art, my classical form and inspiration.

"You will come to my studio Madame Willia Marie. I will show you how to make a rich palette of couleurs and teach you to paint like a master. But first you will model for me my African maiden! Earth Mama! Queen of the Nile!" C'est la vie Auntie. The price I pay for being an artist.

FOR USE IN DISCUSSION

Questions about Substance

1. Compare and contrast *The Picnic at Giverny* with *Matisse's Model.* The word "power" comes up in relation to nudity in both of the figures. How are the representations of nudity consistent? What tension in Ringgold's work do these images illustrate together?
2. How are the gatherings in *Dinner at Gertrude Stein's* and *Le Café Des Artistes* different from those at Giverny and Arles?
3. Examine all of the audience responses to Willia Marie's "Colored Woman's Manifesto of Art and Politics" in *Le Café Des Artistes.* What is their general message? Do any stand out for you? How do these quotes reveal any of Faith Ringgold's artistic intentions in the creation of the scene?

Questions about Structure and Style

1. The written text in these works is in the epistolary form (in the form of letters) from Willia Marie to her Aunt Melissa. Why do you think Ringgold chooses this form rather than merely captioning the paintings, or developing them as the private thoughts of Willia Marie?

2. Why do you think Ringgold paints on quilts rather than traditional canvasses? What does her choice of medium convey about her relationship to tradition, both historical and artistic?
3. Ringgold parodies some of the artists and writers who are featured in her quilts (especially Gertrude Stein and Zora Neale Hurston in *Dinner at Gertrude Stein's*). Are these parodies tributes or criticisms? Explain your answer.

Multimedia Suggestions

1. Faith Ringgold has an interactive Web site at *http://www.faithringgold.com/*. How does the content on and style of this site compare to the quilts in *The French Collection*?
2. Several other contemporary women artists are interested in how the present can provide a lens for "revising" or "rethinking" the past. Barbara Kruger, Cindy Sherman, and Carrie Mae Weems all share Ringgold's interest in simultaneously resisting and continuing traditions. You can look them all up at *http://www.artcyclopedia.com/*, and examine some of their works for comparison with Ringgold's.
3. The film *How to Make an American Quilt* (1995) features a women's quilting circle, and uses the quilt as a metaphor for female experience. View this film and compare its use of the quilt metaphor to Ringgold's.

SUGGESTIONS FOR WRITING AND RESEARCH

1. Choose one of the European artists represented in Ringgold's work—Édouard Monet, Pablo Picasso, Vincent Van Gogh, Henri Matisse, or even Leonardo da Vinci. Familiarize yourself with the hallmarks of his works, his life, and his contribution to art history. What influence does this artist seem to have had on Faith Ringgold, in both substance and form? What elements of his work does she seem to be rejecting?

   Alternately, research one of the African-American figures represented in *Picnic at Giverny, The Sunflowers Quilting Bee at Arles, Dinner at Gertrude Stein's,* or *Le Café Des Artistes.* How does Ringgold implicitly compare Willia Marie to the figure you've chosen? What influence do you think this figure has had on Faith Ringgold?
2. Write about a work that has been remade in some way (e.g., a novel made into a movie, a movie made into a new movie, a movie made into a television show, a piece of music sampled in a new composition, artwork used in advertising, fashions brought back as new trends, etc.). Discuss the choices that the revisionist has made. Is the new work faithful or unfaithful to the old? How? Why? Do a small amount of research on the original so that you can speak with authority. See if the revisionist has made any statements about his/her revision. In your opinion, does he or she seem to be continuing to add to a tradition, or

is the new work merely exploiting the success of the old? How does this revision compare to the artistic "revisions" of Faith Ringgold?

3. The writer Alice Walker is interested in the symbol of the quilt for African American women. Read her story "Everyday Use" and her essay "In Search of Our Mother's Gardens," and develop a theory about the purpose of art that is informed by both Walker and Ringgold. Is there a significant difference between the practice of a craft and the making of art?
4. Some of Faith Ringgold's work could be labeled "utopian," presenting a personal fantasy of Ringgold's that doesn't approximate the reality for African Americans in general, much less African American women artists specifically. Is a utopian vision appropriate and/or effective, in your opinion, with respect to social and political progress for African Americans? Does Ringgold's art condemn enough the exclusion of African American women from European tradition and history while it fantasizes about their inclusion?

WORKING WITH CLUSTERS

Cluster 2: Constructing and Corrupting the Feminine
Cluster 6: The Race for Representation
Cluster 11: The Art of Irony
Cluster 12: Visual Language
Cluster 16: Imagination and Experience
Discipline: The Humanities
Rhetorical Mode: Narration

"Reclaiming Our Ancient Self" (from *The Debt: What America Owes to Blacks*)

by Randall Robinson

Randall Robinson earned a bachelor's degree from Virginia Union University and a juris doctor from Harvard Law School. Robinson served as assistant to two U.S. congressmen—Charles Diggs in 1976–1977, and William Clay in 1975–1976—and was a leader in the Civil Rights Movement. As a Ford Foundation fellow, Robinson lived in Africa for one year (1970–1971) conducting research on the application of European law in Dar es Salaam, Tanzania. Robinson is president of the Washington, DC-based TransAfrica Forum, a private, nonprofit organization that promotes enlightened U.S. policies toward Africa and the Caribbean. Before writing The Debt: What America Owes to Blacks, *from which this selection is drawn, he published* Defending the Black Spirit—The Black Life in America. *In 2002, Robinson published a follow-up to* The Debt, *called* The Reckoning: What Blacks Owe Each Other.

When I discover who I am, I'll be free.

—**Ralph Ellison**

I was born in 1941, but my black soul is much older than that. Its earliest incarnations occurred eons ago on another continent somewhere in the mists of prehistory. Thus, there are two selves: one born a mere fifty-eight years ago; the other, immortal, who has lost sight of the trail of his long story. I am this new self and an ancient self. I need both to be whole. Yet there is a war within, and I feel a great wanting of the spirit.

1. In Your Journal: Why does Robinson say he has "two selves"?

The immortal self—the son of the shining but distant African ages—tells the embattled, beleaguered, damaged self, the modern self, what he needs to remember of his ancient traditions. But the modern self simply cannot remember and thus cannot believe. The modern self has desperately tried, but the effort has been only marginally fruitful. Maliciously shorn of his natural identity for so long, he can too easily get lost in another's.

2. In Your Journal: Why does Robinson refer to "The immortal self" rather than "My immortal self"?

> *It is at* **Heliopolis** *that the most learned of the Egyptian antiquaries are said to be found. . . . As to practical matters, they are all agreed in saying that the Egyptians by their study of astronomy discovered the solar year and were the first to divide it into twelve parts. . . . They also told me that the Egyptians first brought into use the names of the twelve gods, which the Greeks took over from them, and were the first to assign altars and images and temples to the gods, and to carve figures in stone.*
>
> —**Herodotus** (circa 450 B.C.)

3. In Your Journal: Where do you think Robinson might be going with this quote about Egyptians and Greeks?

In any case, in America, there is little space for *before.*
Before the Mayflower . . .

Ralph Ellison: from *Invisible Man* (1952), which chronicles the migration of a nameless young Southern black man to New York (and into the attempted homogeneity of the communist party); uses themes of anonymity and groundlessness to articulate the plight of pre-civil rights blacks in America

Heliopolis: ancient northern Egyptian city, known for philosophy and astronomy, as well as the obelisks called "Cleopatra's Needles"

Herodotus: (484?-425? B.C.) Greek historian known as the "father of history"

Before that Dutch man-o'-war docked at Jamestown Landing in August 1619 with twenty Africans in its belly . . . *Before* the **Middle Passage** . . .

And when *before* is on view, invariably it is white. Sight lines to the *before* that I require, that I crave, are blocked.

4. *In Your Journal:* How does the list of "*Befores*" clarify the previous paragraph about the "modern self"?

From the times of ancient scribes, history has been written and studied, traditions honored, gods worshiped, monuments to the greater glory erected, institutions sustained in countless cultures coursing humanity's mosaic of peoples across the millennia like life-giving rivers. These are not extraneous behaviors. They are essential to the health of any people's spirit. They are givers of collective self-worth, cheaters of mortality, binding frail short lives into a people's ongoing, epic cumulative achievement.

5. *In Your Journal:* How are history-related activities "givers of collective self-worth" and "cheaters of mortality"?

> *They [i.e., the Greek historians relied upon by the writer] say also that the Egyptians are colonists sent out by the Ethiopians [i.e., not the modern Ethiopians, but, the black peoples from inner Africa south of Egypt],* ***Osiris*** *having been the leader of the colony. For speaking generally, what is now Egypt, they maintain, was not land but sea when in the beginning the universe was being formed; afterwards, however, as the Nile during the times of its inundating carried down the mud from [the land of the black peoples], land was gradually built up from the deposit. . . . And the larger part of the customs of the Egyptians are, they [i.e., the Greek historians] hold, Ethiopian, the colonists still preserving their ancient manners.*
>
> —**Diodorus Siculus** (circa 50 B.C.)

6. *In Your Journal:* Does it surprise you that Ethiopia might have "colonized" Egypt?

> *We spent the night on the island [of* ***Mombasa****] and then set sail for Kilwa, the principal town on the [East African] coast, the greater part of whose inhabitants are* ***Zanj*** *of very black complexion. . . . A merchant told me that* ***Sofala*** *is half a month's march from Kilwa, and that between Sofala and* ***Yufi*** *in the country of the Limiin is a month's march. Powdered gold is brought from Yufi to Sofala. . . .*

- **Middle Passage:** portion of the triangular trade route that brought slaves from West Africa to North America, South America, and the Caribbean on 5- to 12-week trips
- **Osiris:** Egyptian god of underworld
- **Diodorus Siculus:** (c. 21 B.C.) Sicilian historian; wrote a world history in 40 volumes, including a history of North Africa
- **Mombasa:** Kenya's chief port and an important commercial and industrial center
- **Zanj:** East African slave laborers in Iraq who fought a 15-year rebellion (868–883) called the "Revolt of Zanj"
- **Sofala:** city in Mozambique; early Arab trading post, settled by the Portuguese in 1505
- **Yufi:** source of gold dust in Zimbabwe; Battuta identified it as a city hostile to whites

7. In Your Journal: In what ways does it seem Robinson thinks "Americans grow less knowledgeable by the day"?

8. In Your Journal: Why do you think Robinson lists many places in Africa that he believes Americans to be unaware of without glossing the geography or historical significance of those places? What point does he make by *not* explaining to the reader what she might be ignorant of?

9. In Your Journal: Why can't a lot of "individual career success" add up to a positive "group morale" or collective identity, according to Robinson's logic?

10. In Your Journal: Compare this use of "soul" to the previous use of the word on page 871.

Kilwa is one of the most beautiful and well-constructed towns in the world. The whole of it is elegantly built.

—**Ibn Battuta** (1331)

Though it would appear that Americans grow less knowledgeable by the day, there are still many American school-children who recognize the Roman Colosseum, the Great Wall of China, the **Parthenon,** the Tower of London. From Africa, only the great pyramids of Egypt enjoy such broad recognition, and they are popularly and wrongly attributed to a civilization not spawned from Africa's interior. By and large, only behind the most obscure doors of high academe can one unearth a mention of the great African empires and polities of antiquity like **Kush, Benin, Meroë, Djenné, Ghana,** and **Songhay.** Few Americans, if shown photographs of the stone walls of **Monomatapa** or the magnificent ruins at **Axum,** would be able to identify these ancient African survivals.

Far too many Americans of African descent believe their history starts in America with bondage and struggles forward from there toward today's second-class citizenship. The cost of this obstructed view of ourselves, of our history, is incalculable. How can we be *collectively* successful if we have no idea or, worse, the wrong idea of who we were and, therefore, are? We are history's amnesiacs fitted with the memories of others. Our minds can be trained for individual career success but our group morale, the very soul of us, has been devastated by the assumption that what has not been told to us about ourselves does not exist to be told.

- **Ibn Battuta:** see page 524
- **Parthenon:** sacred temple in Athens, built 447-432 B.C.
- **Kush:** ancient kingdom in Sudan; first African civilization after Egypt (flourished in the 11th-4th century B.C.); controlled parts of Egypt in the 8th century
- **Benin:** republic in West Africa; colluded in the slave trade during the 16th and 17th centuries
- **Meroë:** ancient city in northern Sudan
- **Djenné:** city in south central Mali; agricultural market center; prosperous Muslim culture
- **Ghana:** republic in West Africa, important to the gold and slave trades; developed use of camels for transport and labor
- **Songhay:** former Islamic empire in the Sudan
- **Monomatapa:** city in Zimbabwe
- **Axum:** mixed people of Ethiopian and southern Arabian extraction with one of the oldest literate traditions in Africa; thriving kingdom in 1st century A.D.

> *Previous European scholarship knew that the foundations of European civilization derived from classical Greek civilization. That scholarship further accepted what the Greeks had laid down as patently obvious: that classical Greek civilization derived in its religion, its philosophy, its mathematics and much else, from the ancient civilizations of Africa above all from Egypt of the Pharaohs. To those 'founding fathers' in classical Greece, any notion that Africans were inferior, morally or intellectually, would have seemed silly.*
>
> —Basil Davidson, *Africa in History* (1991)

This then is the nub of it. America's contemporary racial problems cannot be solved, racism cannot be arrested, achievement gaps cannot be fully closed until Americans—*all Americans*—are repaired in their views of Africa's role in history.

Like it or not, the races are fixed in their views of each other. While restrained by the **diaphanous fetters** of polite hypocrisy, most in the world, including Africa and her progeny, perceive Africa and blacks generally to be lagging the field in achievement. This was not always the case, and has only *been* the case for the merest moment in the long march of human progress. To be made large and formidable and masterful again—to be whole again—blacks need to know the land of their forebears when its civilizations were verifiably equal to any in the world.

diaphanous: sheer; filmy

fetters: shackles; restraints

Blacks, and no less whites, need to know that in the centuries preceding the Atlantic slave trade and the invention of a virulent racism to justify it, the idea of black inferiority did not exist.

> *I say with the fullest confidence that you could strike out every single reference to [**Othello's**] black skin and the play would be essentially the same. Othello's trouble is that be is an outsider. He is not a Venetian. He is a military bureaucrat, a technician, hired to fight for Venice, a foreign country. The Senate has no consciousness whatever of his color. That is a startling fact but true. They haven't to make allowances for it. It simply has no place in their minds.*
>
> —**C. L. R. James**

William Shakespeare wrote *Othello* between 1602 and 1604. Had Shakespeare lived and written in the eighteenth century, *Othello* would

---

❖ ***Othello:*** tragedy by William Shakespeare (1602) about a Moorish army hero who weds a white noblewoman (Desdemona), and is convinced by a jealous, conniving and racist colleague (Iago) that Desdemona has been unfaithful, which leads to Othello's killing of both Desdemona and himself

❖ **C.L.R. James:** (1901–1989) born in Trinidad; novelist, playwright, American literature scholar, and political activist (most noted for support of Leon Trotsky's views)

never have had a **Moor** as the protagonist. The sea change in global racial perceptions, principally occasioned by the Atlantic slave trade and its justifiers, was that pervasive.

In the modern social context of spoken and unspoken assumptions about race, the apparent nonexistence of race as a basis for prejudgment during the early and middle ages may strain credulity for many. As does the truth of individual black achievement and prominence in the far past.

Take, for instance, an edition of the CBS News program *60 Minutes* that aired September 20, 1998. A segment of the program focused on who might succeed Pope John Paul II as head of the Roman Catholic Church. Cardinal Francis Arinze, a Nigerian, was described as having a reasonable chance of becoming the next pope.

Would Catholics bolt the church *en masse* if the **College of Cardinals** were to select Cardinal Arinze as the next pope? Could the church politically afford to name an African pope? Catholic hierarchs and historians reviewed four centuries of Vatican history and puzzled with CBS's Morley Safer over such questions and the chances for a revolutionary breakthrough. The discussion had a milestone-aborning feel to it. But, oh, how misleading this was.

Never once was it mentioned that in the first millennium the Catholic Church had three popes who were either from Africa or of African descent; **Saint Victor I** (189–99), **Saint Miltiades** (311–14), and Saint Gelasius I (492–96) of whom, in his 1996 book *Popes through the Ages*, James Brusher wrote, "Although a great writer, Gelasius made his strongest impression as a man of holiness. . . . He was outstanding for his sense of justice and above all for his charity to the poor." Born in Rome, but described in the *Oxford Dictionary of Popes* to have been of African descent and in P. G. Maxwell-Stuart's *Chronicle of the Popes* as African by nationality, Gelasius was remembered as "great even among the saints." Much is written in the literature of the episcopates of these three African popes, but nothing that would suggest controversy about their ethnic identity. The three popes were selected, they served with distinction, and that was that. Such would be hard to imagine in today's climate.

Was *60 Minutes*'s omission of Saints Victor, Miltiades, and Gelasius an oversight? Certainly, in preparing for the segment, the *60 Minutes* researchers

---

Moor: Muslim of Berber and Arabic extraction in northwest Africa

College of Cardinals: body of Cardinals that elects the pope

Saint Victor I: born in Africa, died in 199; 13th pope who decreed allowance for emergency baptism, established the practice of celebrating Easter on a Sunday, and facilitated a lull in the persecution of the Catholic Church

Saint Miltiades: African pope elected in 311; oversaw controversy among bishops in North Africa during his three-year reign must have come upon the early African popes. What were the researchers thinking?

Giving them the benefit of the doubt, they had either: (1) looked directly upon, but not seen, the voluminous references in the early church texts; (2) misread the early church texts; or (3) elected not to believe the early church texts.

11. In Your Journal: Which of the three reasons that Robinson provides for *60 Minutes'* oversight do you think he favors? What is your guess as to why they neglected the previous African popes?

As I write this, I picture my immortal soul in the body of a man in the year 1831 A.D. living out my time in West Africa. I am eighty years old by then. I grow poorer by the day and wish to die before my resources are fully depleted. The physical decline of my village parallels the long, slow decline of my material living conditions. I am weak, but that is to be expected at my age. I am more troubled by the **ineffable** and unascribable sadness that I suffer of late. I sometimes cry for no reason. My kinspeople are mystified and saddened for me. Our family compound is deteriorated but **commodious**. It mirrors the problems of our troubled land.

ineffable: deep; beyond words

commodious: spacious; comfortable

Great age affords me a long view of past events. It is that view that fills me with pride. The view's dimming light, I believe, may be one source of this unshakable **disconsolacy** as well.

disconsolacy: cheerlessness

In the 1750s my grandparents filled my small child's head with stories about our people when we were a great power in the world. My grandfather was a much respected scholar who knew the stories of ancient empire well and told them to my siblings and me more out of duty than pleasure. He knew things that few others knew, sometimes things that had happened long ago and beyond the great sea. I cannot remember the stories so well anymore and that too saddens me. I think that I am failing our young, who will have no memory of our greatness if I can no longer recall the far past for them.

12. In Your Journal: Why does Robinson emphasize the "duty" rather than the "pleasure" of telling ancient stories?

Was Meroe the place of the sumptuous stone buildings? I think but I'm not sure anymore.

There are times, though increasingly further apart, when my memory works as it once did, when I can remember well Grandfather's stories and the rigorous studies of my youth under his tutelage. Grandfather had read all the works of the ancient scholars. The scholars whose writings I could not read for myself, Grandfather told me about. Many who wrote about my region were from faraway places, like al-Bakri of **Cordoba** who had, seven hundred years before, chronicled the empire of Ghana. Mahmud Kati and Abd al-Rahman were scholars who were born in this region and lived in nearby **Timbuktu.** They too had written much about the great kingdom of Ghana, which had been succeeded in wealth and power by my own **Mali,**

⁂ **Cordoba:** Spanish city; center of Muslim Spain

⁂ **Timbuktu:** central Mali; major commercial center; great center of Muslim education

⁂ **Mali:** republic in West Africa; 90% Muslim; known as the "French Sudan" which in turn had given way to the even more powerful empire of Songhay. My country and Songhay together were as large, I had learned, as the whole of western Europe. Ibn Battuta, the Moroccan scholar who had traversed Africa and visited Turkey and traveled as far east as China, wrote of us in the year 1352: "One of the good features [of the government and people of Mali] is their lack of oppression. They are the farthest removed from it. Another of their good features is the security which embraces the whole country. Neither the traveler nor the man who stays at home has anything to fear from thief or from usurper."

The Mandinka people, to which I belong, formed the core of our empire. The greatest of our emperors was Mansa Musa, who rose to power in 1312 and died in 1337. It was under him that the cities of Timbuktu and Djenne launched their long eras of scholarship and learning, with notice of the excellence of their schools of law and theology reaching far into Muslim Asia.

The emperor erected great mosques of brick, expanded the military, and built a trade network so vast that in 1375, thirty-eight years after his death, the Majorcan cartographer Cresques depicted traders from all of North Africa marching to our markets. The Muslim dinar, the gold coin that had supplanted the *denarius aureus* of **Byzantium** as the most respected standard of value in much of the world, was minted from our region's gold, Asia Minor's sources having long since been exhausted.

In those times, our empires were world powers. It was our gold that undergirded the world trading system. Europe was only just emerging from the poverty and chaos that followed the **collapse of the Western Roman Empire.** Their new money would be based on our gold. No other sources existed anywhere.

littoral: near or relating to the sea

I knew less about the coastal people who lived to the unfathomable east, beyond the great lake, along the **littoral** of the *Sea of the Zanj* (sea of the black people), as the Arab writers called it. But Grandfather had read of them in a very old book that he prized more than any other single thing he owned. As its parchment was powdery and fragile, I was allowed to read the book only in his presence. It had been written in 925 A.D. by Abu al-Hasan al-Masudi. I remember that the name of the book was *The Meadows of Gold and Mines of Gems.* It told of the kingdom of the Zanj and a leader who bore the title of *waqlimi,* which means "supreme lord." The Zanj, al-Masudi wrote, "give this title to their sovereign because he has been chosen to govern them with equity. But once he becomes tyrannical and departs from the rules of justice, they cause him to die and exclude his posterity from succession to

---

Byzantium: successor state to the Roman Empire (after centuries as Constantinople); now Istanbul, Turkey

---

collapse of the Western Roman Empire: 476 A.D., due to poor leadership and military decline the throne, for they claim that in behaving thus he ceases to be the son of the Master, that is the king of heaven and earth."

Grandfather said that in the year 1414 the leader of **Malindi** along the same coast to the east made a gift of a giraffe to China. The Chinese emperor, having never seen one, had thought the giraffe to be a mythical creature and demonstrated his appreciation by sending an ocean-sailing ship that bore away to China Malindi's ambassador to be thanked personally by the emperor in the year 1417. The ship had been under the command of an Admiral Cheng-Ho. Grandfather showed this reference to me in another of his countless books.

Not long after this, the sun went out across the whole of our land. For it was around the year 1500 that the Portuguese arrived along the coast to the east. They seemed a curious people, simultaneously looting and admiring. One of their chroniclers, a Duarte Barbosa, wrote of the coastal city-state of Kilwa that it "has many handsome houses of stone and mortar, with many windows such as our own houses have, and very well arranged streets." Of Mombasa, further north along the coast, Barbosa had described "a very handsome place with tall stone and mortar houses well aligned in streets as they are in Kilwa, as well as being a place of much traffic with a good harbor where are always moored boats of many kinds, and also great ships." It is strange, I think, that this Barbosa man would write such things about *buildings* while, not three score years before his account, his people, the Portuguese, had begun stealing our people.

13. In Your Journal: Why does Robinson quote Barbosa's description of Kilwa here? Why does his imagined ancient self find Barbosa's description strange?

> *. . . our men had very great toil in the capture of those who were swimming, for they dived like* **CORMORANTS**, *so that they could not get hold of them, and the capture of the second man caused them to lose all the others. For he was so valiant that two men, strong as they were, could not drag him into the boat until they took a boatbook and caught him above one eye, and the pain of this made him abate his courage, and allow himself to be put inside the boat.*
>
> —Gomes Eannes de Zurara, *Chronicle of the Discovery and Conquest of Guinea*, 1444

cormorants: large aquatic birds found mostly in temperate and tropical regions

You might have thought that today had been a good day for me, inasmuch as my mind has been clear. But such days, mercifully rare, leave me more, rather than less, depressed.

For the whole of my life and a time before, many of those I have known, including my sister and two brothers, have been captured and (I later learned) boarded on ships at the coast. My family did not know where the ships went and never heard word about my sister and brothers again.

Are they alive somewhere and old like me? I wish I could know only that. I am crying again. This practice of stealing our people continues to

---

Malindi: town in southeast Kenya; founded in the 10th century by Arab traders this day. Our young people cannot sit still to listen to tales of glory from a dying old man while they fear being stolen.

Grandfather had hoped that those who had been captured would, as is the custom here, be set free or become a member of the new tribe. But none who had been taken away were ever seen again.

I am old and broken now and I cry. I cry for all who have been abducted, for this empty broken land, for Grandfather's stories that are fading in my memory, for the souls of my ancestors who gave art and craft and science to the whole of the world.

The American writer Thomas Paine would likely have sympathized with my imagined Malian soul-sharer and his scholarly eighteenth-century grandfather. Before slavery, Paine had seen Africa as a fertile land of industrious, quiet-living, peace-loving people. On March 8, 1775, Paine, soon to be one of the leaders of the American Revolution, published "African Slavery in America" in the *Pennsylvania Journal and Weekly Advertiser*. He wrote:

> That some desperate wretches should be willing to steal and enslave men by violence and murder for gain is rather lamentable than strange. . . . The managers of that trade themselves, and others, testify that many of these African nations inhabit fertile countries, are industrious farmers, enjoy plenty and lived quietly, averse to war, before the Europeans debauched them with liquors, and bribed them against one another, and that these inoffensive people are brought into slavery, by stealing them, tempting kings to sell subjects, which they have no right to do, and hiring one tribe to war against another to catch prisoners. By such wicked and inhuman ways the English are said to enslave toward one hundred thousand yearly; of which thirty thousand are supposed to die by barbarous treatment in the first year; besides all that are slain in the unnatural wars excited to take them. So much innocent blood have the managers and supporters of this inhuman trade to answer for to the common Lord of all.

In 1434, when the Portuguese approached the land mass of Africa, they were to discover in the regions south of the Sahara peoples who had long since developed complex economic, political, and social systems. Cities along the Niger River, such as Segu, Kankan, Timbuktu, Djenne, and Gao, ranged from ten to thirty thousand people. Katsina and Kano, Hausa cities, had each as many as a hundred thousand inhabitants. Iron and steel of high quality were **smelted**. Copper was a fruit of local industry. Knives, spears, axes, and hoes were produced by Africans for African households. Such was the quality of goldsmithery that a Dutch captain would write: "The thread and texture of their hatbands and chaining is so fine that . . . our ablest European artists would find it difficult to imitate them." Africans

smelted: fused or melted

had made finely decorated pottery for centuries. They wove, wore, and traded linen and cotton.

All of this—centuries of economic and social development—was about to change.

On August 8, 1444, six hundred-ton caravels made port in the Algarve region of Portugal and unloaded a cargo of 235 African slaves, who were displayed in an open field. The Portuguese chronicler Gomes Eannes de Zurara was to describe the scene: "What heart could be so hard as not to be pierced with piteous feeling to see that company? For some kept their heads low, and their faces bathed in tears, looking one upon another. Others stood groaning very **dolorously**, looking up to the height of heaven, fixing their eyes upon it, crying out loudly, as if asking help from the Father of Nature; others struck their faces with the palms of their hands, throwing themselves at full length upon the ground; while others made lamentations in the manner of a **dirge**, after the custom of their country."

dolorously: so as to express grief

dirge: funeral hymn

By 1448 the Portuguese had carried off a thousand Africans. The number would grow exponentially over the next century.

King Affonso of Kongo (Congo) wrote to King João of Portugal in 1526: "Each day the traders are kidnapping our people—children of this country, sons of our nobles and vassals, even people of our own family. [King Affonso's nephews and grandchildren had been kidnapped while en route to Portugal for religious education and sent into slavery in Brazil.] . . . This corruption and depravity are so widespread that our land is entirely depopulated. . . . It is our wish that this Kingdom not be a place for the trade or transport of slaves."

King João wrote back: "You . . . tell me that you want no slave-trading in your domains, because this trade is depopulating your country. . . . The Portuguese there, on the contrary, tell me how vast the Congo is, and how it is so thickly populated that it seems as if no slave has ever left."

While King Affonso was no stranger to slavery, which was practiced throughout most of the known world, he had understood slavery as a condition befalling prisoners of war, criminals, and debtors, out of which slaves could earn, or even marry, their way. This was nothing like seeing this wholly new and brutal commercial practice of slavery where tens of thousands of his subjects were dragged off in chains. When the king sent emissaries on a long and arduous sea voyage to appeal to the pope in Rome, the emissaries were arrested upon their arrival in **Lisbon.**

By 1831 the Africans who had been sold into slavery numbered in the millions. America, along with Europe, had fallen in behind a leading

---

Lisbon: capital of Portugal

German thinker, **Georg Hegel,** in justifying slavery to itself and to the world. Declared Hegel:

> The Negro exhibits the natural man in his completely wild and untamed state. We must lay aside all thought of reverence and morality—all that we call feeling—if we could rightly comprehend him: there is nothing harmonious with humanity to be found in his type of character. . . . [Africa] is no historical part of the world; it has no movement or development to show.

14. In Your Journal: Robinson suggests that Hegel's view held a good deal of power. Do you think he means Hegel to be representative of others?

Africans would henceforth be seen as without worth or history.

Darkness. Opaque, impenetrable darkness. Africa's past before the slave trade, quite literally, had disappeared. And that continent's chattel issue, for a limitless future the world around, would become history's orphans. Languages, customs, traditions, rituals, faiths, mores, taboos—all vitals of the immortal larger self—gone, extinguished. A seeming eternal identity, a people's whole memory, crushed under the remorseless commerce of slavery.

No people can live successfully, fruitfully, triumphantly without strong memory of their past, without reading the future within the context of some reassuring past, without implanting reminders of that past in the present. Consider the following passage from David S. Ariel's 1995 book *What Do Jews Believe?*:

15. In Your Journal: Why would Robinson compare the plight of the African diaspora to that of Jews?

> Each generation retells the sacred myths of the Jewish people. In each telling of the story, we relate to the narratives told by previous generations while modifying and changing them. For example, the sacred myth of the Exodus from Egypt became the basis of the Passover Seder and the Haggadah, the written account of the Exodus. Each Passover, the story of how God freed the ancient Israelites from Egypt in order to give them the Torah is retold.

> *There are in Timbuktu numerous judges, doctors [of letters] and priests [i.e., learned Muslims]. [The ruler] greatly bonors scholarship. Here too they sell*

⁖ **Georg Hegel:** (Wilhelm Friedrich) (1770–1831) German philosopher who influenced the development of existentialism and socialism and posited the concept of "dialectical logic"—where thesis and antithesis lead to synthesis—as a method of understanding human life and activity *many bandwritten books that arrive from Barbary [i.e., North Africa]. More profit is had from their sale than from any other merchandise.*

—**Leo Africanus** (1550)

Jews, Arabs, Turks, Russians, Finns, Swedes, Czechs, Uzbeks, Macedonians, Estonians, Malayans, Cathayans, Japanese, Sinhalese—one and all planetwide—have a nurturing access to the fullness of their myriad histories, histories that often seem as old as time.

African Americans must spiritually survive from the meager basket of a few mean yesterdays. No chance for significant group progress there. None. For we have been largely over-whelmed by a majority culture that wronged us dramatically, emptied our memories, undermined our self-esteem, implanted us with palatable voices, and stripped us along the way of the sheerest corona of self-definition. We alone are presumed pastless, left to cobble self-esteem from a vacuum of stolen history.

By default, we must define ourselves by our ongoing tribulations and those who **mete** them out to us. Otherwise, we have little in the way of a long-held interior idea of who we are.

mete: to portion or measure

While I am anything but the passionate conspiracy-phobic, the contemporary social results seem anything but accidental.

Leo Africanus: (1526–1554) born in Moorish Granada; expelled by Ferdinand and Isabella in 1492; studied in Morocco, captured by Christian pirates and made a slave to Pope Leo X, who freed him and commissioned him to write a history of Africa in Italian; converted back to Islam before his death

FOR USE IN DISCUSSION

Questions about Substance

1. Robinson talks of a warring self, struggling to connect the immediate self and the immortal self (518). Do you think this predicament is specific to African Americans, or do you think Robinson's point is universal? Explain your answer.
2. Given Robinson's struggle with the legacies of African American history (both what is and is not lost), what do you think his general opinion of history is? Is it, as Robinson overtly suggests, liberating, or is it a burden that obscures individual identity?

3. "This then is the nub of it. America's contemporary racial problems cannot be solved, racism cannot be arrested, achievement gaps cannot be fully closed until Americans—*all Americans*—are repaired in their views of Africa's role in history" (521). How could whites and other Americans who are not African Americans benefit from this "repair" that Robinson alludes to?
4. How much use did you make of the footnotes in this text? Do you think that Robinson ought to have provided more of the glossary information that the editors have added to this text? What could Robinson's point have been in making so many allusions to remote, ancient, and obscure references without taking the time to define them for his readers?

Questions about Structure and Style

1. Robinson integrates a linear narrative style of discussion with quoted material from various historical sources. Does he try to synthesize these two features in any direct or indirect way? How is this structure meant to convey an overall point about learning and/or history? How does this point relate to the argument contained in the linear narrative?
2. There is a bit of fantasy created in this essay. Robinson imagines himself a 19th century African and uses that fantasy to make logical and emotional points. What are those points? How does Robinson's fanciful style contribute to his overall goal?

Multimedia Suggestions

1. David Horowitz responded passionately to the reparations movement by publishing "Ten Reasons Why Reparations for Blacks Is a Bad Idea," which caused an intense debate on college campuses across the country. Read Horowitz's article at *http://www.frontpagemag.com/Articles/ReadArticle.asp?ID= 1153* and one of the major responses to it at *http://www.umass.edu/afroam/hor.html.*

SUGGESTIONS FOR WRITING AND RESEARCH

1. Write a response to Robinson's argument, using his style of linear exposition interspersed with personal anecdotes and dreams. How does this structure contribute to Robinson's substantive point? Is he suggesting that history and personal understanding are always inextricable? What is your thought about how connected collective history is to the individual present? How do your personal experiences and fantasies affect your impression of Robinson?
2. View the mini-series *Roots* (1977) or the film *Amistad* (1997) to examine a work that attempts to fill in some of the gaps in African-American history. Read Ralph Ellison's novel *Invisible Man,* from which Robinson takes his epigraph, and read more of Robinson's book *The Debt,* from which this essay is drawn. Ellison's nameless protagonist, too, struggles with finding both himself and his

place in history. How does Robinson's analytical book read like Ellison's fiction? How does Ellison's fiction have characteristics of history? What is the relationship between fiction and history?

3. Malcolm X once said: "History is a people's memory, and without memory man is demoted to the lower animals." Apply this quote to Robinson's essay and to your knowledge of African American history. How does it apply to the institution of slavery? How does it apply to the Civil Rights Movement?

WORKING WITH CLUSTERS

Cluster 6: The Race for Representation
Cluster 18: Ethnicity and Conflict
Discipline: The Humanities
Rhetorical Mode: Cause and Effect

"The Triad of Alexis de Tocqueville" (from *Brown: The Last Discovery of America*)

by Richard Rodriguez

Richard Rodriguez is a prominent writer, associate editor with the Pacific News Service in San Francisco, contributing editor of Harper's *and the* Los Angeles Times, *and regular essayist on the* Jim Lehrer News Hour. *Born and raised in California, Rodriguez earned a B.A. at Stanford University and then spent two years studying with leading Protestant and Jewish theologians at the Union Theological Seminary. He later attended London's Warburg Institute and Oxford before earning a Ph.D. in Renaissance Literature at the University of California, Berkeley. Rodriguez's books include* Hunger of Memory *and* Days of Obligation: An Argument with My Mexican Father. *He received one of television's highest accolades, the George Foster Peabody Award, for his* News Hour *essays on American life and in recognition of his "outstanding achievement in broadcast and cable." Rodriguez's other awards include the Frankel Medal from the National Endowment for the Humanities and the International Journalism Award from the World Affairs Council of California. This essay is taken from Rodriguez's most recent book,* Brown: The Last Discovery of America.

glade: an open space surrounded by woods

1. *In Your Journal:* What is Rodriguez's physical characterization of de Tocqueville meant to suggest about the traveler-philosopher's account of the new world?

motif: recurrent thematic element

2. *In Your Journal:* Summarize the contrast between the Indian and the Negress that de Tocqueville presents.

Two women and a child in a **glade** beside a spring. Beyond them, the varnished wilderness wherein bright birds cry. The child is chalk, Europe's daughter. Her dusky attendants, a green Indian and a maroon slave.

The scene, from *Democracy in America,* is discovered by that most famous European traveler to the New World, Alexis de Tocqueville, aristocratic son of the **Enlightenment,** liberal, sickly, gray, violet, lacking the vigor of the experiment he has set himself to observe.

"I remember . . . I was traveling through the forests which still cover the state of Alabama. . . . "

In a clearing, at some distance, an Indian woman appears first to Monsieur, followed by a "Negress," holding by the hand "a little white girl of five or six years."

The Indian: "A sort of barbarous luxury" set off her costume; "rings of metal were hanging from her nostrils and ears, her hair, which was adorned with glass beads, fell loosely upon her shoulders. . . . " The Negress wore "squalid European garments."

Such garments are **motifs** of de Tocqueville's pathos. His description intends to show the African and the Indian doomed by history in corresponding but opposing ways. (History is a coat cut only to the European.)

"The young Indian, taking the child in her arms, lavished upon her such fond caresses as mothers give, while the Negress endeavored, by various little artifices, to attract the [child's] attention. . . . "

The white child "displayed in her slightest gestures a consciousness of superiority that formed a strange contrast with her infantine weakness; as if she received the attentions of her companions with a sort of condescension."

Thus composed: The Indian. The Negress. The white child.

" . . . In the picture that I have just been describing there was something peculiarly touching; a bond of affection here united the oppressors with the oppressed, and the effort of Nature to bring them together rendered still more striking the immense distance placed between them by prejudice and the laws."

Enlightenment: 18th century movement in Europe and the American colonies emphasizing an emergence from darkness and ignorance into an age of reason, science, and respect for humanity

At Monsieur's approach, this natural **colloquy** is broken. He becomes the agent of history. Seeing him, the Indian suddenly rises, "push[es] the child roughly away and, giving [Monsieur] an angry look, plunge[s] into the thicket."

colloquy: conversation or dialogue

The Negress rests; awaits de Tocqueville's approach.

Neither response satisfies the European. The African, de Tocqueville writes, has lost the memory of ancestors, of custom and tongue; the African has experienced degradation to his very soul, has become a true slave. "Violence made him a slave, and the habit of servitude gives him the thoughts and desires of a slave; he admires his tyrants more than he hates them, and finds his joy and his pride in the servile imitation of those who oppress him."

The bejeweled Indian, alternately, is "condemned . . . to a wandering life, full of inexpressible sufferings," because European interlopers have unbalanced the **provender** of Nature.

provender: provisions

And, de Tocqueville remarks (a fondness for fable), whereas the Negro's response to mistreatment is canine, the Indian's is feline. "The Negro makes a thousand fruitless efforts to insinuate himself among-men who repulse him. . . . " The Indian is filled with **diffidence** toward the white, "has his imagination inflated with the pretended nobility of his origin, and lives and dies in the midst of these dreams of pride." The Indian refuses civilization; the African slave is rendered unfit for it.

3. In Your Journal: Why does de Tocqueville call the Negro "canine" and the Indian "feline" in describing their responses to the European?

diffidence: lacking self-confidence; shy

But cher Monsieur: You saw the Indian sitting beside the African on a drape of **baize.** *They were easy together. The sight of them together does not lead you to wonder about a history in which you are not the narrator?*

baize: felt-like, woolen fabric

These women are but parables of your interest in yourself. Rather than consider the nature of their intimacy, you are preoccupied alone with the meaning of your intrusion. You in your dusty leather boots, cobbled on the rue du Faubourg St.-Honoré. Your tarnished silver snuffbox, your saddlebag filled with the more ancient dust of books. You in your soiled ***cambric. Vous-même.***

4. In Your Journal: Why does Rodriguez question de Tocqueville's "role as narrator"?

cambric: a fine, thin white linen fabric

vous-même: (French) yourself

A boy named Buddy came up beside me in the schoolyard. I don't remember what passed as prologue, but I do not forget what Buddy divulged to me:

If you're white, you're all right;
If you're brown, stick around;
If you're black, stand back.

It was as though Buddy had taken me to a mountaintop and shown me the way things lay in the city below.

In Sacramento, my brown was not halfway between black and white. On the leafy streets, on the east side of town, where my family lived, where Asians did not live, where Negroes did not live, my family's Mexican shades passed as various. We did not pass "for" white; my family passed among white, as in one of those old cartoons where Clarabelle the Cow goes shopping downtown and the mercantile class of dogs does not remark her exception. As opposed to **Amos and Andy,** whose downtown was a parallel universe of no possible **admixture.** And as I easily pass in these pages between being an American and regarding America from a distance.

admixture: compound substance

5. In Your Journal: What is the significance of Rodriguez' neighborhood?

As opposed, also, to the famous photograph of a **girl in Little Rock in the pages of *Life* magazine.** A black girl, no older than Alice, must pass alone through the looking glass. I remember wondering what my brown would have meant to Little Rock, how my brown would have withstood Little Rock.

6. In Your Journal: Based on this paragraph, how would you describe the status of "Brown" in 1950's Sacramento?

In the Sacramento of the 1950s, it was as though White simply hadn't had time enough to figure Brown out. It was a busy white time. Brown was like the skinny or fat kids left over after the team captains chose sides. "You take the rest"—my cue to wander away to the sidelines, to wander away.

In those years, I recall seeing a movie called *The Defiant Ones.* Two convicts—Sidney Poitier and Tony Curtis—were shackled to each other. The movie did not occur to me racially or politically but erotically. The child's obvious question concerned privacy. By comparison, the pairing of **The Lone Ranger** and Tonto on television did occur to me racially. They were twin **scourges**, upholders of the law of the West. They were of compatible mind and they were of complementary skill—one sneaky, one full-charge. I noticed Tonto had no vocabulary but **gravitas**. Of more immediate interest to me was that each wore the symbol of his reserved emotion—the mask; the hair in a bun. I didn't identify with Tonto any more than with Lone, or less. I identified with their pairing.

scourge: instrument of punishment or criticism

gravitas: high seriousness in a person's bearing

7. In Your Journal: Why does Rodriguez identify with the "pairing" of the Lone Ranger and Tonto?

My parents had come from Mexico, a short road in my imagination. I felt myself as coming from a caramelized planet, an upside-down planet, pineapple-cratered. Though I was born here, I came from the other side of the looking glass, as did Alice, though not alone like Alice. Downtown I saw lots of brown people. Old men on benches. Winks from Filipinos. **Sikhs** who worked in the fields were the most mysterious brown men, their

- **Amos and Andy:** (1950's) African American characters in a comical radio show narrated by two white men; made into a television series with African American actors, but canceled after only two years because of the controversy of white writers behind the African American actors
- **girl in Little Rock in the pages of *Life* magazine:** refers to the famous photo of Elizabeth Eckford trying to enter Little Rock Central High School, and being verbally harassed by other students; result of uproar over *Brown* v. *Board of Education,* which required integration of public schools
- **The Lone Ranger:** 1950's western television drama, pairing a cowboy and an American Indian
- **Sikhs:** believers of Sikhism, a monotheistic Hindu tradition that espouses the universal acceptance of all humanity and stresses the practice of meditation

heads wrapped in turbans. They were the rose men. They looked like roses. And the Palestinian communist bookie—entirely hearsay—who ran a tobacco store of pungent brownness (the smell of rum-soaked cigars and cheap, cherry-scented pipe tobacco) was himself as brown as a rolled cigar, but the more mysterious for having been born in Bethlehem.

And as we passed, we passed very close to the young man, close enough for me to smell him, something anointing his hair. He was the most beautiful man (my first consciousness of the necessity for oxymoron) I remember seeing as a boy. He wore a suit-vest over his naked torso. He wore a woman's gold locket, with a dark red stone. He was petting a dog in the street. His pant knees were dirty. He smelled of coconut. He smiled brilliantly as we passed.

> ***8. In Your Journal:*** How does Rodriguez come to understand the concept of "oxymoron"?

The missing tooth.

Heepsie, my mother whispered, taking me firmly by the hand, refusing his blazing notice with an averted nod.

I had seen the gypsy's mother—she must be his mother—dozens of times, sitting on a lawn chair outside her "office" on H Street, near my father's work. There was a sign in the window beneath which she sat, a blank hand outlined in neon. She never sought or met my gaze. She looked Mexican to me. Not Mexican, my parents assured me. My brother said, *Watch out, Ricky, she's sitting there reading your tombstone.*

A boy with a face as dark as mine, but several years older, stepped out of the crowd at the state fair to press a warm dime into my hand. Said nothing; wanted nothing, apparently; disappeared. His curious **solemnity**. But I interpreted—because I remember—the transaction as one of brown eyes.

> **solemnity:** sobriety in manner or aspect

A friend of mine, born and raised in Hong Kong, remembers attending British schools in Hong Kong; remembers being constrained to learn about India. My friend learned nothing about China; instead, the ***Gita*** and ***Only connect,*** **Lord Curzon, Mother Ganga, mulligatawny**, Mahatma Gandhi. The British obsession with India—as its **existential** opposite—seemed to my friend an affront to China. But surely there was also a kind of freedom in growing up without the Briton's attention?

> **mulligatawny:** Anglo-Indian soup; name means "pepper water"

> **existential:** expressing the fact of existence; branch of philosophy concerned with the meanings of existence

My uncle from India was several times called "nigger" by strangers downtown in Sacramento. His daughter, Delia, forbade the rhyme I learned

> ***9. In Your Journal:*** How are the Chinese in Hong Kong similar to the Indians de Tocqueville describes? Do you think Rodriguez intends this analogy?

Gita: (*Bhagavad-Gita*) ancient Hindu scripture used as a guide to self realization through selfless action, knowledge, and devotion to god

Only connect: phrase from Indian-born English novelist E.M. Forster's *Howard's End;* a call to be true to one's passions but also sometimes suggested as an allusion to Forster's homosexuality

Lord Curzon: a viceroy sent from England to address India's problems through reform and to strengthen the British Empire in India from 1899 to 1905

Mother Ganga: river running through India, believed by the Hindu religion to have healing and other holy properties at school. ***Eenie, meenie, mynie, moe. . . .*** But her eyes softened as she corrected me and her mouth softened.

Brown is a bit of a cave in my memory. Like Delia's eyes.

Lights up, then, on **"Theme from a Summer Place,"** on blue and gold and electric guitar strings. A decade on. I am staying for a month of summer in Laguna Beach with the family of my best friend, Larry Faherty. I am covered with a cool film of Sea & Ski, as is Larry, though I suspect the insistence on this precaution by Larry's mother is **gratuitous** in my case. Larry's mother is sitting on the deck with a neighbor, a red-faced woman with protuberant pale blue eyes, penciled eyebrows. The bug-eyed woman burbles into her tomato juice cocktail, "some niggers . . . " (ah, ah, ah, I can feel the hairs lift on the back of my neck) " . . . some niggers came onto the beach over the weekend . . . " (she glances at me while she is saying this; her eyes are needles; I am the camel) " . . . we let them know they weren't welcome." It is not clear where I fit into her use of the first-person plural. Finally, however, my presence does not disturb her narrative.

gratuitous: unwarranted

10. In Your Journal: Why doesn't Rodriguez's presence "disturb the narrative" of Mrs. Flaherty? What would it mean if his presence did disturb her narrative?

Years later, the same story, a different summer—Columbia, South Carolina. A different storyteller—a lawyer in New York rehearses his famous anecdote, "The Hawaiian Stranger," in three passages; two tumblers of scotch.

1. It is summer, 1944; World War II is coming to an end. (There is no tragic coast to this story; the boys in it will not taste the tin can of death.) The lawyer's mother, **gallantly streaming,** has decided to invite a bevy of "boys so far from home" from a nearby army base onto her lawn for a Fourth of July picnic. Of course a complement of young ladies has been invited as well, Sallys and Dorothys, women from town and from the college.

2. The day dawns golden. Syrup and mosquitoes. The hired help arrive first, disinterested capable hands. By and by, the young men arrive. Smiles, sweat rings, aftershave. The young women arrive also, in summer dresses. There will be games to put the gentlemen at ease. The women arrange themselves in wicker chairs, sip cool drinks and appraise the gentlemen from the shade of the porch.

Volleyball.

But, "South Carolina in summer . . . ," the lawyer sighs, five decades later, rattling the ice in his glass.

Eenie, meenie, mynie, moe . . . : refers to child's rhyme "Eenie, meenie, mynie, moe/catch a tiger (or piggy) by the toe/if he hollers let him go/eenie, meenie, mynie, moe" often sung with the word "nigger" in the place of "tiger" during the pre-civil rights era

"Theme from a Summer Place": 1960's song written by Percy Faith and sung by The Letterman; *A Summer Place* (1959) starred Sandra Dee and Troy Donohue, the biggest white teen idols of their day

gallantly streaming: reference to the national anthem

3. Scotch #2. Conspicuous among the young recruits is a tall brown man with short-cropped hair. The Hawaiian. "Poor Mama. 'Another Coca-Cola, Mr. Cooke?' (She could just about manage that one.) But, during the volleyball game, Mr. Cooke sheds first his shirt, then his T-shirt." The narrator remembers the sight of brown shoulders, brown nipples, a navel that tempted vertigo—"Why do we remember such things, and not who invented the cotton gin?"—and the sweat streaming down Mr. Cooke's rib cage; his flared nostrils.

(Poor Mama.)

Poor Narrator. Nevertheless, Mama keeps her stride, marching her fruit-bobbling sandals into the house and back out to the yard. More potato salad? Key lime pie. Lemonade. "Each time she'd pass me—I was sitting alone under the shade tree—she'd detour; she'd come around the trunk of the tree, bend down so close I could smell her powder—she pretended to be fixing my collar or working on my cowlick—but her whisper came down furious as a flyswatter: 'He isn't either a nigger, you mind yourself, he's Hawaiian."

> ***11. In Your Journal:*** Why does Rodriguez refer to himself as "Poor Narrator"? Why does it matter to "Poor Mama" that the shirtless man is Hawaiian?

Stories darken with time, some of them.

The first book by an African American I read was Carl T. Rowan's memoir, *Go South to Sorrow.* I found it on the bookshelf at the back of my fifth-grade classroom, an adult book. I can remember the quality of the morning on which I read. It was a sunlit morning in January, a Saturday morning, cold, high, empty. I sat in a rectangle of sunlight, near the grate of the floor heater in the yellow bedroom. And as I read, I became aware of warmth and comfort and optimism. I was made aware of my comfort by the knowledge that others were not, are not, comforted. Carl Rowan at my age was not comforted. The sensation was pleasurable.

Only a few weeks ago, in the year in which I write, Carl T. Rowan died. Hearing the news, I felt the sadness one feels when a writer dies, a writer one claims as one's own—as potent a sense of implication as for the loss of a body one has known. Over the years, I had seen Rowan on TV. He was not, of course he was not, the young man who had been with me by the heater—the photograph on the book jacket, the voice that spoke through my eyes. The muscles of my body must form the words and the chemicals of my comprehension must form the words, the windows, the doors, the Saturdays, the turning pages of another life, a life simultaneous with mine.

It is a kind of possession, reading. Willing **the Other** to abide in your present. His voice, mixed with sunlight, mixed with Saturday, mixed with my going to bed and then getting up, with the pattern and texture of the

---

the Other: term used by cultural critics to mean any being that is "not you"; especially in the context of race, gender, or sexuality, "the Other," as a proper noun, suggests that all beings that are "not you" can be put into one large official category blanket, with the envelope from a telephone bill I used as a bookmark. With going to Mass. With going to the toilet. With my mother in the kitchen, with whatever happened that day and the next; with clouds forming over the Central Valley, with the flannel shirt I wore, with what I liked for dinner, with what was playing at the Alhambra Theater. I remember Carl T. Rowan, in other words, as myself, as I was. Perhaps that is what one mourns.

In the Clunie Public Library in Sacramento, in those last years of a legally segregated America, there was no segregated shelf for Negro writers. Frederick Douglass on the same casement with Alexis de Tocqueville, Benjamin Franklin. Today, when our habit is willfully to confuse literature with sociology, with sorting, with trading in skins, we imagine the point of a "life" is to address some sort of numerical average, common obstacle or persecution. Here is a book "about" teenaged Chinese-American girls. So it is shelved.

12. In Your Journal: Why is Rodriguez so concerned about the shelves on which his favorite authors are found?

I found this advice, the other day, in an essay by Joseph Addison, his first essay for the *Spectator,* the London journal, Thursday, March 1, 1711. "I have observed, that a reader seldom puruses a Book with Pleasure, 'til he knows the writer of it be a black or a fair Man, of a mild or cholerick Disposition, Married or a Bachelor, with other particulars of the like nature, that conduce very much to the right understanding of an Author. To gratifie this Curiosity, which is so natural to a Reader. . . . "

It is one thing to know your author—man or woman or gay or black or paraplegic or president. It is another thing to choose only man or woman or et cetera, as the only quality of voice empowered to address you, as the only class of sensibility or experience able to understand you, or that you are able to understand.

13. In Your Journal: Can you think of any writers, singers, political leaders, or other cultural figures by whom you feel "empowered" because of their social identity (i.e., race, gender, sexuality, class)? How do you respond to Rodriguez's criticism of this kind of identification?

How a society orders its bookshelves is as telling as the books a society writes and reads. American bookshelves of the twenty-first century describe fractiousness, reduction, hurt. Books are isolated from one another, like gardenias or peaches, lest they bruise or become bruised, or, worse, consort, confuse. If a man in a wheelchair writes his life, his book will be parked in a blue-crossed zone: "Self-Help" or "Health." There is no shelf for bitterness. No shelf for redemption. The professor of Romance languages at **Dresden,** a convert to Protestantism, was tortured by the Nazis as a Jew—only that—a Jew. His book, published sixty years after the events it recounts, is shelved in my neighborhood bookstore as "Judaica." There is no shelf for irony.

14. In Your Journal: What does Rodriguez mean when he says that "Books should confuse"?

Books should confuse. Literature abhors the typical. Literature flows to the particular, the mundane, the greasiness of paper, the taste of warm beer, the smell of onion or quince. **Auden** has a line: "Ports have names

Dresden: southeastern German city; cultural and industrial center; heavily bombed by the Allies in World War II

Auden: (Wystan Hugh) (1907–1973) American writer/poet; remembered most for his range of forms and techniques; won a Pulitzer Prize in 1947 for *The Age of Anxiety*

they call the sea." Just so will literature describe life familiarly, regionally, in terms life is accustomed to use—high or low matters not. Literature cannot by this impulse betray the grandeur of its subject—there is only one subject: What it feels like to be alive. Nothing is irrelevant. Nothing is typical.

It was only from the particular life—a single life, a singular voice named Frederick Douglass, a handsome man, anybody can see that, a tall man, a handsome man, who lived and died in another century, another place, another skin, another light, the light changing every hour, every day, within a room; he did not choose the room or the hour or the skin—that a brown boy in Sacramento could sense the universality of dissimilarity. The offense of slavery (the lure of literature) was that Douglass's life was precisely different from mine in California, a century later.

15. In Your Journal: What does Rodriguez mean by the "universality of dissimilarity"? Is this phrase an oxymoron?

Now I am a writer, and now that my writing so often runs close to the boundaries of social science, I must remember it is the reader alone who decides a book's universality. One cannot arrange a classic. It is the reader's life that opens a book. I am dead. Only a reader can testify to the ability of literature to open; sometimes this opening causes pain.

16. In Your Journal: According to Rodriguez, what power does a reader have over a book?

I mean to put you in company with the young African-American girl who discovers she is like Jane Austen. How so? In temperament, in sensibility, in some way she recognizes and approves. Then this thrilling recognition brings a cloud of shame to her spontaneity—I write of myself, of course—shame for what she intuits, shame for what she cannot share: that a novel from some unenlightened world is not fit for her. She is discouraged. Why it is unfit she cannot completely account for. (Because the sensibility she reads would be cruelly amused at the spectacle of her interest?) She notices her absence. Another girl her age, or a girl from another age, would not notice; would not need to notice.

The **nescience** of a book can undermine its clarity, can spoil our pleasure in it. Our age looks for exclusion. And there is a certain gumption missing from our age as a result, and from the literature of our age.

nescience: lack of knowledge or awareness

Helen Keller wrote that dust spoiled the feel of things for her. **Simone Weil** wrote that the music and the pageantry of a Nazi youth parade were viscerally thrilling to her.

Already in grammar school there were rooms in my reading life into which I would have been reluctant to admit Frederick Douglass, for I knew in those rooms he was mocked. *You must wait here, Mr. Douglass.* I made

Helen Keller: (1880–1968) deaf, mute, and blind as result of serious illness, but gained knowledge and a sense of the world by having things spelled on her hands; first blind person to enroll in a school of higher learning and to earn a bachelor's degree in art at Radcliffe College, Keller was a well-known pacifist, feminist, and socialist

Simone Weil: (1909–1943) native Parisian; teacher, philosopher, political activist, mystic and convert to Roman Catholicism who searched for ways to solve the injustices in the world (through intellecturalism, socialism, and spiritualism, most notably)

> ***17. In Your Journal:*** For whom is Rodriguez the "go-between"? What makes him assume this role?

myself the go-between. I must come to the conclusion that the suite of mockery, though refined, though pleasing to me in most ways—a room of **Thackeray's** perhaps—retained poisonous vapors of another age, and would not have admitted me. And yet these apartments existed uniquely in my imagination, nowhere else. In books, you say. But books must be reimagined, misunderstood, read. Readers repair to books as men and women to monasteries, none with an identical motive. I was the reader of Thackeray. These rooms, these weathers, these confidences from the dust must burn my ears if they were read out loud. But in my privacy I could regret they could not be revised. I strained to restore them to the conditional. Clouds that might pass. The authors could not know what Frederick Douglass would have taught them. Were they damned? Was the crudeness of their imaginations commensurate with the way they made toast? Were books a sort of limbo, characterized by unchangeability? Books! They were damned, authors, not to know that what they dropped could not be revised.

> ***18. In Your Journal:*** What difference does Keats's accent make to Rodriguez?

cockney: working class dialect of London

I did not know until this year that **Keats** spoke with a **cockney** accent.

My reading was a thicket, a blind, from which I observed. (Addison: "Thus I live in the world, rather as a spectator of mankind than as one of the species. . . . ")

> ***19. In Your Journal:*** What does Rodriguez mean when he says that "whites were emancipating themselves"? How does this compare with the emancipation of African Americans at the end of slavery?

A scholarship boy, and sexually secretive, I was deaf to the rock-n-roll blaring from the radio. I did not know that the great drama of integration—White with Black—was playing itself out under the guise of the Top 40. I did not realize, as my younger sister did—she watched **Dick Clark's *American Bandstand*** each afternoon—that whites were emancipating themselves by dancing to **Little Richard.** I do remember that song called **"The Name Game"**—my sister could do it, I never could—in which an

---

Thackeray: (William Makepeace) (1811–1863) white English novelist whose *Vanity Fair* is a satire of upper middle class Londoners

Keats: (John) (1795–1821) English poet; considered one of three great Romantic poets; known for sensuous imagery; his most famous works are "Ode on a Grecian Urn" (which includes the famous line "Beauty is truth, truth beauty . . . ") and "Ode to a Nightingale"

Dick Clark's *American Bandstand:* started in 1952; in 1956, Clark became host; kids from South Philadelphia were let on to the show every day along with the "regulars" to dance on television to new music

Little Richard: (1935-) laid foundation for rock and roll with raspy shrieking voice, explosive piano playing, and outrageous costumes

"The Name Game": song by Shirley Ellis that created rhymes with first names (e.g., "Shirley, Shirley bo Birley Bonana fanna fo Firley/Fee fy mo Mirley, Shirley!")

African-American voice (*Come on now, you try it . . .*) cheerfully played havoc with the American tongue. I remember laughing, dizzied by the freedom of the voice to play.

The Indian plunges into the thicket. The Negress awaits the white man's approach.

That part of America where I felt least certain about the meaning of my brown skin was also the part of the country I came to know best in my reading.

> ***20. In Your Journal:*** Does it make sense to you that Rodriguez knew best the literature that confused him the most about his skin? Is this a logical or ironic outcome?

While my sister danced, I sat on shellacked benches on the Colored side of the Memphis bus station, felt underneath with my hand for dried gum. I drank from the Colored fountain. The fountain tasted of rust, and rust stained the basin and made it unpleasant. I could see where the White fountain was. There was no one about. I was human. I was thirsty. I was quick. As I bent my head to the fount, a hand grabbed me from behind, pulled back my head by its hair, my arms flaying for a purchase on my tormentor. I felt the knuckle—Oh my Jesus. I felt the gold ring boring into my scalp. I knew the ring from a thousand observations. I had seen it setting down coin, raising a glass, grasping the reins of that red-eyed bay. I had seen it, often enough, raised in anger. I said his name out loud, *Please, mister. . . .* (All I know of life is this: Hair is amazingly strong, and I went with my hair, backward. If I had parted from my hair, I might have saved my life.)

> ***21. In Your Journal:*** What does Rodriguez mean when he says that "if [he] had parted from his hair, [he] might have saved [his] life"?

While my sister danced, I watched Malcolm X interviewed on KCRA-TV, Sacramento. I noticed a fierceness in him and a criticism of White that made no distinction between good readers and bad. Something in his manner, something I recognized, rhymed with the scholarship boy I was.

> ***22. In Your Journal:*** Why does Rodriguez use the word "rhyme" when he compares himself to Malcolm X?

I went alone. My evenings out in Sacramento were secretive. Insofar as they were experiments with adulthood, I wouldn't have considered bringing anyone else along. I went to hear Malcolm X alone, as I went alone to hear **Marian Anderson.** (Her red velvet gown. A baby's little blue cry pierced the golden disk she had spun. Silence. Shame for Sacramento! A nod to her pianist to resume.) When I went to hear Malcolm X, I felt as invisible, as anonymous, as safe as I have ever felt. The audience was overwhelmingly male. It was a busy black time. No one seemed to notice my brown in the crowd.

Malcolm X stood in a circle of light. He was not possessed of a theatrical power to transfigure himself. His voice was nothing at all like what I expected. I expected the near-singing of ministers I had heard broadcast from the South. His voice was high, nasal, a scold's voice. A hickory stick. But for all his thin structure, there was something generous about this

---

Marian Anderson: (1897–1993) African American opera singer; considered world's best contralto during her career man, something of **Benjamin Franklin**—his call to brothers to better themselves. In his black mortician's suit, Malcolm X spoke of his early life, his years as a con, a hustler; cruel toward women because false to himself. His glasses flared in the spotlight.

What about that summer night was so thrilling to me?

There is shattered glass in the street. I am transported by **James Baldwin** to Harlem in the aftermath of a race riot. ("On the morning of the 3rd of August, we drove my father to the graveyard through a wilderness of smashed plate glass.") Among Baldwin's plays, I knew only *The Amen Corner* (Beah Richards played it in San Francisco). Among the novels, I favored *Go Tell It on the Mountain*. Most, I loved Baldwin's essays. There was to a Baldwin essay a **metropolitan** elegance I envied, a refusal of the livid. In Baldwin I found a readiness to rise to prophetic wrath, something like those ministers, and yet, once more, to bend down in tenderness, to call grown men and women "baby" (a whiff of the theater). Watching Baldwin on television—I will always consider the fifties to have been a sophisticated time—fixed for me what being a writer must mean. Arching eyebrows intercepted ironies, parenthetically declared fouls; mouthfuls of cigarette smoke shot forth ribbons of exactitude.

metropolitan: sophisticated

23. In Your Journal: Why does Rodriguez admire what he calls James Baldwin's "refusal of the livid"?

The Freedom March of 1965, from Selma to Montgomery, marked the turning point for the Civil Rights movement in the South. It became clear to America that the spiritual momentum of the march would carry the day; the South would bend.

Then the Negro Civil Rights movement, the slow sad movement of moral example, veered north, cooled, hardened as it climbed, to a secular anger. The Watts riots in Los Angeles of 1965 were the worst U.S. riots in twenty years. Young Negroes with no time to waste, no patience for eternal justice, renamed themselves "black." Their proclamation began a project of redefinition, not only of themselves and of their political movement, but of power, of glamour. The Name Game was at once fierce and dazzling. Black America led white America through the changes. The equation of desire was going to be reversed.

24. In Your Journal: What is the "equation of desire" that is "going to be reversed"?

Within the new insistence on blackness was a determination on the part of blacks to transform into boast all that whites had, for genera-

Benjamin Franklin: (1706–1790) statesman, printer, scientist, and philosopher; his *Poor Richard's Almanack* (1732–1757) illustrates the common sense perspective for which he was famous

James Baldwin: (1924–1987) African American expatriate author of *Go Tell It on the Mountain* (1953), about his experiences as a young preacher, and *Giovanni's Room* (1956), about his homosexuality tions, made jest: curly hair, orange polyester, complexion, dialect, spiritual ecstasy.

When I was in high school, white boys inhaled black voices like helium. The Christian Brothers' Gaels drove off to a football game in the big yellow bus, windows lowered, the crew-cuts singing a Little Stevie Wonder song in **falsetto** for the pure pleasure and novelty of squeezing their thighs to the highest pitch.

falsetto: an artificially high voice

But the necessity, for a new black generation, of transposing shame into pride led to a dangerous romanticism. Segregation, **de facto** and legal, was transformed into self-willed exclusion—also a point of pride. Perhaps it was that the Negro Civil Rights movement of the South had been governed by a Protestant faith in conversion, whereas the northern black movement cared nothing for conversion.

de facto: in reality

Despite laws prohibiting black literacy in the nineteenth century, the African in America took the paper-white English and remade it (as the Irish and the Welsh also took their English), wadded it up, rigmarolled it, rewound it into a **llareggub** rap, making English theirs, making it idiosyncratically glamorous (*Come on now, you try it*), making it impossible for any American to use English henceforward without remembering them; making English so cool, so jet, so festival, that children want it only that way.

The only voices as blatant as black voices, as contentious, as alive in American air and literature, are those first-generation Jewish voices, skeptical, playful, dicing every assertion. The black-Jewish conversation was inevitable, for reasons of rhetoric, of history, of soul. As the American Indian had also been drawn, the Jew must have felt drawn to the African American from some recognition of exclusion, expectation of exclusion. Unlike the Indian, however, the Jew had been shaped by a theology of **the Word**—a schooling that became, like the African's, a strategy for survival. And for a time, theirs was a brilliant alliance, the Black with the Jew. But the genius for verbal survival uniting Black and Jew would undermine their alliance.

The Word: "the word of God" or the Bible

"You cannot imagine how many times I need to squirt my eyes with Visine just to get through ***Othello.*** (So rage won't dry them out.)" An African-American graduate student addressed a roomful of English professors and graduate students at Berkeley. (This was late in the 1970s.) A

Llareggub: mythical Welsh village in Dylan Thomas's play *Under Milk Wood;* name spells "bugger all" backwards

Othello: tragedy by William Shakespeare (1602) about a Moorish army hero who weds a white noblewoman (Desdemona), and is convinced by a jealous conniving and racist colleague (Iago) that Desdemona has been unfaithful, which leads to Othello's killing of both Desdemona and himself

Jewish professor immediately joined with "You can't imagine how difficult it is for me to read ***The Merchant of Venice***" (assuming the alliance).

"Well, goddamn!" snarled the black woman in a stage whisper, her topknot vibrating, her eyes lashed to the notebook on her desk, "Jews always have to feel exactly what we are feeling, only more so."

Did you ever cross over to Snedens . . . ?

Snedens Landing is a pre-revolutionary town upstate. I was fifty before I heard a recording of **Mabel Mercer** singing that brittle song. I don't care for the song. I like Mabel Mercer. She was a black Englishwoman who grew up in a theatrical family. She went to Paris at nineteen; she sang in bars, mainly for expatriate audiences, James Baldwin and others. From Paris, Mabel Mercer came to New York, became a fixture of the supper clubs there. She sat in a straight-backed chair, in a spot-light, her hands folded in her lap. She leaned slightly forward, as if imparting a confidence to her audience. The confidence she imparted was that hers was the most refined lyric sensibility in Manhattan of the 1950s.

melanin: dark pigment in hair or skin

minstrelsy: stage entertainment featuring whites playing blacks, with exaggerated physical features and mannerisms

Mabel Mercer performed the songs of **Porter and Coward** and such with a perfect mid-Atlantic pronunciation, which is to say, without a trace of **melanin** in her voice. This was not ventriloquism or **minstrelsy** or parody—I was disappointed to learn it wasn't—but the voice was authentic to Mercer because she had been educated by British nuns who insisted upon public-school elocution. Another cabaret singer of that time, **Anita O'Day,** quoted in a book I can't find, described Mabel Mercer thus: "That chick has the weirdest fucking act in show business."

25. In Your Journal: Are you surprised when Rodriguez confesses that he would "like [his] act to be as weird" as Mabel Mercer's? What does he mean by this?

I would like my act to be as weird. An old brown man walking the beach, singing "**The Love Song of J. Alfred Prufrock.**" I have, throughout my writing life, pondered what a brown voice should sound like.

The Merchant of Venice: comedy by William Shakespeare (1600) that features the character Shylock, a money lender with exaggerated anti-semitic characteristics; Shylock is famous for the soliloquy that includes the line "If you prick us, do we not bleed?"

Mabel Mercer: (1900–1984) African American cabaret singer whose influence on American music earned her the Presidential Medal of Freedom (highest award a civilian can receive from the U.S. government)

Porter and Coward: (Cole and Noel) successful gay songwriters of the 1930's

Anita O'Day: (1919-   ) American big band jazz singer

"The Love Song of J. Alfred Prufrock": poem by T.S. Elliot about Prufrock's feeling of isolation and inability to act

I have pondered what a black voice should sound like.

On September 16, 1966—contemporary newspaper accounts reported a cool evening—the new Metropolitan Opera House opened in New York City. President Johnson and Mrs. Johnson were in attendance, as were President and Mrs. Marcos of the Philippines, as was U Thant, Secretary-General of the United Nations. The opera house, designed by Wallace K. Harrison, was a modernist pavilion with an arched façade, retractable chandeliers, murals by **Marc Chagall.**

The opera commissioned for the opening was *Antony and Cleopatra* by American composer Samuel Barber. **Leontyne Price** sang the role of Cleopatra. The **Franco Zeffirelli** production fused disparate motifs of colonial adventure in the manner of a seventeenth-century print. Zeffirelli's Egyptians were Elizabethan-Floridian. Leontyne Price wore an enormous feathered, beribboned headdress reminiscent of Amazonia, and a gown of Renaissance cut. She was costumed to appear bare-breasted, a **caryatid** of continental allegory—at once the African and the Indian of Alexis de Tocqueville's notice. At least that is how I remember the photograph of Leontyne Price in *Time* magazine; that is the image that comes to mind as I reread de Tocqueville.

26. In Your Journal: How is Leontyne Price "at once the African and the Indian of Alexis de Tocqueville's notice"?

caryatid: sculpture of a woman used as a supporting column

You are probably too young to remember or perhaps you have forgotten what a pride for America that evening was—the most modern opera house in the world to prolong the heart-beat of the nineteenth century, and with Leontyne Price, the reigning dramatic soprano of her day, enshrined at the center. And yet, the Metropolitan Opera seemed at that moment—eight o'clock, September 16, 1966—to mark the very crossroads of American history, the division of the old era and the new. Leontyne Price seemed the **apotheosis** of African America, of new America, as if uncountable degradations inflicted upon African Americans might be ransomed by a single, soaring human voice.

apotheosis: glorified personification of a principle or idea

That same year, 1966, there were thirty-eight race riots in American cities. And thirty-five years later, Lincoln Center looks irrelevant; there is talk in the papers about pulling it down.

That same year, 1966, I was in college. I typed, on erasable onionskin paper: "White southern writers had earlier preoccupied themselves with

---

Marc Chagall: (1887–1985) French painter; painted with strong bright colors to create dreamlike simplicity

Leontyne Price: (1927-   ) African-American opera singer (soprano); has earned 15 Grammys during her career

Franco Zefirelli: (1923-   ) Italian director; produced many adaptations of Shakespeare; recognized for attention to detail and extravagant productions the deconstruction of the South along **Grecian** lines, a lament for pride brought low and a contrition for the sins of the Fathers, all the while insisting upon kinship—the black maid's sigh, the white child's 'Why?' "

27. In Your Journal: What is so troublesome to Rodriguez about his phrasing in: the "Black maid's sign, the white child's Why"?

Black maid's sigh? White child's Why?

My forehead began to pain me remarkably, to throb; a sort of mockery seized upon my temples, then billowed from my ears, like black smoke from a stovepipe. A figment stood before me:

Naw.
Listen, ***Hiawatha,*** *honey, sittin by yo heatah,*
Cradlin' little ninny books, playin' ***Little Eva***—
Doodah mantchuns fulla haunted crackahs,
Long-face mens pullin' sacks a 'baccas,
Clean white aprons wid dese fairytale patchas!
The sky is the skin o'yo eye, Hiawatha!
Peel that skin off yo eye!

jerkin: sleeveless jacket

pinafore: sleeveless garment fastened in the back worn as an apron or dress

sclera: white of the eye

The figment was clothed with a red calico shirt and a voluminous apron with many pockets and colored patches sewn on, like the patches on **jerkins** and **pinafores** in a child's picture book. It wore a sort of turban on its head. The head was a tablespoonful of black wax, the size of a chunk of coal. It had eyes—large, lidless **sclera** with black balls painted in. But no mouth.

With one hand—a glob of glue stuck to its sleeve—it extended a tambourine which it brandished menacingly (ah, ah, ah).

Ol' man ***Faulkner*** *make me sigh,*
Meek as Ella Cinder. Sigh?
Black maid's sigh?
Naw. Black maid's thighs was blackberry pies,
'Sall it was,
Coolin' on the winder.

Grecian: in the style of Greek art, culture, or thought; according to principles of classical Greek literature.

Hiawatha: (c. 1550) Chief of Onodaga tribe; one of the organizers of the Iroquois Confederacy

Little Eva: (Eva Boyd) (1946-) asked to record "The Locomotion" by songwriters Carole King and Gerry Goffin (for whom she worked as a babysitter); the song became a number one hit

Faulkner: (William) (1897–1962) American novelist and Nobel Prize winner who primarily examined the decay of the post-Civil War South, employing a highly symbolic and technical style; most well-known for *The Sound and the Fury* (1929)

No mouth, and yet it spoke. The voice had lips and tongue and breath and also a kind of history—each utterance was accompanied by a hissing, sparkling, ambient air, like that of an old recording with a gold tooth. The voice was parody, the only voice the figment owned, and as patented as wild rice.

Listen, Little Elbow Grease,
Peckin' on your pica,
Readin' Mod'n Library's
Bad as breathin' ether.
Ol' man Faulkner make you nod?
(Drunk in his ***mimesis****.)*
But don't you goddamn dare to try
Amanuensis *me!*

28. In Your Journal: Rodriguez's figment has "no mouth, and yet it spoke." What is this contradiction meant to symbolize?

mimesis: imitation of nature

amanuensis: one who takes dictation

Reproach. This was Denial of Imagination. Copyright Infringement. Fear of Offending. Appropriation of Voice. Objection Sustained. Willful Misunderstanding. **Preclusion.** Scandal. Minstrelsy. Ah, I knew exactly what it was. This was a New Orleans doll manufactured in wax, in 1922, by Madame Granger, a Creole; this was Luther's doll, a figure of speech; my friend Luther's phrase, the phrase that elicited nervous laughter from me when I heard him use it in public: *You want I should pull nigger out the bag?* (As he addressed a recalcitrant store clerk.)

preclusion: something ruled out in advance

I bent once more to my typewriter. I wrote: "Faulkner strained to find the cadence of black patience and faith, creating his own forgiveness in the person of **Dilsey**—Dilsey hovering over her lost white charges."

Here he come, ol'skinny ***whey,***
Sobbin'in his 'kerchief—
Whiney, piney, woe is me—
"The South, the South," he constant say;
He longin' for de dear ol'days.
And you as bad as he is. Why?
White child's Why?
You confusin'grief with biscuits.
—Why ain't there biscuits?—
'Sall it was.
Ain't enough I'm bought and sold,
Ain't enough I'm weak and old,
Still you goin' make me up—
Say I smell like copper-gold;
Pour me in some nigger mold—

29. In Your Journal: Why does the figment object to Rodriguez's analysis?

whey: the watery part of milk

Dilsey: black servant of Compson household in William Faulker's *The Sound and the Fury* (1929)

malaprop: unintentional misuse or distortion of a word

Some ***malaprop,*** *some black tar soap,*
Some hangin' rope, some 'bacca smoke—
You make me up, you make me up,
I don't exist, goddamn you.
'Cept
Some 'Mimah flapjack mix,
Some Cream o'Wheat steam
Risin' swift to ol'whey's
Quiv'rin' nostril.
Soon
I free the slaves that lick my pots
And bubble the swill that fill you—
Slave as plain as buttercup,
Slave as hot as forget-me-not,
Slave as shrill as daffodil—
Slaves wear them yella jackets.

"Faulkner strained to reproduce the cadence of Negro patience."

. . . *Shoulda noticed the fire. Fiah. FIAH!*

As a young man, I was more a white liberal than I ever tried to put on black. For all that, I ended up a "minority," the beneficiary of affirmative action programs to redress black exclusion. And, harder to say, my brown advantage became a kind of embarrassment. For I never had an adversarial relationship to American culture. I was never at war with the tongue.

30. In Your Journal: How is Rodriguez's disadvantage actually an advantage?

Brown was no longer invisible by the time I got to college. In the white appraisal, brown skin became a coat of disadvantage, which was my advantage. Acknowledgment came at a price, then as now. (Three decades later, the price of being a published brown author is that one cannot be shelved near those one has loved. The price is segregation.)

I remain at best ambivalent about those Hispanic anthologies where I end up; about those anthologies where I end up the Hispanic; about shelves at the bookstore where I look for myself and find myself. The fact that my books are published at all is the result of the **slaphappy** strategy of the northern black Civil Rights movement.

slaphappy: recklessly carefree

Late in the 1960s, the university complied with segregation—the notion that each can only describe and understand her own, that education is a deeper **solipsism**, that pride is the point of education, that I would prefer to live among my kind at a separate theme-house dormitory; that I would prefer to eat with my kind at the exclusive cafeteria table where all conversation conforms to the implicit: *You Can't Know What I'm Feeling Unless You Are Me.*

solipsism: theory that all knowledge is subjective and therefore one can only know one's self

In college, I revisited James Baldwin, seeking to forestall what I feared was the disintegration of my reading life, which had been an unquestioned faith in Signet Classics. My rereading of "**Stranger in a Village**" discovered a heavy hand. In the Swiss Alps, humorless **frauen** with crackled eyes go in and out their humorous houses, while on the twisting streets of the village, towheaded children point to Baldwin and shout after him *Neger! Neger!* ("From all available evidence no black man had ever set foot in this tiny Swiss village before I came.") So what is the point of the essay? It seemed to me Baldwin had traveled rather far to get himself pointed at, to arrange such an outlandish contrast; to describe himself as an outsider. And, too, the Alps seemed to represent Baldwin's obsession, an obsession that now seemed to stand between us.

frauen: title for married women in Germany

This was not a generous assessment on my part, not a generous moment in my life. As a young reader, I would never have noticed or objected to Baldwin's preoccupation with White to the exclusion of all other kind. In the 1950s it would have seemed to me that a Negro writer was writing about the nation in which I was a part, regardless of whether my tribe was singled out for mention. But when the American university began to approve, then to enforce fracture, and when blood became the authority to speak, I felt myself rejected by black literature and felt myself rejecting black literature as "theirs."

31. In Your Journal: What price does Rodriguez have to pay for the American university's approval?

Neither did I seek brown literature or any other kind. I sought Literature—the deathless impulse to explain and describe. I trusted white literature, because I was able to attribute universality to white literature, because it did not seem to be written for me.

William Makepeace Thackeray mocks my mother's complexion. And mine. My smell. My fingers. My hair. Cunning little savage. Little Jew. Little milkmaid. Little Cockney. Really, how can I laugh?

The gym I attend in San Francisco is the whitest, the most expensive. Men and women read the *Wall Street Journal,* climb perpetual stairs pursued by grimacing voices.

Thump, thump, thump, thump. Stanzas, paragraphs, pages, hours, days, days, nights, days, *thump, thump, thump.*

Only **Bach** is as relentless, as monotonous, as cat's-cradled as hip-hop. Hip-hop is not music, in my estimation. (If music resolves.) Hip-hop does not progress, it revolves, replicates, sticks to the floor. It is not approximate emotion. It is approximate obsession. The "voice," the bard, the oracle, the messenger, the minister of propaganda intricately, saucily rhymes, chugs, foreshortens, sneers, insinuates, retreats. The voice betrays no emo-

"Stranger in a Village": (1955) work by James Baldwin about his experiences as an African-American traveling in the Swiss Alps

Bach: (Johann Sebastian) (1685–1750) Baroque composer and organist; best known for the Brandenburg concertos, the *Well-Tempered Clavier* and various religious compositions

32. *In Your Journal:* What does music "resolve" and why does hip-hop not accomplish this, in Rodriguez's opinion? Do you share Rodriguez's definition of music?

masonic: of or related to a secret society

tion; has none; this is not rage, but cleverness. Too wise. Too sly. A dictatorship of rhyme. There is a message; the message is **masonic;** the conveyance too dense; deep as a trance. The voice is preoccupied and always in the present. It is the voice of schizophrenia. It is bad advice. It is the voice of battle—**Beowulf, Edda,** the madder psalms—the voice justifies endlessly. What is going to happen if you don't stop this! On and on and on. Slamming the table. It is the post-lude to music. Long after emotion has been flung from the bone, the beat remains. The beat plows through the rubble of music, turning under the broken arches of melody, stabbing about for rhyming shards—raising them, rubbing them together rhythmically—trying to ignite.

And what of the gym? They of the gym, we of the gym? Where is our allegiance? Is it to **Queen Latifah** or **Gertrude Himmelfarb?** And if we of the gym are somehow, unconsciously, and in thrall to madder music, arming ourselves, it is for a battle against what?

A few weeks ago, in the newspaper (another day in the multi-cultural nation), a small item: Riot in a Southern California high school. Hispanic students protest, then smash windows, because African-American students get four weeks for Black History month, whereas Hispanics get one. The more interesting protest would be for Hispanic students to demand to be included in Black History month. The more interesting remedy would be for Hispanic History week to include African history.

33. *In Your Journal:* Why does Rodriguez chastise the Hispanic students who worry that Blacks are only preoccupied with White? Why does he then write an article saying the very same?

Hispanic students I meet on my speaking rounds complain of African-American students in their high schools or colleges. The complaint is that Black is preoccupied only with White; neither Black nor White will be dissuaded from a mutual vanity. I pretend not to understand the complaint. I play the adult. I answer the question with a question: *Why should they?* And then I turn around to write an op-ed about how the *New York Times* compiles a series on "race in America" that is preoccupied with Black and White.

I have not previously taken a part in the argument, the black-white argument, but I have listened to it with diminishing interest for forty years. It is like listening to a bad marriage through a thin partition, a civil war replete with violence, recrimination, mimicry, slamming doors.

Beowulf: oldest English epic (8th century) recounting Beowulf's struggle with the monster Grendel

Edda: collection of Norse tales dating to Viking times featuring the god Thor

Queen Latifah: (Dana Owens) (1970-) African-American rapper, rhythm and blues singer, and actress

Gertrude Himmelfarb: (1922-) Professor Emeritus at the Graduate school of the City of New York; Victorian history scholar

I am not who I was. All the cells of my body have changed since I cradled Carl T. Rowan's book in my lap. I remain too much a cultural **xenophobe**, but also too convinced a **mestizo** to permit myself to claim any simple kinship with Black, with partition America. African Americans remain at the center of the moral imagination of America, which, I agree, is a very spooky place to be. Nobody else wants to be there, except by analogy. For it was there Africans were enslaved. It was there African Americans hung by their throats from trees. ***Agnus Dei, qui tollis peccáta mundi, miserére nobis.*** And what has emerged from the cocoon of African-American suffering, cut down from the tree, buried for half a century?

xenophobe: one afraid of people of foreign origin

mestizo: of mixed European and Native American ancestry

The boom. The boom. Superfly. Ropes of gold surround his resurrected neck. The glamour of the dead-eyed man.

34. In Your Journal: What does Rodriguez mean when he calls African-Americans the "center of the moral imagination in America"? What does imagination have to do with morality?

I dislike to hear hip-hop at my gym. I am unfair. Do I object to the restriction of the form—as strict as a **villanelle**? Do I object to an outlaw romanticism? Do I object to the cadence of the pulpit given over to **quixotism**? Do I object to the immoral lyric chugging along a rhythm track, only concerned with finding the rhyme for muthafucka?

But then I admit I've never wanted to bite the tongue. I may have mastered the tongue, but I have never felt the need—or the love, incidentally—to invent a new one.

villanelle: 19-line poem with strictly defined structure

quixotism: tendency to be foolishly impractical

. . . Shoulda noticed the fiah!

Yes, I should have. But shut up for a minute. A few years ago, on a book tour, I found myself in a radio booth, the disappointed author (having just read a dismissive review of my second book in the *Washington Post*). I put the review aside. Played eager-to-please. *Thank you for having me.*

You didn't have me. And you didn't want me. Not that it matters; it was a whorish transaction, I knew that. The movie director Spike Lee had preceded me onto the program in the previous hour, promoting his movie about Malcolm X. The African-American radio host suffered from time warp—***esprit d'escalier***—something he had said or left unsaid, I don't know.

esprit d'escalier: (French) spirit of the staircase; refers to the experience of thinking of exactly the right remark/response when it is too late to use it

So we remained shadows to each other, the interviewer and I. Departed Spike Lee was the only substance. At every break in the program, the interviewer would rise to pace the tiny studio, his body jerking with involuntary darns and double-damns—if only he'd thought to ask this or that.

35. In Your Journal: Why is Rodriguez so disappointed by this radio interview?

Agnus Dei, qui tollis peccáta mundi, miserére nobis: (Latin) "lamb of God, who takes away the sins of the world: have mercy on us"; part of a Catholic mass, related to the sacrament of communion

He hadn't read my book. I watched the second hand of the clock on the wall. I didn't expect him to have read my book. I don't listen to his program.

I have been pondering what a black voice should sound like. A Baptist minister? An opera singer? A café artiste? Only to come to the conclusion a black voice should sound like **parody**? A brown voice should sound like **rue**?

rue: regret

parody: ridicule or mockery

No, that is not my conclusion. My conclusion is a measure of thankfulness: I cannot imagine myself a writer, I cannot imagine myself writing these words, without the example of African slaves stealing the English language, learning to read against the law, then transforming the English language into the American tongue, transforming me, rescuing me, with a **coruscating** nonchalance.

coruscating: glittering

Come on now, you try it.

FOR USE IN DISCUSSION

Questions about Substance

1. When Rodriguez calls history "a coat cut only to the European" (534), how is he playing off of de Tocqueville's observations?
2. "The Indian refuses civilization; the African slave is rendered unfit for it" (535) is the argument Rodriguez infers from de Tocqueville's description. On what evidence does Rodriguez base this inference?
3. What contrasting reactions does Rodriguez have to the convicts in *The Defiant Ones* and the Lone Ranger and Tonto (536)?
4. What did Rodriguez mourn when Carl T. Rowan died? What does he use this example of mourning to say about reading?
5. "There is only one subject," Rodriguez argues, "What it feels like to be alive" (541). Do you agree or disagree with this assertion?
6. Rodriguez says that the "genius for verbal survival uniting Black and Jew would undermine their alliance" (545). What does he mean by this?
7. A mysterious figment begins to speak to Rodriguez while he is writing a college paper on white southern writers (548–550). Who do you think this figment is? What role does this figment play in shaping Rodriguez's perceptions of racial difference?
8. Why does the young Rodriguez "trust white literature even though it "mocks" him (551)?
9. What is Rodriguez's response to the Hispanic students' protest of Black History month (552)?

Questions about Structure and Style

1. The introduction to this essay is highly visual. What are some of the images Rodriguez wants to show the reader early in the essay? Why do you think he takes this approach?
2. Rodriguez presents three "Brown" men from his childhood in succession: the Palestinian bookie, the gypsy man, and the boy who gave Rodriguez a dime at the state fair (537). How are these illustrations of the same idea? How do they differ? Why does Rodriguez need all three of them to make his point?
3. Why does Rodriguez juxtapose his discussion of "The Name Game" with a repeated passage from de Tocqueville ("*The Indian plunges into the thicket. The Negress awaits the white man's approach*") (542–543)?
4. Why does Rodriguez employ the anecdote of the African-American student and the Jewish professor on page 545–546? Why does he quote rather than paraphrase or summarize here?
5. Analyze the style of the following paragraph: "Reproach. This was Denial of Imagination. Copyright Infringement. Fear of Offending. Appropriation of Voice. Objection Sustained. Willful Misunderstanding. Preclusion. Scandal. Minstrelsy" (549). What effect is Rodriguez trying to achieve with this list of offenses he has committed in writing his college paper?
6. Why do you think Rodriguez's conclusion includes a reproach of hip-hop music and the anecdote about his unsatisfying radio interview?

Multimedia Suggestions

1. View Spike Lee's *Do the Right Thing* (1989), a film about the very "black and white" nature of racial dialogue and tension in the United States. Examine the way the film portrays the characters who are neither white nor black. How does this film relate to Rodriguez's argument? How do you think Rodriguez would react to this film?
2. Rodriguez makes a number of references to black opera singers, and other musical artists. Listen to some of the artists he refers to, and try to find some reviews of their work. Why does Rodriguez use the particular examples you've examined? Do they represent something larger than themselves? Pay attention to their choice of material (including lyrics and themes, as well as sound), and note how they are "categorized" in music criticism or in a music store.

SUGGESTIONS FOR WRITING AND RESEARCH

1. Examine the following passage: "The nescience of a book can undermine its clarity, can spoil our pleasure in it. Our age looks for exclusion. And there is a certain gumption missing from our age as a result, and from the literature of our age" (541). Explain what Rodriguez means by this and respond to it in an

essay. Refer to books of "our age" that you find "nescient" or the opposite (aware), and refer to other passages from Rodriguez's text for further support of your argument or for the purposes of challenging Rodriguez's argument.

2. While he is recounting some important events taking place in the 1960's, Rodriguez intersperses quotes from a paper he wrote in college, and quotes from a figment of his imagination criticizing the paper (548–550). Do you find this passage difficult to follow? Is there some purpose to the wandering structure? (Remember that Rodriguez believes that "books should confuse" (550). Write an essay that explains the effect of this technique and attempts to explain Rodriguez's intentions in using it.
3. Read James Baldwin's story "Stranger in the Village" and explain why you think the story had the effect it did on Rodriguez. Compare Baldwin's study of race to Rodriguez's. What are the primary similarities? What are the primary differences?

WORKING WITH CLUSTERS

Cluster 3: Reading Meaning, Achieving Literacy

Cluster 6: The Race for Representation

Cluster 18: Ethnicity and Conflict

Discipline: The Humanities

Rhetorical Mode: Analysis

"The Ladies Have Feelings, So . . . Shall We Leave It to the Experts?" (from *Power Politics*)

by Arundhati Roy

Born in Bengal, Arundhati Roy grew up in Kerala, India. She trained as an architect at the Delhi School of Architecture, but became better known as the author of complex and politically pointed film scripts. She wrote and starred in the film In Which Annie Gives it Those Ones, *and she composed the script for Pradip Kishen's* Electric Moon. *Her first book,* The God of Small Things, *won Britain's premier book prize, the Booker McConnell award. The author is also known for her famous mother, Mary Roy, a woman who challenged Indian inheritance laws and won, leading to the revision of these laws in favor of women's rights.* Power Politics, *from which this selection (based on a talk given at Hampshire College in 2001) is drawn, was published in 2001.*

India lives in several centuries at the same time. Somehow we manage to progress and regress simultaneously. As a nation we age by pushing outward from the middle—adding a few centuries on to either end of our extraordinary **c.v.** We greaten like the maturing head of a hammerhead shark with eyes looking in diametrically opposite directions. I have no doubt that even here in North America you have heard that Germany is considering changing its immigration laws in order to import **Indian software engineers.** I have even less doubt that you've heard of **the Naga Sadhu at the Kumbh Mela** who towed the District Commissioner's car with his penis while the Commissioner sat in it solemnly with his wife and children.

c.v.: curriculum vitae; academic work history or résumé

> ***1. In Your Journal:*** What could Roy mean when she talks about adding "a few centuries on to either end of our extraordinary c.v."?

As Indian citizens we subsist on a regular diet of **caste** massacres and nuclear tests, mosque breakings and fashion shows, church burnings and expanding cell phone networks, bonded labor and the digital revolution, female infanticide and the **NASDAQ** crash, husbands who continue to burn their wives for **dowry** and our delectable stockpile of Miss Worlds. I don't mean to put a simplistic value judgment on this peculiar form of "progress" by suggesting that Modern is Good and Traditional is Bad—or vice versa. What's hard to reconcile oneself to, both personally and politically, is the schizophrenic nature of it. That applies not just to the ancient/modern conundrum, but to the utter illogic of what appears to be the current national enterprise. In the lane behind my house, every night I walk past road gangs of emaciated laborers digging a trench to lay fiber-optic cables to speed up our digital revolution. In the bitter winter cold, they work by the light of a few candles.

caste: class; social group

dowry: bridal purse; money from bride's in-laws

> ***2. In Your Journal:*** What is so illogical to Roy about the road gangs working behind her house?

Indian software engineers: India has extremely competitive programs in engineering (degrees from the Indian Institute of Technology are, in fact, more competitive than those from American Ivy League colleges); India's engineers are thus highly marketable internationally, and so many emigrate for high paying jobs

Naga Sadhu at the Kumbh Mela: Naga Sadhu are holy Hindu priests who live devout, austere existences without any material possessions; Kumbh Mela is a Hindi river worship festival; some sadhus hang heavy weights to the penis to conquer sexual desire

NASDAQ: National Association of Securities Dealers Automated Quotations; allows computerized trading on domestic and international levels

It's as though the people of India have been rounded up and loaded onto two convoys of trucks (a huge big one and a tiny little one) that have set off resolutely in opposite directions. The tiny convoy is on its way to a glittering destination somewhere near the top of the world. The other convoy just melts into the darkness and disappears. A cursory survey that tallies the caste, class, and religion of who gets to be on which convoy would make a good Lazy Person's Concise Guide to the History of India. For some of us, life in India is like being suspended between two of the trucks, one in each convoy, and being neatly dismembered as they move apart, not bodily, but emotionally and intellectually.

Of *course* India is a microcosm of the world. Of *course* versions of what happens there happen everywhere. Of *course,* if you're willing to look, the parallels are easy to find. The difference in India is only in the scale, the magnitude, and the sheer proximity of the disparity. In India your face is slammed right up against it. To address it, to deal with it, to not deal with it, to try and understand it, to insist on not understanding it, to simply survive it—on a daily, hourly basis—is a fine art in itself. Either an art or a form of insular, inward-looking insanity. Or both.

> ***3. In Your Journal:*** How would *not* dealing with something or *not* understanding something be a "fine art"?

To be a writer—a supposedly "famous" writer—in a country where three hundred million people are illiterate is a dubious honor. To be a writer in a country that gave the world Mahatma Gandhi, that invented the concept of nonviolent resistance, and then, half a century later, followed that up with nuclear tests is a ferocious burden. (Though no more ferocious a burden, it has to be said, than being a writer in a country that has enough nuclear weapons to destroy the earth several times over.) To be a writer in a country where something akin to an undeclared civil war is being waged on its subjects in the name of "development" is an onerous responsibility. When it comes to writers and writing, I use words like **"onerous"** and "responsibility" with a heavy heart and not a small degree of sadness.

onerous: oppressive

> ***4. In Your Journal:*** Why does Roy "use words like 'onerous' and 'responsibility' with a heavy heart"?

This is what I'm here to talk to you, to think aloud with you, about. What is the role of writers and artists in society? Do they have a definable role? Can it be fixed, described, characterized in any definite way? Should it be?

Personally, I can think of few things more terrifying than if writers and artists were charged with an immutable charter of duties and responsibilities that they had to live and work by. Imagine if there was this little black book—a sort of Approved Guide to Good Writing—that said: All writers shall be politically conscious and sexually moral, or: All writers should believe in God, globalization, and the joys of family life . . . .

Rule One for a writer, as far as I'm concerned, is There Are No Rules. And Rule Two (since Rule One was made to be broken) is There Are No Excuses for Bad Art. Painters, writers, singers, actors, dancers, filmmakers, musicians are meant to fly, to push at the frontiers, to worry the edges of the human imagination, to conjure beauty from the most unexpected things, to find magic in places where others never thought to look. If you limit the trajectory of their flight, if you weight their wings with society's existing notions of morality and responsibility, if you truss them up with preconceived values, you subvert their endeavor.

> ***5. In Your Journal:*** What might be some of the "Excuses for Bad Art" that Roy alludes to here?

A good or great writer may refuse to accept any responsibility or morality that society wishes to impose on her. Yet the best and greatest of them know that if they abuse this hard-won freedom, it can only lead to bad art. There is an intricate web of morality, rigor, and responsibility that art, that writing itself, imposes on a writer. It's singular, it's individual, but nevertheless it's there. At its best, it's an exquisite bond between the artist and the medium. At its acceptable end, it's a sort of sensible co-operation. At its worst, it's a relationship of disrespect and exploitation.

> ***6. In Your Journal:*** How does this argument relate to the point in the previous paragraph about society's values?

esoteric: obscure; mysterious

arcane: secret, deep, or unknowable

> ***7. In Your Journal:*** Why doesn't "the absence of external rules" simplify rather than "complicate" things?

putative: supposed; commonly accepted

The absence of external rules complicates things. There's a very thin line that separates the strong, true, bright bird of the imagination from the synthetic, noisy bauble. Where is that line? How do you recognize it? How do you know you've crossed it? At the risk of sounding **esoteric** and **arcane**, I'm tempted to say that you just know. The fact is that nobody—no reader, no reviewer, agent, publisher, colleague, friend, or enemy—can tell for sure. A writer just has to ask herself that question and answer it as honestly as possible. The thing about this "line" is that once you learn to recognize it, once you see it, it's impossible to ignore. You have no choice but to live with it, to follow it through. You have to bear with all its complexities, contradictions, and demands. And that's not always easy. It doesn't always lead to compliments and standing ovations. It can lead you to the strangest, wildest places. In the midst of a bloody military coup, for instance, you could find yourself fascinated by the mating rituals of a purple sunbird, or the secret life of captive goldfish, or an old aunt's descent into madness. And nobody can say that there isn't truth and art and beauty in that. Or, on the contrary, in the midst of **putative** peace, you could, like me, be unfortunate enough to stumble on a silent war. The trouble is that once you see it, you can't unsee it. And once you've seen it, keeping quiet, saying nothing, becomes as political an act as speaking out. There's no innocence. Either way, you're accountable.

> ***8. In Your Journal:*** What kind of "innocence" is Roy alluding to here?

Today, perhaps more so than in any other era in history, the writer's right to free speech is guarded and defended by the civil societies and state establishments of the most powerful countries in the world. Any overt attempt to silence or muffle a voice is met with furious opposition. The writer is embraced and protected. This is a wonderful thing. The writer, the actor, the musician, the filmmaker—they have become radiant jewels in the crown of modern civilization. The artist, I imagine, is finally as free as he or she will ever be. Never before have so many writers had their books published. (And now, of course, we have the Internet.) Never before have we been more commercially viable. We live and prosper in the heart of the marketplace. True, for every so-called success there are hundreds who "fail." True, there are myriad art forms, both folk and classical, myriad languages, myriad cultural and artistic traditions that are being crushed and cast aside in the stampede to the big bumper sale in Wonderland. Still, there have never been more writers, singers, actors, or painters who have become influential, wealthy superstars. And they, the successful ones, spawn a million imitators, they become the torchbearers, their work becomes the benchmark for what art is, or ought to be.

Nowadays in India the scene is almost **farcical**. Following the recent commercial success of some Indian authors, Western publishers are desperately prospecting for the next big Indo-Anglian work of fiction. They're doing everything short of interviewing English-speaking Indians for the post of "writer." Ambitious middle-class parents who, a few years ago, would only settle for a future in Engineering, Medicine, or Management for their children, now hopefully send them to creative writing schools. People like myself are constantly petitioned by computer companies, watch manufacturers, even media magnates to endorse their products. A boutique owner in Bombay once asked me if he could "display" my book *The God of Small Things* (as if it were an accessory, a bracelet or a pair of earrings) while he filmed me shopping for clothes! **Jhumpa Lahiri,** the American writer of Indian origin who won the Pulitzer Prize, came to India recently to have a traditional Bengali wedding. The wedding was reported on the front page of national newspapers.

farcical: ludicrous; mocking

Now where does all this lead us? Is it just harmless nonsense that's best ignored? How does all this ardent wooing affect our art? What kind of lenses does it put in our spectacles? How far does it remove us from the world around us?

There is very real danger that this **neoteric** seduction can shut us up far more effectively than violence and repression ever could. We have free speech. Maybe. But do we have Really Free Speech? If what we have to say doesn't "sell," will we still say it? Can we? Or is everybody looking for Things That Sell to say? Could writers end up playing the role of palace entertainers? Or the subtle twenty-first-century version of court eunuchs attending to the pleasures of our incumbent CEOs? You know—naughty, but nice. Risqué perhaps, but not risky.

neoteric: new; recent in origin

9. In Your Journal: How does political repression compare to the market pressures, according to Roy?

10. In Your Journal: What's the difference between "risqué" and "risky"?

It has been nearly four years now since my first, and so far only, novel, *The God of Small Things,* was published. In the early days, I used to be described—introduced—as the author of an almost freakishly "successful" (if I may use so vulgar a term) first book. Nowadays I'm introduced as something of a freak myself. I am, apparently, what is known in twenty-first-century vernacular as a "writer-activist." (Like a sofa-bed.)

11. In Your Journal: How is the term "writer-activist" like the term "sofa-bed," in terms of meaning?

Jhumpa Lahiri: daughter of Bengali parents, author of *Interpreter of Maladies,* Pulitzer Prize winner for short fiction in 2000, which featured stories about the alienation of American immigrants from India

Why am I called a "writer-activist" and why—even when it's used approvingly, admiringly—does that term make me flinch? I'm called a writer-activist because after writing *The God of Small Things* I wrote three political essays: "The End of Imagination," about India's nuclear tests, "The Greater Common Good," about Big Dams and the "development" debate, and "Power Politics: The Reincarnation of Rumpelstiltskin," about the privatization and corporatization of essential infrastructure like water and electricity. Apart from the building of the temple in **Ayodhya,** these currently also happen to be the top priorities of the Indian government.

Now, I've been wondering why it should be that the person who wrote *The God of Small Things* is called a writer, and the person who wrote the political essays is called an activist? True, *The God of Small Things* is a work of fiction, but it's no less political than any of my essays. True, the essays are works of nonfiction, but since when did writers forgo the right to write nonfiction?

My thesis—my humble theory, as we say in India—is that I've been saddled with this double-barreled appellation, this awful professional label, not because my work is political, but because in my essays, which are about very contentious issues, I take sides. I take a position. I have a point of view. What's worse, I make it clear that I think it's right and moral to take that position, and what's even worse, I use everything in my power to flagrantly solicit support for that position. Now, for a writer of the twenty-first century, that's considered a pretty uncool, unsophisticated thing to do. It skates uncomfortably close to the territory occupied by political party ideologues—a breed of people that the world has learned (quite rightly) to mistrust. I'm aware of this. I'm all for being **circumspect.** I'm all for discretion, prudence, tentativeness, subtlety, ambiguity, complexity. I love the unanswered question, the unresolved story, the unclimbed mountain, the tender shard of an incomplete dream. Most of the time.

> *12. In Your Journal:* Why do you think it's considered "uncool" and "unsophisticated" for a contemporary writer to solicit support for a political position?

circumspect: cautious

But is it mandatory for a writer to be ambiguous about everything? Isn't it true that there have been fearful episodes in human history when prudence and discretion would have just been euphemisms for **pusillanimity?** When caution was actually cowardice? When sophistication was disguised decadence? When circumspection was really a kind of **espousal?**

> *13. In Your Journal:* What "episodes in human history" might Roy allude to here?

pusillanimity: cowardliness

espousal: support; siding with

Isn't it true, or at least theoretically possible, that there are times in the life of a people or a nation when the political climate demands that we—even the most sophisticated of us—overtly take sides? I believe that such times are upon us. And I believe that in the coming years intellectuals and artists in India will be called upon to take sides.

⁘ **Ayodhya:** center of pilgrimage in northern India; history of Muslim-Hindu tensions

And this time, unlike the struggle for Independence, we won't have the luxury of fighting a colonizing "enemy." We'll be fighting ourselves.

14. *In Your Journal:* Why does Roy call "fighting a colonizing 'enemy'" a "luxury"?

We will be forced to ask ourselves some very uncomfortable questions about our values and traditions, our vision for the future, our responsibilities as citizens, the legitimacy of our "democratic institutions," the role of the state, the police, the army, the judiciary, and the intellectual community.

15. *In Your Journal:* What is the "cultural insult" Roy alludes to here?

Fifty years after independence, India is still struggling with the legacy of colonialism, still flinching from the "cultural insult." As citizens we're still caught up in the business of "disproving" the white world's definition of us. Intellectually and emotionally, we have just begun to grapple with communal and caste politics that threaten to tear our society apart. But in the meanwhile, something new looms on our horizon.

It's not war, it's not genocide, it's not ethnic cleansing, it's not a famine or an epidemic. On the face of it, it's just ordinary, day-to-day business. It lacks the drama, the large-format, epic magnificence of war or genocide or famine. It's dull in comparison. It makes bad TV. It has to do with boring things like jobs, money, water supply, electricity, irrigation. But it also has to do with a process of barbaric dispossession on a scale that has few parallels in history. You may have guessed by now that I'm talking about the modern version of globalization.

What is globalization? Who is it for? What is it going to do to a country like India, in which social inequality has been institutionalized in the caste system for centuries? A country in which seven hundred million people live in rural areas. In which eighty percent of the landholdings are small farms. In which three hundred million people are illiterate.

Is the corporatization and globalization of agriculture, water supply, electricity, and essential commodities going to pull India out of the stagnant morass of poverty, illiteracy, and religious bigotry? Is the dismantling and auctioning off of elaborate public sector infrastructure, developed with public money over the last fifty years, really the way forward? Is globalization going to close the gap between the privileged and the underprivileged, between the upper caste and the lower castes, between the educated and the illiterate? Or is it going to give those who already have a centuries-old head start a friendly helping hand?

Is globalization about "eradication of world poverty," or is it a mutant variety of **colonialism,** remote controlled and digitally operated? These are huge, contentious questions. The answers vary depending on whether they come from the villages and fields of rural India, from the slums and shantytowns of urban India, from the livingrooms of the burgeoning middle class, or from the boardrooms of the big business houses.

colonialism: system where one nation maintains control over foreign, dependent nations

Today India produces more milk, more sugar, more food grain than ever before. This year government warehouses are overflowing with forty-two million tons of food grain. That's almost a quarter of the total annual food grain produce. Farmers with too much grain on their hands were driven to despair. In regions that wielded enough political clout, the government went on a buying spree, purchasing more grain than it could possibly store or use. While the grain rots in government warehouses, three hundred and fifty million Indian citizens live below the poverty line and do not have the means to eat a square meal a day. And yet, in March 2000, just before President Clinton's visit to India, the Indian government lifted import restrictions on one thousand four hundred commodities, including milk, grain, sugar, cotton, tea, coffee, and palm oil. This despite the fact that there was a glut of these products in the market.

From April 1—April Fool's Day—2001, according to the terms of its agreement with the **World Trade Organization (WTO),** the Indian government will have to drop its quantitative import restrictions. The Indian market is already flooded with cheap imports. Though India is technically free to export its agricultural produce, in practice most of it cannot be exported because it doesn't meet the first world's "environmental standards." (You don't eat bruised mangoes, or bananas with mosquito bites, or rice with a few weevils in it. Whereas we don't mind the odd mosquito and the occasional weevil.)

Developed countries like the United States, whose hugely subsidized farm industry engages only two to three percent of its total population, are using the WTO to pressure countries like India to drop agricultural subsidies in order to make the market "competitive." Huge, mechanized corporate enterprises working thousands of acres of farmland want to compete with impoverished subsistence farmers who own a couple of acres of land.

garroted: strangled

In effect, India's rural economy, which supports seven hundred million people, is being **garroted**. Farmers who produce too much are in distress, farmers who produce too little are in distress, and landless agricultural laborers are out of work as big estates and farms lay off their workers. They're all flocking to the cities in search of employment.

"Trade Not Aid" is the rallying cry of the headmen of the new Global Village headquartered in the shining offices of the WTO. Our British colonizers stepped onto our shores a few centuries ago disguised as traders. We all remember the **East India Company.** This time around, the colonizer doesn't even need a token white presence in the colonies. The CEOs and their men don't need to go to the trouble of tramping through the tropics, risking malaria, diarrhea, sunstroke, and an early death. They don't have to

---

World Trade Organization (WTO): established in 1995; monitors national trade to eliminate discriminatory treatment in international commerce

---

East India Company: (1606-1874) highly profitable British trading company established in India; eventually began to control India's commercial policy until the Indian mutiny of 1857-1858

maintain an army or a police force, or worry about insurrections and mutinies. They can have their colonies and an easy conscience. "Creating a good investment climate" is the new euphemism for third world repression. Besides, the responsibility for implementation rests with the local administration.

> *16. In Your Journal:* How does Roy see the early colonists as similar to today's CEO's of globalization?

In India, in order to clear the way for "development projects," the government is in the process of amending the present Land Acquisition Act (which, ironically, was drafted by the British in the nineteenth century) and making it more draconian than it already is. State governments are preparing to ratify "anti-terrorist" laws so that those who oppose development projects (in **Madhya Pradesh,** for example) will be counted as terrorists. They can be held without trial for three years. They can have their lands and cattle seized.

Recently, globalization has come in for some criticism. The protests in Seattle and Prague will go down in history. Each time the WTO or the **World Economic Forum** wants to have a meeting, ministers have to barricade themselves with thousands of heavily armed police. Still, all its admirers, from Bill Clinton, **Kofi Annan,** and A.B. Vajpayee (the Indian prime minister) to the cheering brokers in the stalls, continue to say the same lofty things. If we have the right institutions of governance in place—effective courts, good laws, honest politicians, participatory democracy, a transparent administration that respects human rights and gives people a say in decisions that affect their lives—then the globalization project will work for the poor, as well. They call this "globalization with a human face."

> *17. In Your Journal:* In this paragraph, how does Roy counter the logic of Bill Clinton, Kofi Annan, and A.B. Vajpee, summarized above?

The point is, if all this were in place, almost *anything* would succeed: socialism, capitalism, you name it. Everything works in Paradise, a Communist State as well as a Military Dictatorship. But in an imperfect world, is it globalization that's going to bring us all this bounty? Is that what's happening in India now that it's on the fast track to the free market? Does any one thing on that lofty list apply to life in India today?

> *18. In Your Journal:* What is Roy suggesting here about what proponents of globalization see as the "right institutions of governance"?

Are state institutions transparent? Have people had a say, have they even been informed—let alone consulted—about decisions that vitally affect their lives? And are Mr. Clinton (or now Mr. Bush) and Prime Minister Vajpayee doing everything in their power to see that the "right institutions of governance" are in place? Or are they involved in exactly the opposite enterprise? Do they mean something else altogether when they talk of the "right institutions of governance"?

Madhya Pradesh: one of the largest states in (central) India; popular tourist destination

World Economic Forum: independent international organization of national leaders and business executives

Kofi Annan: seventh Secretary-General of the United Nations, who began his term in 2001

On October 18, 2000, in one of the most extraordinary legal decisions in post-independence India, the Supreme Court permitted the construction of the Sardar Sarovar Dam on the Narmada river to proceed. The court did this despite indisputable evidence placed before it that the Sardar Sarovar Project did not have the mandatory environmental clearance from the central government. Despite the fact that no comprehensive studies have ever been done on the social and ecological impact of the dam. Despite the fact that in the last fifteen years not one single village has been resettled according to the project's own guidelines, and that there was no possibility of rehabilitating the four hundred thousand people who would be displaced by the project. In effect, the Supreme Court has virtually endorsed the violation of human rights to life and livelihood.

Big Dams in India have displaced not hundreds, not thousands, but millions—more than thirty million people in the last fifty years. Almost half of them are **Dalit and Adivasi,** the poorest of the poor. Yet India is the only country in the world that refused permission to the World Commission on Dams to hold a public hearing. The government in Gujarat, the state in which the Sardar Sarovar Dam is being built, threatened members of the commission with arrest. The World Commission on Dams report was released by Nelson Mandela in November 2000. In February 2001, the Indian government formally rejected the report. Does this sound like a transparent, accountable, participatory democracy?

Recently the Supreme Court ordered the closure of seventy-seven thousand "polluting and nonconforming" industrial units in Delhi. The order could put five hundred thousand people out of work. What are these "industrial units"? Who are these people? They're the millions who have migrated from their villages, some voluntarily, others involuntarily, in search of work. They're the people who aren't supposed to exist, the "noncitizens" who survive in the folds and wrinkles, the cracks and fissures, of the "official" city. They exist just outside the net of the "official" urban infrastructure.

19. In Your Journal: Do you think this migration is related to the downturn in agriculture discussed on pages 563–564?

Close to forty percent of Delhi's population of twelve million—about five million people—live in slums and unauthorized colonies. Most of them are not serviced by municipal services—no electricity, no water, no sewage systems. About fifty thousand people are homeless and sleep on the streets. The "noncitizens" are employed in what economists rather stuffily call the "informal sector," the fragile but vibrant parallel economy. That both shocks and delights the imagination. They work as hawkers, **rickshaw** pullers, garbage recyclers, car battery rechargers, street tailors, transistor

rickshaw: transport vehicle powered by a person on foot or riding a bicycle

---

Dalit and Adivasi: the Dalit are a non-acquisitive tribal society in Kerala, displaced by the Indian government in recent years; the Adivasi are low-caste Christian "untouchables"

knob makers, buttonhole stitchers, paper bag makers, dyers, printers, barbers. These are the "industrial units" that have been targeted as nonconforming by the Supreme Court. (Fortunately I haven't heard *that* knock on my door yet, though I'm as nonconforming a unit as the rest of them.)

The trains that leave Delhi these days carry thousands of people who simply cannot survive in the city. They're returning to the villages they fled in the first place. Millions of others, because they're "illegal," have become easy meat for the **rapacious**, bribe-seeking police and predatory government officials. They haven't yet been driven out of the city but now must live in perpetual fear and anticipation of that happening.

rapacious: greedy; gluttonous

In India the times are full of talk of the "free market," reforms, deregulation, and the dismantling of the "license **raj**"—all in the name of encouraging entrepreneurship and discouraging corruption. Yet when the state, supported by the judiciary, curbs freedom and obliterates a flourishing market, when it breaks the backs of numerous imaginative, resourceful, small-scale entrepreneurs, and delivers millions of others as fodder to the doorstep of the corruption industry, few comment on the irony.

raj: ruler; office

No doubt it's true that the informal sector is polluting and, according to a colonial understanding of urban land use, "nonconforming." But then we don't live in a clean, perfect world. What about the fact that sixty-seven percent of Delhi's pollution comes from motor vehicles? Is it conceivable that the Supreme Court will come up with an act that bans private cars? The courts and the government have shown no great enthusiasm for closing down big factories run by major industrialists that have polluted rivers, denuded forests, depleted and poisoned ground water, and destroyed the livelihoods of hundreds of thousands of people who depend on these resources for a living. The Grasim factory in Kerala, the Orient Paper Mill in Madhya Pradesh, the "sunrise belt" industries in Gujarat. The uranium mines in Jadugoda, the aluminum plants in Orissa. And hundreds of others.

20. In Your Journal: Why do you think neither the court nor the government has any "great enthusiasm for closing down big factories run by major industrialists" responsible for large-scale polluting?

This is our in-house version of first world bullying in the global warming debate: i.e., We pollute, you pay.

In circumstances like these, the term "writer-activist" as a professional description of what I do makes me flinch doubly. First, because it is strategically positioned to diminish both writers and activists. It seeks to reduce the scope, the range, the sweep of what a writer is and can be. It suggests somehow that the writer by definition is too **effete** a being to come up with the clarity, the explicitness, the reasoning, the passion, the grit, the audacity, and, if necessary, the vulgarity to publicly take a political position. And, conversely, it suggests that the activist occupies the coarser, cruder end of the intellectual spectrum. That the activist is by profession a "position-taker" and therefore lacks complexity and intellectual sophistication, and is instead fueled by a crude, simple-minded, one-sided understanding of things. But the more fundamental problem I have with the

effete: soft or delicate

term is that professionalizing the whole business of protest, putting a label on it, has the effect of containing the problem and suggesting that it's up to the professionals—activists and writer-activists—to deal with.

The fact is that what's happening in India today is not a *problem,* and the issues that some of us are raising are not *causes.* They are huge political and social upheavals that are convulsing the nation. One is not involved by virtue of being a writer or activist. One is involved because one is a human being. Writing about it just happens to be the most effective thing I can do. I think it's vital to de-professionalize the public debate on matters that vitally affect the lives of ordinary people. It's time to snatch our futures back from the "experts." Time to ask, in ordinary language, the public question and to demand, in ordinary language, the public answer.

21. In Your Journal: Why do you think Roy rejects the terms "problem" and "causes"?

22. In Your Journal: What would it mean to "de-professionalize" a public debate?

Frankly, however trenchantly, however angrily, however combatively one puts forward one's case, at the end of the day, I'm only a citizen, one of many, who is demanding public information, asking for a public explanation. I have no axe to grind. I have no professional stakes to protect. I'm prepared to be persuaded. I'm prepared to change my mind. But instead of an argument, or an explanation, or a disputing of facts, one gets insults, invective, legal threats, and the Expert's Anthem: "You're too emotional. You don't understand, and it's too complicated to explain." The subtext, of course, is: Don't worry your little head about it. Go and play with your toys. Leave the real world to us.

It's the old **Brahminical** instinct. Colonize knowledge, build four walls around it, and use it to your advantage. The Manusmriti, the Vedic Hindu code of conduct, says that if a Dalit overhears a **shloka** or any part of a sacred text, he must have molten lead poured into his ear. It isn't a coincidence that while India is poised to take its place at the forefront of the Information Revolution, three hundred million of its citizens are illiterate. (It would be interesting, as an exercise, to find out how many "experts"—scholars, professionals, consultants—in India are actually Brahmins and upper castes.)

Brahminical: relating to the social elite (the highest four major castes in Indian society)

shloka: Sanskrit prayer

If you're one of the lucky people with a berth booked on the small convoy, then Leaving it to the Experts is, or can be, a mutually beneficial proposition for both the expert and yourself. It's a convenient way of shrugging off your own role in the circuitry. And it creates a huge professional market for all kinds of "expertise." There's a whole ugly universe waiting to be explored there. This is not at all to suggest that all consultants are **racketeers** or that expertise is unnecessary, but you've heard the saying—There's a lot of money in poverty. There are plenty of ethical questions to be asked of those who make a professional living off their expertise in poverty and despair.

23. In Your Journal: What is Roy's perception of "expertise"?

24. In Your Journal: How can there be "a lot of money in poverty"?

racketeer: one who commits extortion, loansharking, or ...vice

For instance, at what point does a scholar stop being a scholar and become a parasite who feeds off despair and dispossession? Does the source of your funding compromise your scholarship? We know, after all, that World Bank studies are among the most quoted studies in the world. Is the World Bank a dispassionate observer of the global situation? Are the studies it funds entirely devoid of self-interest?

Take, for example, the international dam industry. It's worth thirty-two to forty-six billion U.S. dollars a year. It's bursting with experts and consultants. Given the number of studies, reports, books, PhDs, grants, loans, consultancies, EIAs—it's odd, wouldn't you say, that there is no really reliable estimate of how many people have been displaced by Big Dams in India? That there is no estimate for exactly what the contribution of Big Dams has been to overall food production in India? That there hasn't been an official audit, a comprehensive, honest, thoughtful, post-project evaluation of a single Big Dam to see whether or not it has achieved what it set out to achieve? Whether or not the costs were justified, or even what the costs actually were?

25. In Your Journal: How do you think Roy would differentiate between herself and the "parasite" scholars she refers to here?

What *are* the experts up to?

If you manage to ignore the **invective**, shut out the din of the Expert's Anthem, and keep your eye on the ball, you'll find that a lot of dubious politics lurks inside the stables of "expertise." Probe further, and it all precipitates in a **bilious** rush of abuse, intimidation, and blind anger. The intellectual equivalent of a police baton charge. The advantage of provoking this kind of unconstrained, spontaneous rage is that it allows you to get a good look at the instincts of some of these normally cautious, supposedly "neutral" people, the pillars of democracy—judges, planners, academics. It becomes very clear that it's not really a question of experts versus laypersons or of knowledge versus ignorance. It's the pitting of one value system against another, one kind of political instinct against another. It's interesting to watch so many supposedly "rational" people turn into irrational, instinctive political beings. To see how they find reasons to support their views, and how, if those reasons are argued away, they continue to cling to their views anyway. Perhaps for this alone, provocation is important. In a crisis, it helps to clarify who's on which side.

invective: abusive language

bilious: bad-tempered; irritable

A wonderful illustration of this is the Supreme Court's reaction to my essay "The Greater Common Good," which was published in May 1999. In July and August of that year, the monsoon waters rose in the **Narmada** and submerged villages. While villagers stood in their homes for days together in chest-deep water to protest against the dam, while their crops were submerged, and while the NBA—Narmada Bachao Andolan, the people's movement in the Narmada valley—pointed out (citing specific instances) that government officials had committed perjury by signing false affidavits claiming that resettlement had been carried out when it hadn't, the three-judge bench in the Supreme Court met over three sessions. The only sub-

Narmada: turbulent river in Madya Pradesh, sacred to Hindus but ill-suited for navigation ject they discussed was whether or not the dignity of the court had been undermined. To assist them in their deliberations, they appointed what is called an *amicus curiae* (friend of the court) to advise them about whether or not they should initiate criminal proceedings against the NBA and me for **contempt of court.** The thing to keep in mind is that, while the NBA was the petitioner, I was (and hopefully still am) an independent citizen. I wasn't present in court, but I was told that the three-judge bench ranted and raved and referred to me as "that woman." (I began to think of myself as the hooker who won the **Booker.**)

On October 15, 1999, they issued an elaborate order. Here's an extract:

contumacious: rebellious

stultification: ridiculousness; stupidity

> . . . Judicial process and institution cannot be permitted to be scandalised or subjected to **contumacious** violation in such a blatant manner in which it has been done by her [Arundhati Roy] . . . vicious **stultification** and vulgar debunking cannot be permitted to pollute the stream of justice . . . we are unhappy at the way in which the leaders of NBA and Ms. Arundhati Roy have attempted to undermine the dignity of the Court. We expected better behaviour from them . . . After giving this matter thoughtful consideration . . . we are not inclined to initiate contempt proceedings against the petitioners, its leaders or Arundhati Roy. . . . after the 22nd of July 1999 . . . nothing has come to our notice which may show that Ms. Arundhati Roy has continued with the objectionable writings insofar as the judiciary is concerned. She may have by now realised her mistake . . .

26. In Your Journal: What is the Supreme Court's main objection to Roy's writing?

dissent: disagreement; opposition

What's **dissent** without a few good insults?

Anyway, eventually, as you can see, they let me off. And I continued with my Objectionable Writings. I hope in the course of this lecture I've managed to inspire at least some of the students in this audience to embark on careers as Vicious Stultificators and Vulgar Debunkers. We could do with a few more of those.

On the whole, in India, the prognosis is—to put it mildly—Not Good. And yet one cannot help but marvel at the fantastic range and depth and wisdom of the hundreds of people's resistance movements all over the country. They're being beaten down, but they simply refuse to lie down and die.

Malayali: Keralan language group

Their political ideologies and battle strategies span the range. We have the maverick **Malayali** professor who petitions the president every day against the communalization of history texts, Sunderlal Bahugana,

---

❖ **contempt of court:** act of interfering with the legal process

❖ **Booker:** England's biggest book prize, the Booker McConnell who risks his life on indefinite hunger strikes protesting the **Tehri Dam,** the Adivasis in **Jadugoda** protesting uranium mining on their lands, the Koel Karo Sanghathan resisting a mega-dam project in Jharkhand, the awe-inspiring **Chattisgarh Mukti Morcha,** the relentlessly dogged **Mazdoor Kisan Shakti Sangathan,** the **Beej Bachao Andolan** in **Tehri-Garhwal** fighting to save biodiversity of seeds, and of course, the Narmada Bachao Andolan, the people's movement in the Narmada valley.

India's redemption lies in the inherent anarchy and **factiousness** of its people, and in the legendary inefficiency of the Indian state. Even our heel-clicking, boot-stamping Hindu fascists are undisciplined to the point of being chaotic. They can't bring themselves to agree with each other for more than five minutes at a time. Corporatizing India is like trying to impose an iron grid on a heaving ocean and forcing it to behave.

factiousness: divisiveness

27. In Your Journal: What does Roy suggest by using this "heaving ocean" image?

My guess is that India will not behave. It cannot. It's too old and too clever to be made to jump through the hoops all over again. It's too diverse, too grand, too **feral**, and—eventually, I hope—too democratic to be lobotomized into believing in one single idea, which is, ultimately, what globalization really is: Life Is Profit.

feral: untamed

What is happening to the world lies, at the moment, just outside the realm of common human understanding. It is the writers, the poets, the artists, the singers, the filmmakers who can make the connections, who can find ways of bringing it into the realm of common understanding. Who can translate cash-flow charts and scintillating boardroom speeches into real stories about real people with real lives. Stories about what it's like to lose your home, your land, your job, your dignity, your past, and your future to an invisible force. To someone or something you can't see. You can't hate. You can't even imagine.

28. In Your Journal: How does Roy suggest artists can help in the resistance to globalization?

It's a new space that's been offered to us today. A new kind of challenge. It offers opportunities for a new kind of art. An art which can make the impalpable palpable, make the intangible tangible, and the invisible vis-

- **Tehri Dam:** civil works project in northern India; opposed by environmentalists and civil rights activists
- **Jadugoda:** east Indian site where a uranium mine, allegedly poisoning local tribal families
- **Chatisgarh Mukti Morcha:** political people's trade union movement whose leader and founder was mysteriously murdered
- **Mazdoor Kisan Shakti Sangathan:** grassroots movement advocating the right to access government information
- **Beej Bachao Andolan:** movement to revive traditional agricultural practices and conserve indigenous seeds
- **Tehri-Garhwal:** sacred district in the Himalayas

incorporeal: disembodied; intangible

ible. An art which can draw out the **incorporeal** adversary and make it real. Bring it to book.

Cynics say that real life is a choice between the failed revolution and the shabby deal. I don't know . . . maybe they're right. But even they should know that there's no limit to just how shabby that shabby deal can be. What we need to search for and find, what we need to hone and perfect into a magnificent, shining thing, is a new kind of politics. Not the politics of governance, but the politics of resistance. The politics of opposition. The politics of forcing accountability. The politics of slowing things down. The politics of joining hands across the world and preventing certain destruction. In the present circumstances, I'd say that the only thing worth globalizing is dissent. It's India's best export.

FOR USE IN DISCUSSION

Questions about Substance

1. Roy says, "To be a writer—a supposedly "famous" writer—in a country where three hundred million people are illiterate is a dubious honor" (559). What does she mean by this? How do you think this idea informs this essay's argument?
2. When Roy says the she's "all for being circumspect," and that she loves "the unanswered question, the unresolved story; the unclimbed mountain, the tender shard of an incomplete dream" (562), she suggests these things are incompatible with political activism. How so? How might the values of art and the values of politics be antithetical? Are there any values these two endeavors share?
3. Illiteracy comes up again and again in this essay (see 559, 563, and 568). While Roy does not formally explain what she sees as the connection between illiteracy in India and her roles as writer and activist, there is surely a connection. What does illiteracy have to do with globalization? What does it have to do with Roy's politics? Why would a novelist be so interested in the illiterate?
4. Roy is very interested in political euphemism—the use of gentler, more ambiguous terms to put unsavory political issues in a positive light. She uses quotation marks to denote the euphamisms she wishes to call into question: "progress" (558); "environmental standards" and "competitive" (564); "creating a good investment climate," and "globalization with a human face" (565); "right institutions of government" (565); "industrial units" and "the informal sector" (556); and "experts" (568). How does this interest grow out of Roy's perspective as a writer? How does it relate to her political activism?

Questions about Structure and Style

1. What, if anything, does the title of this essay have to do with its contents? What do you think the title is meant to impress upon the reader?
2. Examine the diffuse list of conditions Roy suggests she lives with: a "dubious honor," a "ferocious burden," and an "onerous responsibility." (559). What stylistic effect does this list illustrate?
3. Roy explains that she got into trouble with the Indian government for writing political essays because she "takes sides," "takes a position," and "has a point of view" (956). Why does she express this point with three examples of a similar idea? Are the examples precisely synonymous or do they have subtle differences?
4. What point does Roy make by juxtaposing the Indian government's protection of Big Dam projects and the court ordered closure of "'polluting and nonconforming' industrial units" (566)?

Multimedia Review

1. Read a few issues of *The Times of India,* available at *http://timesofindia.indiatimes.com/cms.dll/html/uncomp/default?xml=0&*, or *All India News,* available at *http://www.allindianews.com/*. Look for updates on some of the issues that concern Roy in this essay (e.g., The Tehri Dam project or the Jadugoda mine, for example). Has any progress been made that would suggest a less eager rush toward globalization?
2. Read the interview with Roy about her writing and her feelings about India at Salon.com (*http://www.salon.com/sept97/00roy.html*). Does this interview provide any context that further informs your understanding of Roy's essay here?
3. Roy makes almost no reference to "Bollywood," India's hugely successful film center. You can get a sense of India's filmmaking tradition at *http://www.planetbollywood.com/*, where, among lots of other information, you will find reviews of many popular Bollywood films. Evaluate some of these reviews, thinking about whether you think the trends in Bollywood would help or hurt Roy's argument in any way.

SUGGESTIONS FOR WRITING AND RESEARCH

1. Examine the definition of art that Roy seems to be developing in this essay. She says that artists are "meant to fly, to push the frontiers, to worry the edges of the human imagination, to conjure beauty from the most unexpected things, to find magic in places where others never thought to look." Then she argues that we should not "weight their wings with society's existing notions of morality and responsibility" (560) or they will not be able to fulfill their promises. What is the relationship then, in Roy's opinion, between the artist and society? Who has the bigger responsibility in this relationship?

2. Before finally naming "globalization" as the subject she wants to introduce, Roy lists the subjects she is not getting at: war, genocide, ethnic cleansing, or epidemic (563). She also characterizes globalization as "ordinary" and "boring" before arguing that its barbarism is unparalleled in history. The word "globalization" at last appears as the last word in the paragraph that alludes to it so descriptively. What effect is this delay and the preceding description of what globalization is *not* meant to have on the reader? How does this strategy relate to Roy's career as a fiction writer? How does it affect the effectiveness of her argument? Examine Roy's analysis of globalization and the manner in which she presents that analysis.
3. Do a comparative study on the poverty in the United States with that of India. Research economics, civil rights, health, literacy and education, or whatever aspect of poverty interests you. Since both the United States and India are democratic, would you expect there to be more similarities or differences? Do you think the methods of addressing (or not addressing) poverty in both countries is the same? What about the attitudes of the poor toward their government?

WORKING WITH CLUSTERS

Cluster 10: Interpretation and/as Ideology
Cluster 13: Global Knowledge
Discipline: The Social Sciences
Rhetorical Mode: Cause and Effect

Safe Area Goražde: The War in Eastern Bosnia 1992–95

by Joe Sacco

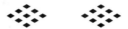

Joe Sacco is a native of Malta, but he has spent much of the last twenty-five years in the United States and traveling to various countries in the Middle East and Europe while working as a reporter, editor, illustrator, and graphic novelist. He earned a Bachelor's degree in journalism from University of Oregon in 1981. His work has been nominated for a Harvey Award, and he won an American Book Award in 1996. In addition to his work on war and international relations, Sacco has written frequently about music and musicians. He was recently featured in exhibits at the Buffalo Art Gallery and the Pittsburgh Art Gallery, and his work has been highly praised by The Utne Reader, Entertainment Weekly, Men's Journal, The Nation *columnist Christopher Hitchens, noted Columbia University literature scholar Edward Said, and Pulitzer Prize winner Art Spiegelman. Sacco is the author of* Palestine *(1992–1995), "Christmas with Karadzic" (1997),* Soba *(1998) and* Safe Area Goražde: The War in Eastern Bosnia, 1992–95 *(2000), from which these excerpts are drawn. His earlier works on the Gulf War and other subjects are collected in* Notes from a Defeatist.

GO AWAY
No-man's-land
nearing Gorazde
In the fall of 1995, the future of Gorazde and its 57,000 inhabitants was by no means clear...
UN

- **separatist:** one who advocates secession or separation from an established order or institution
- **safe area:** place declared by the United Nations to be effectively off limits to military offense, and to be guarded by designated peacekeepers
- **Srebrenica and Zepa:** other designated "safe areas," meant to be protected by the United Nations, but both invaded by Serbs

❖ **Dayton, Ohio:** eventually these peace talks led to the Dayton Peace Accords, a treaty that would end the conflict and establish the Bosnian Federation (of Muslims and Croats) and the Serbian Republic

"I wish Gorazde would go away," I heard one American correspondent say...

1. In Your Journal: Describe the tone of this American correspondent's comment. How does this comment set the general tone for the story Sacco is about to tell?

Brother-hood and Unity
Edin
I SPENT A VERY NICE CHILD-HOOD...
"I didn't make any distinction between Serb, Croat, and Muslim children. We were always together... fishing, in forests, on the playground, the stadium...
"It was a mixed population here. On the left of my house were Serbs, across the street Muslims, on the right Muslims...
"At one point, I was mostly with a Serb friend. He was at my house during the day. During the evening hours... if my mother wanted me to eat, she'd call him over and he'd eat with me...
"I spent all my life with [my Serb friends] Boban, Miro, Goran... I was drunk with them so many times... We were together at every party, at every place. We didn't make any distinction."

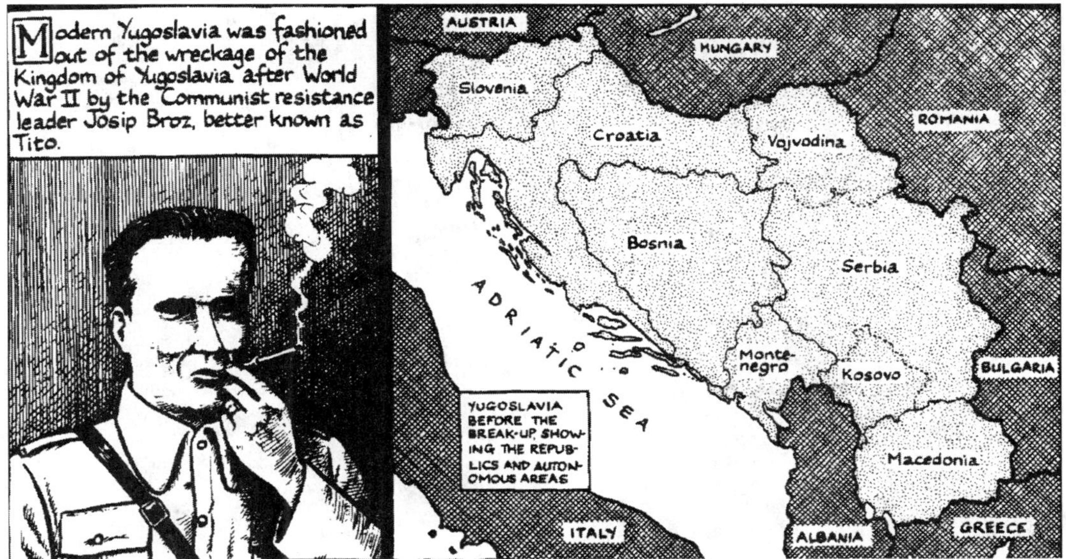

2. ***In Your Journal:*** Make note of the maps provided. Sacco will make subsequent references to most of the places listed on the maps, and they will help you to understand the logistics of the story. Additionally, consider this level of detail in Sacco's work. What preconceptions did you have of cartooning before reading this selection? How much geographic and/or historical information would you have expected from a comic strip?

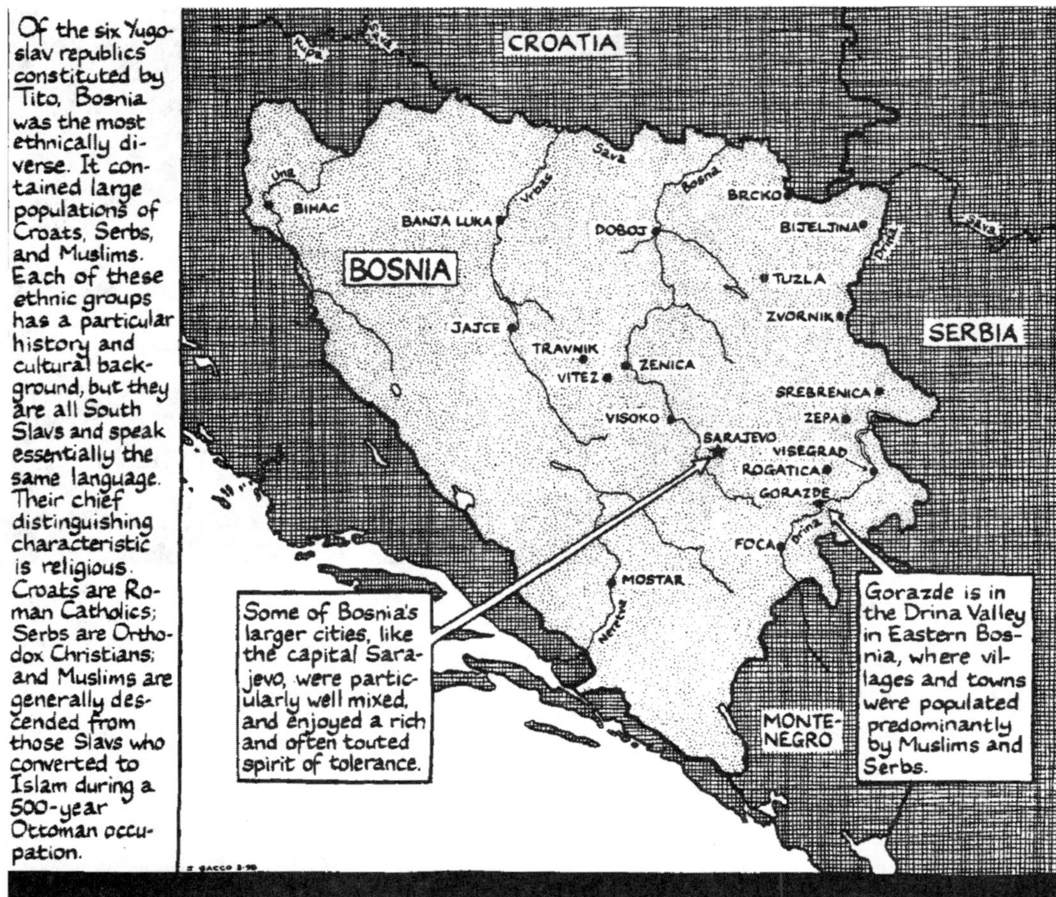

Of the six Yugoslav republics constituted by Tito, Bosnia was the most ethnically diverse. It contained large populations of Croats, Serbs, and Muslims. Each of these ethnic groups has a particular history and cultural background, but they are all South Slavs and speak essentially the same language. Their chief distinguishing characteristic is religious. Croats are Roman Catholics; Serbs are Orthodox Christians; and Muslims are generally descended from those Slavs who converted to Islam during a 500-year Ottoman occupation.
CROATIA
BOSNIA
SERBIA
MONTENEGRO
BIHAC
BANJA LUKA
DOBOJ
BRCKO
BIJELJINA
TUZLA
ZVORNIK
JAJCE
TRAVNIK
VITEZ
ZENICA
VISOKO
SREBRENICA
ZEPA
SARAJEVO
VISEGRAD
ROGATICA
GORAZDE
FOCA
MOSTAR
Sava
Una
Vrbas
Bosna
Drina
Neretva
Kupa
Some of Bosnia's larger cities, like the capital Sarajevo, were particularly well mixed, and enjoyed a rich and often touted spirit of tolerance.
Gorazde is in the Drina Valley in Eastern Bosnia, where villages and towns were populated predominantly by Muslims and Serbs.

✧ **500-year Ottoman occupation:** the Ottoman Empire was a vast state founded in the 13th century by Turks, and ruled by descendents of Osmani I until after World War I, when it was dissolved and Yugoslavia was formed

3. In Your Journal: Does it surprise you to see this praise of an "authoritarian" style of government? What does this perspective suggest about the period after Tito's rule?

More than a million Yugoslavs died in the war, mostly at the hands of other Yugoslavs.
When the Axis powers occupied and dismembered the Kingdom of Yugoslavia in 1941, they installed Croatian fascists, the Ustasha, in their own state, which was expanded to include Bosnia. The fury with which the Ustasha carried out their genocidal program of wholesale slaughter, forced religious conversion, and expulsion of the Serb population left even the Nazis aghast. Ustasha victims fed the ranks of two competing resistance groups, the Chetniks and the Partisans.
The Chetniks were a somewhat loose alliance of groups of Serb nationalists and royalists who typically sought the establishment of a Greater Serbia cleansed of non-Serbs. The Chetniks waged a ruthless war against Bosnia's Croat and Muslim citizenry, whom they viewed as Ustasha collaborators, and against the Partisans, whom they saw as likely post-war rivals.
The Partisans, the Communist resistance force led by Tito, also were a predominantly Serb group (Tito himself was half-Croatian, half-Slovenian), but they welcomed a growing number of Muslim and Croatian recruits as disillusionment with the Ustasha regime increased and Chetnik outrages continued. The Partisans fought a generally defensive war against Axis forces and waged an aggressive campaign against the Chetniks, whom they eventually crushed.

⁘ **Axis powers:** coalition of countries in World War II headed by Germany, Italy, and Japan; Hitler enlisted the Utasha after invading Yugoslavia because the Axis powers were not yet militarily prepared to occupy the area

Bosnia's Muslims could be found on all sides of the conflict. A few even allied themselves with the Chetniks. Others joined in the Ustasha persecution of the Serbs. Several thousand volunteered with the Germans for a Muslim S.S. division which carried out anti-Serb atrocities.

4. *In Your Journal:* What is remarkable about the Muslims who aligned themselves with the Chetniks?

As chaos spread, some Muslims formed autonomous defense units for protection against any and all threats, and in greater and greater numbers Muslims joined the multi-ethnic Partisans, which led to more Chetnik reprisals.

Hundreds of thousands of Serbs were killed in the war, mostly by the Ustasha, but the Muslims lost a greater percentage of their population, mostly in Chetnik attacks and massacres, many of which took place in Eastern Bosnia.

THERE WAS PLENTY OF KILLING IN THE WAR, MUSLIMS BY CHETNIKS.

"They were coming and going whenever they liked, in small groups, burning houses, killing people, raping women... Muslims in this area did not have anything to defend themselves with.

"The Chetniks raped and slaughtered... so many of my cousins and Muslims in this area. The worst things happened in Foca. The village of my family, Bucije ...over the River Drina, the Chetniks completely blew up, and whomever they found they killed. We're talking about the men...

"When people heard that these groups were coming, as fast as possible they were hiding themselves or escaping somewhere. My grandfather hid himself with the help of his wife for nearly one year under the cows' shed in the ground...

5. In Your Journal: Does Edin's grandparents' story of survival seem familiar in any way?

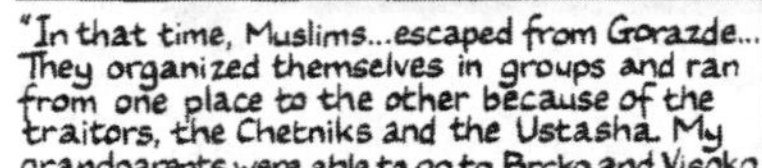

"In that time, Muslims...escaped from Gorazde... They organized themselves in groups and ran from one place to the other because of the traitors, the Chetniks and the Ustasha. My grandparents were able to go to Brcko and Visoko.

"My grandfather and grandmother sometimes tried to explain to me what happened during World War II, but I did not listen, or listened with one ear."

6. *In Your Journal:* Sacco describes the Goražde residents as seeing "promise" in the "outsideness" of the foreign journalists. What does he mean by this? Is the word choice ironic in any way, given the context of ethnic conflict?

---

he started belting: lyrics presented here are from the Eagles' "Hotel California," Simon and Garfunkel's "The Boxer," and Bruce Springsteen's "Born in the USA"

7. *In Your Journal:* Describe the tone of Sacco's aside here ("He meant bombing the Serbs").

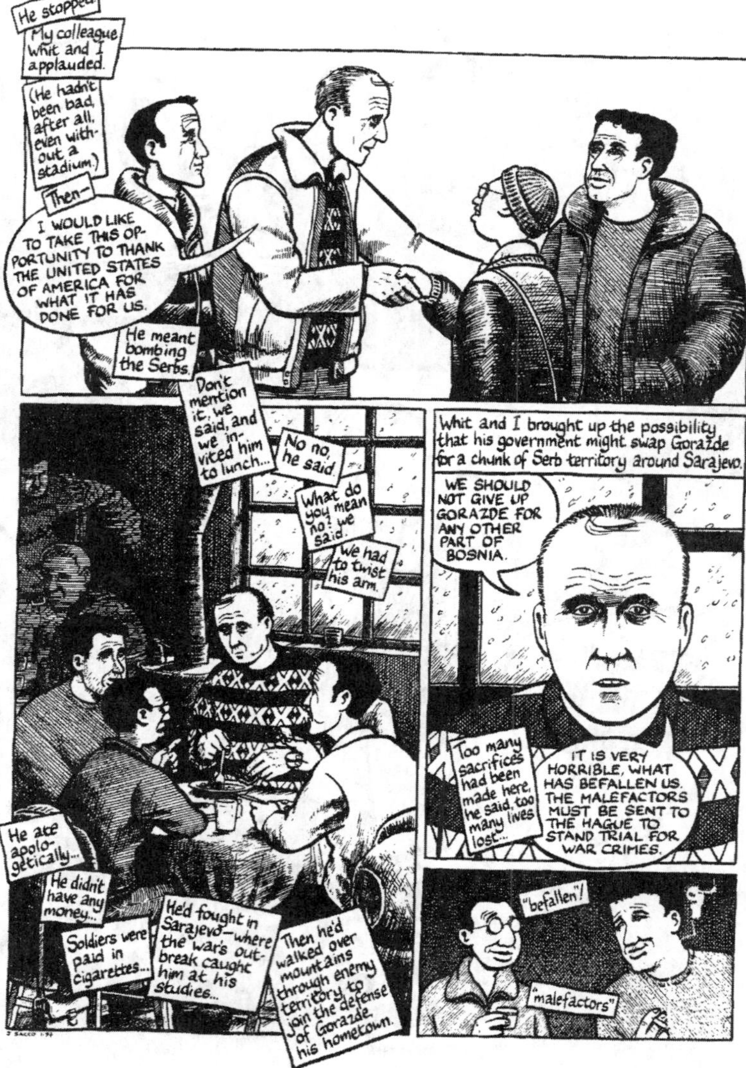

8. *In Your Journal:* Why does Sacco show himself and his colleague making fun of Riki's use of English?

The Hague: city in Holland which is the seat of the International Court of Justice (the legal arm of the United Nations), formed by the countries fighting against the Axis powers during World War II; the International Court of Justice hears disputes among member states relating to breaches of international obligations, among other matters

reticent: reserved; restrained; quiet

- **making love . . . :** from Simon and Garfunkel's "Cecelia"
- **Turkish journalist:** though the majority of the population is Muslim, Turkey is a very diverse country ethnically

Then he and Edin regaled us with Bosnian folk and patriotic songs...
They'd been roommates before the war at the University of Sarajevo where both had studied mechanical engineering...
It got late and we were quieting down...
the three of us who were outsiders began speculating about Gorazde's future...
their future...
land swap?
evacuation?
Like most foreigners in Bosnia, we enjoyed weaving our theories...

Then Serif, perhaps the most charming journalist in all of Bosnia, who, as a Turkish national, had passed through Serb territory to reach Gorazde at some peril, began a gentle, sleepy summation of how she'd come to cover the war for ten days and stayed two years...

9. In Your Journal: Is the juxtaposition of tragic stories and syrupy pop lyrics here meant to be funny or sad? Why does Sacco emphasize Riki's love of pop music?

wo wo yay yay . . . : from Leo Sayer's "More Than I Can Say"

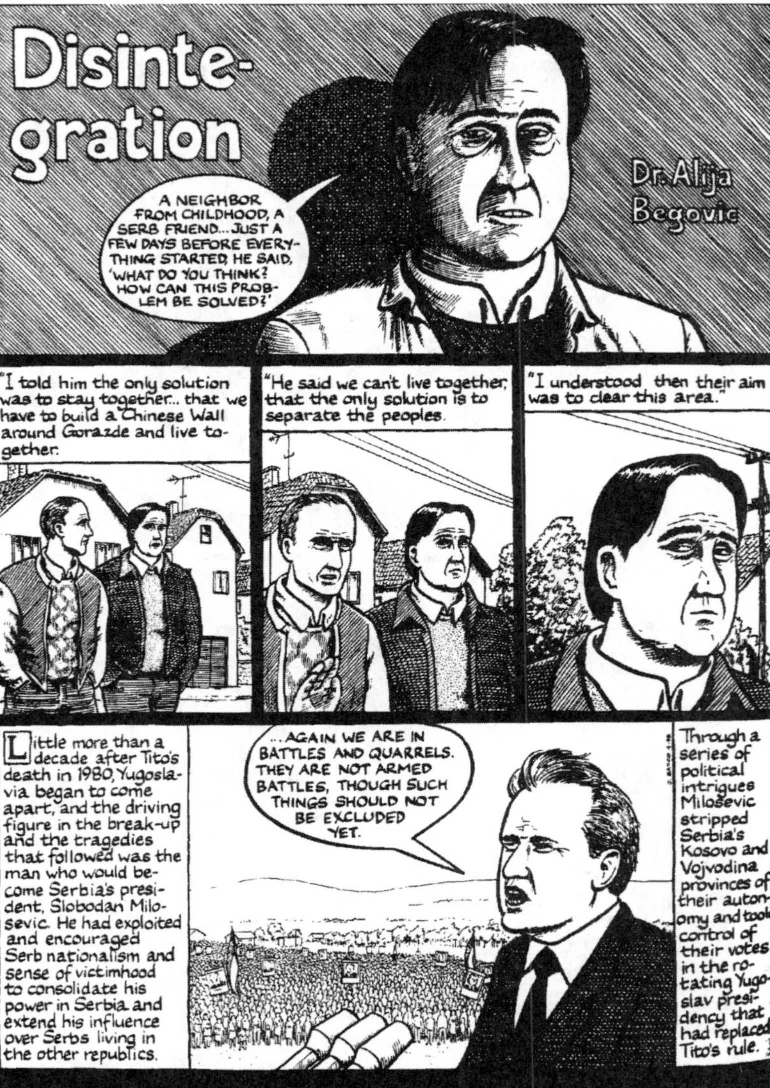

10. In Your Journal: Does the warning of Dr. Begovic's friend seem to be threatening or protective in this scene?

Slobodan Milosevic: (1941–) President of Serbia (1989–1997), and (the new) Yugoslavia (1997–2000); charged in 1999 with crimes against humanity by the International Criminal Tribunal for the former Yugoslavia, and in 2002 with war crimes by the U.N. International War Crimes Tribunal in the Hague for his actions in Bosnia, Croatia, and Kosovo

Slovenia and Croatia, their own nationalism roused and wary of Milosevic's growing power, declared their independence from Yugoslavia in 1991. Slovenia, which did not have a significant Serb population, was permitted to leave the federation after a ten-day conflict. In Croatia, however, a brutal war broke out as a large Serb minority—whose interests and sensitivities had been run roughshod by the Croatian leadership—carved out its own statelet.
In this they were supported by Milosevic and the heavy guns of the JNA (Yugoslav People's Army), which had evolved from a federal institution into an instrument for achieving a Greater Serbia, a state that would encompass Serbs living beyond Serbia's borders.
In the territory they consolidated, the Serbs brutally cleansed themselves of Croatian civilians.
The Serbs were convinced they were preempting their own victimization by what they perceived to be a resurgent Ustasha state. Their nationalist leaders had used the ethnic crimes of the past to fuel a new cycle of ethnic violence in order to shatter the notion of "brotherhood and unity" forever.

---

cleansed themselves: "ethnic cleansing" was a term coined during this conflict, and widely used as a euphemism for the genocide of Bosnian Muslims and Kosovar Albanians

Radovan Karadzic: commander-in-chief of the Bosnian Serbs during the war; formally indicted by the International War Crimes Tribunal in 1995 for genocide and crimes against humanity; has been a fugitive for over seven years

HIS WORDS AND MANNERS ILLUSTRATE WHY OTHERS REFUSE TO STAY IN THIS YUGOSLAVIA. NOBODY ELSE WANTS THE KIND OF YUGOSLAVIA THAT MR. KARADZIC WANTS ANY MORE. NOBODY EXCEPT PERHAPS THE SERBS...
I WANT TO TELL THE CITIZENS OF BOSNIA-HERZEGOVINA NOT TO BE AFRAID, BECAUSE THERE WILL BE NO WAR...
THEREFORE, SLEEP PEACEFULLY.
The SDS left the Bosnian assembly and established its own Serb parliament. The Bosnian government, meanwhile, continued to pursue sovereignty, and the European Community recognized Bosnia as independent on April 6, 1992. That night, the separatist Serbs declared their own independent state, which they later called Republika Srpska.
I SPENT FIVE YEARS AT THE COLLEGE [IN SARAJEVO]... I HEARD THERE WOULD BE TROUBLE. IF THERE WOULD BE WAR, I THOUGHT IT WOULD BE BETTER IF I WERE WITH MY PARENTS. I TOOK A BUS AND CAME BACK TO GORAZDE.
"I had a good Serb friend living three houses from me. He was with me eight years at the primary school. I called him. I asked if we could go out together.
NO, IT'S NOT POSSIBLE... MAYBE ANOTHER TIME... I CAN'T GO WITH YOU. MY PEOPLE WILL POINT AT ME.
OKAY, IF YOU DON'T WANT TO GO WITH ME, NEVER MIND, BUT I WANT US TO BE GOOD NEIGHBORS...
"In my neighborhood, there were guards with arms, together, Muslims and Serbs because it wasn't safe. Anything was possible. Maybe somebody would come from outside, from Visegrad, from another part of town and kill my Serb neighbor. They would think a Muslim neighbor had done that.
"Or maybe somebody would come and kill a Muslim, and Muslims would think it was by a Serb neighbor. It was better that we would... patrol the neighborhood together...over the night.

11. In Your Journal: Edin uses the word "maybe" several times here. Are these hypothetical examples or real examples that Edin for some reason cannot state directly?

"Every day it was the same, ordinary life, but it was possible to feel something in the air — trouble.
"Every day tensions increased... because leaders of this town argued on the radio...trying to find a solution for both nationalities.
"In some coffee bars, all the people were Muslim, and 15 meters away another coffee bar was full of Serbs.... I didn't feel comfortable going alone into a Serb coffee bar.
"I asked a lot of Serbs ... good friends, others... for the reason... and always it was answered, 'Why don't you want to live with us in the same country, with Montenegro and Serbia?'
"My friend said to me—
YOU CAN'T EXPECT GOOD RELATIONS BETWEEN US IN THE NEAR FUTURE. YOU WILL TRY TO KILL ALL THE SERBS IN BOSNIA AND MAKE A MUSLIM COUNTRY.
"I told him that wasn't true, and if it was true, I didn't want to live in a Muslim country.
"The last days before the war you didn't hear, 'Hello, how are you, neighbor?'"

War broke out in north-eastern Bosnia in the towns of Bijeljina and Zvornik in early April 1992. In a pattern already established in Croatia, paramilitary groups from Serbia, Milosevic's JNA, and local Serb nationalists began ethnically cleansing areas of their non-Serb inhabitants. The Bosnian government was totally unprepared to fight a war and further hampered by a standing U.N. arms embargo on the former Yugoslavia.
The Serb bombardment of Sarajevo had begun, but Gorazde was still quiet.
Bahra
BEFORE THE WAR I SAW A LOT OF SERBS PUTTING THEIR FAMILIES ON BUSES TO BELGRADE, AND I SAID TO MY HUSBAND, 'SOMETHING IS GOING TO HAPPEN.'
NO, DON'T BE FOOLISH, THERE WON'T BE ANYTHING. THERE IS GOING TO BE NO WAR HERE.
"I was working in a factory and I asked my manager, who was a Serb, 'Is something going to happen? Have you sent your family somewhere?'
NO.
I WISH I HAD A PLACE TO SEND THEM—
BECAUSE THERE IS GOING TO BE NO LIFE TOGETHER BETWEEN SERBS AND MUSLIMS, NOT JUST HERE IN GORAZDE, BUT EVERYWHERE IN BOSNIA.
SO, IF YOU CAN, SEND YOUR FAMILY ANYWHERE, JUST TO BE SAFE.
"We had guards in our neighborhood...to keep out infiltrators. One of those guards saw a Serb neighbor... taking crates of guns from a truck and putting them into his cellar.

" But he said the crates had meat and cheese for the market, not to be afraid.
"(The daughter and son-in-law of that guy later turned out to be snipers in Gorazde.)
"After that the Muslims of the neighborhood had a meeting and decided to remove their families to Sarajevo.... We went in buses.
"We came to a JNA checkpoint in Ustipraca, and... they checked our documents and our luggage and let us go.
"When we got to Rogatica Serb police checked us again and let us go.
"In the center of town we were stopped again. Again they entered — the Serb police — and asked for our documents.
"They saw a young couple, a husband and wife.... They took them from the bus.... They never came back.
"Our driver was a Serb, so we decided to collect money and give it to him so that he'd manage that no one would stop us again. So there were checkpoints, but no one was stopping us....

"Only at Sokolac, one guy... from Arkan's unit*... entered and asked for documents.
"He saw my mother's ID was from Visegrad.
DO YOU HAVE A HOUSE IN VISE-GRAD?
NOT ONE. TWO HOUSES.
WHAT IF SOMEONE BURNS YOUR HOUSES?
I THINK I WAS GOOD WITH ALL MY NEIGHBORS, AND NO ONE WILL BURN MY HOUSES.
HOPEFULLY THERE ARE STILL PEOPLE LIKE THAT.
"We continued... and all the forest around the road was full of Chetniks and JNA soldiers. They were together.
"So my mother said to my son, 'Hide behind the curtains of the bus, and if they ask how old you are, say you are 11....'
WHY?
BECAUSE THEY CAN TAKE YOU FROM THE BUS.
"I couldn't believe it when we came to Sarajevo, when I put my foot on the ground... I said, 'Dear God, has it finally happened that we are saved?'
"We went to a relative of ours.... After that house was shelled...we moved to a refugee center.
"Then the first list of killed people from Gorazde came, and the first name on the list was my husband's."

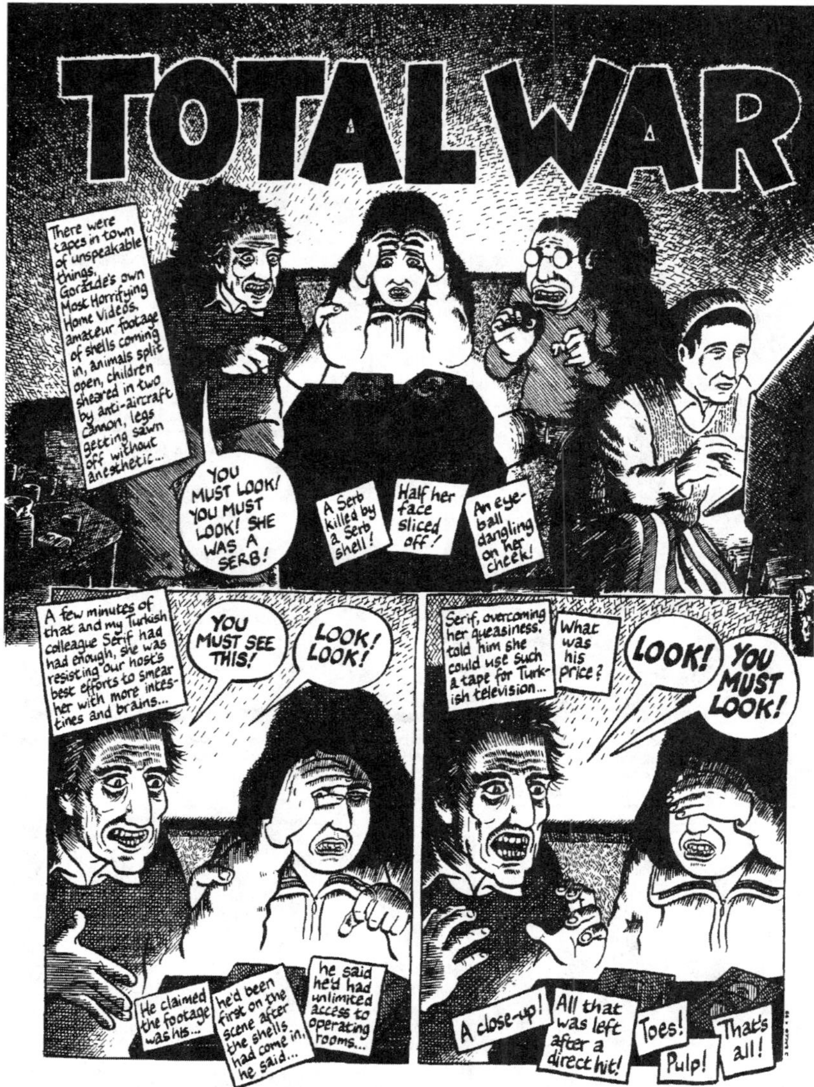

12. In Your Journal: What effect is this caricature of the human appetite for violence meant to have on his readers? Is Sacco merely criticizing the host who shows him and Serif the videos, or is his critique broader than that?

Most Horrifying Home Videos: word play on the popular American television show, *America's Funniest Home Videos*

And in that way he beat around the bush for half an hour...
an hour...
an hour and a half...
while the video procession of dead children and shrieking parents went on and on...
He himself had been wounded seven, eight times!
And look at that!
Not even Serif's abundant charm could withstand the barrage!
and the heat in there!
the heat!
the wood stove roaring all out,
melting what remained of Serif's pleasant disposition!
LOOK!
and only when we'd finally forced our way out the door and into the outside chill did he name his price—
a figure so outrageous that it seemed to disgust Serif as much as all those full-color images of the dismembered and the disemboweled.

13. In Your Journal: How does this scene compare to the previous scene, which also involves watching videos of war footage?

White Eagles: armed paramilitary formations, equipped by the Serbian Ministry of Internal Affairs during the war; largely involved in the "ethnic cleansing" of Bosnian Muslims

In the fall of 1992 a couple of trained surgeons walked over mountains through Serb lines to reach Goražde, and over the next few months, before this route was cut, a few more medical personnel made it in with a limited amount of supplies.
NOW IT'S NOT VERY GOOD, BUT IT'S BETTER...
ONLY IN THE LAST FEW WEEKS, WITH THE OPENING OF THE BLUE ROAD, CAN WE BREATHE A LITTLE EASIER.
I CAN EVEN OFFER YOU A JUICE.
He watched the video absently.
There were plenty of distractions.
Staff, patients, others popped in...
Someone investigating war crimes plopped into a chair and began leafing through evidence...
He needed to go over a few incidents with the doctor.
His wife, also a physician, stopped by to whisper into his ear.
Even I had a visitor, and Dr. Begovic was good enough to translate.
YOU ARE TO MEET EDIN AT HIS COUSIN'S COFFEE BAR AT 11 O'CLOCK.

As I got up to leave, the doctor seemed genuinely bewildered by the broader implications of the video we'd just watched.
I CAN'T UNDERSTAND WHY THE REST OF THE WORLD HASN'T INTERVENED MORE FORCEFULLY. THE U.N. IS ALWAYS POINTING OUT ITS NEUTRALITY, EVEN NOW.
NEUTRAL IN WHAT?
IN A SLAUGHTER OF LAMBS BY THE WOLVES?
I SIMPLY CAN'T BELIEVE SUCH PEOPLE EXIST —SOMEONE WHO WOULD FORCE A GRANDFATHER TO EAT THE LIVER OF HIS GRAND-SON.
I wasn't sure what he was referring to, and I didn't ask. Maybe it was one of those apocryphal stories going around about the enemy, remarkably far fetched even in a war like this...
or maybe not.
I let the doctor gather his thoughts, and I went away to dissipate my own.
PART III
DO YOU WANT TO MEET ONE OF GORAZDE'S BIGGEST WAR CRIMINALS?
He said he'd been an inductee in the Yugoslav People's Army in 1991 when his artillery unit was sent to intervene on behalf of Serbs fighting to remove themselves from newly independent Croatia.
He and his unit had taken part in the notorious bombardment of Vukovar, which killed hundreds.

apocryphal: of questionable authorship or authenticity; dubious

---

Vukovar: city in Croatia, site of the worst destruction of the Croatia-Serbia war in 1991/92

14. In Your Journal: What is the distinction Sacco is making here between suffering on camera and suffering off camera?

Dubrovnik: city in Croatia attacked by Serbs in 1991

94 Offensive: 3-week attack of Goražde in 1994 by Serbian forces; thousands were killed or wounded, despite Goražde's "safe-area" designation

15. *In Your Journal:* Do you think K. is exaggerating when he says the "front line and the town are the same"? What point is he trying to make about this war?

∴ **Medivac:** medical evacuation out of a military conflict, usually by helicopter

That's how her brother got out.
He'd been taken to Britain to recover from his wounds.
HE JUST WROTE TO SAY HIS LEG WAS AMPUTATED.
At the Piramida one night a woman approached me to tell me "the truth about the medical situation in Gorazde."
I NEED TO BE MEDIVAC'D.
I NEED TO GO TO A HOSPITAL IN SARAJEVO FOR A BRAIN SCAN.
THERE IS SOMETHING WRONG WITH MY BRAIN.
I AM 25, I HAVE A TWO YEAR OLD, MY HUSBAND WAS KILLED.
SOMETHING IS WRONG... I LOSE MYSELF. I GO INTO A STATE.
SOMETIMES I BEGIN TO TAKE MY CLOTHES OFF AT COFFEE BARS. I THROW MY DAUGHTER TO THE GROUND.
BUT THE DOCTORS HERE DON'T WANT TO MEDIVAC ME.
I told her maybe civilians would be traveling the Blue Road to Sarajevo soon.
Then she could get treated.
WE DON'T BELIEVE IN THE BLUE ROAD.
WE DON'T BELIEVE IT WILL BE OPEN TO CIVILIANS.
I KNOW HEALTHY PEOPLE WHO'VE BEEN MEDIVAC'D.
IT'S ALL ABOUT MONEY.
WITH MONEY YOU CAN GET TO NEW YORK.

gratis: free of charge

⁂ **no-fly zone:** area in the skies through which any unauthorized travel is prohibited by the U.N.

16. *In Your Journal:* What comment is made here about the interests of the Western media?

17. *In Your Journal:* Why does Sacco include this anecdote about the bon-bons? How does it relate to the larger themes of his work?

CAN YOU LIVE WITH
TOO MUCH HAS HAPPENED, TOO MANY FAMILY MEMBERS KILLED. I USED TO HAVE MANY SERB FRIENDS... I HAD A CLOSE FRIEND NAMED MIRO, AND IT'S POSSIBLE HE WAS A SNIPER SHOOTING AT MY DAUGHTER, THAT HE WAS ONE OF THOSE PEOPLE WHO RAPED AND SLAUGHTERED...
I CAN NEVER TRUST THOSE SERBS AGAIN, THAT'S OBVIOUS, AND NOT ONLY THAT, MY RELATIONSHIP WITH SERBS WHO REMAINED IN GORAZDE HAS CHANGED, TOO...
THINGS CAN NEVER BE THE SAME.
I DON'T WANT TO HEAR ANYTHING ABOUT THEM. I THINK MY FORMER SERB FRIENDS ARE DEAD, METAPHORICALLY. WE HAD A GOOD PAST. THIS WAR HAS LASTED ALMOST FOUR YEARS AND MANY THINGS HAVE CHANGED... OF COURSE BOSNIA CAN ONLY BE A SINGLE STATE WITH SERBS AND CROATS, BUT I WOULD LIKE TO LIVE WITHOUT THEM...
MY ROOMMATE IN THE DORMITORY IN ZENICA WAS A SERB, A GOOD GUY. HE WENT TO BELGRADE, HE DIDN'T WANT TO FIGHT FOR KARADZIC. I COULD LIVE WITH SOMEONE LIKE HIM, BUT HE LEFT. IN SARAJEVO, IT'S OKAY TO LIVE TOGETHER WITH SERBS, BUT IN EASTERN BOSNIA IT'S IMPOSSIBLE. WE ARE UNABLE TO DISTINGUISH BETWEEN NORMAL SERBS AND THE KILLERS.
THE SERBS CAN'T BE TRUSTED, THEY LIE. THE ONLY REASON SOME SERBS REMAINED IN GORAZDE WAS BECAUSE THEY WERE AFRAID OF LOSING THEIR HOMES.
I CAN LIVE WITH THE SERBS AGAIN, BUT NOT THOSE GUILTY OF CRIMES. I'M QUITE AWARE OF THE LOYAL SERBS LIVING IN SARAJEVO...
I CAN'T UNDERSTAND IT. ABOUT 90 PERCENT OF MY FRIENDS WERE SERBS. OLDER PEOPLE SAID THAT SERBS HATED MUSLIMS, BUT WE DIDN'T BELIEVE THEM.
I UNDERSTAND SERBS LIVED WITH US DURING THE WAR, ESPECIALLY IN SARAJEVO, BUT I'M SUSPICIOUS OF THEM. I CAN'T HELP IT. I DON'T HAVE THE SAME FEELINGS FOR THEM I HAD BEFORE... THEY CAN VISIT ME IF THEY WANT, BUT I CAN'T FEEL COMFORTABLE WITH THEM AGAIN.

> ***18. In Your Journal:*** Can any generalizations be made about the various responses to Sacco's question?

---

mini-centrale: hydroelectric power source; water-fed generator

---

Ratko Mladic: former commander of Yugoslav National Army and Radovan Karadzic's Army chief throughout the war in Bosnia; indicted for genocide and crimes against humanity by the U.N. War Crimes Tribunal in 1995 and a fugitive for over seven years

contravene: violate; infringe; counter

Mladic's first target was Srebrenica, whose fighters had waged an aggressive war against neighboring Serb villages early in the conflict. Their attacks often were followed by a wave of desperate, hungry Muslim civilians—many of whom had been cleansed from their own communities—looting and burning homes and exacting vengeance on the Serbs they caught.
After an overwhelming Serb offensive in 1993, the enclave's defenders had agreed to a U.N.-monitored demilitarization,* and Srebrenica had become the first U.N. safe area.
Mladic launched his attack on Srebrenica in July 1995. His forces brushed aside the Dutch peacekeepers stationed there and took some of them hostage. The Dutch put up no resistance themselves but called for air support to halt the Serbs six times.
Their requests were turned down or postponed by top U.N. officers, including Janvier personally, even after the Dutch themselves came under attack.
Finally, five days after the first request, two NATO planes made bombing runs. They were ineffective.
The Serbs threatened to kill their Dutch hostages and shell panicked civilians if NATO attacked again.
In any case, it was too late. Bosnian soldiers, who had believed the U.N. would defend the safe area, put up an ineffectual defense.
The Serbs entered Srebrenica.
THERE WAS A VERY BIG PANIC.
Nermin
"I left Srebrenica with other soldiers. The civilians went to Potocari, the main base of U.N. forces..."
THE DE-MILITARIZATION WAS ONLY PARTIALLY FULFILLED.

⁘ **Potocari:** town near Srebrenica with a U.N. peacekeeping camp, where thousands of Muslims fled during the massacre at Srebrenica; the Serbs notoriously began to ship the men out of Potocari for execution, with the apparent compliance of peacekeepers, so many men fled into the woods, attempting to reach Tuzla and Bosnian territory

gantlet (or gauntlet): two facing lines of armed men who attack the person(s) forced to run between them

Konjevic Polje: municipality of Bratunac, north of Srebrenica, near the Bosnian border with Serbia; area where thousands of Muslims were allegedly executed

Over the next few days, the men from Srebrenica, only a third of whom were armed, fell into ambush after ambush as they tried to break through 40 kilometers of Serb-controlled territory.
TUZLA
Drina
KILOMETER SCALE
BOSNIAN-GOVERNMENT CONTROLLED TERRITORY
BOSNIAN-SERB CONTROLLED TERRITORY
KONJEVIC POLJE
BRATUNAC
POTOCARI
SREBRENICA
ZEPA
Both Nermin and Haso claimed the Serbs attacked the column with what they called "combat gas."
Perhaps the incapacitating chemical agent BZ, a benzilate compound, "combat gas" rendered its victims disoriented and hallucinatory, among other effects, they said.*
HASO: "The firing had been going on for 20 minutes. Bosnian soldiers were surrendering to the Serbs. They were not behaving normally—crazy because of the combat gas.
"My neighbor was captured with a large group...more than 3- or 400 soldiers. They were forced to say—
WE ARE SERB SOLDIERS.
WE ARE THE SERB ARMY.
"They were taken away, and I didn't see what happened to them."
NERMIN: "I was with a group of soldiers who'd survived those ambushes and mines. The Chetniks saw us.
SURRENDER! WE'LL MAKE YOU A CORRIDOR TO TUZLA!
"Some people started surrendering. Some started carrying the wounded toward the Chetniks. A lot of them were crazy from combat gas.
"I stayed there in the field... My brother and a couple of friends were with me...
"I wasn't feeling normal...I was suffering from combat gases.
"I didn't know what was happening around me.
"The Chetniks approached and started firing...
* DESPITE MANY EYEWITNESS ACCOUNTS, HUMAN RIGHTS WATCH FOUND EVIDENCE OF GAS ATTACKS "INCONCLUSIVE" THOUGH SUCH ATTACKS "CANNOT BE RULED OUT."

19. *In Your Journal:* How much difference do you think it makes whether the Serbs used "combat gas"?

"Two guys approached me...I didn't know them.
"We were together all night.
"The Chetniks were moving around us.
"I heard crying and screaming in the field. And Chetnik voices. They were shouting–
WHY ARE YOU CRY-ING?
FUCKING ALIJA*!
"We stayed till early morning...The Chetniks called on us to go toward Tuzla.
YOU KNOW THE ROAD...
"The two guys agreed to go with some Serbs—they didn't know they were Serbs.
"I knew so I stayed hidden.
"The Chetniks discovered me.
"One Chetnik started shooting in the air. I pretended nothing was happening.
"They thought the combat gas had damaged my mind...so they left me.
"After 15 minutes I realized there wasn't anyone around...I started moving toward Žepa."
Nermin had given up on reaching Tuzla and joined other stragglers retracing their steps to get to the safe area directly south of Srebrenica.
"I found about 200 men searching for Chetniks to surrender to. I was in a group of 15 people, and they asked if we were surrendering.
"We saw what the Serbs had done. I tried to persuade them not to surrender...
*A REFERENCE TO THE PRESIDENT OF BOSNIA,
IZETBEGOVIC

"The 15 of us moved toward Zepa, but, the rest of them started surrendering."
HASO: "We found another group in the forest and we stayed there for 12 days. I ate only apples for seven days.
"We made the decision to go back toward Srebrenica.
"We saw many dead people. They were soldiers, some old people...
"It was the field of an ambush. They were lying where they were killed.
"The Serbs had put bodies in the forest. Probably they had captured them, killed them, and put them in the forest. One beside another. Some had been killed by gunfire, others by slaughtering."
Nermin and Haso reached Zepa separately after long and dangerous trips.
Back in the Srebrenica enclave, General Mladic and Serb soldiers had walked among Muslim civilians gathered for protection at the U.N. compound.
YOU HAVE NO REASON TO BE AFRAID.
His men dispensed sweets.
The Serbs transported the Muslim women and children to Bosnian government territory. However, while disarmed Dutch peacekeepers watched, hundreds of men in the civilian group were separated and led away.

20. In Your Journal: Are you surprised at all by the level of neutrality of the peacekeepers?

21. *In Your Journal:* Does this scene of carnage seem more or less alarming to you in an illustrated form than it would in a photograph? Explain.

⁘ **Janvier:** (General Bernard) commander of U.N. troops in former Yugoslavia during the war

Many of Zepa's men hid in caves around the town before trekking to Bosnian government territory or technically neutral Serbia.
Nermin and Haso spent almost a month and a half in a cave before joining a group that crossed Serb territory to Gorazde.
That's where I met them.
I asked Nermin if he knew what happened to his brother, from whom he'd been separated in the break-out from Srebrenica.
I DON'T HAVE ANY INFORMATION ABOUT HIM.
I DON'T KNOW IF HE'S DEAD.
The Serbs trucked Haso's mother and sister from Srebrenica to Bosnian government lines, but—
MY FATHER WAS TAKEN FROM THE CONVOY IN BRATUNAC.
I DON'T KNOW WHAT'S HAPPENED TO HIM.
At the end of July 1995, Gorazde was the last remaining U.N.-designated safe area in eastern Bosnia. Said Mladic—
BY THE AUTUMN WE'LL TAKE GORAZDE, BIHAC, AND, IN THE END, SARAJEVO, AND WE'LL FINISH THE WAR IN BOSNIA.
ALL OF US THOUGHT WE WERE NEXT.
"After Srebrenica and Zepa fell, we expected an attack from the other side. We knew what was going on. We were getting Radio Sarajevo and Voice of America.
"During a very heavy shelling of 10 or 15 days, the British soldiers left Gorazde and hid themselves in the deep forest...
"People realized. We didn't have any protection from them.

quagmire: difficult predicament; impossible situation

Yasushi Akashi: U.N. special envoy to Bosnia; accused by the Bosnian government of appeasing the Serbs in order to prevent casualty to U.N. forces

On Aug. 19, the U.N. announced its peacekeepers would soon start withdrawing from Gorazde.
To many in Gorazde, it seemed they were about to be abandoned.
On Aug. 28, one Serb shell killed 38 people in Sarajevo, which earlier had been afforded the same protection guaranteed Gorazde at the London conference.
The next day, the U.N. essentially ceded its authority over air power to U.S.-dominated NATO, which now had a pretext it couldn't pass up.
I WAS IN THE CAMP. IT WAS AFTER-NOON.
"The British had already prepared themselves for a fast evacuation. A captain came and ordered the soldiers to be ready to leave in two hours.
WE HAVE PER-MISSION FROM THE SERB SIDE TO LEAVE THROUGH THEIR TERRI-TORY.
WHAT DOES THIS MEAN? IS THE SAME THING GOING TO HAPPEN TO US THAT HAPPENED TO SREBRENICA AND ZEPA?
NO. IT'S BETTER THIS WAY. NOW OUR AIRPLANES CAN HIT SERB LINES.
"I didn't believe him.
"The British left the camp.
"And people heard. They approached the camp. There was a mass of people. They wanted to take food, gasoline.
"And I told myself, 'The Serbs can see everything. They'll start shelling. They'll kill everyone...'

"I was the first one who could have taken sugar, salt, coffee, batteries for cars, fuel, but I didn't...
"because I thought everything was going to end for us.
"I took my portion of food and left.
"The people came in, started to grab. Behind them came our soldiers, military police, who pushed them away to keep everything for the military.
"It was only a couple of hundred meters to the Serb lines But they didn't shell."
THE NEXT DAY THE AIR STRIKES STARTED.
On Aug. 30, with the Gorazde peacekeepers out of harm's way—and no longer potential hostages—NATO began a two-week bombing campaign against the Bosnian Serbs.
More than the damage they caused, the air attacks demonstrated to the Serbs that the NATO states had unambiguously lined up against them.

Suddenly the military balance in the former Yugoslavia was shifting. Earlier in August the Croatian army had overrun a separatist Serb statelet and chased tens of thousands of Serb refugees into a Serbia worn down by years of U.N. sanctions.

Then, in September and October, a combined Croatian and Bosnian offensive recaptured large amounts of territory from the Serbs in northern Bosnia.

The Bosnian Serbs were reeling and came under pressure from Serbian President Slobodan Milosevic to make peace. A country-wide cease-fire went into effect on Oct. 12. Among its provisions, the Serbs were required to allow U.N. and relief-organization convoys unhindered access to Gorazde.

It was on one of these convoys that I first entered Gorazde.

Final peace talks were set for November in Dayton, Ohio, but the U.S. had already floated ideas for a settlement. The elimination of the Srebrenica and Zepa enclaves played into the hands of those who advocated simplifying the map, including National Security Adviser Anthony Lake. He wanted the Bosnian government to make the map even simpler by swapping Gorazde for Serb-controlled suburbs of Sarajevo.

EVERYONE WAS TALKING ABOUT IT.

"Were they going to trade us for Brcko? Or Banja Luka? Nobody knew exactly what would happen. It was a period when people were confused... nervous.

"At that time, TV crews and everybody were coming with the same question: 'What do you think about that? About being traded?'"

YOU WERE ASKING THOSE QUESTIONS.

22. In Your Journal: Why would the sight of strangers be so upsetting to Sarajevans at this point?

23. In Your Journal: How do you perceive Benetton's opening in Sarajevo after the war? Is it a good sign or bad? What do you think Sacco makes of it?

24. In Your Journal: Why does Sacco include this anecdote about ordering wine? What is it meant to reveal?

25. *In Your Journal:* Compare Edin's resignation to the prospect of future conflicts with his desire to "get on with things." Is there a contradiction here, or can his feelings be reconciled somehow?

BIBLIOGRAPHY

I never intended this book to be a comprehensive overview of the break-up of Yugoslavia and the war in Bosnia. However, I found it necessary to provide some context in order to tell the story of Goražde. I leaned heavily on a number of books for background information.

Noel Malcolm's *Bosnia, A Short History* (New York University Press, 1994) is widely considered a masterpiece of scholarship, and rightly so. I had the pleasure to listen to Mr. Malcolm talk in Sarajevo in late 1995. Unfortunately, he was introduced for an hour by a professor, a parliament member, and a minister and only got 20 minutes to speak himself. He downplayed the role of the historian — his own role — saying that he'd heard a number of British politicians had read his book (Mr. Malcolm is himself British), but that Britain had changed its policy in Bosnia only after America had told it to do so. Anyway, I found Malcolm's section on World War II particularly helpful.

As far as World War II goes, I was also greatly helped by Matteo J. Milazzo's *The Chetnik Movement & The Yugoslav Resistance* (The Johns Hopkins University Press, 1975), which describes the different factions and changing allegiances in excruciating detail. I relied on the very readable *Tito And the Rise and Fall of Yugoslavia* (Carroll & Graf Publishers, Inc., 1994), by Richard West, for information about the Partisans and Tito's post-war Yugoslavia.

Mark Thompson's *A Paper House, The Ending of Yugoslavia* (Vintage, 1992) gave me a good overall feel for Yugoslavia and the thoughts of Yugoslavs at the time of the break-up.

As far as the politics of the disintegration of Yugoslavia, there is no better reference than *Yugoslavia, Death of a Nation* (TV Books, Inc., 1995 and 1996), by Allan Little and Laura Silber, which accompanied a television documentary. Little and Silber interviewed most all the major political players and their book is a triumph of reporting. It was on my desk at all times. I had the pleasure of meeting Ms. Silber in New York City, but she didn't come to a party I invited her to. Another excellent book on the break-up is Misha Glenny's *The Fall of Yugoslavia, The Third Balkan War* (Penguin Books, 1992 and 1993). Glenny has a real understanding of how the Balkans tick, though I read an essay or two by him during the war that pissed me off. I can't remember why.

I did need specific help in understanding the history of the arrangement between the U.N. and NATO in Bosnia and how that arrangement affected the safe areas. Chuck Sudetic's *Blood and Vengeance* (Norton, 1998) and David Rohde's *Endgame* (Farrar, Straus and Giroux, 1997) were more than a little helpful. Both these books, which I consider two of the best to come out of the war, tell the story of the fall of the Srebrenica safe area. Another useful book on Srebrenica is Jan Willem Honig and Norbert Both's *Srebrenica, Record of a War Crime* (Penguin Books, 1996).

For information on the end of the war and the backroom negotiations at the Dayton, Ohio, peace talks, I turned to Richard Holbrooke's *To End a War* (Random House, 1998). Holbrooke was a U.S. assistant secretary of state at the time of Dayton accords, which he helped design.

I am also indebted to the *New York Times* and the *Guardian* newspapers which provided me a day-by-day account of the war in Bosnia.

FOR USE IN DISCUSSION

Questions about Substance

1. Describe the "brotherhood and unity" policy forged by Tito (Josip Broz) in the post-World War II period. What does Edin think of this policy? What does Sacco seem to think of it?
2. Sacco goes into great detail about the complexity of the various conflicts, rather than generalizing about Yugoslavia's political history. What role does all of this detail play in explaining or presenting the war in Bosnia?
3. Do any of the groups in the modern history of Yugoslavia that Sacco presents (e.g., Utasha, the Chetniks, the Partisans, the Serbs, or the Croats) seem particularly innocent in the way they are portrayed? Do there seem to be any clear villains and/or victims among the different factions?
4. Sacco frequently features several non-Yugoslavian reporters speculating about the potential outcomes of the conflict and their ramifications. What point do you think he is trying to make with this theme?
5. Edin, Riki, and Serif are prominently figured characters in Sacco's story. What do they all have in common? How does each character serve an individual purpose in the story?
6. Why do you think Sacco chose to tell this very complicated war history through the lens of a "safe area"? Wouldn't the front lines have provided a more relevant picture?
7. Does this work involve the traditional comic book theme of good versus evil? Explain your answer.

Questions about Structure and Style

1. Review the illustration of the crowds on page 579. How do you think this illustration conveys the setting of this story? How would the imagery have a different effect if conveyed by a photograph rather than an illustration? Describe Sacco's style of illustration in general. What do you like or dislike about it? How is it similar to or different from other illustration styles you may be familiar with?
2. The reader is never able to see Sacco's eyes through his glasses. Why do you think Sacco presents himself in this manner?
3. There are many minor characters (including soldiers, civilian, and journalists) in this book, all of whom get to tell the story of this war from their individual perspectives. Does this technique clarify or confuse the situation for you? Do you think Sacco intends to clarify or complicate the story for his readers?
4. In an interview featured on his publisher's website (*www.fantagraphics. com*), Sacco explains that comics make things "REAL in the reader's eye," in a way that traditional photojournalism may not be capable of (since photojournalism

often relies on one image to sum up an entire story). Do you agree or disagree with this assessment? Explain your response.

5. How does the dialogue between characters interact with the narrator's comments? Is there tension between the two different kinds of texts in Sacco's work, or are they more complementary?
6. Facial expressions seem to be emphasized in Sacco's drawings of the characters here. Find several frames where you think the facial expressions are especially effective. Describe the emotions those expressions convey and how they are conveyed.

Multimedia Suggestions

1. Find the lyrics for or listen to some of the songs Riki sings (the Eagles' "Hotel California," Simon and Garfunkel's "The Boxer," Bruce Springsteen's "Born in the USA," Simon and Garfunkel's "Cecelia," or Leo Sayer's "More Than I Can Say"). Do you find any particular ironies in the lyrics or music in any of Riki's favorite pop tunes?
2. You can get information about the post-war legal activities by the International Court of Justice at *http://www.icj-cij.org/icjwww/idecisions.htm*, and the International War Crimes Tribunal at *http://www.un.org/icty/*. You may be interested in following up on the events you have read about in Sacco's account of the conflict to see who has been indicted and/or convicted of war crimes and/or crimes against humanity.
3. Several films about the war in the former Yugoslavia are available on either VHS or DVD, including *No Man's Land; Welcome to Sarajevo; Shot through the Heart; Yugoslavia: Death of a Nation; Vukovar; Pretty Village, Pretty Flame; While America Watched: The Bosnia Tragedy;* and *The Wounds.* View one or more of these films, and note the way the visual imagery in the film(s) compare(s) to the illustrations in Sacco's work.
4. The United Colors of Benetton—which rushed to establish a new store in Sarajevo right after the war—is a highly controversial clothing company, mostly due to their provocative advertising campaigns. Visit *www.benetton.com* and view the "photo gallery" of advertisements and the "press room" clips featured there. What do you think of Benetton's techniques? Do they have an important social mission or are they merely opportunistic?

SUGGESTIONS FOR WRITING AND RESEARCH

1. In the introduction to Joe Sacco's *Palestine,* Edward Said comments:

> In ways that I still find fascinating to decode, comics in their relentless foregrounding . . . [seem] to say what couldn't otherwise be said, perhaps what [isn't] permitted to be said or imagined, defying

> the ordinary processes of thought, which are policed, shaped and re-shaped by all sorts of pedagogical as well as ideological pressures . . . comics [free] me to think and imagine and see differently.

Apply these comments to this selection of Sacco's work. What kind of "foregrounding" does it involve? How does Sacco "defy" the kind of "policed" thinking to which Said refers? Develop an essay that addresses the ways that the genre of comics is freed from "pedagogical" and/or "ideological pressures," using Sacco's work as an illustration of this freedom.

2. Compare Sacco's work to that of another graphic novelist or comic book author of your choosing. Some potentially rich comparisons could be found in Art Spiegelman's *Maus,* Joe Kubert's *Fax from Sarajevo,* or Marjane Satrapi's *Persepolis.* Consider especially issues related to the subject matter (the particular conflict or plot), the illustrations (level of intricacy, level of realism, tone and mood, etc.), and to the character development. What are the similarities and differences between the artists, and what do these similarities and differences suggest about the subject matter, the genre, or the artists themselves?
3. The main objective of the Serb offensive was seemingly "ethnic cleansing," a term we now know to mean the genocide of an entire population, but which could easily be applied to the Holocaust during World War II, to other "genocides," such as the Hutu murder of Tutsis in Rwanda in 1994, or the massacre of Armenians by the Young Turks in 1915. Do you see much of a difference between a Holocaust, a genocide, an ethnic cleansing campaign, or a mass murder? Or are they all essentially the same thing? How important is the language we use to describe such actions? What is it we are trying to achieve by putting all of these atrocities into different categories? And how do you think that graphic illustrators perceive such linguistic distinctions? What can we learn about *language* from illustrators like Joe Sacco?

WORKING WITH CLUSTERS

Cluster 4: Conceiving Death

Cluster 7: Holocausts and Histories

Cluster 12: Visual Language

Discipline: The Humanities

Rhetorical Mode: Narration

"Some Kind of Cleansing" (from *Welcome to My Country: A Therapist's Memoir of Madness*)

by Lauren Slater

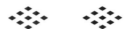

Lauren Slater is a psychotherapist and writer living in the Boston area. She received an M.A. in Psychology from Harvard University and a Ph.D. from Boston University. In addition to Welcome to My Country: A Therapist's Memoir of Madness *(from which this select is drawn), her books include:* Prozac Diary, Lying: A Metaphorical Memoir, *and* Love Works Like This: Moving from One Kind of Life to Another. *She has won the New Letters Literary Award, The Missouri Review Award, and has been chosen five times for The Best American Essays. She has also been published in* Rosie, Elle, Self, New York Times Magazine, Nerve.com, Salon.com, *and several other periodicals. Most of her work can be characterized as either memoir or creative non-fiction, and she has been both lauded and criticized for pushing the boundaries of those genres.*

No one knows for sure why the **schizophrenic** has such a hard time with words, why so little of his language makes sense. Ask him how the weather is and he might tell you, *Frogs be flying a green way.* Ask him about the Yankees game he stares at on the TV screen and he could well respond, *Pastimes that glump up are good.* Is this mumbo jumbo due to a dysfunction of the parietal lobe, that crescent of gray matter in the center of our skulls, or to some other kind of **neuronal** collapse? Or is it due to the schizophrenic's mother, who, early on, tongue-tied him with an overbearing love? People cannot definitively say. And we cannot go to the sources themselves, the actual schizophrenics, because they will babble or write a reason so jumbled it will hurt our own heads. I touch my own head, feel its spherical shape, feel the pulse of my voice pass from axon to dendrite and finally emerge from my mouth in blessed sentences. I watch as I press a series of separate keys on this computer and up through the gas plasma screen drifts a story for you. And for me. In this way we join. The ability to use words, to tell a story, is so central to having human relationships that I find myself wondering how someone with schizophrenic illness survives the loss. When the men I work with weep or scream or clench their hands, I think they are mourning their muteness. There's frustration on their faces. As they attempt to talk, I sometimes try to catch glimpses of their tongues, expecting to see not the limber red scalpel that shapes a sentence, but a flapping gray thing, loose and dead.

neuronal: pertaining to nerve cells, which control the basic functioning of the nervous system

Of all the tongue-tied schizophrenics I know, Joseph D'Agostino stands out for me as an **effigy** of suffering. Joseph is forty-six years old. He has a mangy black beard in which lice like to live, and on some days he wears a floppy bow tie, on other days an army helmet and a green shirt with fake medals of honor dangling from the pockets. Although he claims to have crouched in the foxholes of World War I and sloshed through the jungles of Vietnam, Joseph, in actuality, has never been to war in the way we know it. The terrors live within him; the bombs are bursts of dopamine that sting the raw ravines of his brain.

effigy: image that embodies the essence or epitome of something; model

1. In Your Journal: What sense is there in Joseph's claim to have served in World War I and Vietnam?

·⁘· **schizophrenia:** severe psychiatric disorder affecting the coherence of the personality, with symptoms of emotional instability, detachment from reality, and withdrawal into the self. Symptoms can include psychosis, delusions, hallucinations, disorganized thinking and speech, catatonic behavior, trouble with basic life activities (e.g., work, hygiene), and heightened symptoms during stressful times

I encountered Joseph—with whom I was to do individual therapy—during my first week on the ward. He was also one of the six men in my group, which had just gathered for the first time. I was slowly starting to adjust to the place, to the long scrubbed corridors and the drone of the TV perched high in a corner of the kitchen. To the patients who, in their free time, sat on the deck smoking endless packs of cigarettes and lecturing to invisible students. The ward was, of course, bizarre, the banal noise of daytime TV game shows mixed in with shrieks and fantastic tales about harems of wives who climbed through windows each night.

Before he got sick, Joseph lived out much of his life in Boston's **North End,** that small Italian community crammed into one corner of the city. As a neighborhood, the North End is known for its coherence; families stay together, oftentimes great aunts and grandparents living in the same apartments as their younger offspring. Joseph's upbringing was that way. I didn't learn these details from him, of course, but from his sister, Vickie, who sometimes came to visit him, and from the voluminous hospital charts kept in the locked cabinet of the staff room.

> ***2. In Your Journal:*** What contrast do you think Slater might be trying to draw between the hospital ward and the North End of Boston?

He applied and was accepted to Princeton, the first child in his immigrant family to go off to college. I do not know how he felt, with such a load of expectations on his back. I do not know if the duffel bags he carried off that first semester were weighted more with the family's hopes than with his clothes. Grandmothers, aunts, siblings, neighbors, saw him off at the bus terminal. And it must have seemed like a slash, like a cruel sort of severance, one moment lodged in the tiny nest of some city, the next moment released into the ivy air, facing a sprawling green campus and kids who owned their own cars. He wanted to be a literary critic or a social psychologist.

Instead, four weeks into that first semester at Princeton, he started to stare at things and laugh. ("In one class, the professor told us, he kept flapping his hand in front of his face, over and over again.") By the eighth week he was smoking several joints a day and not coming out of his room. He got into a fight with a dorm mate and put his fist through a window. Just before Christmas, when the ivy had fallen, stripped veins clinging to the sides of buildings, he confided to a friend that there were microphones hidden inside the stems.

He left on a bus for Christmas break. I wonder what he saw, driving back through the countryside, dry clouds scraping the sky. I feel great fear

---

❖ **North End:** the oldest neighborhood in Boston, covering one densely populated square mile and dating back to the 17th century; by 1920, its population was 90 percent Italian-American, and it remains a world-renowned center for Italian cuisine; often characterized as a close-knit community with very strong family relationships, an emphasis on Catholic traditions, and a commitment to historical preservation

3. *In Your Journal:* Why does Slater try to imagine Joseph's ride home for Christmas break? How is this description intended to help the reader?

for him at this point in our story. I think about the brown blades of winter in the barren fields, maybe the first snow starting to fall, each flake, in his eyes, articulated to the point of pain, white prongs, a dazzle of frozen lace.

Was he looking for warmth, for a way to connect with a world that had suddenly slipped from him? Is that why, once home, he walked into his family's living room and, in front of mother, father, aunts, unbuckled his pants and exposed himself? "Look at me," he wailed, tugging at his penis. His father leapt up and slapped him. The mother wept. His report card came a few days later, a slew of D's, and F's.

He never went back to Princeton. For a long time after that he did not go out of the North End at all. He was overcome by delusions and hallucinations, and his speech deteriorated. His clothes got grungy and he would tramp home at two A.M. smelling of booze and back alleys. The family sought professional help, frequently had him hospitalized, but nothing worked. Years passed. Horrified, the father shunned him, would not allow this disheveled son into the family's restaurant. The mother drew even closer to him, bathing her boy, combing his matted hair, and dressing him in a neat black suit to wear to the father's funeral when Salvatore finally passed away. After that, with the other children grown and gone, the oldest son now running the restaurant, just Joseph and his mother lived together, she doing everything for him while he paced and ranted in his room. He lost the ability to wash his hair, make a meal. Down in the kitchen, she fried eggs for him, smooth white globes of wholeness she would crack against the side of a pan, watch the shocking yellow innards spill, sizzle.

After Joseph's mother died and there was no one to take care of him, the sister and brother placed him here, in this inner-city residential unit located four trolley stops from the North End. Because the unit is open, the men—unless they are suicidal—can come and go as they please, without escort. Without escort, then, Joseph, in between groups and individual therapy, often likes to ride the trolley back to his old neighborhood. Perhaps he even goes to the house where he once lived, sees in the windowpane's reflection the fragile face of his mother. At work, when I look at him sitting in that spare bedroom, I try to imagine who he could have been. I focus on his chapped wet mouth, and in my mind I sculpt its lines smooth. I bend over and blow the duff from his fogged eyes. For me, it is hard to match the Joseph I now know—the frustrated, word-bound man—with the bright boy who so loved language, who, with a **Boston Latin High School** pencil, could shape letters into moving compositions.

Like other schizophrenics, Joseph suffered from overinclusion, so that his stories contained bits of everything that came to nothing. Sometimes his sentences were so broad they spanned eons of time, as in: "Wind mov-

---

Boston Latin High School: prestigious, highly competitive public exam school ing the grass where daddy rooster goes licking the skyscraper. I once rode up to the top and looked way down. Hi!" But Joseph's tendency toward overinclusion showed itself best in the way he packed for a camping trip the ward manager took the boys on late in August, about a year after I'd started on the unit. Going away for only two days, Joseph took it upon himself to pack five suitcases, four duffel bags, and a tower of crates. He brought all of his blankets, every pair of shoes, the pillows on his bed, the light-bulbs from the lamp, a fan, a hammer, a hole puncher, and two quarts of antifreeze. He appeared in front of the van with all of this stuff, and it took staff two hours to return the excess, marching up and down the unit's stairs.

How can you understand and connect to a man through whom the whole world sweeps and speaks, and how can that man understand and connect to you? That was the question informing my therapy with Joseph. Despite the plethora of words, ours was a silent journey, static everywhere we turned. Joseph wrote continually, compulsively. If I tried to get him to put down his pencil and speak with me, he would moan and pick it back up again. If I asked him to write me how he was feeling, he produced a tome of chaos. Why was he doing this? Was his **hypergraphia** some mere neurological twitch, or a way to contain anxiety, or, what I most believed, a desperate and perpetually failing plea to become what he once was, a storyteller, a social participant whose words would break the barrier of isolation and thrust him into community? That is what we all want our stories, however meager, to do. With Joseph it didn't work.

> ***4. In Your Journal:*** How does this essay begin to examine the general relationship between story and community through the example of Joseph?

hypergraphia: syndrome causing a compulsive need to write

Sometimes I stared and stared at his sentences. And I could find within them half-formed ideas, a growing pattern of thought that aborted itself in messy clots. All of our sessions took place in that spare bedroom, he bent over the desk, I standing by his side, watching powerlessly as he, because of some undefined illness, wrote walls and walls of babel around his body.

> ***5. In Your Journal:*** Slater describes Joseph's sentences as miscarriages ("aborted . . . messy clots"). What do you think is the connection in her mind?

Until at last, one day, frustrated by the hypergraphia that kept me so severed from him, I leaned forward, plucked up the pencil, and scrawled my way right onto his page.

"The church," Joseph had written in his tilted letters, "is where the peropper people go. Worms sleep inside of me, all clouds and test tubes."

"I once went to church," I wrote back in careful large script. "I was only six, and I remember seeing Jesus on a cross on the wall."

Joseph turned his head and looked up at me, his mouth agape. He stared at me holding his pencil, and then he swiveled himself slowly and peered at the page where I had put my writing next to his. The room got strangely silent. I waited to see what would happen. I had been trying to begin a correspondence, somehow cross into his space. My gesture didn't have quite the effect I'd hoped for. Joseph kept staring and staring at my sentences, his eyes widening. Instead of writing back, he uncurled one grimy index finger and started to stroke the letters, my plump *o,* the sophisticated shape of my *s.* I was reminded of the way some ladies will stroke diamonds on the jeweler's velvet trays or put pearls to their powdered cheeks, longing in every movement. My letters next to Joseph's, I then realized, were jewels to him, crafted shapes that gleamed with sense. He kept tracing and retracing them, as though through touch he might absorb their gifts. "You are a doctor," he murmured, still fingering the shapes, "Pretty pretty."

He looked up at me then. "I once could," he said. He stopped.

"Could what, Joseph?"

He set his mouth in a bitter line and shook his head. He went back to patting my sentences. "I once could," he said again. Sadness in his voice. "You went to school, Doctor," he said.

I nodded my head yes.

"Harvard," Joseph said. "Your school was Harvard."

And I nodded again, because he happened to be right.

He snatched away his hand then, shoved it between his knees. "Harvard," Joseph said. "Harvard Harvard Harvard." He chanted and rocked, the rocking motions strengthening and I, suddenly scared, wondering what I'd set off in him.

"I, too," he shouted.

"I know," I said.

"I, too!" he bellowed, and he leaned back over the page to fondle my letters. "Bloomsbury," he spit. **"Bloomsbury in bedlam."**

With misgivings, but because Joseph had agitated for several weeks to go back to a university, we finally, with funding from the Massachusetts Rehabilitation Commission, helped him register for two courses at an open-admissions school known for the diversity of its students—Admiral's Hill Community College. Located in a rough section of Charlestown, this community college boasted "an acceptance of students from all walks of life, from all over the globe. English and non-English speakers, old and young, handicapped people of all persuasions, are welcome here." We hoped Joseph would be welcome. We were not at all convinced. He wouldn't sign releases allowing us to talk to the school about his particular disabilities. And he chose, not surprisingly, some of the most demanding courses in social psychology and creative writing, two disciplines based on narrative, its creation and interpretation.

> ***6. In Your Journal:*** What is the significance of Joseph's choice of courses based on *narrative*?

"Bloomsbury in bedlam": The Bloomsbury Group was a social club in London in the early 20th century which included Modernist writers like Virginia Woolf and E.M. Forster, as well as artists and other intellectuals. Bedlam was the nickname for England's first mental institution (Bethlehem Royal Hospital) founded in Kent in the 13th century

In the four days before classes started, Joseph stayed busy. He spent his entire Social Security disability check on a briefcase, a suit, a pair of shoes, and, finally, an Aladdin lunch box. On the Tuesday after Labor Day he came downstairs for breakfast scrubbed and shining, the *first time* in years. He sported a fresh white shirt, Italian leather loafers, and a corduroy coat, and carried a brown briefcase and the lunch box, full to bursting not with food but with his fake army medals.

Eventually, I examined the papers Joseph wrote for his classes. Of course, on most of them were mad scribbles, but some of them were stories he had tried to write, stories marred by a teacher's red pen. As I had so many times before, I peered at his sentences and paragraphs and saw glimmers of coherence in some of them, half-uttered themes that bled away into chaos. How could I tease sense from the shambles? And the shambles themselves, they did have a kind of haunting poetry that, I suspected, was so unsatisfying to Joseph because he appeared to have no control over it. The man could, without quite meaning to, write a tilted e. e. cummings–type paragraph, but not a simple shopping list. An odd kind of curse, no doubt. And then I saw that one of the papers was a multiple-choice quiz from the social psychology class. The grade was an F. "You have to pick one," the teacher had written across the top of the paper, and, looking down the columns, I saw that Joseph, too much in love with the world—the man through whom the whole world sweeps and speaks—had circled every choice, all possibilities existing.

7. *In your Journal:* Describe Slater's reaction to Joseph's multiple choice test. How does she interpret his incorrect answers?

"Yes, I am failing," he said when we asked him the next morning.

"Do you want to stop? You can always stop."

"I want to stop failing," he said.

Again, I looked over some of his writings. One of his sentences read, "Going back to school is a keyboard to the excellence exciting and I want to walk down the paths to the black flag beating blackboard."

8. *In your Journal:* How does Slater reveal a change in her attitude toward Joseph's writing here? Why do you think this change is significant?

Instead of looking at this sentence as crazy gibberish, I inspected it with the assumption that it was a coherent, meaningful unit, fallen victim to the break-through of mental dust.

Acting as Joseph's filter, I cleaned up the sentence without changing any words. The sentence now read, "Going back to school is (a keyboard to the excellence) exciting and I want to walk down the paths to the (black flag beating) blackboard."

The parentheses enclosed what I took to be the mental detritus. Further scrubbing would give us: "Going back to school is exciting. I want to walk to the blackboard."

I was excited. I felt I had found something, made some sort of small discovery. A strong swath of sense really might run through many of Joseph's writings, the sediment and digressions giving them the appearance of chaos when in fact the writings were merely unedited. I tried this editing with another group of sentences, but it didn't work so easily. I had to change a lot. The sentences originally read:

> I have trouble structuring my time but I will be a gift wrapper at Jordan Marsh maybe. That's because going to Welfare is being on a treasure hunt where I eat fish and popsicles. Very confusing. Sophie got it for me. Having a job is so I don't fall into the void. It makes me feel luckyish.

Here the meaning was harder to find and, unless one knew the details of Joseph's life, reconstructing the narrative would have been difficult, if not impossible. I, however, happened to know that one of the aides had been telling Joseph that he had difficulty with free time and, because of this, she was trying to get him a job at Jordan Marsh gift wrapping for the Christmas season. I suspected that Welfare, where he went to get his check each month—a building full of labyrinthine corridors and ticking clocks—somehow symbolized for Joseph a chaotic, unstructured experience. Thematically, then, the whole narrative did actually fit together. If I, acting as a bit more than a filter now, cut the welfare part and added a few left-out details and some syntactical structure, the "story" jumped into view. After I worked with it, clearing up the cluttered grammar while trying to preserve the meaning, it read:

> **9. *In your Journal:*** What does Slater's editing of Joseph reveal about herself? Would you edit Joseph's work any differently?

> I have trouble structuring my time and that's why I will get a job being a gift wrapper at Jordan Marsh. My counselor Sophie will help me. I don't fall into the void if I have a job. That makes me feel luckyish.

During our session that day, I asked Joseph to write me about the things he most feared. He grabbed his pen and started his frantic scribbling, and it looked like this:

> I fear fear is fear fear fear itself fear and the invisible people in the Teddy Bear Lounge. They have all kinds of colors and I fear they are around me everywhere to go back and forth on a dream eddie talking. Where the water goes and a high cliff comes. Church is a living crab. About me and talking back at me. Everyone. They enter my mind and distract me. And I've yes always wanted to enhance myself in the present tense. They have heads and a line for a neck. Two arms and two legs. Like a geeeee!!! Charlie Brown Character!!! Their shape is distorted by . . .

And here Joseph stopped writing, started to rock. "By what, Joseph?" I asked. "Go on. Their shape is distorted by what?"

By reds and greens and white and yellllowing the people have a girl curve feminine adventure and are GHOSSTLEY.

I had to struggle for the meaning in this one too. I had to make some assumptions about what was parenthetical and could be cut, and what was central. I had to build some verbal bridges. The work was similar to translation when the translator does not know the native language completely, and so has to guess from context. Nevertheless, I believed that, primarily by cutting and cleaning, I had allowed the spirit of the piece to emerge intact, and after I'd shaped it into stanzas, it read:

I fear fear itself
I fear invisible people
They have all kinds of colors
I fear they are around me, talking back at me
They enter my mind and
Distract me
They have heads
A line for a neck
Two arms
Two legs
Like a Charlie Brown Character
Their shape is distorted
By reds and greens, whites and yellows
The people have a girl curve
Feminine adventure and are
Ghostly

A beautiful poem, I thought, written, I thought, by Joseph. He later titled it "Secret Illusion." The next day I showed it to him. "Here," I said. "Here is what you did." He took the page I'd written on, scanned it, and his mouth dropped as he recognized his words, cleaned and shaped. "Oh," he said. "Oh. My. Mine." He smiled.

"Yes, yours. Another?"

"Yes."

"Your earliest memory," I said. "Write me about your earliest memory."

And again, later on that night at my desk, I took his scrambled prose and this time, instead of using a pen, I typed it up. As I cut and cleaned I felt invigorated, and close to Joseph for the first time during our treatment. The wall of **babel** separating him from me was gone for a while. I could see him. His pain and hopes came clear to me. Joseph.

babel: confusion of sounds or languages

Pruned, his memory piece read:

I remember being washed in the sink. It's my very first realization. It's the first memory I have of being in my family's house, being my mother's son. She washed me in the sink. I remember a few of the things she said as she washed me. "Son, please beware of bad things." She said that. And that's when I was taught right from wrong. It was some kind of cleansing. She washed me in the sink every Tuesday. My mother used to give me a lot of comfort when raising me. My mother gave me a cat called Buffy. I have a picture of him and I lost it. I'm sorry I lost it.

My mom has black hair, curly. She looks like me. My mother would test me for a headache and a fever when I was young. She took very good care of me. She looked out for colds and toothaches. She always touched me. I ran in my mother's bed when I had nightmares and we would sleep together with the cat Buffy too. Dad was in the restaurant.

My mother took a heart attack a few years ago. I found her in the room, on the floor. I gave her mouth to mouth and then I called the police. I said, "My mother's on the floor." That's when my mind got worse. I got even more confused and needed structure. I started to hallucinate, the illusory things.

When I was in the sink, being washed, it was always dark. I think I felt safe in that darkness.

I don't know where she went.

10. *In your Journal:* How do you suppose Slater would answer these questions she puts to the reader?

Is this Joseph's real work? Can such a scrambled man take credit for a piece of prose so simplified, so smoothed? Who is *really* the author of this tale, that poem, Joseph or me? And another question: The chunks I've cut out, are they not important too, raw bits of his id tossed away like the thick fat the butcher prunes with his blades?

perjury: willingly false assertion

And while he did finally have to drop his social psychology course, he stayed with the creative writing, passing it at the end of the semester. Sometimes I wondered what his teacher would have thought had she known my role in his writings. Would she have accused him—and me—of artistic **perjury**? I don't know at what point one can call a story truly one's own, where the boundaries between one mind and another's meet. I can't say that the pages you have before you here come from only me, for at every point the words—which pass from *my* axons to *my* dendrites and finally emerge in blessed sentences—are tangled in Joseph's rhythms and history, as well as in my own. Perhaps narratives are the one realm that cannot ever—despite the consumerism and capitalism in the publishing industry—be confidently claimed by any individual. I am not sure.

What I am sure of, though, is the expression on Joseph's face when I showed him the edited version of the tale Joseph called "Culture of My Mother." "You typed it up, you typed it up," he cried, as though seeing his words in print, his words graced by the daisy wheel real authors use, meant as much to him as the words themselves. "You typed it up, you typed it up," he kept chanting, and then suddenly he stopped. He held the paper up to the light as, a long time ago, his father had held up his report cards, inspecting their wondrous contents. For a second, then, he was his father and his son; he was tossed back to a past where there was hope and a wider world. And at the same time I noticed the paper I'd used was very fine—onion-skin—and the light in the spare bedroom filtered through it, showing us the grains and watermarked stamp that ran like crazy currents beneath the ordered words, all that commotion threatening to well up through the streamlined sentences.

"Hello," Joseph said to the page. "Hello, my mother. My words."

Then he began to cry, softly, his face turning a tender shade of red. I wanted to hold him as his mother might have, but there is only so much you can do for a patient, only so much hurt you can heal. This is what is hard about my work, knowing when to exit, knowing there are times you must take a soft touch, fingers formed into a strainer, and bring them back to your own body. Separate again.

> ***11. In your Journal:*** Why does Joseph greet his words as if they are people ("Hello, my words")?

FOR USE IN CLASS DISCUSSION

Questions about Substance

1. On page (638), Slater describes the language problem that many schizophrenics experience. Does she reveal her own relationship to language while doing so?
2. Slater uses a lot of metaphors. Locate some of the more vivid metaphors she creates and analyze their significance.
3. Examine the way Slater describes what she imagines Joseph's first moments at Princeton to be like. What further details about Joseph's first semester at college would you like to have?
4. Slater includes anecdotes and other concrete details that she could not possibly know about (e.g. the image of Joseph's mother frying eggs on (640). What purpose do such inclusions serve, in your best estimation?
5. Twice Slater describes Joseph as someone "through whom the whole world sweeps and speaks" (641 and 643). Why is this image so important to her? What does it signify?
6. Examine the list of supplies with which Joseph arms himself when he is going back to school (643). What do you think each of the items might represent, in terms of Joseph's past and his hopes for the future?
7. "Perhaps narratives are the one realm that cannot ever—despite the consumerism and capitalism in the publishing industry—be confidently claimed by any individual" (646). What does this passage mean? How does it relate to Slater's own writing?

8. Slater shapes one of Joseph's pieces into a poem he calls "Secret Illusion" (645). Does the poetic form seem particularly appropriate to Joseph's ideas? Why or why not?

Questions about Structure and Style

1. Analyze Slater's opening paragraph. What first impression of her subject matter would she like the reader to have? Explain your answer.
2. At what points in her narrative does Slater provide samples of Joseph's writing? Describe the function these samples provide in a structural sense. In what ways do the samples help you understand Joseph better? In what ways do the samples make him even more difficult to know?
3. Many times this essay reminds us that Joseph is not its only subject. Slater frequently refers to her own feelings, she calls her essay "our story" (640), Joseph's ideas her "discovery" (643). Who do you think this essay is about? Who is it written for?
4. How would you characterize the Slater's ability/intention to organize her story about (Joseph's) disorganization? Does she intend for you to see a contrast in the structure she uses to present Joseph's lack of structure?

Multimedia Suggestions

1. View the HBO film *The Living Museum* (1998) to see how some mentally ill artists talk about the way they express themselves. The director of the museum calls art "therapeutic . . . in that it can change your identity from a mental patient to that of an artist." How is this kind of art therapy similar to what Slater was trying to accomplish with her patient? Since artists do not have "editors," is their work inherently more authentic than Joseph's? How is writing different from visual art? How is it similar?
2. Listen to the music of Sepultura's album *Schizophrenia* and think about how it may or may not evoke the experience of a schizophrenic. Do you see indications of "overinclusion" or other illustrations of the "word salad" Slater refers to? Can non-schizophrenics write effectively about the experience of this disease? Lyrics available at: *www.darklyrics.com*, *www.purelyrics.com*, or *www.rocklyricsonline.com*.
3. Watch the film *A Beautiful Mind* (2001). Compare John Nash's relationship to mathematics with Joseph's relationship to language.

SUGGESTIONS FOR WRITING AND RESEARCH

1. E.L. Doctorow said that "Writing is a socially acceptable form of schizophrenia." Many others have used schizophrenia as a metaphor for the experience of having a divided personality or mind. Is this a fair or accurate use of metaphor? Is Slater's use of her subject in any way metaphoric? Write an essay presenting

your opinion of the use of mental disorders as metaphors for more universal experiences.

2. Write an essay in which you trace and analyze the editing job that Slater does for Joseph. Examine the "before" and "after" excerpts, and describe the substantive and thematic differences between the two. Does Slater "find" Joseph's true meaning or does she make her own? Support your argument with lots of evidence from the text.
3. What is Slater's definition of language? Review the ways she discusses and *uses* language before answering. Do you think her relationship to language (and thus the way she perceives other people's relationships to language) is enigmatic or commonplace? Use examples from the text to support your answer.

WORKING WITH CLUSTERS

Cluster 3: Reading Meaning, Achieving Literacy
Cluster 8: Metaphor and Truth
Cluster 17: Dis-Ability and Dis-Ease
Cluster 19: Structuring Chaos
Discipline: The Social Sciences
Rhetorical Mode: Narration

"The Daily Me" and "The Neighborhood Me" (from *Republic.com*)

by Cass Sunstein

A Professor at University of Chicago Law School, Cass Sunstein is the author and editor of copious books and articles related to issues of Constitutional law, including Republic.com, *from which these excerpts are taken. His work spans topics from free speech to cloning to economic policy, but all address the relationship between law and human behavior. His most recent book is* Risk and Reason: Safety, Law, and the Environment.

THE DAILY ME

It is some time in the future. Technology has greatly increased people's ability to "filter" what they want to read, see, and hear. General interest newspapers and magazines are largely a thing of the past. The same is true of broadcasters. The idea of choosing "channel 4" or instead "channel 7" seems positively ***quaint.*** *With the aid of a television or computer screen, and the Internet, you are able to design your own newspapers and magazines. Having dispensed with broadcasters, you can choose your own video programming, with movies, game shows, sports, shopping, and news of your choice. You mix and match.*

quaint: charmingly old-fashioned

1. In Your Journal: What do you think of Sunstein's vision of the future presented in this introduction?

2. In Your Journal: Respond to Sunstein's description of customized newspapers: "Without any difficulty, you are able to see exactly what you want to see, no more and no less." Does this appeal to you? Why or why not?

You need not come across topics and views that you have not sought out. Without any difficulty, you are able to see exactly what you want to see, no more and no less.

Maybe you want to focus on sports all the time, and to avoid anything dealing with business or government. It is easy for you to do exactly that. Perhaps you choose replays of famous football games in the early evening, live baseball from New York at night, and college basketball on the weekends. If you hate sports, and want to learn about the Middle East in the evening and watch old situation comedies late at night, that is easy too. If you care only about the United States, and want to avoid international issues entirely, you can restrict yourself to material involving the United States. So too if you care only about New York, or Chicago, or California, or Long Island.

Perhaps you have no interest at all in "news." Maybe you find "news" impossibly boring. If so, you need not see it at all. Maybe you select programs and stories involving only music and weather. Or perhaps you are more specialized still, emphasizing opera, or Beethoven, or the Rolling Stones, or modern dance, or some subset of one or more of the above.

If you are interested in politics, you may want to restrict yourself to certain points of view, by hearing only from people you like. In designing your preferred newspaper, you choose among conservatives, moderates, liberals, vegetarians, the religious right, and socialists. You have your favorite columnists; perhaps you want to hear from them, and from no one else. If so, that is entirely feasible with a simple "point and click." Or perhaps you are interested in only a few topics. If you believe that the most serious problem is gun control, or global warning, or lung cancer, you might spend most of your time reading about that problem, if you wish, from the point of view that you like best.

Of course everyone else has the same freedom that you do. Many people choose to avoid news altogether. Many people restrict themselves to their own preferred points of view—liberals watching and reading mostly or only liberals; moderates, moderates; conservatives, conservatives; neo-Nazis, neo-Nazis. People in different states, and in different countries, make predictably different choices.

> *3. In Your Journal:* What do you think "what you like" has to do with what is news or what is newsworthy?

The resulting divisions run along many lines—of race, religion, ethnicity, nationality, wealth, age, political conviction, and more. Most whites avoid news and entertainment options designed for African-Americans. Many African-Americans focus largely on options specifically designed for them. So too with Hispanics. With the reduced importance of the general interest magazine and newspaper, and the flowering of individual programming design, different groups make fundamentally different choices.

> *4. In Your Journal:* Sunstein says that in terms of news seeking, "different groups make fundamentally different choices." Why doesn't Sunstein approve of this practice?

The market for news, entertainment, and information has finally been perfected. Consumers are able to see exactly what they want. When the power to filter is unlimited, people can decide, in advance and with perfect accuracy, what they will and will not encounter. They can design something very much like a communications universe of their own choosing.

PERSONALIZATION AND DEMOCRACY

Our communications market is rapidly moving in the direction of this apparently utopian picture. As of this writing, many newspapers, including the *Wall Street Journal*, allow readers to create "personalized" electronic editions, containing exactly what they want, and excluding what they do not want. If you are interested in getting help with the design of an entirely personalized paper, you can consult an ever-growing number of Websites, including individual.com (helpfully named!) and crayon.com (a less helpful name, but evocative in its own way).

In reality, we are not so very far from complete personalization of the system of communications. Consider just a few examples.

- Broadcast.com has "compiled hundreds of thousands of programs so you can find the one that suits your fancy. . . . For example, if you want to see all the latest fashions from France twenty-four hours of the day you can get them. If you're from Baltimore living in Dallas and you want to listen to WBAL, your hometown station, you can hear it."[1]
- Sonicnet.com allows you to create your own musical universe, consisting of what it calls "Me Music." Me Music is a "place where you can listen to the music you love on the radio station YOU create . . . A

place where you can watch videos of your favorite artists and new artists."

- Zatso.com allows users to produce "a personal newscast." Its intention is to create a place "where you decide what's news." Your task is to tell "what TV news stories you're interested in," and Zatso.com turns that information into a specifically designed newscast. From the main "This is the News I Want" menu, you can choose stories with particular words and phrases, or you can select topics, such as sports, weather, crime, health, government/politics, and much more.
- Info Xtra offers "news and entertainment that's important to you," and it allows you to find this "without hunting through newspapers, radio and websites." Personalized news, local weather, and "even your daily horoscope or winning lottery number" will be delivered to you once you specify what you want and when you want it.

5. In Your Journal: Describe how you presently take "ultimate control over your viewing" of news, entertainment, and information.

- TiVo, a television recording system, is designed, in the words of its Website, to give "you the ultimate control over your TV viewing." It does this by putting "you at the center of your own TV network, so you'll always have access to whatever you want, whenever you want." TiVo "will automatically find and digitally record your favorite programs every time they air" and will help you create "your personal TV line-up." It will also learn your tastes, so that it can "suggest other shows that you may want to record and watch based on your preferences."
- Intertainer, Inc. provides "home entertainment services on demand," not limited to television but also including music, movies, and shopping. Intertainer is intended for people who want "total control" and "personalized experiences." It is "a new way to get whatever movies, music, and television you want anytime you want on your PC or TV."
- George Bell, the chief executive officer of the search engine Excite, exclaims, "We are looking for ways to be able to lift chunks of content off other areas of our service and paste them onto your personal page so you can constantly refresh and update that 'newspaper of me.' About 43 percent of our entire user data base has personalized their experience on Excite."[2]

6. In Your Journal: What would your "newspaper of me" contain?

If you put the words "personalized news" in any search engine, you will find vivid evidence of what is happening. And that is only the tip of the iceberg.[3] Thus MIT technology specialist Nicholas Negroponte prophecies the emergence of "the Daily Me"—a communications package that is personally designed, with each component fully chosen in advance.[4]

Many of us are applauding these developments, which obviously increase individual convenience and entertainment. But in the midst of the applause, we should insist on asking some questions. How will the increasing power of private control affect democracy? How will the Internet, the new forms of television, and the explosion of communications options alter the capacity of citizens to govern themselves? What are the social preconditions for a well-functioning system of democratic deliberation, or for individual freedom itself?

> *7. In Your Journal:* How would you respond to Sunstein's questions here?

My purpose is to cast some light on these questions. I do so by emphasizing the most striking power provided by emerging technologies: *the growing power of consumers to filter what they see.* In the process of discussing this power, I will attempt to provide a better understanding of the meaning of freedom of speech in a democratic society.

A large part of my aim is to explore what makes for a well-functioning system of free expression. Above all, I urge that in a diverse society, such a system requires far more than restraints on government censorship and respect for individual choices. For the last decades, this has been the preoccupation of American law and politics, and indeed the law and politics of many other nations as well, including, for example, Germany, France, England, and Israel. Censorship is indeed a threat to democracy and freedom. But an exclusive focus on government censorship produces serious blind spots. In particular, a well-functioning system of free expression must meet two distinctive requirements.

> *8. In Your Journal:* Can you imagine what Sunstein alludes to by suggesting that there are non-governmental forms of censorship?

First, people should be exposed to materials that they would not have chosen in advance. Unplanned, unanticipated encounters are central to democracy itself. Such encounters often involve topics and points of view that people have not sought out and perhaps find quite irritating. They are important partly to ensure against fragmentation and extremism, which are predictable outcomes of any situation in which like-minded people speak only with themselves. I do not suggest that government should force people to see things that they wish to avoid. But I do contend that in a democracy deserving the name, people often come across views and topics that they have not specifically selected.

Second, many or most citizens should have a range of common experiences. Without shared experiences, a heterogeneous society will have a much more difficult time in addressing social problems. People may even find it hard to understand one another. Common experiences, emphatically including the common experiences made possible by the media, provide a form of social glue. A system of communications that radically diminishes the number of such experiences will create a number of problems, not least because of the increase in social fragmentation.

> *9. In Your Journal:* Do you agree that "shared experiences" are necessary in a heterogeneous society? Why or why not?

As preconditions for a well-functioning democracy, these requirements hold in any large nation. They are especially important in a heterogeneous nation, one that faces an occasional risk of fragmentation. They have all the more importance as each nation becomes increasingly global and each citizen becomes, to a greater or lesser degree, a "citizen of the world."[5]

nostalgia: longing reminiscence

idyllic: peaceful, heavenly

An insistence on these two requirements should not be rooted in **nostalgia** for some supposedly **idyllic** past. With respect to communications, the past was hardly idyllic. Compared to any other period in human history, we are in the midst of many extraordinary gains, not least from the standpoint of democracy itself. For us, nostalgia is not only unproductive but also senseless. Nor should anything here be taken as a reason for "optimism" or "pessimism," two great obstacles to clear thinking about new technological developments. If we must choose between them, by all means let us choose optimism. But in view of the many potential gains and losses inevitably associated with massive technological change, any attitude of "optimism" or "pessimism" is far too general to make sense. What I mean to provide is not a basis for pessimism, but a lens through which we might understand, a bit better than before, what makes a system of freedom of expression successful in the first place. That improved understanding will equip us to appreciate a free nation's own aspirations and thus help in evaluating continuing changes in the system of communications. It will also point the way toward a clearer understanding of the nature of citizenship and toward social reforms if emerging developments disserve our aspirations, as they threaten to do.

10. In Your Journal: Why are "optimism" and "pessimism" too general to be useful in this discussion, according to Sunstein?

As we shall see, it is much too simple to say that any system of communications is desirable if and because it allows individuals to see and hear what they choose. Unanticipated, unchosen exposures, and shared experiences, are important too.

PRECURSORS AND INTERMEDIARIES

Unlimited filtering may seem quite strange, perhaps even the stuff of science fiction. But it is not entirely different from what has come before. Filtering is inevitable, a fact of life. It is as old as humanity itself. No one can see, hear, or read everything. In the course of any hour, let alone any day, every one of us engages in massive filtering, simply to make life manageable and coherent.

tyrannies: autocracies, dictatorships

With respect to the world of communications, moreover, a free society gives people a great deal of power to filter out unwanted materials. Only **tyrannies** force people to read or to watch. In free nations, those who read newspapers do not read the same newspaper; some people do not read any newspaper at all. Every day, people make choices among magazines based on their tastes and their point of view. Sports enthusiasts choose sports magazines, and in many nations they can choose a magazine focused on the sport of their choice, *Basketball Weekly,* say, or the *Practical Horseman;* conservatives can read *National Review* or the *Weekly Standard;* countless magazines are available for those who like cars; *Dog Fancy* is a popular item for canine enthusiasts; people who are somewhat left of center might like the *American Prospect;* there is even a magazine called *Cigar Aficionado.*

These are simply contemporary illustrations of a long-standing fact of life in democratic countries: a diversity of communications options and a range of possible choices. But the emerging situation does contain large differences, stemming above all from a dramatic increase in available options, a simultaneous increase in individual control over content, and a corresponding decrease in the power of *general interest* ***intermediaries.***[6] These include newspapers, magazines, and broadcasters. An appreciation of the social functions of general interest intermediaries will play a large role in this argument.

intermediary: mediators, disinterested party

People who rely on such intermediaries have a range of chance encounters, involving shared experiences with diverse others, and also exposure to materials and topics that they did not seek out in advance. You might, for example, read the city newspaper and in the process find a range of stories that you would not have selected if you had the power to do so. Your eyes might come across a story about ethnic tensions in Germany, or crime in Los Angeles, or innovative business practices in Tokyo, and you might read those stories although you would hardly have placed them in your "Daily Me." You might watch a particular television channel—perhaps you prefer channel 4—and when your favorite program ends, you might see the beginning of another show, perhaps a drama that you would not have chosen in advance but that somehow catches your eye. Reading *Time* or *Newsweek,* you might come across a discussion of endangered species in **Madagascar,** and this discussion might interest you, even affect your behavior. maybe even change your life, although you would not have sought it out in the first instance. A system in which individuals lack control over the particular content that they see has a great deal in common with a public street, where you might encounter not only friends, but also a heterogeneous array of people engaged in a wide array of activities (including perhaps bank presidents and political protesters and panhandlers).

11. In Your Journal: What is the value of the "public street," according to the author?

Some people believe that the mass media are dying—that the whole idea of general interest intermediaries, providing both shared experiences for millions and exposure to diverse topics and ideas, was a short episode in the history of human communications. As a prediction, this view is probably over-stated. But certainly the significance of the mass media has been decreasing over time. We should not forget that from the standpoint of human history, even in industrialized societies, general interest intermediaries are relatively new, and far from inevitable. Newspapers, radio stations, and television broadcasters have particular histories with distinctive beginnings and possibly distinctive endings. In fact the twentieth century should be seen as the great era for the general interest

Madagascar: island country of the southeast coast of Africa intermediary, providing similar information and entertainment to millions of people.

The twenty-first century may well be altogether different on this score. Consider one small fact: In 1948, daily newspaper circulation was 1.3 per household, a rate that had fallen by 57 percent by 1998—even though the number of years of education, typically correlated with newspaper readership, rose sharply in that period.[7] At the very least, the sheer volume of options, and the power to customize, are sharply diminishing the social role of the general interest intermediary.

12. In Your Journal: Does the recent decline in newspaper distribution surprise you? Why or why not?

I seek to defend a particular conception of democracy—a deliberative conception—and to evaluate, in its terms, the outcome of a system with the power of perfect filtering. I also mean to defend a conception of freedom, associated with the deliberative conception of democracy, and to oppose it to a conception that sees consumption choices by individuals as the very embodiment of freedom.

13. In Your Journal: What do you think Sunstein means when he suggests he wants to be "deliberative" about democracy?

My claim is emphatically not that street corners and general interest intermediaries will or would disappear in a world of perfect filtering. To what extent the market will produce them, or their equivalents, is an empirical issue. Many people like surprises. Some people have a strong taste for street corners and for their equivalent on the television and on the Internet. Indeed, new technological options hold out a great deal of promise for exposure to materials that used to be too hard to find, including new topics and new points of view. If you would like to find out about different forms of cancer, and different views about possible treatments, you can do so in less than a minute. If you are interested in learning about the risks associated with different automobiles, a quick search will tell you a great deal. If you would like to know about a particular foreign country, from its customs to its politics to its weather, you can do better with the Internet than you could have done with the best of encyclopedias.

14. In Your Journal: What is the relationship between consumption and freedom?

Most parents of school-age children are stunned to see how easy all this is. From the standpoint of those concerned with ensuring access to more opinions and more topics, the new communications technologies can be a terrific boon. But it remains true that many apparent street corners, on the Internet in particular, are highly specialized. Consider Townhall.com, a street corner-type site, as befits its name, through which you can have access to dozens of sites. But unlike at most real townhalls, only conservative views can be found at Townhall.com. Each site is a conservative political organization of one sort or another, including, among many others, the American Conservative Union, the **Oliver North** Radio Show,

15. In Your Journal: What is the paradoxical role of technology in information consumption?

⁂ **Oliver North:** retired Marine Lt. Col. North is best known for the role he played in the Iran-Contra affair in Central America in the 1980's; in May 1988, he retired in order to defend himself against a special prosecutor investigating the events in Central America; he is a featured writer at *Townhall.com*

Protect Americans Now, Conservative Political Action Conference, Citizens Against Government Waste, and the ***National Review***—each with a site of its own, most with many links to like-minded sites, and few with links to opposing views.

It is not that people lack curiosity or that street corners will disappear but instead that there is an insistent need for them, and that a system of freedom of expression should be viewed partly in light of that need. There are serious dangers in a system in which individuals bypass general interest intermediaries and restrict themselves to opinions and topics of their own choosing. In particular, the risks posed by any situation in which thousands or perhaps millions or even tens of millions of people are mainly listening to louder echoes of their own voices. A situation of this kind is likely to produce far worse than mere fragmentation.

I want to stress problems on the "demand" side on the speech market. These are problems that stem not from the actions of *producers*—Microsoft, Netscape, and the like—but instead from the choices and preferences of *consumers*. I am aware that on the standard view, the most important emerging problems come from large corporations, and not from the many millions, indeed billions, of individuals who make communications choices. In the long run, however, I believe that the more serious risks, and certainly the most neglected ones, are consumer driven. This is not because consumers are usually confused or irrational or **malevolent.** It is because choices that seem perfectly reasonable in isolation may, when taken together, badly disserve democratic goals.

malevolent: wicked, evil, malicious

THE NEIGHBORHOOD ME

The changes now being produced by new communications technologies are understated, not overstated, by the thought experiment with which I began. What is happening goes far beyond the increasingly customized computer screen.

For countless people, the Internet is producing a substantial decrease in unanticipated, unchosen interactions with others. Many of us telecommute rather than going to work; this is a rapidly growing trend. Rather than visiting the local bookstore, where we are likely to see a number of diverse people, many of us shop for books on Amazon.com. Others avoid the video store or the grocery because Kosmo.com is entirely delighted to deliver ***Citizen Kane*** and a pizza. Because of MP3 technology, a visit to the local music store may well seem a hopeless waste of time. Thus communications specialist **Ken Auletta** enthuses, "I can sample music on my

Citizen Kane: Orson Welles' film (1941) about a media magnate who was based on William Randolph Hearst; the film comments masterfully on the emtiness of materialism and consumerism

National Review: conservative weekly periodical

Ken Auletta: "Annals of Communication" columnist for the *New Yorker* since 1992

computer, then click and order. I don't have to go to a store. I don't have to get in a car. I don't have to move. God, that's heaven."[1]

If you are interested in anything at all—from computers to linens to diamonds to cars—Buy.com, or MySimon.com, or Bloomingdales.com, or productopia.com, or pricecan.com, or any one of hundreds of others, will be happy to assist you. Indeed, if you would like to attend college, or even to get a graduate degree, you may be able to avoid the campus. College education is already being offered on line.[2] A recent advertisement for New York University invites people to attend "the Virtual College at NYU" and emphasizes that with virtual education, you can take a seat "anywhere" in the class—and even sit alone.

> ***16. In Your Journal:*** Why would some want to "avoid the [college] campus" or "sit alone" in class?

It would be foolish to claim that this is bad, or a loss, in general or on balance. On the contrary, the dramatic increase in convenience is a wonderful blessing for consumers. Driving around in search of gifts, for example, can be a real bother. (Can you remember what this used to be like? Is it still like that for you?) For many of us, the chance to point-and-click is an extraordinary improvement. And many people, both rich and poor, take advantage of new technologies to "go" to places that they could not in any sense have visited before—South Africa, Germany, Iran, stores and more stores everywhere, an immense variety of specialized doctors' offices (with some entertaining surprises as you search; for example, lungcancer.com is a law firm's Website, helping you to sue, rather than a doctor's site, helping you to get better). But it is far from foolish to worry that for millions of people, the consequence of this increased convenience is to decrease the set of chance encounters with diverse others—and also to be concerned about the consequence of the decrease for democracy and citizenship.

> ***17. In Your Journal:*** Is the deception practiced by *lungcancer.com* specific to the online environment?

Or consider the concept of *collaborative filtering*—an intriguing feature on a number of sites, and one that is rapidly becoming routine. Once you order a book from Amazon.com, for example, Amazon.com is in a position to tell you the choices of other people who like that particular book. Once you have ordered a number of books, Amazon.com knows, and will tell you, what other books—and compact discs and movies—you are likely to like based on what people like you have liked. Other Websites, such as Qrate.com and Movielens, are prepared to tell you which new movies you'll enjoy and which you won't—simply by asking you to rate certain movies, then matching your ratings to those of other people, and then finding out what people like you think about movies that you haven't seen. Collaborative filtering is used by CDnow, Moviefinder.com, Firefly, and increasingly many others. We have seen that TiVo, the television recording system, is prepared to tell you what other shows you'll like, based on what shows you now like.

Collaborative filtering is only the beginning. "Personalized shopping" is becoming easily available, and it is intended, in the words of a typical account, to "match the interests and buying habits of its customers, from fabric preferences to room designs to wish lists."[3] Or consider the suggestion that before long we will "have virtual celebrities. . . . They'll look terrific. In fact, they'll look so terrific that their faces will be exactly what *you* think is beautiful and not necessarily what your neighbor thinks, because they'll be customized for each home."[4] (Is it surprising to hear that at least one Website provides personalized romance stories? That it asks you for information about "your fantasy lover," and then it designs a story to suit your tastes?)

In many ways what is happening is quite wonderful, and some of the recommendations from Amazon.com and analogous services are miraculously good, even uncanny. (Thousands of people have discovered new favorite authors through this route.) But it might well be disturbing if the consequence is to encourage people to narrow their horizons, or to cater to their existing tastes rather than to form new ones. Suppose, for example, that people with a certain political conviction find themselves learning about more and more authors with the same view, and thus strengthening their existing judgments, only because most of what they are encouraged to read says the same thing. In a democratic society, might this not be troubling?

18. In Your Journal: Do you think a Web site like Amazon would prefer to narrow or expand consumers' tastes? Does collective filtering seem to be in their best interest in the long run?

The underlying issues here are best approached through two different routes. The first involves an unusual and somewhat exotic constitutional doctrine, based on the idea of the **"public forum."** The second involves a general constitutional ideal, indeed the most general constitutional ideal of all: that of deliberative democracy. A decline in common experiences and a system of individualized filtering might compromise that ideal. As a corrective, we might build on the understandings that lie behind the notion that a free society creates a set of public forums, providing speakers' access to a diverse people, and ensuring in the process that each of us hears a wide range of speakers, spanning many topics and opinions.

THE IDEA OF THE PUBLIC FORUM

In the common understanding, the free speech principle is taken to forbid government from "censoring" speech of which it disapproves. In the standard cases, the government attempts to impose penalties, whether civil or criminal, on political dissent, libelous speech, commercial advertising, or sexually explicit speech. The question is whether the government has a legitimate, and sufficiently weighty, reason for restricting the speech that it seeks to control.

This is indeed what most of the law of free speech is about. But in many free nations, an important part of free speech law takes a quite different form. In the United States, for example, the Supreme Court has ruled

---

public forum [doctrine]: set of formal regulations that defines the scope of protections under the First Amendment that streets and parks must be kept open to the public for expressive activity. In the leading case, from the early part of the twentieth century, the Court said, "Wherever the title of streets and parks may rest, they have immemorially been held in trust for the use of the public and time out of mind, have been used for the purposes of assembly, communicating thought between citizens, and discussing public questions. Such use of the streets and public places has, from ancient times, been a part of the privileges, immunities, rights, and liberties of citizens."[5] Hence governments are obliged to allow speech to occur freely on public streets and in public parks—even if many citizens would prefer to have peace and quiet, and even if it seems irritating to come across protesters and dissidents when you are simply walking home or to the local grocery store.

19. In Your Journal: Why does the public forum doctrine value a citizen's expression more than her comfort or privacy?

To be sure, the government is allowed to impose restrictions on the "time, place, and manner" of speech in public places. No one has a right to set off fireworks or to use loudspeakers on the public streets at 3:00 A.M. to complain about global warming or the size of the defense budget. But time, place, and manner restrictions must be both reasonable and limited. Government is essentially obliged to allow speakers, whatever their views, to use public property to convey messages of their choosing.

A distinctive feature of the public forum doctrine is that it creates a *right of speakers' access, both to places and to people.* Another distinctive feature is that the public forum doctrine creates a right, not to avoid governmentally imposed *penalties* on speech, but to ensure government *subsidies* of speech. There is no question that taxpayers are required to support the expressive activity that, under the public forum doctrine, must be permitted on the streets and parks. Indeed, the costs that taxpayers devote to maintaining open streets and parks, from cleaning to maintenance, can be quite high. Thus the public forum represents one area of law in which the right to free speech demands a public subsidy to speakers.

20. In Your Journal: Why does the public forum doctrine provide "subsidies" for the speech of its citizens while also reserving the right to impose "penalties" on speech? Is this a contradiction?

JUST STREETS AND PARKS? OF AIRPORTS AND THE INTERNET

As a matter of principle, there seems to be good reason to expand the public forum well beyond streets and parks. In the modern era, other places have increasingly come to occupy the role of traditional public forums. The mass media, including the Internet, have become far more important than streets and parks as arenas in which expressive activity occurs.

21. In Your Journal: How is the space of the mass media different from streets and parks? How is it similar?

Nonetheless, the Supreme Court has been wary of expanding the public forum doctrine beyond streets and parks. Perhaps the Court's wariness stems from a belief that once the historical touchstone is abandoned, lines will be extremely hard to draw, and judges will be besieged with requests for rights of access to private and public property. Thus the Court has rejected the seemingly convincing argument that many other places should be seen as public forums. In particular, it has been urged that airports, more than streets and parks, are crucial to reaching a heterogeneous public; airports are places where diverse people congregate and where it is important to have access if you want to speak to large numbers of people. The Court was not convinced, responding that the public forums idea should be understood by reference to historical practices. Airports certainly have not been treated as public forums from "ancient times."[6]

22. In Your Journal: Why aren't airports considered "public forums"?

But at the same time, members of the Court have shown considerable uneasiness with a purely historical test. In the most vivid passage on the point, Supreme Court Justice Anthony Kennedy wrote: "Minds are not changed in streets and parks as they once were. To an increasing degree, the more significant interchanges of ideas and shaping of public consciousness occur in mass and electronic media. The extent of public entitlement to participate in those means of communication may be changed as technologies change."[7] What Justice Kennedy is recognizing here is the serious problem of how to "translate" the public forum idea into the modern technological environment. And if the Supreme Court is unwilling to do any such translating, it remains open for Congress and state governments to do exactly that. In other words, the Court may not be prepared to say, as a matter of constitutional law, that the public forum idea extends beyond streets and parks. But even if the Court is unprepared to act, Congress and state governments are permitted to conclude that a free society requires a right to access to areas where many people meet. Indeed, Websites, private rather than public, might reach such conclusions on their own, and take steps to ensure that people are exposed to a diversity of views.

23. In Your Journal: What do you think are the differences between having the Supreme Court taking action on a Constitutional issue and the Congress or state governments taking action?

WHY PUBLIC FORUMS? OF ACCESS, UNPLANNED ENCOUNTERS, AND IRRITATIONS

The Supreme Court has given little sense of why, exactly, it is important to ensure that the streets and parks remain open to speakers. This is the question that must be answered if we are to know whether, and how, to understand the relationship of the public forum doctrine to contemporary problems.

We can make some progress here by noticing that the public forum doctrine promotes three important goals.[8] First, it ensures that speakers can have access to a wide array of people. If you want to claim that taxes are too high or that police brutality against African-Americans is widespread, you are able to press this argument on many people who might otherwise fail to hear the message. The diverse people who walk the streets and use the parks are likely to hear speakers' arguments about taxes or the police; they might also learn about the nature and intensity of views held by their fellow citizens. Perhaps some people's views will change because of what they learn; perhaps they will become curious, enough so to investigate the question on their own. It does not much matter if this happens a little or a lot. What is important is that speakers are allowed to press concerns that might otherwise be ignored by their fellow citizens.

24. In Your Journal: Who does it benefit that "speakers are allowed to press concerns that might otherwise be ignored by their fellow citizens"?

On the speakers' side, the public forum doctrine thus *creates a right of general access to heterogeneous citizens.* On the listeners' side, the public forum creates not exactly a right but an opportunity, if perhaps an unwelcome one: *shared exposure to diverse speakers with diverse views and complaints.* It is important to emphasize that the exposure is shared. Many people will be simultaneously exposed to the same views and complaints, and they will encounter views and complaints that some of them might have refused to seek out in the first instance. Indeed, the exposure might well be considered, much of the time, irritating or worse.

25. In Your Journal: Why is it important to Sunstein that "exposure is shared"?

Second, the public forum doctrine allows speakers not only to have general access to heterogeneous people, but also to specific people and specific institutions with whom they have a complaint. Suppose, for example, that you believe that the state legislature has behaved irresponsibly with respect to crime or health care for children. The public forum ensures that you can make your views heard by legislators, simply by protesting in front of the state legislature itself.

26. In Your Journal: How are the two types of access—"general" and "specific"—different in the benefits they have for citizens?

The point applies to private as well as public institutions. If a clothing store is believed to have cheated customers or to have acted in a racist manner, protestors are allowed a form of access to the store itself. This is not because they have a right to trespass on private property—no one has such a right—but because a public street is highly likely to be close by, and a strategically located protest will undoubtedly catch the attention of the store and its customers. Under the public forum doctrine, speakers are thus permitted to have access to particular audiences, and particular listeners cannot easily avoid hearing complaints that are directed against them. In other words, listeners have a sharply limited power of self-insulation.

Third, the public forum doctrine increases the likelihood that people generally will be exposed to a wide variety of people and views. When you go to work or visit a park, it is possible that you will have a range of unexpected encounters, however fleeting or seemingly inconsequential. On your way to the office or when eating lunch in the park, you cannot easily wall yourself off from contentions or conditions that you would not have sought out in advance, or that you would have avoided if you could have. Here too the public forum doctrine tends to ensure a range of experiences that are widely shared—streets and parks are public property—and also a set of exposures to diverse views and conditions. What I mean to suggest is that these exposures help promote understanding and perhaps in a sense freedom. As we will soon see, all of these points can be closely connected to democratic ideals.

We should also distinguish here between exposures that are *unplanned* and exposures that are *unwanted*. In a park, for example, you might encounter a baseball game or a group of people protesting the conduct of the police. These might be unplanned experiences; you did not choose them and you did not foresee them. But once you encounter the game or the protest, you are hardly irritated; you may even be glad to have stumbled across them. By contrast, you might also encounter homeless people or beggars, asking you for money and perhaps trying to sell you something that you really don't want. If you could have "filtered out" these experiences, you would have chosen to do so. For many people, the category of unwanted—as opposed to unplanned—exposures includes a great deal of political activities. You might be bored by those activities, and wish that they were not disturbing your stroll through the street. You might be irritated or angered by such activities, perhaps because they are disturbing your stroll, perhaps because of the content of what is being said, perhaps because of who is saying it.

> ***27. In Your Journal:*** How are "unplanned" and "unwanted" exposures different? If you wanted exposure to something, wouldn't you "plan" it?

It is also important to distinguish between exposures to *experiences* and exposures to *arguments*. Public forums make it more likely that people will not be able to wall themselves off from their fellow citizens. People will get a glimpse, at least, of the lives of others, as for example through encountering people from different social classes. Some of the time, however, the public forum doctrine makes it more likely that people will have a sense, however brief, not simply of the experiences but also of the arguments being made by people with a particular point of view. You might encounter written materials, for example, that draw attention to the problem of domestic violence. The most ambitious uses of public forums are designed to alert people to arguments as well as experiences—though the latter sometimes serve as a kind of shorthand reference for the former, as when a picture or a brief encounter has the effect of thousands of words.

> ***28. In Your Journal:*** Why does Sunstein insist on differentiating between "experiences" and "arguments"?

> ***29. In Your Journal:*** Do you think the domestic violence example illustrates exposure to an "experience" or an "argument"? How does Sunstein categorize it?

In referring to the goals of the public forum doctrine, I aim to approve of encounters that are unwanted as well as unplanned, and also of exposure to experiences as well as arguments. But those who disapprove of unwanted encounters might also agree that unplanned ones are desirable, and those who believe that exposure to arguments is too demanding, or too intrusive, might also appreciate the value, in a heterogeneous society, of exposure to new experiences.

GENERAL INTEREST INTERMEDIARIES AS UNACKNOWLEDGED PUBLIC FORUMS (OF THE WORLD)

Of course there is a limit to how much can be done on streets and in parks. Even in the largest cities, streets and parks are insistently *local*. But many of the social functions of streets and parks, as public forums, are performed by other institutions too. In fact society's general interest intermediaries—newspapers, magazines, television broadcasters—can be understood as public forums of an especially important sort.

> ***30. In Your Journal:*** What does Sunstein mean when he categorizes streets and parks as "insistently *local*"?

The reasons are straightforward. When you read a city newspaper or a national magazine, your eyes will come across a number of articles that you would not have selected in advance. If you are like most people, you will read some of those articles. Perhaps you did not know that you might have an interest in minimum wage legislation, or Somalia, or the latest developments in the Middle East; but a story might catch your attention. What is true for topics is also true for points of view. You might think that you have nothing to learn from someone whose view you abhor. But once you come across the editorial pages, you might well read what they have to say, and you might well benefit from the experience. Perhaps you will be persuaded on one point or another, or informed whether or not you are persuaded. At the same time, the front page headline, or the cover story in *Newsweek*, is likely to have a high degree of **salience** for a wide range of people.

salience: recognizability; relevance

Unplanned and unchosen encounters often turn out to do a great deal of good, both for individuals and for society at large. In some cases, they even change people's lives. The same is true, though in a different way, for unwanted encounters. In some cases, you might be irritated by seeing an editorial from your least favorite writer. You might wish that the editorial weren't there. But despite yourself, your curiosity might be **piqued,** and you might read it. Perhaps this isn't a lot of fun. But it might prompt you to reassess your own view and even to revise it. At the very least, you will have learned what many of your fellow citizens think and why they think it. What is true for arguments is also true for topics, as when you encounter, with some displeasure, a series of stories on crime or global warming or same-sex marriage or alcohol abuse, but find yourself learning a bit, or more, from what those stories have to say.

piqued: annoyed

Television broadcasters have similar functions. Maybe the best example is what has become an institution in many nations: the evening news. If you tune into the evening news, you will learn about a number of topics that you would not have chosen in advance. Because of the speed and immediacy of television, broadcasters perform these public forum–type functions even more than general interest intermediaries in the print media. The lead story on the networks is likely to have a great deal of public saliency, helping to define central issues and creating a kind of shared focus of attention for many millions of people. And what happens after the lead story—dealing with a menu of topics both domestic and international—creates something like a **speakers' corner** beyond anything ever imagined **in Hyde Park.**

31. In Your Journal: Does the "speed and immediacy of television" change the definition of public forum somewhat?

None of these claims depends on a judgment that general interest intermediaries always do an excellent job, or even a good job. Sometimes

speaker's corner . . . in Hyde Park: public gathering place in London, where people can express their opinions publicly (i.e., on a "soap box") such intermediaries fail to provide an adequate understanding of topics or opinions. Sometimes they offer a watered-down version of what most people already think. Sometimes they suffer from prejudices of their own. Sometimes they deal little with substance and veer toward sound bites and sensationalism, properly deplored trends in the last two decades. What matters for present purposes is that in their best forms, general interest intermediaries expose people to a range of topics and views at the same time that they provide shared experiences for a heterogeneous public. Indeed, general interest intermediaries of this sort have large advantages over streets and parks precisely because most of them tend to be so much less local and so much more national, even international. Typically they expose people to questions and problems in other areas, even other nations. They even provide a form of modest, back-door **cosmopolitanism,** ensuring that many people will learn something about diverse areas of the world, regardless of whether they are much interested, initially or ever, in doing so.

cosmopolitanism: feeling or theory of being at home anywhere in the world

Of course general interest intermediaries are not public forums in the technical sense that the law recognizes. These are private rather than public institutions. Most important, members of the public do not have a legal right of access to them. Individual citizens are not allowed to override the editorial and economic judgments and choices of private owners. In the 1970s, a sharp constitutional debate on precisely this issue resulted in a resounding defeat for those who claimed a constitutionally guaranteed access right.[9] But the question of legal compulsion is really incidental. Society's general interest intermediaries, even without legal compulsion, serve many of the functions of public forums. They promote shared experiences; they expose people to information and views that would not have been selected in advance.

32. In Your Journal: If general interest intermediaries are not public institutions then how can they be considered public forums?

REPUBLICANISM, DELIBERATIVE DEMOCRACY, AND TWO KINDS OF FILTERING

The public forum doctrine is an odd and unusual one, especially insofar as it creates a kind of speakers' access right, subsidized by taxpayers, to people and places. But the doctrine is closely associated with a longstanding constitutional ideal, one that is very far from odd: that of republican self-government.

From the beginning, the U.S. constitutional order was designed to be a republic, as distinguished from a monarchy or a direct democracy. We cannot understand the system of freedom of expression, and the effects of new communications technologies and filtering, without reference to this ideal. It will therefore be worthwhile to spend some space on the concept of a republic, and on the way the American constitution understands this concept, in terms of a deliberative approach to democracy. The general ideal is hardly limited to America; it plays a role in many nations committed to self-government.

In a republic, government is not managed by any king or queen; there is no sovereign operating independently of the people.[10] The American Constitution represents a firm rejection of the monarchical heritage, and the framers self-consciously transferred **sovereignty** from any monarchy (with the explicit constitutional ban on "titles of nobility") to "We the People." This represents, in **Gordon Wood's** illuminating phrase, the "radicalism of the American revolution."[11] At the same time, the founders were extremely fearful of popular passions and prejudices, and they did not want government to translate popular desires directly into law. Indeed, they were sympathetic to a form of filtering, though one very different from that emphasized thus far. Rather than seeking to allow people to filter what they would see and hear, they attempted to create institutions that would "filter" popular desires so as to ensure policies that would promote the public good. Thus the structure of political representation, and the system of checks and balances, were designed to create a kind of filter between people and law, so as to ensure that what would emerge would be both reflective and well-informed. At the same time, the founders placed a high premium on the idea of "civic virtue," which required participants in politics to act as citizens dedicated to something other than their self-interest, narrowly conceived.

sovereignty: power; rule

33. In Your Journal: Why wouldn't the founders want "popular desires" to translate "directly into law"?

This form of republicanism involved an attempt to create a "deliberative democracy." In this system, representatives would be accountable to the public at large. But there was also supposed to be a large degree of reflection and debate, both within the citizenry and within government itself.[12] The aspiration to deliberative democracy can be seen in many places in the constitutional design. The system of **bicameralism,** for example, was intended as a check on insufficiently deliberative action from one or another legislative chamber; the Senate, in particular, was supposed to have a "cooling" effect on popular passions. The long length of service for senators was designed to make deliberation more likely; so too for large election districts. The **Electoral College** was originally a deliberative body, ensuring that the president would result from some combination of popular will and reflection and exchange on the part of representatives. Most generally, the system of checks and balances had, as its central purpose, the creation of a mechanism for promoting deliberation within the government as a whole.

bicameralism: system based on having two legislative branches

34. In Your Journal: What is "deliberative democracy"?

35. In Your Journal: By what means do you think the "citizenry" were meant by the founders to have "a large degree of reflection and debate"?

Gordon Wood: Professor of History at Brown University, who won a Pulitzer Prize for his book *The Radicalism of the American Revolution* in 1993 which traces the transformation of American society from its deferential origins to its democratic fruition

Electoral College: body of electors appointed by each state to choose the President and Vice-President

From these points it should be clear that the Constitution was not rooted in the assumption that direct democracy was the ideal, to be replaced by republican institutions only because direct democracy was impractical in light of what were, by modern standards, extremely primitive technologies for communication. Many recent observers have suggested that, for the first time in the history of the world, something like direct democracy has become feasible. It is now possible for citizens to tell their government, every week if not every day, what they would like it to do.[13] Indeed, Websites have been designed to enable citizens to do precisely that (vote.com is an example). We should expect many more experiments in this direction. But from the standpoint of constitutional ideals, this is nothing to celebrate, indeed it is a grotesque distortion of founding aspirations. It would undermine the deliberative goals of the original design. Ours has never been a direct democracy, and a good democratic system attempts to ensure informed and reflective decisions, not simply snapshots of individual opinions, suitably aggregated.[14]

36. In Your Journal: Why wouldn't "direct democracy" be an ideal form of government?

HOMOGENEITY, HETEROGENEITY, AND A TALE OF THE FIRST CONGRESS

There were articulate opponents of the original constitutional plan, whose voices have echoed throughout American history; and they spoke in terms that bear directly on the communications revolution. The antifederalists believed that the Constitution was doomed to failure, on the ground that deliberation would not be possible in a large, heterogeneous republic. Following the great political theorist **Montesquieu,** they urged that public deliberation would be possible only where there was fundamental agreement. Thus **Brutus,** an eloquent antifederalist critic of the Constitution, insisted, "In a republic, the manners, sentiments, and interests of the people should be similar. If this be not the case, there will be a constant clashing of opinions; and the representatives of one part will be continually striving against those of the other."[15]

37. In Your Journal: What was the "antifederalist" position?

It was here that the Constitution's framers made a substantial break with conventional republican thought, focusing on the potential uses of diversity for democratic debate. For them, heterogeneity, far from being an obstacle, would be a creative force, improving deliberation and producing

---

Monstesquieu: (Charles Louis, II) (1689–1755) French jurist and political philosopher, known for promoting the "separation of powers" structure of government

Brutus: pseudonym for Robert Yates, whose essays inspired Alexander Hamilton, James Madison, and John Jay, authors of *The Federalist* papers, written during the debates over ratifying the Constitution

38. In Your Journal: How does diversity turn out to be an asset to our democracy rather than a problem to overcome?

39. In Your Journal: Why wouldn't the Bill of Rights grant citizens the right to instruct their representatives on how to vote?

better outcomes. If everyone agreed, what would people need to talk about? Why would they want to talk at all? Alexander Hamilton invoked this point to defend discussion among diverse people within a bicameral legislature, urging, in what could be taken as a direct response to Brutus, that "the jarring of parties . . . will promote deliberation."[16] And in an often forgotten episode in the very first Congress, the nation rejected a proposed part of the original Bill of Rights, a "right" on the part of citizens to "instruct" their representative on how to vote. The proposed right was justified on republican (what we would call democratic) grounds. To many people, it seemed a good way of ensuring accountability on the part of public officials. But the early Congress decided that such a right would be a betrayal of republican principles. **Senator Roger Sherman's** voice was the clearest and most firm:

> The words are calculated to mislead the people, by conveying an idea that they have a right to control the debates of the Legislature. This cannot be admitted to be just, because it would destroy the object of their meeting. I think, when the people have chosen a representative, it is his duty to meet others from the different parts of the Union, and consult, and agree with them on such acts as are for the general benefit of the whole community. If they were to be guided by instructions, there would be no use in deliberation.[17]

40. In Your Journal: What does Sunstein mean by the phrase "republic of reasons"?

Sherman's words reflect the founders' general receptivity to deliberation among people who are quite diverse and who disagree on issues both large and small. Indeed, it was through deliberation among such persons that "such acts as are for the general benefit of the whole community" would emerge. Of course the framers were not naive. Sometimes some regions, and some groups, would gain while others would lose. What was and remains important is that the resulting pattern of gains and losses would themselves have to be defended by reference to reasons. Indeed, the Constitution might well be seen as intended to create a "republic of reasons" in which the use of governmental power would have to be justified, not simply supported, by those who asked for it.

We can even take Sherman's conception of the task of the representative as having a corresponding conception of the task of the idealized citizen in a well-functioning republic. Citizens are not supposed to press their self-interest, narrowly conceived, nor are they to insulate themselves from the judgments of others. Even if they are concerned with the public good, they might make errors of fact or of value, errors that can be reduced or corrected through the exchange of ideas. Insofar as people are acting in

---

❖ **Senator Roger Sherman:** (1721–1793) Connecticut senator, signer of the Declaration of Independence and member of the Constitutional Convention their capacity as citizens, their duty is to "meet others" and "consult," sometimes through face-to-face discussions or if not through other routes as, for example, by making sure to consider the views of those who think differently.

This is not to say that most people should be devoting most of their time to politics. In a free society, people have a range of things to do. But to the extent that both citizens and representatives are acting on the basis of diverse encounters and experiences, and benefiting from heterogeneity, they are behaving in accordance with the highest ideals of the constitutional design.

E PLURIBUS UNUM AND MADISON VS. JEFFERSON

Any heterogeneous society faces a risk of fragmentation. This risk has been serious in many periods in American history, most notably during the Civil War, but often in the twentieth century as well. The institutions of the Constitution were intended to diminish the danger, partly by producing a good mix of local and national rule, partly through the system of checks and balances, and partly through the symbol of the Constitution itself. Thus the idea of *e pluribus unum* (from many, one) can be found on ordinary currency, in a brief, frequent reminder of a central constitutional goal.

Consider in this regard the instructive debate between Thomas Jefferson and **James Madison** about the value of a bill of rights. In the founding era, Madison, the most important force behind the Constitution itself, sharply opposed such a bill, on the ground that it was unnecessary and was likely to sow confusion. Jefferson thought otherwise, and insisted that a bill of rights, enforced by courts, could be a **bulwark** of liberty. Madison was eventually convinced of this point, but he emphasized a very different consideration: the unifying and educative functions of a bill of rights.

bulwark: fortification

In a letter to Jefferson on October 17, 1788, Madison asked, "What use, then, it may be asked, can a bill of rights serve in popular Government?" His basic answer was that the "political truths declared in that solemn manner acquire by degrees the character of fundamental maxims of free Government, and as they become incorporated with the National sentiment, counteract the impulses of interest and passion."[18] In Madison's view, the Bill of Rights, along with the Constitution itself, would eventually become a source of shared understandings and commitments among extremely diverse people. The example illustrates the founders'

James Madison: (1751–1836) 4th President of the United States (1809–1817), often called the "father of the Constitution"

41. In Your Journal: How does the Madison example illustrate the need for "common experiences"?

belief that for a diverse people to be self-governing, it was essential to provide a range of common experiences.

TWO CONCEPTIONS OF SOVEREIGNTY, AND HOLMES VS. BRANDEIS

We are now in a position to distinguish between two conceptions of sovereignty. The first involves consumer sovereignty, the idea behind free markets. The second involves political sovereignty, the idea behind free nations. The notion of consumer sovereignty underlies enthusiasm for the "Daily Me"; it is the underpinning of any utopian vision of the unlimited power to filter. Writing in 1995, Bill Gates cheerfully predicted, "Customized information is a natural extension. . . . For your own daily dose of news, you might subscribe to several review services and let a software agent or a human one pick and choose from them to compile your completely customized 'newspaper.' These subscription services, whether human or electronic, will gather information that conforms to a particular philosophy and set of interests."[19] Or recall the first epigraph to this book, Gates's celebratory words in 1999: "When you turn on DirectTV and you step through every channel—well, there's three minutes of your life. When you walk into your living room six years from now, you'll be able to just say what you're interested in, and have the screen help you pick out a video that you care about. It's not going to be 'Let's look at channels 4, 5, and 7.'" This is the principle of consumer sovereignty in action.

The notion of political sovereignty underlies the democratic alternative, which poses a challenge to Gates's vision on the ground that it may well undermine both self-government and freedom, properly conceived. Recall here **John Dewey's** words: "Majority rule, just as majority rule, is as foolish as its critics charge it with being. But it never is *merely* majority rule. . . . The important consideration is that opportunity be given ideas to speak and to become the possession of the multitude. The essential need is the improvement of the methods and constitution of debate, discussion and persuasion. That is *the* problem of the public."

42. In Your Journal: What, according to Dewey, is a more important problem for the public than "majority rule"?

Consumer sovereignty means that individual consumers are permitted to choose as they wish, subject to the constraints provided by the price system, and also by their current holdings and requirements. This idea plays a significant role in thinking not only about economic markets, but also about both politics and communications. When we talk as if politi-

---

John Dewey: (1859–1952) American philosopher, proponent of "instrumentalism," the theory that since human problems always change, the instruments used to address them must also change cians are "selling" a message, and even themselves, we are treating the political domain as a kind of market, subject to the forces of supply and demand. And when we act as if the purpose of a system of communications is to ensure that people can see exactly what they "want," the notion of consumer sovereignty is very much at work.

The idea of political sovereignty stands on different foundations. It does not take individual tastes as fixed or given. It prizes democratic self-government, understood as a requirement of "government by discussion," accompanied by reason-giving in the public domain. Political sovereignty comes with its own distinctive preconditions, and these are violated if government power is not backed by justifications, and represents instead the product of force or simple majority will.

Of course the two conceptions of sovereignty are in potential tension. A commitment to consumer sovereignty may well compromise political sovereignty if, for example, free consumer choices result in insufficient understanding of public problems, or if they make it difficult to have anything like a shared or deliberative culture. We will create serious problems if we confound consumer sovereignty with political sovereignty. If the latter is our governing ideal, for example, we will evaluate the system of free expression partly by seeing whether it promotes democratic goals. If we care only about consumer sovereignty, the only question is whether consumers are getting what they want. The distinction matters for policy as well. If the government takes steps to increase the level of substantive debate on television or in public culture, it might well be undermining consumer sovereignty at the same time that it is promoting democratic self-government.

43. In Your Journal: How can consumer sovereignty be maintained within the context of political sovereignty? Does Sunstein's argument make them incompatible?

With respect to the system of freedom of speech, the conflict between consumer sovereignty and political sovereignty can be found in an unexpected place: the great constitutional dissents of Supreme Court Justices **Oliver Wendell Holmes** and **Louis Brandeis.** In the early part of the twentieth century, Holmes and Brandeis were the twin heroes of freedom of speech, dissenting, usually together, from Supreme Court decisions allowing the government to regulate political dissent. Sometimes Holmes wrote for the two dissenters; sometimes the author was Brandeis. But the two spoke in quite different terms. Holmes wrote of "free trade on ideas," and treated speech as part of a great political market, with which

---

Oliver Wendell Holmes: (1841–1935) Associate Justice for the Supreme Court, known as the "Great Dissenter," and known for arguing that speech should be curbed or regulated only when there is "clear and present danger" to the public

---

Louis Brandeis: (1856–1941) Associate Justice for the Supreme Court, considered an enemy of industrial and financial monopoly government could not legitimately interfere. Consider a passage from Holmes' greatest free speech opinion.

> When men have realized that time has upset many fighting faiths, they may come to believe even more than they believe the very foundations of their own conduct that the ultimate good desired is better reached by free trade in ideas—that the best test of truth is the power of the thought to get itself accepted in the competition of the market, and that truth is the only ground upon which their wishes safely can be carried out. That at any rate is the theory of our Constitution.[20]

Brandeis's language, in his greatest free speech opinion, was quite different.

> Those who won our independence believed that the final end of the state was to make men free to develop their faculties; and that in its government the deliberative forces should prevail over the arbitrary. . . . They believed that . . . without free speech and assembly discussion would be futile; . . . that the greatest menace to freedom is an inert people; that public discussion is a political duty; and that this should be a fundamental principle of the American government.[21]

Note Brandeis's suggestion that the greatest threat to freedom is an "inert people," and his insistence, altogether foreign to Holmes, that public discussion is not only a right but "a political duty." Brandeis sees self-government as something dramatically different from an exercise in consumer sovereignty. On Brandeis's self-consciously republican conception of free speech, unrestricted consumer choice is not an appropriate foundation for policy in a context where the very formation of preferences, and the organizing processes of the democratic order, are at stake.

In fact Brandeis can be taken to have offered a conception of the social role of the idealized citizen. For such a citizen, active engagement in politics, at least some of the time, is an obligation, not just an entitlement. If citizens are "inert," freedom itself is at risk. This does not mean that people have to be thinking about public affairs all or most of the time. But it does mean that each of us has rights and duties as citizens, not simply as consumers. As we will see, active citizen engagement is necessary to promote not only democracy but social well-being too. And in the modern era, one of the most pressing obligations of a citizenry that is not inert is to ensure that "deliberative forces should prevail over the arbitrary." For this to happen, it is indispensable to ensure that the system of communications

44. In Your Journal: How does Sunstein characterize the main difference between Holmes's and Brandeis's dissents? Whose model does Sunstein seem to prefer?

promotes democratic goals. Those goals emphatically require both unchosen exposures and shared experiences.

REPUBLICANISM WITHOUT NOSTALGIA

These are abstractions; it is time to be more concrete. I will identify three problems in the hypothesized world of perfect filtering. These difficulties would beset any system in which individuals had complete control over their communications universe and exercised that control so as to decrease *shared communications experiences* and *exposure to materials that would not have been chosen in advance but that nonetheless are beneficial,* both to the person who is exposed to them and to society at large.

The first difficulty involves fragmentation. The problem here comes from the creation of diverse speech communities, whose members make significantly different communications choices. A possible consequence is considerable difficulty in mutual understanding. When society is fragmented in this way, diverse groups will tend to polarize, in a way that can breed extremism and even hatred and violence. New technologies, emphatically including the Internet, are dramatically increasing people's ability to hear echoes of their own voices and to wall themselves off from others. An important result is the existence of *cybercascades*—processes of information exchange in which a certain fact or point of view becomes widespread, simply because so many people seem to believe it.

The second difficulty involves a distinctive characteristic of information. Information is a public good in the technical sense that once some person knows something, other people are likely to benefit as well. If you learn about crime in the neighborhood or about the problem of global warming, you will probably tell other people, and they will benefit from what you have learned. In a system in which each person can "customize" his own communications universe, there is a risk that people will make choices that generate too little information, at least to the extent that individual choices are not made with reference to their social benefits. An advantage of a system with general interest intermediaries and with public forums—with broad access by speakers to diverse publics—is that it ensures a kind of social spreading of information. At the same time, an individually filtered speech universe is likely to underproduce what I call *solidarity goods*—goods whose value increases with the number of people who are consuming them.[22] A presidential debate is a classic example of a solidarity good.

> ***45. In Your Journal:*** Why is a presidential debate an example of "solidarity good[s]"? Can you think of any other examples?

The third and final difficulty has to do with the proper understanding of freedom and the relationship between consumers and citizens. If we believe in consumer sovereignty, and if we celebrate the power to filter, we are likely to think that freedom consists in the satisfaction of private preferences—in an absence of restrictions on individual choices. This is a widely held view about freedom. Indeed, it is a view that underlies much current thinking about free speech. But it is badly misconceived. Freedom consists not simply in preference satisfaction but also in the chance to have preferences and beliefs formed under decent conditions—in the ability to have preferences formed after exposure to a sufficient amount of information, and also to an appropriately wide and diverse range of options. There can be no assurance of freedom in a system committed to the "Daily Me."

46. In Your Journal: Why can there be "no assurance of freedom in a system committed to the "Daily Me"?

NOTES

The Daily Me

1. Alfred C. Sikes, *Fast Forward* 204, 211 (2000).
2. Id. at 25.
3. Numbers go quickly out of date, but as of 2000, nearly thirty million people have personalized a Web page, over ten times the number from 1998. Of those who use the Internet, fully 71 percent personalize a Website to receive more relevant content, often involving local topics; 65 percent personalize a site so as to allow it to "remember" their "preferences and interests, based on their inputs." See Kevin Mably, *Private vs. Personalization* 5 (2000), available at *http://www.cyberdialogue.com.*
4. See Nicholas Negroponte, *Being Digital* 153 (1995). See also Robert Putnam, *Bowling Alone* 177–79 (2000) for a brief but helpful discussion of "cyberbalkanization," which draws in turn on an illuminating paper by Marshall Van Alstyne and Erik Brynjolfsson, *Electronic Communities: Global Village or Cyberbalkans,* available at *http://wed.mit.edu/marshall/www/Abstracts.html.*
5. See, e.g., Martha Nussbaum, *For Love of Country* (1998).
6. The point is emphasized in Andrew Shapiro, *The Control Revolution* (1999), from which I have learned a great deal, and many of whose concerns, including fragmentation and self-insulation, are the same as those stressed here.
7. See Putnam, *Bowling Alone* at 218.

The Neighborhood Me

1. Alfred C. Sikes, *Fast Forward* 210 (quoting Ken Auletta).
2. In some ways these developments are entirely continuous with other important social changes. The automobile, for example, has been criticized for "its extreme unsociability," especially compared with the railway, "which tended to gather together . . . all activity that was in any way related to movements of freight or passengers into or out of the city." George Kennan, *Around the Cragged Hill* 161, 160 (1993). Far more important in this regard has been what may well be the dominant technology of the twentieth century: television. In the words of political scientist Robert Putnam, the "single most important consequence of the television revolution has been to bring us home." Putnam, *Bowling Alone* 221. And the result of the shift in the direction of home has been a dramatic reduction—perhaps as much as 40 percent—in activity spent

on "collective activities, like attending public meetings or taking a leadership role in local organizations." Id. at 229.

3. See Air Technology Groups Powers living.com, available at *http://industry.java.sun.com/javanews/stories/story2/0,1072,17512,00.html.*
4. Sikes, *Fast Forward* 208 (quoting Alvin Toffler).
5. *Hague* v. *CIO,* 307 US 496 (1939). For present purposes, it is not necessary to discuss the public forum doctrine in detail. Interested readers might consult Geoffrey Stone et al., *The First Amendment* 286–330 (1999).
6. See *International Society for Krishna Consciousness* v. *Lee,* 505 US 672 (1992).
7. See *Denver Area Educational Telecommunications Consortium, Inc.* v. *FCC,* 518 US 727, 802–3 (1996) (Kennedy, J., dissenting).
8. See the excellent discussion in Noah D. Zatz, *Sidewalks in Cyberspace: Making Space for Public Forums in the Electronic Environment,* 12 Harv. J Law and Tech. 149 (1998).
9. See *Columbia Broadcasting System* v. *Democratic National Committee,* 412 US 94 (1973).
10. An especially illuminating elaboration of republican ideals is Philip Pettit, *Republicanism: A Theory of Freedom and Government* (1999).
11. See Gordon Wood, *The Radicalism of the American Revolution* (1993).
12. From the standpoint of American history, the best discussion of deliberative democracy is William Bessette, The *Mild Voice of Reason* (1984). There are many treatments of deliberative democracy as a political ideal. For varying perspectives, see Amy Gutmann and Dennis Thompson, *Democracy and Disagreement* (1998); Jurgen Habermas, *Between Facts and Norms* (1997); and *Deliberative Democracy* (Jon Elster ed. 1998).
13. A popular treatment is Dick Morris, *Vote.com* (2000).
14. To be sure, one of the central trends of the last century has been a decrease in the deliberative features of the constitutional design, in favor of an increase in popular control. As central examples, consider direct primary elections, initiatives and referenda, interest group strategies designed to mobilize constituents, and public opinion polling. To a greater or lesser extent, each of these has diminished the deliberative functions of representatives, and increased accountability to public opinion at particular moments in time. Of course any evaluation of these changes would require a detailed discussion. But from the standpoint of the original constitutional settlement, as well as from the standpoint of democratic principles, reforms that make democracy less deliberative are at best a mixed blessing. Government by initiatives and referenda are especially troubling insofar as they threaten to create ill-considered law, produced by soundbites rather than reflective judgments by representatives, citizens, or anyone at all. For valuable discussion, see James Fishkin, *The Voice of the People* (1995).
15. 2 *The Complete Antifederalist* 369 (H. Storing ed. 1980).
16. *The Federalist* No. 81.
17. I *Annals of Cong.*733–45 (Joseph Gale ed. 1789).
18. *The Mind of the Founder* 156–60 (M. Meyers ed. 1981).

19. Bill Gates, *The Road Ahead* 167–68 (1995).
20. *Abrams* v. *United States,* 250 US 616, 635 (Holmes, J., dissenting).
21. *Whitney* v. *California,* 274 US 357, 372 (1927) (Brandeis, J., concurring).
22. For more detailed discussion, see Cass R. Sunstein and Edna Ullmann-Margalit, *Solidarity in Consumption,* available at *http://papers.SSRN.com/paper.taf?ABSTRACT_ID=224618.*

FOR USE IN DISCUSSION

Questions about Substance

1. What value is inherent in the unchosen or the unexpected? How is that related to the values of democracy (655)?
2. Do you think that technology has made us "citizens of the world" (655) or key-board consumers?
3. Sunstein argues that people in a democracy should be exposed to a diversity of voices and ideas (657). Do you agree? Why or why not?
4. Explain Sunstein's metaphoric use of translation when he discusses the founding fathers and modern citizenry (663).
5. What does it mean that "the question of legal compulsion is really incidental"? Does this problematize Sunstein's general argument? (667)
6. How is the filtering performed by "political representation" different from the filtering of a specialty publication by an individual consumer? (668)
7. How can the Web be suited to "direct democracy" while it is a "grotesque distortion of founding aspirations" (669)? How is citizenship affected by consumerism?
8. Why does political sovereignty require "government by discussion" and "reasongiving" (673)?

Questions about Structure and Style

1. When Sunstein describes the different customizing Web sites available to us now (653–654), why do you think he uses a bulleted list rather than paragraph form?
2. On page 655, Sunstein alludes to a relationship between a "well-functioning system of democracy" and a "well-functioning system of free expression." Do you have any idea how those things are meant to work together according to his logic?
3. Why does Sunstein include Bill Gates's specific comment, "It's not going to be 'Let's look at channels 4, 5, and 7' " (672)? Could he have made the same point without quoting the CEO of Microsoft?

4. Does Sunstein offer any proof that customization leads to a decline in information? Does he need to provide evidence or is this argument self-evident (see 675)?

Multimedia Suggestions

1. Create your own news source at one of the following Web sites and describe the rationale for your choices:
   http://www.crayon.net/
   http://www.newsalert.com/
   http://www.newsindex.com/
2. Examine one of the Web sites below and describe its democracy quotient—both in your own opinion and in the context of Sunstein's argument:
   http://www.csmonitor.com/
   http://www.buzzflash.com/
   http://www.mediawhoresonline.com/
   http://www.adbusters.org/
   http://www.adot.com/
   http://www.townhall.com/
   http://www.mediaresearch.org/
   http://www.wsws.org/
3. See the recent movie *Simone* (2002, directed by Andrew M. Niccol), in which an actress is digitally created based on a predetermined set of appealing characteristics. Does this movie parallel Sunstein's argument in any way?

SUGGESTIONS FOR WRITING AND RESEARCH

1. Write an essay about what you see to be the relationship between free speech and civic duty. Do these concepts necessarily conflict with each other? Use Sunstein's terminology, but feel free to explore other contexts. For example, do pornographers have a civic duty to keep their materials away from minors? Do racists have a right to hang offensive material on their property or to parade it in public spaces?
2. Find an ad in a magazine with whose content you are very familiar (even if you do not read it regularly). For example, if you are a car fanatic you might choose *Car and Driver*, or if you are from New York you might choose *New York Magazine*. Analyze the content and placement of the ad to determine its "target audience." Then relate your findings to Sunstein's argument, assessing the issues of consumerism, heterogeneity, and democracy in relation to this target market. Be sure to turn in the ad with your essay.

3. Examine another kind of "customization" experience that is similar to the news services Sunstein refers to (e.g., your Internet service provider home page, make your own music CD services) or one that is subtler (e.g., choosing a major in college, pledging a fraternity/sorority, or even creating a speed-dial list on your telephone). Compare and contrast your choice with Sunstein's example: is your example as important as news consumption? Why or why not?

WORKING WITH CLUSTERS

Cluster 3: Reading Meaning, Achieving Literacy

Cluster 13: Global Knowledge

Cluster 15: Spatial Realities

Cluster 20: The Burdens of Modernity

Discipline: The Social Sciences

Rhetorical Mode: Argument

Darkness in El Dorado: How Scientists and Journalists Devastated the Amazon

by Patrick Tierney

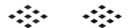

Patrick Tierney is a freelance journalist who has spent many years investigating the impact of anthropologists upon native peoples. He holds a B.A. from the University of California at Los Angeles in Latin American Studies. Tierney is author of The Highest Altar: The Story of Human Sacrifice *and* Darkness in El Dorado: How Scientists and Journalists Devastated the Amazon *(Chapters 1–3 excerpted here), which was a finalist for the 2000 National Book Award in Non-Fiction. He is also a Center Associate/Visiting Scholar in the Center for Latin American Studies at the University of Pittsburgh Center for International Studies.*

El Dorado: a legendary city thought to be in South America, known for its wealth of gold and jewels.

1. In Your Journal: What is this photograph meant to reveal about the figures in it?

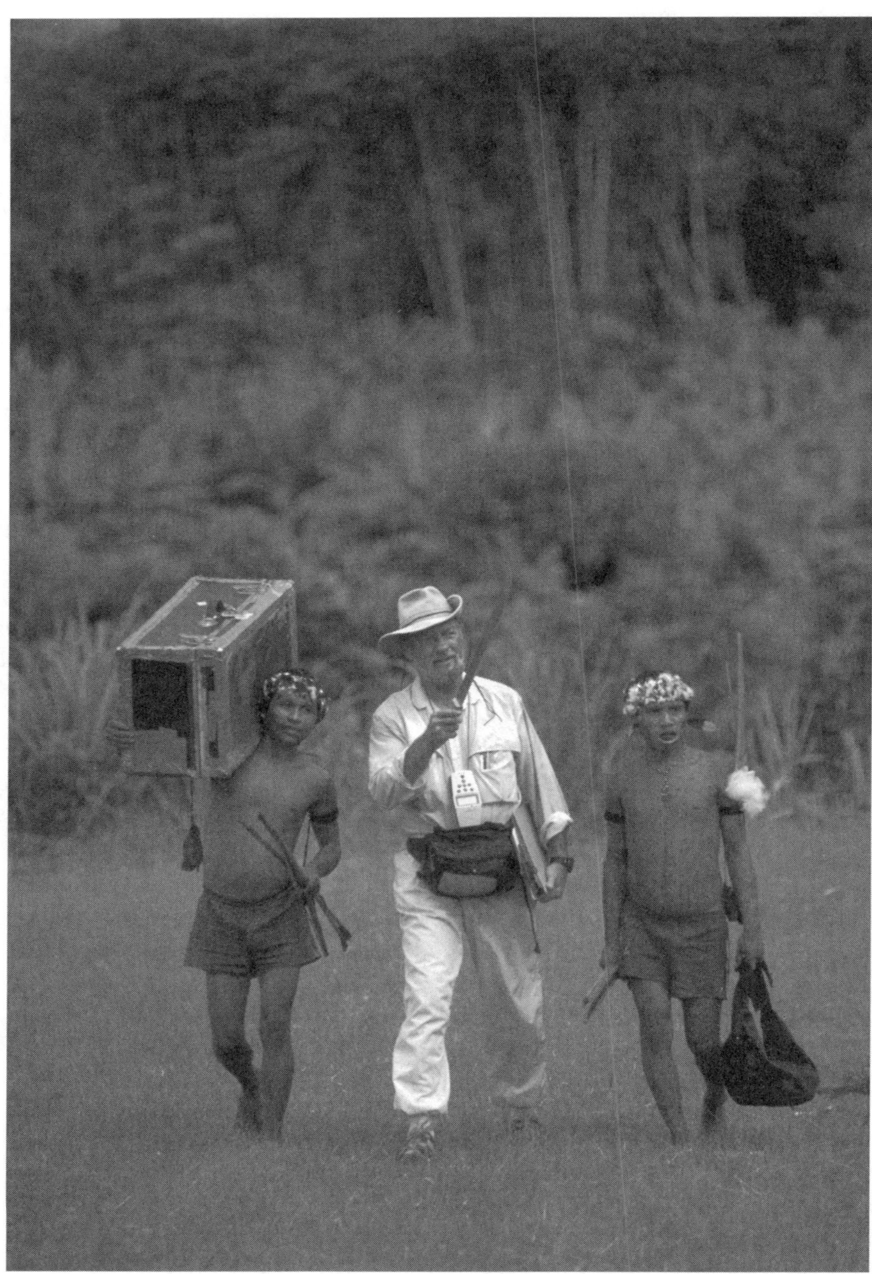

Napoleon Chagnon and assistants at Abruwa-teri, Brazil, 1995 (photo by Antonio Mari)

SAVAGE ENCOUNTERS

Every time we are making a contact, we are spoiling them.

—Charles Brewer Carías[1]

The thunderous descent of the military helicopter at the village of Dorita-teri drove Yanomami Indian women and children screaming into the surrounding plantain gardens. Out in the jungle, panic also reigned, as macaws and parrots, deer and **tapirs** scrambled to escape the machine. When the dust cleared, twenty Yanomami warriors were standing in a semicircle, yelling at seven white men and one white woman who had descended from the helicopter with television cameras and sound equipment. Most of the warriors held enormous bows and arrows. The headman waved an ax.[2]

tapir: large, chiefly nocturnal animal from Central America, which has a heavy body, short legs and a fleshy upper lip

2. In Your Journal: There will be many dates to keep track of in this selection. You may want to begin creating a timeline in your notes to be able to infer cause-and-effect relationships from all of the events.

The tumultuous landing in Dorita-teri, on May 17, 1991, created an impressive spectacle for the Venezuelan television crew, which was doing a special on "the purest human groups in existence."[3] The community was located in the little-explored Siapa Highlands on the Brazil-Venezuela border, the Amazon's last frontier. These remote mountains also concealed the last intact cluster of aboriginal villages in the world—whose inhabitants were considered living relics of prehistoric culture. The seminomadic Yanomami spent their time hunting and trekking in much the same way humanity had done for countless generations. The anthropologist directing the expedition called them "our contemporary ancestors."[4]

3. In Your Journal: What do you think the Venezuelan television crew meant by "'the purest human groups in existence'"?

Although it was a novelty for the television journalists to be welcomed into an Indian village with axes and arrows in 1991, the expedition leaders Napoleon Chagnon and Charles Brewer Carías had been taking risks like this for decades. Chagnon, an anthropologist at the University of California at Santa Barbara, and Brewer, a naturalist, then associated with the New York Botanical Garden, claimed first contact with 3,500 Yanomami Indians in the Siapa region alone.[5] In August 1990, their "discovery of 10 Yanomami villages they say had never been visited before by anyone except other tribal members" set off a frenzy of media competition and scientific congratulation.[6] "Stone Age Villages Found" ran a typical headline.[7]

4. In Your Journal: What is a frontier? What images does this word conjure in your mind?

5. In Your Journal: Why would anyone want to "claim first contact" with a tribe? What does this phrase suggest about the relationship between anthropologists and the groups they study?

In the economics of exoticism, the more remote and more isolated a tribal group is, the greater its market value. As the last intact aboriginal group, the Yanomami were in a class by themselves, poster people whose naked, photogenic appeal was matched by their unique genetic inheritance. Their blood was as coveted by scientists as their image was by photographers.[8] Technically, the Yanomami were defined as a virgin soil

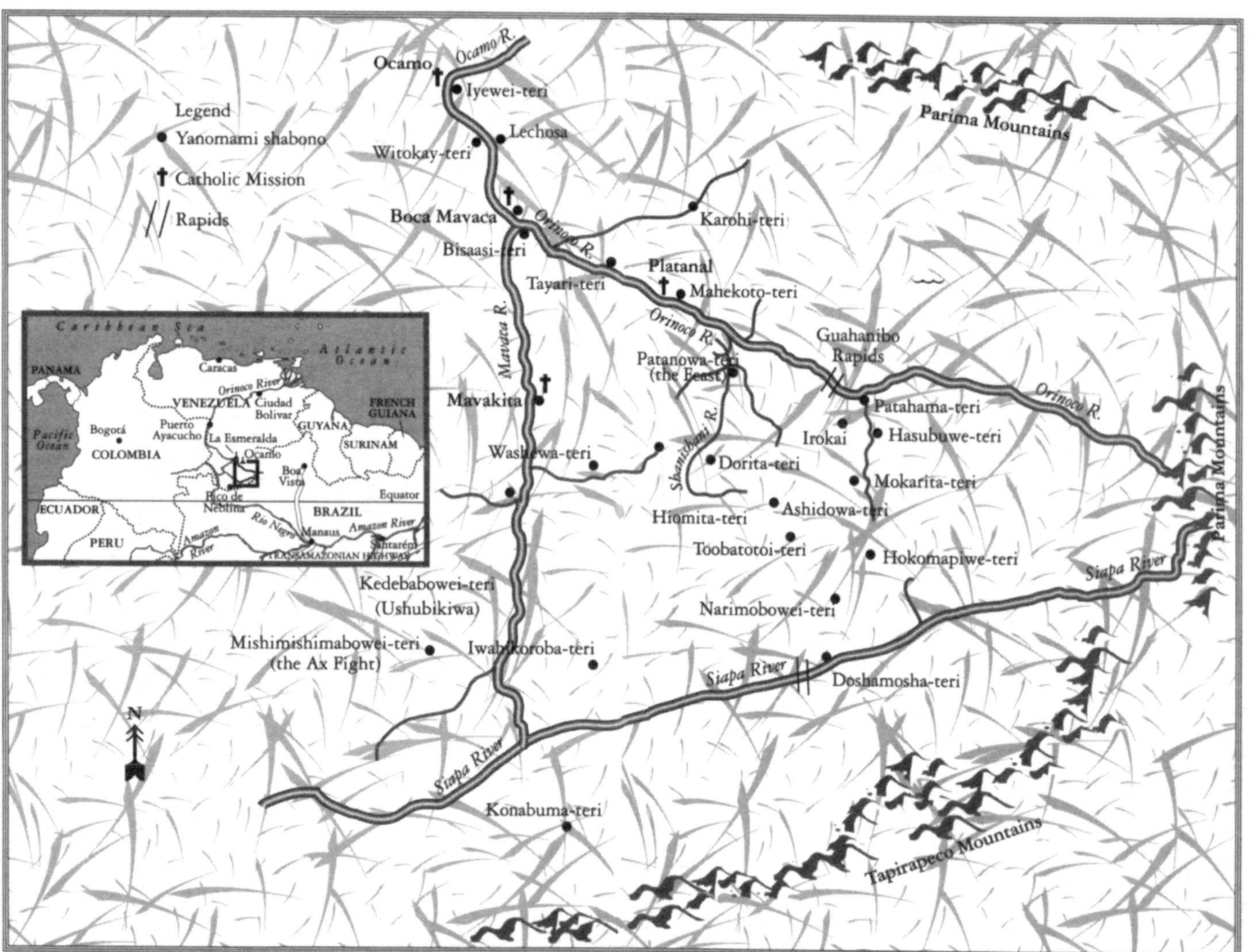

The Siapa Highlands

population, and there was a trace of feudal privilege in the way the visitations were doled out: ABC's *Prime Time* got one village,[9] *Newsweek* another,[10] and so it went. The *New York Times* got two villages,[11] but had to share one of them with the Associated Press.

Sometimes the media's own arrival was the real scoop. Just before visiting Dorita-teri, the same Venevisión crew had gotten exciting footage at a neighboring village, Shanishani-teri, where the helicopter landed in the middle of the circular communal house, or *shabono*. The round house's roofing was whisked up and away, like Dorothy's house in a Kansas tornado, while the Yanomami's possessions—bark hammocks, gourds, woven baskets, and bamboo arrows—splintered and shattered like Tinkertoys. The on-camera journalist, Marta Rodríguez Miranda, said, "They kindly accepted our landing in the middle of the *shabono* even though their whole roof would collapse with the downblast."[12]

Similar scenes were repeated elsewhere with different media teams. At one village, the helicopter was driven off with a hail of rocks and sticks;[13] at another, five Yanomami were injured by falling roof poles.[14] During all these adventures, only ABC's John Quiñones asked the most obvious question, one that might have occurred to any grade-school student educated about the tragic history of Indian tribes since the European discovery of America in the fifteenth century. "Aren't we doing some harm, spoiling this culture, even by coming here today?" Quiñones asked Charles Brewer, who at fifty-two, looked fit, handsome, and baby-faced behind his sprawling mustache.

> ***6. In Your Journal:*** What do you think "spoiling" means to Brewer? Does all anthropology "spoil" people?

"Definitely," Brewer answered. "Every time we are making a contact, we are spoiling them."[15]

In spite of the "first contact" craze, almost all of these extraordinarily remote communities had been visited before and were being reharvested after a suitable interval. In fact, Chagnon and Brewer had visited the Yanomami of Dorita-teri at another location in 1968, where they made two award-winning documentaries, which went on to become staples of anthropology classes around the world.[16] One film, *Yanomama: A Multidisciplinary Study,* dramatically illustrated the scientists' **altruism** in rescuing the Dorita-teri's parent village from a deadly measles epidemic.[17] The second documentary—*The Feast*—showcased Yanomami ferocity and won first prize at every film festival in which it was entered.[18] Everyone praised these films except the Dorita-teri, who apparently had a different interpretation of the scientists' camera work.

> **altruism:** unselfish concern for others

Despite their previous acquaintance, the Dorita-teri were not enthusiastic about seeing Chagnon and Brewer again. The village headman, Harokoiwa, greeted them with an ax. Swaying from side to side, Harokoiwa upbraided the scientists for driving away game with their helicopter. He also accused them of bringing *xawara*—evil vapors that, in the Yanomami conception of disease, cause epidemics. Harokoiwa angrily claimed that Chagnon had killed countless Yanomami with his cameras.[19] In reality, many of the Yanomami who starred in *The Feast* died of mysterious illnesses immediately afterward—new sicknesses the Indians had attributed to the scientists' **malefic** filmmaking.[20] The Yanomami abandoned the village where *The Feast* was made and never returned. Later they shot arrows into a palm **effigy** of the film's anthropologist—Napoleon Chagnon.[21]

malefic: having evil influence

effigy: crudely representative figure

Now, on Chagnon's return, the headman began swinging his ax tantalizingly close to the anthropologist's head. Harokoiwa yelled that he did not want outsiders to poison any more rivers,[22] a reference to Brewer's huge open-pit gold mines on Indian lands.[23]

Suddenly, one of the chief's sons, wielding another ax, rushed Chagnon. As the weapon arced through the air, it appeared to be on its way to splitting Chagnon's skull when Brewer deftly intercepted the ax with one hand and, with the other, knocked the man to the ground. Adding to the confusion were screams by some of the Dorita-teri women, who begged their men not to kill Chagnon and Brewer, "because they had always brought so many presents."[24]

7. In Your Journal: How does the women's plea to spare Chagnon contribute to Tierney's characterization of them?

Under the circumstances, the scientists and television crew thought it best to leave. On returning to Caracas, Venevisión's producers shelved the footage of this confrontation,[25] though not without some pain. It was a great little scene. But it raised nagging questions that could not be answered, at least not on a show about Stone Age ancestors.

AT PLAY IN THE FIELD

> *For many years now anthropologists have been saying how exotic we Yanomami are. But when we finally tell our story the world will find out who is truly exotic.*
>
> —Davi Kopenawa[1]

Almost every anthropology student has experienced the horror of Napoleon Chagnon's first encounter with South America's Yanomami Indians. Chagnon stumbled into a village while Yanomami **shamans** were blowing hallucinogenic snuff up their noses. Deeply drugged, the Indians drew their six-foot bows. "I looked up and gasped when I saw a dozen burly, naked, sweaty, hideous men staring at us down the shaft of their drawn arrows! Immense wads of green tobacco were stuck between their lower teeth and lips making them look even more hideous, and strands of dark-green slime dripped or hung from their nostrils. . . ."[2]

shaman: medicine man in tribal societies who are thought to possess magic healing powers and control over natural events

Yanomamo: The Fierce People, which Chagnon first published in 1968, quickly became the all-time best-seller in anthropology.[3] Four million students bought the book,[4] which is both a riveting account of warfare among

Stone Age people and a sobering assessment of what life may have been like for much of prehistory. *The Fierce People* made the Yanomami the most famous tribe in the world—a model for primitive man and a synonym for aggression.[5] It made Napoleon Chagnon the best-known American anthropologist since **Margaret Mead.**

By the time I began studying the Yanomami, in 1989, they were caught in the middle of the Amazon gold rush, the largest gold migration in history.[6] Forty-five thousand miners were flying in and out of **clandestine** airstrips, bringing epidemics, alcohol, guns, and prostitution.[7] Malaria, influenza, and hepatitis were out of control: fifteen hundred Yanomami had died of infectious diseases.[8] Although I contracted malaria, my worst moments came after being robbed at gunpoint, when I found myself sleeping on the jungle floor without food and negotiating rapids in a leaky boat with gold miners who were as hungry and desperate as I was.

clandestine: secret

Before going into the jungle, I had read and admired *The Fierce People.* So it was surprising to see that the Yanomami—so terrifying and "burly" in Chagnon's text—were, in fact, among the tiniest, scrawniest people in the world.[9] Adults averaged four feet seven inches in height,[10] and children had among the lowest weight-height ratios on the planet.[11] They seemed decidedly timid compared to several other Amerindian groups with whom I had lived. The Yanomami welcomed me effusively, as they welcomed missionaries, anthropologists, gold miners, and anybody else who brought them steel, medicine, or food. But the real shock came when I visited a village on the Mucajaí River in Brazil, where Chagnon claimed to have discovered a Yanomami group that embodied the tribe's ultimate form of "treachery."[12] In reality, these Indians had lived in relative harmony for half a century.[13] I was amazed to find that Chagnon had even created his own **topography**—moving a mountain where one did not exist and landing cargo planes where they had never touched down[14]—while quoting people he could never have spoken to in this part of the jungle.[15] It was the Mucajaí of Chagnon's mind.[16]

topography: detailed physical description of a place or region

When I went into the jungle, Chagnon was embroiled in an academic dispute that, like the rumblings and lightning of a distant storm, was already setting fire to anthropology journals around the world. Many of the anthropologists in Yanomami studies were denouncing Chagnon. They had accused him of inventing quotations and creating nonexistent villages—of fabricating lurid stories about Yanomami violence that were being enthusiastically broadcast by pro-mining forces to justify the ***conquista*** of Yanomamiland.[17] The titles of the articles alone suggested the bitterness of

conquista: defeat; claiming

⁘ **Margaret Mead:** (1901-1978) American anthropologist who studied child-rearing, adolescents, and sexual behavior in primitive cultures; her most famous work is *Coming of Age in Samoa* (1928)

ethnography: branch of anthropology dealing with scientific descriptions of specific human cultures

the debate: "**Ethnography** and Ethnocide"; "The Academic Extermination of the Yanomami"; "To Fight over Women and to Lose Your Lands: Violence in Anthropological Writing and the Yanomami of Amazonia"; "Bias in Ethnographic Reporting."[18] In the end, the journal *Science,* which had twice published articles by Chagnon, despite opposition by Yanomami field experts,[19] was forced to run a new article on the imbroglio: "Warfare over Yanomamo Indians."[20]

But no one was prepared for Chagnon's next move—which brought anthropology's war and the gold war together. In 1990, he began campaigning to turn the Yanomami's homeland into the world's largest private reserve, to be administered by himself and two controversial allies, both of whom had their own gallery of enemies inside Venezuela. One was the naturalist turned gold miner Charles Brewer, who had a police record of clandestine gold diggings on Indian lands.[21] Charlie, as everyone called him, certainly had a history as wild as that of any ***conquistador***—Olympic swimmer, scientist, explorer, government minister—and these were just a few of his incarnations.[22] Like Chagnon, he had started off as a disciple of the great geneticist James Neel at the University of Michigan's Department of Human Genetics, where he began his romance with violent competition.[23] Like Chagnon, he loved guns and fighting.[24] Brewer ferried a surprising variety of celebrities into the forest, from **Margot Hemingway** to **David Rockefeller,**[25] and even arranged a tuxedo dinner catered by helicopters atop a magnificent, 10,000-foot *meseta.*[26] One of Brewer's jungle companions was the London *Times* editor Redmond O'Hanlon, who made Charlie the hero of his classic jungle book, *In Trouble Again.*[27] The editor of ***Geo*** was even more impressed. He called Brewer "the **Alexander Humboldt** of our time."[28]

conquistador: *(Spanish)* conqueror; especially a Spanish conqueror of Mexico and Peru in the 16th century

Meanwhile, Brewer led the Amazon gold stampede.

Brewer introduced Chagnon to President Carlos Andrés Pérez's mistress, Cecilia Matos.[29] Together, they planned to control Yanomamiland—all under the auspices of Cecilia Matos's foundation, FUNDAFACI.[30] In retrospect, the bold decision to seize control of Yanomamiland—an area the size of Maine, with immense scientific and mineral resources—was the most fateful of Chagnon's career. But it made sense, from Chagnon's perspective. By 1990, he could not get research permits. South American anthropologists, Indian Agency bureaucrats, indigenous leaders, and mis-

Margot Hemingway: actress and granddaughter of Ernest Hemingway; died of a drug overdose in 1996

David Rockefeller: the honorary chairman of the Trilateral Commission who served as officer of the Chase Manhattan bank from 1946 to 1981; engaged in major economic and philanthropic activities in Latin America

Geo: geography and nature monthly magazine (German and French)

Alexander Humboldt: see page 691

sionaries wanted him, and the legacy of *The Fierce People,* to disappear.[31] Of course, Chagnon might have rested on his laurels, allowing his books and films to roll onward, conquering by their sheer mass and momentum. But refusing a challenge would have been contrary both to Chagnon's personality and to his theory of violence. According to him, murderers reproduced prolifically. Aggressive villages prospered. Evolution punished passivity and rewarded predation. Chagnon had no choice but to attack.

8. In Your Journal: Why does Chagnon have "no choice but to attack"?

And it had to be a total war. Chagnon hoped to construct the biggest tropical research station ever in the Yanomami wilderness.[32] It would have given him unprecedented power, but it required overthrowing the legal structure already established in Yanomami territory, which in turn required a public-relations campaign. Chagnon managed this brilliantly by handing out "first contact" scoops in the hitherto-unmolested Siapa Highlands in exchange for promoting his plan and denouncing the missionaries and Yanomami leaders who opposed it. In this agile ***quid pro quo,*** reporters plugged Chagnon's plan while claiming the Yanomami were dying out at the missions at several times the rate of the remote villages—an inversion of reality.[33] Thanks to Chagnon's ability at sound bites, the plan almost worked. But that was the trouble with all the plans to create a kingdom in El Dorado country. They always almost worked.

quid pro quo: (Latin) "this for that" exchange

The immediate cause of Chagnon's downfall was Charles Brewer, who wanted to "administer" the same area where he had been planning one of the largest tin mines in the world.[34] The Yanomami rebelled against the proposed FUNDAFACI **biosphere.** And, after Pérez was impeached and jailed for corruption, Matos herself became a fugitive from justice. Among other things, the police and congress investigated her use of government helicopters to fly her friends—including Chagnon—around Yanomami territory,[35] junkets that cost millions of dollars[36] and apparently violated the law.[37]

biosphere: closed, self-regulating ecological system

Judge Nilda Aguilera expelled Brewer and Chagnon from Yanomami territory on September 30, 1993,[38] following public demonstrations and petitions from seventeen Indian tribes.[39] Venezuelan anthropologist Nelly Arvelo Jiménez, who has a Ph.D. from Cornell University, publicly asked about Chagnon what many privately wondered: "How could he dare become associated with . . . environment[al] predators and economic gangsters?"[40]

The aftermath convulsed the Venezuelan congress, courts, and media. Chagnon was also charged with spreading diseases through large, reckless expeditions to vulnerable, uncontacted Yanomami villages in the Siapa Highlands of Venezuela,[41] and with provoking conflict among them—to the point of setting off battles in which his own guides were killed.[42]

The scandal created concentric circles of violence, starting among the least-contacted Yanomami villages and spreading to Venezuelan national politics, where it culminated in a failed **putsch,** led by tanks and attack planes, against the presidential palace.[43] When I arrived in Caracas, the doors of the palace, with their bronze lions, were all shattered, and tank tracks ran down the mansion's marble stairs like the footsteps of a Hollywood star.

putsch: (German) sudden attempt to overthrow the government

The fallout has also shaken American anthropology since the late 1980s. Chagnon's writings were a blessing to the gold miners invading Yanomami lands and a curse to the Yanomami political organizations trying to expel these so-called *garimpeiros* (hill bandits). Chagnon did nothing to distance himself from crude attacks against the Yanomami that utilized quotations from his books and articles—quotations so long they appeared to infringe on copyright laws.[44] He had always been a militant anti-Communist and free-market advocate.[45] Now Chagnon began lumping "leftwing anthropologists," "leftwing politicians," and "survival groups" into the same dismissive sentences,[46] while calling the Yanomami's most visible spokesman, Davi Kopenawa, "a parrot of human rights groups."[47] In the eyes of most human rights workers, Chagnon became, as a French anthropologist put it, "an intellectual accomplice of the gold miners."[48] The *Chronicle of Higher Education* now called it "Bitter Warfare in Anthropology."[49]

Terence Turner, an Amazon expert from the University of Chicago who headed a commission on the fate of the Yanomami, told colleagues in December 1994, "We have no right to castigate the gold miners, the military, the missionaries, or the governments of South America if we're afraid to look at the role of our own anthropologists in the Yanomami tragedy. Unfortunately, Napoleon Chagnon has caused a great deal of harm to the Yanomami and their chances of survival."[50]

What began as a debate about human nature has become a dispute about science at the service of ethnocide. "This is by far the ugliest controversy in the history of anthropology," commented Lesley Sponsel, a professor at the University of Hawaii who headed the American Anthropological Association's Human Rights Committee. "Nothing else even comes close."[51]

Chagnon's influence has often been compared to that of Margaret Mead,[52] whose own classic, *Coming of Age in Samoa,* was surpassed in sales and influence only by *The Fierce People.* In some ways, the current controversy started off like the one that brought discredit to Mead's writings. Mead conjured up an idyllic society in the South Pacific, whose sexual freedom coincided with the theories of her mentor, Franz Boas of Columbia University and appealed to Mead personally. Mead managed to ignore the fact that the Samoans had one of the highest indices of violent rape on the planet.[53]

Whereas Mead continued **Rousseau's** tradition of pressing idealized natives into service for the left, Chagnon picked up where **Social**

⁘ **Rousseau:** (Jean Jacques) (1712-1778) Swiss philosopher and writer who reasoned that the individual is essentially good, but usually becomes corrupted by his society; Rousseau's *The Social Contract* (1762) became the textbook for the French Revolution

---

⁘ **Social Darwinist:** believer in the idea that one group achieves an advantage over others as a result of genetic or biological superiority

Darwinists left off. He emphasized the necessity of lethal competition in nature and the inevitable dominance of murderous men in a prehistoric society. Chagnon's ethnographic image of the ferocious Yanomami matched his own reputation for bar fighting[54] and also echoed the views of his sponsor, the great geneticist James Neel of the University of Michigan. Neel believed that modern society was going soft. From the Amazon's unspoiled inheritance, Neel hoped to find a genetic basis for male dominance—"the Index of Innate Ability"—a kind of **elixir** to the gene pool.[55] It was Neel who selected the Yanomami as experimental subjects and sent Chagnon to find evidence for his **quixotic** theory.[56]

elixir: a substance or medicine believed to have the power to cure illness

quixotic: idealistic; foolishly impractical

That is how Chagnon initially found himself in remote rain forest highlands surrounded by ancient mountains of granite, called the Guiana Shield, which divide the immense Amazon-Orinoco watersheds. When Chagnon arrived in 1964, this remained one of the last unmapped areas of the Americas; the origins of rivers and the boundaries between Venezuela and Brazil were still uncertain. The highest peak, Cerro Neblina (9,889 feet), had been discovered only in 1953. White-water rapids, 3,000-foot cliffs, and swamps the size of European states had frustrated conquerors of all countries since the sixteenth century, making these **redoubts** a perfect blank slate for wilder hopes than the leadership gene. Here, **Sir Walter Raleigh** unsuccessfully searched for a second **Cuzco** and then wrote a popular book in 1601 about an Inca city of solid gold, Gran Manoa, built next to "a mountain of crystal."[57]

redoubts: temporary refuge

The **tectonic** plates of all European empires collided here, too, creating the splinter states of the **Guyanas,** and a cartographer's dream labeled El Dorado. Spectacular tabletop mountains added to the mystery. **Sir Arthur Conan Doyle** used one of them, Mount Roraima, for his fictional Lost World, an Edwardian Jurassic Park inhabited by ape-men, continuing Raleigh's image of Indians "who dwell upon the trees."[58] The German naturalist Alexander von Humboldt concluded that delusions came with the territory. "Above the great cataracts of the Orinoco a mythical land begins, the soil of fable and fairy vision."

tectonic: relating to structural deformation of the Earth's crust; architectural

---

- **Sir Walter Raleigh:** (1552–1618) English navigator, colonizer and writer who introduced tobacco and the potato to Europe; convicted of treason by James I and later executed

- **Cuzco:** city in southern Peru in the Andes mountains; according to the legend, it was the center of the vast Incan empire in the 12th century and was later rebuilt by the Spanish

- **Guyanas:** republic in northeastern South America; officially English-speaking

- **Sir Arthur Conan Doyle:** (1859–1930) British author and creator of the stories of Sherlock Holmes, who solved seemingly impossible cases with his brilliant deductive reasoning skills

But the reality Chagnon described was in some ways stranger than the tradition of projection and fantasy. He focused on the seemingly compulsive violence of the Yanomami, whose 25,000 members made up the world's largest intact aboriginal culture. As Chagnon went farther into uncharted territory, he had a **Conradian** sense of going backward in evolutionary time to an awful, almost apelike existence. The foreword to *The Fierce People* characterized the Yanomami as a "brutal, cruel, treacherous" people whose morality was the antithesis of "the ideal **postulates** of the Judaic-Christian tradition."[59]

postulate: assumption of truth

metallurgy: process of creating useful tools from metal

The Yanomami had no **metallurgy** and little social hierarchy. They slung bark hammocks around the periphery of communal round houses with open centers, called *shabonos*. Personal possessions were almost nonexistent. Although the Yanomami practiced slash-and-burn gardening, they spent much of their time on long treks hunting and gathering, the way of life that predominated for most of humanity's prehistory. The Yanomami did not use canoes and had little use for clothes, other than a cotton waistband for women and a penis string for men. They practiced ritual combats that no other Amazonian group shared—a graded series of exchanges starting with chest pounding and followed by duels with long poles.[60] Even their blood was different. The Yanomami have a private gene mutation not found in any other human population. They also lack the Diego factor, an **antigen** found in all other **Mongoloid** peoples, including other Amerindians.[61]

antigen: substance that stimulates the production of antibodies

Mongoloid: ethnic division including various Asian groups, Eskimos, and American Indians

paleo: prehistoric

Caucasoid: relating to the Caucasian or white racial classification

enigma: something thoroughly puzzling or inexplicable

Presumably, the Yanomami are also of Asiatic origin, but their skin is often lighter and their eyes are hazel, characteristics that have earned them the name White Indians. Some scientists believe they are descended from the first **paleo** hunters who crossed the **Bering Strait** at least thirteen thousand years ago[62] (and whose few skeletal remains suggest **Caucasoid** features). In Chagnon's evocative writing, the Yanomami became both unique and normative, a one-of-a-kind tribe held up as a model for humanity's earliest type of warfare, sexual competition, and economy. It was as close as an anthropologist could come to discovering El Dorado.

The Yanomami may always remain an **enigma.** But James Neel certainly picked the wrong place and the wrong people to try and prove his quirky ideas about hierarchies of violence and genetic selection. The Yanomami have a low level of homicide by world standards of tribal cul-

---

Conrad: (Joseph)(1857–1924) British novelist noted as a master of atmosphere and narrative technique; most famous works are *Lord Jim* (1900), *Heart of Darkness* (1902), and *Nostromo* (1904); referred to here because the themes of *Heart of Darkness* (e.g., the clash of primitive cultures and modern civilization) relate somewhat to the activities of Chagnon

---

Bering Strait: narrow stretch of water between Alaska and Siberia connecting the Artic Ocean to the Bearing Sea; believed to have formed a land bridge between North America and Asia in prehistoric times ture and a very low level by Amazonian standards. Compared to other tribes, they are fearful of outsiders, especially when it comes to dealing with aggressors like gold miners. As Chagnon noted in his Ph.D. thesis, "the Yanomamo are not brave warriors."[63]

The attempt to portray the Yanomami as **archetypes** of ferocity would be pathetic were it not for its political consequences—and for the fabulous distortions this myth has perpetrated in biology, anthropology, and popular culture. The ripple consequences of the Yanomami fantasy can be seen from the film *The Emerald Rain Forest* (where an apelike group called "the Fierce People" create indiscriminate mayhem), to the Harvard primatologist Richard Wrangham's recent book *Demonic Males,* which has a whole section about "Yanomamo Indians and Gombe chimpanzees."[64] Just as Mead's beliefs about sexual freedom and child rearing worked their way into public-policy debates, Chagnon's ferocious Yanomami have become proof to some social scientists that ruthless competition and sexual selection cannot be legislated away by idealistic do-gooders. The Yanomami are the Cold Warriors who never came in from the cold.

Unraveling this academic distortion might have been as significant, say, as Derek Freeman's book *Margaret Mead and Samoa: The Making and Unmaking of an Anthropological Myth.* But, as I began investigating on the Upper Orinoco, I found that things were both stranger and more complicated than I had expected.

One of the oddest things I uncovered among the most remote Yanomami villages was a pattern of choreographed violence, dating back to the early, internationally acclaimed films of the Yanomami made by Chagnon and **Timothy Asch,** and continued to the present by *Nova* and the BBC. As a missionary who accompanied me said, "It's amazing how many alliances were created and villages were built just to satisfy the film crews."[65]

A case in point was the recent *Nova*/BBC documentary "Warriors of the Amazon," which has aired many times in the United States in the late 1990s. The hour-long piece was a dramatic narrative about an unnamed *shabono* that was said to be ceaselessly warring against another unnamed *shabono.*[66]

In reality, the hosts had not had any wars in years, until the film crew arrived and built a new *shabono,* negotiated a new alliance, and helped create a feud that has split the former community apart.[67]

Anthropologists have left an indelible imprint upon the Yanomami. In fact, the word *anthro* has entered the Indians' vocabulary, and it is not a term of endearment. For the Indians, *anthro* has come to signify something like the opposite of its original Greek meaning, "man." The

---

Timothy Asch: (1932–1994) well-known ethnographic filmmaker whose works include various documentaries on the Yanomani as well as the diverse cultures of the Indonesian archipelago

Yanomami consider an *anthro* to be a powerful nonhuman with deeply disturbed tendencies and wild eccentricities—an Olympian in a funk.[68]

It is no exaggeration to say that the Yanomami are ethnographic experts on the madness of anthropologists. A German anthropologist from a prestigious Max Planck Institute near Munich committed suicide at the Yanomami village of Patanowa-teri after his Yanomami lover deserted him.[69] A French *anthro* in the Parima Mountains had to be disarmed, tied up, and carried off by parachutists after he tried to kill one of his colleagues with a knife.[70] Chagnon, according to videotaped testimony by his own principal informant, played the role of a shaman who took hallucinogens and incorporated the most fearsome entities of the Yanomami's spirit **pantheon.**[71]

pantheon: a temple dedicated to all gods

And these were the normal anthropologists.

Well, yes, when compared with Jacques Lizot, a University of Paris anthropologist and disciple of Claude Lévi-Strauss. Lizot lived for thirty years with the Yanomami, far longer than any other anthropologist, and served as principal consultant for *Nova*'s recent documentary. Yet, in some ways, the Yanomami he conjures up would appear utterly alien to the Fierce People. Lizot has portrayed the Yanomami as sexual innovators of stunning sophistication, an Erotic People—a product better appreciated in the French cultural sphere.[72]

According to the author Mark Ritchie, Lizot was not altogether lacking in sexual imagination himself. Through transcribed testimonies from a variety of Yanomami sources, Ritchie recounts, in his book *Spirit of the Rainforest,* Lizot's exotic career. Lizot was identified by his Yanomami name, Bosinawarewa—which Ritchie renders as Ass Handler[73] (literally, Anus Eater). At the same time that Lizot became the acknowledged expert on Yanomami language, the French scientist indirectly expanded the Yanomami lexicon. In some villages, the Yanomami word for anal intercourse is *Lizo-mou:* "to do like Lizot."[74]

Not even the most inventive chronicler could have envisioned a mythology as **florid** as that which scientists and filmmakers have scripted for the Yanomami and enacted for themselves. Above the great **cataracts** of the Orinoco is the strangest story in the history of social science—the Bermuda Triangle of anthropology.

florid: ornate

cataract: waterfall

"We started calling the Upper Orinoco **'Macondo,' the surreal world of Gabriel García Márquez**," says Jesús Cardozo, president of the Venezuelan Foundation for Anthropological Investigation (FUNVENA). "When I first started doing research among the Yanomami, I was told, 'Lizot is going to kill you.' I thought it was a joke, you know. But I found out that the most insane things were going on. I mean, anthropologists were chasing each other around with shotguns. Each had his own fiefdom. Villages were

---

Macondo . . . : the village in Marquez's novel *One Hundred Years of Solitude,* famous for its epic scope and use of magical realism named for Lizot and Chagnon, as though they were great Yan chiefs. And the anthropologists' villages took on their persor Chagnon's Yanomami were more warlike than any other group; Liz lage became the capital of homosexuality. Of course, there's a question of human rights violations. But what interests me is not t Lizot or Chagnon before an international tribunal. I just think it's in for anthropology, for the history of science, to understand how tl pened, and what role the media played in creating this strange nev Because the more weird Chagnon and Lizot became, the more they were worshiped as celebrities."[75]

In the discourse of the Upper Orinoco, words like "paranoid,"[76] "sociopath,"[77] "loathsome,"[78] and "criminal"[79] are commonplace—especially when anthropologists talk about Chagnon. Chagnon, for his part, has written that one of his critics is "fucked,"[80] and he has dismissed the rest as skunks.[81]

"I think so many anthropologists went bonkers among the Yanomami because there were no limits, no rules among the Yanomami," says the missionary Michael Dawson, who has spent forty years among the Indians. "With their tools and guns, they were like **Connecticut Yankees at King Arthur's court.** They could become whatever they wanted to become. They became gods."[82]

For the Yanomami, as for the Greeks, a proof of a god's power was the ability to bring epidemics. This is unquestionably the most impressive legacy of scientists and journalists on the Upper Orinoco. On the basis of the scientists' own detailed records, hundreds of Yanomami died in the immediate wake of exploration and filming.[83]

I was surprised to learn that the **Atomic Energy Commission** (AEC) had lavishly funded the earliest and deadliest expeditions. As I requested AEC documents through the **Freedom of Information Act,** I found that the AEC had used the Yanomami as a control group, comparing their rate of genetic mutation with that of the survivors of the atomic bombs in Hiroshima and Nagasaki. The Department of Energy wrote to me, "The results of this research have contributed to our understanding of the natural development of gene mutations in man and have helped to bridge the gap between **mutagenesis** studies in experimental animals and observations in people."[84]

mutagenisis: development of an alteration; biological mutation

---

Connecticut Yankees at King Arthur's court: refers a novel by Mark Twain, which juxtaposes values of different cultures and centuries; the "modern" Hank is shown to be more helpless and ignorant than the medieval characters, and his representation implicitly criticizes what Twain thought was a tendency toward "destructive progress" in American culture

Atomic Energy Commission: American agency (from 1947 to 1977) that was responsible for research into atomic energy

Freedom of Information Act: law that provides individual citizens with access to government records and documents

To complete these unique studies, which helped the AEC set radiation standards in the United States, the AEC needed great amounts of Yanomami blood, all purchased with steel goods. The researchers were particularly interested in Yanomami responses to disease pressure: "How disease as well as warfare decimates the population."[85]

The Venezuelan Yanomami experienced the greatest disease pressure in their history during a 1968 measles epidemic. The epidemic started from the same village where the geneticist James Neel had scientists inoculate the Yanomami with a live virus that had proven safe for healthy American children but was known to be dangerous for immune-compromised people.[86] The epidemic seemed to track the movements of the vaccinators. An estimated 15 to 20 percent of the Venezuelan Yanomami died of measles in the months following vaccination.[87]

I sensed that the injustice done to the Yanomami was matched by the distortion done to science and the history of human evolution. Yet the incredible faith the sociobiologists had in their theories was admirable. Like the old Marxist missionaries, these zealots of biological determinism sacrificed everything—including the lives of their subjects—to spread their gospel. A fascination with this fanaticism led me to places I did not intend to go—including the National Film Archives in Washington. After a week of searching through a collection no one else had ever examined, I found a dusty box labeled "Very valuable. Original sound tracks of 1968 expedition." I also found myself trekking, *shabono* by *shabono,* mountain range by mountain range, into the Siapa Highlands, and into an Amazonian heart of darkness where scientists and journalists were the chief protagonists.

The risks of such a crusade should have been obvious. After all, plenty of cautionary tales dotted the Yanomami landscape. "You really have to really feel sorry for the Yanomami," said the anthropologist Kenneth Good, a former Ph.D. student of Chagnon's who has lived longer among the Yanomami than any other American anthropologist. "The United States sent Chagnon. France sent Lizot. In Caracas they added on Charlie Brewer. *Jesus.* You better be careful down there yourself. Yanomami studies make people crazy."[88]

Was it heredity or the environment? Did the Yanomami's culture, or something in the Orinoco's water, drive researchers mad? Or was it a self-selecting group of born misfits? Luckily, I did not have time to worry about such trifles as I conducted censuses and advanced farther into the jungle, always making good progress. After a particularly exhausting trudge through the Siapa wilderness, I was only slightly disconcerted when the Yanomami at the village of Mokarita-teri all dispersed in terror at my arrival. The first man who returned came back warily, as if approaching one of the dangerous ghosts, called *bore,* who show themselves to the Yanomami at night.

> ***9. In Your Journal:*** How do you read Tierney's tone here? What is Tierney revealing about himself in this paragraph?

"Are you Chagnon?" he asked.[89]

THE NAPOLEONIC WARS

The village I'm living in really thinks I am the be-all and end-all.

—Napoleon Chagnon, 1965[1]

The wars that made Chagnon and the Yanomami famous—the ones he wrote about with such relish in *The Fierce People*—began on November 14, 1964, the same day the anthropologist arrived with his shotguns, outboard motor, and a canoe full of steel goods to give away.[2]

"A war started between groups which had been at peace for some time on the very first day Chagnon got there, and it continued until he left," said Brian Ferguson, a Rutgers anthropologist who is an expert on violence in primitive societies. "I don't think that was an accident." Ferguson's book *Yanomami Warfare,* published in 1995, is perhaps the most comprehensive account ever written about tribal conflict. Two of its chapters are devoted to Chagnon's own role in fomenting warfare among the Yanomami.[3] "I originally considered calling my book *The Napoleonic Wars,*" Ferguson said.[4]

Ferguson's work is part of a growing consensus that Westerners, including scientists, profoundly disrupt tribal health, life, and politics on arrival. The 1998 Pulitzer Prize for nonfiction went to the UCLA medical researcher Jared Diamond and his book *Guns, Germs, and Steel: The Fates of Human Societies,*[5] a meditation on the worldwide spread of Eurasian war, disease, and trade goods. No tribal society could withstand their onslaught. Historians who have revisited the role of European scientists in the exploration of Africa (in *Dark Safari*) and New Guinea (in *First Contact*) have documented widespread devastation, caused almost unconsciously by specialists convinced of their own objectivity. In some cases, an expedition was not needed. Diamond, who did field research in the South Pacific, recounted how a single British sailor, Charlie Savage, drastically altered **Fiji** society in 1808 with the help of a couple of old muskets. "The aptly named Savage proceeded single-handedly to upset Fiji's balance of power. . . . His victims were so numerous that surviving villages piled up the bodies to take shelter behind them, and the stream beside the village was red with blood."[6]

Far-traveled Carib tribes that gave their name to the Caribbean once settled the Orinoco. They lived in large, fortified towns and plied the great river in hundred-foot canoes. The wars and disease that accompanied

---

❖ **Fiji:** country in the southwest Pacific comprised of about 320 islands, mainly populated by Melanesian and Peloponnesian groups spasmodic efforts of Europe's colonial empires to locate El Dorado exterminated their civilization. An enterprising Dutch governor of **Suriname,** Gravesande, launched the final quest in the first half of the eighteenth century. He formed a military-slaving alliance with a **Rio Negro** tribe, the Manau, whose leader, Ajuricaba, styled himself king of Gran Manoa (an alias for El Dorado) while flying the Dutch flag.[7] Brazil's colonial authorities sent an army that crushed the Manau, captured Ajuricaba (who committed suicide by leaping into a river in chains), and supplanted the Dutch as the leading entrepreneurs in the slave business. The Portuguese kidnapped or purchased over five thousand Indian slaves between 1725 and 1750 on the Upper Orinoco alone.[8]

The earliest mention of the Yanomami came from a multidisciplinary expedition of engineers, surveyors, naturalists, and artists who worked for the Portuguese boundary commission. In 1786, Lobo de Almada described the Yanomami as the "remnant" of a "nation," whose survivors were "still living" in the inaccessible headwaters between Venezuela and Brazil. Almada, who brilliantly directed the collection of new plant species and the cataloging of Indian cultures, contributed to genocide by relocating the Yanomami's eastern neighbors, the Macuxi, to a reservation a thousand miles away, where most of them died in what the historian John Hemming styled "a grotesque experiment."[9]

Other experiments were also underway. In 1784, Alexandre Rodrigues Ferreira, whom Hemming called "the first great naturalist to study the Amazon," began an ambitious scientific enterprise that conscripted hundreds of native guides, porters, paddlers, and servants. "Such navigation is fatal to the Indians, most of whom generally die or are incapacitated for life," a local bishop complained. Thousands perished or fled from the main rivers to escape Ferreira's botanical enthusiasm, leaving whole stretches of the Rio Negro on the Yanomami's southern border devoid of inhabitants.[10]

The Yanomami's strategy of hiding in the hills was more successful—reportedly some three thousand managed to escape the slavers and naturalists and the plagues that accompanied both of them.[11] It was an accident of geography. Europeans failed to reach the source of the Orinoco because the river narrowed to a swift, stone channel—a granite flume only six feet wide in stretches, with wild waters broken by impassable cataracts.[12] Farther upriver, after the **portaging** of a dozen waterfalls but still far from the source, the going became excruciatingly slow. The Orinoco spilled out into a labyrinthine swamp, choked by rotting logs and densely matted vegetation, where navigation was out of the question. It was miserable going.

portage: carry boats and supplies over land

Suriname: country in northeastern South America on the Atlantic Ocean

Rio Negro: river in South America that flows from eastern Colombia to the Amazon River in Brazil

Even in the so-called dry season, from January to March, downpours fell forty-eight days out of fifty.[13] There were few stands of rubber or cacao trees, nothing to excite collectors. And, along the Orinoco's final stages, the only thing that obviously glittered was mica, fool's gold. Given the surfeit of pain and the apparent absence of reward, every European expedition for two centuries turned back without reaching the Orinoco's source. It was actually a tiny catch basin, a few feet in diameter, situated on the rim of a dark, steep gorge above granite escarpments, and it was finally located in 1951 by a Franco-German expedition. Nevertheless, earlier explorers left their mark and contributed to the creation of a Yanomami myth of unbridled ferocity.

The first American to attempt the Orinoco's origin was the noted geographer Hamilton Rice, on assignment for the Royal Geographical Society. He camped above the turbulent Guaharibo Rapids, considered the border of Yanomamiland, on January 21, 1921. There, seeing his abundant supplies, a group of about sixty Yanomami came begging for food and trade goods. This was the Yanomami's typical approach to outsiders,[14] but it startled Rice, who decided to take no chances. He opened fire with his Thompson machine gun and did not bother to count the dead. The Rice expedition fled downriver. He later wrote in Royal Geographical Society's *Journal* that the Yanomami were cannibals who ate raw flesh and that, given the danger of becoming dinner, it had been "necessary to fire to kill."[15]

The next incursion of Americans on the Upper Orinoco came during World War II. A team of U.S. Army engineers and surveyors did a feasibility study on a super-canal to join the Amazon and Orinoco watersheds.[16] Although the canal, which would have dwarfed Panama's, was never built, the friendly engineers got along well with the Indians. The Yanomami eagerly ate the army people's leftovers and shared their cigarettes before returning home with priceless machetes—and deadly contagion. The new respiratory diseases decimated *shabonos* far from the Orinoco, while sparking wars over witchcraft accusations, the double whammy that outside infections have historically brought to Amazon tribes.[17]

The wars and epidemics that shadowed these expeditions profoundly altered the Yanomami landscape. According to local colonists, Rice's machinegun "massacre against unarmed Indians"[18] provoked Yanomami raids against the only remaining settlements on the Upper Orinoco between 1921 and 1931.[19] Although the Yanomami did not kill any whites, they stole all the steel goods they could find and wreaked so much havoc that colonists abandoned the area altogether. For the first time since the Spaniards arrived in 1750, there were no **garrisons** or trading posts within hundreds of miles. The jungle reclaimed old towns, missions, and forts. Another American geographer, Earl Hanson, reported on the **phantasmagoric** victory of the rain forest. "It is probable that the present regression of the region is the most complete in its history since the first advent of the

garrison: military post

phantasmagoric: of or related to a fantastic sequence of imagery, as seen in dreams

Spanish," he wrote. "An interesting spectacle is taking place . . . affording an opportunity for some ethnologist to record a brand-new primitive culture in the making."[20]

There was no one better equipped than Chagnon to record this "brand new primitive culture in the making." *The Fierce People* was written in a fresh, unfettered voice. After giving an account of a man who beat his brother with the blunt edge of an ax, Chagnon confided that the victor was "one of few Yanomami that I feel I can trust."[21] The anthropologist admitted he would have preferred studying some other, kinder group, but cautioned, "This is not to state that primitive man everywhere is unpleasant."[22] He described Yanomami women over the age of thirty as having "a vindictive and caustic attitude toward the external world." There was no puritanical preaching, no concession to the ideal of the Noble Savage. Another reason for the book's popularity was that Chagnon combined two favorite undergraduate themes—violence and sex—into a single theory about Yanomami warfare: Yanomami men fought over women, a message that has resonated on American campuses.

Chagnon survived a nighttime murder attempt by his hosts, whom he frightened off with his flashlight, and a close encounter with a jaguar, which sniffed him in his hammock. He hollowed out his own log canoe to ride down the Mavaca River, after a Yanomami guide abandoned him, and pushed on into unknown territory in spite of repeated death threats. You had to admire his courage—though it was harder to admire the Yanomami as Chagnon depicted them. By the end of the story, many readers concluded the Yanomami were, well, pretty awful.

Perhaps Chagnon's most brilliant achievement was fitting his grimly fascinating adventures into a clear, simple Darwinian framework that seemed to shed new light on human origins. *Time* magazine summarized Chagnon's theory: "the rather horrifying Yanomami culture makes some sense in terms of animal behavior. Chagnon argues that Yanomami structures closely parallel those of many primates in breeding patterns, competition for females and recognition of relatives. Like baboon troops, Yanomami villages tend to split into two groups after they reach a certain size."[23] You had to be fierce to survive and reproduce.

Chagnon said he had to become fierce himself in order to survive among the Yanomami: "I soon learned that I had to become very much like the Yanomamo to be able to get along with them on their terms: sly, aggressive, and intimidating." Otherwise, they would have pushed him around unmercifully and stolen him blind. He learned to shout at them "as loudly and as passionately as they shouted at me." "I had to establish my position in some sort of pecking order of ferocity at each and every village."[24]

Pecking orders of violence were popular in the 1960s, in part because of Konrad Lorenz's influential book *On Aggression,* published in 1966. Lorenz, a Nobel Prize–winning biologist at the Max Planck Institute, made many crucial contributions to understanding the behavior of rats and geese—two very aggressive animals—and a few equally crucial mistakes in applying his laboratory observations to human behavior. He concluded that humans were a simian species gone awry, great apes deformed by hunting and technology to kill without inhibition unlike any other animal.[25] Thus, **original sin** was reinvented, and man became known as a killer ape. Chagnon's Fierce People resembled killer apes: Amazonian primates, similar to baboons, whose perfect **amorality** turned murder and treachery into tribal ideals.

10. In Your Journal: What does Tierney mean when he says that "original sin was reinvented"? How does the Lorenz study compare with the standard narrative of "original sin"?

amorality: lacking moral judgment

Today even Chagnon's strongest supporter, the Harvard sociobiologist Edward O. Wilson, recognizes that humans are probably less violent than any other species, at least as measured by common homicide and infanticide: "The murder rate is far higher than for human beings, even taking into account our wars."[26] Humans are not killer apes, nor are the Yanomami "fierce people."

There are Amazonian tribes, like the Huarani and Achuar, that have levels of violence far higher than that of the Yanomami.[27] Among the Huarani, for example, over 60 percent of all men are killed,[28] compared with 30 percent among the Yanomami Chagnon studied.[29] But the Yanomami have four regional dialects and are spread out over 80,000 square miles. All other Yanomami subgroups have homicide levels much lower than those Chagnon recorded.[30] The adult male homicide rate for the entire tribe might be 12–14 percent. There are villages where no one has been killed in generations and others where a high percentage of the men have been slain.[31] Therefore, rates of adult male war deaths could be engineered in a range from zero to over 40 percent, depending on the village and the time frame. And, if the approximate Yanomami homicide rate appears high when compared with *domestic* rates for wealthy, democratic societies, it is unfair to say, as Chagnon often does, that the Yanomami have a higher homicide rate than the city of Detroit.[32] Such comparisons are **dubious,** not only because the data is so uneven but because tribal violence **conflates** war and common murder—categories that modern societies keep strictly separate. (If murder rates for the Soviet Union or Poland were computed like the Yanomami's—tallying *all killings* over several generations—they would also be high, since they would include millions of male "murders" during World Wars I and II.) In any case, the overall level of violence among the Yanomami is undoubtedly modest for a tribal society without written laws or police.[33]

dubious: uncertain

conflate: combine (somewhat carelessly)

11. In Your Journal: Why are the homicide rates of Chagnon's Yanomami so important, in Tierney's opinion?

The question is no longer why the Yanomami are so fierce, but why Chagnon's Yanomami have homicide rates so much higher than those of

---

original sin: in Christian theology, the sin that marks all humans as a result of Adam's first act of disobedience; suggests we are all born in need of redemption and with a tendency to be tempted towards sin other Yanomami groups. Although Chagnon has portrayed his home village, Bisaasi-teri, as a "typical Yanomamo village,"[34] it was exceptional. By the time Chagnon met the Bisaasi-teri, they were living at the juncture of the Orinoco (400 yards wide) and the Mavaca River (100 yards wide). From the air, the area looks lovely, with its riverine forests shading the muddy Orinoco's banks and granite foothills fingering their way out of the luxuriant growth. But the aerial view is deceiving, for this is a miserable, sticky, malaria-ridden place. No traditional Yanomami village was located anywhere near such a wide stretch of river.[35] Archaeological excavations at Bisaasi-teri have uncovered pottery shards and **manioc** strainers commonly used in Carib cultures but unknown in the Yanomami's mountain redoubt.[36] The Yanomami penetrated this far down the Orinoco only because the Carib tribe that traditionally dwelt there was driven off or enslaved. Two thousand Carib speakers were pressed into servitude by a band of adventurers while an energetic Frenchman set up a trading village in the 1830s at the same spot where Chagnon met the Bisaasi-teri.[37]

manioc: tropical South American plant grown for its roots

All experts, including Napoleon Chagnon, agree that the existing Yanomami groups originated in the Parima and Siapa highlands, which they populated "during untold centuries." The first scientist to live with the highland Yanomami was a University of Pittsburgh geographer, William Smole. After experiencing the Yanomami in their ancestral habitat in 1969–70, Smole began to publicly dispute the "fierce people" appellation for the Yanomami. In the Parima Mountains, Smole settled near a large village that had been at peace for two generations. There were no headmen to speak of, and much less squabbling over marriageable females. Whereas Chagnon's villages had a dramatic shortage of women, the highland villages had a slight surplus. Sorcery was the main cause of what warfare did occur; capturing women was secondary.[38] Smole concluded that Chagnon's Yanomami differed so markedly from the villages in the tribes' more tranquil homeland that they could not be considered traditional Yanomami at all.

12. In Your Journal: What does Smole's conclusion that Chagnon's Yanomami were "not traditional" say about the geographer's attitude toward Chagnon?

Even within the subgroup where Chagnon worked, there is a sharp split between highland and lowland villages. In fact, when Chagnon surveyed five mountain *shabonos* from his own linguistic group in 1990–91, he learned that only about one-fourth as many men had participated in killings as among the lowland groups (11 percent as opposed to 44 percent).[39] Chagnon has yet to reveal the actual homicide statistics for these mountain villages contiguous to the Mavaca River. Nevertheless, his more recent findings confirm what William Smole has been saying for decades—that violence is spacially variable in the Yanomami world, the villages living at low elevations along the Orinoco-Mavaca drainage being the most violent known. These dozen *shabonos,* with a population of 1,394,[40] comprise less than 6 percent of the 25,000 Yanomami alive today. As Smole put it, "Certainly the Yanoama who have moved to sites on or near navigable water are not representative. They are outside their niche in the broadest sense, caught in a squeeze between various adverse influences of 'civilization.' "[41] Smole believed that steel goods, disease, and the divisive influence of outsiders altered such émigré groups beyond recognition. Ferocity and fighting over women "might apply to a lowland zone of acculturation and acute cultural instability."[42]

Almost all subsequent researchers have echoed Smole's criticisms, including most of Chagnon's own students. Chagnon blamed these attacks on romantics trying to create a prettified version of Yanomami culture. Having met with some assaults myself for graphic description of violence among Amerindian groups, I initially sympathized with Chagnon. Once I reached Yanomamiland, however, I found it increasingly difficult to accept Chagnon's version of their culture.

Brazil's nomadic gold miners, whose cross-continental wanderings have brought them into contact with dozens of tribes, have often remarked on how friendly the Yanomami are compared with other Amazonian Indians. The Yanomami at first welcomed me with a kindness that was disconcerting—tied my hammock, brought me food and water, lugged my heavy equipment, and lit lights all around me at night. I soon realized they were desperate for medicines and for someone to take their dying children upriver to a medical clinic.

> ***13. In Your Journal:*** Why does Tierney find the kindness of the Yanomami disconcerting?

Later, I was robbed at gunpoint by several young Yanomami who were working with gold miners. Had I wanted to render a heroic, Chagnonian version of the incident, it might have gone like this:

> When we came to the big curve of the Mucajaí River, white water sprayed us as we dodged in and out of eddy currents. Just after escaping the last whirlpools, we confronted a new danger: a canoe of belligerent warriors heading straight toward us. They pulled even. Then a vicious and powerfully built man leapt into our boat and pointed a shotgun at my head. "I kill gold miners!" he shouted as he beat his chest to establish his dominance. He swayed from side to side, proclaiming his murderous intentions. I stared him down, knowing that a true warrior will never display fear. I also knew the real motive for the treacherous assault: the Yanomami's perpetual suspicion that outsiders wanted to steal their women.

Actually, I had happened on a Yanomami funeral ritual, in which the ashes of the dead are taken out and shared in a tribal communion, a time when the feared ghosts from the past are honored and when old scores can be settled. My boat was boarded in midstream by a twenty-year-old who was drunk on imported whiskey, and he was soon supported by other drunken youngsters with guns of their own. The gold miner, named Cícero Hipólito dos Santos, and I were forced out of the boat at gunpoint, and, as a crowd of warriors and women gathered around, there ensued a debate about whether they should kill us. The surprising thing was that the Yanomami did not kill the gold miner, or me, for that matter; they just stole all our stuff. The local chief, painted red and black, with macaw feathers in his ears, planted himself between the adolescents' guns and me. He yelled, "Go away! Go down the river! The Indians here are all drunk. Indians are very dangerous when they're drunk."

I realized that my own actions, as well as the Yanomami's needs and the bizarre twists of the gold rush, had created situations from which I could have fashioned either a romantic or a Darwinian image of the Yanomami. Of course, either one would have been a distortion, like the portrait in *The Fierce People.*

The Yanomami I met on the Mucajaí were certainly no proverbial saints. But in sixty years they launched only two raids; on two other occasions, a few Mucajaí men joined allied raiding parties. That was it. Yet Chagnon took one of the two raids that the Mucajaí people initiated, and turned it into both the prime example of Yanomami treachery and a case study of a war fought exclusively to capture women. In *The Fierce People,* he claimed that the Mucajaí Borabuk "had a critical shortage of women" and proceeded to describe "the treacherous means by which the group alleviated its problem":

> The headman of the group organized a raiding party to abduct women from a distant group. They went there and told these people that they had machetes and cooking pots from the foreigners, who prayed to a spirit that gave such items in answer to the prayers. They then volunteered to teach these people how to pray. When the men knelt down and bowed their heads, the raiders attacked them with their machetes and killed them. They captured their women and fled.
>
> Treachery of this kind, called nomohori (dastardly trick) is the ultimate from of violence.[43]

But the demographer John Early and the sociologist John Peters, who spent over eight years on the Mucajaí, have put this raid into a wholly different perspective. In the first place, the Mucajaí Borabuk (People of the Waterfall) were not trying to capture women. "They did not view themselves as having a sex ratio problem as such."[44] It is true that they had fewer women than men, but they were not overly concerned about it, because the Yanomami can acquire wives through trade and bride service (such as providing game for a marriageable woman's parents). So the temporary imbalance, common in tribal populations, was taken in stride. In the meantime, they simply shared wives. Chagnon perceived "a critical shortage of women," but the Borabuk did not. In fact, they had not raided anyone in over twenty years.

What really disturbed them were the devastating illnesses that came with first contact, which had arisen from their desire for steel goods. "Previously such tools had been obtained by exchange with or raids upon other indigenous groups." But the Mucajaí group had been isolated since their last raids to obtain steel in the mid-1930s. "The tools they had were wearing out and in need of replacement. They had moved to the banks of the Mucajaí River in the hope of making contact with Brazilians from whom they could obtain the tools. At the time of contact this appeared to be their most preoccupying problem."[45]

In 1955, an amazing event changed their lives: missionaries flew a small plane over the Mucajaí Borabuk and dropped fishhooks. The Borabuk sent a party of men in search of the source of steel. They built canoes for the first time and dispatched them far downstream; where, in late 1957 and again in late 1958, they made contact with Brazilian peasants and received some trade goods. Unfortunately, on both occasions the Mucajaí people also "contracted respiratory infections from the Brazilians and many died after they returned upstream. They had no immunity due to their previous isolation." "The resulting sickness and death was a new and frightening experience for the Mucajaí community."[46]

Two months after the second wave of imported illness, the missionaries arrived, who treated the sick and contained the epidemics. Then the second act in the tragedy of contact began. On the pretext of going on a long hunt, the Mucajaí Borabuk borrowed a gun from the unsuspecting missionaries and traveled upriver, searching for the sorcerers who they believed had caused all the deaths. They investigated the Marashi-teri, on the Couto de Magalhẽs River, who accused another distant group, the Shiri-teri, of being the agents of witchcraft against the Borabuk. Finally, in a confused encounter characterized by mutual misunderstanding, the Borabuk and the Marashi-teri attacked the Shiri-teri, although they did not kill them with machetes as Chagnon reported. One Shiri-teri was actually shot with a gun, showing how radically the impact of first contact had changed warfare on the Mucajaí. Their tricking the Shiri-teri into "praying" for metal goods also underscored what a strange new brew of outside influences was working on the Borabuk.[47]

Shortly afterward, the Borabuk sent peace offerings to the Shiri-teri, and they have been on good terms for the last thirty-five years. Although the Borabuk live in some half-dozen different *shabonos* spread out over a wide area of the Mucajaí River, with a population of over three hundred, there have been no raids between any of these *shabonos*. Between about 1935 and 1985, a total of three Borabuk men were killed violently; two others disappeared.[48] By the standards of the Amazon, or the world, the Borabuk form a fairly peaceful tribal society.

I also visited over thirty Yanomami *shabonos,* including several in the Parima Mountains. Of all the varied landscapes of Yanomamiland, I loved

altiplano: high plateau

these inaccessible highlands best. The **altiplano** has majestic scenery, splendid waterfalls, and a blessedly temperate climate. Mosquitoes are not as horrible a nuisance there as elsewhere. Until recently, the Parima Yanomami did not suffer from colds or malaria.[49]

Why, then, did the Bisaasi-teri end up at a malaria trap exposed to Western diseases on the main course of the Orinoco?

The Bisaasi-teri splintered from a larger block, the Namowei, which had been torn apart by the respiratory infections that coincided with the U.S. Army expedition of 1942–43. The outbreak killed off most of the tribal elders, giving power to immature and aggressive young men—like the ones who robbed me on the Mucajaí—who plunged the Bisaasi-teri into a fratricidal war. As usual, the killing started over suspicions that rival Yanomami had sent lethal new diseases through witchcraft. But the strife also involved competition to secure the trading routes to a new Protestant mission—the first permanent source of steel goods in Yanomamiland—which opened in 1948.[50]

coalesce: grow together or fuse

Defeated by both disease and war, the Bisaasi-teri relocated and adapted to river life, learning canoe travel and line fishing. As upland Yanomami, they did not even know how to swim. Nor did they have any clothes to keep off the clouds of gnats and dive-bomber mosquitoes. Bisaasi-teri was a village created by the catastrophe of first contact, and it first **coalesced,** six years before Chagnon's arrival, in 1958, around a government malaria post, without whose medicine the Bisaasi-teri could never have survived the unhealthy lowlands.[51]

Chagnon's exciting narrative edited out these unfortunate details. Prior to the arrival of the U.S. Army and Protestant missionaries in the 1940s, the Namowei Yanomami had lived in peace for a generation. Their only raiding parties had gone out searching for whites in order to steal machetes. But since there were no whites in the area, nothing happened. Other Yanomami journeyed three hundred miles to the Rio Negro in order to steal *madohe* (stuff): axes, machetes, knives, pots, and cloth.[52]

On one of these epic forays near the Rio Negro, the raiders captured a young white girl, Helena Valero, while she was traveling with her family on a hunting trip. "It was not to rob women but to seize the goods my family was carrying; they were not interested in women," Valero recalled. "They carried me off because they found me abandoned. But the Indians did not want to capture women, just *madohe*."[53]

During her twenty-four years as a wife and mother among the Indians, from 1932 to 1956, Valero witnessed the epidemics that carried off the Namowei leaders and the subsequent killings over sorcery suspicions. She described how the Namowei's young men had to be trained in the art of raiding because they had never fought anyone. In the beginning, they were comically incompetent, unable even to locate enemy *shabonos*.[54] But in the terrible struggle that followed the arrival of the first missionaries, Helena Valero's husband became the Namowei war chief. He was murdered in 1949; the other war leaders were all killed by 1951. The group split up into two villages—Bisaasi-teri and Patanowa-teri. Peace ensued.

After settling on the Orinoco, the Bisaasi-teri gained fitful access to Western manufactures. They traded a trickle of metal goods to villages in the hill country and received a bounty of young brides in exchange. From 1951 to 1964, no Namowei were killed in warfare. Then Chagnon arrived.

During Chagnon's brief, thirteen-month residence, ten Yanomami were killed in a war that once again pitted the people of the Bisaasi-teri alliance against their old Namowei cousins, the Patanowa-teri. These deaths constituted a third of all the war fatalities over a fifty-year period for the Namowei villages, according to Chagnon's Ph.D. thesis. All of the remaining male war deaths in these villages occurred during another brief period, 1949–51, when Protestant missionaries first established their bases on the Upper Orinoco.

14. In Your Journal: Why does Tierney keep bringing up Chagnon's Ph.D. thesis?

The missionaries initially made serious mistakes. They distributed machetes to win converts and unknowingly provoked bloody battles for monopoly rights to their supplies. But they eventually brought stable trading relations and good medical care to the Indians. They also actively intervened to stop fighting.

Chagnon could not provide ongoing medical attention or stable terms of trade, not because his intentions were less good but because his research, which will be examined in the next chapter, required him to collect thousands of genealogies and blood samples in a short period of time. He had to buy the Yanomami's cooperation in scores of villages across an area larger than New York State.

Chagnon arrived with a boatload of machetes and axes, which he distributed within twenty-four hours; the delighted recipients of this instant wealth immediately left the village unattended and went to trade with equally delighted allies. For the steel-poor villages of the Yanomami hill country, Chagnon was a one-man treasure fleet. The remote villages of Patanowa-teri and Mishimishimabowei-teri began sending messengers begging Chagnon to come and visit,[55] but their ambassadors were driven away by Bisaasi-teri and its closer allies, who fought to maintain their monopoly of Chagnon's steel wealth.

Within three months of Chagnon's sole arrival on the scene, three different wars had broken out, all between groups who had been at peace for some time and all of whom wanted a claim on Chagnon's steel goods. "Chagnon becomes an active political agent in the Yanomami area." said Brian Ferguson. "He's very much involved in the fighting and the wars. Chagnon becomes a central figure in determining battles over trade goods and machetes. His presence, with a shotgun and a canoe with an outboard motor, involves him in war parties and factionalism. What side he takes makes a big difference."[56]

15. In Your Journal: What do you think Chagnon means by the "'bad breath' theory of tribal warfare"?

Chagnon has dismissed this charge as "the 'bad breath' theory of tribal warfare."[57] Yet Chagnon brought more than breath with him into

Yanomami territory. He introduced guns, germs, and steel across a wide stretch of Yanomamiland—and on a scale never seen before. The Yanomami's desire for steel is as intense as our longing for gold. Westerners became the Yanomami's metal mines, local El Dorados that dispensed machetes, axes, and fishhooks that instantly increased agricultural production by 1,000 percent and protein capture by huge amounts. Yanomami groups made heroic odysseys in search of a single secondhand machete. Remote groups traded their daughters for a worn machete or a blunt ax. Villages with more steel always acquired more women. The sociologist John Peters, who lived among the Brazilian Yanomami for eight years, was offered two young girls in exchange for a couple of stainless steel pots. He refused the offer.

Chagnon did not wait to be asked, according to his closest friend and main informant—Kaobawa, the Bisaasi-teri headman, who was videotaped by Mark Ritchie, author of the 1995 book *Spirit of the Rainforest*. Kaobawa's picture formerly graced the cover of *The Fierce People,* where he held a pole with his right hand and jabbed an angry right index finger at the world. Chagnon has long considered this "unobstrusive, calm, modest, and perceptive" man as "the wise leader" of the Bisaasi-teri. Kaobawa's decision to help Chagnon sort out his interviews with dozens of informants "was perhaps the most important single event in my fieldwork," Chagnon wrote, adding, "Kaobawa's familiarity with his group's history and his candidness were remarkable. His knowledge of details was almost encyclopedic."[58]

Therefore, Kaobawa's videotaped statements raised a number of questions—about both men. Kaobawa claimed that Chagnon offered him a special deal. "That's my picture there," Kaobawa said when Mark Ritchie showed him a copy of *The Fierce People*. "When he was taking my picture he said, 'If you'll really help me, I'll give you a motor.' . . . He said, 'Father-in-law, I'm going to really be a Yanomami and you're going to get me a wife.' That's what he said. But although he said that, he just left. . . ."[59]

According to Ritchie, "The story of Chagnon trying to get a wife from Kaobawa is a comedy of errors. As Kaobawa explains it, Shaki—Chagnon—wanted to buy a wife from a distant village, and Kaobawa kept trying to stop him because Kaobawa didn't want Chagnon and his trade goods to move away. Apparently, Chagnon wanted a Yanomami wife, but far enough away from the missionaries so that they wouldn't find out."[60]

Chagnon suddenly went from being an impoverished Ph.D. student at the bottom of the totem pole to being a figure of preternatural power. His first letter from the field revealed this: "The village I'm living in really thinks I am the be-all and the end-all. I broke the final ice with them by participating in their dancing and singing one night. That really impressed them. They want to take me all over Waicaland to show me off. Their whole attitude toward me changed dramatically. Unfortunately, they want me to dance all the time now. You should have seen me in my feathers and loincloth! They were so anxious to show me off that they arranged to take me to the first Shamatari village so that I could dance with them."[61]

Chagnon's status was enhanced by a pair of shotguns. The geneticist James Neel described Chagnon firing off his gun preemptively to scare off young men they suspected might steal some goods. "At dusk Nap casually blasted the tips of a tree branch overhanging the *shabono* where we were sleeping, and we retired with the shotgun leaning against his hammock—to a quiet night."[62] Of course, this was an old conquistador strategy, one employed over the centuries to keep the natives cowed. In 1531, when Francisco Pizarro reached his first Inca city, Tumbes, at the Bay of Guayaquil, a soldier named Pedro de Candia "astounded the inhabitants by firing an **arquebus** at a target."[63] For the Spaniards, it became a standard technique of forced entrance.

arquebus: long barreled gun from the 15th century

The American Anthropological Association first got word of Chagnon's shotgun diplomacy when, in 1991, the anthropologist Terence Turner, head of its Yanomami survival commission, interviewed Davi Kopenawa, the Yanomami's most visible spokesperson and a winner of the UN Global 500 Award for defending the rain forest. Kopenawa told of reports that had come to his community of Chagnon's threatening behavior—walking around villages brandishing firearms and showing himself as a warrior. "Chagnon is fierce," Kopenawa said. "Chagnon is very dangerous. He did crazy things. *Ele tem a própria briga dele.*" This literally means "He has his own personal war."[64]

That is what Brian Ferguson concluded.

"Chagnon's role is a strange thing for me," admitted Ferguson, whose *Yanomami Warfare* breaks a professional taboo by scrutinizing a fieldworker as though he were a native. "One of the things I'm saying is that anthropologists need to be looked at. Anthropologists have been trained to screen out their own effects on their subjects. Their behavior is also a fit subject for investigation. The influence of Chagnon in the Yanomami area is a fit subject for investigation."[65]

Chagnon found himself in a difficult predicament, having to collect genealogical trees going back several generations. This was frustrating for him because the Yanomami do not speak personal names out loud. And the names of the dead are the most taboo subject in their culture.

"To name the dead, among the Yanomami, is a grave insult, a motive of division, fights, and wars," wrote the **Salesian** Juan Finkers, who has lived among the Yanomami villages on the Mavaca River for twenty-five years.[66]

Chagnon found out that the Yanomami "were unable to understand why a complete stranger should want to possess such knowledge [of personal names] unless it were for harmful magical purposes."[67] So Chagnon

Salesian: member of a Roman Catholic congregation founded in 1845 and dedicated chiefly to education and missionary work had to parcel out "gifts" in exchange for these names. One Yanomami man threatened to kill Chagnon when he mentioned a relative who had recently died. Others lied to him and set him back five months with phony genealogies. But he kept doggedly pursuing his goal.

Finally, he invented a system, as ingenious as it was divisive, to get around the name taboo. Within groups, he sought out "informants who might be considered 'aberrant' or 'abnormal,' outcasts in their own society," people he could bribe and isolate more easily. These pariahs resented other members of society, so they more willingly betrayed sacred secrets at others' expense and for their own profit. He resorted to "tactics such as 'bribing' children when their elders were not around, or capitalizing on animosities between individuals."[68]

Chagnon was most successful at gathering data, however, when he started playing one village off against another. "I began traveling to other villages to check the genealogies, picking villages that were on strained terms with the people about whom I wanted information. I would then return to my base camp and check with local informants the accuracy of the new information. If the informants became angry when I mentioned the new names I acquired from the unfriendly group, I was almost certain that the information was accurate."[69]

When one group became angry on hearing that Chagnon had gotten their names, he covered for his real informants but gave the name of another village nearby as the source of betrayal. It showed the kind of dilemmas Chagnon's work posed. In spite of the ugly scenes he both witnessed and created, Chagnon concluded, "There is, in fact, no better way to get an accurate, reliable start on genealogy than to collect it from the enemies."[70]

His divide-and-conquer information gathering exacerbated individual animosities, sparking mutual accusations of betrayal. Nevertheless, Chagnon had become a prized political asset of the group with whom he was living, the Bisaasi-teri. He took a Bisaasi-teri raiding party partway to their enemies' *shabono* with his outboard motor; later he helped Bisaasi-teri's allies leapfrog their enemies and avoid an ambush. By making one man, Kaobawa, the principal funnel of his largesse, Chagnon effectively created him "headman," a pattern he would repeat at other villages. With Chagnon established at Bisaasi-teri, minding the store with his shotguns, the Bisaasi-teri could raid other groups at a much greater distance because Chagnon made them immune to attack. Chagnon gave one of his shotguns to a Bisaasi-teri guide who was afraid of traditional foes nearby. "I had two shotguns. . . . I gave one of them to Bakotawa, along with a dozen or so cartridges and a quick lesson in how to load and shoot a gun."[71]

Another time Chagnon helped his Bisaasi-teri allies recapture a woman, Dimorama, whose abusive husband, Shiborowa, had shot her in the stomach with a barbed arrow. "They were going to Momaribowei-tedi to take Dimorama away from her protectors by force, if necessary, and asked me to come along knowing that I always traveled with a gun, presuming that my presence, with a gun, would aid in their objective." Their presumption was correct. They recaptured the girl and gave her back to Shiborowa.[72]

Although any Westerner bringing piles of steel goods would have disrupted Yanomami culture, Chagnon's role was arguably unique. Not only did the Bisaasi-teri have first choice of Chagnon's seemingly endless supply of steel goods; they also had a Western chief of sorts. "Dancing in another village is a part of politics—one way of displaying strength," Ferguson noted. "The participation of a white man in feathers and loincloth, virtually declaring his identification with Bisaasi-teri in intervillage relations, would represent a major coup." He added, "And it was during these first months of Chagnon's fieldwork that the Bisaasi-teri's conflicts with the Shamatari and Mahekoto-teri transpired. . . . But while he was behaving more like a Yanomami big man in his interpersonal relations, his other actions—his quest for the taboo names of the dead ancestors, his moving back and forth between antagonistic villages, and, above all, his being the source of Western goods that every village wanted to monopolize—created a very different and 'un-Yanomami' context for his behavior. Chagnon thus became something of a wild card on the local political scene."[73]

It is precisely the "un-Yanomami" context of the Napoleonic wars that makes them so problematic. Chagnon now recognizes that Yanomami violence is "actually quite low" by world standards of tribal culture.[74] And it is undeniably connected to the fluctuating impact of Western technology and disease. Whatever else can be said about Yanomami warfare, it is not "chronic," as hundreds of articles, documentaries, and books still insist. All of the violence among Chagnon's subjects can be spelled out in two stark spikes, both corresponding to outside intrusion. This is the picture of Yanomami ferocity that actually emerges from Chagnon's own Ph.D. thesis, the only complete accounting of Yanomami war deaths he has published for any group.[75]

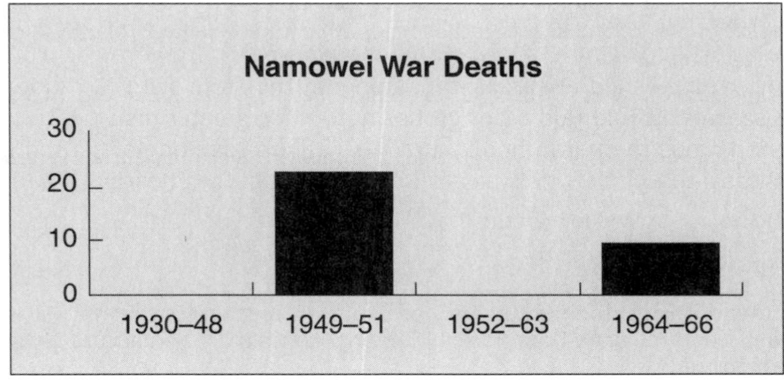

An **"uncertainty principle"** pertains to these wars. Would they have occurred at all without the germs, steel, and guns brought by strangers?

NOTES

Savage Encounters

1. Charles Brewer Carías, quoted in John Quiñones, "A Window on the Past," *Prime Time Live,* July 26, 1991.
2. Issam Madi, *Conspiración al sur del Orinoco* (Caracas: self-published, 1998), pp. 71–72.
3. Marta Rodríguez, Venevisión, Caracas, Fundación Cultural Venevisión, "Los Yanomami," July 24, 1991. Charles Brewer Carías stated, "Los grupos humanos más puros que existen son estos." Padre Nelson, camcorder interview with Marta Miranda, Ocamo, May 13, 1991.
4. Napoleon Chagnon, *Yanomamo: The Fierce People,* 3d ed. (New York: Holt, Rinehart and Winston, 1983), p. 214.
5. James Brooke, "In an Almost Untouched Jungle, Gold Miners Threaten Indian Ways," *NYT,* Sept. 19, 1990.
6. James Brooke, "Reserve for Primitive Tribe Promised in 6 Months," *NYT,* Sept. 25, 1990.
7. James Brooke, "Stone Age Villages Found: Venezuela to Protect Yanomami Indians," *Gazette* (Canada), Sept. 27, 1990.
8. "Their primitive state and considerable isolation have made them ideal for studies from a biological and genetic standpoint." David Atkins and Timothy Asch, *Yanomamo: A Multidisciplinary Study, Field Notes* (Somerville, Mass.: DER, 1975), p. 2.
9. Quiñones, "A Window on the Past."
10. Spencer Reiss, "The Last Days of Eden: The Yanomamo Indians Will Have to Adapt to the 20th Century—or Die," *Newsweek,* Dec. 3, 1990, pp. 40–42.
11. Charles Brewer Carías, Napoleon Chagnon, and Brian Boom, "Forest and Man" (MS; Caracas: Fundación Explora, 1993), pp. 10–19.
12. "Gentilmente aceptaron el aterrizaje del helicóptero en el centro del *shabono* a pesar de que todos sus techos caerían con el viento." Marta Miranda, Venevisión.
13. Napoleon Chagnon, "To Save the Fierce People," *Santa Barbara* magazine, Jan.–Feb: 1991, p. 36.
14. America Perdamo, head of Malariologia, interview, Puerto Ayacucho, Venezuela, June 16, 1996.
15. Quiñones, "A Window on the Past."

"uncertainty principle": theory of quantum mechanics that says it is impossible to measure both time and energy completely and accurately at the same time

16. "Because Napoleon's book is so popular, the films are used with the book in almost every University and College in the United States and also in Japan, Australia, England, Italy, France, etc." Timothy Asch, personal correspondence, Jan. 17, 1991, NAA.
17. James Neel, Timothy Asch, and Napoleon Chagnon, *Yanomama: A Multidisciplinary Study,* 43 min. (DOE, 1971).
18. Timothy Asch and Napoleon Chagnon, *The Feast,* 29 min. (DOE, 1970).
19. "Harokoiwa began rocking rhythmically sideways, violently denouncing me for killing their babies and causing epidemics among them, slapping his thighs as he rocked from side to side. . . . All the mysterious deaths in their village since I began visiting them were due to my ID photographs. They wanted to kill me to avenge all these deaths." Chagnon, *Yanomamo,* 4th ed. (Fort Worth: Harcourt Brace, 1992), pp. 236–237. See also Madi, *Conspiración al sur del Orinoco,* p. 71.
20. "The members of the Mahekototeri who feasted with the Patanowateri the next week were not inoculated and many of the members of this village died." Atkins and Asch, *Yanomamo,* p. 14. "Doritateri 15 de mayo de 1991: . . . que por causa de nuestras fotografías . . . éramos los causantes de enfermedades y culpables de la muerte de todos los Yanomami en las últimas dos décadas." Brewer Carías, Chagnon, and Boom, "Forest and Man," p. 15.
21. Napoleon Chagnon, *Studying the Yanomamo* (New York: Holt, Rinehart and Winston, 1974), p. 172.
22. Chagnon, *Yanomamo,* 4th ed., p. 237.
23. ". . . Charles Brewer-Carías, the man who has accompanied Chagnon for some years now on his trips into Yanomami territory, is indeed the owner of goldmines in Venezuela. It is more than understandable that a Yanomami, who is informed about the threats of goldmining on his own people's territory be alarmed about somebody like Brewer-Carías. . . ." Irenaus Eibl-Eibesfeldt and Gabriele Herzog-Schroder, "In Defense of the Mission" (paper, Forschungsstelle für Humanetheologie in der Max-Planck Gesellschaft, Feb. 28, 1994), pp. 6–7.
24. Madi, *Conspiración al sur del Orinoco,* p. 72.
25. Brewer Carías, "Teocracia y soberanía de Amazonas."

At Play in the Field

1. Davi Kopenawa, interview, Boa Vista, Brazil, Nov. 3, 1990.
2. Napoleon Chagnon, *Yanomamo: The Fierce People,* 3d ed. (New York: Holt, Rinehart and Winston, 1983), p. 10.
3. Timothy Asch, "Bias in Ethnographic Reporting" (MS), p. 4.
4. "Between 3 and 4 million students of anthropology, just in the United States, have read one of my books about the Yanomami." Chagnon, quoted in Eurípides Alcántara, "Indio também é gente," *Veja,* Dec. 6, 1995, p. 8.
5. Peter Monaghan, "Bitter Warfare in Anthropology," *Chronicle of Higher Education,* Oct. 26, 1994.
6. David Cleary, *The Anatomy of the Amazon Gold Rush* (Oxford: Macmillan and St. Antony, 1990), p. 1.

7. Rubens Esposito, *Yanomami: Um povo ameacado de extinção* (Rio de Janerio: Qualitymark Editora, 1998), pp. 1–35.
8. Brian Ferguson, *Yanomami Warfare: A Political History* (Santa Fe: School of American Research Press, 1995), p. 374.
9. Darna L. Dufour, "Diet and Nutritional Status of Amazonian People," in *Amazonian Indians,* ed. Anna Roosevelt (Tucson: Univ. of Arizona Press, 1994), pp. 151–76; William J. Smole, *The Yanoama Indians: A Cultural Geography* (Austin: Univ. of Texas Press, 1976), p. 19.
10. In the Parima Mountains, the Yanomami's most densely populated heartland, men were 145 mm; women, 136 mm. R. Holmes, "Nutritional Status and Cultural Change in Venezuela's Amazon Territory," in *Change in the Amazon Basin* ed. J. Hemming (Manchester: Univ. of Manchester, 1985), p. 251.
11. Kim Hill, phone interview, Jan. 17, 1995.
12. Napoleon Chagnon, *Yanomamo,* 4th ed. (Fort Worth: Harcourt Brace, 1992), pp. 189–90.
13. John D. Early and John F. Peters, *The Population Dynamics of the Mucajaí Yanomama* (San Diego; Academic Press, 1990), pp. 67–76.
14. Chagnon, *Yanomamo,* 4th ed., p. 220.
15. Napoleon Chagnon, "The Guns of Mucajaí: The Immorality of Self-deception" (MS, Sept. 1992, part of Chagnon's press kit), pp. 1–3.
16. He had also completely altered the geography of their warfare and multiplied it by using a single incident in three different contexts. See pp. 24–26, 210–14, Yanomamo Warfare, Social Organization, Village Alliance, pp. 196–99.
17. Jacques Lizot, "On Warfare: An Answer to N. A. Chagnon," trans. Sarah Dart, *American Ethnologist* 21 (1994): 845–62.
18. Jeffrey Rifkin, "Ethnography and Ethnocide," *Dialectical Anthropology* 19 (1994): 295–327; Bruce Albert and Alcida Rita Ramos, "O exterminio academico dos Yanomami," *Humanidades* (Brasília), 18 (1988): 85–89; Chris J. Van Vuner, "To Fight for Women and Lose Your Lands: Violence in Anthropological Writings and the Yanomami of Amazonia," *Unisa Largen* 10, no. 2 (July 1994): 10–20; Asch, "Bias in Ethnographic Reporting."
19. The first article, on protein consumption—Napoleon Chagnon and Raymond Hames, "Protein Deficiency and Tribal Warfare in Amazonia: New Data," *Science,* 203 (1979): 910–13—is covered in Chapter 16. The second, on homicide—Napoleon Chagnon, "Life Histories, Blood Revenge, and Warfare in a Tribal Population." *Science* 239 (1988): 985–92—is the subject of Chapter 10. Two Yanomami experts from Chagnon's field research area. Kenneth Good and Jacques Lizot, objected to Chagnon's protein article on the grounds that it falsely presented a Maquiritare Indian village, Toki, as a traditional Yanomami community. See Kenneth Good and Jacques Lizot, letter to *Science,* appended to Marvin Harris, "Culture Materialist Theory of Band and Village Warfare," in *Warfare, Culture, and Environment,* ed. R. B. Ferguson (Orlando, Fla.: Academic Press, 1984), pp. 111–40. Their letter was never published. Nor were they, or any other expert from Chagnon's Yanomami subgroup—the Yanomami of the Upper Orinoco—consulted about the publication of the controversial homicide study. At the time of the publication of the protein study, Good and Lizot were

the only other anthropologists in Chagnon's immediate research area. At the time of the second publication, there was a Salesian anthropologist, María Eguillor García, and a Venezuelan, Jesús Cardozo. None of these individuals was a reviewer for *Science.*

20. William Booth, "Warfare over Yanomamo Indians." *Science* 243 (1989): 238–40.
21. See Chapter 9 for a full account of the police, congressional, and NGO reports on Brewer's illegal mining operations. Mayor Sergio Rafael Milano (Jefe). Teniente Luis Alberto Godoy y Geraldi Antonio Villaroel (Secretario), Expediente de la Comisión de la Guardia Nacional. Fuerzas Armadas de Cooperación, Comando Regional 6, Destacamento de Frontera No. 61, Puerto Ayacucho, April 18, 1984.
22. E. S., "Charles Brewer Carías: Inventario de supervivencia," *ExcesO,* April 1990, p. 65.
23. James V. Neel. *Physician to the Gene Pool: Genetic Lessons and Other Stories* (New York: John Wiley, 1994), p. 408, n. 8, 134–200, 310.
24. Redmond O'Hanlon, *In Trouble Again* (London: Hamish Hamilton, 1988), p. 15.
25. There is a two-page photograph of Brewer smiling and swimming with David Rockefeller and two of Venezuela's richest men in the shadow of a tabletop mountain, in E.S., "Charles Brewer Carías," p. 65.
26. Colonel Sergio Milano, IVIC, phone interview, Dec. 12, 1994. Milano, an anthropologist who worked on frontier security from 1984 to 1993, before taking a job at IVIC, described Brewer's mountaintop parties to me: "El hace un turismo muy exclusivo. Ultimamente ha estado pidiendo permiso para ir con helicóptero y comida muy fina arriba de los tepuis—Auyantepui, Roraima—para hacer fiestas, cosas eccentricas con millionarios Venezolanos y Americanos."
27. O'Hanlon, *In Trouble Again,* pp. 1–40.
28. E.S., "Charles Brewer Carías," p. 65.
29. "For a while, from 1990 till May 1993, they enjoyed a lot of power and let the rest of the world know it should keep off Yanomami territory which for research purposes and applied work was only theirs (Chagnon, Brewer, Matos): The Salesian missionaries were appalled by the abuses of Matos, the illegal extraction of gold from Yanomami territory in military airplanes; perhaps they were also fearful of the power Chagnon and Brewer had acquired via Cecilia Matos. . . . 2) the airforce pilots were also mad and outraged (or envious, I do not know) to be forced to fly airplanes full of gold following orders given by Cecilia Matos. Those pilots, or some of them at least, came to hate Brewer for his association with Matos and the abuse of power. The two aborted military coup-d'etats of 1992 were carried out by junior army people who were fed up by the economic and political abuses committed by Pérez' friends, including his lover Cecilia Matos." Nelly Arvelo Jiménez. "The Repudiation of Brewer Carías and Chagnon Is Due to Their Intimate Association with Goldmining" (Caracas: IVIC, 1994), p. 7.
30. John Quiñones, "A Window on the Past," *Prime Time Live,* July 26, 1991. This segment featured a map of the 18,000-square-mile area that FUNDAFACI would have administered.

31. César Dimanawa, "Carta abierta a Napoleon Chagnon,." *La Iglesia en Amazonas,* March 1990, p. 20.
32. James Brooke, "In an Almost Untouched Jungle, Gold Miners Threaten Indian Ways," *NYT,* Sept. 19, 1990.
33. Venevisión's account was fairly typical: the television show claimed that mortality at the Salesian missions was two and a half times higher than that of the "purer" Indians of the Siapa Highlands. Marta Miranda, Venevisión, Caracas, Fundación Cultural Venevisión, July 24, 1991.
34. Charles Brewer Carías, "Una futura zona en reclamación," *El Nacional,* May 10, 1987.
35. Edgar López, in *El Diario de Caracas,* Sept. 2, 1993.
36. Misioneros del Alto Orinoco, "Consideraciones a un documento de Charles Brewer Carías" (Mavaca: Salesian Mission, 1991), p. 12.
37. Napoleon Chagnon has maintained that because President Pérez knew about the flights and tacitly approved them, they were legal. The *Fiscalía,* the attorney general's office, maintained that these flights were simply one more illegal activity that Pérez permitted. The legal argument seems to favor the *Fiscalía.* Federal Law 250 required scientists to receive approval for any expeditions to indigenous reserves. Although it would have been within President Pérez's power to issue a new federal decree empowering Chagnon, Brewer, and Matos, there is no record in the Official Gazette of his ever having done so. These expeditions and their fallout are the subject of chapter 1.
38. They were expelled from the village of Haximu-teri on Sept. 29, but flew out of the reserve on a small plane the next day from a nearby military base. Josefa Camargo, assistant attorney general for indigenous affairs, phone interview, Dec. 23, 1995; Terence Turner, "The Yanomami: Truth and Consequences," *Anthropology Newsletter,* May 1994, p. 48.
39. "Indígenas del Amazonas rechazan presencia de Brewer Carías y Chagnon." *El Nacional,* Sept. 14, 1993.
40. Arvelo Jiménez. "The Repudiation of Brewer Carías and Chagnon." p. 3.
41. María Yolanda García, "Cecilia Matos no iba a proteger indígenas sino a sacar oro del Amazonas," *El Nacional,* Jan. 15, 1993; Leda Martins, "Ciúme na floresta: Chagnon viola a ética médica (1990–1992)," *A Gazeta de Roraima,* March 18–24; 1996, p. 7.
42. "The promise of many presents caused some Indians to collaborate with Mr. Chagnon. This caused a division between communities: those who were on Mr. Chagnon's side and those who were against his visit. It reached the point where they fought a war resulting in three deaths, including Antonio and his brother, collaborators of Chagnon. Of course, the widows of Antonio are still waiting for the outboard motor promised to their dead husband." Juan Finkers, "Aclaraciones al Sr. Chagnon," *La Iglesia en Amazonas,* Dec. 1994. pp. 7–10.
43. "Tuvimos la oportunidad de leer las escandalosas declaraciones que dieron algunos de los pilotos que participaron en la bochomosa intentona golpista . . . para justificarse frente a la opinión pública, cuando señalaron desde su refugio en Perú, que habían participado en el intento de golpe 'indignados' porque

Charles Brewery Cecilia Matos sacaban oro en unos bidones desde Amazonas." Issam Madi, *Conspiración al sur del Orinoco* (Caracas: self-published, 1998), p. 72.

44. Janer Cristaldo, "Os Bastidores do Ianoblefe," *A Fôlha de S,o Paulo,* April 24, 1994.
45. Barry Bortnick, "From Amazon Jungle to Ivory Tower," *Santa Barbara News-Press,* April 19, 1999.
46. Napoleon Chagnon, "Killed by Kindness?" *TLS,* Dec. 24, 1993, p. 11.
47. Monaghan, "Bitter Warfare in Anthropology," A19.
48. Jacques Lizot, "N.A. Chagnon, o sea: Un presidente falsificador," *La Iglesia en Amazonas,* March 1994, p. 14.
49. Monaghan, "Bitter Warfare in Anthropology," A10.
50. Terence Turner, interview, Pittsburgh, March 29, 1995. Turner was recalling his statements to colleagues at the American Anthropological Association's annual meeting in Atlanta, Dec. 1994.
51. Lesley Sponsel, Univ. of Hawaii, phone interview, Aug. 22, 1995.
52. Asch, "Bias in Ethnographic Reporting," p.4.
53. Geoffrey W. Wrangham and Dale Peterson, *Demonic Males: Apes and the Origins of Human Violence* (Boston: Houghton Mifflin, 1996), chap. 5.
54. Kenneth Taylor, an anthropologist who received his Ph.D. at the Univ. of Wisconsin-Madison, told me that Chagnon's reputation for bar fighting was still remembered several years afterward. Phone interview, Jan. 27, 1995. See Chapter 7 for Chagnon's bar-fighting abilities at Penn State.
55. James V. Neel, "On Being Headman," *Perspectives in Biology and Medicine* 23 (1980): 277–94.
56. Neel, *Physician to the Gene Pool,* p. 134.
57. Walter Raleigh, *The Discoverie of the Large, Rich, and $$$Bewtifal Empire of Guiana,* ed. V.T. Harlow. (London: Haklyut Society, 1928), p. 5.
58. Alain Gheerbrant, *The Amazon: Past, Present and Future* (London: Thames and Hudson, 1992), pp. 39–58.
59. Napoleon Chagnon, *Yanomamo: The Fierce People,* 2d ed. (New York: Holt, Rinehart and Winston, 1977), pp. vii–viii.
60. Ibid., pp. 113–24.
61. Johannes Wilbert, *Survivors of El Dorado: Four Indian Cultures of South America* (New York: Praeger, 1972), p. 4.
62. Smole, *The Yanoama Indians,* p. 18.
63. Napoleon Chagnon, "Yanomamo Warfare, Social Organization and Marriage Alliances" (Ph.D. diss., Univ. of Michigan, 1966), p. 137.
64. Wrangham and Peterson, *Demonic Males,* chap. 4.
65. Jodie Dawson, interview at Platanal, with Mahekoto-teri and Patanowa-teri elders, June 11, 1996.
66. Andy Jillings, director, *Warriors of the Amazon, Nova,* WGBH, Boston, 1996.
67. Interviews at Karohiteri, June and Sept. 1996. See chapter 13.

68. *Anthro* now means anyone who seems more dedicated to studying the Yanomami than to helping them—anyone who goes around with a notepad or camera or blood-collecting equipment. See chapter 3.
69. Kenneth Good, *Into the Heart: One Man's Pursuit of Love and Knowledge among the Yanomama* (New York: Simon & Schuster, 1991), pp. 313–14.
70. E.S., "Charles Brewer Carías," p. 66.
71. Mark Ritchie. *Spirit of the Rainforest: A Yanomamo Shaman's Story* (Chicago: Island Lake Press, 1995), pp. 246–50; Mark Ritchie, video interview with Kaobawa, Padamo River, Jan. 1995.
72. Alcida Rita Ramos, "Reflecting on the Yanomami: Ethnographic Images and the Pursuit of the Exotic," *Cultural Anthropology* 2 (1987): 284–304.
73. " 'Turkey's village [Bisaasi-teri] finally got a smart naba to help them and he thinks he can reproduce himself from the back-end of boys?' . . . That's how the naba became known as A.H., meaning Ass Handler." Ritchie. *Spirit of the Rainforest,* p. 144.
74. Gary Dawson, head of the Padamo mission, a translator for Mark Ritchie and also for *National Geographic Explorer,* interview, June 4, 1996.
75. Jesús Cardozo, president of the Venezuelan Anthropological Institute, phone interview, Aug. 31, 1995.
76. Bortnick, "From Amazon Jungle to Ivory Tower."
77. Frank Salamone, *The Yanomami and Their Interpreters: Fierce People or Fierce Interpreters* (Lanham, Md.: (Univ. Press of America, 1997), p. 15.
78. Jesus Cardozo, phone interview, Dec. 20, 1994.
79. Colonel Sergio Milano, IVIC, interview, Dec. 12, 1994.
80. Napoleon Chagnon, "Conversation with Jesús Cardozo," March 23, 1994, p. 6.
81. Bortnick, "From Amazon Jungle to Ivory Tower."
82. Michael Dawson, interview. Padamo mission, June 4, 1996.
83. See chapters 5 and 6 for the deaths of people filmed in *The Feast* and *The Ax Fight:* Napoleon Chagnon and Thomas Melancon, "Epidemics in a Tribal Population," in *The Impact of Contact: Two Yanomamo Case Studies,* ed. K. Kensinger (Cambridge: Cultural Survival, 1983), pp. 53–78.
84. David Thomassen, DOE, Office of Energy Research, personal correspondence in reply to FOIA request No. 9501260003. March 13, 1994, p. 3.
85. James Neel, Timothy Asch, and Napoleon Chagnon, *Yanomama: A Multidisciplinary Study,* 43 min. (DOE, 1971).
86. Anna Mitus, Ann Holoway, Audrey Evans, and John Enders, "Attenuated Measles Vaccine in Children with Acute Leukemia," AJDC 103 (1962): 413–17.
87. The Yanomami population in Venezuela was ten thousand at this time, and measles had a mortality rate of 25–30 percent outside the immediate mission stations of Ocamo, Mavaca, and Kosh. As I show in chapter 5, the epidemic swept the whole Orinoco from the Padamo confluence to above the Guaharibo Rapids—more than a hundred miles—and ran into the heart of the Parima Massif on the Padamo, Ocamo, and Manaviche tributaries. See also Smole, *The Yanoama Indians,* p. 50, and Ferguson, *Yanomami Warfare,* p. 309.

88. Kenneth Good, phone interview, Feb. 27, 1998.
89. Mokarita-teri, Sept. 7, 1996.

The Napoleonic Wars

1. Napoleon Chagnon, letter from the field, in *The Human Condition in Latin America,* ed. Eric Wolf and Edward Hansen (New York: Oxford Univ. Press, 1972), p. 67.
2. "This particular war got started the day I arrived in the field (cause: woman stealing), and it is getting hotter and hotter." Ibid., p. 68.
3. Brian Ferguson, *Yanomami Warfare: A Political History* (Santa Fe: School of American Research Press, 1995), chaps. 13–14.
4. Brian Ferguson, phone interview, Jan. 3, 1995.
5. Jared Diamond, *Guns, Germs, and Steel: The Fates of Human Societies* (New York: W. W. Norton, 1997).
6. Ibid., p. 76.
7. John Hemming, *The Search for El Dorado* (New York, E.P. Dutton, 1978), p. 441.
8. Felipe Salvador Gilij, *Ensayo de historia americano,* vol. 2 (Caracas: Biblioteca de la Academia Nacional de Historia. 1965), p. 289.
9. John Hemming, *Amazon Frontier: The Defeat of the Brazilian Indians* (Cambridge: Harvard Univ. Press, 1987), pp. 36–37.
10. Ibid., p. 29.
11. Jacques Lizot. "Population, Resources, and Warfare among the Yanomami," *Man* 12 (1977): 497–517.
12. "For many miles the Orinoco is confined within a narrow bed of stone. Only short stretches are navigable." Inga Steinvorth Goetz, *Uriji Jami!: Life and Belief of the Forest Waika in the Upper Orinoco,* trans. Peter Furst (Caracas: Asociación Cultural Humboldt, 1969), p. 139.
13. Ibid., pp. 196–97, 194.
14. William J. Smole, *The Yanoama Indians: A Cultural Geography* (Austin: Univ. of Texas Press, 1976), pp. 220–21, n. 36.
15. Hamilton A. Rice, "The Rio Negro, the Casiquiare Canal, and the Upper Orinoco, September 1919–April 1920," *Geographical Journal* 58 (1921): 340–41.
16. Charles Hitchcock, *La región Orinoco-Ventuari: Relato de la expedición Phelps al Cerro Yavi* (Caracas: Ministerío de Educación. Nacional Directión de Cultura, 1948), p. 34.
17. Ettore Biocca, *Yanoama* (New York: Kodansha International, 1996), pp. 206–28.
18. Luis Cocco, *Iyewei-teri: Quince años entre los Yanomamas* (Caracas: Editorial Salesiana, 1973), p. 60.
19. "Las dificultades comenzaron con Hamilton Rice, quien por miedo, los ametrallóo. Hamilton les ofreció desde leios unas baratijas los guaharibos corrieron a tomarlas sin abandonar las flechas entonces aquel creyéndose atacado, hizo funcionar la ametralladora que en su lancha llevaba. Muchos guaharibos murieron en la oportunidad, y desde esa época Rodríguez Franco y yo

sũrrimos las consecuencias. De tiempo en tiempo pretenden prender fuego a nuestros poblados." Carlos Alamo Ibarra. *Rio Negro* (Caracas: Tipografia Vargas, 1950), quoted in Cocco, *Iyewei-teri,* p. 60.

20. Earl Hanson, "Social Regression in the Orinoco and Amazon Basins: Notes on a Journey in 1931 and 1932," *Geographical Review* 23 (1933): 588.
21. Napoleon Chagnon, *Yanomamo: The Fierce People,* 3d ed. (New York: Holt, Rinehart and Winston, 1983), p. 29.
22. Ibid., pp. 8–9. Attitude of women, p. 114.
23. "Beastly or Manly," *Time,* May 10, 1975.
24. Napoleon Chagnon, *Yanomamo: The Fierce People,* 2d ed. (New York: Holt, Rinehart and Winston, 1977), p. 9.
25. Konrad Lorenz, *On Aggression* (New York: Harcourt Brace Jovanovich, 1966), pp. 232–34.
26. Wilson, quoted in Barbara Burke, "Infanticide," *Science* 84, May 1984, p. 31.
27. Michael Harner, *The Jivaro: People of the Sacred Waterfall* (Berkeley: Univ. of California Press, 1984), pp. 134–169.
28. J. Larrick et al., "Patterns of Health and Disease among Waorani Indians of Eastern Ecuador," *Medical Anthropology* 3 (1979): 147–89.
29. Napoleon Chagnon, "Life Histories, Blood Revenge, and Warfare in a Tribal Population," *Science* 239 (1988): 985.
30. Bruce Albert, "Yanomami 'Violence': Inclusive Fitness or Ethnographer's Representation?" *Current Anthropology* 30 (1989): 631.
31. "A major difficulty in characterizing rates of violence in tribal societies with this kind of statistic is the fact that violence waxes and wanes radically over relatively short periods of time in most tribal societies, and grossly different estimates of homicide rates for the same population can be obtained from studies done of the same local group at two different periods of time, or neighboring groups at the same point in time." Chagnon, "Life Histories," p. 991, n. 24.
32. Napoleon Chagnon, "Chronic Problems in Understanding Tribal Violence and Warfare," in *Genetics of Criminal and Antisocial Behavior,* ed. G. R. Bock and J. A. Goode (Chichester, N.Y.: John Wiley, 1996), p. 217; Napoleon Chagnon, "To Save the Fierce People," *Santa Barbara* magazine, Jan.–Feb. 1991, p. 36.
33. Albert, "Yanomami 'Violence,' " p. 631.
34. Frederic Golden, "Scientist a Fierce Advocate for a Fierce People," *Los Angeles Times,* May 15, 1997.
35. "Figure 9: A Yanomamo village on a large river, atypical of their settlement locations." Napoleon Chagnon, *Yanomamo Interactive User's Guide,* p. 10.
36. Smole, *The Yanomama Indians,* p. 52.
37. Ferguson, *Yanomami Warfare,* p. 101.
38. Smole, *The Yanoama Indians,* pp. 50–1, 72, 76.
39. The five mountain villages had 7.7, 21.4, 15.4, 0, and 12.5 percent, respectively, of *unokai* (killers) among adult men. This averages to 11 percent, though the exact number of *unokai* per village is not available. Chagnon, "Chronic Problems in Understanding Tribal Violence and Warfare," p. 224.

40. Chagnon, "Life Histories," p. 986.
41. Smole, *The Yanomama Indians,* pp. 31–32.
42. Ibid., p. 233, n. 94.
43. Napoleon Chagnon. *Yanomamo,* 3d. ed., p. 175.
44. John D. Early and John F. Peters, *The Population Dynamics of the Mucajai Yanomama* (San Diego: Academic Press, 1990), p. 23.
45. Ibid., p. 24.
46. Ibid., pp. 67, 74.
47. Ibid., pp. 67–68.
48. Ibid., pp. 79–80.
49. Smole, *The Yanoama Indians,* p. 51.
50. Ferguson, *Yanomami Warfare,* pp. 224–54.
51. "The government malaria post invited the Bisaasi-teri to move to Boca Mavaca, where they were joined in 1959 by New Tribes missionaries down from Platanai." Ibid., p. 265.
52. Helena Valero, *Yo soy Napeyoma: Relato de una mujer raptada por los indígenas Yanomami* (Caracas: Fundación La Salle de Ciencias Naturales, 1984), pp. 24–30.
53. Ibid., pp. 12–13.
54. Ibid., pp. 140–51.
55. Chagnon, *Yanomamo,* 2d ed., p. 79, n. 17; 3d ed., p. 38.
56. Brian Ferguson, phone interview, Jan. 3, 1995.
57. Napoleon Chagnon, *Yanomamo: Last Days of Eden* (San Diego: Harcourt Brace Jovanovich, 1992), p. xv.
58. Chagnon, *Yanomamo,* 2d ed., pp. 96, 14, 13.
59. Kaobawa, video interview by Mark Ritchie, trans. Michael Dawson, Padamo mission, Jan. 1995.
60. Mark Ritchie, phone interview, Feb. 6, 1995.
61. Chagnon, in *The Human Condition in Latin America,* p. 67.
62. James V. Neel, *Physician to the Gene Pool: Genetic Lessons and Other Stories* (New York: John Wiley, 1994), p. 146.
63. John Hemming, *The Conquest of the Incas* (New York: Harcourt Brace Jovanovich, 1970), p. 26.
64. Terence Turner, unedited tape from an interview with Davi Kopenawa, "I fight because I am alive," Boa Vista, Brazil, 1991. Other portions of this interview were published in *Cultural Survival Quarterly* 15, no. 3 (1991): 59–64, and in the *AAA Newsletter* 32, no. 6 (1991): 52.
65. Brian Ferguson, phone interview, Jan. 3, 1995.
66. Juan Finkers, "Aclaraciones al Sr. Chagnon," *La Iglesia en Amazonas,* Dec. 1994. pp. 7–10.
67. Napoleon Chagnon, "Yanomamo Warfare, Social Organization and Marriage Alliances" (Ph.D. diss., Univ. of Michigan, 1966), p. 17.
68. Napoleon Chagnon, *Studying the Yanomamo* (New York: Holt, Rinehart and Winston, 1974), p. 91.

69. Chagnon, *Yanomamo,* 2d ed., p. 12.
70. Chagnon, *Studying the Yanomamo,* pp. 29, 95.
71. Ibid., p. 23.
72. Chagnon, "Yanomamo Warfare," p. 213.
73. Ferguson, *Yanomami Warfare,* pp. 286–88.
74. Chagnon, "Chronic Problems in Understanding Tribal Violence and Warfare," p. 217.
75. Chagnon, "Yanomamo Warfare," p. 62. Eight deaths occurred in fighting over the Shihota garden, a conflict that coincided with James Barker's arrival at Platanal in 1949, according to Helena Valero, whose chronology I am following here. Chagnon has offered two distinct chronologies, one in his Ph.D. thesis and one in the later editions of his text, *Yanomamo.* I consider both chronologies in more detail in chapter 16. However, in Chagnon's current construction, the violence that I have portrayed here between 1949 and 1951 would be an even sharper spike—all condensed into the year 1950–51. The picture for war deaths also differs substantially in Valero's and Chagnon's accounts. For the purpose of this analysis, I am accepting Chagnon's account only. "The raiders killed one of the Wanidima-tedi men, but in doing so angered both the Hasabowa-tedi and their cognate group, the Ashadowa-tedi. With the aid of the last two villages, the Wanidima-tedi [Valero and Fusiwe's Nomowei splinter] raided the Shihota-tedi [Rashawe and the young Kaobawa's Namowei splinter] and killed a younger brother of Makuwa. The Shihota-tedi reciprocated by raiding the Wanidima-tedi, killing Husiwa (Nabayoma's husband), Hoari, and Siayeikema. This in turn was followed by raids from the Wanidima-tedi in which the Shihota-tedi lost Ushuenawa and the two younger brothers of Paruriwa, and had one of their women, Bhiomi, seized." Ibid., p. 155. "In 1950 these villages [Bisaasi-teri and Monou-teri, western Namowei] were victimized by the Mowaraoba-tedi and the Iwahikoroba-tedi in a treacherous feast. They lost approximately 15 men." Ibid., p. 60. The actual date of the massacre was Feb. 1951, which Chagnon gives elsewhere in the same chapter (p. 21). The important point is that the number of deaths, in Chagnon's Ph.D. thesis history of the Namowei, comes to 23 by 1951. During Chagnon's fieldwork, the Patanowa-teri "suffered about eight deaths." Ferguson, *Yanomami Warfare,* p. 303. In Jan. 1965, the Mounou-teri killed one Patanowa-teri man, Bosibrei. Chagnon, "Yanomamo Warfare," p. 178. The Patanowa-teri retaliated by killing Damowa, the Monou-teri headman, in March 1965. Ibid., p. 179. The Bisaasi-teri and Monou-teri then united to kill another Patanowa-teri man, unnamed, at the Shihota garden, in late April 1965. Ibid., p. 181. Sometime between Nov. 1965 and Feb. 1966, the Bisaasi-teri and Monou-teri, who now formed one group, killed one additional Patanowa-teri man. Ibid., p. 189. There were about nine war deaths among the Namowei—which included Bisaasi-teri, Monou-teri, and Patanowa-teri. Since one victim was a woman, the total male death count, which is what Chagnon gives, stood at eight. Ferguson, *Yanomami Warfare,* pp. 300–306.

FOR USE IN DISCUSSION

Questions about Substance

1. Tierney says the Yanomami were "in a class by themselves" when it comes to the "economics of exoticism" (683). What does he mean by this? What does "economics" have to do with science?
2. Why does Venevisión shelve the footage of the Yanomami threatening Chagnon (686)? What kinds of unanswerable questions—alluded to by Tierney—do you think the footage raises?
3. While *anthro* means "man" for Westerners, for the Yanomami it has come to be associated with "a powerful nonhuman with deeply disturbed tendencies and wild eccentricities" (693–694). How are these connotations emblematic of Tierney's main argument?
4. How does Chagnon present his attitude about studying the Yanomami, according to Tierney (700)? Why did his attitude resonate with his audiences for *The Fierce People?*
5. Chagnon often used the testimony of cultural outsiders and enemies to gather genealogical data. In fact, he said there was "no better way to get accurate, reliable" data than to turn to "enemies" (710). What is the logic behind this argument? What are the weaknesses of this logic?

Questions about Structure and Style

1. Why does Tierney describe the Royal Geographic Society's and Army engineers' incursions into Yanomamiland before providing the details of Chagnon's endeavors?
2. What purpose does Tierney have in presenting an imagined "Chagnonian" account of his experience on the Mucajaí River (703)? What is so "Chagnonian" about the account?
3. Tierney describes the relationships and conflicts among the Namowei in some detail (706–707), providing much of it through the account of Helena Valero. What purpose does this section serve in the context of Tierney's larger argument about Chagnon? Why is Helena Valero's account highlighted?

Multimedia Suggestions

1. Tierney's book caused an uproar in the anthropology community. In fact, before it was even published, supporters of Chagnon started a campaign denouncing the book as an unsubstantiated polemic. Examine Chagnon's response to Tierney's accusations at *www.anth.ucsb.edu/chagnon.html.*
2. At the *http://randomplace.com/index-a.html* you can view an art collection of works by the children of the Yanomami, which include responses to the

ongoing deforestation of their land. Do any of these sketches illustrate the kind of cross-cultural anxieties that Tierney's work suggests?

3. If available at your institution, watch *The Feast* (1970) or *The Ax Fight* (1975), films directed by Timothy Asch and Napoleon Chagnon that examine various aspects of the Yanomami culture. Are you more or less skeptical of Chagnon after watching the film(s)?

SUGGESTIONS FOR WRITING AND RESEARCH

1. "The question is no longer why the Yanomami are so fierce, but why Chagnon's Yanomami have homicide rates so much higher than those of other Yanomami groups" (702), write Tierney, revealing his main goal in this work. Do you whink "the question" is so decidedly about Chagnon? Is Tierney's intense focus on Chagnon's work the strength or the weakness of *Darkness in El Dorado*? Explain your answer in an essay that analyzes Tierney's characterization of Chagnon to support your position.
2. Because anthropologists are collectively engaged in such a huge project—the study of human culture from its origin to the present—both documentation of sources and cooperation among scientists are crucial. Footnotes, therefore, are among the most important features of an anthropological study. Now that you have read Tierney's text, read (or re-read) his footnotes. Do they strike you as central to his argument, or do they seem extraneous? If this work did not contain the footnotes, would it be less compelling to you? Write an essay that describes and explores the relationship between Tierney's text and footnotes, citing examples where the footnotes add to or change your understanding of the text.
3. Susan Sontag has written that the anthropologist "submits himself to the exotic to confirm his own inner alienation as an urban intellectual," suggesting that anthropologists are more interested in their own character than in the cultures of the people they study. How does this concept apply to Chagnon? How does it apply to Tierney? Which of the two anthropologists do you think is more implicated in Sontag's assertion? Use passages of the text to support your response.

WORKING WITH CLUSTERS

Cluster 10: Interpretation and/as Ideology

Cluster 13: Global Knowledge

Cluster 15: Spatial Realities

Discipline: The Social Sciences

Rhetorical Mode: Analysis

Working with Clusters

Working with clusters of readings can provide the most challenging and productive discussions and assignments. By concentrating on more than one essay at a time, one learns that academic writing involves a great deal of inter-textual synthesis and that argument construction is a highly complex and ultimately open-ended process (i.e., a new text always sheds new light on previous ideas and discussions). While almost any group of readings in this anthology could be the basis for such clustered discussions and assignments, *Information and Meaning* suggests twenty possible thematic clusters, which include brief introductions and several writing assignments involving some combination of works in the cluster.

The clusters are made up of three to six essays, and while the themes are more open than those of a thematically organized reader, you will find that each selection in the cluster is directly relatable to the cluster theme as well as to the other selections. The writing assignments are diverse and flexible enough that one could certainly choose to delete or add on to a cluster as desired. These clusters should be used as models for creating additional groupings that suit the particular needs of a class or curricula, rather than strict guidelines for using this text. A limited number of clusters around discipline and clusters around rhetorical terms are suggested at the end of this section.

CLUSTER 1: SENSORY KNOWLEDGE

Diane Ackerman	*A Natural History of the Senses*
Charles Bowden	"The Bone Garden of Desire"
Annie Dillard	*The Writing Life*

The first and last information we receive in life is sensory. The senses inform and shape everything we know, yet we have a tendency to separate the intellect from the senses, and thus meaning from feeling. These selections put the senses in front of intellect, and ask the reader what kind of meaning is created through touch, taste, smell, sight, and hearing. The excerpts from Diane Ackerman's *A Natural History of the Senses* offer a microcosm of Ackerman's book: snippets of sensory experience that mimic the ebb and flow of the senses themselves. In concert, these snippets—like our senses—create a chaotic symphony of information and meaning that cannot be quite as ordered as our intellectual knowledge, but which nonetheless cues and tunes the intellect continually. Charles Bowden, in "The Bone Garden of Desire," expresses a desire to subordinate the intellect to the senses completely, and thus to allow sensory chaos to take up the space of meaning rather than to be displaced by language. Food and flowers can explain the life cycle better than any language or philosophy can, in his opinion. Annie Dillard, on the other hand, would reject the notion that language is less organic than food or flora. In this excerpt from *The Writing Life,* words are not only capable of personifying the inanimate, they are themselves the animate. In each selection, sensory imagery is emphasized and the notion of cerebral superiority is rejected (the organic structure of each selection is further evidence of this substantive point). The cluster as a whole makes a case for trusting a kind of knowledge often thought unstable at best. *Cluster 9: Bodies of Knowledge* and *Cluster 12: Visual Language* could work well with this cluster during the course of a semester.

SUGGESTIONS FOR WRITING

1. In *The Writing Life,* Annie Dillard says that "the written word is weak." Charles Bowden argues throughout his essay, "The Bone Garden of Desire," that language is no comfort in the face of death. Diane Ackerman, too, in *A Natural History of the Senses,* cites the failure of words to describe sensory experience. What does it mean for writers to discredit language in this way? Examine the ways these writers talk about the inadequacy of language and try to explain why they turn to language despite that inadequacy.
2. All three of these authors make frequent reference to biological facts, usually with some intent to aestheticize them (i.e., make them beautiful or examine their creative/artistic quality). Each seems to use a slightly different version of this technique, however. For example, Ackerman compares the senses to elegant mechanical processes (e.g., cartography, photography, or orchestra conducting); Bowden uses nature to stand in for desire and grief—for example, describing the biology of the *Selenicereus plerantus* as if he were describing a lover; finally, Dillard uses the mysteriousness of nature to help articulate the capricious character of the artistic process (e.g., watching an inchworm crawl across the grass is like watching oneself create a story). Write an essay in which you explain the usefulness of nature in writing. Using at least two of the three authors in this cluster, describe the ways they put nature to work in the service of language and beauty.

3. Some of us may find the writing style of these authors difficult to follow. Ackerman uses a style that wanders, Bowden presents an elusive argument, and Dillard uses metaphor so extensively that one might lose sight of her subject. Write an essay about the purpose of this kind of difficulty, citing examples from the text where you felt lost or challenged. What point are the writers trying to get across by making the reading experience so complicated?

CLUSTER 2: CONSTRUCTING AND CORRUPTING THE FEMININE

Natalie Angier	"Circular Reasonings: The Story of the Breast"
Kimberlé Crenshaw	"Whose Story Is It, Anyway? Feminist and Antiracist Appropriations of Anita Hill"
Colette Dowling	"Closing the Strength Gap"
Wendy Ewald	"Saudi Arabia 1997"
Faith Ringgold	*The French Collection*

The tennis world has been irrevocably unsettled by sisters Venus and Serena Williams for several reasons: they're muscular, they're sexy, they're black, and they have a sense of entitlement that seems impossible given the demographics of professional tennis players and fans. In this regard, they embody the "problems" presented in this unit. What it means to be feminine (including what it means to be beautiful or desirable) isn't as clear as it used to be. During the 18th and 19th centuries when the "cult of true womanhood" was in full force, the phenomenon of the Williams sisters would have been inconceivable. It's inconceivable even now. The ways science has encouraged such limited definitions of womanhood is Natalie Angier's interest. In the selection "Circular Reasonings: The Story of the Breast," she explores evolutionary theory around a single female body part and questions the rigid interpretations of biological data related to the breast. Kimberlé Crenshaw is also interested in interpretation in her essay "Whose Story Is It, Anyway? Feminist and Antiracist Appropriations of Anita Hill." Crenshaw argues that the rhetorics of anti-racism and feminism competed for credibility during the Clarence Thomas confirmation hearings, and as a result Anita Hill became invisible as a woman. Colette Dowling, like Angier and Crenshaw, puts forward the notion that the female body is an inherent threat to patriarchal cultures, but in her case she turns to the world of sports. In "Closing the Strength Gap" she argues that today's female athletes are redefining sports *and* gender by surpassing all social and physical expectations of women. The expectations of women in Islam is a focus of Wendy Ewald's work in "Saudi Arabia 1997." The women in these photographs attempt to both fulfill and challenge the social and religious constraints of the veil.

Finally, Faith Ringgold sends an imaginary black woman from the Jim Crow south to Paris during the height of modernism. In paintings from Ringgold's *French Collection,* the character of Willia Marie Simone calls the notion of the female muse into question (suggesting that the models of the "masters" were merely using their role as objects to further their goals of becoming creative subjects). Like Crenshaw, Ringgold examines the intersection of gender and race, and like Dowling and Angier, she is acutely aware of the cultural power of the female body. The cluster as a whole offers a fresh, complicated perspective on the meanings of femininity and the female body. It would work well in conjunction with *Cluster 10: Interpretation and/as Ideology* and *Cluster 17: Dis-Ability and Dis-Ease.*

SUGGESTIONS FOR WRITING

1. Why do you think the female body and definitions of femininity cause such uproar? Angier examines the kind of controversies they cause in science, Crenshaw in politics, Dowling in sports, and Ewald and Ringgold in art. Why don't we have the same tendency to ascribe meaning to the male body and masculinity? Is our anxiety related to sin (i.e., the temptress Eve), to pregnancy and childbirth, or is it all about the human nature to have control over others? Put forward your theory of what all the fuss is about when it comes to the female body, and use the texts to support your claim.
2. Natalie Angier and Colette Dowling both write about a generic female body—one that crosses cultures and races—whereas Crenshaw and Ringgold focus on the black female body, suggesting that race plays a big role in conceptions of the feminine. Does it? Do you think Angier and Dowling should be more attentive to race, or do you think that race is unrelated to their concerns? Where do Ewald's subjects fit into the discussion? Write an essay about the relevance of race in discussions about gender, and use the essays in this unit to provide support for your position.
3. Historically, emotion has been thought to be the purview of women, whereas logic is most commonly characterized as belonging in the male realm. Examine the ways these essays do or do not address the topic of emotion as it relates to gender stereotypes, and also look for signs of emotion in the work of the writers themselves. Do any of them seem to be making "emotional" arguments, or are they primarily using logic to press their points?

CLUSTER 3: READING MEANING, ACHIEVING LITERACY

Sven Birkerts	"MahVuhHuhPuh"
Richard Rodriguez	"The Triad of Alexis de Tocqueville"
Lauren Slater	"Some Kind of Cleansing"
Cass Sunstein	"The Daily Me" and "The Neighborhood Me"

Got Books? In today's visually charged and technologically frenetic society, it appears that books have gone the way of milk, while television and the Web take their place with Coca-Cola as the sustenance of choice. How is meaning gathered by reading different from that obtained by other information delivery methods? Is reading unique as a means of learning? Sven Birkerts perceives a destructive generation gap and cultural shift resulting from a decrease in patience for and pleasure in the act of reading. His "MahVuhHuhPuh" advocates for the meandering prose of Henry James and Virginia Woolf as an antidote to the flashy films and harassing hypertext most young readers are reared on. Richard Rodriguez also has a complicated relationship to reading. Throughout his life, Rodriguez has been an avid consumer of the western canon of literature. But as much as he identified with white European authors, his culture(s) never let him forget his Mexican-American origins. Lauren Slater's schizophrenic patient has lost his hold on language, and struggles to regain it and the attendant sense of community that comes from literacy. In "Some Kind of Cleansing," Slater advocates the shared sense of narrative that language facilitates. In "The Daily Me" and "The Neighborhood Me," Cass Sunstein explores the potential loss of such joint constructions due to the over-customization of reading material, especially news. He wonders what will happen to democracy when readers are able to filter out anything they don't already see in the mirror. This is a flexible cluster, but all of the essays examine the personal and collective values of reading and literacy. *Cluster 9: Bodies of Knowledge* and *Cluster 12: Visual Language* would provide interesting partners for this cluster.

SUGGESTIONS FOR WRITING

1. Compare and contrast the conceptions of "literacy" presented in this unit. Not all of the authors use this term explicitly, so you will need to infer a definition more carefully from those texts that do not provide one. Choose three of the essays to work with and begin by articulating and supporting the definitions of literacy you see developing in each. Then address the similarities and differences

in the way literacy (or illiteracy) is illustrated by these essays. Are there different kinds of literacy, different uses for literacy, and/or different levels of literacy represented?

2. Write a critique of one of these essays from the point of view of one of the other essays' authors. For example, how would Lauren Slater perceive Sven Birkerts's attitude toward his students? What would Sven Birkerts say about Cass Sunstein's argument? Use ample evidence from the text to support your response.
3. Re-examine the way that Lauren Slater presents Joseph's isolation and its relationship to language and compare this image to Sven Birkerts's description of his students reading Henry James. How do these examples call to mind the role language and story play in the formation of community? How do they relate to Richard Rodriguez's sense of isolation *because* of his reading?
4. Joseph's experience of "overinclusion" provides us with an apt metaphor for the problem of living in our information age. Apply this term to Birkerts's and Sunstein's texts, and discuss the ways we filter out the relevant from the irrelevant. Slater filters Joseph's language, allowing him to speak coherently for the first time in years. What kinds of filters would Birkerts like to loan his students? How would Sunstein distinguish what Slater does from what a customized news service does?
5. Both Birkerts and Rodriguez refer to many works of literature to illustrate the abstract points they want to convey. Compare the role this type of illustration plays—in terms of both structure and substance—in each author's general argument.

CLUSTER 4: CONCEIVING DEATH

Charles Bowden	"The Bone Garden of Desire"
Dave Eggers	*A Heartbreaking Work of Staggering Genius*
Atul Gawande	"Final Cut"
Philip Gourevitch	*We Wish to Inform You that Tomorrow We Will Be Killed with Our Families*
Joe Sacco	*Safe Area Goražde: The War in Eastern Bosnia 1992-95*

There are only two certainties, as they say, and death is the main one. Yet, at least in American culture, the subject of death is almost entirely relegated to the small worlds of Hallmark and Hollywood. Outside of debating the theoretical merits of capital punishment or the ethics of the estate tax, we avoid serious discussion of death entirely. What do we know about death, and how does it shape our view of the world? This cluster provides several essays that deal directly with death and the cultural (mis)understandings that are created in our efforts to cope with death, whether individually or collectively. Charles Bowden loses many friends to death in a short space of time, and he finds that only the sensual pleasures of eating and gardening can begin to compensate for the loss. "The Bone Garden of Desire" examines the life cycle in its most unromanticized form. Dave Eggers, in struggling to overcome the loss of his parents, has written a memoir/novel that also *appears* to avoid romanticization—in favor of neurotic self-examination. In the introductory material for *A Heartbreaking Work of Staggering Genius,* Eggers grieves the loss of his parents by birthing a genre: romantic post-modernism. In "Final Cut," Atul Gawande looks at death from a different perspective—that of the medical establishment. He is perplexed by the decline of the autopsy, which can provide so much information to medical science—perhaps more information than we can bear. Philip Gourevitch finds death "beautiful" rather than clinical in *We Wish To Inform You That Tomorrow We Will Be Killed with Our Families.* He wonders at his inability to accept or even imagine the terrible specter of death in the aftermath of the Rwandan genocide, even as he sees it for himself. This disbelief is shared by Joe Sacco's subjects, who attempt to grapple with the massacre of Bosnian Muslims in the UN declared "safe areas" Sacco reports on. In *Safe Area Goražde: The War in Eastern Bosnia 1992–95,* Sacco uses comic illustration to relate a tragic reality. How *real* is the result? *Cluster 1: Sensory Knowledge* and *Cluster 17: Dis-Ability and Dis-Ease* would pair well with this cluster.

SUGGESTIONS FOR WRITING

1. Bowden asks, "What can death mean in the face of all this drive?" Apply this thought to Gourevitch's Rwanda. How do Bowden and Gourevitch express a similar view of death? How is their view different? Examine these two essays in terms of their context, use of language, and the overall sense of purpose that each exhibits.
2. All of these selections at some point describe a need for comfort in the face of loss. Discuss this theme in relation to each author, citing examples from each text where the theme is most apparent. Do you find more comfort in one of the essays than the others? If so, why?
3. As Gawande states, the word "autopsy" literally means "to see for oneself." Apply the concept of autopsy to Gourevitch's investigation in Rwanda and Sacco's "comic" news reporting. In what ways do their texts perform a kind of literary autopsy? Where appropriate, make references to Gawande's defense of the purpose and results of medical autopsies.

4. Bowden and Eggers grapple with the specter of personal loss through the deaths of their loved ones. They also play with genre conventions, using unexpected structures and techniques to articulate the experience of this kind of loss. Explain why you think these authors find the conventions of typical essays or memoirs inadequate for their purposes.
5. Bowden argues that language is an inadequate tool for expressing or facilitating grief, preferring instead the comforts of food and gardening. Do any other authors in this cluster have non-verbal ways of experiencing grief? Compare and contrast another text with Bowden's in conjunction with the inadequacy of language. What do you think it means for writers to be so disappointed in the power of language?

CLUSTER 5: THE LAW AND THE PUBLIC

Clay Calvert	"Free Press, Free Voyeurs?"
Kenneth Cole	"Where Would We Be without Our Rights?"
Kimberlé Crenshaw	"Whose Story Is It, Anyway? Feminist and Antiracist Appropriations of Anita Hill"
E.J. Graff	"Inside Out or Outside In: Who Says You're Married?"

The *least* educated layperson is expected to follow the law; the *most* educated constitutional scholar has trouble explaining it. This paradox affects all citizens and permeates many major social debates in today's world. As the general public inhales the McLaw of daytime small claims television and sexy cable-produced trials, the "truth" of the law is diluted to the point of absurdity. But then again, aren't some of our attachments to the law in themselves absurd? Clay Calvert's "Free Press, Free Voyeurs?" wonders if the First Amendment has run amok by affording corporate press conglomerates the same rights as individual citizens. Privacy is increasingly violated as must-see TV wins more and more legal privilege. Kenneth Cole's "Where Would We Be without Our Rights?" ad series also meditates on constitutional issues, however sarcastically. Mocking both the fashion industry and the political apathy of today's consumers, the ads demand to know why viewers are reading clothing catalogues rather than the transcripts of congressional hearings and Supreme Court cases. "Whose Story Is It, Anyway? Feminist and Antiracist Appropriations of Anita Hill" by Kimberlé Crenshaw brings readers directly into a congressional hearing and exposes the ideological circus underneath. As Crenshaw explains, the Hill–Thomas hearings exposed to the public the ways ideology affects legal status. Finally, E.J. Graff worries the boundary between the personal and legal definitions of marriage in "Inside Out or Outside In: Who Says You're

Married?" Is the law sometimes just a state of mind? In the case of marriage, it's tough to tell where social definitions of love end and laws begin. What all of these selections share is an urgent sense that the lay public plays a much bigger role in legal interpretation and application than it imagines. *Cluster 10: Interpretation and/as Ideology* and *Cluster 13: Global Knowledge* could provide interesting curricular complements to this cluster.

SUGGESTIONS FOR WRITING

1. "Where Would We Be without Our Rights" offers a critique of consumers' relationship to privacy by suggesting that we want privacy only when it suits us ("if we see fit"). How much privacy do you think citizens legally deserve? How are the law and American culture at odds when it comes to notions of privacy? Reread Calvert and Graff and compare their notions of privacy with each other's and Kenneth Cole's. Does either essay resonate more with your own opinion? How much responsibility do you think the law has to protect an individual's privacy?
2. Calvert, Cole, and Crenshaw all examine different ways the popular media can affect the law. How is the law represented and defined by the popular media? Do you think the media tries to inform the public of its legal rights and responsibilities, or do you think it exploits public ignorance to raise its own status? Would you distinguish among the different types of media (e.g., television, advertising, news, Internet, etc.) in terms of how much or little effect they have on the public's understanding of the law? Take a legal topic from one of the essays in this unit (e.g., free speech, constitutional rights, race and gender discrimination, or marriage rights) and discuss how you think the media influences our understanding of the law around that topic. Make references to the texts and to specific media representations of your topic as necessary.
3. An ideology is a collection of beliefs that result from self-interest (usually of a group). Feminism, for example, is an ideology that expresses interest in and advocates for the rights of women. How do Crenshaw and Graff examine ideology's relationship with the law in their essays? Do they see ideology as harmful to the law or helpful? What role do you think ideology should play in the law?

CLUSTER 6: THE RACE FOR REPRESENTATION

Kimberlé Crenshaw	"Whose Story Is It, Anyway? Feminist and Antiracist Appropriations of Anita Hill"
Faith Ringgold	*The French Collection*
Randall Robinson	"Reclaiming Our Ancient Self"
Richard Rodriguez	"The Triad of Alexis de Tocqueville"

As with most identity issues, the more we discuss the topic of race, the less we seem to know about it. While we seem finally to have moved beyond the essentialism versus constructivism debate (a politicized version of the nature versus nurture debate) into a more holistic discussion of lived experience and collective consciousness, American society still refuses to acknowledge that the riddle of race will never be solved. The more directly we approach it, the more quickly it recedes. Perhaps its elusiveness is all we need to know. If we accept our inability to apprehend race as a concept, perhaps we will be comforted by its chimerical nature. Kimberlé Crenshaw tries to get at one aspect of the confusion by examining the ideological intersection of race (and anti-racism) and gender (and feminism), as illustrated by the Clarence Thomas confirmation hearing in 1991. In "Whose Story Is It, Anyway? Feminist and Antiracist Appropriations of Anita Hill," Crenshaw demonstrates the ways that Anita Hill's race was obscured by her gender, which prevented her allegations of Thomas's sexual harassment from being heard. Faith Ringgold is also interested in the ways race and gender intersect, but her concern is artistic rather than political expression. She imagines a young black woman onto the art scene of modernist Paris in her *French Collection,* and wonders through the voice of her heroine how racial identity might be able to fuel more than it impedes her art. In "Reclaiming Our Ancient Self," Randall Robinson examines the way the legacy of slavery impedes progress on multiple levels, sharing with Ringgold an interest in the need to understand and be a part of tradition. His creative essay weaves personal fantasies of the past he wishes he knew with the collective past he demonstrates has been excised from the history books, irrevocably changing the identity of blacks in America. Blacks in America, Richard Rodriguez demonstrates, have provided an important model and foil for Latinos in America. Rodriguez is at once baffled by his outsiderness and boosted by it. He argues, in "The Triad of Alexis de Tocqueville," that *brown* is both informed by black and white and yet isolated from them. All of the selections in this unit resist simple platitudes and reductionism; all of the authors are unsettled and their arguments unsettling. This cluster would interact well with *Cluster 10: Interpretation and/or Ideology* and *Cluster 18: Ethnicity and Conflict.*

SUGGESTIONS FOR WRITING

1. In "Whose Story Is It, Anyway? Feminist and Antiracist Appropriations of Anita Hill," Kimberlé Crenshaw states that "Once [the] ideologically formed character assignments are made, 'the story' tells itself." Unpack her theory of social "storytelling" as it relates to the Anita Hill/Clarence Thomas case, and then relate it to

Randall Robinson and Richard Rodriguez. What ideologies are behind the character assignments in their conceptions of history? What narratives are forced into action by the establishment of those characters?

2. Examine the representations and definitions of tradition as expressed by Ringgold, Robinson, and Rodriguez. Create a fictional dialogue between the three authors on the role tradition plays in the formation of identity. Think about how the authors would interpret and discuss each other's works. Develop a series of questions that you (the moderator) would ask this panel about their own sense of belonging to or being excluded from a tradition, and imagine how they would respond to the comments of their colleagues.
3. Crenshaw, Ringgold, and Rodriguez all struggle to different extents with the intersection of race and gender in their understandings of their identities. Compare and contrast the three versions of this intersection and see if you can find commonalities among all three texts. Are two of the texts more alike than the third? Are all three more different than similar? Whose version resonates most with your own experience or knowledge?

CLUSTER 7: HOLOCAUSTS AND HISTORIES

Don DeLillo	*White Noise*
Robert Eaglestone	"Postmodernism and Holocaust Denial"
Philip Gourevitch	*We Wish To Inform You That Tomorrow We Will Be Killed with Our Families*
Joc Sacco	*Safe Area Goražde: The War in Eastern Bosnia 1992–95*

As the numbers of its survivors and contemporaries dwindle, the burden to remember and learn from the Holocaust grows more complicated. Reinvigorated Holocaust deniers and more recent atrocities make some wonder whether we have indeed learned. Some writers and artists have turned to post-modernism—a belief in multiple perspectives, even in the context of history—to examine how atrocities morph into more modern memories, critiques, or allegories of the Holocaust. Others emphasize the need to bear witness, to report, as much as possible, the truth(s) of new atrocities in our midst. The only thing that remains clear is that the historical specter of the Holocaust has not dampened our human tendency toward violent hatred. Each of the works in this unit explores the legacies of the Holocaust or the shocking outrage resulting from subsequent "holocausts." In *White Noise,* Don DeLillo explores the way Hitler's legacy becomes watered down or commodified as time passes. His fictional "Hitler Studies" department and its inventor could seem like an unthinkable joke, a critique of academic detachment, or an examination of consumer culture depending on one's perspective. The notion of perspective is also central to Robert Eaglestone's "Postmodernism and Holocaust Denial" which follows the slander suit against Holocaust scholar Deborah Lipstadt brought by a Holocaust denier in a British court. Eaglestone argues that rigorous historical method requires acknowledgement of the subjective nature of history rather than a pretense of objectivity. Philip Gourevitch, in *We Wish To Inform You That Tomorrow We Will Be Killed with Our Families,* also encounters some "deniers." His account of the Hutu massacre of Tutsis in Rwanda emphasizes the incredulity of both the victims and perpetrators of the slaughter. During roughly the same period, another reporter covered another slaughter, turning to graphic illustration to communicate the incredible events to his readers. Joe Sacco, in *Safe Area Goražde: The War in Eastern Bosnia 1992–95,* chronicles the various betrayals of Bosnian Muslims in UN sanctioned "safe areas" during that war. All four of the pieces suggest that while history often inspires violence, it is also one of the keys to preventing it. *Cluster 8: Metaphor and Truth, Cluster 10: Interpretation and/or Ideology,* and *Cluster 20: The Burdens of Modernity* would combine with this cluster for a provocative and challenging semester of work.

SUGGESTIONS FOR WRITING

1. Explore the concept of denial (historical, psychological, political) in these works. While Eaglestone's work is most explicitly centered on the act of denial, both Gourevitch and Sacco look at the capacity of both implicitly examine the ways both perpetrators and victims engage in denial, and DeLillo's characters seem to engage in denial as a kind of play. Why do humans have such a strong tendency to deny truth, to deny responsibility, to deny their own ability to intervene in conflict?
2. The philosopher Theodor Adomo famously said that, "After Auschwitz . . . to write a poem is barbaric." Did he mean that art—all aesthetic pleasure—is undeserved and possibly meaningless in a world that can produce the Holocaust? Or did he want to suggest that art *about* atrocity is unconscionable? In either case, where does his critique leave Joe Sacco, Don DeLillo, or even Philip Gourevitch, who all take up somewhat aesthetic concerns within the context of murderous atrocities? Write an essay in which you respond to this quote as it pertains to these works, in which the aesthetic concerns and power of the imagination threaten to overshadow the literal histories of human violence their works present.

3. Each of these writers has strong relationships with the "characters" they present in their works, but despite their status as news reporters, Gourevitch and Sacco seem to be the most intimately involved with the people they feature. Is this the real nature of journalism or do the reporters cross a line of objectivity that they should respect more? How could any reporter be expected to present the kinds of events Gourevitch and Sacco cover without getting personally involved in the lives of those affected by the events? Write an essay about your expectations of news reporters and assess whether or not these reporters meet those expectations.
4. How does the concept of postmodernism, as defined and analyzed by Robert Eaglestone, apply to Don DeLillo's writing? Would Deborah Lipstadt approve of DeLillo's *White Noise*? How would DeLillo develop the characters involved in the libel trial Eaglestone presents and where would those characters fit into the context of his novel?

CLUSTER 8: METAPHOR AND TRUTH

Natalie Angier	"Circular Reasonings: The Story of the Breast"
Charles Bowden	"The Bone Garden of Desire"
Annie Dillard	*The Writing Life*
Lauren Slater	"Some Kind of Cleansing"

Metaphors are both whimsical inventions and essential tools of communication. They lead a reader away from and closer to one's intended meaning simultaneously. To call one's coworker a "gnat," for instance, would instantly evoke several precise personality characteristics (intrusiveness, tenaciousness, lack of self-consciousness, etc.) without even the slightest attempt to describe the coworker directly. The metaphor user conveys what she perceives to be an essential "truth" about her subject by comparing it to something familiar. Additionally, the writer who uses extended or multiple metaphors reveals a great deal about herself. The selections in this cluster all employ and explore the use of metaphor to convey some truth of experience. In "Circular Reasonings: The Story of the Breast," Natalie Angier uses unexpected metaphors to describe breasts, supplanting the more familiar breast metaphors employed by mainstream society. Charles Bowden uses processes of nature to articulate grief and his understanding of death. In "The Bone Garden of Desire," Bowden relies heavily on the aphrodisiacal effects of his favorite flower to explain the capricious nature of death, the way that death feeds life, and the desire that anticipating death creates. Annie Dillard, like Bowden, writes with particular attention to nature, in an attempt to reveal the organic process of writing. In *The*

Writing Life, Dillard compares writing to such varied things as mining, slicing out a chunk of one's flesh, an inchworm clinging to a blade of grass, and collecting honey, to prove that writing is no mundane or mechanical task. Lauren Slater also looks at subject that many would find unpleasant (treating a severely schizophrenic patient) and through the use of metaphor she helps the reader work through that unpleasantness to a deeper and more inspiring meaning. While covering a broad range of topics, each of these essays provides the opportunity to study the construction of effective metaphors and the important role they play in communication. Combine this cluster with *Cluster 12: Visual Language* and *Cluster 16: Imagination and Experience* for a layered examination of indirect use of language.

SUGGESTIONS FOR WRITING

1. Examine the ways these authors use metaphor to present subject matter that is banal or unpleasant in order to redeem or redefine it. How do these essays give you a new or unexpected perspective on breasts, death, writing, or mental illness? Compare at least two of the essays' effects on you, drawing specific examples from the texts as much as possible.
2. Nature provides an endless resource of rich metaphors. It seems that the more knowledge one has about the natural world (whether through scientific study or personal experience), the more metaphoric imagery one has at one's disposal. Which of these essays do you think uses nature metaphors most effectively? Whose subject matter seems best articulated through the lens of nature (or science)? In making your choice, you ought also to explain why the others are less effective or "natural," in your opinion, citing evidence from each text as you go.
3. Annie Dillard and Lauren Slater both seem to use metaphor to figure their way through professional problems—for Dillard the problem of writing and for Slater the problem of treating her patient. How does comparing their problems to unrelated experiences or processes help them to find solutions to what's in front of them? Does this practice go against your intuition about how one generally solves a problem? What does this process say about the nature of the relationship between problems and solutions? How do you think Dillard and Slater would have solved each other's problems?

CLUSTER 9: BODIES OF KNOWLEDGE

Natalie Angier	"Circular Reasonings: The Story of the Breast"
Colette Dowling	"Closing the Strength Gap"
Atul Gawande	"Final Cut"
John Hockenberry	"The Next Brainiacs"
Cindy Patton	"Media, Testing, and Safe Sex Education: Controlling the Landscape of AIDS Information"

The common phrase "body of knowledge" is interesting and problematic on many levels. First, it presumes a clear demarcation between the body under question and the world in which that body functions. Secondly, it suggests that a collection of knowledge, like a body, functions coherently and harmoniously. Thirdly, it expresses a bias towards meaningfulness in terms of the physical body; in other words, it suggests that the physical body *must* carry some sort of abstract meaning beyond its own mundane existence. The writers in this unit all examine the human body as emblematic of a particular body of scientific, social, medical, or political knowledge, questioning the possibilities of containment, cohesion, and stability of meaning therein. In "Circular Reasonings: the Story of the Breast," for example, Natalie Angier traces the evolutionary theories developed around the biology of the human breast, and suggests that the theories say more about their inventors than about the breast itself. Like Angier, Colette Dowling is interested in misinterpretations of the female body. In "Closing the Strength Gap," she explores the way sexism rather than physical weakness kept women from developing their athletic potential until recently, and she wonders how ideology will change as women athletes approach and even surpass the physical abilities of men. While he does not discuss gender in "Final Cut," Atul Gawande is also interested in biological and institutional questions. He argues that the decline of the autopsy is evidence that modern medicine denies its human fallibility. While the evisceration of a loved one's body creates disturbing images and evokes difficult emotions in most people, Gawande argues that the consequences of avoiding autopsy are far more disturbing. John Hockenberry also thinks about the general public's need to keep bodies intact and contained. When he explores new assistive technology for the disabled in "The Next Brainiacs," he questions the notion of the natural body as preferred "interface," and advocates broader definitions of functionality and humanness in our technological age. Finally, Cindy Patton asks us to think about the gay body as a site of contestation over moral and political issues, especially at the height of the AIDS crisis. In "Media, Testing, and Safe Sex Education: Controlling the Landscape of AIDS Information," she argues that mythologies about how AIDS or HIV testing assessed the body developed in the service of moral and political agendas, thus neglecting the very bodies the tests were ostensibly designed to help. This is a broad and diverse cluster, but all of the authors here offer fresh complicated ways of exploring the body and the knowledge it can produce or challenge. *Cluster 1: Sensory Knowledge* and *Cluster 10: Interpretation and/or Ideology* together with this cluster could inspire an interesting extended dialogue on the limits of abstract interpretation over the course of a semester.

SUGGESTIONS FOR WRITING

1. Natalie Angier questions the authoritative manner in which evolutionary biologists have interpreted the female body. Atul Gawande posits the idea that doctors are ordering fewer autopsies nowadays because they have too much confidence in new technology, but that this is erroneous thinking. Meanwhile, John Hockenberry shows us that "The Cure" gets copious funding and attention despite the inability of its researchers to produce any real results so far. How are these responses to scientific fallibility with respect to the human body different? How are they similar?
2. Colette Dowling and Cindy Patton are concerned with the way normative categories of gender and sexuality affect interpretations of the female body and the homosexual body, respectively. Compare and contrast their way of using politics to read biology.
3. Both Gawande and Hockenberry are interested in the way that science views and works with the human body. Compare and contrast the way that autopsies and assistive technologies serve and yet intrude on what it means to be human. Do we have too much reverence for our bodies? Do we have too little? What does it mean to be human in an increasingly technological age?
4. Individual illustrations are central to Dowling, Gawande, and Hockenberry's works. How do the stories of individual experience contribute to the more general arguments these authors make? Do the authors present enough illustrations to be able to generalize to the extent that they do? How do the authors use other elements (statistics, logic, expert testimony) to complement their emphasis on individual experience? Do they provide enough of a balance to be persuasive?

CLUSTER 10: INTERPRETATION AND/AS IDEOLOGY

Robert Eaglestone	"Postmodernism and Holocaust Denial"
Stephen Jay Gould	"A Tale of Two Work Sites"
Avishai Margalit and Ian Buruma	"Occidentalism"

Cindy Patton	"Media, Testing, and Safe Sex Education: Controlling the Landscape of AIDS Information"
Arundhati Roy	"The Ladies Have Feelings, So . . . Shall We Leave It to the Experts?"
Patrick Tierney	*Darkness in El Dorado: How Scientists and Journalists Devastated the Amazon*

When you look at a work of art in a museum, how do you formulate a theory about its meaning? Are you more likely to respond to color, theme, mood, or some other aesthetic preference? Does a representation of landscapes, animals, or a human figure appeal to you more than other images? Do you compare it to works you have seen before? When you read the title and description of the work and artist, perhaps you respond to the information you find there—including the country of origin, the historical period, or the artist's intentions. In any case, your interpretation is necessarily informed by your own knowledge, experience, emotions, and character. Interpretation is generally a highly subjective process that cannot be separated from your own perspective or subjectivity. But what if instead of a work of art the object is history, politics, or scientific phenomena? Does one have an obligation to suppress that subjectivity—to put aside one's self-interest? And how much subjectivity can you tolerate in the interpretations of others? The texts in this cluster each present and/or examine the ways ideology—a belief system based on self-interest—influences interpretation of an event, a practice, or even of another ideological belief system. In "Postmodernism and Holocaust Denial," Robert Eaglestone deconstructs the insidious ideology of Holocaust deniers who insist that their "interpretation" of the events of the Holocaust is legitimate because they falsely label their propaganda "history." Stephen Jay Gould, in "A Tale of Two Work Sites," examines the ways that class and moral ideology can affect scientific and political interpretation. Avishai Margalit and Ian Buruma are also interested in moral and political ideology in their essay "Occidentalism." They discuss the ways cultural ideology has been used as camouflage for anti-Western sentiments and actions. Cindy Patton, like Eaglestone and Margalit and Buruma, sees harmful propaganda as the logical outcome when ideological interpretation is allowed to develop unchecked. In "Media, Testing, and Safe Sex Education: Controlling the Landscape of AIDS Information," Patton traces the "(dis)information" campaign that erroneously suggested one's HIV antibody status revealed both the past and future sexual behaviors of the tested individual, thus exacerbating homophobia more than it curbed the spread of the disease. Arundhati Roy also examines a national information campaign in "The Ladies Have Feelings, So . . . Shall We Leave It to the Experts?" where she critiques the Indian government's rush to embrace the ideology of globalization at the expense of the vast majority of poor Indian citizens. In the excerpt from Patrick Tierney's *Darkness in El Dorado: How Scientists and Journalists Devastated the Amazon,* we can see a somewhat related critique of paternalism. Tierney blasts fellow anthropologist Napoleon Chagnon's paternalistic relationship with the Venezuelan Yanomamo tribe. All of these authors underscore the way that ideological interests can affect or infect the process of interpretation. This cluster, in combination with *Cluster 18: Ethnicity and Conflict* and/or Cluster *20: The Burdens of Modernity* would provide for an intensive investigation of the complicated relationship between perspective and persuasion.

SUGGESTIONS FOR WRITING

1. Explore the relationship between anti-Semitism and interpretation in the works of Eaglestone, Gould, and Margalit and Buruma. How does the ideology of anti-Semitism lead to specific kinds of interpretations according to these essays?
2. Authority often leads to a particular kind of control over interpretation. Cindy Patton, Arundhati Roy, and Patrick Tierney all present situations in which political, social, or intellectual authority allows for particular interpretations to be deemed "the truth," or at least conventional wisdom. The authors in each case dismantle the assumed authority in their essays. Explore the similarities and differences in their negative critiques of assumed authority.
3. Stephen Jay Gould and Arundhati Roy are both interested in the conditions of the working class. How do their professions (scientist and novelist, respectively) affect their interpretations of the conditions they examine? Are they more alike or more different?
4. Reread Margalit and Buruma's and Patrick Tierney's essays to examine the way that ideology contributes to conflict between Eastern and Western value systems.

CLUSTER 11: THE ART OF IRONY

Don DeLillo	*White Noise*
Dave Eggers	*A Heartbreaking Work of Staggering Genius*
Jedediah Purdy	"Avoiding the World"
Faith Ringgold	*The French Collection*

When pop star Alanis Morisette sang "Isn't It Ironic?" in describing "rain on your wedding day" or "a fly in your Chardonnay," the only real irony was her inability to identify a single example of it. Such is the world of popular culture. Young entertainers and consumers have a sincere desire to understand and comment on complicated tricks like irony, but they often want to get to that understanding by quick and dirty methods. Strangely, our culture (high and low) is awash in irony, and young people seem to adore it implicitly, despite the frequency of misinterpretations like Morisette's. Don DeLillo uses irony with great skill in *White Noise,* as in his description of "the most photographed barn in the world" or the professor who wants to raise Elvis Presley to the same academic stature as Adolf Hitler. This excerpt of the novel dares the reader to take irony seriously by pushing irony's inclination toward humor to the extreme. Dave Eggers also uses irony for comic effect, sneaking serious insights into the spaces between the punch lines that pummel the reader continually. For example, in his "rules for reading" *A Heartbreaking Work of Staggering Genius*, he lists many sections that needn't be read, calling into question the very significant relationship between author and audience by mocking his own text. Jedediah Purdy, unlike DeLillo and Eggers, feels confined by irony rather than liberated by it. In his essay "Avoiding the World," he laments the popularity of the "ironist's view" that nothing really matters as much as previously thought. He ties irony to the decline of sincerity and community, and argues that even its ostensible antidote (sincere spirituality) has been degraded into a superficial worship of cartoon angels. In Faith Ringgold's *French Collection,* the artist explores a highly ironic fantasy. Her character Willia Marie Simone moves to Paris during the modernist movement, becoming an ironic presence among artists and writers who would count African and American artists as influences and the female "exotic" as a subject worthy of representation, but who cannot fathom the presence of an African American woman in the flesh. *Cluster 3: Reading Meaning, Achieving Literacy* and *Cluster 8: Metaphor and Truth* together with this cluster would create a useful unit on literary and artistic devices and how they convey meaning to their audiences.

SUGGESTIONS FOR WRITING

1. Write a critique of Dave Eggers's work from the point of view of Jedediah Purdy. How would Purdy employ his argument in favor of sincerity and community to Eggers's super-ironic self-exploration? Use as much of Purdy's terminology and as many illustrations from Eggers as you can.
2. Don DeLillo and Faith Ringgold both examine particular traditions with a certain amount of ironic distance. DeLillo implicitly critiques the traditions of academia and the study of history by using the ironic figure of Jack Gladney and his "Hitler Studies" program. Ringgold revises the tradition of European painting by toying with many famous canonical images from the masters of modernism. Does their irony signify contempt in your view? Do DeLillo and Ringgold have any particular affection for the subjects they critique? Compare

and contrast their use of irony, and assess the level of approval or disapproval for their subject matter you think that irony reveals.

3. Contemporary popular culture, according to DeLillo, Eggers, and Purdy, seems to go hand in hand with the use of irony, though each author seems to have a different relationship to pop culture. Examine the different references to popular culture in each text (e.g., popular books, movies, television shows, commercials, strip malls, and supermarket trends). Is the irony conveyed meant to offer criticism of popular culture in general or just of the individual examples of pop culture? Are the things themselves ironic, or are they ironic because of the context of the author's argument or story? What does all of this irony suggest to you about the general nature of popular culture?

CLUSTER 12: VISUAL LANGUAGE

Kenneth Cole	"Where Would We Be without Our Rights?"
Wendy Ewald	"Saudi Arabia 1997"
Faith Ringgold	*The French Collection*
Joe Sacco	*Safe Area Goražde: The War in Bosnia 1992–95*

Written language began with pictographs and other symbolic drawings. Thousands of years later, we seem on some level to have grown nostalgic for a primarily visual means of communicating. From corporate "branding" to music videos to myriad applications for digital photography, our culture wants to leave no expression left unillustrated. Some critics worry that younger generations are losing verbal literacy skills to our image-centric society, but others suggest there are many types of literacy, and that visual literacy is as useful and meaningful as its verbal counterpart. In this unit, various visual texts illustrate the power of the visual image, its relationship to verbal narrative, and the skills involved in visual literacy. In a series of images from a Kenneth Cole accessories catalogue, which asks consumers of trendy fashions to consider their constitutional rights, we see the way images can convey as much irony and criticism to a reader as a verbal text. "Where Would We Be without Our Rights?" attracts and critiques its audience simultaneously. Wendy Ewald's work also offers a critique, but with a more poignant effect. In "Sandi Arabia 1997," photographs composed by and featuring Muslim women illustrate the gravity with which some cultures still perceive photographic portraits, especially of women. Faith Ringgold's images similarly convey a sociopolitical message. The paintings in her *French Collection* present a complex visual conversation about race, tradition, and art by de-familiarizing familiar images and historical contexts with elements of fantasy and whimsy. Joe Sacco's work in *Safe Area Goražde: The War in Eastern Bosnia 1992–95* also explores notions of familiarity, both in form and content. His illustrations convey the shocking betrayal of friends and neighbors during the Bosnian War. In combination, these selections speak to the power of the visual image, not as a substitute for verbal language, but as a crucial supplement. *Cluster 1: Sensory Knowledge* and *Cluster 3: Reading Meaning, Achieving Literacy* would pair well with this unit over the course of a semester.

SUGGESTIONS FOR WRITING

1. How does each of these selections characterize the relationship between pictures and words? Do words supplement the pictures, or vice versa? Do the words and pictures ever complicate or conflict with each other? Could you imagine any of these selections being able to convey its message without using pictures and words together? Refer to specific images and texts to make your argument.
2. Joe Sacco uses what might be considered a children's genre to convey a very adult subject matter, whereas both Wendy Ewald and Faith Ringgold introduce elements of "play," into their very adult media. How do these inversions contribute to the overall effectiveness of each artist/author? How would Sacco convey the message of Ewald's Muslim women? How would Ewald or Ringgold represent Sacco's Bosnian story?
3. Faith Ringgold, Joe Sacco, and Kenneth Cole resist the conventions of their genres in some way. How does their resistance suggest an historic or political agenda in their work? What ideas are they rethinking and revising in the course of this resistance?
4. Each of these visual/verbal texts plays with a familiar structure or order (the Constitution, the portrait, the artistic canon, and history, respectively). Do you think the selections mean to suggest a substitute structure or order, or do they mean to criticize the concept of order itself? In either case, why is it important for the selections to use both the visual and the verbal in the service of their critique of conventional structures?

CLUSTER 13: GLOBAL KNOWLEDGE

Thomas Friedman	"Tourist with an Attitude"
Philip Gourevitch	*We Wish To Inform You That Tomorrow We Will Be Killed with Our Families*
Avishai Margalit and Ian Buruma	"Occidentalism"

Arundhati Roy	"The Ladies Have Feelings, So . . . Shall We Leave It to the Experts?"
Cass Sunstein	"The Daily Me" and "The Neighborhood Me"
Patrick Tierney	*Darkness in El Dorado: How Scientists and Journalists Devastated the Amazon*

"All politics is local," the late Massachusetts Speaker of the House Tip O'Neill famously quipped, and there is a lot of truth in the idea that the biggest effect one can have on the world is through influencing one's immediate environment. But how do our provincial interests affect the community next door, or the state, country, or continent next door to that? How often do you think about issues brewing outside of your own sphere of reference, and how has that sphere expanded with the development of new technologies and the movement towards "globalization"? The authors in this unit are determined to see the larger connections among nations and cultures, and all of them write on some level about the potential boons and busts of globalization. Thomas Friedman, for examples, argues enthusiastically in favor of globalization in "Tourist with an Attitude." He contrasts the international ties globalization can facilitate with the divisions the Cold War perpetuated, arguing that a new type of education and experience is necessary if one wants to thrive in this new system. Philip Gourevitch shows readers the opposite of globalization—extreme provincialism. In this excerpt from *We Wish To Inform You That Tomorrow We Will Be Killed with Our Families,* Gourevitch deconstructs the Rwandan Hutu massacre of their Tutsi compatriots, vilifying not only the violence that results from extreme prejudice, but also exposing the industrial world's refusal to acknowledge or come to the aid of the doomed Tutsi population. Avishai Margalit and Ian Buruma are also interested in cultural conflict. In "Occidentalism," they trace the development of anti-Western sentiments from World War II Shintoists to present day Islamic extremists, exposing a resistance to industrial urbanization underneath the apparent racial/ethnic agenda. Urbanization figures significantly in Arundhati Roy's essay as well. In "The Ladies Have Feelings, So . . . Shall We Leave It to the Experts?" Roy recounts the hypocrisy she perceives in the Indian government's desire to crack down on environmental pollution while simultaneously promoting large-scale industrial efforts to compete in the global marketplace. Cass Sunstein has his own problem with the marketplace. In "The Daily Me" and "The Neighborhood Me," Sunstein theorizes about the ways individualized (customized) news outlets will dampen the purposes of democracy. While customized news services may have begun to isolate individuals in the industrial world, the industrial world has begun to force other cultures out of isolation for the ostensible purpose of educating itself. Patrick Tierney looks at a specific example of this anthropological problem in an excerpt from *Darkness in El Dorado: How Scientists and Journalists Devastated the Amazon.* Tierney criticizes Napoleon Chagnon and his dangerously manipulative tactics for procuring information about the Yanomamo Indians, arguing that the anthropologist intentionally introduced aggressive violence and disease to the Yanomami in order to then "discover" and treat those problems in his academic research. All of the texts in this unit ask readers to think more seriously about the way our own cultural beliefs, practices, and oversights affect the rest of the world, even if we do have the most "local" of intentions. Group this cluster with *Cluster 14: Epistemologies* and *Cluster 19: Structuring Chaos* for an interesting unit on the relationship between microcosms and macrocosms.

SUGGESTIONS FOR WRITING

1. Using Friedman, Roy, and Sunstein for support, make an argument about the relationship between globalization and democracy. Do you see a complementary or conflicting relationship between the two systems?
2. Tierney and Roy use an approach that could be called "negative critique," where they analyze and criticize the ideas and practices of those with whom they disagree. The other essays do not lack criticism, but they seem to examine social forces and belief systems more than specific individuals or groups. Do you find either approach more persuasive? Is either more vulnerable to countercriticism? Discuss Tierney, Roy and at least two of the others in your analysis.
3. Margalit and Buruma and Friedman use very broad perspectives in their arguments, taking on virtually the whole world in the course of their essays. The other selections in this cluster have a more "local" emphasis, though they clearly do not ignore the international ramifications of their arguments. How "global" can an essay's focus be without losing its resonance; how narrow can an essay's focus be without losing its relevance? In other words, do you find the broader arguments more or less persuasive than the more local arguments?

CLUSTER 14: EPISTEMOLOGIES

Natalie Angier	"Circular Reasonings: The Story of the Breast"
Atul Gawande	"The Final Cut"
E.J. Graff	"Inside Out or Outside In: Who Says You're Married?"
Cindy Patton	"Media, Testing, and Safe Sex Education: Controlling the Landscape of AIDS Information"

Epistemology is a branch of philosophy that investigates the nature and origin of knowledge. Its root word is "*epistanai,*" which means to "stand upon," suggesting that knowledge is a constructed platform on which one may place and present oneself. Knowledge is thus both foundational and subordinate—we create it so that it will support us, but we can also rebuild it when it becomes unstable. To be interested in epistemology is to be interested in just how stable and supportive our knowledge platforms are. Who built the knowledge you depend on? Is it still secure? Can it support us all, or is it designed to reveal only one specific perspective? Are there other platforms encroaching on its territory or does it stand in isolation from all other knowledge? These are abstract questions illustrated by specific concrete means in the texts in this cluster. Natalie Angier attempts to pull the platform out from under evolutionary biology's theories of the human breast, arguing in "Circular Reasonings: The Story of the Breast" that such theories have been developed and disseminated through a cultural and possibly ideological lens masquerading as a scientific view. Also interested in scientific knowledge, Atul Gawande questions the wisdom of modern medicine and its tendency to ignore its fallibility. In "Final Cut," he reveals how the decline of the autopsy has significantly destabilized medical knowledge, even if the instability has not become overtly apparent yet. In "Inside Out or Outside In: Who Says You're Married?" E.J. Graff examines the history of our knowledge about marriage—as an institution and an experience—making room for multiple platforms and demonstrating that none has had a particularly more permanent structure. Cindy Patton presents an epistemology of "AIDS testing," itself a misnomer, in order to demonstrate the way a respected body of knowledge can turn out to be little more than an optical illusion. In "Media, Testing, and Safe Sex Education: Controlling the Landscape of AIDS Information," Patton asserts that many AIDS education programs produced false knowledge to win a short-term public relations battle, choosing to ignore the negative consequences such falsehoods would have on the long-term war against the disease. This cluster will provide useful opportunities for discussing the means by which knowledge is created, depended upon, and challenged and it would work well in concert with *Cluster 2: Constructing and Corrupting the Feminine* and *Cluster 6: The Race for Representation.*

SUGGESTIONS FOR WRITING

1. What is the nature of scientific knowledge? On one hand, we tend to think that the rigors of the scientific method make scientific discovery impervious to critique. On the other hand, scientists are human just like the rest of us—they have subjective experience and individual perspective, too. Using Angier, Gawande, and Patton, develop an essay about the stability (or lack thereof) of scientific discovery. How do ideology, social forces, and/or politics challenge our belief in the scientific method?

2. How do we understand the nature of gender? Do we understand gender instinctively or are we taught to see it? How does our knowledge of gender affect other epistemological questions? Discuss the nature of our "gender knowledge"—where it comes from, how it gets articulated, and how it changes—using Angier, Graff, and Patton's work.
3. Epistemology has a lot to do with history. Knowledge changes with time, though not always in the direct linear fashion of "progress" we like to think it does. Look at the kinds of historical "progress" examined by Angier, Gawande, and Graff. Are we moving exclusively forward in your opinion, in the realms of evolutionary biology, medicine, and marriage?

CLUSTER 15: SPATIAL REALITIES

Charles Bowden	"The Bone Garden of Desire"
Thomas Friedman	"Tourist with an Attitude"
Stephen Jay Gould	"A Tale of Two Work Sites"
Cass Sunstein	"The Daily Me" and "The Neighborhood Me"

How does the space we inhabit affect our consciousness, and vice versa? When you feel connected to a specific place, is it because of the memories you hold in your mind about the place, or is it truly the place itself that speaks to you? Does the world feel "smaller" because of the power of technology to "transport" us metaphorically across countries and continents without our ever having to leave the spaces in front of our computers or televisions? In "The Bone Garden of Desire," Charles Bowden meditates in and on his own garden, pondering the ways he and his friends have become identified with the small plot of land—sharing food, stories, and sickness—by adding to and taking from its life-giving properties. Thomas Friedman, in contrast, travels the world in "Tourist with an Attitude," seeming to make the case that all places are becoming more and more part of the same space because of the connective tissue of globalization. Stephen Jay Gould reflects on the way time and history affect space as he recounts the capricious twists in his personal history, and how his fate was determined by two seemingly unrelated places. In "A Tale of Two Work Sites," Gould demonstrates the relationships between place and time, past and present. Finally, Cass Sunstein's "The Daily Me" and "The Neighborhood Me" look at the loss of public space and interaction that result from mass media technology. As cyberspace becomes more populated, our physical public forums lose their inhabitants and thus, as Sunstein argues, we lose some of the benefits of democracy. Use *Cluster 5: The Law and the Public* and *Cluster 19: Structuring Chaos* together with this cluster to examine the difference between individual and collective understandings of space, both physical and intellectual.

SUGGESTIONS FOR WRITING

1. Describe the importance of physical space in each of these essays. Do they seem to have different theories of the relationship between place and experience? Do any of their theories resonate more strongly with your own ideas about space or place?
2. Charles Bowden and Stephen Jay Gould's essays are much more personal than Friedman's or Sunstein's in terms of how they interpret the significance of place. How is place/space different for individuals and communities? Do you think place is more important in defining individual experience or communal values?
3. How does technology affect our relationship to physical space? Friedman and Sunstein comment on this issue directly, with very different effects. Given your own experiences with technology, do you feel more like Friedman, who sees technology as minimizing the spaces between us, or more like Sunstein, who sees it as further alienating us from each other?

CLUSTER 16: IMAGINATION AND EXPERIENCE

Diane Ackerman	*A Natural History of the Senses*
Don DeLillo	*White Noise*
Faith Ringgold	*The French Collection*
Joe Sacco	*Safe Area Goražde: The War in Eastern Bosnia 1992–95*

Does imagination help us escape reality, or is imagination what we use to apprehend and absorb reality? In either case, society tells us that there are appropriate uses for imagination, and that sometimes we're better off facing the facts rather than chasing a reverie. But isn't imagination itself a real experience? Do we not learn from and act upon the substance of what we imagine? Imagination provides scientists with important hypotheses, it helps policy analysts to debate the potential outcomes to a change in the law, it allows people to form sympathetic bonds with others who are different from them, and it inspires artists to interpret, criticize, or otherwise comment on the world around them. So where does imagination end and experience begin? All of the selections in this cluster make some sort of comment on the relationship between imagination and experience. Diane Ackerman writes about the way sensory experiences inform and are fueled by the imagination in these excerpts from *A Natural History of the Senses.* In *White Noise,* Don DeLillo imagines an extreme version of academia, apparently as a way to both embrace and critique a profession that sometimes appears to examine Adolf Hitler and Elvis Presley with the same sense of purpose and seriousness. Faith Ringgold seems to equalize historical figures in a different way. In the selections from her *French Collection,* Ringgold imagines a black American woman from Jim Crow times into the same Parisian cafes and salons inhabited by modernism's most renowned artists and writers. Finally, Joe Sacco imagines (and helps his readers to imagine) the terrors of war and ethnic cleansing in his *Safe Area Goražde: the War in Eastern Bosnia 1992-95.*

All of these selections value highly the power of imagination to teach, to inspire, and to represent the "reality" of our experiences in a meaningful and memorable way. With *Cluster 4: Conceiving Death* and *Cluster 20: The Burdens of Modernity,* this cluster could facilitate a semester's-worth of discussion and writing about the role and resonance of the imagination in our contemporary society.

SUGGESTIONS FOR WRITING

1. What is the role of the imagination in the creation and use of history? If we must, in some sense, *imagine* the past to document it, how authentic or accurate can the historical record be? Look at the ways Faith Ringgold and Joe Sacco use a combination of historical imagination and present experience in their work. Are the resulting texts "authentic" and/or accurate? How would their work change if it emphasized the imagination less and the historical record more?
2. All of these authors use imagination to show you familiar subjects (the senses, academia, racism, war) in surprising ways. Ironically, their imaginative twists may bring you closer to those subjects by first de-familiarizing you with them. How does imagination (the ability to envision what has not or what might happen) allow us to see the truth of what has happened?

CLUSTER 17: DIS-ABILITY AND DIS-EASE

John Hockenberry	"The Next Brainiacs"
Cindy Patton	"Media, Testing, and Safe Sex Education: Controlling the Landscape of AIDS Information
Lauren Slater	"Some Kind of Cleansing"

The prefix "dis-" denotes a negation or an invalidation of some kind. Therefore, at least from a semantic point-of-view, "disability" and "disease" both partially negate or invalidate the individuals they label. As John Hockenberry points out, semantics aren't evidence of much. The disabled individuals he features in "The Next Brainiacs" are not only not invalids, they in some ways surpass their able-bodied counterparts with the use of assistive technologies. Hockenberry argues that the technologies they employ make them no more dependent (no more disabled) than a baby is on a mother's hip or a senior is on a cane. In "Media, Testing, and Safe Sex Education: Controlling the Landscape of AIDS Information," Cindy Patton advocates for a more precise definition of disease rather than rejecting the label altogether. She demonstrates that the media (in the service of political forces) dumbed down the science behind AIDS research in order to define the label "HIV positive" in a way that suited the public relations agenda of certain institutional forces. In the name of "AIDS education," the label "disease" ended up having less to do with biology than morality. Finally, Lauren Slater looks at a condition that might be categorized as both a disability *and* a disease: mental illness. Her patient, Joseph D' Agostino, suffers from further permutations of the disease, namely "hypergraphia" and "overinclusion," which cause him to write copious tracts of incoherence and cause Slater to vow to translate at least some of his tomes. Translation turns out to be the default purpose of all of these authors—translation of labels, translation of experience, and translation of public judgment. This cluster, grouped with *Cluster 1: Sensory Knowledge, Cluster 9: Bodies of Knowledge,* and *Cluster 16: Imagination and Experience* would form a rich semester-long study of the human body.

SUGGESTIONS FOR WRITING

1. In her academy award–winning documentary *Breathing Lessons: the Life and Work of Mark O'Brien,* Jessica Yu features the inspiring story of a man confined to an iron lung since the age of six, when he contracted polio. O'Brien (who died in 1999) was a poet and journalist determined not to let his predicament overpower him. "Disability causes me to believe more strongly in a duality between body and spirit," he said in *Breathing Lessons,* ". . . cause if I'm a soul, I'm just as good as you. And if I'm a body, then I'm up shit creek, ain't I?" Does this belief in duality apply in any ways to Joseph D'Agostino or the people featured in Hockenberry's essay? Use the texts to construct an argument about the duality O'Brien describes. Is disability largely a matter of perception? Is it a concrete reality that can be transcended by abstract concepts like "spirit" and "soul"? Use the texts to support your theory of *what disability is* in relation to body and soul.
2. These texts provide some unconventional definitions of disease. Try to identify or infer the working definition of disease used by each of the authors. Compare

and contrast those definitions until you can come up with a working synthesis of all three. What could society learn from these essays about how to think about or understand the experience of disease?

3. John Hockenberry is very concerned that readers not take pity on the disabled, while Cindy Patton is more interested in teaching readers not to judge either gay men or those with HIV-positive status. Does Lauren Slater have a similar project with regard to the schizophrenic (i.e., to prevent pity or judgment)? Furthermore, does any of the three authors seem a more effective spokesperson for the group he or she champions? Explain your answer.

CLUSTER 18: ETHNICITY AND CONFLICT

Philip Gourevitch	*We Wish To Inform You that Tomorrow We Will Be Killed with Our Families*
Avishai Margalit and Ian Buruma	"Occidentalism"
Randall Robinson	"Reclaiming Our Ancient Self"
Richard Rodriguez	"The Triad of Alexis de Tocqueville"

German scholar and Harvard Professor Werner Sollors asserts that there are two facets to or manifestations of ethnicity—descent and consent. One's *descent*—comprised of one's ancestry, race, first language, and even first culture—is not a choice, whereas one's *consent* can lead to the formation of a new identity, or a more or less emphatic version of one's descent. One can choose new languages (including new accents and dialects), new clothing, new cultural interests, new religions, and new communities if one so desires or has the means to. Often descent and consent are at odds within a community or even within a single individual. Conflict arises from the tension between the unchangeable facts and the desire for self-definition. All of the essays in this unit explore ethnicity—some in the form of descent or consent, some in the form of the tension between the two. For example, in *We Wish To Inform You that Tomorrow We Will Be Killed with Our Families,* Philip Gourevitch reveals the tragic consequences for a world that becomes singly preoccupied with descent. The journalist chronicles the events of the senseless Rwandan Hutu massacre of their compatriot Tutsi neighbors. Avishai Margalit and Ian Buruma are similarly interested in the potential destructiveness of ideologies based on descent. They examine the ways that "East" and "West" have come to symbolize irreconcilable descents. Occidentalists blame the Judeo-Christian West for the world's ills and Orientalists blame the East (including the Middle East). But in some way the conflict between Occidentalism and Orientalism is also consensual, in that ideology can always be manipulated in the service pursuing power—especially international political power. On a much more personal note, Richard Rodriguez looks at the ways descent can be imposed on an individual who prefers to choose his own identity. In "The Triad of Alexis de Tocqueville," Rodriguez pieces together his "brown" identity by including white and black influences that were both forced on and chosen by him, rejecting the notion that one's identity must either follow a coherent blueprint provided by society or be wholly self-determined. Randall Robinson, in contrast, craves coherence, but perceives it to be lost to the vestiges of slavery. He argues in "Reclaiming Our Ancient Self" that the large-scale loss of history and ancestry for African Americans makes an authentic sense of identity (via descent or consent) nearly impossible. Ethnicity is in many ways a hackneyed topic in our culture today, and yet it is more important than ever that we come to some understanding of the importance of ethnicity, both in the formation of individual identity and in the administration of world affairs. *Cluster 2: Constructing and Corrupting the Feminine, Cluster 6: The Race for Representation,* and *Cluster 17: Dis-Ability and Dis-Ease* could combine with this cluster to form an intensive investigation into the politics of identity.

SUGGESTIONS FOR WRITING

1. Examine the role of imperialism and colonization in the work of Margalit and Buruma, Rodriguez, and Robinson. How is ethnicity both the source and the result of the kinds of conflicts these essays describe?
2. Compare and contrast Richard Rodriguez and Randall Robinson's views on African-American history. Are their views primarily oppositional or do you see more parallels than conflict? How would Robinson view Rodriguez's theory about the effect of African-American culture on "brown" identity and American culture in general? What do you think Rodriguez would say to Robinson's lament that African-American identity was irrevocably damaged by slavery?
3. In Philip Gourevitch's *We Wish To Inform You That Tomorrow We Will Be Killed with Our Families,* ethnicity seems to have different connotations than in the other three pieces. Or are the obvious racial and national differences examined by the other authors just easier to acknowledge and theorize about? The Hutus and Tutsis in Rwanda seem to share the most similarities, from a racial or ethnic point-of-view, and yet the violence expressed in the Rwandan massacre is one of the most extreme and concentrated examples in all of history. Does the example of Rwanda suggest that all ethnic conflict is largely socially constructed, or does it just mean that race is less a factor in ethnic conflict than we think?

CLUSTER 19: STRUCTURING CHAOS

Sven Birkerts	"MahVuhHuhPuh"
Dave Eggers	*A Heartbreaking Work of Staggering Genius*
Thomas Friedman	"Tourist with an Attitude"
Lauren Slater	"Some Kind of Cleansing"

For a physicist, "chaos theory" attempts to uncover predictability in events that may on the surface seem somewhat unpredictable. For example, the flapping of certain butterfly wings in a region of East Africa can potentially be shown to precipitate a series of atmospheric changes that eventually will cause a hurricane in the southern United States. What if those butterflies in East Africa are forced into extinction by the expansion of human settlements? Will a subsequent (albeit subtle) fluctuation in weather patterns change the physical environment in Florida? If so, will another species' habitat be threatened? And how will that in turn affect the human habitat? Imagine the power of butterfly wings! You can see from this single example that formerly undiscovered connections can have a radical effect on the natural world. Chaos theory can also lead to important insights outside of the hard sciences. Historians, psychologists, political theorists, and cultural theorists also have a vested interest in the connections among seemingly random entities. The selections in this cluster all suggest that the most disparate forces, events, and images can be shown to have relationships to each other, or at least that sometimes things thought to be random or tangential can in fact turn out to be quite central. For example, Sven Birkerts defends a style of writing that favors tangents and "distractions," arguing that important insights are gained in the process of reading through another's mental wanderings. In "MuhVuhHuhPuh," Birkerts laments the loss of writing and reading styles that value unpredictable inferences and unexpected connections. In an excerpt from his memoir, *A Heartbreaking Work of Staggering Genius,* Dave Eggers creates a reading experience that certainly involves surprises, though perhaps not those Birkerts has in mind. He closely associates seemingly "random" elements of form (e.g., the copyright page of a book) with the central themes of his story, such as self-explanation and fear of loss. This might be an example of the kind of "information arbitrage" Thomas Friedman advocates in his essay "Tourist with an Attitude." Friedman extols the benefits of globalization, a system in which the Cold War sense of order and stability has no more relevance, and where the unexpected connection is itself expected. Believing that there is some kind of order even in a system that appears chaotic is also the subject of Lauren Slater's essay "Some Kind of Cleansing." Slater makes a conscious decision to find order in her schizophrenic patient Joseph's writing, and thus she does find it, unscrambling the apparently senseless babblings of the would-be writer. All of these selections are interested in connections and logic that lie beneath a chaotic surface, and provide a fresh look at the ways humans can construct order in even the most disorderly situations. *Cluster 15: Spatial Realities* and *Cluster 20: The Burdens of Modernity* would work well in connection with this cluster, but you may want to choose more "random" pairings to test the foundations of chaos theory in your own classroom.

SUGGESTIONS FOR WRITING

1. In each of these essays, the author pieces together fragments until a kind of whole is achieved, though you might find more coherence in one or two of the essays than the others. Try to identify the mechanisms by which each author pieces the fragments together. Is there a chronological structure, a least-to-most significant or least-to-most complex structure, a random accumulation, or some other means by which each author gets to the "whole" of what he or she is trying to say? Write an essay comparing and contrasting the strategies of two to three of the authors, explaining how the content of their work is related to the cohering structures.
2. Eggers and Slater both emphasize a kind of personal chaos or confusion in their work, though Eggers writes about himself and Slater writes largely about her patient Joseph. While they use the first-person point of view, there seem to be different kinds of intimacy in each piece. As a reader, do you feel closer to Eggers or to Slater (or Joseph)? Whom do you feel you learn more about? Why? Lastly, do you think the intimacy created by either of these writers is somewhat constructed (false) or do both seem to invite the reader into their stories without any kind of defense or self-protection?
3. There are generational conflicts presented in both Birkerts's and Friedman's essays, though while Birkerts is nostalgic, Friedman is eager to move with the trends of the times. How would these writers respond to the other's arguments? Do you think Birkerts could be persuaded by Friedman's argument or that Friedman could see Birkerts's point of view? For which author do you feel more empathy, and why?

CLUSTER 20: THE BURDENS OF MODERNITY

Sven Birkerts	"MahVuhHuhPuh"
Clay Calvert	"Free Press, Free Voyeurs?"
Jedediah Purdy	"Avoiding the World"
Cass Sunstein	"The Daily Me" and "The Neighborhood Me"

Every generation thinks it improves human society, from its communities and quality of life to its innovations and general intelligence. However, most progress comes at a price. For example, many would agree that the Internet has provided people with greater access to information and much faster and more efficient methods of communication. But it also widens the information gap between those with access to a computer and those without, a gap that can lead to all kinds of other gaps—in education, employment, wealth, and even political power. Furthermore, it keeps those who do have access tied to their desks for many more hours per day, which can lead to eye problems, repetitive stress injuries, weight gain, personal isolation, and fatigue, to name a few things. So when lauding progress, we must also keep our eyes on the drawbacks, as the authors in this cluster insist on doing. In "MahVuhHuhPuh," Sven Birkerts warns about the cultural effects of the decline of reading—especially the reading of difficult material that takes considerable time and effort to work through. Birkerts feels that the increasing dependence on television and other media that provide a more passive experience than reading does is causing a problematic generation gap and a loss of creativity among today's youth. Clay Calvert is also fearful of the effects of television, though his concern is with the voyeuristic practices of investigative journalism. In "Free Press, Free Voyeurs?" Calvert argues that an increasingly corporate-owned media is beginning to press the limits of the First Amendment to the U.S. Constitution, which grants "freedom of the press." The corporate world is also one of Jedediah Purdy's interests. In "Avoiding the World," Purdy examines the contemporary tendency toward extreme irony, which he argues positions itself against sincerity, excluding the personal growth and fulfillment promised by corporate America. Finally, Cass Sunstein warns that both personal growth and the growth of democracy are hampered by the kinds of customized products most media now provide. He suggests technology's ability to "filter" unwanted or unanticipated experiences or information will have a negative effect on democracy, which is partially grounded in the concept of pluralism and antithetical to the kind of isolation media filtering can cause. All of these selections caution against an overly enthusiastic embrace of modern progress, and entreat readers to be more skeptical of modernity in general. *Cluster 7: Examining the Holocaust* and *Cluster 13: Global Knowledge* would combine well with this cluster to create a semester's course on the major events of the 20th century.

SUGGESTIONS FOR WRITING

1. All of the selections in this unit refer or allude to the popular media as a primary source of our cultural decline or depravity. Are these authors merely elitists who don't want to be associated with the popular culture around them, or

do they justifiably see the popular media as corrupting cultural progress? Quoting the texts where necessary, develop a critique or defense of the popular media and its value to society (or lack thereof).

2. Clay Calvert and Cass Sunstein are both lawyers interested in the ways that the media affect the legal and political ideals of American society. While Calvert is interested in a specific constitutional amendment and Sunstein is more interested in the general processes of democracy, both worry that the media are not regulated effectively. Compare and contrast their arguments and see if you can develop an argument that synthesizes their agendas.
3. Jedediah Purdy is perhaps the type of young person Sven Birkerts wishes he had in his literature classes. How do you think these two authors would respond to each other's essays? Are they in full agreement, or do their analyses have significant differences? Would Birkerts find Purdy's argument too linear or simplistic? Would Purdy think Birkerts's ideas "sincere" enough to be useful to his own thinking? Write a response from the point of view of one these authors about the other's essay.

Additional Cluster Work Suggestions

CLUSTERS BY DISCIPLINE

While many of these essays are interdisciplinary and could fit into more than one category, all are listed according to what appear to be the selections' primary disciplinary affiliations.

The Natural Sciences

- Diane Ackerman (Biology, Anatomy and Physiology)
- Natalie Angier (Evolutionary Biology)
- Atul Gawande (Medicine)
- Stephen Jay Gould (Evolutionary Biology, History)
- John Hockenberry (Technology)
- Cindy Patton (Epidemiology, Politics)

The Social Sciences

- Clay Calvert (Law)
- Kimberlé Crenshaw (Politics, Law)
- Colette Dowling (Sociology, Psychology)

- Thomas Friedman (Economics, Politics)
- E.J. Graff (Sociology, Law, History)
- Avishai Margalit and Ian Buruma (International Relations, History)
- Arundhati Roy (Politics)
- Lauren Slater (Psychology, Memoir)
- Cass Sunstein (Sociology, Law, Cultural Studies)
- Patrick Tierney (Anthropology)

The Humanities

- Sven Birkerts (Literary Criticism, Cultural Studies)
- Charles Bowden (Memoir)
- Kenneth Cole (Advertising)
- Don DeLillo (Fiction)
- Annie Dillard (Creative Non-fiction)
- Robert Eaglestone (Cultural Studies, Law, History)
- Dave Eggers (Memoir, Fiction)
- Wendy Ewald (Photography)
- Philip Gourevitch (Journalism)
- Jedediah Purdy (Cultural Studies)
- Faith Ringgold (Studio Art, Historical Fiction)
- Randall Robinson (Cultural Studies, History, Personal Essay)
- Richard Rodriguez (Personal Essay, Cultural Studies, Literary Criticism)
- Joe Sacco (Graphic Art, History, Journalism)

CLUSTERS BY RHETORICAL MODE

All of the selections use more than one rhetorical technique, but each is categorized according to its primary effect.

Description

- Diane Ackerman
- Don DeLillo
- Annie Dillard
- Dave Eggers

Narration

- Charles Bowden
- Philip Gourevitch
- Faith Ringgold

- Lauren Slater
- Joe Sacco

Illustration

- Sven Birkerts
- Clay Calvert
- Kenneth Cole
- Wendy Ewald

Definition

- Natalie Angier
- Robert Eaglestone
- E.J. Graff

Compare and Contrast

- Kimberlé Crenshaw
- Colette Dowling
- Thomas Friedman

Cause and Effect

- Stephen Jay Gould
- Avishai Margalit and Ian Buruma
- Randall Robinson
- Arundhati Roy

Analysis

- Cindy Patton
- Richard Rodriguez
- Patrick Tierney

Argument

- Atul Gawande
- John Hockenberry
- Jedediah Purdy
- Cass Sunstein

Credits

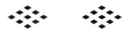

Page 1—From *A Natural History of the Senses,* by Diane Ackerman. Copyright © 1990 by Diane Ackerman. Reprinted by permission of Random House, Inc.

Page 25—"Circular Reasonings: The Story of the Breast," from *Woman: An Intimate Biography* by Natalie Angier. Copyright © 1999 by Natalie Angier. Reprinted by permission of Houghton Mifflin Company. All rights reserved.

Page 47—"MahVuhHuhPuh" from *The Gutenberg Elegies: The Fate of Reading in an Electronic Age,* by Sven Birkerts. Copyright © 1994 by Sven Birkerts. Reprinted by permission of Faber & Faber, Inc. an affiliate of Farrar, Straus & Giroux, LLC.

Page 71—Reprinted from *Esquire,* August 2000. Copyright © 2000 Charles Dowden. Reprinted by permission.

Page 89—Calvert, Clay. *Voyeur Nation: Media, Privacy, and Peering in Modern Culture*. Copyright © 2000 Westview Press. Reprinted by permission of Westview Press, a member of Perseus Books. LLC.

Page 123—Copyright © Kenneth Cole. Reprinted by permission.

Page 139—"Whose Story Is It Anyway?" Copyright © 1992 by Kimberle Crenshaw, from *Race-ing Justice, En-gendering Power*, edited by Toni Morrison. Used by permission of Pantheon Books, a division of Random House, Inc.

Page 167—From *White Noise*, by Don DeLillo. Copyright © 1984, 1985 by Don DeLillo. Used by permission of Viking Penguin, a division of Penguin Group (USA) Inc.

Page 187—From *The Writing Life*, by Annie Dillard. Copyright © 1989 by Annie Dillard. Reprinted by permission of HarperCollins Publishers, Inc.

Page 201—From *The Frailty Myth*, by Colette Dowling. Copyright © 2000 by Colette Dowling. Used by permission of Random House, Inc.

Page 227—Eaglestone, Robert. "Postmodernism and Holocaust Denial." Copyright © 2001 Totem Books. Reprinted by permission.

Page 257—Reprinted with the permission of Simon & Schuster Adult Publishing Group from *A Heartbreaking Work of Staggering Genius*, by Dave Eggers. Copyright © 2000 by Dave Eggers.

Page 295—From *Secret Games: Collaborative Works with Children 1969–1999*, by Wendy Ewald. Copyright © 1997 Wendy Ewald. Reprinted by permission.

Page 307—"Tourist with an Attitude," from *The Lexus and the Olive Tree* by Thomas Friedman. Copyright © 1999, 2000 by Thomas L. Friedman. Reprinted by permission of Farrar, Strauss & Giroux, LLC.

Page 331—"Final Cut" from *Complications: A Surgeon's Notes on an Imperfect Science*, by Atul Gawande. Copyright © 2002 by Atul Gawande. Reprinted by permission of Henry Holt & Company, LLC.

Page 345—From *The Lying Stones of Marrakech: Penultimate Reflections in Natural History*, by Stephen Jay Gould. Copyright © 2000 by Turbo, Inc. Used by permission of Harmony Books, a division of Random House, Inc.

Page 365—Excerpt from *We Wish To Inform You That Tomorrow We Will Be Killed with Our Families: Stories from Rwanda* by Philip Gourevitch. Copyright © 1998 by Philip Gourevitch. Reprinted by permission of Farrar, Strauss & Giroux, LLC.

Page 387—Graff, E.G. *What is Marriage For?* Copyright © 1999 Beacon Press. Reprinted by permission.

Page 405—*Wired*, August 2001. Copyright © 1991 Conde Nast Publications. Reprinted by permission.

Page 423—*The New York Review of Books*, January 17th, 2002. Copyright © 2002 New York Review of Books. Reprinted by permission.

Page 441—Patton, Cindy. *Inventing AIDS*. Copyright © 1990 Routledge. Reprinted by permission of Taylor & Francis Group.

Page 475—Purdy, Jedediah. *For Common Things: Irony, Trust and Commitment in America Today*. Copyright © 2000 Alfred A. Knopf. Reprinted by permission of Alfred A. Knopf, a division of Random House, Inc.

Page 495—Ringgold, Faith. *Dancing at the Louvre: Faith Ringgold's Collection and Other Story Quilts*. Copyright © 1998 University of California Press. Reprinted by permission.

Page 517—Robinson, Randall N. *The Debt: What America Owes to Blacks*. Copyright © 2001 Plume Publishing. Reprinted by permission.

Page 533—Rodriguez, Richard. *Brown: The Last Discovery of America*. Copyright © 2002 Viking Press, a division of Random House, Inc. Reprinted by permission.

Page 557—Roy, Arundhati. *Power Politics*. Copyright © 2002 South End Press. Reprinted by permission.

Page 575—Sacco, Joe. *Safe Area Goražde*. Copyright © 2000, 2001 by Joe Sacco. Reprinted by permission of Fantagraphic Books.

Page 637—From *Welcome to My Country* by Lauren Slater. Copyright © 1996 by Lauren Slater. Reprinted by permission.

Page 651—Excerpts from *Republic.com* by Cass Sunstein. Reprinted by permission.

Page 681—Tierney, Patrick. *Darkness in El Dorado: How Scientists and Journalists Devasted the Amazon*. Copyright © 2002 W.W. Norton & Company. Reprinted by permission.

Page 682—Copyright © 1995 Antonio Mari. Used by permission.